Lecture Notes in Computer Science   11140

Commenced Publication in 1973
Founding and Former Series Editors:
Gerhard Goos, Juris Hartmanis, and Jan van Leeuwen

More information about this series at http://www.springer.com/series/7407

Věra Kůrková · Yannis Manolopoulos
Barbara Hammer · Lazaros Iliadis
Ilias Maglogiannis (Eds.)

Artificial Neural Networks and Machine Learning – ICANN 2018

27th International Conference on Artificial Neural Networks
Rhodes, Greece, October 4–7, 2018
Proceedings, Part II

 Springer

Editors
Věra Kůrková
Czech Academy of Sciences
Prague 8
Czech Republic

Yannis Manolopoulos
Open University of Cyprus
Latsia
Cyprus

Barbara Hammer
CITEC Bielefeld University
Bielefeld
Germany

Lazaros Iliadis
Democritus University of Thrace
Xanthi
Greece

Ilias Maglogiannis
University of Piraeus
Piraeus
Greece

ISSN 0302-9743   ISSN 1611-3349 (electronic)
Lecture Notes in Computer Science
ISBN 978-3-030-01420-9   ISBN 978-3-030-01421-6 (eBook)
https://doi.org/10.1007/978-3-030-01421-6

Library of Congress Control Number: 2018955577

LNCS Sublibrary: SL1 – Theoretical Computer Science and General Issues

This Springer imprint is published by the registered company Springer Nature Switzerland AG
The registered company address is: Gewerbestrasse 11, 6330 Cham, Switzerland

Preface

Technological advances in artificial intelligence (AI) are leading the rapidly changing world of the twenty-first century. We have already passed from machine learning to deep learning with numerous applications. The contribution of AI so far to the improvement of our quality of life is profound. Major challenges but also risks and threats are here. Brain-inspired computing explores, simulates, and imitates the structure and the function of the human brain, achieving high-performance modeling plus visualization capabilities.

The International Conference on Artificial Neural Networks (ICANN) is the annual flagship conference of the European Neural Network Society (ENNS). It features the main tracks "Brain-Inspired Computing" and "Machine Learning Research," with strong cross-disciplinary interactions and applications. All research fields dealing with neural networks are present.

The 27th ICANN was held during October 4–7, 2018, at the Aldemar Amilia Mare five-star resort and conference center in Rhodes, Greece. The previous ICANN events were held in Helsinki, Finland (1991), Brighton, UK (1992), Amsterdam, The Netherlands (1993), Sorrento, Italy (1994), Paris, France (1995), Bochum, Germany (1996), Lausanne, Switzerland (1997), Skovde, Sweden (1998), Edinburgh, UK (1999), Como, Italy (2000), Vienna, Austria (2001), Madrid, Spain (2002), Istanbul, Turkey (2003), Budapest, Hungary (2004), Warsaw, Poland (2005), Athens, Greece (2006), Porto, Portugal (2007), Prague, Czech Republic (2008), Limassol, Cyprus (2009), Thessaloniki, Greece (2010), Espoo-Helsinki, Finland (2011), Lausanne, Switzerland (2012), Sofia, Bulgaria (2013), Hamburg, Germany (2014), Barcelona, Spain (2016), and Alghero, Italy (2017).

Following a long-standing tradition, these Springer volumes belong to the *Lecture Notes in Computer Science Springer* series. They contain the papers that were accepted to be presented orally or as posters during the 27th ICANN conference. The 27th ICANN Program Committee was delighted by the overwhelming response to the call for papers. All papers went through a peer-review process by at least two and many times by three or four independent academic referees to resolve any conflicts. In total, 360 papers were submitted to the 27th ICANN. Of these, 139 (38.3%) were accepted as full papers for oral presentation of 20 minutes with a maximum length of 10 pages, whereas 28 of them were accepted as short contributions to be presented orally in 15 minutes and for inclusion in the proceedings with 8 pages. Also, 41 papers (11.4%) were accepted as full papers for poster presentation (up to 10 pages long), whereas 11 were accepted as short papers for poster presentation (maximum length of 8 pages).

The accepted papers of the 27th ICANN conference are related to the following thematic topics:

AI and Bioinformatics
Bayesian and Echo State Networks
Brain-Inspired Computing

Chaotic Complex Models
Clustering, Mining, Exploratory Analysis
Coding Architectures
Complex Firing Patterns
Convolutional Neural Networks
Deep Learning (DL)

- DL in Real Time Systems
- DL and Big Data Analytics
- DL and Big Data
- DL and Forensics
- DL and Cybersecurity
- DL and Social Networks

Evolving Systems – Optimization
Extreme Learning Machines
From Neurons to Neuromorphism
From Sensation to Perception
From Single Neurons to Networks
Fuzzy Modeling
Hierarchical ANN
Inference and Recognition
Information and Optimization
Interacting with the Brain
Machine Learning (ML)

- ML for Bio-Medical Systems
- ML and Video-Image Processing
- ML and Forensics
- ML and Cybersecurity
- ML and Social Media
- ML in Engineering

Movement and Motion Detection
Multilayer Perceptrons and Kernel Networks
Natural Language
Object and Face Recognition
Recurrent Neural Networks and Reservoir Computing
Reinforcement Learning
Reservoir Computing
Self-Organizing Maps
Spiking Dynamics/Spiking ANN
Support Vector Machines
Swarm Intelligence and Decision-Making
Text Mining
Theoretical Neural Computation
Time Series and Forecasting
Training and Learning

The authors of submitted papers came from 34 different countries from all over the globe, namely: Belgium, Brazil, Bulgaria, Canada, China, Czech Republic, Cyprus, Egypt, Finland, France, Germany, Greece, India, Iran, Ireland, Israel, Italy, Japan, Luxembourg, The Netherlands, Norway, Oman, Pakistan, Poland, Portugal, Romania, Russia, Slovakia, Spain, Switzerland, Tunisia, Turkey, UK, USA.

Four keynote speakers were invited, and they gave lectures on timely aspects of AI.

We hope that these proceedings will help researchers worldwide to understand and to be aware of timely evolutions in AI and more specifically in artificial neural networks. We believe that they will be of major interest for scientists over the globe and that they will stimulate further research.

October 2018

Věra Kůrková
Yannis Manolopoulos
Barbara Hammer
Lazaros Iliadis
Ilias Maglogiannis

Organization

General Chairs

Věra Kůrková   Czech Academy of Sciences, Czech Republic
Yannis Manolopoulos   Open University of Cyprus, Cyprus

Program Co-chairs

Barbara Hammer   Bielefeld University, Germany
Lazaros Iliadis   Democritus University of Thrace, Greece
Ilias Maglogiannis   University of Piraeus, Greece

Steering Committee

Vera Kurkova   Czech Academy of Sciences, Czech Republic
  (President of ENNS)
Cesare Alippi   Università della Svizzera Italiana, Switzerland
Guillem Antó i Coma   Pompeu Fabra University, Barcelona, Spain
Jeremie Cabessa   Université Paris 2 Panthéon-Assas, France
Wlodzislaw Duch   Nicolaus Copernicus University, Poland
Petia Koprinkova-Hristova   Bulgarian Academy of Sciences, Bulgaria
Jaakko Peltonen   University of Tampere, Finland
Yifat Prut   The Hebrew University, Israel
Bernardete Ribeiro   University of Coimbra, Portugal
Stefano Rovetta   University of Genoa, Italy
Igor Tetko   German Research Center for Environmental Health, Munich, Germany
Alessandro Villa   University of Lausanne, Switzerland
Paco Zamora-Martínez   das-Nano, Spain

Publication Chair

Antonis Papaleonidas   Democritus University of Thrace, Greece

Communication Chair

Paolo Masulli   Technical University of Denmark, Denmark

Program Committee

Najem Abdennour   Higher Institute of Computer Science and Multimedia (ISIMG), Gabes, Tunisia

Tetiana Aksenova	Atomic Energy Commission (CEA), Grenoble, France
Zakhriya Alhassan	Durham University, UK
Tayfun Alpay	University of Hamburg, Germany
Ioannis Anagnostopoulos	University of Thessaly, Greece
Cesar Analide	University of Minho, Portugal
Annushree Bablani	National Institute of Technology Goa, India
Costin Badica	University of Craiova, Romania
Pablo Barros	University of Hamburg, Germany
Adam Barton	University of Ostrava, Czech Republic
Lluís Belanche	Polytechnic University of Catalonia, Spain
Bartlomiej Beliczynski	Warsaw University of Technology, Poland
Kostas Berberidis	University of Patras, Greece
Ege Beyazit	University of Louisiana at Lafayette, USA
Francisco Elanio Bezerra	University Ninth of July, Sao Paolo, Brazil
Varun Bhatt	Indian Institute of Technology, Bombay, India
Marcin Blachnik	Silesian University of Technology, Poland
Sander Bohte	National Research Institute for Mathematics and Computer Science (CWI), The Netherlands
Simone Bonechi	University of Siena, Italy
Farah Bouakrif	University of Jijel, Algeria
Meftah Boudjelal	Mascara University, Algeria
Andreas Bougiouklis	National Technical University of Athens, Greece
Martin Butz	University of Tübingen, Germany
Jeremie Cabessa	Université Paris 2, France
Paulo Vitor Campos Souza	Federal Center for Technological Education of Minas Gerais, Brazil
Angelo Cangelosi	Plymouth University, UK
Yanan Cao	Chinese Academy of Sciences, China
Francisco Carvalho	Federal University of Pernambuco, Brazil
Giovanna Castellano	University of Bari, Italy
Jheymesson Cavalcanti	University of Pernambuco, Brazil
Amit Chaulwar	Technical University Ingolstadt, Germany
Sylvain Chevallier	University of Versailles St. Quentin, France
Stephane Cholet	University of Antilles, Guadeloupe
Mark Collier	Trinity College, Ireland
Jorg Conradt	Technical University of Munich, Germany
Adriana Mihaela Coroiu	Babes-Bolyai University, Romania
Paulo Cortez	University of Minho, Portugal
David Coufal	Czech Academy of Sciences, Czech Republic
Juarez Da Silva	University of Vale do Rio dos Sinos, Brazil
Vilson Luiz Dalle Mole	Federal University of Technology Parana, Brazil
Debasmit Das	Purdue University, USA
Bodhisattva Dash	International Institute of Information Technology, Bhubaneswar, India
Eli David	Bar-Ilan University, Israel
Konstantinos Demertzis	Democritus University of Thrace, Greece

Antreas Dionysiou	University of Cyprus, Cyprus
Sergey Dolenko	Lomonosov Moscow State University, Russia
Xiao Dong	Chinese Academy of Sciences, China
Shirin Dora	University of Amsterdam, The Netherlands
Jose Dorronsoro	Autonomous University of Madrid, Spain
Ziad Doughan	Beirut Arab University, Lebanon
Wlodzislaw Duch	Nicolaus Copernicus University, Poland
Gerrit Ecke	University of Tübingen, Germany
Alexander Efitorov	Lomonosov Moscow State University, Russia
Manfred Eppe	University of Hamburg, Germany
Deniz Erdogmus	Northeastern University, USA
Rodrigo Exterkoetter	LTrace Geophysical Solutions, Florianopolis, Brazil
Yingruo Fan	The University of Hong Kong, SAR China
Maurizio Fiasché	Polytechnic University of Milan, Italy
Lydia Fischer	Honda Research Institute Europe, Germany
Andreas Fischer	University of Fribourg, Germany
Qinbing Fu	University of Lincoln, UK
Ninnart Fuengfusin	Kyushu Institute of Technology, Japan
Madhukar Rao G.	Indian Institute of Technology, Dhanbad, India
Mauro Gaggero	National Research Council, Genoa, Italy
Claudio Gallicchio	University of Pisa, Italy
Shuai Gao	University of Science and Technology of China, China
Artur Garcez	City University of London, UK
Michael Garcia Ortiz	Aldebaran Robotics, France
Angelo Genovese	University of Milan, Italy
Christos Georgiadis	University of Macedonia, Thessaloniki, Greece
Alexander Gepperth	HAW Fulda, Germany
Peter Gergel'	Comenius University in Bratislava, Slovakia
Daniel Gibert	University of Lleida, Spain
Eleonora Giunchiglia	University of Genoa, Italy
Jan Philip Goepfert	Bielefeld University, Germany
George Gravanis	Democritus University of Thrace, Greece
Ingrid Grenet	University of Côte d'Azur, France
Jiri Grim	Czech Academy of Sciences, Czech Republic
Xiaodong Gu	Fudan University, China
Alberto Guillén	University of Granada, Spain
Tatiana Valentine Guy	Czech Academy of Sciences, Czech Republic
Myrianthi Hadjicharalambous	KIOS Research and Innovation Centre of Excellence, Cyprus
Petr Hajek	University of Pardubice, Czech Republic
Xue Han	China University of Geosciences, China
Liping Han	Nanjing University of Information Science and Technology, China
Wang Haotian	National University of Defense Technology, China
Kazuyuki Hara	Nihon University, Japan
Ioannis Hatzilygeroudis	University of Patras, Greece

Stefan Heinrich	University of Hamburg, Germany
Tim Heinz	University of Siegen, Germany
Catalina Hernandez	District University of Bogota, Colombia
Alex Hernández García	University of Osnabrück, Germany
Adrian Horzyk	AGH University of Science and Technology in Krakow, Poland
Wenjun Hou	China Agricultural University, China
Jian Hou	Bohai University, China
Haigen Hu	Zhejiang University of Technology, China
Amir Hussain	University of Stirling, UK
Nantia Iakovidou	King's College London, UK
Yahaya Isah Shehu	Coventry University, UK
Sylvain Jaume	Saint Peter's University, Jersey City, USA
Noman Javed	Namal College Mianwali, Pakistan
Maciej Jedynak	University of Grenoble Alpes, France
Qinglin Jia	Peking University, China
Na Jiang	Beihang University, China
Wenbin Jiang	Huazhong University of Science and Technology, China
Zongze Jin	Chinese Academy of Sciences, China
Jacek Kabziński	Lodz University of Technology, Poland
Antonios Kalampakas	American University of the Middle East, Kuwait
Jan Kalina	Czech Academy of Sciences, Czech Republic
Ryotaro Kamimura	Tokai University, Japan
Andreas Kanavos	University of Patras, Greece
Savvas Karatsiolis	University of Cyprus, Cyprus
Kostas Karatzas	Aristotle University of Thessaloniki, Greece
Ioannis Karydis	Ionian University, Greece
Petros Kefalas	University of Sheffield, International Faculty City College, Thessaloniki, Greece
Nadia Masood Khan	University of Engineering and Technology Peshawar, Pakistan
Gul Muhammad Khan	University of Engineering and Technology, Peshawar, Pakistan
Sophie Klecker	University of Luxembourg, Luxembourg
Taisuke Kobayashi	Nara Institute of Science and Technology, Japan
Mario Koeppen	Kyushu Institute of Technology, Japan
Mikko Kolehmainen	University of Eastern Finland, Finland
Stefanos Kollias	University of Lincoln, UK
Ekaterina Komendantskaya	Heriot-Watt University, UK
Petia Koprinkova-Hristova	Bulgarian Academy of Sciences, Bulgaria
Irena Koprinska	University of Sydney, Australia
Dimitrios Kosmopoulos	University of Patras, Greece
Costas Kotropoulos	Aristotle University of Thessaloniki, Greece
Athanasios Koutras	TEI of Western Greece, Greece
Konstantinos Koutroumbas	National Observatory of Athens, Greece

Giancarlo La Camera	Stony Brook University, USA
Jarkko Lagus	University of Helsinki, Finland
Luis Lamb	Federal University of Rio Grande, Brazil
Ángel Lareo	Autonomous University of Madrid, Spain
René Larisch	Chemnitz University of Technology, Germany
Nikos Laskaris	Aristotle University of Thessaloniki, Greece
Ivano Lauriola	University of Padua, Italy
David Lenz	Justus Liebig University, Giessen, Germany
Florin Leon	Technical University of Iasi, Romania
Guangli Li	Chinese Academy of Sciences, China
Yang Li	Peking University, China
Hongyu Li	Zhongan Technology, Shanghai, China
Diego Ettore Liberati	National Research Council, Rome, Italy
Aristidis Likas	University of Ioannina, Greece
Annika Lindh	Dublin Institute of Technology, Ireland
Junyu Liu	Huiying Medical Technology, China
Ji Liu	Beihang University, China
Doina Logofatu	Frankfurt University of Applied Sciences, Germany
Vilson Luiz Dalle Mole	Federal University of Technology – Paraná (UTFPR), Campus Toledo, Spain
Sven Magg	University of Hamburg, Germany
Ilias Maglogiannis	University of Piraeus, Greece
George Magoulas	Birkbeck College, London, UK
Christos Makris	University of Patras, Greece
Kleanthis Malialis	University of Cyprus, Cyprus
Kristína Malinovská	Comenius University in Bratislava, Slovakia
Konstantinos Margaritis	University of Macedonia, Thessaloniki, Greece
Thomas Martinetz	University of Lübeck, Germany
Gonzalo Martínez-Muñoz	Autonomous University of Madrid, Spain
Boudjelal Meftah	University Mustapha Stambouli, Mascara, Algeria
Stefano Melacci	University of Siena, Italy
Nikolaos Mitianoudis	Democritus University of Thrace, Greece
Hebatallah Mohamed	Roma Tre University, Italy
Francesco Carlo Morabito	Mediterranean University of Reggio Calabria, Italy
Giorgio Morales	National Telecommunications Research and Training Institute (INICTEL), Peru
Antonio Moran	University of Leon, Spain
Dimitrios Moschou	Aristotle University of Thessaloniki, Greece
Cristhian Motoche	National Polytechnic School, Ecuador
Phivos Mylonas	Ionian University, Greece
Anton Nemchenko	UCLA, USA
Roman Neruda	Czech Academy of Sciences, Czech Republic
Amy Nesky	University of Michigan, USA
Hoang Minh Nguyen	Korea Advanced Institute of Science and Technology, South Korea
Giannis Nikolentzos	Ecole Polytechnique, Palaiseau, France

César Torres-Huitzil	National Polytechnic Institute, Victoria, Tamaulipas, Mexico
Athanasios Tsadiras	Aristotle University of Thessaloniki, Greece
Nicolas Tsapatsoulis	Cyprus University of Technology, Cyprus
George Tsekouras	University of the Aegean, Greece
Matus Tuna	Comenius University in Bratislava, Slovakia
Theodoros Tzouramanis	University of the Aegean, Greece
Juan Camilo Vasquez Tieck	FZI, Karlsruhe, Germany
Nikolaos Vassilas	ATEI of Athens, Greece
Petra Vidnerová	Czech Academy of Sciences, Czech Republic
Alessandro Villa	University of Lausanne, Switzerland
Panagiotis Vlamos	Ionian University, Greece
Thanos Voulodimos	National Technical University of Athens, Greece
Roseli Wedemann	Rio de Janeiro State University, Brazil
Stefan Wermter	University of Hamburg, Germany
Zhihao Ye	Guangdong University of Technology, China
Hujun Yin	University of Manchester, UK
Francisco Zamora-Martinez	Veridas Digital Authentication Solutions, Spain
Yongxiang Zhang	Sun Yat-Sen University, China
Liu Zhongji	Chinese Academy of Sciences, China
Rabiaa Zitouni	Tunis El Manar University, Tunisia
Sarah Zouinina	Université Paris 13, France

Keynote Talks

Cognitive Phase Transitions in the Cerebral Cortex – *John Taylor Memorial Lecture*

Robert Kozma

University of Massachusetts Amherst

Abstract. Everyday subjective experience of the stream of consciousness suggests continuous cognitive processing in time and smooth underlying brain dynamics. Brain monitoring techniques with markedly improved spatio-temporal resolution, however, show that relatively smooth periods in brain dynamics are frequently interrupted by sudden changes and intermittent discontinuities, evidencing singularities. There are frequent transitions between periods of large-scale synchronization and intermittent desynchronization at alpha-theta rates. These observations support the hypothesis about the cinematic model of cognitive processing, according to which higher cognition can be viewed as multiple movies superimposed in time and space. The metastable spatial patterns of field potentials manifest the frames, and the rapid transitions provide the shutter from each pattern to the next. Recent experimental evidence indicates that the observed discontinuities are not merely important aspects of cognition; they are key attributes of intelligent behavior representing the cognitive "Aha" moment of sudden insight and deep understanding in humans and animals. The discontinuities can be characterized as phase transitions in graphs and networks. We introduce computational models to implement these insights in a new generation of devices with robust artificial intelligence, including oscillatory neuromorphic memories, and self-developing autonomous robots.

On the Deep Learning Revolution in Computer Vision

Nathan Netanyahu

Bar-Ilan University, Israel

Abstract. Computer Vision (CV) is an interdisciplinary field of Artificial Intelligence (AI), which is concerned with the embedding of human visual capabilities in a computerized system. The main thrust, essentially, of CV is to generate an "intelligent" high-level description of the world for a given scene, such that when interfaced with other thought processes can elicit, ultimately, appropriate action. In this talk we will review several central CV tasks and traditional approaches taken for handling these tasks for over 50 years. Noting the limited performance of standard methods applied, we briefly survey the evolution of artificial neural networks (ANN) during this extended period, and focus, specifically, on the ongoing revolutionary performance of deep learning (DL) techniques for the above CV tasks during the past few years. In particular, we provide also an overview of our DL activities, in the context of CV, at Bar-Ilan University. Finally, we discuss future research and development challenges in CV in light of further employment of prospective DL innovations.

From Machine Learning to Machine Diagnostics

Marios Polycarpou

University of Cyprus

Abstract. During the last few years, there have has been remarkable progress in utilizing machine learning methods in several applications that benefit from deriving useful patterns among large volumes of data. These advances have attracted significant attention from industry due to the prospective of reducing the cost of predicting future events and making intelligent decisions based on data from past experiences. In this context, a key area that can benefit greatly from the use of machine learning is the task of detecting and diagnosing abnormal behaviour in dynamical systems, especially in safety-critical, large-scale applications. The goal of this presentation is to provide insight into the problem of detecting, isolating and self-correcting abnormal or faulty behaviour in large-scale dynamical systems, to present some design methodologies based on machine learning and to show some illustrative examples. The ultimate goal is to develop the foundation of the concept of machine diagnostics, which would empower smart software algorithms to continuously monitor the health of dynamical systems during the lifetime of their operation.

Multimodal Deep Learning in Biomedical Image Analysis

Sotirios Tsaftaris

University of Edinburgh, UK

Abstract. Nowadays images are typically accompanied by additional information. At the same time, for example, magnetic resonance imaging exams typically contain more than one image modality: they show the same anatomy under different acquisition strategies revealing various pathophysiological information. The detection of disease, segmentation of anatomy and other classical analysis tasks, can benefit from a multimodal view to analysis that leverages shared information across the sources yet preserves unique information. It is without surprise that radiologists analyze data in this fashion, reviewing the exam as a whole. Yet, when aiming to automate analysis tasks, we still treat different image modalities in isolation and tend to ignore additional information. In this talk, I will present recent work in learning with deep neural networks, latent embeddings suitable for multimodal processing, and highlight opportunities and challenges in this area.

Contents – Part II

Kernel

Reinforcement

Pattern Recognition/Text Mining/Clustering

Optimization/Recommendation

Computational Neuroscience

SOM/SVM

Anomaly Detection/Feature Selection/Autonomous Learning

Signal Detection

Long-Short Term Memory/Chaotic Complex Models

Wavelet/Reservoir Computing

Similarity Measures/PSO - RBF

ELM/Echo State ANN

Rank-Revealing Orthogonal Decomposition in Extreme Learning Machine Design

Jacek Kabziński$^{(\boxtimes)}$

Lodz University of Technology, Stefanowskiego 18/22, Lodz, Poland
jacek.kabzinski@p.lodz.pl

Abstract. Extreme Learning Machine (ELM), a neural network technique used for regression problems, may be considered as a nonlinear transformation (from the training input domain into the output space of hidden neurons) which provides the basis for linear mean square (LMS) regression problem. The conditioning of this problem is the important factor influencing ELM implementation and accuracy. It is demonstrated that rank-revealing orthogonal decomposition techniques can be used to identify neurons causing collinearity among LMS regression basis. Such neurons may be eliminated or modified to increase the numerical rank of the matrix which is pseudo-inverted while solving LMS regression.

Keywords: Neural networks modelling · Extreme learning machine
Nonlinear systems

1 Introduction

An Extreme Learning Machine (ELM) [1, 2] – a neural network with one fixed hidden layer and adjustable output weights - is able to solve complicated regression or classification problems. In this paper, application of ELMs for modeling multivariable, nonlinear functions with batch data processing is considered. The main ideas behind the standard ELM approach are that: the weights and biases of the hidden nodes are generated at random, without 'seeing the data', and are not adjusted, so 'training' means that the output weights are determined analytically, solving a linear mean square (LMS) problem. Therefore, the training is reduced to one step and the training time is very short comparing to iterative training.

The numerical round-off errors of linear mean square regression are the main reasons for ELMs' modeling errors and are strictly connected with the number of neurons in the hidden layer. When the number of hidden layer nodes is small, the ELM may not be able to transform the input into the feature space effectively and the approximation error may be unacceptably large. When the number of hidden layer nodes is large, it increases the computation complexity, may lead to an ill-conditioned LMS regression problem and may even result in overfitting of the ELM. The necessity of improving the numerical properties of ELM was noticed in several recent publications [3–6]. Neurons pruning techniques were proposed in [7, 8] and incremental learning was used in [9, 10]. Both methods try to get the optimal number of hidden layer nodes. But, with every change of hidden layer nodes, the output weights need to

© Springer Nature Switzerland AG 2018
V. Kůrková et al. (Eds.): ICANN 2018, LNCS 11140, pp. 3–13, 2018.
https://doi.org/10.1007/978-3-030-01421-6_1

be recalculated, so these techniques considerably increase the computation complexity of ELM. In [11], the method called orthogonal projections to latent structures, which is a combination of orthogonal signal correction and partial least squares, is proposed, but it still leads to a tedious iterative procedure. Complicated methods of probability distribution optimization are proposed in [12].

The main contribution of this paper is to show that rank-revealing transformations, known since the previous century, are effective tools to indicate neurons responsible for numerical collinearity among the LSM regression basis. Such "non-contributing" neurons may be eliminated or modified so that they are useful in the approximation. In any case, the final basis for LMS regression is orthogonal and the output weights may be obtained by solving well-conditioned LMS problem.

The standard ELM is described in Sect. 2. Instead of the most popular random generation of weights, the application of low discrepancy sequences (LDS) [13, 14] is considered. Rank-Revealing Orthogonal Decomposition is introduced and applied in Sect. 3, while the proposed neuron modification procedure is presented in Sect. 4. The paper ends with numerical experiments and conclusions.

2　Basic Extreme Learning Machine

The standard Extreme Learning Machine applied for modelling (regression) problems may be considered as a combination of a nonlinear mapping from the input space into the feature space and a linear least-squares regression. The training data for a n-input ELM form a batch of N samples:

$$\{(x_i, t_i), \quad x_i \in R^n, \, t_i \in R, \, i = 1, \ldots, N\}, \tag{1}$$

where x_i denote the inputs and t_i denote the desired outputs, which form the target (column) vector $T = \begin{bmatrix} t_1 & \cdots & t_N \end{bmatrix}^T$. It is assumed that each input is normalized to the interval [0,1].

The nonlinear mapping is performed by a single layer of hidden neurons with infinitely differentiable activation functions. The "projection-based neurons" are used most commonly. Each n-dimensional input is projected by the input layer weights $w_k^T = [w_{k,1} \ldots w_{k,n}]$, $k = 1, \ldots M$ and the bias b_k into the k-th hidden neuron input. Next, a nonlinear transformation h_k, called activation function (AF) of the neuron is applied to obtain the neuron output. The transformation of a batch of N samples by the hidden layer is represented as an $N \times M$ matrix:

$$H = H_{N \times M} = \left[h_i \left(w_i^T x_j + b_i \right) \right]_{\substack{j = 1, \ldots, N \\ i = 1, \ldots, M}}. \tag{2}$$

It is assumed that the number of samples is greater than the number of neurons: $N > M$. The impact of the selected type of AFs on the network performance is limited, and therefore sigmoid AFs remain among the most widely used.

According to the standard approach, the weights and biases are generated at random, using any continuous probability distribution [2]. Using the uniform distribution in $[-1, 1]$ to generate the weights and the biases is the standard procedure. Recently, an application of Low-Discrepancy Sequences (LDS) [13, 14] was proposed to replace the random generation of neurons' parameters. The discrepancy measures the uniformity of a sequence X of N points in the hypercube $P = [0, 1]^n$, and is defined as

$$D_N(X) = \sup_B \left| \frac{N_o(X, B)}{N} - L(B) \right|, \tag{3}$$

where B is any hypercube $[a_1, b_1] \times \ldots \times [a_n, b_n] \subset P$, $N_o(X, B)$ denotes the number of points from X belonging to B and $L(B)$ is the Lebesgue measure (volume) of B [13]. So, low discrepancy means that the number of points in a subset is as proportional as possible to the volume. Numerical procedures to generate various LDSs are offered by popular software packages. For example, easy generation of Halton and Sobol sequences [13, 14] is possible in Matlab. The distance among any LDS and a random set tends to zero if the number of points increases (Fig. 1), so the universal approximation property of a standard (randomly-generated) ELM [15] is generalized to the deterministic case with weights and biases taken from an LDS [16] (Fig. 2).

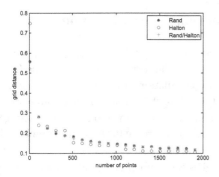
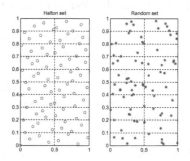

Fig. 1. Maximal distance (mean in 20 experiments) to the nearest neighbour: * - inside the random set, o – inside the Halton set, + from the Halton set to the random set. Points are generated in the 3-dimensional cube.

Fig. 2. 80 points generated from Halton sequence and from uniform distribution in 2 dimensions.

Hence, deterministic creation of neurons' weights and biases from an LDS is an interesting alternative and allows to describe features of an ELM without repeating numerous experiments.

The output weights β are found by minimizing the approximation error

$$E_C = \|\beta\|^2 + C\|H\beta - T\|^2, \tag{4}$$

where $C > 0$ is a design parameter added to improve the conditioning of the problem. This approach is called 'Tikhonow regularization' [17]. For $C \to \infty$ the problem becomes equivalent to the minimization of

$$E_\infty = \|H\beta - T\|^2. \tag{5}$$

The output weights, which minimize the regularized criterion (4) are

$$\beta_{Copt} = \left(\frac{1}{C}I + H^T H\right)^{-1} H^T T, \tag{6}$$

while (5) is minimized by

$$\beta_{opt} = H^+ T, \tag{7}$$

where H^+ is the Moore–Penrose generalized inverse of matrix H:

$$H^+ = \left(H^T H\right)^{-1} H^T. \tag{8}$$

3   ELM with Rank-Revealing Orthogonal Decomposition

When a large number of hidden layer neurons is selected, high correlations and multicollinearity always exist among the columns of the hidden layer output matrix H. It may lead to ill-condition of the Moore–Penrose calculation or cause overfitting of the final model. The high condition number of $H^T H$ is the main reason of numerical difficulties in ELM implementation. The Tikhonov regularization is supposed to improve this situation - the coefficient C is selected to decrease the condition number of $\frac{1}{C}I + H^T H$, but unavoidably degrades the approximation accuracy.

The "numerical rank" of a matrix is defined as the number of singular values larger than a certain threshold r.

Rank-Revealing Orthogonal Decomposition, introduced in [18, 19] allows to eliminate multicollinearity among columns of H. Rank-revealing decomposition provides information about the numerical rank of the matrix. For any numerical rank threshold r, the algorithm called RRQR (Rank-Revealing Q-R factorization) allows to represent the column-permuted matrix H as

$$H[P_1 \quad P_2] = [Q_1 \quad Q_2 \quad Q_3] \begin{bmatrix} R_1 & R_2 \\ 0 & R_3 \\ 0 & 0 \end{bmatrix}, \tag{9}$$

where P_1, P_2 are permutation matrices, $Q = [Q_1 \quad Q_2 \quad Q_3]$ is an orthogonal matrix, R_1, R_3 are upper-triangular matrices and R_1 is a full-numerical-rank matrix with respect to the threshold r, while maximal singular value of R_3 is not bigger than r. Therefore, after calculation of the rank-revealing QR factorization, the orthogonal matrix

$$Q_1 = HP_1R_1^{-1} \tag{10}$$

may be used to replace H. The multiplication by the permutation matrix P_1 represents selection of the neurons that contribute to the numerical rank. Then, the multiplication by R_1^{-1} provides normalization such that $cond\ Q_1^T Q_1 = 1$. Finally, the optimal output weights are obtained from

$$\beta_{opt} = \left(Q_1^T Q_1\right)^{-1} Q_1^T T. \tag{11}$$

Some neurons are eliminated permanently from the initial set of neurons, hence, the final number of neurons may be smaller than the initially planned. Therefore, the effort to select parameters of excluded neurons is spoiled, but all remaining neurons contribute to the effective approximation. The final form of the network is presented in Fig. 3.

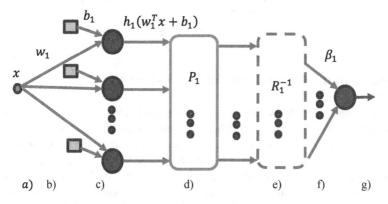

Fig. 3. The modified ELM: (a) input, (b) weights and biases, (c) hidden neurons, (d) elimination of neurons, (e) normalization, (f) output weights, (g) output.

The applied algorithms (RRQR and triangular matrix inversion) are available in various software packages. The computational complexity of the proposed modification is $O(M^3)$. All operations are done "without seeing the data" and the final training of the network (calculation of β_{opt}) is done in one step. The only additional parameter is the numerical rank threshold r.

The proposed procedure may lead to stagnation of the number of neurons, limited by the numerical rank condition, in spite of the user's plan to use more neurons. Therefore RRQR factorization may be used to recognize "non-contributing" neurons. Such neurons are indicated by the permutation matrix P_2 and their parameters must be modified. The modification is discussed in the next section, and the pseudo-code for the complete design procedure is presented in Fig. 4.

1. Select weights and biases for M hidden neurons.
2. Select the numerical rank threshold r.
3. Calculate the matrix H using neurons parameters and input samples.
4. While **LoopCounter** < **Max** do
   4.1 Perform the RRQR factorization of the matrix H with the numerical rank threshold r.
   4.2 Use the permutation matrix P_2 to recognize the non-contributing neurons.
   4.3 Modify the weights and biases of the non-contributing neurons.
   4.4 Calculate the new matrix H using new neurons' parameters and input samples.
   4.5 Increment the **LoopCounter** and go to 4.1.
5. Perform the RRQR factorization of the matrix H with the numerical rank threshold r.
6. Eliminate the non-contributing neurons and calculate the optimal output weights from (11).

Fig. 4. The pseudo-code for the modified ELM

4   Modification of Non-contributing Neurons

According to step 4.3 of the design procedure presented in Fig. 4, weights and biases of the selected neurons need to be modified. The aim of this modification is to change columns of the matrix H which do not contribute to the numerical rank for the given threshold, i.e. the columns in HP_2. The modification has to preserve the nature of weights selection – at random, using a continuous probability distribution, or from an LDS, in a compact hypercube. Several approaches are possible, but it is well-known that multicollinearity of columns in the matrix H may be caused by an insufficient variance of the AFs. The easy way to enhance the variance of sigmoid AFs was proposed in [4–6] and may be applied to modify the weights and biases of the non-contributing neurons.

The first step to enlarge variation of sigmoid activation functions is to increase the range of weights. The weights must be large enough to expose the nonlinearity of the sigmoid AF, and small enough to prevent saturation. Therefore, the already selected weights of non-contributing neurons will be multiplied by a random factor taken from the interval $[q, p]$. The values $[q, p] = [3, 10]$ are suitable.

Next, the biases are selected to guarantee that the range of a sigmoid function is sufficiently large. The minimal value of the sigmoid function

$$h_k(x) = \frac{1}{1 + exp\left(-\left(w_k^T x + b_k\right)\right)}, x \in [0, 1]^n, \tag{12}$$

is achieved at the vertex selected according to the following rules:

$$w_{k,i} > 0 \Rightarrow x_i = 0, w_{k,i} < 0 \Rightarrow x_i = 1 \ i = 1, \ldots, n, \tag{13}$$

and equals

$$h_{k,min} = \frac{1}{1 + exp\left(-\left(\sum_{i:w_{k,i}<0} w_{k,i} + b_k\right)\right)}. \tag{14}$$

The maximal value is attained at the vertex defined by

$$w_{k,i} > 0 \Rightarrow x_i = 1, w_{k,i} < 0 \Rightarrow x_i = 0 \ i = 1, \ldots, n, \tag{15}$$

and is

$$h_{k,max} = \frac{1}{1 + exp\left(-\left(\sum_{i:w_{k,i}>0} w_{k,i} + b_k\right)\right)}. \tag{16}$$

Therefore, to get $h_{k,min} < r_1, h_{k,max} > r_2$ for given $0 < r_1 < r_2 < 1$ requires to have

$$\bar{b} := -\sum_{i:w_{k,i}>0} w_{k,i} - ln\left(\frac{1}{r_2} - 1\right) < b_k < -ln\left(\frac{1}{r_1} - 1\right) - \sum_{i:w_{k,i}<0} w_{k,i} := \tilde{b}. \tag{17}$$

As the initial bias $b_{k\,old}$ was selected from the interval $[-1,1]$, it is modified according to the linear transformation

$$b_{k\,new} = \frac{1}{2}(\tilde{b} - \bar{b})b_{k\,old} + \frac{1}{2}(\tilde{b} + \bar{b}), \tag{18}$$

providing the chance for $\bar{b} < b_{k\,new} < \tilde{b}$.

5 Numerical Examples

The two-dimensional function

$$z = sin(2\pi(x_1 + x_2)), x_1, x_2 \in [0, 1] \tag{19}$$

is considered. 200 samples selected at random constitute the training set, and 100 samples are use as the test set. The surface (18) is plotted in Fig. 5.

In all experiments, the initial values of the hidden layer neurons weights and biases are selected from the Halton sequence. First, only orthogonalization-based elimination of the non-contributing neurons is applied, and this approach (Orthogonalized Extreme Learning Machine - OELM) is compared with the standard ELM. The numerical rank

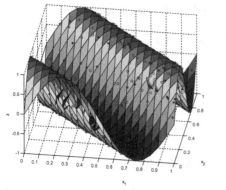

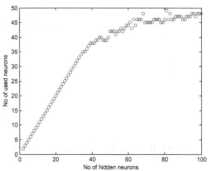

Fig. 5. The surface (18) with with the training (*circles*) and the testing (*stars*) data.

Fig. 6. Reduction of non-contributing neurons.

threshold is 10^{-9}. As it is presented in Fig. 6, the number of the finally used neurons is stabilized below 50, although up to 100 neurons were planned to be used initially. The achieved modeling accuracy is almost the same as obtained with the standard approach with 100 neurons (Fig. 7) and the conditioning of the output weights calculation is far better (Fig. 8).

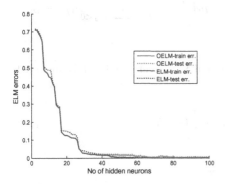

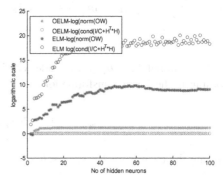

Fig. 7. Training and test errors of the ELM with reduced number of neurons (OLM) and the standard ELM.

Fig. 8. The condition coefficient and the norm of output weights in OELM and standard ELM.

Of course, the increase of the numerical rank threshold reduces the number of the finally used neurons and the approximation errors increase. If the threshold equals 10^{-3} the number of neurons is reduced below 15 and the errors stabilize at ~ 0.5, which is far too large. Applying the procedure enhancing the variation of the AFs ($r_1 = 0.1$, $r_2 = 0.9$), it is possible to increase the number of finally used neurons and to reduce the approximation errors, preserving numerical rank threshold of 10^{-3}. In Fig. 9 the number of finally used neurons is presented after the first, second and third application of the variation enhancing procedure. In this case, the errors of the modified ELM are smaller

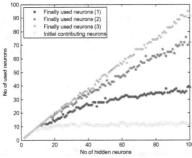

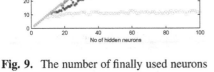

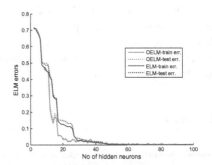

Fig. 9. The number of finally used neurons after the first, second and third application of enhancing variation procedure.

Fig. 10. Training and test errors of the ELM with reduced number of neurons and enhancing variation procedure (OLM) and the standard ELM.

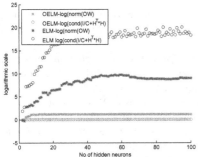

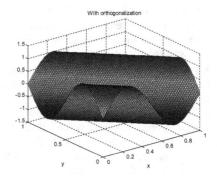

Fig. 11. The condition coefficient and the norm of output weights in ELM with neurons reduction and enhancing variation modification (OELM) compared with the standard ELM.

Fig. 12. The surface generated by the trained ELM.

than the standard ELM (Fig. 10), while it is still guaranteed that the condition number equals 1 and the norm of the output weights is minimized (Figs. 11 and 12).

6 Conclusions

The rank-revealing QR decomposition is an effective tool to indicate the neurons in ELM which do not contribute to the effective approximation due to multicollinearity of the columns in matrix H. The indicated neurons may be eliminated and the remaining neurons may be linearly transformed to get the orthogonal basis for the final linear mean square problem, which provides the output weights. If this procedure generates a too small number of neurons to get the desired approximation accuracy, the indicated non-contributing neurons may be modified to enhance variation of AFs. The approach presented in Sect. 4 re-scales previously chosen weights and biases and increases the number of contributing neurons. The numerical rank threshold is the only additional parameter of the ELM design and it allows to control numerical properties of the network training effectively.

References

1. Huang, G., Huang, G.-B., Song, S., You, K.: Trends in extreme learning machines: a review. Neural Netw. **61**(1), 32–48 (2015)
2. Huang, G.-B., Zhu, Q.-Y., Siew, C.-K.: Extreme learning machine: theory and applications. Neurocomputing **70**(1–3), 489–501 (2006)
3. Akusok, A., Bjork, K.M., Miche, Y., Lendasse, A.: High-performance extreme learning machines: a complete toolbox for big data applications. IEEE Access **3**, 1011–1025 (2015)
4. Kabziński, J.: Extreme learning machine with enhanced variation of activation functions. In: IJCCI 2016 - Proceedings of the 8th International Joint Conference on Computational Intelligence, vol. 3, pp. 77–82 (2016)
5. Kabzinski, J.: Extreme learning machine with diversified neurons. In: CINTI 2016 - 17th IEEE International Symposium on Computational Intelligence and Informatics: Proceedings, pp. 181-186 (2016)
6. Kabziński, J.: Is extreme learning machine effective for multisource friction modeling? In: Chbeir, R., Manolopoulos, Y., Maglogiannis, I., Alhajj, R. (eds.) AIAI 2015. IAICT, vol. 458, pp. 318–333. Springer, Cham (2015). https://doi.org/10.1007/978-3-319-23868-5_23
7. Miche, Y., Sorjamaa, A., Bas, P., Simula, O., Jutten, C., Lendasse, A.: OP-ELM: optimally pruned extreme learning machine. IEEE Trans. Neural Netw. **21**(1), 158–162 (2010)
8. Rong, H.J., Ong, Y.S., Tan, A.H., Zhu, Z.X.: A fast pruned-extreme learning machine for classification problem. Neurocomputing **72**(1–3), 359–366 (2008)
9. Huang, G.-B., Chen, L.: Enhanced random search based incremental extreme learning machine. Neurocomputing **71**(16–17), 3460–3468 (2008)
10. Feng, G., Bin Huang, G., Lin, Q., Gay, R.: Error minimized extreme learning machine with growth of hidden nodes and incremental learning. IEEE Trans. Neural Netw., **20**(8), 1352–1357 (2009)
11. Zhang, R., Xu, M., Han, M., Li, H.: Multivariate chaotic time series prediction using based on improved Extreme Learning Machine. In: Proceedings of the 36th Chinese Control Conference, 26–28 July 2017, Dalian, China, pp. 4006–4011 (2017)
12. Han, H., Gan, L., He, L.: Improved variations for Extreme Learning Machine: space embedded ELM and optimal distribution ELM. In: 20th International Conference on Information Fusion, Fusion 2017 - Proceedings, no. 2 (2017)
13. Dick, J., Pillichshammer, F.: Digital Nets and Sequences: Discrepancy Theory and Quasi-Monte Carlo Integration. Cambridge University Press (2010)
14. Niederreiter, H.: Random Number Generation and Quasi-Monte Carlo Methods. SIAM, Philadelphia (1992)
15. Bin Huang, G., Chen, L., Siew, C.K.: Universal approximation using incremental constructive feedforward networks with random hidden nodes. IEEE Trans. Neural Netw. **17**(4), 879–892 (2006)
16. Cervellera, C., Macciò, D.: Low-discrepancy points for deterministic assignment of hidden weights in extreme learning machines. IEEE Trans. Neural Netw. Learn. Syst. **27**(4), 891–896 (2016)

17. Tikhonov, A.N., Goncharsky, A., Stepanov, V.V., Yagola, A.G.: Numerical Methods for the Solution of Ill-posed Problems. Kluwer Academic Publishers, Dordrecht (1995)
18. Fierro, R.D., Hansen, P.Ch.: Low-rank revealing UTV decompositions. Numer. Algorithms, **15**, 37–55 (1997)
19. Chan, T.F.: Rank revealing QR factorizations. Linear Algebra Appl. **88**(89), 67–82 (1987)

An Improved CAD Framework for Digital Mammogram Classification Using Compound Local Binary Pattern and Chaotic Whale Optimization-Based Kernel Extreme Learning Machine

Figlu Mohanty[✉], Suvendu Rup, and Bodhisattva Dash

Image and Video Processing Laboratory, IIIT Bhubaneswar, Bhubaneswar, India
figlu92@gmail.com, suvendu@iiit-bh.ac.in, bdash.fac@gmail.com

Abstract. The morbidity and mortality rate of breast cancer still continues to remain high among women across the world. This figure can be reduced if the cancer is identified at its early stage. A Computer-aided diagnosis (CAD) system is an efficient computerized tool used to analyze the mammograms for finding cancer in the breast and to reach a decision with maximum accuracy. The presented work aims at developing a CAD model which can classify the mammograms as normal or abnormal, and further, benign or malignant accurately. In the present model, CLAHE is used for image pre-processing, compound local binary pattern (CM-LBP) for feature extraction followed by principal component analysis (PCA) for feature reduction. Then, a chaotic whale optimization-based kernel extreme learning machine (CWO-KELM) is utilized to classify the mammograms as normal/abnormal and benign/malignant. The present model achieves the highest accuracy of 100% and 99.48% for MIAS and DDSM, respectively.

Keywords: Mammograms · Compound local binary pattern
Chaotic map · Whale optimization algorithm
Kernel extreme learning machine

1 Introduction

According to the statistics of cancer, the incidence and mortality scenario of breast cancer is increasing day by day. The world health organization [17] makes an estimation of 21 million cancer cases by the year 2030 which was only 12.7 million in 2008. 0.537 millions of women and 0.477 millions of males in India were diagnosed with breast cancer in the year 2012 [19]. So, it becomes utmost necessary to design an efficient detection and diagnosis tool in order to reduce the mortality rates among women and men. In this context, mammography is the most effective and reliable tool to detect the abnormalities in the breast at its

© Springer Nature Switzerland AG 2018
V. Kůrková et al. (Eds.): ICANN 2018, LNCS 11140, pp. 14–23, 2018.
https://doi.org/10.1007/978-3-030-01421-6_2

earliest stage. A computer-aided diagnosis (CAD) system combines various principles of image analysis, machine learning, and pattern recognition approaches to examine the crucial information present in the mammograms. CAD is a fast and cost-effective system to assist the medical practitioners or radiologists to detect and diagnose cancer. Designing a CAD system with high efficiency is important as well as a challenging task.

Various researchers have developed different CAD models to detect or diagnose the abnormalities in the mammograms. Yasser *et al.* [21] proposed a CAD system which extracts features using discrete wavelet transform (DWT), contourlet transform (CT), and local binary pattern (LBP) reporting the best accuracy of 98.63%. Bajaj *et al.* [4] proposed a novel approach using bi-dimensional empirical mode decomposition (BEMD) and least-square SVM for mammogram classification. Chithra *et al.* [5] used wavelet entropy and ensemble classifiers using k-nearest neighbor (k-NN) and SVM. Singh *et al.* [24] proposed a wavelet-based center-symmetric local binary pattern technique to extract the features from the mammograms yielding an accuracy of 97.3%. Few more recently proposed CAD systems can be referred in [8,14,20,26]. Motivated by the previously developed CAD schemes, the proposed work aims at designing an efficient and robust CAD system for accurate diagnosis of breast cancer.

The structure of the remaining article is as follows: Sect. 2 elaborates the proposed CAD model. Section 3 analyses the results obtained with the proposed model. Lastly, Sect. 4 presents the concluding remarks.

2   Proposed Methodology

In the present work, initially, the desired ROIs are generated from the original mammograms using simple cropping approach. In case of abnormal mammograms, the cropping is done using the given ground truth information about the position and radius of the abnormal regions. However, for normal mammograms, cropping is done on any arbitrary location to get the ROI. Once the ROIs are obtained, the next step is to apply the CM-LBP technique to extract the texture features from the ROIs. Thereafter, PCA is applied to reduce the size of the feature vector followed by CWO-KELM to classify the mammograms as normal or abnormal, and further, benign or malignant. A detailed diagram of the proposed CAD model is illustrated in Fig. 1.

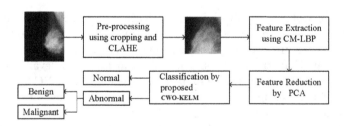

Fig. 1. Block diagram of the proposed CAD model

2.1   Pre-processing Using CLAHE

Pre-processing of the ROIs is considered to be a vital step before performing any further modules in a CAD system. As some of the images collected from the datasets are of low contrast, so it is required to enhance the contrast of such images. Hence, in the present work, contrast limited adaptive histogram equalization (CLAHE) [18] is utilized to improve the quality of the low-contrast images.

2.2   Feature Extraction Using Compound Local Binary Pattern (CM-LBP)

The original local binary pattern operator ignores the magnitude of the difference between the center pixel value and its neighboring pixel values resulting in an inconsistent code. So, to overcome the issues of LBP, CM-LBP is introduced [1]. In CM-LBP, a 2-bit code is utilized to encode the local texture information of an image where the first bit indicates the sign of the difference between the center pixel and its neighboring pixel values, and the second bit represents the magnitude of the difference with respect to a threshold value T_{avg}. The term T_{avg} is the average magnitude of the difference between the center pixel and its corresponding neighbors in the local neighborhood window. If P_n is one of the neighboring pixels, and P_c is the center pixel, then the mathematical expression of the 2-bit code is as follows:

$$s(i_n, i_m) = \begin{cases} 00 & P_n - P_c < 0 \ and \ |P_n - P_c| \le T_{avg} \\ 01 & P_n - P_c < 0 \ and \ |P_n - P_c| > T_{avg} \\ 10 & P_n - P_c \ge 0 \ and \ |P_n - P_c| \le T_{avg} \\ 11 & otherwise \end{cases} \qquad (1)$$

This $C(P_n, P_c)$ generates 16-bit codes for the eight neighbors which is again split into two 8-bit codes, one for the diagonal neighbors and another for non-diagonal neighbors. Then, two different histograms are plotted for the two different groups and are combined for generating the CLBP.

2.3   Feature Reduction Using PCA

The number of features obtained from the feature extraction module is quite large and to prevent the 'curse of dimensionality' issue, it is needed to lessen the size of the feature vector which also makes the task of classifier simple. In addition, out of all the features, some of them are not relevant. To obtain the set of relevant features, the PCA technique is employed. PCA generates a reduced set of features by transforming the high-dimensional data to a set of data having low dimension retaining maximum variance of the original data. This transforms produces a set of linearly uncorrelated data which are called as principal components (PCs). A deep insight about PCA can be referred in [6,9].

2.4   Classification Using CWO-KELM

Chaotic Whale Optimization: The whale optimizer proposed in [16] is an optimization approach based on the hunting behaviour of the humpback whales, known as bubble-net hunting. The WOA technique considers the current best solution to be the prey or is near to the optimal solution. When the target prey is defined, the rest of the whales hence update their locations to move towards the best search candidate with the increment of the iterations. This can be mathematically represented as:

$$\overrightarrow{W}(i+1) = \overrightarrow{W^*}(i) - \overrightarrow{A}.\overrightarrow{D} \tag{2}$$

where

$$\overrightarrow{D} = \left| \overrightarrow{C}.\overrightarrow{W^*(i)} - \overrightarrow{W(i)} \right| \tag{3}$$

$\overrightarrow{A}$ and $\overrightarrow{C}$ are the two coefficient vectors and can be defined using Eqs. (4) and (5). W^* and W represent the location of the prey and the whale, respectively at the current iteration i.

$$\overrightarrow{A} = 2a.\overrightarrow{r}.a \tag{4}$$

$$\overrightarrow{C} = 2.\overrightarrow{r} \tag{5}$$

where $\overrightarrow{r}$ is a random vector ranging between [0,1]. a linearly decreases from 2 to 0 during the iterations and can be represented using Eq. (6).

$$a = 2 - i.\frac{2}{maxiter} \tag{6}$$

However, the humpback whales move around the target prey through a shrinking circle and also along a spiral-like pathway at the same time. Hence, a probability of 0.5 is assumed to select either the shrinking path or the spiral path in order to update the location of the whales. The mathematical representation of this behaviour can be expressed as follows:

$$W(i+1) = \begin{cases} \overrightarrow{W^*}(i) - \overrightarrow{A}.\overrightarrow{D} & p \leq 0.5 \\ \overrightarrow{D'}.e^{bt}.cos(2\pi t) + \overrightarrow{W^*}(i) & p \geq 0.5 \end{cases} \tag{7}$$

where

$$\left| \overrightarrow{D'} = \overrightarrow{W^*(i)} - \overrightarrow{W(i)} \right| \tag{8}$$

b represents a constant which defines the shape of the logarithmic spiral, t symbolizes a random number ranging between $[-1, 1]$ whereas p is taken randomly between $[0, 1]$.

The value of the parameter $\overrightarrow{A}$ can be randomly initialized with $\overrightarrow{A} > 1$ or $\overrightarrow{A} < -1$ to find the target prey (exploration stage) and to make the search candidates go away from a reference whale. The mathematical formulation for this exploration stage can be defined as:

$$\overrightarrow{D} = \left| \overrightarrow{C}.\overrightarrow{W_{rand}(i)} - \overrightarrow{W(i)} \right| \tag{9}$$

$$\vec{W}(i+1) = \overrightarrow{W_{rand}}(i) - \vec{A}.\vec{D} \tag{10}$$

where $\overrightarrow{W_{rand}}$ is a random whale's position vector selected from the current population of whales. For detail understanding of WOA, readers are referred to [16].

Though the convergence rate of WOA is considerably good, it still cannot perform well in searching the global optimum solution which influences the convergence speed of the technique. Hence, to overcome such issue, in this article, a chaos-based WOA technique is adopted. The chaotic sequence has three important properties, namely, ergodicity, quasi-stochastic, and sensitivity to original conditions which helps to search the solution at a higher speed as compared to that of the stochastic search [22]. The dynamic property of the chaotic maps makes them acceptable in various optimization algorithms to explore the search more robustly [27]. Almost every meta-heuristic technique achieves randomness of the stochastic components by utilizing a probability distribution. However, it can be more promising if such random values are replaced with the chaotic sequences. In the present work, a logistic chaotic function [2] is incorporated in the WOA algorithm. The mathematical representation of the logistic chaos is given by:

$$L_{i+1} = cL_i(1 - L_i), \quad c = 4 \tag{11}$$

Classification Using Proposed CWO-KELM: Extreme learning machine (ELM) is a type of single hidden layer feed-forward network (SLFN) proposed by Huang et al. [13], which has been utilized in many research domains [3,10, 23]. Unlike other traditional algorithms like BPNN [15] and SVM [7], ELM is capable of achieving higher classification accuracy with faster convergence rate. In this work, one of the variants of ELM referred to as kernel ELM (KELM) is used as it is capable of proving improved results than that of the conventional ELM [12]. In KELM, the kernel function replaces the random feature mapping of the traditional ELM and thus results in more stable output weights. The kernel ELM uses two important parameters, namely, penalty parameter (C) and the kernel parameter (γ) to obtain the final output weights. However, finding the optimal values for the aforementioned parameters is a challenging task. This motivates the authors to exploit an evolutionary algorithm to get the optimal values for these two parameters to obtain better convergence. In the present work, a chaotic whale optimization algorithm is incorporated with KELM to find the optimized values of C and γ.

Prior to the classification module, the whole dataset is divided into training, validation, and testing set using a 10-fold stratified cross-validation (SCV) to prevent the over-fitting problem. The flowchart of the working principle of the proposed CWO-KELM model is represented in Fig. 2. In addition to this, the steps involved in the proposed CWO-KELM are given in the following:

1. Start the process with random initialization of candidate solution in the population so that each solution has a set of C and γ as

$$K = [C_1, C_2, ..., C_j, \gamma_1, \gamma_2, ..., \gamma_j] \tag{12}$$

C and γ are initialized in a range of $[2^{-8}, 2^{-6}, 2^{-4}, ..., 2^8]$.
2. Initialize the values of A, p, C, a, and t.
3. For each of the candidate solutions, determine the fitness value (classification accuracy) using KELM. The fitness value is calculated on the validation set in order to prevent the over-fitting issue.
4. Sort the whales in descending order and select the best whale position having the highest fitness value.
5. Update the values of A and p using the chaotic map using Eq. 11.
6. Update the position of candidate whales based on values of A and p and find the position of the best whale.
   - If $p < 0.5$ and $|A| < 1$, then update the position of the current whale using Eq. 2.

   - If $p < 0.5$ and $|A| \geq 1$, then find a random whale and update the position of the current whale with respect to the random whale using the Eq. 10.

   - If $p \geq 0.5$, then update the position of then current whale using the Eq. 7.
7. Generate the new best whale as

$$W(i+1) = \begin{cases} W(i+1) \; if f(W(i+1)) > f(W(i)) \\ W(i) \qquad\qquad otherwise \end{cases} \tag{13}$$

where $f(W(i+1))$ and $f(W(i))$ denote the fitness value of the updated whale and previous whale, respectively.
8. Find the out-of-bound cases in the new solution and limit them in a range of $[2^{-8}, 2^8]$ as

$$W(i+1) = \begin{cases} 2^{-8} \; if \; W(i+1) < 2^{-8} \\ 2^8 \quad if \; W(i+1) > 2^8 \end{cases} \tag{14}$$

9. Repeat steps 3–8 till the predefined number of iterations. Finally, the optimal values of C and γ are obtained and validated on the test set to get the overall performance of the proposed CWO-KELM-based model.

3 Experimental Results and Analysis

The proposed CAD model is experimented on two standard benchmark datasets, namely, MIAS [25] and DDSM [11]. A total of 314 and 1500 images are collected from MIAS and DDSM, respectively. The collected images are first classified as normal or abnormal, and further, benign or malignant using the proposed CAD system. The performance of the proposed model is evaluated in terms of different performance metrics, namely, accuracy, sensitivity, specificity, area under curve (AUC), and receiver operating characteristics (ROC) curve. In addition to this, the proposed scheme is compared against some of the recently designed CAD schemes.

Prior to the feature extraction module, ROIs are segmented from the unnecessary background regions using cropping. Using the ground truth information regarding the coordinates of the abnormalities in the images, ROIs of

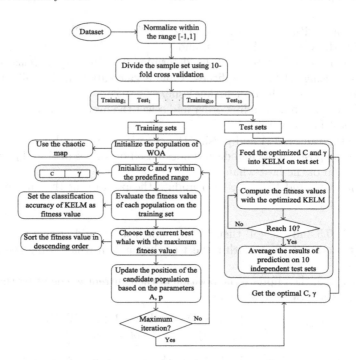

Fig. 2. Flowchart of the proposed CWO-KELM

size 256×256 are generated. After cropping, the ROIs are pre-processed using CLAHE to enhance the contrast. Then, CLBP technique is applied on the extracted ROIs to obtain the feature matrix. Applying CLBP, a feature matrix of size $s \times F$ is obtained, where s and F indicate the number of ROIs and the number of generated features, respectively. In this work, 512 number of features (F) are generated from CLBP which is quite large. So, to reduce the size of the feature vector and make the classification simpler, PCA is utilized which reduces the number of features from 512 to 14 preserving 99% of the variance of the original data. The reduced features are passed to the proposed CWO-KELM classifier for classifying the mammograms as normal or abnormal followed by benign or malignant.

Table 1 depicts the various performance results attained with the proposed CAD model. From the table, it can be noticed that the highest accuracy achieved for MIAS dataset is 100% in both normal-abnormal and benign-malignant classifications. Similarly, for the DDSM dataset, an accuracy of 99.48% and 98.61% is achieved for normal-abnormal, and benign-malignant classification, respectively. Additionally, the ROC graphs generated by the proposed classifier are plotted in Figs. 3 and 4 showing the corresponding values of AUC for MIAS and DDSM datasets, respectively.

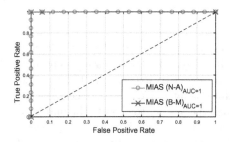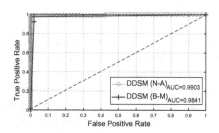

Fig. 3. ROC of MIAS   **Fig. 4.** ROC of DDSM

Further, to add more justification, the proposed CAD model is compared with five recently developed CAD schemes. The comparison against the other schemes is made in terms of classification accuracy and is depicted in Table 2.

Table 1. Performance measures obtained by the proposed CWO-KELM-based model; N-Normal, A-Abnormal, B-Benign, M-Malignant

Dataset	Performance measures	CLAHE+CLBP+ PCA+CWO-KELM	
		N-A	B-M
MIAS	Sensitivity	1	1
	Specificity	1	1
	Accuracy (%)	100	100
DDSM	Sensitivity	0.9945	0.9886
	Specificity	0.9912	0.9869
	Accuracy (%)	99.48	98.61

Table 2. Comparison with some of the other existing CAD schemes

Reference	Proposed scheme	Classification accuracy (%)
[21]	Statistical Features+LBP+SVM	98.63 (DDSM)
[26]	Firefly+ANN	95.23 (DDSM)
[14]	Parasitic metric learning	96.7 (MIAS), 97.4 (DDSM)
[4]	BEMD+SVM	95 (MIAS)
[24]	WCS-LBP+SVM-RFE+Random Forest	97.25 (MIAS)
Proposed	**CLAHE+CLBP+PCA+CWO-KELM**	**100 (MIAS), 98.61 (DDSM)**

4 Conclusion

In the present work, an enhanced CAD system has been proposed for breast cancer classification in digital mammograms. Initially, CLAHE is used to enhance the low-contrast images. Then, CLBP is employed to extract the texture features followed by a feature reduction module using PCA. The reduced feature set is then passed through a CWO-KELM-based classifier to classify the mammograms. The proposed model has been experimented on two benchmark datasets, namely, MIAS and DDSM. Furthermore, the performance of the proposed model has been compared with five recent schemes and it has been noticed that the proposed model with only 14 features achieves improved results over the competent schemes. The high success rate with respect to the accuracy of the proposed scheme helps radiologists to make an accurate diagnosis decision to reduce unnecessary biopsies.

References

1. Ahmed, F., Hossain, E., Bari, A., Hossen, M.S.: Compound local binary pattern (CLBP) for rotation invariant texture classification. Int. J. Comput. Appl. **33**(6), 5–10 (2011)
2. Alatas, B.: Chaotic bee colony algorithms for global numerical optimization. Expert. Syst. Appl. **37**(8), 5682–5687 (2010)
3. Bai, Z., Huang, G.B., Wang, D., Wang, H., Westover, M.B.: Sparse extreme learning machine for classification. IEEE Trans. Cybern. **44**(10), 1858–1870 (2014)
4. Bajaj, V., Pawar, M., Meena, V.K., Kumar, M., Sengur, A., Guo, Y.: Computer-aided diagnosis of breast cancer using bi-dimensional empirical mode decomposition. Neural Comput. Appl. 1–9 (2017)
5. Chithra Devi, M., Audithan, S.: Analysis of different types of entropy measures for breast cancer diagnosis using ensemble classification. Biomed. Res. **28**(7), 3182–3186 (2017)
6. Christopher, M.B.: Pattern Recognition and Machine Learning. Springer, New York (2016)
7. Cortes, C., Vapnik, V.: Support-vector networks. Mach. Learn. **20**(3), 273–297 (1995)
8. Dhahbi, S., Barhoumi, W., Kurek, J., Swiderski, B., Kruk, M., Zagrouba, E.: False-positive reduction in computer-aided mass detection using mammographic texture analysis and classification. Comput. Meth. Prog. Biomed. **160**, 75–83 (2018)
9. Duda, R.O., Hart, P.E., Stork, D.G.: Pattern Classification. Wiley, New York (2012)
10. Han, M., Liu, B.: Ensemble of extreme learning machine for remote sensing image classification. Neurocomputing **149**, 65–70 (2015)
11. Heath, M., Bowyer, K., Kopans, D., Moore, R., Kegelmeyer, W.P.: The digital database for screening mammography. In: Proceedings of the 5th International Workshop on Digital Mammography, pp. 212–218. Medical Physics Publishing (2000)
12. Huang, G.B., Wang, D.H., Lan, Y.: Extreme learning machines: a survey. Int. J. Mach. Learn. Cybern. **2**(2), 107–122 (2011)

13. Huang, G.B., Zhu, Q.Y., Siew, C.K.: Extreme learning machine: theory and applications. Neurocomputing **70**(1–3), 489–501 (2006)
14. Jiao, Z., Gao, X., Wang, Y., Li, J.: A parasitic metric learning net for breast mass classification based on mammography. Pattern Recogn. **75**, 292–301 (2018)
15. Junguo, H., Guomo, Z., Xiaojun, X.: Using an improved back propagation neural network to study spatial distribution of sunshine illumination from sensor network data. Ecol. Model. **266**, 86–96 (2013)
16. Mirjalili, S., Lewis, A.: The whale optimization algorithm. Adv. Eng. Softw. **95**, 51–67 (2016)
17. World Health Organization: Burden: mortality, morbidity and risk factors. Global Status Report on Noncommunicable Diseases 2011 (2010)
18. Pizer, S.M., Johnston, R.E., Ericksen, J.P., Yankaskas, B.C., Muller, K.E.: Contrast-limited adaptive histogram equalization: speed and effectiveness. In: Proceedings of the First Conference on Visualization in Biomedical Computing, pp. 337–345. IEEE (1990)
19. Raj, P., Muthulekshmi, M.: Review of cancer statistics in India. Int. J. Adv. Signal Image Sci. **1**(1), 1–4 (2015)
20. Rampun, A., Scotney, B.W., Morrow, P.J., Wang, H., Winder, J.: Breast density classification using local quinary patterns with various neighbourhood topologies. J. Imaging **4**(1), 14 (2018)
21. Reyad, Y.A., Berbar, M.A., Hussain, M.: Comparison of statistical, LBP, and multi-resolution analysis features for breast mass classification. J. Med. Syst. **38**(9), 100 (2014)
22. dos Santos Coelho, L., Mariani, V.C.: Use of chaotic sequences in a biologically inspired algorithm for engineering design optimization. Expert Syst. Appl. **34**(3), 1905–1913 (2008)
23. Silvestre, L.J., Lemos, A.P., Braga, J.P., Braga, A.P.: Dataset structure as prior information for parameter-free regularization of extreme learning machines. Neurocomputing **169**, 288–294 (2015)
24. Singh, V.P., Srivastava, S., Srivastava, R.: Effective mammogram classification based on center symmetric-LBP features in wavelet domain using random forests. Technol. Health Care **25**(4), 709–727 (2017)
25. Suckling, J., et al.: The mammographic image analysis society digital mammogram database. In: Exerpta Medica. International Congress Series, vol. 1069, pp. 375–378 (1994)
26. Thawkar, S., Ingolikar, R.: Classification of masses in digital mammograms using firefly based optimization. Int. J. Image Graph. Sig. Process. **10**(2), 25 (2018)
27. Yang, D., Li, G., Cheng, G.: On the efficiency of chaos optimization algorithms for global optimization. Chaos Solitons Fractals **34**(4), 1366–1375 (2007)

A Novel Echo State Network Model Using Bayesian Ridge Regression and Independent Component Analysis

Hoang Minh Nguyen, Gaurav Kalra, Tae Joon Jun, and Daeyoung Kim[✉]

School of Computing, Korea Advanced Institute of Science and Technology (KAIST),
291 Daehak-ro, Yuseong-gu, Daejeon 34141, Republic of Korea
{minhhoang,gvkalra,taejoon89,kimd}@kaist.ac.kr

Abstract. We propose a novel Bayesian Ridge Echo State Network (BRESN) model for nonlinear time series prediction, based on Bayesian Ridge Regression and Independent Component Analysis. BRESN has a regularization effect to avoid over-fitting, at the same time being robust to noise owing to its probabilistic strategy. In BRESN we also use Independent Component Analysis (ICA) for dimensionality reduction, and show that ICA improves the model's accuracy more than other reduction techniques. Furthermore, we evaluate the proposed model on both synthetic and real-world datasets to compare its accuracy with twelve combinations of four other regression models and three different choices of dimensionality reduction techniques, and measure its running time. Experimental results show that our model significantly outperforms other state-of-the-art ESN prediction models while maintaining a satisfactory running time.

Keywords: Echo State Network · Bayesian Ridge Regression Independent Component Analysis · Nonlinear time series prediction

1 Introduction

Analyzing time-dependent data and forecasting future values has been widely studied and applied in a multitude of domains, including economics, engineering, and natural and social sciences. A practical application of time-series involves both univariate and multivariate analysis, with linear and nonlinear dynamics [7,11]. Consequently, various neural network and support vector machine (SVM) based models have been proposed, such as multilayer perceptrons (MLP) [8], radial basis function (RBF) neural network [9], extreme learning machine (ELM) [4], and echo state network (ESN) [6].

ESN is a type of recurrent neural network (RNN) designed to solve vanishing and exploding gradient problems, with the core idea of driving a large and fixed number of randomly generated neurons (called the reservoir) with the input signal to induce a nonlinear response in each neuron [5]. In other words, ESN

© Springer Nature Switzerland AG 2018
V. Kůrková et al. (Eds.): ICANN 2018, LNCS 11140, pp. 24–34, 2018.
https://doi.org/10.1007/978-3-030-01421-6_3

avoids the gradient problem by training only the output weights; this allows ESN to have significantly faster training time compared to other multi-layer RNNs (e.g. Long Short Term Memory (LSTM)), which typically require powerful Graphics Processing Units (GPUs).

In this paper, we propose a novel ESN model, namely Bayesian Ridge Echo State Network (BRESN), to improve the prediction capability of existing ESN models. Firstly, BRESN uses Bayesian Ridge Regression, which adds a probabilistic perspective and the 'prior' concept to help with the regularization of the classical ridge, and overall provides higher robustness. Secondly, we have introduced Independent Component Analysis for dimensionality reduction in BRESN, and shown that it provides more accurate prediction results with Bayesian Ridge Regression than previous reduction techniques. Finally, we have evaluated our BRESN model on both synthetic and real-world datasets, and shown that our model significantly outperforms other state-of-the-art models in term of accuracy while maintaining a satisfactory running time.

The rest of the paper is organized as follows. Section 2 provides information on related work, and Sect. 3 gives an overview on ESN architecture. Section 4 explains the components of our BRESN model, while Sect. 5 presents and discusses our experimental setup and results. Finally, concluding remarks are provided in Sect. 6.

2   Related Work

In training the output weights of ESN, pseudoinverse is a commonly used method. However, in practical applications, pseudoinverse can easily lead to ill-posed problems and cause weak generalization capability of the model. To resolve these problems, regularization methods such as Tikhonov regularization can be used. The traditional Tikhonov regularization, or ridge regression, penalizes high coefficient values in order to 'simplify' the trained model as much as possible. This allows the method to avoid over-fitting by minimizing the impacts of irrelevant features. Noise injection is an alternative, but it is not as stable as the standard Tikhonov regularization [1].

In addition to Ridge Regression, still one of the most widely applied and well performed ESN output regression techniques, there have been various other works on different ESN variants. This includes using Support Vector Regression (SVR) together with ESN to replace 'kernel trick' with 'reservoir trick' in dealing with nonlinearity; in other words, to perform linear SVR in the high-dimension 'reservoir' state space [12]. Another notable work is from [3], where a probabilistic instead of regularization approach is applied in training ESN output weights.

As ESN often deals with high dimensional data, dimensionality reduction techniques have been proposed and evaluated in [10]. In this work, Principal Component Analysis (PCA) and kernel Principal Component Analysis (kPCA) have been shown to consistently provide improvements in ESN prediction accuracy. This work has also experimented and shown promising results when using ν-SVR, a SVR variant that uses a hyperparameter ν to control the number of support vectors, together with PCA and kPCA.

3   Basics of Echo State Network

The architecture of Echo State Network (without feedback, for purely input-driven dynamical pattern recognition) is depicted in Fig. 1. The circles depict input u, reservoir state x, and output y. The gray dashed squares depict the input-to-reservoir weight matrix W_i^r and the reservoir weight matrix W_r^r. These two matrices are randomly initialized with real values sampled from a uniform distribution in the $[-1, 1]$ interval. The solid squares depict the reservoir-to-output weight matrix W_r^o and the input-to-output weight matrix W_i^o. The diamond shape with z^{-1} depicts the unit delay operator, and the polygon illustrates the non-linear transformation performed by the neurons of the network.

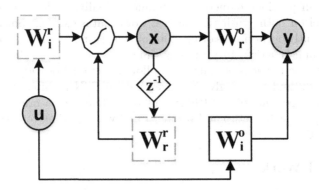

Fig. 1. Echo State Network architecture

The system and output equations of the discrete-time ESN are as follow:

$$x[n] = f(W_r^r x[n-1] + W_i^r u[n]) + \nu(n-1) \tag{1}$$
$$y[n] = W_r^o x[n] + W_i^o u[n] \tag{2}$$

where f is a sigmoid function (usually the logistic sigmoid or tanh function), and ν is a noise vector added to the reservoir states.

By definition, the two weight matrices W_i^r and W_r^r are randomly initialized and not trained, while W_r^o and W_i^o of the readout are optimized for specific tasks. To begin with, supposed we have a training set T_{tr}; from this training set input-output pairs can be formed:

$$(u[1], y[1]), ..., (u[T_{tr}], y[T_{tr}]) \tag{3}$$

In the training phase, or *state harvesting*, the reservoir states $x[1],...,x[T_{tr}]$ can be *harvested* using Eq. 1, and the target outputs are used for Eq. 2. The inputs, reservoir states, and outputs can be stacked into a matrix S, and the target outputs can be stacked into a vector Y in order to train the ESN readout layer:

$$S = \begin{bmatrix} x^T[1], u^T[1] \\ \vdots \\ x^T[T_{tr}], u^T[T_{tr}] \end{bmatrix}, Y = \begin{bmatrix} y[1] \\ \vdots \\ y[T_{tr}] \end{bmatrix} \tag{4}$$

4   Bayesian Ridge Echo State Network (BRESN)

The overall architecture of our Bayesian Ridge Echo State Network (BRESN) model is shown in Fig. 2.

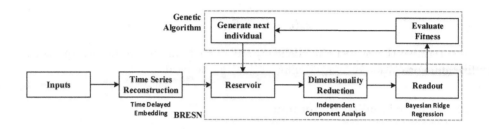

Fig. 2. Bayesian Ridge Echo State Network (BRESN) architecture

The input time series data is firstly reconstructed using time delayed reconstruction method and put into BRESN. As there are a variety of hyperparameters necessary to be optimized for BRESN, genetic algorithm is utilized for this purpose. Individuals from genetic algorithm are created, and the individual with the best cross-validation fitness result is chosen for testing of the model.

4.1   Time Series Reconstruction

In order to provide quality predictions, identifying the original phase space of observed time series data is necessary. This can be done by converting observations into state vector by a process known as phase space reconstruction. Takens' Embedding Theorem [14] shows that with a suitable dimension, we can obtain a topologically equivalent structure to the original 'attractor' of the time series.

Given a time series $[\boldsymbol{X}_1, \boldsymbol{X}_2, ..., \boldsymbol{X}_N]$, where $\boldsymbol{X}_i = [x_1(i), x_2(i), ..., x_d(i)]^T$ (d dimensions) and $i = 1, 2, ..., N$, suppose we set the time delay vector as $\boldsymbol{M} = [m_1, m_2, ..., m_d]$, where $m_j(j = 1, 2, ..., d)$ is the jth embedding dimension, and $\tau_j(j = 1, 2, ..., d)$ is the time delay. Then a time delayed phase space reconstruction can be created as follow:

$$
\begin{aligned}
\boldsymbol{V}(k) =& \big[x_1(k), x_1(k - \tau_1), ..., x_1(k - (m_1 - 1)\tau_1), \\
& x_2(k), x_2(k - \tau_2), ..., x_2(k - (m_2 - 1)\tau_2), \\
& ... \\
& x_d(k), x_2 d(k - \tau_d), ..., x_d(k - (m_d - 1)\tau_d)\big]
\end{aligned}
\tag{5}
$$

The time series dimension after phase space reconstruction is $m_1 + m_2 + ... + m_d$. Suppose that ρ is the prediction horizon, then according to Takens'

Embedding Theorem, with suitable time delay and embedding dimension parameters, generally there exists a function F such that:

$$
\begin{aligned}
x_1(k + \rho) &= F_1(\mathbf{V}(k)) \\
x_2(k + \rho) &= F_2(\mathbf{V}(k)) \\
&\cdots \\
x_d(k + \rho) &= F_d(\mathbf{V}(k))
\end{aligned}
\tag{6}
$$

To determine the correct time delay τ_j and embedding dimension m_j, methods like autocorrelation or mutual information can be used.

4.2 Dimensionality Reduction

To deal with very high dimensional data in readout layer (Eq. 4), we have employed dimensionality reduction techniques to overcome the multicollinearity problem. Independent Component Analysis (ICA) is chosen for this purpose. For matrix $\mathbf{S}$ (Eq. 4), using ICA we consider the source $\mathbf{S}$ to be a linear combination of independent non-Gaussian components. ICA attempts to 'un-mix' the source into $\mathbf{S} = \mathbf{S}_i \mathbf{A}$ where $\mathbf{S}_i$ contains the independent components and $\mathbf{A}$ is the mixing matrix. In other words, ICA searches for $\mathbf{A}$ that maximizes the non-Gaussianity of the sources; as a result, it can also be used for dimensionality reduction with the resulting $\mathbf{S}_i$ being the reduced version of $\mathbf{S}$.

At the center of the ICA algorithm, neg-entropy ($\mathbf{J}$) can be used to measure non-Gaussianity, which is fast to compute and more robust than kurtosis-based method. The approximation of neg-entropy for a variable s in case of one quadratic function $\mathbf{G}$ is of the form:

$$
\mathbf{J}(s) \simeq [\mathbf{E}\{\mathbf{G}(s)\} - \mathbf{E}\{\mathbf{G}(v)\}]^2
\tag{7}
$$

where $\mathbf{E}$ denotes expectation, s is assumed to be of mean 0 and unit variance, and v is a random variable following a normal distribution of mean 0 and unit variance. In this work, we have chosen $\mathbf{G}$ to be log cosh function; more specifically, function $\mathbf{G}$ for a variable u has the form $\mathbf{G}(u) = \frac{1}{c}\log(\cosh(cu))$ where c is some suitable constant (c is set to 1 in this work).

4.3 Bayesian Ridge Regression (BayeRidge)

To train ESN readout layer, linear regression can be used; however, this method can easily cause overfitting problem. This is because both reservoir states and inputs (with increased dimensions from reconstruction) are stacked into matrix $\mathbf{S}$ of Eq. 4, making it very high dimensional and easy to overfit. As a result, one common approach to resolve this problem is ridge regression, which penalizes high coefficient values by solving the following regularized least-square problem:

$$
\mathbf{W}_{ls}^* = \underset{\mathbf{W}}{argmin}(||\mathbf{Y} - \mathbf{SW}||^2 + \lambda||\mathbf{W}||^2)
\tag{8}
$$

where λ is the L_2 regularization coefficient, and $\boldsymbol{W} = [\boldsymbol{W}_i^o \boldsymbol{W}_r^o]$. Larger values of λ will cause the components of $\boldsymbol{W}$ to shrink more towards zero. In matrix terms, the calculation in the right hand side of Eq. 8 is the same as:

$$(\boldsymbol{Y} - \boldsymbol{SW})^T(\boldsymbol{Y} - \boldsymbol{XW}) + \lambda \boldsymbol{W}^T \boldsymbol{W} \tag{9}$$

where $\boldsymbol{W}^T$ denotes the transpose of the matrix form of $\boldsymbol{W}$.

Solving Eq. 9 we get the Ridge estimator as follows:

$$\boldsymbol{W} = (\boldsymbol{S}^T \boldsymbol{S} + \lambda \boldsymbol{I})^{-1} \boldsymbol{S}^T \boldsymbol{Y} \tag{10}$$

where $\boldsymbol{I}$ is the identity matrix.

For the Ridge Regression discussed above, we can obtain a Bayesian view of it by considering the standard regression model $Y = \boldsymbol{SW} + \epsilon$ with two following conditions: (i) the error ϵ has a normal distribution with mean 0 and known variance matrix $\sigma^2 \boldsymbol{I}$, and (ii) $\boldsymbol{W}$ has a prior normal distribution with known mean α and known variance matrix $\boldsymbol{Z}$. Posterior probability of $\boldsymbol{W}$ can be obtained using Bayes' theorem:

$$p(\boldsymbol{W}/Y) \sim \mathcal{N}\big[(\boldsymbol{Z}^{-1} + (1/\sigma^2)\boldsymbol{S}^T \boldsymbol{S})^{-1}(\boldsymbol{Z}^{-1}\alpha + (1/\sigma^2)\boldsymbol{S}^T \boldsymbol{Y});$$
$$(\boldsymbol{Z}^{-1} + (1/\sigma^2)\boldsymbol{S}^T \boldsymbol{S})^{-1}\big] \tag{11}$$

Using Eq. 11, if we set $\alpha = 0$ and $\boldsymbol{Z} = (\sigma^2/\lambda)\boldsymbol{I}$, the posterior mean of $\boldsymbol{W}$ is equal to $(\boldsymbol{S}^T \boldsymbol{S} + \lambda \boldsymbol{I})^{-1} \boldsymbol{S}^T \boldsymbol{Y}$, which is the same as the Ridge estimator in Eq. 10. In other words, the penalization by weighted L_2 coefficient is equivalent to setting a Gaussian prior on the weights $\boldsymbol{W}$.

Also, in order to complete the priors' specification, the priors for the variances of ϵ and $\boldsymbol{W}$ need to be defined. Suppose $\varphi_\epsilon = 1/\sigma^2$ and $\varphi_w = \lambda/\sigma^2$ are the precisions of ϵ and $\boldsymbol{W}$, respectively, then their priors can be suitably defined by the following Gamma distributions [2]:

$$p(\varphi_\epsilon) \sim Gamma(\alpha_1, \alpha_2) \tag{12}$$

$$p(\varphi_w) \sim Gamma(\lambda_1, \lambda_2) \tag{13}$$

As a result, the hyperpriors α_1, α_2, λ_1, and λ_2 are the hyperparameters necessary to be estimated for Bayesian Ridge Regression.

The key difference between **Ridge** and **BayeRidge** is that the Bayesian approach makes predictions by integrating over the distribution of model parameter ($\boldsymbol{W}$), instead of using a specific estimated value. This key property allows Bayesian Ridge Regression to reduce overfitting (as its predictions are basically averaged over many possible solutions), as a result improve predictive capability compared to the classical Ridge Regression.

4.4   Hyperparameters Optimization Using Genetic Algorithm

In order to optimize the set of hyperparameters for BRESN, genetic algorithm is used with Gaussian mutation, random crossover, tournament selection, and elitism. The genetic algorithm is ran for 20 generations, population size of 50, number of offsprings of 30 in each generation, mutation probability of 0.2, and crossover probability of 0.5. To select the best individual, the genetic algorithm attempts to minimize the following fitness function:

$$\boldsymbol{Fit}(\boldsymbol{\theta}) = (1 - r)Err(\boldsymbol{Y}) + r * d/N_r \tag{14}$$

where $\boldsymbol{\theta}$ is an individual, and the ratio r is set to 0.9 for this work.

The fitness function not only tries to minimize prediction errors (for targeted outputs $\boldsymbol{Y}$) but also penalizes models with high complexity of dimension $\boldsymbol{d}$.

5 Results and Discussion

5.1 Experimental Setup

Benchmark Models: In this work we compare BRESN against 12 combinations of 4 other regression models and 3 other dimensionality reduction technique choices. The 4 benchmark regression models include Ridge Regression (**Ridge**), Linear Support Vector Regression (**SVR**), ν-Support Vector Regression (ν-**SVR**), and Bayesian Regression (**Bayesian**). The 3 benchmark dimensionality reduction technique choices are no reduction (**Identity**), Principal Component Analysis (**PCA**), and kernel Principal Component Analysis (**kPCA**).

Datasets: To evaluate the accuracy of prediction models, we have used 2 synthetic and 2 real-world datasets. The 2 synthetic datasets include Lorenz (**Lorenz**) and Rossler (**Rossler**) chaotic time series generated for 4000 time steps, while the 2 real-world datasets include daily closing prices between January 1st, 2000 and December 31st, 2017 of Standard and Poor's 500 stock data[1] (**SP500**) and the 13-month smoothed monthly total international sunspot number between July 1749 and September 2017 (**Sunspots**) [13]. In each dataset, the first 50% of data is used for training, the next 20% is for cross-validation, and the last 30% is for testing. For time series reconstruction, the time delay and embedding dimension (τ, m) for **Lorenz**, **Rossler**, **SP500**, and **Sunspots** are $(10, 1)$, $(3, 13)$, $(10, 1)$, and $(10, 1)$, respectively.

Accuracy Metric: To evaluate the prediction accuracy of models and for the error function Err in Eq. 14, we use Normalized Root Mean Squared Error (**NRMSE**). For a testing set T_{te} with real values $\boldsymbol{Y} = [y[1], ..., y[T_{te}]]$ and prediction results $\boldsymbol{P} = [p[1], ..., p[T_{te}]]$, then NRMSE is defined as follow:

$$NRMSE(\boldsymbol{P}, \boldsymbol{Y}) = \frac{\sqrt{\frac{1}{T_{te}} \sum_{i=1}^{T_{te}} (p[i] - y[i])^2}}{std(\boldsymbol{Y})} \tag{15}$$

where $std(\boldsymbol{Y})$ is the standard deviation of $(\boldsymbol{Y})$.

---

[1] https://finance.yahoo.com/quote/SPY/history/.

Hyperparameter Optimization: The hyperparameters necessary to be optimized by genetic algorithm is shown in Table 1; each hyperparameter is searched within the interval $[min, max]$ with resolution Δ, except reservoir sparsity/connectivity is fixed at 0.25 to maintain sparse weights of ESN.

Table 1. Hyperparameter intervals and resolutions. For general ESN: number of neurons in reservoir (N_r), state update noise (ξ), input scaling (w_i), teacher/output scaling (w_o), spectral radius (ρ); for Ridge Regression: regularization (λ); for Linear- and Nu-SVR: error term penalty (C), epsilon-insensitive loss function hyperparameter (ϵ), nu hyperparameter (ν), kernel coefficient (γ); for Bayesian Ridge: shape and inverse scale parameters for Gamma distribution $(\lambda_1, \lambda_2, \alpha_1, \alpha_2)$; for PCA, kPCA, ICA: dimensionality reduction ratio $(\frac{d}{N_r})$

	ESN					Ridge	SVR, ν-SVR				BayeRidge				PCA, kPCA, ICA
	N_r	ξ	w_i	w_o	ρ	λ	C	ϵ	ν	γ	λ_1	λ_2	α_1	α_2	$\frac{d}{N_r}$
min	100	0.0	0.1	0.1	0.5	0.001	0.001	0.001	0.001	0.001	0.001	0.001	0.001	0.001	0.001
max	500	0.1	0.9	0.9	1.4	1.0	10.0	2.0	1.0	1.0	1.0	1.0	1.0	1.0	1.0
Δ	5	0.01	0.08	0.08	0.09	0.1	1.0	0.1	0.1	0.1	0.1	0.1	0.1	0.1	0.1

5.2 Dimensionality Reduction Technique

There have been experimental results showing the effectiveness of using dimensionality reduction techniques, including PCA and kPCA to train ESN readout layer [10]. Thus, in order to demonstrate the reason for our choice of ICA for dimensionality reduction, we have shown the accuracy comparison across 4 datasets for Bayesian Ridge Regression with different dimensionality reduction techniques in Table 2.

Table 2. NRMSE of different dimensionality reduction techniques for Bayesian Ridge Regression (lowest NRMSE results in bold blue text)

	Identity	PCA	kPCA	ICA
Lorenz	$6.54 * 10^{-6}$	$4.29 * 10^{-8}$	$3.78 * 10^{-8}$	$\mathbf{3.62 * 10^{-8}}$
Rossler	$1.92 * 10^{-5}$	$3.13 * 10^{-7}$	$4.34 * 10^{-5}$	$\mathbf{2.80 * 10^{-7}}$
SP500	$3.95 * 10^{-1}$	$1.65 * 10^{-1}$	$1.37 * 10^{-1}$	$\mathbf{4.19 * 10^{-2}}$
Sunspots	$2.59 * 10^{-2}$	$2.28 * 10^{-2}$	$2.29 * 10^{-2}$	$\mathbf{2.19 * 10^{-2}}$

The effectiveness of applying dimensionality reduction can clearly be seen from Table 2, in which almost all dimensionality reduction techniques perform better than 'identity' (no reduction) with only one exception of kPCA for Rossler dataset. Also, even though kPCA provides a kernel extension to PCA, it does not always perform better when using together with Bayesian Ridge Regression (PCA is better in Rossler, and similar results between the two in Sunspots). Finally, the results in Table 2 clearly shows that ICA outperforms all other dimensionality reduction techniques in all 4 datasets.

5.3   Accuracy Comparison

In order to evaluate the accuracy of our BRESN model, we have compared it to 4 other regression models, including Ridge, SVR, ν-SVR, and Bayesian, and 3 other dimensionality reduction approaches, including Identity (no dimensionality reduction), PCA, and kPCA. As the 2 synthetic datasets (Lorenz, Rossler) are generated from well-defined equations thus having less noise than the 2 real-world datasets (SP500, Sunspots), all the models provide better prediction results for the first 2 than the last 2. It is also worth noting that Ridge and Bayesian models consistently perform better than SVR and ν-SVR given the same dimensional reduction techniques.

Table 3. NRMSE of different models (lowest NRMSE results in bold blue text)

	Ridge			SVR		
	Identity	PCA	kPCA	Identity	PCA	kPCA
Lorenz	$2.72 * 10^{-5}$	$9.90 * 10^{-7}$	$1.02 * 10^{-6}$	$2.90 * 10^{-3}$	$5.50 * 10^{-4}$	$8.56 * 10^{-4}$
Rossler	$1.35 * 10^{-4}$	$1.56 * 10^{-4}$	$5.52 * 10^{-5}$	$1.68 * 10^{-3}$	$6.08 * 10^{-3}$	$1.27 * 10^{-3}$
SP500	$4.49 * 10^{-1}$	$1.03 * 10^{-1}$	$6.04 * 10^{-2}$	$6.35 * 10^{-1}$	$4.33 * 10^{-1}$	$4.91 * 10^{-2}$
Sunspots	$2.22 * 10^{-2}$	$2.24 * 10^{-2}$	$2.44 * 10^{-2}$	$3.39 * 10^{-2}$	$4.17 * 10^{-2}$	$3.11 * 10^{-2}$

	ν-SVR			Bayesian			
	Identity	PCA	kPCA	Identity	PCA	kPCA	BRESN
Lorenz	$3.76 * 10^{-3}$	$4.87 * 10^{-3}$	$2.16 * 10^{-3}$	$1.30 * 10^{-4}$	$1.96 * 10^{-4}$	$2.34 * 10^{-4}$	$\mathbf{3.62 * 10^{-8}}$
Rossler	$2.56 * 10^{-4}$	$3.04 * 10^{-4}$	$2.51 * 10^{-4}$	$2.09 * 10^{-4}$	$8.12 * 10^{-7}$	$2.90 * 10^{-5}$	$\mathbf{2.80 * 10^{-7}}$
SP500	$7.00 * 10^{-1}$	$5.84 * 10^{-1}$	$6.97 * 10^{-1}$	$4.81 * 10^{-1}$	$1.40 * 10^{-1}$	$8.67 * 10^{-2}$	$\mathbf{4.19 * 10^{-2}}$
Sunspots	$3.32 * 10^{-2}$	$3.74 * 10^{-2}$	$3.37 * 10^{-2}$	$2.21 * 10^{-2}$	$2.27 * 10^{-2}$	$2.26 * 10^{-2}$	$\mathbf{2.19 * 10^{-2}}$

From the results of the 12 benchmark models, it is clear that dimensionality reduction (PCA, kPCA) offers improvement in prediction capability of ESN models. When applying either PCA or kPCA, the NRMSE results either stay at similar levels or decrease, even significantly decrease compared to Identity in cases like Ridge model for Lorenz dataset, or Bayesian for Rossler dataset. Furthermore, except in the case of Bayesian for Rossler dataset, generally kPCA either offers improvements or at least provides similar accuracy results to that of PCA.

The NRMSE results from Table 3 clearly show that our BRESN model with Bayesian Ridge Regression and Independent Component Analysis outperforms all other 12 models in all 4 datasets. By combining both the regularization and probabilistic aspects of Ridge and Bayesian, BRESN demonstrates both its high accuracy and robustness in non-linear time series prediction.

5.4   Running Time

We have also measured the running time of different regression models and dimensionality reduction techniques, by varying the number of neurons in the ESN reservoir while keeping all other hyperparameters fixed. For each model, the running time has been obtained by averaging over 20 runs, with number of neurons ranging from 100 to 1000 at step size of 100 (Fig. 3).

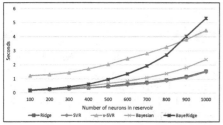
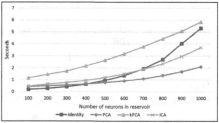

(a) Different regression models with no dimensionality reduction

(b) Different dimensionality reduction techniques for Bayesian Ridge Regression

Fig. 3. Running time of different regression models and dimensionality reduction techniques. BayeRidge denotes Bayesian Ridge Regression (used in BRESN), and all hyperparameters except number of neurons in reservoirs are fixed, including spectral radius ρ at 0.9 and dimensionality reduction ratio $\frac{d}{N_r}$ at 0.1.

As can be seen from the figure, our BRESN model maintains a satisfactory running time. Even without ICA to reduce dimensionality, one run still takes a reasonable amount of 5.31 s, while a 'full' BRESN with all components and 1000 neurons in reservoir reduces the number to 3.69 s per run. Also, it is worth noting that in this work we have experimented with a maximum of 500 neurons in reservoir for all ESN models, and we have run the models concurrently for multiple times of training and testing. These factors reduce the average running time even further, thus making BRESN's training and testing speed satisfactory for real-world use.

6   Conclusion

In this paper, we have proposed a novel Bayesian Ridge Echo State Network (BRESN), which introduces Bayesian Ridge Regression for regression and Independent Component Analysis (ICA) for dimensionality reduction in ESN readout training. We have evaluated and shown that ICA provides higher accuracy improvements than other dimensionality techniques. Also, we have tested BRESN on both synthetic and real-world datasets, compared it with 12 combinations of 4 other regression models and 3 other dimensionality reduction technique choices, and measured its running time. The results show that BRESN significantly outperforms other state-of-the-art models in term of accuracy while still having satisfactory running time.

Acknowledgments. This research was supported by the MSIT (Ministry of Science, ICT), Korea, under the ITRC (Information Technology Research Center) support program (IITP-2018-2018-1-00877) supervised by the IITP (Institute for Information & communications Technology Promotion), and International Research & Development Program of the National Research Foundation of Korea (NRF) funded by the Ministry of Science, ICT & Future Planning of Korea (2016K1A3A7A03952054).

References

1. Bishop, C.M.: Training with noise is equivalent to Tikhonov regularization. Neural Comput. **7**(1), 108–116 (1995)
2. Bishop, C.M., Tipping, M.E.: Bayesian regression and classification. Nato Science Series sub Series III Computer And Systems Sciences, vol. 190, pp. 267–288 (2003)
3. Han, M., Mu, D.: Multi-reservoir echo state network with sparse Bayesian learning. In: Zhang, L., Lu, B.-L., Kwok, J. (eds.) ISNN 2010. LNCS, vol. 6063, pp. 450–456. Springer, Heidelberg (2010). https://doi.org/10.1007/978-3-642-13278-0_58
4. Huang, G.B., Zhu, Q.Y., Siew, C.K.: Extreme learning machine: theory and applications. Neurocomputing **70**(1–3), 489–501 (2006)
5. Jaeger, H.: The "echo state" approach to analysing and training recurrent neural networks-with an erratum note. German National Research Center for Information Technology GMD, Bonn, Germany, Technical report, vol. 148(34), p. 13 (2001)
6. Jaeger, H., Haas, H.: Harnessing nonlinearity: predicting chaotic systems and saving energy in wireless communication. Science **304**(5667), 78–80 (2004)
7. Kantz, H., Schreiber, T.: Nonlinear Time Series Analysis, vol. 7. Cambridge University Press, Cambridge (2004)
8. Koskela, T., Lehtokangas, M., Saarinen, J., Kaski, K.: Time series prediction with multilayer perceptron, FIR and Elman neural networks. In: Proceedings of the World Congress on Neural Networks, pp. 491–496. Citeseer (1996)
9. Leung, H., Lo, T., Wang, S.: Prediction of noisy chaotic time series using an optimal radial basis function neural network. IEEE Trans. Neural Netw. **12**(5), 1163–1172 (2001)
10. Løkse, S., Bianchi, F.M., Jenssen, R.: Training echo state networks with regularization through dimensionality reduction. Cogn. Comput. **9**(3), 364–378 (2017)
11. Reinsel, G.C.: Elements of Multivariate Time Series Analysis. Springer, New York (2003)
12. Shi, Z., Han, M.: Support vector echo-state machine for chaotic time-series prediction. IEEE Trans. Neural Netw. **18**(2), 359–372 (2007)
13. SILSO World Data Center: The international sunspot number. International Sunspot Number Monthly Bulletin and online catalogue (1749-2017). http://www.sidc.be/silso/
14. Takens, F.: Detecting strange attractors in turbulence. In: Rand, D., Young, L.-S. (eds.) Dynamical Systems and Turbulence, Warwick 1980. LNM, vol. 898, pp. 366–381. Springer, Heidelberg (1981). https://doi.org/10.1007/BFb0091924

Image Processing

A Model for Detection of Angular Velocity of Image Motion Based on the Temporal Tuning of the Drosophila

Huatian Wang[1], Jigen Peng[2], Paul Baxter[1], Chun Zhang[3], Zhihua Wang[3], and Shigang Yue[1(✉)]

[1] The Computational Intelligence Lab (CIL), School of Computer Science, University of Lincoln, Lincoln LN6 7TS, UK
16626432@students.lincoln.ac.uk, {pbaxter,syue}@lincoln.ac.uk
[2] School of Mathematics and Information Science, Guangzhou University, Guangzhou 510006, China
jgpeng@mail.xjtu.edu.cn
[3] Institute of Microelectronics, Tsinghua University, Beijing 100084, China
{zhangchun,zhihua}@tsinghua.edu.cn

Abstract. We propose a new bio-plausible model based on the visual systems of Drosophila for estimating angular velocity of image motion in insects' eyes. The model implements both preferred direction motion enhancement and non-preferred direction motion suppression which is discovered in Drosophila's visual neural circuits recently to give a stronger directional selectivity. In addition, the angular velocity detecting model (AVDM) produces a response largely independent of the spatial frequency in grating experiments which enables insects to estimate the flight speed in cluttered environments. This also coincides with the behaviour experiments of honeybee flying through tunnels with stripes of different spatial frequencies.

Keywords: Motion detection · Insect vision · Angular velocity Spatial frequency

1 Introduction

Insects though with a mini-brain have very complex visual processing systems which is the fundamental of the motion detection. How visual information are processed, especially how insects estimate flight speed have been met with strong interest for a long time. Here we use Drosophila as instance whose visual processing pathways have been researched the most among insects by using both anatomy, two-photon imaging and electron microscope technologies, to explain generally how signals are processed in insects' visual systems, inspiring us to build up new bio-plausible neural network for estimating angular velocity of image motion.

© Springer Nature Switzerland AG 2018
V. Kůrková et al. (Eds.): ICANN 2018, LNCS 11140, pp. 37–46, 2018.
https://doi.org/10.1007/978-3-030-01421-6_4

Drosophila have tens of thousands of ommatidia, each of which has its small lens containing 8 photoreceptors R1-R8 sending their axons into the optic lobe to form a visual column. Optic lobe, as the most important part of the visual system, consists of four retinotopically organized layers, lamina, medulla, lobula and lobula plate. The number of columns in optic lobe is the same with the number of ommatidia [1]. Each column contains roughly one hundred neurons and can process light intensity increments (ON) and decrements (OFF) signals in parallel way simultaneously [2]. In each column, visual signals of light change can be transformed to motion signals by this visual system with ON and OFF pathways [3] (see Fig. 1). Visual signals of light change can be transformed to motion signals by these two pathways in each column [3] (see Fig. 1).

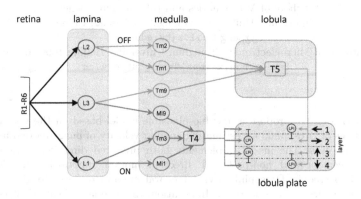

Fig. 1. Visual system of Drosophila with ON and OFF pathways. In each column of the visual system, the motion information are mainly captured by photoreceptors R1-R6, and processed by lamina cells L1-L3, medulla neurons (Mi1, Mi9, Tm1, Tm2, Tm3, Tm9) and T4, T5 neurons. The lobula plate functioning as a map of visual motion which has four layers representing four cardinal directions (front to back, back to front, upward and downward). T4 and T5 cells showing both preferred motion enhancement and non-preferred direction suppression are first to give a strong directional selectivity [5]. This figure referenced Takemura and Arenz's figures [3,4].

How the visual system we describe above detects motions has been researched for a long time. Hassenstein and Richardt proposed an elementary motion detector (EMD) model to describe how animals sense motion [6]. This HR detector uses two neighbouring viewpoints as a pair to form a detecting unit. The delayed signal from one input multiplies the signal from another without delay to get a directional response (Fig. 2a). This ensures the motion of preferred direction have a higher response than non-preferred direction. Another competing model called BL model, proposed by Barlow and Levick implements the non-preferred direction suppression instead [7]. BL detector uses signal from one input without delay to divide the input from another delayed arm located on preferred side to get a directional selective response (Fig. 2b). Both models can be implemented in Drosophila's visual system since patch-clamp recordings showed a temporal delay for Mi1 regard to Tm3 in ON pathway and Tm1 with regard to Tm2 in OFF pathway [8]. This also provides the neural fundamental for delay and correlation mechanism.

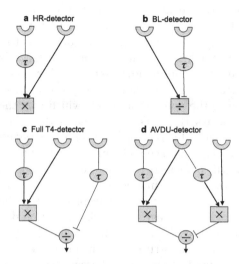

Fig. 2. Contrast of the Motion detectors. (a) In Hassenstein-Reichardt detector, a delayed signal from left photoreceptor multiplies the signal from right to give a preferred direction enhancement response. (b) In Barlow-Levick detector, a delayed signal from right divides the signal from left to suppress null direction response. (c) A recently proposed Full T4 detector combines both PD enhancement and ND suppression. (d) Proposed angular velocity detecting unit (AVDU) detector combines the enhancement and suppression with a different structure.

Recently, a HR/BL hybrid model called Full T4 model has been proposed based on the finding that both preferred enhancement and non-preferred suppression is functioning in Drosophila's visual circuits [9]. The motion detector they proposed consists of three input elements. The delayed signal from left arm multiplies the undelayed signal from middle arm, and then the product is divided by the delayed signal from right arm to give the final response (Fig. 2c). Circuits connecting T4 or T5 cells that are anatomically qualified to implement both two mechanisms also give a support to this hybrid model [3]. According to their simulation, this model structure can produce a stronger directional selectivity than HR model and BL model. However, one problem of the models we mentioned above is that they prefer particular temporal frequency and cause the ambiguity that a response could correspond to two different speeds. Though they can give a directional response for motion, it's hard to estimate the motion speed. So these models can only explain part of the motion detection, while some of the descending neurons, according to Ibbotson's records, shows that the response grows monotonically as the angular velocity increases [10]. What's more, the response is largely independent with the spatial frequency of the stimulus, which is also coincident with the corridor behaviour experiments of honeybee [11].

In order to solve this problem, Riabinina presents a angular velocity detector mainly based on HR model [12]. The key point of this model is that it uses the summation of the absolute values of excitation caused by differentiation of signal intensity over time, which is strongly related to the temporal frequency and independent of the angular velocity, as the denominator to eliminate the temporal dependence of the final output. Cope argues that this model simulates a circuit that separates to the optomotor circuit which requires more additional neurons and costs more energy. Instead, Cope proposes a more bio-plausible model as an extension to the optomotor circuit which uses the ratio of two HR model with different delays [13]. The main idea is that the ratio of two bell shaped response curves with different optimal temporal frequencies can make a monotonic response to eliminate the ambiguity. The problem is that the delays is chose by undetermined coefficients method, and need to be finely tuned which may weaken the robustness of the model.

Neural structure under recent researches inspires us building up a new angular velocity detection model. We agree that visual motion detection systems is complex and should have three or more input elements like Full T4 model as the new researches indicate. But the structure of the models with both enhancement and suppression implemented can be very different from Full T4 model. Here we give an example AVDU (Fig. 2d) for reference. AVDU (angular velocity detector unit) uses the product of the delayed signal from left arm and undelayed signal from middle arm to divide by the product of the delayed signal from middle arm and undelayed one from right arm. This structure combines the HR and BL model together to give a directional motion response. What's more, according to our simulation, AVDU is suitable as a fundamental unit for angular velocity detection model that is largely independent to spatial frequency of the grating pattern.

2 Results

Based on proposed AVDU detector, we build up the angular velocity detecting model (AVDM) to estimate visual motion velocity in insects' eyes. AVDM consists of an ommatidial pattern with 27 horizontal by 36 vertical ommatidia per eye to cover the field of view which is 270° horizontally by 180° vertically. Each 3 adjacent ommatidia in the horizontal direction form a detector for horizontal progressive image motion. And each detector consists of two AVDUs with different sampling rates to produce a directional response for preferred progressive motion (i.e. image motion on left eye when flying backward). The ratio of two AVDUs with different sampling rates then produce a response largely independent of the spatial frequencies of the sinusoidal grating. The output of all detectors then are summed and averaged to give a response representing the velocity of the visual image motion (see Fig. 3).

We simulated the OFF pathway of the Drosophila's visual neural circuits when the sinusoidal grating moving in preferred direction. The normalized

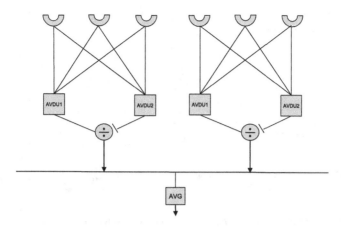

Fig. 3. Angular velocity detecting model. The model use three neighbouring photoreceptors as a unit and each unit contains two AVDUs with different sampling rates. The output is then averaged over the whole visual field to give the final response.

responses of AVDM over different velocities and spatial periods in contrast of experimental results [14] can been seen from Fig. 4. The response curves of AVDM are generally in accordance with the experimental data. Especially when the spatial period is 14°, the curve shows a notable lower response than other spatial periods. This might be caused by the suppression of high temporal frequency of T4/T5 cells [4] since the descending neurons are located downstream of optomotor circuit. This can also be explained by Jonathan's research on spatial frequency tuning of bumblebee Bombus impatiens which indicates that high spatial frequency affects the speed estimation [15]. And this will be discussed in later researches.

In order to get a more general results, the spatial period of the grating and the angular velocity of the image motion are chosen widely (Fig. 5). All response curves under different periods show nearly monotonic increasing potential. And the responses weakly depend on the spatial period of the grating. This coincides with the responses of the descending neurons according to Ibbotson's records [10,14]. And this is important for insects estimating flight speed or gauging distance of foraging journey in a clutter environment.

Though the results of Riabinina's model use different velocity and spatial frequency metric and Cope's model use spikes as the final output, the trend of the curves can show the performances of the models. So we give their results here as reference (Fig. 6). In general, AVDM performs better than Riabinina's model whose response curves of 4 different spatial frequencies are separate from each other [12]. Cope's model is more bio-plausible than Riabinina's model which is based on optomotor circuit. But it only performs well when the speed is around 100 deg/s, and the semilog coordinate outstands that part, while honeybee mainly maintains a constant angular velocity of 200–300 deg/s in open flight [16]. Another problem of Cope's model is that the response of grating with

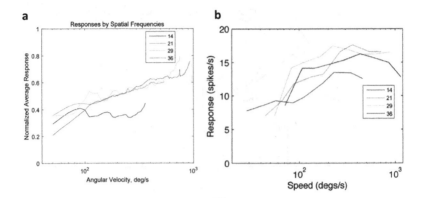

Fig. 4. Contrast of AVDM and experimental records under different angular velocities. (a) The responses of AVDM over different spatial periods. (b) The responses of one type of descending neuron (DNIII$_4$) over different spatial periods based on Ibbotson's records [14].

very high frequency should be lower rather than maintain spatial independence according to Ibbotson's records on descending neuron [10,14]. Our model AVDM uses a bandpass temporal frequency filter simulated by experimental data [4] to deal with this problem. As you can see, AVDM produces a lower response when the spatial period is 14° and shows response largely independence on spatial period ranging from 36° to 72° (Fig. 5).

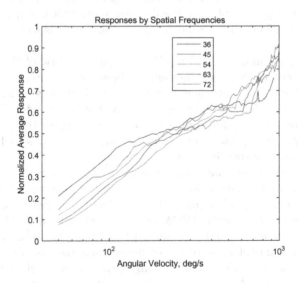

Fig. 5. Responses of AVDM over different spatial periods under different angular velocities.

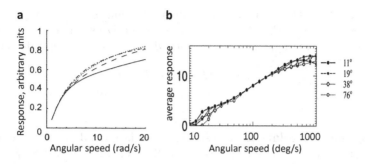

Fig. 6. Contrast of responses of two other models. (a) Riabinina's model uses rad/s as the velocity metric and the spatial frequencies is $10\,\mathrm{m}^{-1}$ (solid), $20\,\mathrm{m}^{-1}$ (dashed), $30\,\mathrm{m}^{-1}$ (dotted) and $40\,\mathrm{m}^{-1}$ (dot-dashed) [12]. (b) Cope's model uses spikes to represent the model response and uses method of undetermined coefficients to decide the two delays of the correlation system [13].

3   Methods

All simulations were carried out in Matlab (© The MathWorks, Inc.), And the layout of the AVDM neural layers is given below.

3.1   Input Signals Simulation

The input signal is simulated using two dimensional images frames with sinusoidal grating moving across the vision. AVDU1 processes all input images while AVDU2 only samples half the total images. The spatial period λ (deg) of the grating and the moving speed V (deg/s) are treated as variables. This naturally induces a temporal frequency of V/λ (Hz) and an angular frequency $\omega = 2\pi V/\lambda$.

   Considering the sinusoidal grating moving in visual field of the detecting unit with three receptors A, B and C, let I_0 be the mean light intensity, then the signal in receptor A can be expressed as $I_0 + m \cdot sin(\omega t)$. Let $\Delta\phi$ denotes the angular separation between the neighbouring receptors, then the signal of receptor B is $I_0 + m \cdot sin(\omega(t - \Delta\phi/V))$, and the signal of receptor C is $I_0 + m \cdot sin(\omega(t - 2\Delta\phi/V))$. So the input signal of one eye can be expressed as:

$$I_{x,y}(t) = I_0 + m \cdot sin(\omega(t - y\Delta\phi/V)), \qquad (1)$$

where (x, y) denotes the location of the ommatidium.

3.2   AVDM Neural Layers

(1) Photoreceptor. The first layer of the AVDM neural network receiving the input signals of light intensity change to get the primary information of visual motion:

$$P_{x,y}(t) = I_{x,y}(t) - I_{x,y}(t - 1). \qquad (2)$$

(2) ON & OFF Pathways. The luminance changes are separated to two pathways according to the neural structures of the Drosophila visual systems, with ON representing light increments and OFF representing light decrements:

$$P_{x,y}^{ON}(t) = (P_{x,y}(t) + |P_{x,y}(t)|)/2,$$
$$P_{x,y}^{OFF}(t) = |(P_{x,y}(t) - |Px,y(t)|)|/2. \tag{3}$$

(3) Delay and Correlation. The signals are delayed and correlated following the structure of AVDU. Here we take one AVDU as example, let S_1, S_2, S_3 donate the input signal of photoreceptor A (left), B (middle), C (right), and S_1^D, S_2^D donate the temporal delayed signal of A and B, then we have the following expression:

$$S_1^D(t) = m \cdot [sin(\omega(t + \Delta T)) - sin(\omega(t - 1 + \Delta T))] \approx M \cdot cos[\omega(t + \Delta T)], \tag{4}$$

similarly we can get $S_2 \approx M \cdot cos[\omega(t - \Delta\phi/V)]$, $S_2^D \approx M \cdot cos[\omega(t - \Delta\phi/V + \Delta T)]$ and $S_3 \approx M \cdot cos[\omega(t - 2\Delta\phi/V)]$, where ΔT is the temporal delay of the model. According to the structure of AVDU, the response of the detector can be expressed as $\overline{(S_1^D \cdot S_2)}/\overline{(S_2^D \cdot S_3)}$, where the bar means the response is averaged over a time period to remove fluctuation caused by oscillatory input. What's more, we set a lower bound of 0.01 on denominator to avoid the output being too high. This also can be explained by the tonic firing rate of neurons.

(4) Ratio and Average. If we set temporal delay as 6ms, and take two sampling rates as 1ms per frame and 2ms per frame, then we can get the responses of AVDU under different angular velocities, spatial periods and sampling rates. According to our simulation, though the response curves of different sampling rates have different values, the shapes are very similar. That means that using the ratio of the responses under different sampling rates can largely get rid of the influence of spatial frequency. The output of detectors each composed of three neighboring photoreceptors are then summed up and averaged over the whole visual field.

(5) Band-Pass Temporal Frequency Filter. We use the records of temporal tuning of the Drosophila to simulate the band-pass temporal frequency filter here [4]. According to Arenz's experiments, the tuning optimum of the temporal frequency will shift from 1 Hz to 5 Hz with application of the octopamine agonist CDM (simulating the Drosophila shifts from still to flying). So we set the temporal frequency filter as a bell-shaped response curve which achieves its optimum at 5 Hz under semilog coordinate. In fact HR completed model can naturally be a temporal frequency filter with little modification since it has a particular temporal frequency preferred bell-shaped curve.

4 Discussion

We proposed a bio-plausible model, the angular velocity detecting model (AVDM), for estimating the image motion velocity using the latest neural circuits discoveries of the Drosophila visual systems. We presented a new structure AVDU as a part of the model to implement both preferred direction motion enhancement and non-preferred direction motion suppression, which is found in Drosophila's neural circuits to make a stronger directional selectivity. And we use the ratio of two AVDUs with different sampling rates to give spatial frequency independent responses for estimating the angular velocity. In addition this can be used as the fundamental part of the visual odometer by integrating the output the AVDM. This also provides a possible explanation about how visual motion detection circuits connecting the descending neurons in the ventral nerve cord.

Using the ratio of two AVDUs with different sampling rates is twofold. One of the reason is that it can be realized in neural circuits naturally since one AVDU only needs to process part of the visual information while the structure and even the delay of two AVDUs are the same. It's easier than using the ratio of two HR-detectors with different delays as Cope's model did [13], because signals are passed with two different delays means there should have two neurotransmitters in one circuit or there are two circuits. Another reason is that the response of individual AVDU is largely dependent on the spatial frequency of the grating, and the ratio of different sampling rates, according to our simulation, can get rid of the influence of the spatial frequency.

Here we only simulate ON pathway of the visual systems with T4 cells. OFF pathway dealing with brightness decrements is similar. Further, models for forward, upward and downward motion detector can be constructed using the same structure since they can be parallel processed.

Acknowledgments. This research is supported by EU FP7-IRSES Project LIV-CODE (295151), HAZCEPT (318907) and HORIZON project STEP2DYNA (691154).

References

1. Fischbach, K.F.: Dittrich APM: the optic lobe of drospholia melanogaster. I. A Golgi analysis of wild-type structure. Cell Tissue Res. **258**(3), 441–475 (1989). https://doi.org/10.1007/BF00218858
2. Joesch, M., Weber, F., Raghu, S.V., Reiff, D.F., Borst, A.: ON and OFF pathways in Drosophila motion vision. Nature **17**(1), 300–304 (2011). https://doi.org/10.1038/nature09545
3. Takemura, S.Y., Nern, A., Chklovskii, D.B., Scheffer, L.K., Rubin, G.M., Meinertzhagen, I.A.: The comprehensive connectome of a neural substrate for 'ON' motion detection in Drosophila. eLife **6**, e24394 (2017). https://doi.org/10.7554/eLife.24394
4. Arenz, A., Drews, M.S., Richter, F.G., Ammer, G., Borst, A.: The temporal tuning of the Drosophila motion detectors is determined by the dynamics of their input elements. Curr. Biol. **27**, 929–944 (2017). https://doi.org/10.1016/j.cub.2017.01.051

5. Haag, J., Mishra, A., Borst, A.: A common directional tuning mechanism of Drosophila motion-sensing neurons in the ON and in the OFF pathway. eLife **6**, e29044 (2017). https://doi.org/10.7554/eLife.29044

6. Hassenstein, B., Reichardt, W.: Systemtheoretische analyse der zeit-, reihenfolgen- und vorzeichenauswertung bei der bewegungsperzeption des rüsselkäfers chlorophanus. Zeitschrift Für Naturforschung B **11**(9–10), 513–524 (1956). https://doi.org/10.1515/znb-1956-9-1004

7. Barlow, H.B., Levick, W.R.: The mechanism of directionally selective units in rabbit's retina. J. Physiol. **178**, 477–504 (1965). https://doi.org/10.1113/jphysiol.1965.sp007638

8. Behnia, R., Clark, D.A., Carter, A.G., Clandinin, T.R., Desplan, C.: Processing properties of ON and OFF pathways for Drosophila motion detection. Nature **512**, 427–430 (2014). https://doi.org/10.1038/nature13427

9. Haag, J., Arenz, A., Serbe, E., Gabbiani, F., Borst, A.: Complementary mechanisms create direction selectivity in the fly. eLife **5**, e17421 (2016). https://doi.org/10.7554/eLife.17421

10. Ibbotson, M.R.: Evidence for velocity-tuned motion-sensitive descending neurons in the honeybee. Proc. Biol. Sci. **268**(1482), 2195 (2001). https://doi.org/10.1098/rspb.2001.1770

11. Srinivasan, M.V., Lehrer, M., Kirchner, W.H., Zhang, S.W.: Range perception through apparent image speed in freely flying honeybees. Vis. Neurosci. **6**(5), 519–535 (1991). https://www.ncbi.nlm.nih.gov/pubmed/2069903

12. Riabinina, O., Philippides, A.O.: A model of visual detection of angular speed for bees. J. Theor. Biol. **257**(1), 61–72 (2009). https://doi.org/10.1016/j.jtbi.2008.11.002

13. Cope, A., Sabo, C., Gurney, K.N., Vasislaki, E., Marshall, J.A.R.: A model for an angular velocity-tuned motion detector accounting for deviations in the corridor-centering response of the Bee. PLoS Comput Biol. **12**(5), e1004887 (2016). https://doi.org/10.1371/journal.pcbi.1004887

14. Ibbotson, M.R., Hung, Y.S., Meffin, H., Boeddeker, N., Srinivasan, M.V.: Neural basis of forward flight control and landing in honeybees. Sci. Rep. **7**(1), 14591 (2017). https://doi.org/10.1038/s41598-017-14954-0

15. Dyhr, J.P., Higgins, C.M.: The spatial frequency tuning of optic-flow-dependent behaviors in the bumblebee Bombus impatiens. J. Exp. Biol. **213**(Pt 10), 1643–50 (2010). https://doi.org/10.1242/jeb.041426

16. Baird, E., Srinivasan, M.V., Zhang, S., Cowling, A.: Visual control of flight speed in honeybees. J. Exp. Biol. **208**(20), 3895–905 (2005). https://doi.org/10.1242/jeb.01818

Local Decimal Pattern for Pollen Image Recognition

Liping Han$^{(\boxtimes)}$ ⓘ and Yonghua Xie

School of Computer and Software,
Nanjing University of Information Science and Technology, Nanjing, China
HanLiping93@163.com

Abstract. In this paper, we propose local decimal pattern (LDP) for pollen image recognition. Considering that the gradient image of pollen grains has more prominent textural features, we quantify by comparing the gradient magnitude of pixel blocks rather than the single pixel value. Unlike the local binary pattern (LBP) and its variants, we encoding by counting the pixel blocks on different quantization intervals, which makes our descriptor robust to the rotation of pollen images. In order to capture the subtle textural feature of pollen images, we increase the number of quantization intervals. The average correct recognition rate of LDP on Pollenmonitor dataset is 90.95%, which is much higher than that of other compared pollen recognition methods. The experimental results show that our method is more suitable for the practical classification and identification of pollen images than compared methods.

Keywords: Local decimal pattern · Pollen recognition · Textural feature
Gradient magnitude

1 Introduction

The classification of pollen particles has been widely applied for allergic pollen index forecast, drug research, paleoclimatic reconstruction, criminal investigation, oil exploration and some other fields [1]. The traditional identification of pollen grains is mainly done by artificial inspection under microscopy, which requires the operator to have a rich knowledge of pollen morphology and needs a high level of training to get accurate recognition results. The commonly used discriminate criteria is the visual biological pollen grain morphological appearance, such as shape, polarity, aperture, size, exine stratification and thickness, and so on [2]. It takes operator much of time and effort to observe the appearance of pollen grains, and often causes misrecognition.

With the development of image processing and pattern recognition [3–5], using computer to extract and classify pollen features has become an effective way for pollen recognition. The early pollen recognition algorithms focused on extracting shape features, in which the contour shape is a prominent feature for some pollen grains with slender oval shape or rounded triangular shape. However, most pollen grains always have similar contour shapes, so it is difficult to identify different categories of pollen images only by shape features. Considering that pollen images from different categories have large differences in texture, more and more texture based feature extraction

© Springer Nature Switzerland AG 2018
V. Kůrková et al. (Eds.): ICANN 2018, LNCS 11140, pp. 47–55, 2018.
https://doi.org/10.1007/978-3-030-01421-6_5

methods have been proposed for automatic classification of pollen images. For example, Punyasena et al. [6] extracted the texture and shape features of pollen images using dictionary learning and sparse coding (DLSC), which obtained a recognition rate of 86.13%, however, the recognition performance largely depends on the selection and quantity of sample blocks. Daood et al. [7] decomposed the pollen image into multiple feature layers using clustering, then the texture and geometric features (TGF) of each layer were extracted using LBP and fractal dimension respectively. Finally, the SVM classifier was used to classify pollen images and a recognition rate of 86.94% was obtained. Whereas, the method has little robustness to the rotation of pollen grains, and the decomposition of pollen images increases the dimension of features. Boochs et al. [8] proposed a pollen recognition method combining shape, texture and aperture features (STAF), which extracted 18 shape features, 5 texture features (Gabor Filters, Fast Fourier Transform, Local Binary Pattern, Histogram of Oriented Gradients, and Haralick features) and a surface aperture features of pollen images. The method used a random forest classifier to identify pollen images, and obtained nearly 87% recognition rate. Guru et al. [9] proposed a pollen classification model based on surface texture, which combined local binary pattern (LBP), Gabor wavelet, gray-level difference matrix (GLDM), and gray-level co-occurrence matrix (GLCM) for pollen recognition (LGGG), and obtained 91.66% recognition rate. However, the computation cost of these two methods is large due to high dimension of the combined features, which makes them unpractical for real application. Marcos et al. [10] extracted texture features using Log-Gabor filter (LGF), discrete Tchebichef moments (DTM), local binary patterns (LBP) and gray-level co-occurrence matrix (GLCM), which obtained a recognition rate of 94.83%, whereas, the fused texture feature (LDLG) contains large amounts of redundant information and the computational process is complex.

Local binary pattern is an effective method for representing texture feature, which has been widely used in face recognition and texture classification [11]. The traditional local binary pattern and its variants usually use wide quantization intervals to quantize the neighboring pixels, which enhances the descriptor's robustness to the illumination changes of images, but also loses some detailed textural information at the same time. Unlike the general texture images, the textural variation range of pollen images is relatively small, so it's difficult to capture the subtle textural differences of pollen images from different categories in wide quantization intervals. In order to solve the problem, the local decimal pattern (LDP) was proposed. The advantages of our method are as follows: Quantizing using the gradient magnitude of pixel blocks instead of single pixel value to eliminate the effects of image noise. Encoding by referring to the number of pixel blocks in each quantization interval making the descriptor invariant to the rotation of pollen grains. The combination of LDP features in multiple directions increases the descriptor's discrimination. Experimental results on Pollenmonitor dataset show that the recognition rate and computation speed of our method is higher than that of most pollen recognition methods.

2 Local Decimal Pattern (LDP)

Most of the current methods for extracting pollen features are those combining different single features: LBP and fractal dimension as in [7], and LBP, GLCM, LGF and DTM as in [10], and LBP, Gabor, etc. as in [8, 9]. All of these take advantages of different features to construct the optimal representation of pollen images, but the use of multiple features leads to a higher computational costs.

In order to build pollen feature descriptor with high computational efficiency, and high robustness to rotation and noise, we proposed Local Decimal Pattern (LDP). Figure 1 shows the implementation of LDP feature for representing pollen images, and Fig. 2 presents the step of the algorithm based on LDP for pollen recognition. The specific calculation process of LDP is as follows:

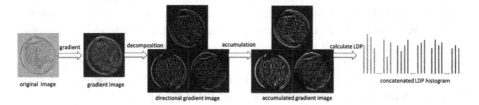

Fig. 1. Implementation of LDP feature for representing pollen.

TRAINING STAGE:
Input: T – Training set(t_i represents the pollen image in training set);
    r – Sampling radius;
    m – Block size;
    L – Quantization interval number;
Output: Trained classifier;
1. **for** t_i **in** T **do**
2.   Calculate the image gradient;
3.   Weighting the gradient into 8 directions and find out the maximum, minimum and median radient directions, which is denoted as D_1, D_2 and D_3 respectively;
4.   **for** D_1 **to** D_3 **do**
5.   Calculate the gradient magnitude of pixel blocks under D_*;
6.   Calculate the LDP under D_* and compute the statistical histogram of LDP;
7.   **end for**
8.   Concatenating the LDP histogram in 3 directions;
9. **end for**
10. Training using SVM classifier;
TEST STAGE:
Input: M– Test set(m_j represents the pollen image in test set);
Output: The predicted category of test image;
11. **for** m_j **in** M **do** 2 - 8
12. Predicting the category of test image using trained SVM classifier;
13. **end for**

Fig. 2. The step of the algorithm based on LDP for pollen recognition.

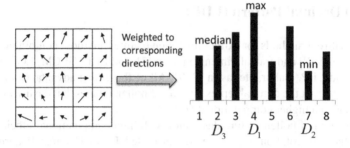

Fig. 3. Calculation of gradient histogram of an image block. The lengths and directions of arrows represent the gradient magnitude and gradient direction of pixels respectively.

First, we calculate the image gradient, the gradient information of each pixel includes gradient magnitude and gradient angle. The gradient angle range from $-\pi$ to π, and we divide $[-\pi, \pi)$ into 8 equal-sized direction intervals. Then, a histogram of gradient is calculated by weighting all pixels' gradient magnitude into corresponding gradient directions, and the directions with maximum, minimum and median gradient are marked as D_1, D_2 and D_3 respectively (as shown in Fig. 3). The gradient magnitude of pixel blocks under different gradient directions is calculated as follows:

$$B_m^D = \sum_{k=1}^{m^2} \left(m_{P_K} \times E^D \left(\theta_{P_k} \right) \right) \tag{1}$$

$$E^D\left(\theta_{P_k} \right) = \begin{cases} 1 & \theta_{P_k} \in D \\ 0 & \theta_{P_k} \notin D \end{cases} \tag{2}$$

Where: D is the gradient direction; m is the pixel block size; m_{P_K} and θ_{P_K} are the gradient magnitude and gradient angle of the pixel P_K.

Second, the number of pixel blocks in ith quantization interval under gradient direction D is counted as follows:

$$N_i^D = \sum_{j=1}^{n} S_i \left(B_{r,n,m,j}^D - B_{m,c}^D \right) \tag{3}$$

$$S_i(x) = \begin{cases} 1 & |x| \in Q_i \\ 0 & |x| \notin Q_i \end{cases} \tag{4}$$

$$Q_i = [l_i, l_{i+1}) \tag{5}$$

Where: n is the number of neighboring pixel blocks; $B_{r,n,m,j}^D$ is the gradient magnitude of the $m \times m$ pixel block in the square neighborhood with sampling radius r; j is the serial number of pixel blocks; $B_{m,c}^D$ is the gradient magnitude of the central pixel block under gradient direction D; Q_i is the ith quantization interval; l_i is the threshold of Q_i.

After counting the number of neighboring pixel blocks located at different quantization intervals, we can define the Local Decimal Pattern (LDP) as follows:

$$LDP^D = \sum_{i=1}^{L} N_i^D \times 10^{i-1} \tag{6}$$

Where L is the total number of quantization intervals.

At last, we calculate the LDP feature histograms under three gradient directions, and the final representation of pollen images is the concatenation of these LDP histograms:

$$LDPH = \left\{ LDPH^{D_1}, LDPH^{D_2}, LDPH^{D_3} \right\} \tag{7}$$

Figure 4 shows the calculation process of LDP of an image block under direction D_1, the color of the square in figure represents the gradient magnitude difference between the neighboring pixel blocks and the central pixel block under the gradient direction D_1, and the same color indicates that the difference of gradient magnitude belongs to the same quantization interval. In Fig. 4, the gradient magnitude of pixel blocks under gradient direction D_1 are quantized into 4 intervals, and the number of pixel blocks under 4 quantization intervals is counted as 4, 2, 1 and 1, respectively. So we can get a local decimal pattern 1124.

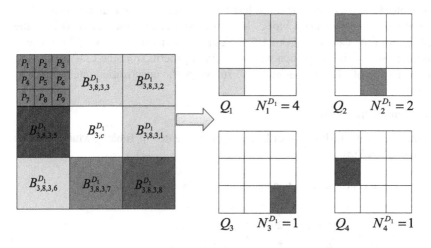

$$LDP^{D_1} = 4 \times 10^0 + 2 \times 10^1 + 1 \times 10^2 + 1 \times 10^3 = 1124$$

Fig. 4. Calculation of LDP of an image block under direction D_1.

3   Pollen Recognition Experiments

To evaluate our method, we performed experiments on pollenmonitor dataset with a computer of Intel(R) Core(TM) i5-3210 M @ 2.50 GHz processor and 6 GB memory, and the software we used is MATLAB R2014a. We randomly selected 60% of the pollen images of each category on pollenmonitor dataset as training images and the rest were used as test images. A SVM classifier [12, 13] was used for the classification and recognition of pollen images, and the correct recognition rate (CRR), recall rate (RR), F1-measure and recognition time (RT) were used to measure the experimental performance, where, F1-measure is the harmonic average of CRR and RR.

3.1 Parameter Selection

(1) Neighbor number, sampling radius and block size:

We use a sampling strategy with fixed number of neighboring pixel blocks ($n = 8$), and different block size and sampling radius ($m = \{2, 3, 4, 5, 6, 7, 8, 9, 10\}$, $r = \{2, 3, 4, 5, 6, 7, 8, 9, 10\}$).

(2) Quantization interval number:

We performed experiments with different number of quantization intervals and find that 2 quantization intervals is not enough to represent pollen texture feature, but too many (more than 4) leads to a higher dimension of LDP histogram. When the number of quantization intervals is 3, 4, the corresponding dimensions of LDP histogram are 8×10^2 and 8×10^3, respectively. In fact, many decimal patterns do not exist, resulting in large columns of LDP histogram are empty. That's because the total number of quantized pixel blocks in the neighborhood is fixed ($n = 8$). Take 3 quantization intervals for instance, if the number of pixel blocks located at first quantization interval is 7, the decimal pattern only can be 107 or 017, and other patterns such as 117, 127, etc. can never appear. So, we delete the nonexistent decimal patterns from the LDP histogram, and the dimension of LDP histogram is 45, 165 when the quantization interval is 3, 4, respectively.

(3) Quantization thresholds:

The quantization thresholds with $L = 3, 4$, are presented in Table 1, which depends on pixel block size (m).

Table 1. The quantization thresholds of different quantization levels

	l_1	l_2	l_3	l_4
$L = 3$	0	2 m	m^3	–
$L = 4$	0	m + 1	$(m+1)^2$	$2(m+1)^2$

3.2 Experimental Results on Pollenmonitor Dataset

The Pollenmonitor dataset comprises air pollen samples from 33 different taxa collected in Freiburg and Zurich in 2006. The number of pollen images in this dataset is about 22700. Affected by the micro-sensors and irregular collection methods, some pollen images have some degrees of deformation and contamination, and the image quality is generally not high.

By varying the pixel block size and sampling radius from 2 to 10, we get the correct recognition rates as presented in Fig. 5. Obviously, 4 quantization intervals ($L = 4$) performs better, and the best recognition rate was obtained with the block size 5.

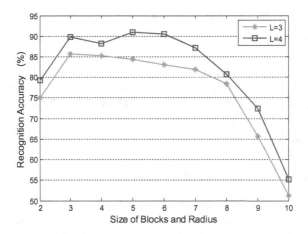

Fig. 5. Recognition results (%) on Pollenmonitor dataset with different block size and quantization intervals.

Figure 6 presents the partial recognition instances of 6 representative pollen categories on Pollenmonitor dataset. It can be seen that most pollen images with clear texture and have not been contaminated and deformed can be correctly identified. The specific recognition results are shown in Table 2, we can find that the correct recognition rates of most pollen categories are more than 90%, and the recall rates of all categories are

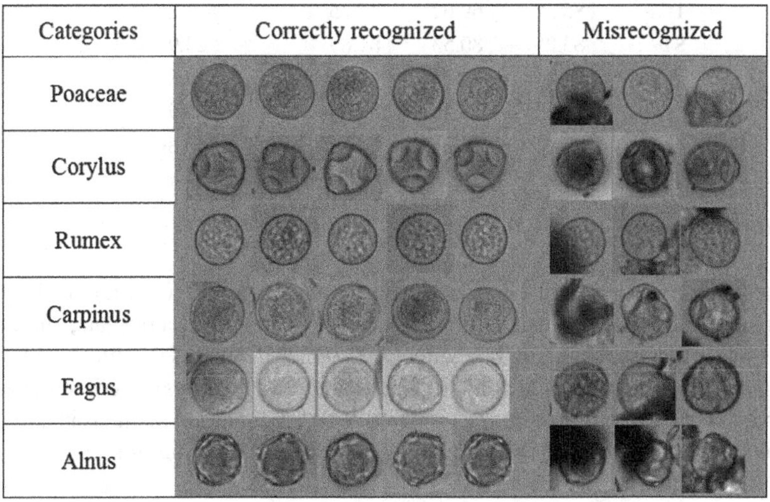

Categories	Correctly recognized	Misrecognized
Poaceae		
Corylus		
Rumex		
Carpinus		
Fagus		
Alnus		

Fig. 6. Recognition instances of 6 classic pollen taxa from the Pollenmonitor dataset.

more than 73%. For Corylus category with varying degrees of rotation, our method achieved 94.02% correct recognition rate. For Fagus category with severe noise, our method can also obtained 83.18% correct recognition rate.

Table 2. Recognition results of 6 classic pollen taxa in Pollenmonitor dataset

Pollen category	CRR/%	RR/%	F1-measure	RT/s
Poaceae	90.33	79.10	84.34	6.5
Corylus	94.02	85.27	89.43	6.4
Rumex	92.15	73.64	81.86	6.4
Carpinus	88.62	78.13	83.05	6.5
Fagus	83.18	76.65	79.78	6.3
Alnus	92.50	88.74	90.58	6.9

3.3   Experimental Comparison and Analysis

We compared the best recognition rates achieved by our method using different block size with state-of-the-art pollen recognition methods, the experimental results on Pollenmonitor datasets are listed in Table 3. The average correct recognition rate of our method on Pollenmonitor datasets is 90.95%, which is on average 6.81 percentage points higher than that of compared pollen recognition methods. The experimental results show that our proposed method has a better recognition performance and the computational efficiency is higher than most of the compared methods.

Table 3. Comparison of the average recognition results of our method and 5 pollen recognition methods on Pollenmonitor dataset

Method	CRR/%	RR/%	F1-measure	ART/s
DLSC	74.83	82.97	78.69	4.1
TGF	85.50	69.62	76.75	7.2
STAF	83.29	80.53	81.89	23.9
LGGG	87.21	70.15	77.76	19.2
LDLG	89.87	75.46	82.04	20.9
LDP	90.95	78.25	84.12	6.8

4   Conclusions

In this paper, we presented a LDP descriptor for pollen image recognition. Unlike most pollen recognition methods fusing different kinds of features in recent years, our method extracts single texture feature in three directions, which decreases the dimensionality of pollen features and increases the discrimination at the same time. Experimental results show that our method outperforms 5 compared pollen recognition methods in extracting pollen texture feature, and has robustness to the noise and rotation of pollen images.

Acknowledgments. This work was partially supported by the grant of the National Natural Science Foundation of China 61375030.

References

1. Treloar, W.J., Taylor, G.E., Flenley, J.R.: Towards automation of palynology 1: analysis of pollen shape and ornamentation using simple geometric measures, derived from scanning electron microscope images. J. Quat. Sci. **19**, 745–754 (2004)
2. Tian, H., Cui W., Wan, T., Chen, M.: A computational approach for recognition of electronic microscope plant pollen images. In: Congress on Image and Signal Processing, CISP 2008, pp. 259–263 (2008)
3. Chen, B., Yang, J., Jeon, B., Zhang, X.: Kernel quaternion principal component analysis and its application in RGB-D object recognition. Neurocomputing **266**, 293–303 (2017)
4. Zhou, Z., Wang, Y., Wu, Q.M.J., Yang, C.N., Sun, X.: Effective and efficient global context verification for image copy detection. IEEE Trans. Inf. Forensics Secur. **12**, 48–63 (2017)
5. Yuan, C., Sun, X., Lv, R.: Fingerprint liveness detection based on multi-scale LPQ and PCA. China Commun. **13**, 60–65 (2016)
6. Kong, S., Punyasena, S., Fowlkes, C.: Spatially aware dictionary learning and coding for fossil pollen identification. In: Computer Vision and Pattern Recognition Workshops, pp. 1305–1314 (2016)
7. Daood, A., Ribeiro, E., Bush, M.: Pollen recognition using a multi-layer hierarchical classifier. In: International Conference on Pattern Recognition, pp. 3091–3096 (2017)
8. Boochs, F., Chudyk, C.: Development of an automatic pollen classification system using shape, texture and aperture features. In: LWA 2015 Workshops: KDML, FGWM, IR, and FGDB (2015)
9. Guru, D.S., Siddesha, S.: Texture in Classification of Pollen Grain Images. Springer India, (2013)
10. Marcos, J.V., et al.: Automated pollen identification using microscopic imaging and texture analysis. Micron. **68**, 36–46 (2015)
11. Wolf, L., Hassner, T., Taigman, Y.: Effective unconstrained face recognition by combining multiple descriptors and learned background statistics. IEEE Trans. Pattern Anal. Mach. Intell. **33**, 1978–1990 (2011)
12. Gu, B., Sheng, V.S., Sheng, S.: A robust regularization path algorithm for v-support vector classification. IEEE Trans. Neural Netw. Learn. Syst. **28**, 1241 (2016)
13. Gu, B., Sheng, V.S., Tay, K.Y., Romano, W., Li, S.: Incremental support vector learning for ordinal regression. IEEE Trans. Neural Netw. Learn. Syst. **26**, 1403–1416 (2017)

New Architecture of Correlated Weights Neural Network for Global Image Transformations

Sławomir Golak, Anna Jama$^{(\boxtimes)}$, Marcin Blachnik, and Tadeusz Wieczorek

Department of Industrial Informatics, Silesian University of Technology, Krasinskiego 8, 40-019 Katowice, Poland
anna.jama@polsl.pl

Abstract. The paper describes a new extension of the convolutional neural network concept. The developed network, similarly to the CNN, instead of using independent weights for each neuron in the network uses related weights. This results in a small number of parameters optimized in the learning process, and high resistance to overtraining. However unlike the CNN, instead of sharing weights, the network takes advantage of weights correlated with coordinates of a neuron and its inputs, calculated by a dedicated subnet. This solution allows the neural layer of the network to perform global transformation of patterns what was unachievable for convolutional layers. The new network concept has been confirmed by verification of its ability to perform typical image affine transformations such as translation, scaling and rotation.

Keywords: Network architecture · Spatial transformation · CNN

1 Introduction

Recent approaches to object recognition make essential use of machine learning methods [1, 2]. To increase their performance, we can collect larger datasets, learn more powerful models, and use better techniques for preventing overfitting [3]. To create network capable to learn to recognize thousands of objects from millions of images, we need to build a model with a large learning capacity. Convolutional neural networks (CNNs) constitute one such class of models. They are powerful visual models which recently enjoyed a great success in large-scale image and video recognition [4–6], what has become possible thanks to the large public image repositories, such as ImageNet, and high performance computing systems, such as GPUs or large-scale distributed clusters [7]. CNN combine three architectural ideas to ensure some degree of shift, scale, and distortion invariance: local receptive fields, shared weights (or weight replication), and spatial or temporal subsampling [8, 9]. The main benefit of using CNNs is the reduced amount of parameters that have to be determined during a learning process. CNN can be regarded as a variant of the standard neural network which instead of using fully connected hidden layers, introduces a special network structure, which consists of alternating so-called convolution and pooling layers [10].

© Springer Nature Switzerland AG 2018
V. Kůrková et al. (Eds.): ICANN 2018, LNCS 11140, pp. 56–65, 2018.
https://doi.org/10.1007/978-3-030-01421-6_6

One of the limitations of CNN is the problem of global pattern transformations such as e.g. rotation or scaling of an image. Convolutional neurons which have spatially limited input field are unable to identify such transformations. They are only capable to local pattern transformations such as detection of local features on the image. The size increase of spatial transformation area would require the enlargement of the neurons input field, therefore the increase of weight vector size and result in the loss of the primary advantage of the CNN network, which is a small number of parameters.

In order to overcome the constraints of CNN in the paper we introduce a new network which can replace the convolutional layer or it can be used as an independent network able to learn any global and/or local transformations. The proposed network consists of two networks. The main network is a single fully connected layer of neurons, aimed at direct performing image transformation. However, weights of this network are not determined directly, instead to limit the number of trainable parameters, the weights of the neurons are obtained by the sub-network, which is relatively small network. The second network takes advantage of the observation that for global transformations particular weights of individual neurons are strongly correlated with one another, hence the entire network is called the Correlated Weights Neural Network (CWNN). Proposed network is a continuation of the earlier idea of using weights calculated by the subnet in a Radial Basis Network (RBF) for pattern classification [11] called the Induced Weights Artificial Neural Network (IWANN). However, in the IWANN the values of weights were determined only based on the input coordinates, consequently the coordinates of the neurons were ignored. This approach was related to different structure and application of the IWANN network.

In the paper we describe and explain the structure of the CWNN network (Sects. 2 and 3), then Sect. 4 describes the training algorithm, and in Sect. 5 we demonstrate its application to train global transformations such as scaling, translation and rotation. We end with a summary of the obtained results and draw further research perspectives.

2 Problem Definition

Neural network presented in this paper is dedicated to global pattern transformations. Figure 1 shows linearized representation of the main network's neurons which are responsible for the input-output transformation, and assume gray scale images. This single layered network consists of linear neurons, witch without the bias, are sufficient to implement the network. Each neuron determine the output value (the gray level of the pixel for output image) as a linear combination of all pixels in the input image. In case of a N size pattern, this operation can be perform by a network which has N output neurons associated to each of the N inputs. Total number of weights for this network is N2, which for relatively small (32 × 32 pixels) images presented in the further part of the article leads to the number of 1 million parameters describing the network. The number of parameters is directly reflected in the complexity of the network learning process, and in the size requirements for training dataset.

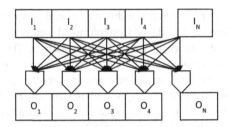

Fig. 1. Neural network for a global transformation of a pattern.

However, in vast majority of global transformation, network weights are correlated with positions of neurons and their inputs. Table 1 presents the values of weights for the network from Fig. 1, which performs translation of one-dimensional pattern, by 2 elements to the right (for simplicity we consider N = 5). The columns in the table correspond to the inputs, and rows to the outputs, so a single row represents weights of a single linear neuron. The final value of each output is determined as the weighted sum of inputs described by weights in particular row.

Table 1. Weights of the neural network translating a linear pattern by two elements.

	I1	I2	I3	I4	5
O1	0	0	0	0	0
O2	0	0	0	0	0
O3	1	0	0	0	0
O4	0	1	0	0	0
O5	0	0	1	0	0

The table content shows a clear regularity in the set of weights. The value of the weight which connects the i-th output's neuron with j-th input, in this network, can be described by simple equation:

$$w_{i,j} = \begin{cases} 1 & j - t = i \\ 0 & j - t \neq i \end{cases} \tag{1}$$

Where: t - size of translation, i-output position, j-input position

This formula replaces 25 network weights, and it's degree of complexity is independent of the size of transformed pattern. The essential idea of the CWNN network can be explained by using this example. It involve the fact that the weights of the network are not stored as static values, but calculated based on the mutual position of neurons and their inputs. The practical use of the relation between neuron weights, requires a subsystem which is able to learn the dependences between neurons and its weights. To address this issue, we utilize additional subnetwork presented in the following section.

3 Network Model

Figure 2 shows the structure of a single-layer network with the Correlated Weights Neural Layer (CWNL). The network has one input layer, which topology results from the size and dimensionality of processed input pattern. Network inputs are described by the coordinates vector, which size is compatible with dimensionality of the input data. The topology of the main, active CWNL layer, which have signals transmitted directly on the network output, is compatible with dimensionality and the size of the output pattern. It should be taken into consideration that both dimensionality and the size of the input and the output can be completely different.

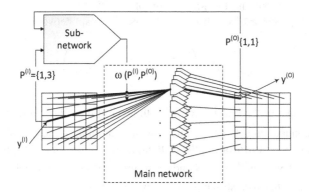

Fig. 2. Structure of the neural network with correlated weights.

It has been assumed that for the neural network performing affine transformations on an image, it is sufficient to use neurons with a linear transition function, that takes as an argument a weighted sum of inputs, without the bias value (2).

$$y_i^{(O)} = \sum_{j=1}^{N^{(I)}} y_j^{(I)} \omega_{i,j,1}^{(M)} \qquad (2)$$

Where: $y_i^{(O)}$ – i-*th* output of the layer with correlated weights, $y_j^{(I)}$ – j-t*h* input of the layer with correlated weights, $N^{(I)}$ – number of inputs for the CWNL layer, $\omega_{i,j,1}^{(M)}$ – output of subnet calculating weights – weight of connection between the i-*th* output with the j-*th* input of the CWNL layer, M - the number of the last subnet layer.

The values of connected weights are calculated by the subnetwork based on the coordinates of neuron in the CWNL layer and the coordinates of neurons inputs. These values are determined many times by the subnet for every combination of input image pixels and output image pixels. The subnetwork inputs are represented by a vector, which consists of coordinates of the CWNL neurons and their inputs:

$$P_{i,j} = P_i^{(I)} \cup P_j^{(O)} \tag{3}$$

where: $P_i^{(I)}$ – coordinates of the i-*th* input of the main network, $P_j^{(O)}$ – coordinates of the j-*th* output (neuron) of the main network

$$\omega_{i,j,k}^{(O)} = P_{i,j}[k] \tag{4}$$

where: the k-*th* input of the subnetwork calculating the weight of the connection between of the i-*th* input and the j-*th* neuron of the CWNL.

The signal is processed by subsequent layers of the subnetwork:

$$\omega_{i,j,k}^{(m)} = f^{(m)} \left(\sum_{l=1}^{O^{(m-1)}} \omega_{i,j,l}^{(m-1)} w_{k,l}^{(m)} + b_k^{(m)} \right) \tag{5}$$

where: $\omega_{i,j,k}^{(m)}$ – output of the k-*th* neuron of m-th layer of the subnetwork calculating the weight for the connection between j-*th* neuron and i-th input of the CWNL layer, $f^{(m)}$ – the transition function of neurons in the m-*th* layer, $O^{(m)}$ – the number of neurons in the m-*th* subnetwork layer, $w_{k,l}^{(m)}$, $b_k^{(m)}$ - standard weight and bias of the subnet neuron.

In the presented network structure, it was proposed to use the multilayer perceptron as a subnetwork. However, this task can be performed by any other approximator.

4   Learning Method

The learning algorithm of the CWNN network is based on the classical minimization of the square error function, defined as:

$$SSE = \frac{1}{2} \sum_{j=1}^{N^{(O)}} \left(y_j^{(O)} - d_j \right)^2 \tag{6}$$

Where: $N^{(O)}$ – number of neurons in the layer with correlated weights, $y_j^{(O)}$ – j-*th* output of the layer with correlated weights, d_j – desired value of the j-*th* output of the CWNN network.

Effective learning of CWNN requires the use of one of the gradient methods to minimalize the error. In case of presented network, the parameters optimized in the learning process include only: weights and biases of the subnetwork, that calculates the main layer weights. This required modification of the classical backpropagation method, to allow for an error transfer to the subnet. The error value for the output neuron of the subnetwork, which calculates the weight of the connection between the j-th output and the i-th input of the main network, is determined by the equation:

$$\sigma_{i,j,k}^{(M)} = \left(y_i^{(O)} - d_i \right) y_j^{(I)} \tag{7}$$

where: $y_j^{(I)}$ – i-th output of the layer with correlated weights, $y_j^{(O)}$ – j-th output of the layer with correlated weights, d_i – value of the i-th input of main network.

In the next stage the error is back propagated from the output through subsequent network layers. The aim of the backpropagation is to update each of the weights in the subnetwork so that they cause the actual output to be closer the target output, thereby minimizing the error for each output neuron and the network as a whole.

$$\sigma_{i,j,k}^{(m)} = \sum_{i=1}^{O^{(m+1)}} \left(\left(\sigma_{i,j,l}^{(m+1)} w_{k,l}^{(m+1)} \right) f' \left(\sum_{l=1}^{O^{(m-1)}} \omega_{i,j,l}^{(m-1)} w_{k,l}^{(m)} + b_k^{(m)} \right) \right) \tag{8}$$

Where: $\omega_{i,j,k}^{(m)}$ – output of the k-th neuron of m-th layer of the subnetwork calculating the weight for the connection between j-th neuron and i-th input of the CWNL layer, $O(m)$ – the number of neurons in the m-th subnetwork layer, $w_{k,l}^{(m)}$, $b_k^{(m)}$ - standard weight and bias of the subnet neuron.

Based on the error value it is possible to determine partial derivative for all parameters (weights and biases) of the subnet. Determination of partial derivative requires summation of derivatives calculated for all weights provided by the subnet:

$$\frac{\partial E}{\partial w_{k,l}^{(m)}} = \sum_{i=1}^{N^{(I)}} \sum_{j=1}^{N^{(O)}} \sum_{l=1}^{O^{(m-1)}} \sigma_{i,j,k}^{(m)} \omega_{k,l}^{(m-1)}; \frac{\partial E}{\partial b_k^{(m)}} = \sum_{i=1}^{N^{(I)}} \sum_{j=1}^{N^{(O)}} \sum_{l=1}^{O^{(m-1)}} \sigma_{i,j,k}^{(m)} \tag{9}$$

where: $\omega_{i,j,k}^{(m)}$ – output of the k-th neuron of m-th layer of the subnetwork calculating the weight for the connection between j-th neuron and i-th input of the CWNL layer, $O^{(m)}$ - the number of neurons in the m-th subnetwork layer, $w_{k,l}^{(m)}$, $N^{(O)}$ – number of neurons in the layer with correlated weights, $N^{(I)}$ – number of inputs for the CWNL layer

For the presented network partial derivatives were computed with the use of the above equations.

5   Results

Effectiveness of the developed neural network has been exanimated by the implementation and analysis of the global image transformations, like scaling, rotation and translation. The popular CIFAR-10 collection was used in the experiments [12]. This dataset was primarily intended for testing classification models, but it can be considered as a useful source of images also for other applications. The collection contains various type of scenes, and consists of 60000 32 × 32 color images.

Due to the large computational complexity of learning process calculations were performed on the PLGRID cluster, which was created as part of the PL-Grid - Polish Science Infrastructure for Scientific Research in the European Research Area project. The PLGRID infrastructure contains computing power of over 588 teraflops and disk storage above 5.8 petabytes.

For each variant of the experiment a collection of images, for both training and testing set, contained only 50 examples. Global image transformations were used to verify the performance of the designed system. The input of the network was a primary image (1024 pixels). The expected response (the output of the network) was an image after the selected transformation. The network was trained in batch mode using the RPROP method (resilient back propagation) [13] due to the resistance of this method to the vanishing gradient problem. This phenomenon occurs in networks with a complex, multilayer structure as in the developed network. For small training sets this method is more effective than the popular group of stochastic gradient descent methods due to a more stable learning process. Weights of the subnetwork were initialized randomly with the use of Nguyen-Widrow method [14]. Due to very low susceptibility to overtraining by the new network, the stop procedure, based on the validation set, was omitted in the learning procedure. The correctness of this decision was confirmed by the obtained results. The quality of the image transformations, for: 50, 100, 1000 and 5000 epochs, was monitored during the learning process, as well as the course of changes in the MSE for both training and testing set. The same network parameters was applied to each variant of the experiment. In the first stage of research the network was trained to perform the image vertical scale transformation. The goal was to resize the image by 50% of height. The main layer with correlated weights, was compatible with the dimensions of the images in the training and test set, and had 1024 inputs and 1024 outputs, so that each neuron correspond to one pixel in 32 × 32 grid. The subnet, calculating weights of the main layer, consisted of 3 layers containing 8, 4, 1 neurons respectively, with a sigmoidal transition function. So a single sigmoid neuron providing the value in the range of [0..1] is present on the output of the sub-network. This is in line with the nature of the mapped transformations in which there are no negative weight values and values greater than 1. The convergence of the learning algorithm was measured using the mean squared error (per pixel) for each training epoch:

$$MSE = \frac{1}{S \cdot N^{(O)}} \sum_{k=1}^{S} \sum_{j=1}^{N^{(O)}} \left(y_{kj}^{(O)} - d_{kj} \right)^2 \qquad (10)$$

where: S – number of examples in the set, $N^{(O)}$ – number of network outputs, $y_{kj}^{(O)}$ – j-th output of the network for k-th example, d_{kj} – desired value of the j-*th* output (pixel brightness) for k-*th* example.

Figure 3 shows the decrease of the MSE during the learning process and a sample of images from the training set with the stages of scaling results during the learning process. It was observed that, after 1000 learning epochs, the outline of correct transformation appeared. After 5000 epochs, the quality of transformed image was satisfactory, although there were still disturbances in case of some images (see the fourth image – the plane). The black stains are areas where pixel values have exceeded the limit value 1. This is the result of a large proportion of bright pixels in the plane image in comparison to other images. Based on the MSE graph it can be concluded that the learning process can still be continued, which should result in further improvement of the quality of the transformation.

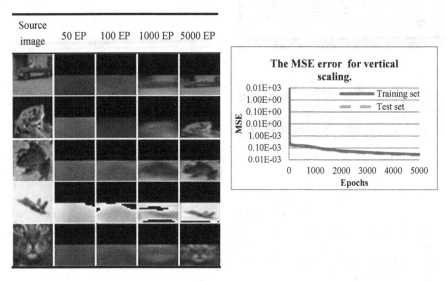

Fig. 3. The MSE error and quality of transformed image for vertical scaling.

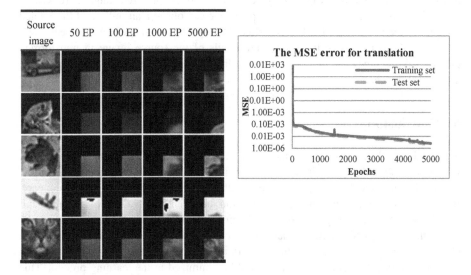

Fig. 4. The MSE error and quality of transformed image for translation.

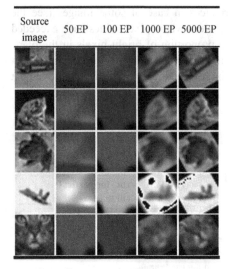

| Source image | 50 EP | 100 EP | 1000 EP | 5000 EP |

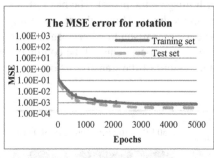

Fig. 5. The MSE error and quality of transformed image for rotation.

The same network was trained to perform an image translation. Quality of obtained results was acceptable after 5000 epochs, so the learning process was terminated. During the learning process the continuous decrease of the MSE was observed (Fig. 4) in both training and testing set. After 1000 learning epochs, the outline of the transformation appeared. The figure also shows stages of the image transformation during the learning process.

Image rotation by 30° was the most difficult challenge for the network due to the necessity of mapping trigonometric relations. During the learning process the decrease of MSE error is similar to the previous cases (Fig. 5). In analyzed range there was no overtraining of the network. After 100 epochs we can observe an outline of the rotated image, but the picture itself is blurry. After 1000 epochs the image become clearer and it is possible to recognize the shape and details of the source image in transformed picture. Like in the previous calculations quality of the obtained results was acceptable after 5000 epochs.

6   Conclusion

Proposed neural network represents a significant extension of the concept of network with convolutional layers. It use the current CNN idea of similarity between the weights for individual neurons in the layer, but breaks with their direct sharing concept. Based on the observation on the correlation between, the values of weights and coordinates of neurons inputs and the coordinates of the neurons themselves, it can be stated that the CWNN network can implement transformations not available for the CNN network. At the same time, the network retains main advantage of CNN, which is the small number of parameters that should be optimized in the learning process. This paper propose a new structure of the neural network and its learning method. The concept of network has been verified by checking its ability to implement typical global pattern transformations. The results confirms the ability of the CWNN to perform any global transformations. Presented research has been conducted based on a single-layer CWNN. Further research will focus on creation of networks with multiple layers, and ability to combine these layers with convolution layers, as well as with standard layers with a full pool of connections. This should give a chance to develop new solutions in the area of deep networks, which will allow to get competitive results in more complex tasks.

Acknowledgments. This research was supported in part by PL-Grid Infrastructure under Grant PLGJAMA2017.

References

1. Jaderberg, M., Simonyan, K., Zisserman, A., Kavukcuoglu, K.: Spatial transformer networks. In: NIPS 2015 (Spotlight), vol. 2, pp. 2017–2025 (2015)
2. Ferreira, A., Giraldib, G.: Convolutional Neural Network approaches to granite tiles classification. Expert Syst. Appl. **84**, 1–11 (2017)
3. Krizhevsky, A., Sutskever I., Hinton, G.E.: Imagenet classification with deep convolutional neural networks. In: NIPS-2012, pp. 1097–1105 (2012)
4. Zhang, Y., Zhao, D., Sun, J., Zou, G., Li, W.: Adaptive convolutional neural network and its application in face recognition. Neural Process. Lett. **43**(2), 389–399 (2016)
5. Radwan, M.A., Khalil, M.I., Abbas, H.M.: Neural networks pipeline for offline machine printed Arabic OCR. Neural Process. Lett. (2017). https://doi.org/10.1007/s11063-017-9727-y
6. Simonyan, K., Zisserman, A.: Very deep convolutional networks for large-scale image recognition. CoRR, abs/1409.1556. http://arxiv.org/abs/1409.1556. Accessed 19 May 2018
7. LeCun, Y., Bottou, L., Bengio, Y., Haffner, P.: Gradient based learning applied to document recognition. IEEE **86**(11), 2278–2324 (1998)
8. Abdel-Hamid, O., Mohamed, A., Jiang, H., Deng, L., Penn, G., Yu, D.: Convolutional Neural Networks for speech recognition. IEEE/ACM Trans. Audio Speech Lang. Process. **22**(10), 1533–1545 (2014)
9. Wang, Y., Zu, C., Hu, G., et al.: Automatic tumor segmentation with Deep Convolutional Neural Networks for radiotherapy applications. Neural Process. Lett. (2018). https://doi.org/10.1007/s11063-017-9759-3
10. Rumelhart, D.E., Hinton, G.E., Williams, R.J.: Learning representations by back-propagating errors. Nature **323**(6088), 533–536 (1986)
11. Golak, S.: Induced weights artificial neural network. In: Duch, W., Kacprzyk, J., Oja, E., Zadrożny, S. (eds.) ICANN 2005. LNCS, vol. 3697, pp. 295–300. Springer, Heidelberg (2005). https://doi.org/10.1007/11550907_47
12. Cire, D., Meier, U., Schmidhuber, J.: Multi-column deep neural networks for image classification. Arxiv preprint arXiv:1202.2745 (2012)
13. Christian, I., Husken, M.: Empirical evaluation of the improved Rprop learning algorithms. Neurocomputing **50**, 105–123 (2003)
14. Nguyen, D., Widrow, B.: Improving the learning speed of 2-layer neural networks by choosing initial values of adaptive weights. In: IJCNN, pp. III-21–26 (1989)

Compression-Based Clustering of Video Human Activity Using an ASCII Encoding

Guillermo Sarasa[1]([✉]), Aaron Montero[1], Ana Granados[2],
and Francisco B. Rodriguez[1]

[1] Grupo de Neurocomputación Biológica, Escuela Politécnica Superior,
Universidad Autónoma de Madrid, Madrid, Spain
guillermo.sarasa@predoc.uam.es, montaaron@gmail.com, f.rodriguez@uam.es
[2] CES Felipe II, Universidad Complutense de Madrid, Aranjuez, Madrid, Spain
ana.granados@ajz.ucm.es
http://arantxa.ii.uam.es/∼gnb/

Abstract. Human Activity Recognition (HAR) from videos is an important area of computer vision research with several applications. There are a wide number of methods to classify video human activities, not without certain disadvantages such as computational cost, dataset specificity or low resistance to noise, among others. In this paper, we propose the use of the Normalized Compression Distance (NCD), as a complementary approach to identify video-based HAR. We have developed a novel ASCII video data format, as a suitable format to apply the NCD in video. For our experiments, we have used the *Activities of Daily Living Dataset*, to discriminate several human activities performed by different subjects. The experimental results presented in this paper show that the NCD can be used as an alternative to classical analysis of video HAR.

Keywords: Data mining · Normalized Compression Distance
Clustering · Dendrogram · Image processing
Human Activity Recognition · Silhouette Coefficient · Similarity

1 Introduction

Human Activity Recognition (HAR) [4,6,31] from videos represent a relevant area of computer vision research. Its utility in many areas has increased the demand of broader analysis in the field, producing an increase of publications related with Computer Vision in HAR [4,26,31]. Some of its applications are: human health care [17], video labeling [27,28], surveillance [21,26]and human-computer interaction [1,24], among others. There are many approaches in the literature to identify human activities from video with remarkable results. However, dealing with video implies solving certain issues that eventually lead to some drawbacks in the final systems of HAR video processing. Some examples are high computational costs, dataset specificity or the dependency of the temporal movement sequence.

© Springer Nature Switzerland AG 2018
V. Kůrková et al. (Eds.): ICANN 2018, LNCS 11140, pp. 66–75, 2018.
https://doi.org/10.1007/978-3-030-01421-6_7

Vision-based HAR can be summarized as a combination of extracting some features from a sequence, and discriminating between activities by means of a classification system. The most important difficulties of feature extraction in video processing are: (i) overlap and variability between and within classes, (ii) temporal differences between samples (iii) impact and complexity of the environment and (iv) quality of the data. As an example of the first problem, a video may contain activities that include similar movements (e.g. reading and using a tablet) but also can include activities that are carried out differently by different people (e.g. cooking). Following this last case we can find others examples of the second problem. Among others, the duration, repetition or even order of execution of an activity can differ greatly, causing variations in the temporal structure, or sequence, of the activity. Finally, the capability to identify the background depends on many factors such as color difference, movement of the camera, or even quality of the recorded video.

There are a considerable variety of methods that aim to solve these problems in the literature [4,6,31]. However, as we introduced before, the inherent drawbacks of these methods require additional adjustments in order to be used in a real-world application. In this work, we aim to use compression algorithms as a parameter free dissimilarity approach (among other reasons, see Sect. 2.1) to identify human activities in video files. The idea behind using a parameter free method is to identify the relevant information without performing any low level analysis on the data. This is to increase the applicability of the method (due to the lack of specificity and parameters) while decreasing its computational costs (that some times make the system prohibitive to real-world implementations). Also, the use of compression distances over video data represents a novel application with remarkable applications for video analysis.

In this work, we have developed a video-to-ASCII processing method to locate and convert the activity of the video files into suitable objects for a compression algorithm. In order to test the capabilities of these methodology, we have performed experiments over the *Activities of Daily Living Dataset* [22] (see Sect. 3). This dataset is composed of different videos of human activities, performed by different subjects. Each video is recorded from a fixed point of view and stored in *Audio Video Interleave* (AVI) format, using the Motion JPEG video codec. In our experiments we try to discriminate between each pair of activities, parsing each video into our ASCII video format and using a widely used compression distance (the so-called Normalized Compression Distance or NCD) together with a hierarchical clustering. The results obtained using our methodology report a good separability between most of the pairs of activities. These results suggest that this measure could be used as an alternative methodology to identify video HAR.

2   Methodology

As mentioned before, we have used the *Activities of Daily Living Dataset* [22]. This data set has been used in several studies on human activity recognition in the literature [2,20]. In this Section we will introduce the compression distances, (as the methodology that we have used in this work) the methodology to convert video streams into ASCII objects and the clustering procedure to measure the identification capabilities of the NCD.

Fig. 1. Video activities examples, obtained from the *Activities of Daily Living Dataset* [22]. The five upper pictures belong to the activities labeled as: "answer phone", "chop banana", "dial phone", "drink water" and "eat banana". The five lower pictures belong to the activities labeled as: "eat snack", "look up in phonebook", "peel banana", "use silverware" and "write on whiteboard".

2.1   Normalize Compression Distances

Compression distances are dissimilarity measures that make use of compression algorithms to identify common properties between objects. These measures search for the information shared between files, and use it, to define how different, in general terms, two objects are. The Normalized Compression Distance (NCD), is a generalization defined in [8,19] that defines the distance between two objects x and y, as the relation between the size of each object compressed alone ($C(x)$ and $C(y)$), and the size of their concatenation (xy) compressed ($C(xy)$). Hence, if the concatenation of two objects can be compressed better than each object alone, it means that the objects share some information. The mathematical formulation of the NCD can be defined as:

$$NCD(x,y) = \frac{\max\{C(xy) - C(x), C(yx) - C(y)\}}{\max\{C(x), C(y)\}} \ ,$$

where C is a compression algorithm and $C(x)$ and $C(xy)$ are the size of the C-compressed versions of x and the concatenation of x and y, respectively. The NCD has been used in different areas of knowledge, with remarkable results, due to its high noise tolerance, wide applicability and capabilities among different types of data (audio, images, text, etc.). Among many others, compression distances have been used from document clustering [13,14] to spyware and phishing detection [7,18], image analysis [10,11,16,29], earth observation [5,15] and music clustering [12,25].

Due to the fact that compression distances are based on the skill of a compressor to identify similar features in big amounts of data, one would expect that video data should not be an exception. However, the video codecs used to store video streams (sequence of images) in video files, already compress the information. In contrast to a text book or a bitmap picture, where the information is fully accessible, a video file contains the information compressed, making its identification by a compression algorithm almost impossible. The way in which the information is compressed, depends on the codec used for the video file. In the data used in this paper, each video sequence is stored using the Motion JPEG codec (one of the few lossless video codecs), which compress each frame individually as a separate image. This however is not the only issue that the NCD has with video objects. Among others, the high percentage of noise or the big heterogeneity of sizes, are examples of other drawbacks to applying NCD directly to the video format. For all these reasons, we propose a novel video ASCII representation, in order to mitigate some of these drawbacks.

2.2 Data Format: From Video to ASCII

In order to transform the activity videos into a format that could be appropriate to be used by compression algorithms, we have developed a video preprocessing method. The aim of this process is to extract the optical flow [3] of the video objects and to obtain the motion signature of each task that takes place in them. This motion signature is the one that will be encoded in ASCII format to be analyzed by the compressor. This encoding allows reducing the size of the original video files from 14.4–211 MBs to a fixed 17 KB for the ASCII format (which also solves the size problem mentioned before).

The video preprocessing consists of the following steps:

1. We extract 10 video frames from the video, equally separated in time, on which we perform a grayscale conversion, see panel (a) in Fig. 2
2. We calculate the optical flow (through Horn–Schunck method [30]) of the selected frames and apply a thresholding to obtain the image points with greater activity, see panel (b) in Fig. 2.
3. We divide the image into binary boxes (1 = movement, 0 otherwise) and calculate the total activity produced in each one of them. This will generate an activity map, see panel (c) of Fig. 2. The dimensions of the boxes used are 16×16 pixels.
4. We obtain the motion signature adding the different activity maps into a unique one, see panel (d) in Fig. 2.
5. We assign identifiers to each of the image boxes using a diagonal zigzag order (used in image encoding such as MPEG [23]), see panel (e) in Fig. 2.
6. Once the boxes are organized by means of the identifiers, we sort them according to the total activity (given by the optical flow) of each of the boxes. This is the information that will be stored into an ASCII file and, later on, analyzed by the NCD, see panel (f) in Fig. 2.

2.3 Clustering of ASCII Objects Using String Compression

Once the video objects have been parsed into our proposed ASCII video objects, it is necessary to define a methodology to measure the effect of the NCD into

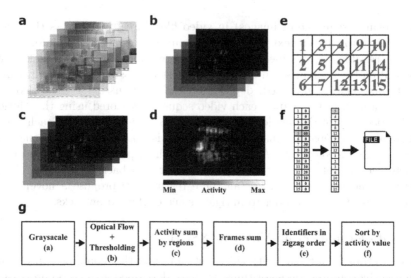

Fig. 2. Video preprocessing for conversion from the original AVI to ASCII format. Firstly, we extract a certain number of video frames and convert them to grayscale, panel (a). Secondly, we calculate the optical flow of these frames and apply a threshold on them to obtain the image points with greater activity, panel (b). Thirdly, we divide the image into boxes and calculate the total activity produced in each of them in order to generate an activity map, panel (c). Subsequently, we make the sum of the different activity maps to obtain the motion signature, panel (d). Finally, we read the image matrix (motion signature) in zigzag order, panel (e), and sort the information as a function of the total activity of each of the boxes, panel (f).

these new ASCII objects. Due to the NCD only reports a distance between two objects, we make use of a hierarchical clustering algorithm (based on the MQTC algorithm [8] from the CompLearn toolkit [9]) to parse the NCDs between objects into a dendrogram. For instance, given the case of a set of ASCII video objects, for two of the classes of Fig. 1, we can measure the NCDs between every pair of files and transform it into a hierarchical dendrogram. Finally, in order to measure how well each class is separated, we have made use of the Silhouette Coefficient (SC) (detailed in [14]) as an unbiased clustering quality measure.

3   Experiments and Results

For our experiments we have taken all the data provided by the Activities of Daily Living Dataset [22] to measure the capabilities of our methodology. This dataset includes 10 different tasks performed by 5 different subjects, 3 times each one of them. The objective in these experiments is to discriminate two sets of 15 objects each, from two classes of the videos of Fig. 1. In this figure, we show a representative frame of each class along with the names of the different tasks to classify. As an example to motivate the complexity of this problem, in Fig. 3, we show 10 samples of processed activity maps before the zig-zag sort (described in Sect. 2.2) and the dendrogram produced by the NCD-driven clustering over the 30 video objects (15 of each class). The left figures are obtained from videos of two activities performed by 5 different subjects. In this figure, one can see that the activity classes have different signatures, but are not easily differentiable at simple sight. In order to identify these signatures we made use of a NCD-driven clustering (described in Sect. 2.3) which, as the right dendrogram of the figure shows, identify the two classes perfectly.

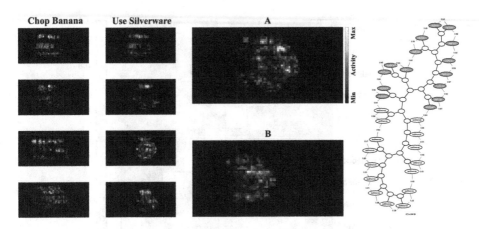

Fig. 3. Sample maps of activity for *Chop banana* and *Use silverware*, for different subjects. Each heatmap is produced by the process described in Sect. 2.2 until the zig-zag sort. This is equivalent to the *d* panel of Fig. 2. The right heatmaps, A and B, belong to *Use silverware* and *Chop banana*, respectively. As we can see, the classes are not easily differentiable at simple sight. The dendrogram of the figure shows how well our method identify each activity for all the subjects samples. The Silhouette Coefficient in this case is 0.51

In Fig. 4 one can see that the proposed format, together with the NCD, report remarkable task identification results for the majority of tasks pairs. However, there is some tasks that are more difficult to identify than others. For example, while "chopBanana" and "eatSnack" are very well separated, "peelBanana" and "eatSnack" are not. Following the first case ("chopBanana" and "eatSnack"), in Fig. 5 we show the dendrogram corresponding to the field marked with an X of Fig. 4, with and without our video-to-ASCII process (right and left dendrograms, respectively). One can see that the clustering is only achieved in the right dendrogram, where all the video objects are processed into the activity ASCII objects. Thus, the conversion of the video objects prove to be essential to the analysis.

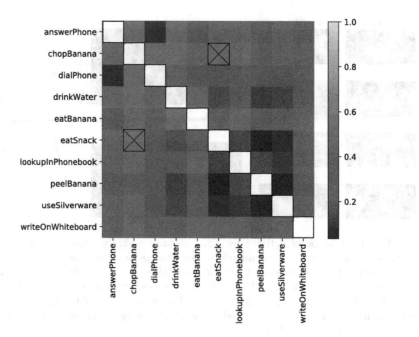

Fig. 4. Color map comparison of the clustering quality obtained from the different experiments. Each point of the map, corresponds to the S.C. obtained from parse the video to our video format (described in Sect. 2.2) and applying a NCD-driven clustering (described in Sect. 2.1). The diagonal of the matrix is not defined due to the fact that a task cannot be compared with itself. The dendrogram of the fields marked with an X is depicted in Fig. 5 right panel.

Original videos (AVI)   Parsed videos (ASCII)
(before our method)   (after our method)

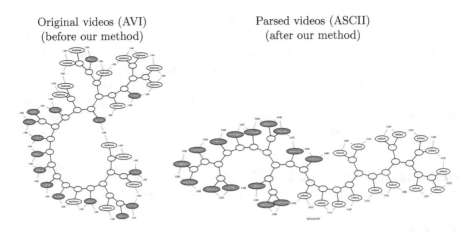

Fig. 5. Sample dendrograms, produced by the clustering of the activities: *Chop banana* and *Eat snack*, for the original files and the processed files. One can easily see that both activities are well separated in the right dendrogram (where the videos are transformed into our proposed format) while the left dendrogram (obtained from the original videos) reports almost no separability. Additionally, the Silhouette Coefficient for these dendrograms is 0.546 and 0.123, respectively. The right dendrogram corresponds to the fields marked with an X of Fig. 4.

4   Conclusions

The approach presented in this work aims to identify different human activities from video sequences addressing some of the drawbacks that classical systems have. The way in which we have performed that consist of adapting a generic, low costly and parameter-free methodology, compression distances, to our specific case by means of a video ASCII format. Particularly, we have used the well-known Normalized Compression Distance (NCD).

In order to use the NCD over video streams we defined a video-to-ASCII conversion methodology. This allows us to make use of compression distances with video objects with successfully results. In this manner, the activity of the video samples is located and casted into text files based on its location in the video frames. Our assumption is that each activity should be expressed with a particular movement signature which, on average, should be shared among various subjects. To corroborate this assumption, we have tested this methodology over different video samples using the *Activities of Daily Living Dataset* [22].

The results presented in this paper show that applying our methodology produces a remarkable clustering along the dataset, which suggests the NCD can be applied to the context of video HAR with success. In the same vein, Fig. 4 shows that the majority of the activities, for this specific database, are fine identified while only a minority are not. This means, that some pairs of activities are too similar to discriminated which videos belong to each activity using this analysis. With this approach, we achieved reasonable results without taking in consideration the particularities of the dataset.

As future work we plan to test and improve our new format over different data sets. In the same vein, we intend to produce alternative video-to-ASCII formats to measure different characteristics of the video activity, and thereby, to add robustness to the system (redundancy). Measuring the vector movement (instead of the activity index) or segmenting the video into multiple ASCII files, are examples of possible alternatives to our method. In summary, we expect to improve the capabilities of the methodology presented in this work exploring different compression algorithms, conversion methodologies and video representations.

Acknowledgment. This work was funded by Spanish project of MINECO/FEDER TIN2014-54580-R and TIN2017-84452-R, (http://www.mineco.gob.es/).

References

1. Akkaladevi, S.C., Heindl, C.: Action recognition for human robot interaction in industrial applications. In: 2015 IEEE International Conference on Computer Graphics, Vision and Information Security (CGVIS), pp. 94–99, November 2015
2. Avgerinakis, K., Briassouli, A., Kompatsiaris, I.: Recognition of activities of daily living for smart home environments. In: 2013 9th International Conference on Intelligent Environments, pp. 173–180, July 2013
3. Beauchemin, S.S., Barron, J.L.: The computation of optical flow. ACM Comput. Surv. **27**(3), 433–466 (1995)
4. Bux, A., Angelov, P., Habib, Z.: Vision based human activity recognition: a review. In: Angelov, P., Gegov, A., Jayne, C., Shen, Q. (eds.) Advances in Computational Intelligence Systems. AISC, vol. 513, pp. 341–371. Springer, Cham (2017). https://doi.org/10.1007/978-3-319-46562-3_23
5. Cerra, D., Datcu, M.: Expanding the algorithmic information theory frame for applications to earth observation. Entropy **15**(1), 407–415 (2013)
6. Chaaraoui, A.A., Climent-Pérez, P., Flórez-Revuelta, F.: A review on vision techniques applied to Human Behaviour Analysis for Ambient-Assisted Living. Expert. Syst. Appl. **39**(12), 10873–10888 (2012)
7. Chen, T.C., Dick, S., Miller, J.: Detecting visually similar web pages: application to phishing detection. ACM Trans. Internet Technol. **10**(2), 5:1–5:38 (2010)
8. Cilibrasi, R., Vitanyi, P.M.B.: Clustering by compression. IEEE Trans. Inf. Theory **51**(4), 1523–1545 (2005)
9. Cilibrasi, R., Cruz, A.L., de Rooij, S., Keijzer, M.: CompLearn Home. CompLearn Toolkit. http://www.complearn.org/
10. Cohen, A.R.: Extracting meaning from biological imaging data. Mol. Biol. Cell **25**(22), 3470–3473 (2014)
11. Cohen, A., Bjornsson, C., Temple, S., Banker, G., Roysam, B.: Automatic summarization of changes in biological image sequences using algorithmic information theory. IEEE Trans. Pattern Anal. Mach. Intell. **31**(8), 1386–1403 (2009)
12. González-Pardo, A., Granados, A., Camacho, D., de Borja Rodríguez, F.: Influence of music representation on compression-based clustering. In: IEEE World Congress on Evolutionary Computation, pp. 2988–2995 (2010)
13. Granados, A., Cebrian, M., Camacho, D., de Borja Rodriguez, F.: Reducing the loss of information through annealing text distortion. IEEE Trans. Knowl. Data Eng. **23**(7), 1090–1102 (2011)

14. Granados, A., Koroutchev, K., de Borja Rodríguez, F.: Discovering data set nature through algorithmic clustering based on string compression. IEEE Trans. Knowl. Data Eng. **27**(3), 699–711 (2015)
15. Gueguen, L., Datcu, M.: A similarity metric for retrieval of compressed objects: application for mining satellite image time series. IEEE Trans. Knowl. Data Eng. **20**(4), 562–575 (2008)
16. Guha, T., Ward, R.K.: Image similarity using sparse representation and compression distance. IEEE Trans. Multimed. **16**(4), 980–987 (2014)
17. Khan, Z.A., Sohn, W.: Abnormal human activity recognition system based on R-transform and kernel discriminant technique for elderly home care. IEEE Trans. Consum. Electron. **57**(4), 1843–1850 (2011)
18. Lavesson, N., Axelsson, S.: Similarity assessment for removal of noisy end user license agreements. Knowl. Inf. Syst. **32**(1), 167–189 (2012)
19. Li, M., Chen, X., Li, X., Ma, B., Vitanyi, P.: The similarity metric. IEEE Trans. Inf. Theory **50**(12), 3250–3264 (2004)
20. Liu, M., Chen, C., Liu, H.: Time-ordered spatial-temporal interest points for human action classification. In: 2017 IEEE International Conference on Multimedia and Expo (ICME), pp. 655–660, July 2017
21. Maddalena, L., Petrosino, A.: A self-organizing approach to background subtraction for visual surveillance applications. IEEE Trans. Image Process. **17**(7), 1168–1177 (2008)
22. Messing, R., Pal, C., Kautz, H.: Activity recognition using the velocity histories of tracked keypoints. In: 2009 IEEE 12th International Conference on Computer Vision, pp. 104–111, September 2009
23. Qiao, L., Nahrstedt, K.: Comparison of MPEG encryption algorithms. Comput. Graph. **22**(4), 437–448 (1998)
24. Roitberg, A., Perzylo, A., Somani, N., Giuliani, M., Rickert, M., Knoll, A.: Human activity recognition in the context of industrial human-robot interaction. In: 2014 Asia-Pacific Signal and Information Processing Association Annual Summit and Conference (APSIPA), pp. 1–10, December 2014
25. Sarasa, G., Granados, A., Rodriguez, F.B.: An approach of algorithmic clustering based on string compression to identify bird songs species in xeno-canto database. In: 2017 3rd International Conference on Frontiers of Signal Processing (ICFSP), pp. 101–104, September 2017
26. Wang, X.: Intelligent multi-camera video surveillance: a review. Pattern Recognit. Lett. **34**(1), 3–19 (2013)
27. Wu, S., Oreifej, O., Shah, M.: Action recognition in videos acquired by a moving camera using motion decomposition of Lagrangian particle trajectories. In: 2011 International Conference on Computer Vision, pp. 1419–1426, November 2011
28. Yan, Y., Ricci, E., Liu, G., Sebe, N.: Egocentric daily activity recognition via multitask clustering. IEEE Trans. Image Process. **24**(10), 2984–2995 (2015)
29. Yu, T., Wang, Z., Yuan, J.: Compressive quantization for fast object instance search in videos. In: 2017 IEEE International Conference on Computer Vision (ICCV), pp. 726–735, October 2017
30. Zhang, G., Chanson, H.: Application of local optical flow methods to high-velocity free-surface flows: validation and application to stepped chutes. Exp. Therm. Fluid Sci. **90**, 186–199 (2018)
31. Zhang, S., Wei, Z., Nie, J., Huang, L., Wang, S., Li, Z.: A review on human activity recognition using vision-based method. J. Healthc. Eng. **2017** (2017)

Medical/Bioinformatics

Deep Autoencoders for Additional Insight into Protein Dynamics

Mihai Teletin[1(✉)], Gabriela Czibula[1], Maria-Iuliana Bocicor[1],
Silvana Albert[1], and Alessandro Pandini[2]

[1] Babes-Bolyai University, Cluj-Napoca, Romania
mihai.teletin@lateral-inc.com,
{gabis,iuliana,albert.silvana}@cs.ubbcluj.ro
[2] Institute of Environment, Health and Societies, Brunel University London, London, UK
alessandro.pandini@brunel.ac.uk

Abstract. The study of *protein dynamics* through analysis of conformational transitions represents a significant stage in understanding protein function. Using molecular simulations, large samples of protein transitions can be recorded. However, extracting functional motions from these samples is still not automated and extremely time-consuming. In this paper we investigate the usefulness of unsupervised machine learning methods for uncovering relevant information about protein functional dynamics. Autoencoders are being explored in order to highlight their ability to learn relevant biological patterns, such as structural characteristics. This study is aimed to provide a better comprehension of how protein conformational transitions are evolving in time, within the larger framework of automatically detecting functional motions.

Keywords: Protein molecular dynamics · Autoencoders
Unsupervised learning

1 Introduction

Proteins are large biomolecules having crucial roles in the proper functioning of organisms. They are synthesized using information contained within the ribonucleic acid (RNA), when by means of the process known as translation, building blocks, the amino acids, are chained together in a sequence. Although this sequence is linear, the protein acquires a complex arrangement in its physiological state, as intramolecular forces between the amino acids and the hydrophobic effect lead to a folding of the protein into its three dimensional shape, which determines the protein's function [27]. The stable three dimensional structure of a protein is unique, however this shape undergoes significant changes to deliver its biological function, according to various external factors from the protein's environment (e.g. temperature, interaction with other molecules). Thus, a protein will acquire a limited number of conformations during its lifetime, having the ability to transition between alternative conformations [26].

The study and prediction of conformational transitions represents a significant stage in understanding protein function [21]. In this paper we investigate protein molecular

© Springer Nature Switzerland AG 2018
V. Kůrková et al. (Eds.): ICANN 2018, LNCS 11140, pp. 79–89, 2018.
https://doi.org/10.1007/978-3-030-01421-6_8

motions and conformational transitions starting from the structural alphabet devised by Pandini et al., a representation which provides a highly informative encoding of proteins [22]. In this description, each fragment consists of 4 residues and is defined by three internal angles: two pseudo-bond angles between the C^α atoms (C^α is the first carbon atom that attaches to a functional group) of residues 1-2-3 and 2-3-4 and one pseudo-torsion angle formed by atoms 1-2-3-4 [22]. These internal angles entirely define each structural fragment which can be also encoded as a letter from a Structural Alphabet (SA) [22]. In addition to the previously mentioned representation based on angles, we investigate whether enhancing the structural alphabet states (represented by the three angles) with relative solvent accessibility information might bring further insight into the matter at hand. Relative solvent accessibility (RSA) of amino acid residues is a value indicating the degree to which the residue is exposed [20], being able to characterize the spatial distribution of amino acids in a folded protein. RSA is significant for predicting protein-interaction sites [20] and it is used in protein family classification [1]. The intuition is that, even if RSA values independently do not offer a unique characterization of a protein, being individually non-specific, new structural states defined by the three angles together with RSA values could bring additional information.

Using molecular simulations, large samples of protein transitions can be recorded. However, extracting functional motions from these samples is still not automated and extremely time-consuming. Therefore, we consider that computational methods such as unsupervised learning could be a well suited solution for better understanding protein dynamics. We are investigating the usefulness of deep autoencoder neural networks to acquire a clearer sense of proteins' structure, with the long term goal of learning to predict proteins' conformational transitions. Several approaches in the literature were proposed for analyzing and modeling protein structural conformations using both supervised and unsupervised machine learning techniques. Support vector machine's performance was tested in [14] by classifying gene function from heterogeneous protein data sets and comparing results with various kernel methods. In [28], a Radial Basis Function Network (RBFN) is proposed for classifying protein sequences. Fifteen supervised learning algorithms were evaluated in [9] by automating protein structural classification from pairs of protein domains and Random Forests were proven to outperform the others. Additional insight into protein molecular dynamics (MD) is gained in [16] by employing L1-regularized reversible Hidden Markov Models. Self-organizing maps have also been used alongside hierarchical clustering in [6], for the purpose of clustering molecular dynamics trajectories. A methodology for detecting similarity between three dimensional structures of proteins was introduced by Iakavidou et al. in [8].

The contribution of the paper is twofold. Our first main goal is to investigate the capability of unsupervised learning models, more specifically of autoencoders, to capture the internal structure of proteins represented by their conformational transitions. Secondly, we propose two internal representations for a protein (one using the structural alphabet states defined by three angle values, as introduced in [22] and one in which these states are extended with RSA information) with the aim of analyzing which of them is more informative and would drive an autoencoder to better learn structural relationships between proteins. The experiments performed are aimed at evaluating the extent by which the combination of a reduced representation and an autoencoder is suitable to compress the complex MD data into a more interpretable representation. With this aim we propose a proof of concept that considers only two similar but unrelated proteins where learning on one can be used on the other. The literature regarding protein data analysis reveals that a study similar to ours has not been hitherto performed. The study can be further extended on a large scale where evolutionary relationship are considered, with the goal of answering how much the "closeness" of proteins in evolutionary space can affect the efficiency of the encoding. To sum up, in this paper we seek answers to the following research questions: **RQ1** What is the potential of autoencoders to unsupervisedly learn the structure of proteins and how does the internal representation for a protein impact the learning process?; and **RQ2** Are autoencoders able to capture biologically relevant patterns? More specifically, are our computational findings obtained by answering **RQ1** and **RQ2** correlated with the biological perspective?

The remainder of the paper is organized as follows. The autoencoder model used in our experiments is described in Sect. 2. Section 3 provides our methodology and Sect. 4 contains the results of our experiments, as well as a discussion regarding the obtained results, both from a computational and biological perspective. The conclusions of our paper and directions for future work are summarized in Sect. 5.

2 Autoencoders

Autoencoders were successfully applied in different complex scenarios such as image analysis [13] and speech processing [5]. An autoencoder [7] is a feed forward neural network. The input of the network is a real numbered vector $x \in R^n$.

An autoencoder is composed of two main components: (1) an encoder: g: $R^n \rightarrow R^m, g(x) = h$ and (2) a decoder: $f:R^m \rightarrow R^n, f(h) = \hat{x}$. The two components are stacked together, hence the goal of the autoencoder is to model a function: $f(g(x)) \approx x$. We notice that the input and the label of the model are the same vector. Thus the autoencoders may be considered self-supervised learning techniques. If $m < n$ then the autoencoder is called undercomplete.

We consider the learning process of autoencoders as minimizing a loss function $L(\hat{x}, x) = \frac{1}{n} \sum_{i=1}^{n} (\hat{x}_i - x_i)^2$. The optimization is performed using stochastic gradient descent with backpropagation. One may notice that the goal of the autoencoder is to copy the input x into the output value. However, such a model would not be useful at all. In fact, the goal of the autoencoder is to come up with useful representation of data in the hidden state, h. Good encoded values may be useful for various tasks such as information retrieval and data representation. A sparse autoencoder is a technique used to help the model avoid the simple copying of the input to the output by introducing a sparsifying penalty to the loss function. Usually this sparsing penalty is the L1 regularization on the encoded state. The penalty term is scaled using a small real number denoted as λ. Thus the employed loss becomes $L(\hat{x}, x) = \frac{1}{n} \sum_{i=1}^{n} (\hat{x}_i - x_i)^2 + \lambda \sum_{i=1}^{n} |h_i|$.

Denoising autoencoders represent another technique to avoid the mere copying of the input data to the output layer, forcing the hidden layers to learn the best defining, most robust features of the input. To achieve this, a denoising autoencoder is fed stochastically corrupted input data and tries to reconstruct the original input data. Thus, in the case of denoising autoencoders the loss function to be minimized is $L(g(f(\tilde{x})), x)$, where the input given to the autoencoder is represented by $\tilde{x}$ - input data corrupted by some form of noise [7]. Therefore, the autoencoder will not simply elicit the input data, but will learn a significant representation of it. Various experiments proved that autoencoders are better than *Principal Component Analysis* (PCA) [7]. This is mainly because autoencoders are not restricted to perform linear mapping. One can consider that a single layer autoencoder with linear activation function has the same capacity as PCA. However, the capacity of autoencoders can be improved by tuning the complexity of the encoder and decoder functions.

3   Methodology

In this section we present the experimental methodology used in supporting our assumption that autoencoders can capture, from a computational viewpoint, biologically relevant patterns regarding structural conformational changes of proteins. With the goal of answering the first research questions formulated in Sect. 1, the experiments will investigate the ability of an autoencoder to preserve the structure of a protein. Two types of representations will be considered in order to identify the one that is best suited for the analysis we are conducting. These representations will be detailed in Sect. 3.1.

3.1   Protein Representations

A protein is a macromolecule with a very flexible and dynamic innate structure [18] that changes shape due to both external changes from its environment and internal molecular forces. The resulting shape is a different conformation. For each conformation of a protein, two different representations of the local geometry of the molecule will be used in our study.

The *first* representation for a protein's conformation, which we call the *representation based on angles* (**Angles**), consists of conformational states given by the three types of angles mentioned in Sect. 1 [22]. In this representation, a conformation of k fragments (letters from the structural alphabet [22]) is represented as *3k* dimensional numerical sequence. This sequence contains three angles for each fragment from the conformation. The *second* way to represent a protein conformation, named in the following the *combined representation* (**Combined**) is based on enhancing the conformational states given by angles with the RSA values of the amino acid residues (see Sect. 1). In our second representation, a conformation of k states is visualized as a *4k* dimensional numerical vector. The first *3k* positions from this vector contain the conformation's representation based on angles, whereas the following k positions contain the RSA values.

3.2 *Autoencoder* Architecture

In the current study we use sparse denoising autoencoders to learn meaningful, lower-dimensional representations for proteins' structures, considering their conformational transitions. Hence, the loss function will be computed as shown in Sect. 2, where $\hat{x} = g(f(\tilde{x}))$ and $\tilde{x}$ represents the corrupted input data. We chose a denoising autoencoder in our experiments, because experimental measurements of biological processes and information generated by particle methods (e.g. MD simulations) can be noisy or subject to statistical errors. We are going to use such an autoencoder in order to reduce the dimensionality of our data. Considering that one of our purposes is to be able to visualize our data sets, all the techniques implied are going to encode the protein representations into 2 dimensional vectors.

The sparse denoising autoencoder learns a mapping function from an n-dimensional space (where n can have different values, according to the employed representation) to a 2 dimensional hidden state. We performed several experiments, with variable numbers of hidden layers and using various activation functions, in order to reduce dimensionality. More specifically, the activation functions we employed for the hidden layers are: rectified linear unit (ReLU), exponential linear unit (ELU) [4] and scaled exponential linear unit (SELU) [12]. As a regularization strategy, we use the dropout technique [24], with dropout rates in $\{0.1, 0.2, 0.3\}$. Since we have only 2 values in the encoded state we are going to use a small value for λ hyperparameter: 10^{-6}. The encoded values are then reconstructed using a similar decoding architecture.

Optimization of the autoencoder is achieved via stochastic gradient descent enhanced with the adam optimizer [11]. We employ the algorithm in a minibatch perspective by using a batch size of 16. The batch size affects the performance of the model. Usually, large batch sizes are not recommended since it may reduce the capacity of the model to generalize. Adam is a good optimizer since it also deals with the adjustment of the learning rate. The data set is shuffled and 10% is retained for validation. We keep the best performing model on the validation phase by measuring the validation loss. The loss obtained on the validation set was 0.555 for 1P1L and 0.378 for 1JT8 for the ReLU activation function, with 0.2 dropout rate. Regarding the encoding architecture, we experimented with 2 and 3 hidden layers, containing different numbers of neurons (depending on the size of the input data), and each of the hidden layers benefit from batch normalization. The decoding architecture is similar, having the same dimensions for the hidden layers, but in reverse.

3.3 Evaluation Measures

In order to determine whether the representation learned by the autoencoder preserves the similarities found in the original protein data we define the intra-protein similarity measure, *IntraPS*, which evaluates the degree of similarity between conformations within a protein and we will use this as an indication of how well the intra-protein conformational relations are maintained in the lower-dimensional representation learned by the autoencoder. *IntraPS* is based on the cosine similarity measure, which is employed to evaluate the likeness between two conformations of a protein.

Cosine similarity (COS) is widely used as a measure for computing the similarity between gene expression profiles. It is a measure of the direction-length similitude between two vectors and is defined as the cosine of the angle between the high dimensional vectors. To define the intra-protein similarity measure, we consider that a protein p is represented as a sequence of n conformations, i.e. $p = \left(c_1^p, c_2^p, \ldots, c_n^p\right)$. Each conformation c_i^p of the protein is visualized as an m-dimensional numerical vector (i.e. the representation based on angles or the combined representation previously described).

The Intra-protein similarity of a protein $p = \left(c_1^p, c_2^p, \ldots, c_n^p\right)$, denoted as *IntraPS(p)*, is defined as the average of the absolute cosine similarities between two consecutive conformations, i.e. $IntraPS(p) = \dfrac{\sum_{i=1}^{n-1} \left| COS\left(c_i^p, c_{i+1}^p\right) \right|}{n-1}$.

In computing the *IntraP* measure, we decided to use the absolute values for the cosine between two conformations, since our assumption was that for protein data the relative strengths of positive and negative cosine values between RSA vectors is the same. This was experimentally confirmed in our experiments. For computing the similarity/dissimilarity between two protein conformational transitions, different methods were investigated (Euclidian distance, Pearson correlation, Biweight midcorrelation) and the *cosine similarity* has proven to be the most appropriate. Since the dimensionality of the original protein conformations is significantly reduced by the autoencoder (i.e. two dimensions), Euclidian, Pearson and Biweight midcorrelation are not good options for measuring the similarity: the Euclidean distance is larger between points in a high dimensional space than in a two dimensional one; Pearson and Biweight are not suitable in 2D (the correlation between two dimensional points is always 1).

4   Results and Discussion

The experiments we performed for highlighting the potential of deep autoencoders to capture the proteins' structure will be further presented, using the experimental methodology presented in Sect. 3.

The proteins used in our study are described in Table 1 which shows a brief depiction of the proteins together with their superfamily and sequence length. The proteins from Table 1 were chosen based on data availability (conformational transitions and RSA values), the fact that they have the same sequence length (which enables us to carry out our investigations related to RQ2 from Sect. 1.

Table 1. Proteins selected for analysis [2].

Protein	Description	Superfamily	Sequence length
1P1L	Component of sulphur-metabolizing organisms	3.30.70.120	102
1JT8	Protein involved in translation	2.40.50.140	102

For both these proteins, *10000* conformational transitions were recovered from the MoDEL database [17] (i.e. $n = 10000$), where each transition consists of a sequence of 99 fragments of the structural alphabet [22]. Thus, as described in Sect. 3.1, in the *representation based on angles*, a conformation has a length of 297, whereas in the *combined representation* a conformation is visualized as a 396-dimensional point. For both proteins, the two representations proposed in Sect. 3.1 will be further used. Before applying the autoencoder, the protein data sets are standardized, i.e. transformed to mean 0 and standard deviation 1. Furthermore, considering that the employed technique is a denoising autoencoder, the input data is corrupted by adding noise (random samples from a standard normal distribution).

4.1 Results

The experiment described below is conducted with the aim of answering our first research question RQ1 and of investigating if and how the internal representation for a protein impacts the learning process. For each protein data set, we trained a number of denoising sparse autoencoders (Sect. 3.2). For the autoencoder we have employed the Keras implementation available at [3]. The autoencoders presented in Sect. 3.2 are used to reduce the dimensionality of our data and to visualize the protein data sets. Figures 1 and 2 depict the visualization of the proteins from our data set using trained sparse denoising autoencoders. The axes on Figs. 1 and 2 represent the range of values obtained within the 2-dimensional encoding of the input data set (the values of the two hidden nodes representing the encoder output). Colours were added to better emphasize the representations of successive conformations).

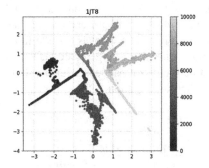 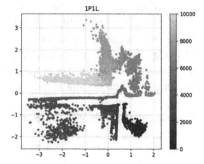

Fig. 1. Visualization of protein 1JT8.   **Fig. 2.** Visualization of protein 1P1L.

The original data fed to the autoencoder for each protein represents a timely evolution of the protein's structure (albeit for an extremely small interval of time - nanoseconds), considering its transitional conformations. From one conformation to another, the protein might remain unchanged, or certain parts of it might incur minor modifications. The autoencoders used to obtain these representations were trained on original data in its *combined representation*, they employ 6 hidden layers (3 for encoding and 3 for decoding), with ReLU as activation function, batch normalization and a dropout rate of 0:2. Nevertheless, we experimented with the *representation based on angles*, as well as with various combinations of parameters (number of neurons, layers, dropout rate, activation functions), as described in Sect. 3.2 and all resulting plots denote an evolution of the data output by the autoencoder (henceforth referred to as encoded data), thus suggesting that autoencoders are able to identify the most relevant characteristics of the original representations.

The two dimensional representations of the proteins as captured by the autoencoders, illustrated in Figs. 1 and 2, reflect the autoencoder's ability to accurately learn biological transitions. Successive conformations in the original data are progressively chained together in the autoencoder's output data thus denoting a visual evolution. Figures 1 and 2 also show that the considered protein data are relevant for machine learning models, as it correctly captures biological chained events, by encoding successive conformations into points that are close in a 2-dimensional space.

Further, to decide whether the autoencoder maintains the relationships found within the original data, we use the *IntraPS* measure. Thus, first we compute these similarities for the original data and then for the two-dimensional data output by the autoencoder, for both considered representations. The results are shown in Table 2. For each protein, in addition to the values for the *IntraPS* measure, we also present the minimum (**Min**), maximum (**Max**) and standard deviation (**Stdev**) of the absolute values of cosine similarities between two consecutive conformations, for both representations. We mention that Min, Max and Stdev were computed using batches of 100 successive conformations. These results are also illustrated in Figs. 3 and 4, which show the comparative evolution of average *IntraPS* values for each 100 conformations in the 10000 conformations that characterize each considered protein. We notice that for both proteins 1JT8 and 1P1L the results output by the autoencoder (denoted by "Encoded data" in the images) are slightly larger, but, on average, particularly similar to the values computed for the original data. All these results suggest that the original proteins' conformations have a high degree of cosine similarity (highlighted in Table 2), which is still preserved in the data resulted from the autoencoder. One observes from Fig. 3 that there is a spike in the encoded data, which is not visible in the original data. Analyzing protein 1JT8, we observed that there is an event in the protein structure, but it happens with about 100 conformations before the spike, thus it needs further investigation.

Table 2. IntraPS for proteins 1JT8 and 1P1L, using the two considered representations.

Protein		Angles	Combined	Min/Max/Stdev (COS)	
				Angles	Combined
1JT8	Original	**0.9960**	**0.9913**	0.9894/0.9995/0.0023	0.9843/0.9962/0.0022
	Encoded	**0.9939**	**0.9985**	0.9213/0.9999/0.0161	0.9573/0.9999/**0.0044**
1P1L	Original	**0.9779**	0.9573	0.9593/0.9896/0.0064	0.9464/0.9695/0.0054
	Encoded	**0.9912**	**0.9962**	0.9315/0.9999/0.0119	0.9661/0.9999/**0.0052**

With regard to the used internal representations, we conclude that these do not seriously influence the learning process. This may be due to the significant reduction of data dimensionality (two dimensions). Still, for the *combined representation* which is richer in information than the *representation based on angles*, slightly better results were obtained. As highlighted in Table 2, for both proteins, IntraPS values are larger for the encoded data and the standard deviation of the cosine similarities between two consecutive conformations is smaller, as well. If the data were reduced to a higher dimensional space, the RSA values might bring additional improvements, which induces an interesting matter for future investigations.

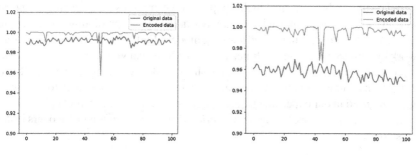

Fig. 3. Protein 1JT8 (combined representation).

Fig. 4. Protein 1P1L (combined representation).

With the aim of answering research question RQ2, we are analyzing in the following the biological relevance of the above presented computational results. The molecular dynamics sampled by the ensemble of structures in the two data sets is consistent with small consecutive changes in the protein structure occurring on the nanosecond time scale. These changes are typical of the first stages of the functional motions and they are generally dominated by local transitions and significant resampling of the conformational space. The autoencoder is able to capture both these features, as demonstrated by the obtained results: changes are encoded in chained events that resample the conformational space effectively. In addition, there is evidence that evolutionary related proteins are also similar in their functional motions [23].

The study performed in this paper with the aim to highlight the ability of *autoencoders* to uncover relevant information about protein dynamics is new. *Autoencoders* have been previously used in the literature for protein structure analysis, but from perspectives which differ from ours.

Autoencoders were proven to be effective for analysis of protein internal structure in [15] where the authors initialized weights, refined them by backpropagation and used each layer's input back to itself in order to predict backbone C^α angles and dihedrals. In [10], autoencoders were employed for improving structure class prediction by representing the protein as a "pseudo-amino acid composition" meaning the model consisted of normalized occurrences of the each of the 20 amino acids in a protein, combined with the order of the amino acid sequence. The algorithm called DL-Pro [19] is designed for classifying predicted protein models as good or bad by using a stacked sparse autoencoder which learns from the distances between two C^α atoms residues. Sequence based protein to protein interaction was also predicted using a sparse *autoencoder* in [25].

5 Conclusions and Further Work

We have conducted in this paper a study towards applying *deep autoencoders* for a better comprehension of protein dynamics. The experiments conducted on two proteins highlighted that *autoencoders* are effective unsupervised models able to learn the structure of proteins. Moreover, we obtained an empirical evidence that autoencoders are able to encode hidden patterns relevant from a biological perspective.

Based on the study performed in this paper and on previous investigations regarding protein data analysis, we aim to advance our research towards predicting protein conformational transitions using supervised learning models. Furthermore, we plan to continue our work by using a two-pronged strategy: from a biological viewpoint we will consider other proteins and examine how their evolutionary relationships are reflected within the resulting data; computationally, we will investigate different architectures for the *sparse autoencoder* used in our experiments (e.g. model's architecture, different optimizers for the gradient descent) and we will apply *variational* and *contractive* autoencoders instead of sparse ones.

References

1. Asgari, E., Mofrad, M.: Continuous distributed representation of biological sequences for deep proteomics and genomics. Plos One (2015). https://doi.org/10.1371/journal.pone.0141287
2. Berman, H., et al.: The protein data bank. Nucleic Acids Res. **28**, 235–242 (2000)
3. Chollet, F., et al.: Deep learning for humans (2015). https://github.com/fchollet/keras
4. Clevert, D.A., Unterthiner, T., Hochreiter, S.: Fast and accurate deep network learning by exponential linear units (ELUS). arXiv preprint arXiv:1511.07289 (2015)
5. Deng, J., Zhang, Z., Marchi, E., Schuller, B.: Sparse autoencoder-based feature transfer learning for speech emotion recognition. In: ACII, pp. 511–516. IEEE (2013)
6. Fraccalvieri, D., Pandini, A., Stella, F., Bonati, L.: Conformational and functional analysis of molecular dynamics trajectories by self-organising maps. Bioinformatics **12**, 1–18 (2011)
7. Goodfellow, I., Bengio, Y., Courville, A.: Deep Learning. MIT Press, Cambridge (2016)
8. Iakovidou, N., Tiakas, E., Tsichlas, K., Manolopoulos, Y.: Going over the three dimensional protein structure similarity problem. Artif. Intell. Rev. **42**(3), 445–459 (2014)
9. Jain, P., Garibaldi, J.M., Hirst, J.: Supervised machine learning algorithms for protein structure classification. Comput. Biol. Chem. **33**, 216–223 (2009)
10. Liu, J., Chi, G., Liu, Z., Liu, Y., Li, H., Luo, X.-L.: Predicting protein structural classes with autoencoder neural networks. In: CCDC, pp. 1894–1899 (2013)
11. Kingma, D., Ba, J.: Adam: a method for stochastic optimization. arXiv preprint arXiv:1412.6980 (2014)
12. Klambauer, G., Unterthiner, T., Mayr, A., Hochreiter, S.: Self-normalizing neural networks. In: NIPS (2017)
13. Le, Q.: Building high-level features using large scale unsupervised learning. In: ICASSP, pp. 8595–8598. IEEE (2013)
14. Lewis, D., Jebara, T., Noble, W.S.: Support vector machine learning from heterogeneous data: an empirical analysis using protein sequence and structure. Bioinformatics **22**(22), 2753–2760 (2006)
15. Lyons, J., et al.: Predicting backbone $C\alpha$ angles and dihedrals from protein sequences by stacked sparse auto-encoder deep neural network. J. Comput. Chem. **35**(28), 2040–2046 (2014)

16. McGibbon, R., Ramsundar, B., Sultan, M., Kiss, G., Pande, V.: Understanding protein dynamics with L1-regularized reversible hidden Markov models. In: ICML. pp. 1197–1205 (2014)
17. Meyer, T., et al.: MoDEL: a database of atomistic molecular dynamics trajectories. Structure **18**(11), 1399–1409 (2010)
18. Moon, K.K., Jernigan, R.L., Chirikjian, G.S.: Efficient generation of feasible pathways for protein conformational transitions. Biophys. J. **83**(3), 1620–1630 (2002)
19. Nguyen, S., Shang, Y., Xu, D.: Dl-PRO: a novel deep learning method for protein model quality assessment. In: IJCNN, pp. 2071–2078. IEEE (2014)
20. Palmieri, L., Federico, M., Leoncini, M., Montangero, M.: A high performing tool for residue solvent accessibility prediction. In: Böhm, C., Khuri, S., Lhotská, L., Pisanti, N. (eds.) ITBAM 2011. LNCS, vol. 6865, pp. 138–152. Springer, Heidelberg (2011). https://doi.org/10.1007/978-3-642-23208-4_13
21. Pandini, A., Fornili, A.: Using local states to drive the sampling of global conformations in proteins. J. Chem. Theory Comput. **12**, 1368–1379 (2016)
22. Pandini, A., Fornili, A., Kleinjung, J.: Structural alphabets derived from attractors in conformational space. BMC Bioinform. **11**(97), 1–18 (2010)
23. Pandini, A., Mauri, G., Bordogna, A., Bonati, L.: Detecting similarities among distant homologous proteins by comparison of domain flexibilities. Protein Eng. Des. Sel. **20**(6), 285–299 (2007)
24. Srivastava, N., Hinton, G., Krizhevsky, A., Sutskever, I., Salakhutdinov, R.: Dropout: a simple way to prevent ANNs from overfitting. J. Mach. Learn. Res. **15**(1), 1929–1958 (2014)
25. Sun, T., Zhou, B., Lai, L., Pei, J.: Sequence-based prediction of protein protein interaction using a deep-learning algorithm. BMC Bioinform. **18**(1), 277 (2017)
26. Tokuriki, N., Tawfik, D.: Protein dynamism and evolvability. Science **324**(9524), 203–207 (2009). https://doi.org/10.1126/science.1169375
27. Voet, D., Voet, J.: Biochemistry, 4th edn. Wiley, Hoboken (2011)
28. Wang, D., Lee, N., Dillon, T.: Extraction and optimization of fuzzy protein sequences classification rules using GRBF neural networks. Neural Inf. Process. Lett. Rev. **1**(1), 53–57 (2003)

Pilot Design of a Rule-Based System and an Artificial Neural Network to Risk Evaluation of Atherosclerotic Plaques in Long-Range Clinical Research

Jiri Blahuta[✉], Tomas Soukup, and Jakub Skacel

Silesian University in Opava, The Institute of Computer Science,
Bezruc Sq. 13, 74601 Opava, Czech Republic
jiri.blahuta@fpf.slu.cz
http://www.slu.cz/fpf/en/institutes/the-institute-of-computer-science

Abstract. Early diagnostics and knowledge of the progress of atherosclerotic plaques are key parameters which can help start the most efficient treatment. Reliable prediction of growing of atherosclerotic plaques could be very important part of early diagnostics to judge potential impact of the plaque and to decide necessity of immediate artery recanalization. For this pilot study we have a large set of measured data from total of 482 patients. For each patient the width of the plaque from left and right side during at least 5 years at regular intervals for 6 months was measured Patients were examined each 6 months and width of the plaque was measured using ultrasound B-image and the data were stored into a database. The first part is focused on rule-based expert system designed for evaluation of suggestion to immediate recanalization according to progress of the plaque. These results will be verified by an experienced sonographer. This system could be a starting point to design an artificial neural network with adaptive learning based on image processing of ultrasound B-images for classification of the plaques using feature analysis. The principle of the network is based on edge detection analysis of the plaques using feed-forwarded network with Error Back-Propagation algorithm. Training and learning of the ANN will be time-consuming processes for a long-term research. The goal is to create ANN which can recognize the border of the plaques and to measure of the width. The expert system and ANN are two different approaches, however, both of them can cooperate.

Keywords: Atherosclerotic plaque · Ultrasound · Expert system
Rule-based system · Image processing with ANN · B-image recognition

1 Atherosclerotic Plaques, Their Risk and Measurement

In general, atherosclerosis is one of the most important causes of mortality. Early diagnostics and prediction of atherosclerosis is a key part of modern medicine.

© Springer Nature Switzerland AG 2018
V. Kůrková et al. (Eds.): ICANN 2018, LNCS 11140, pp. 90–100, 2018.
https://doi.org/10.1007/978-3-030-01421-6_9

This paper has two parts. The first part is focused on a design of rule-based expert system which can be used for decision what next steps are needed depending on progress of the plaque. This system is based on defined rules as a decision-making system. Designed expert system should be a valuable tool for evaluation of the progress of the plaques during series of examinations. Early diagnostics of the plaques and reliable evaluation of their progress are two different, but closely related parts to avoid needless death and for starting the most optimal treatment as well. The second part of the paper is devoted to design of a model of artificial neural network (ANN) which could be able to recognize border of the plaque. ANN should be designed as a feed-forward model with Error Back-Propagation algorithm. In this paper an idea how to create ANN with supervised learning as one of many types of neural network models designed for image processing is discussed.

2   Input Data

For this study a set of measured width of the plaques from total of 482 patients is used. This is a long-term study; each patient was examined for 5 years at regular intervals of 6 months. In this study the data of width of the plaques measured from B-image is used, see Fig. 1. More detailed description of principles of B-imaging of the plaques is available in [1] and a general view of image processing approaches in medicine is available in [2].

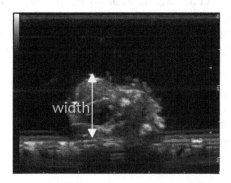

Fig. 1. Measured width of the plaque on B-image

There are different progress models of the plaque during long-term study according to stored data:

- stable plaque with no significant changes
- stable plaque with regular increasing/decreasing, no peaks
- unstable progress of the plaques, peaks
- highly unstable plaques with many peaks and extreme changes between examinations

These four progress models are a starting point for definition of exact rules for the expert system.

3 Design of Rules Used in the Expert System

Input data represent width of the plaque measured from left (L) and right (R) side at regular intervals of 6 months, see Table 1.

Table 1. An example of measured width of the plaque for 4 patients

side / measurement	1	2	3	4	5	6	7	8	9	10	11	12
L	4.6	3.6	4.7	4.1	4.6	4.2	4.9	4.3	4.3	4.3	3.9	4.1
R	3.6	2.5	3.2	3.2	3.4	3.6	3.8	3.9	3.8	3.8	3.2	3.2
L	2.7	4.3	4.1	4.0	4.8	4.8	4.8	5.7	5.7	4.2	N/A	N/A
R	3.1	4.2	4.2	4.2	4.3	4.5	4.5	3.4	5.0	5.5	N/A	N/A
L	3.3	2.3	2.2	2.6	2.2	2.5	2.5	2.7	2.7	2.7	3.4	3.6
R	3.0	3.0	2.5	2.3	2.8	2.7	2.7	2.5	2.5	2.5	2.5	2.7
L	2.0	2.4	2.4	2.3	3.4	2.6	2.6	2.6	2.6	2.6	2.6	2.7
R	4.3	4.3	4.3	4.3	4.3	4.3	4.3	2.8	3.4	3.3	3.3	3.7

Highlighted measurement was visually judged as erroneous. Let $t_1, t_2, t_3, ... t_n$ where $n = 10$ is a series of an examination during 5 years at regular intervals of 6 months. The principle of this system is based on using IF-THEN rules from which the final consequent is decided; it is a rule-based decision system which can be briefly described as follows. The rules are based on the four following criteria:

- maximum and minimum value from all measured data
- difference Δ_t is not considered in absolute value; if $\Delta_t < 0$ width increases and if $\Delta_t < 0$ width decreases
- number of occurrences of difference below or under threshold value
- trend of the progress for 4 consecutive measurements (increasing or decreasing)

The difference Δ_t is not considered in absolute value, thus if $\Delta_t > 0$, the plaque width is growing and if $\Delta_t < 0$, the width of the plaque is decreased.

The expert system is designed using the following exact if-then rules:

- Rule A: IF $\max(\Delta_t) > 2$ mm THEN *ModerateRisk*
- Rule B: IF count of $\Delta_t > 2$ mm at least 2 THEN *ModerateRisk*
- Rule C: IF $\min(\Delta_t) < -2$ mm THEN *ModerateRisk*
- Rule D: IF count of $\Delta_t < -2$ mm at least 2 THEN *ModerateRisk*
- Rule E: IF at least of 4 consecutive differences $\Delta_t < 0$ THEN *ModerateRisk*
- Rule F: IF at least of 4 consecutive differences $\Delta_t > 0$ THEN *HighRisk*

- Rule G: IF $\min(\Delta_t) < -0.8$ mm $\wedge$ $\max(\Delta_t) < 0.8$ mm THEN *LowRisk*
- Rule H: IF no previous rules are applied THEN *LowRisk* (the plaques with no peaks)

So, there are 3 options (output variables) for recommended steps:

- *LowRisk* - no immediate steps are recommended
- *ModerateRisk* - check the plaque progress
- *HighRisk* - check if the measurement is correct (no error), immediate recanalization is strongly recommended

The following rules union produces:

- $A \wedge B$ THEN *HighRisk*
- $E \wedge G$ THEN *LowRisk*
- $F \wedge G$ THEN *ModerateRisk*

The inference engine of the system is designed to produce a reasoning on the rules. In Table 1, there are examples of reasonings. In the past, we have designed a similar expert system to evaluation of substantia nigra hyperechogenicity and the results were published in technical papers [3–5] and also in clinical studies [6,7] (Table 2).

Table 2. Output variables and their reasoning

Variable	Comment
LowRisk	no immediate steps are needed, the plaques seem stable
ModerateRisk	check the progress which could be starting point of a problem
HighRisk	critical growing of the plaque, high risk of stenosis and rupture

However, a sonographer can set more rules, their relations and reasoning; the system is extensible and modular.

4   Evaluation of the Outputs

According to outputs of the expert system immediate recanalization should be recommended. The next step is to verify the reliability of the designed expert system with experienced sonographer. Consider the following example. Let

$$3.1; 3.8; 3.8; 3.8; 3.8; 3.0; 3.0; 3.8; 2.4; 4.1; 3.2; 3.8; 3.8; 3.8; 3.5; 3.6; 3.8$$

be input data of measured width into the system. Maximum difference is 1.7 mm, the minimum difference is -0.3 mm. The plaque does not have at least 4 consecutive differences higher than 0. The Rule H is applied because there are no significant peaks and extreme differences.

In the second example:

$$3; 2.9; 2.8; 2.8; 2.6; 2.6; 2.6; 5.2; 5.2; 5.3$$

the obvious maximum difference is 2.6 mm. The Rule A is applied and the plaque is evaluated as moderately risk (*ModerateRisk*).

4.1 Adaptable Rules to Quality Improvement of the Results

One of the main advantages of this system is adaptability to improving quality of results for more reliable diagnostics. The rules can be modified and/or add new rules. Thus, adding and modifying rules can be useful to create the expert system with high accuracy supported by an experienced sonographer. Another way is to create adjustable expert system; a user can modify rules depending on measurement, e.g. set for high resolution, low resolution, different gamma correction, etc.

5 Using Neural Network in Long-Range Research

The designed expert system should be a helpful software tool to evaluate progress of atherosclerotic plaques using set of IF-THEN rules to decide next steps, i.e. treatment, immediate recanalization, etc. All results must be analyzed by an experienced sonographer. If the system is considered reliable, the next step should be to create a model of artificial neural network (ANN) as a learning platform which will be adapted depending on training set with many examples of outputs and desired outputs. It is a second phase of this study and the second approach; different from Decision-Making expert system. In 2016, the authors published a paper focused on the idea of different approaches how to detect atherosclerotic plaques in B-image [8].

5.1 An Idea How to Design ANN to Classification of Risk of the Plaques

The idea of the ANN is different from the principle of the expert system. The input data are B-images with displayed atherosclerotic plaques in different progress of the plaque instead of stored numerical values. The goal of the ANN is to learn how to classify the plaques according their width and other features. On Fig. 1 the width of the plaque is displayed There are key questions:

- What features should be used?
- How to determine plaque from the artery wall?
- What accuracy of the ANN is acceptable for clinical studies?
- How to define training set to classification learning?

We have the following idea of ANN architecture:

- a feedforward multi-layer network with supervised learning
- Error Back-Propagation algorithm to minimization of the global error
- developed in MATLAB (with NN Toolbox) [9] or similar software for ANN modeling

Figure 2 shows an example of the ANN which could be used.

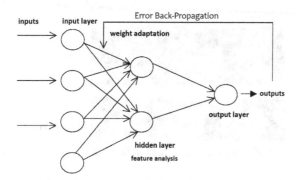

Fig. 2. ANN model with Error Back-Propagation principle

The input is B-image on input layer, each input is multiplied by a weight w; j-th input is multiplied by weight w_j. The principle of the idea is based on weight modification depending on computed network error. The learning of the network is based on comparison of the error for each input.

$$PE = y_j - d_j$$

where y_j is a real output and d_j is a desired output for j-th input. Global error is the sum of all partial errors. Thus, when the large set of examples in training set is available, the network could learn a lot of cases of plaque types. Crucial problem is to determine features which could be used to compute width of the plaque for final output. Designed ANN has the following properties:

- **input** in form of the matrix $m \times n$ of digitized B-image with detected edges
- **hidden layers** computes edge detection algorithm and visibility of the plaque
- **output layer** has 4 neurons to classification the plaque (no visible plaque, low risk plaque, medium risk plaque and high plaque) similarly to output of designed ES

Edge Detection. Images are preprocessed using edge detection. The network is designed to evaluate plaques using features from edge detection.

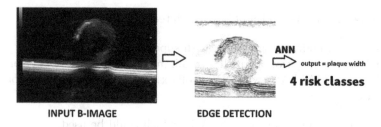

INPUT B-IMAGE   **EDGE DETECTION**

Fig. 3. Input B-image, extract edges with inverted colors) and the output to risk classification

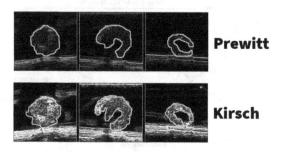

Prewitt

Kirsch

Fig. 4. Prewitt and Kirsch operator with bordered edges to training the network

Edge detection could be an efficient way how to recognize the border of the plaque to measurement of width and evaluation of the risk. There are two major problems:

- isolated pixels which can be considered as a part of the plaque
- artery wall can be also considered as a part of the plaques

Kirsch or Prewitt operator could reach well-bordered shape for training and learning process. On Fig. 4 Prewitt and Kirsch edge detection with border is applied on images from Fig. 3.

Training and Learning Process. The principle is based on a training set in which the input-desired output pairs are paired, i.e. for each input the desired output to learn the network is known. The training set should be supplemented by new examples. The learning of the network is based on error minimization depending on an improvement of the training set. A sonographer must determine error threshold for acceptable accuracy. To determine network error MSE (Mean Squared Error) is used in many applications to learn accuracy evaluation of the network. For simplification, the following preconditions are required:

- all images with the same resolution, zoom level and section
- all images from the same section, e.g. cross-sectional
- all images have the same zoom level

Nevertheless, the design of the ANN is a time-consuming process till the network is useful with reliable results for clinical studies. The most difficult part is selection of the most appropriate features in B-images due to many different types of the plaques caused by fibrosis, calcification, inflammation and other factors, see Fig. 5.

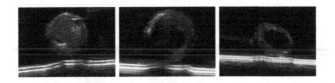

Fig. 5. Different types of the plaques on B-image

The Goal of the Learning. The goal of the learning process is to minimize the network error. For each input desired output is assigned. It is computed partial error PE and the global error. The training set contains well-bordered plaques of many types. The goal is to learn ANN to recognize border and measure width depending on scale axis. To reach better accuracy the training set is supplemented with new examples. When global error is lower than a determined value, the learning process is ended and ANN will work with required accuracy.

5.2 First Experimental Results with ANN

As the first step, we constructed a simple feed-forward ANN with implemented algorithm to border detection. We used a set of 20 images with significant plaque and for each image well-bordered plaque shape determined by experienced sonographer was used. When testing, we use these images to check if the border as output from ANN is considered as well or not to correct classification, see Table 3. The results represent the first run of the network without training/learning process with a large set of patterns.

Table 3. Experimental first results using untrained ANN

Edge/image	1	2	3	4	5	6	7	8	9	10	11	12	13	14	15	16	17	18	19	20
Prewitt	T	T	F	F	T	T	F	F	F	F	F	T	T	F	T	F	F	T	T	F	F
Kirsch	T	F	F	F	F	T	T	F	T	F	F	T	F	T	T	F	F	F	F	T

where T (true) is an acceptable result and F (false) is a rejected result by sonographer. Correctness of edge detection is key for reliable risk classification of the plaque. Untrained ANN shows error rate > 50 % for both edge detection operators. It is strongly unsatisfactory for a clinical study. The aim is to train the network to reach reliability > 85 % with determined partial error between each output and desired output. To training the network we need to use at least 482 B-images from which the data for designed expert system is extracted. Edge detection must be trained to recognize the shape of the plaque and how to separate artery wall, see Fig. 6. Brief description of the functionality of the ANN model:

- input $m \times n$ neurons according the image resolution
- transfer function is logistic sigmoid
- initial uniform weight distribution
- 100 epochs of training

Until the accuracy is not reached, ANN must be modified (weights, number of hidden layers) or another ANN architecture must be used [10], e.g. convolutional neural network (CNN) based on deep learning using GPU acceleration [11]. CNN could be a very perspective solution how to recognize shape of the plaque but it is a time-consuming problem. There is also possibility to use fuzzy neural network FUZNET [12] which could be used as fuzzy-neural system for classification of the plaques. However, after trying many ANN models could be decided that the plaques cannot be recognized with adequate accuracy.

5.3   Cooperation of the ANN with Expert System

Even though the expert system and the ANN are considered as different approaches, these systems can be closely related.

- designed ES is focused on evaluation of progress risk of the plaque from measured data for 5 years
- designed ANN is focused on recognition of the plaque on B-image and evaluation of the risk based on edge detection (width of the plaque)

When the risk level is decided by using expert system, the same plaque can be compared by output from ANN (concordance of measured width).

6   Conclusions and Future Work

This study is focused on application of two different approaches in neurology for early diagnostics of atherosclerosis. The first part is to design rule-based expert system focused on decision of risk level of the progress of atherosclerotic plaques from a large set of measured data. This system can be modular with option to add and/or modify the rules for better decisions. All outputs must be validated by an experienced sonographer. The second part is to design the artificial neural network based on Error Back-Propagation algorithm. The goal of the network is to compute width of the plaque from B-image using image feature analysis from edge detection. ANN can learn a lot of cases of the plaques using large training set with examples of "good" and "bad" plaques. Well-learned neural network should be a useful tool to fast and reliable decisions depending on the width of the plaque. This long-range research is at the beginning. Design of the expert system is relatively fast; the rules are determined by a sonographer and will be adaptable in the future. Design of the neural network is time-consuming due to complexity of image analysis of ultrasound B-images, i.e. selection of suitable architecture and features for computing of the width of the plaque. This research is a challenge for a large team of experts how to create a helpful software to early diagnostics of the atherosclerosis from measured data and from ultrasound B-images.

Acknowledgments. This work was supported by The Ministry of Education, Youth and Sports from the National Programme of Sustainability (NPU II) project IT4Innovations excellence in science - LQ1602.

References

1. Saijo, Y., van der Steen, A.F.W.: Vascular Ultrasound. Springer, Japan (2012). https://doi.org/10.1007/978-4-431-67871-7. (softcover reprint from 2003)
2. Dougherty, G.: Digital Image Processing for Medical Applications, 1st edn. Cambridge University Press (2009). ISBN 978-0-521-86085-7
3. Blahuta, J., Soukup, T. Cermak, P., Rozsypal, J., Vecerek, M.: Ultrasound medical image recognition with artificial intelligence for Parkinson's disease classification. In: Proceedings of the 35th International Convention, MIPRO 2012 (2012)
4. Blahuta, J., Cermak, P., Soukup, T., Vecerek, M.: A reproducible application to B-MODE transcranial ultrasound based on echogenicity evaluation analysis in defined area of interest. In: 6th International Conference on Soft Computing and Pattern Recognition (2014)
5. Blahuta, J., Soukup, T., Martinu, J.: An expert system based on using artificial neural network and region-based image processing to recognition substantia nigra and atherosclerotic plaques in b-images: a prospective study. In: Rojas, I., Joya, G., Catala, A. (eds.) IWANN 2017. LNCS, vol. 10305, pp. 236–245. Springer, Cham (2017). https://doi.org/10.1007/978-3-319-59153-7_21
6. Blahuta, J., et al.: A new program for highly reproducible automatic evaluation of the substantia nigra from transcranial sonographic images. Biomed. Papers, **158**(4), 621–627 (2014)
7. Skoloudik, D., et al.: Transcranial Sonography of the Insula: Digitized Image Analysis of Fusion Images with Magnetic Resonance. Ultraschall in der Medizin, Georg Thieme Verlag KG Stuttgart (2016)
8. Blahuta, J., Soukup, T., Cermak, P.: How to detect and analyze atherosclerotic plaques in B-MODE ultrasound images: a pilot study of reproducibility of computer analysis. In: Dichev, C., Agre, G. (eds.) AIMSA 2016. LNCS (LNAI), vol. 9883, pp. 360–363. Springer, Cham (2016). https://doi.org/10.1007/978-3-319-44748-3_37
9. Marvin, L.: Neural Networks with MATLAB. CreateSpace Independent Publishing Platform (2016). ISBN 978-1539701958
10. Herault, J.: Vision: Images, Signals and Neural Networks: Models of Neural Processing in Visual Perception (Progress in Neural Processing) 1st edn. World Scientific Publishing Company (2010). ISBN 978-9814273688

11. Hijazi, S., Kumar R., Rowen, Ch.: Using Convolutional Neural Networks for Image Recognition. Cadence (2016)
12. Cermak, P., Pokorny, P.: The fuzzy-neuro development system FUZNET. In: 18th International Conference on Methods and Models in Automation and Robotics (MMAR), vol. 75, no. 80, pp. 26–29 (2013). ISBN 978-1-4673-5506-3

A Multi-channel Multi-classifier Method for Classifying Pancreatic Cystic Neoplasms Based on ResNet

Haigen Hu[1], Kangjie Li[1], Qiu Guan[1(✉)], Feng Chen[2(✉)], Shengyong Chen[1], and Yicheng Ni[3]

[1] College of Computer Science and Technology, Zhejiang University of Technology, Hangzhou 310023, People's Republic of China
gq@zjut.edu.cn
[2] The First Affiliated Hospital, College of Medicine, Zhejiang University, Hangzhou 310006, People's Republic of China
chenfengbe@aliyun.com
[3] Department of Imaging and Pathology, KU Leuven, Leuven, Belgium

Abstract. Pancreatic cystic neoplasm (PCN) is one of the most common tumors in the digestive tract. It is still a challenging task for doctors to diagnose the types of pancreatic cystic neoplasms by using Computed Tomography (CT) images. Especially for serous cystic neoplasms (SCNs) and mucinous cystic neoplasms (MCNs), doctors hardly distinguish one from the other by the naked eyes owing to the high similarities between them. In this work, a multi-channel multiple-classifier (MCMC) model is proposed to distinguish the two pancreatic cystic neoplasms in CT images. At first, multi-channel images are used to enhance the image edge of the tumor, then the residual network is adopted to extract features. Finally, the multiple classifiers are applied to classify the results. Experiments show that the proposed method can effectively improve the classification effect, and the results can help doctors to utilize the CT images to achieve reliable non-invasive disease diagnosis.

Keywords: Non-invasive disease diagnosis · Multi-channel images Multi-classifier · ResNet · Pancreatic cystic neoplasms (PCNs)

1 Introduction

Pancreatic cystic neoplasm (PCN) [1–4], mainly characterized by the proliferation of pancreatic ductal (or acinar epithelial cells) and the secretion of cysts, is a type of pancreatic cystic lesions (PCLs). According to the histopathological criteria, Pancreatic cystic neoplasms (PCNs) are loosely grouped into non-mucinous tumors and mucinous tumors by World Health Organization (WTO) in 2010, which mainly contain serous cystic neoplasms (SCNs) and mucinous cystic neoplasms (MCNs), respectively. Generally speaking, the levels of CEA and CA199

© Springer Nature Switzerland AG 2018
V. Kůrková et al. (Eds.): ICANN 2018, LNCS 11140, pp. 101–108, 2018.
https://doi.org/10.1007/978-3-030-01421-6_10

are firstly detected by adopting fine-needle aspiration biopsy through the endoscopic ultrasonography or biopsies, and then the detection results are used to identify the benign and malignant neoplasms during the process of preoperative diagnosis. However, there are still some problems and limitations in these methods. For example, there are improper puncture techniques, the cyst is too small to be accurately located, and the puncture specimens are contaminated. All these problems come down to identifying accurately the pathological types of PCNs before operating, and these limitations have resulted in prohibiting the widespread use of the techniques. Therefore, it is of great importance and value for doctors to accurately diagnosis PCNs by image examination in determining the treatment and operation chance of patients. Figure 1 shows two different kinds of PCNs: SCNs and MCNs. According to clinical statistics, SCNs belong to a kind of benign neoplasms, and the patients with SCNs do not need surgery immediately. In contrast, MCNs have a high probability of malignant transformation. For instance, as shown in Figs. 1(c) and (d), it is hardly distinguished from the other by the naked eyes owing to the high similarities between SCNs and MCNs. Therefore, it is essential to explore some computer-aided diagnosis methods to help clinicians to achieve reliable non-invasive disease diagnosis and to improve the objectivity and rationality of treatment.

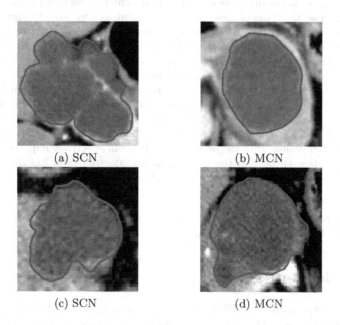

(a) SCN   (b) MCN

(c) SCN   (d) MCN

Fig. 1. Two different kinds of PCNs. (c) and (d) are almost indistinguishable, but they belong to different kinds of PCNs.

With the development of computer vision technology, the above issue attracts more and more attention in the society of medical image process. For example,

Li et al. [5] verify the effectiveness of additional information from the spectral CT for distinguishing serous oligocystic adenomas from mucinous cystic neoplasms using machine-learning algorithms. In [7], a method is proposed based on a Bayesian combination of a random forest classifier and a CNN to make use of both clinical information about the patient and fine imaging information from CT scans. However, The above mentioned methods require the segmentation of images in advance, then the obtained cysts or pancreas are classified by using classifiers. In recent years, the deeplearning-based [6] methods are proposed for classification [8–10], detection [11] and segmentation in the area of medical image process. In 2017, Esteva et al. [12] applies deep learning in skin cancer classification, and the effect of skin cancer classification can reach the level of a dermatologist.

The rest of the paper is organized as follows. In Sect. 2, a MCMC method is proposed by integrating multiple channels and multiple classifiers based on ResNet. Section 3 describes the experimental results and discussions of the proposed method on PCNs datasets. Finally Sect. 4 presents conclusions and future Work.

2   Methods

2.1   ResNet

ResNet [13] is a 'shortcut connection', and as shown in Fig. 2, one or more layers can be skipped in the network. Each skip-connected computation is called a residual block, and its output y_l is defined as

$$y_l = y_{i-1} + H(y_{i-1}) \tag{1}$$

where H contains convolution, batch normalization (BN) [14] and rectified linear units (ReLU) [15].

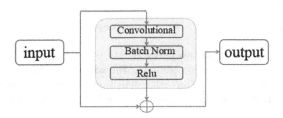

Fig. 2. The structure of the residual block. The convolutional layer is an important layer in CNNs, and it realizes partial receptive fields. Relu is the most popular activation function in DNNs owing to its simplicity and efficiency, and it can partly avoid and rectifies vanishing gradient problem. With the network deepening, the characteristic distribution gradually shifts or changes, and the convergence g slows down during the training process. The essential cause is that the gradient of the low-level neural network disappears in the backward propagation. Therefore, the above problem is solved by batch normalization layer.

In this work, a ResNet-50 model is used to extract features and classify PCNs with a Softmax classifier by the end-to-end training. The ResNet-50 model includes 16 residual blocks, through these residual blocks, the feature information is transmitted to avoid the gradient disappearing.

2.2 MCMC

In this section, a multi-channel multi-classifier method is proposed for the classification of PCNs in detail, and the corresponding framework is illustrated in Fig. 3. Firstly, a single-channel image is converted into a multi-channel image by adjusting the window width and window level of the original single-channel image, by using the Canny edge detection, and by calculating the gradient magnitude, respectively. In this way, the original image can be clearer and obtain enhanced edge information. Secondly, the residual network is used for end-to-end training to classify images and extract features. And then, the 2048-dimensional features obtained from the residual network are classified by adopting Bayesian classifier [16] and k-Nearest Neighbor (KNN) classifier [17]. Significantly, the outputs from the residual network and the two classifier are probability values of a class. Finally, the obtained probability values are classified by adopting a random forest method [18].

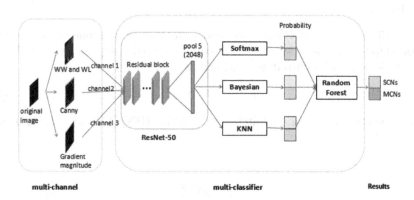

Fig. 3. The structure consists of two parts: (i) Multi-channel and (ii) Multi-classifier. The multi-channel is constructed by adjusting the window width and window level of the original image, by using the Canny edge detection, and by calculating the gradient magnitude, respectively. The multi-classifier includes Softmax, Bayesian, KNN and random forest.

3 Experiments and Results

3.1 Datasets and Experiments

The dataset comes from the First Affiliated Hospital of Zhejiang University, China. It contains 3,076 CT images of PCNs, and consists of the two most common PCNs: 1763 SCN images and 1313 MCN images. Thereinto, 615 PCNs (about 20%) are randomly selected as a testing data set, among them including 340 SCNs and 275 MCNs. All experiments are implemented on a computer with a E5-494 2620 2.0 GHz processor, and six nuclear of CPU, 32 GB RAM, and single tesla K20 graphics cards.

3.2   Results and Discussions

The results are shown in Table 1, and the accuracies obtained by using traditional methods [19, 20] are all less than 80%, meanwhile, the accuracies obtained by using convolutional neural networks is greatly improved due to the extraction ability of features. By comparing the results among SC-Resnet and MCMC, it shows that adding edge features in the multi-channel image can effectively improve the evaluation index of each classification result. The number of invalid feature values extracted from single-channel images is twice that of multi-channel images through the statistics for the 2048-dimensional features extracted from ResNet-50. Therefore, the increase of valid features obviously contributes to the improvement of multi-channel image classification effect.

Table 1. Results of different methods

Methods	Sensitive	Specificity	Precision	Accuracy	F-score
Gabor-KNN	**94.12%**	9.09%	56.14%	56.10%	70.33%
Gabor-Bayesian	75.00%	30.91%	57.30%	55.28%	64.97%
GLCM-KNN	72.65%	46.55%	62.69%	60.98%	67.30%
GLCM-Bayesian	85.29%	30.55%	60.29%	60.81%	70.64%
SC-ResNet	92.06%	68.73%	78.45%	81.63%	84.71%
MCMC	92.65%	**85.45%**	**88.73%**	**89.43%**	**90.65%**

From the results, the integrated multi-classifier (i.e., MCMC) can obtain good effects in many performance indicators. The sensitivity by adopting the proposed MCMC method is not the best among all these methods, but multiple performance indicators are the best, such as specificity, precision, F-score and accuracy.

Compared with Gabor-KNN, Gabor-Bayesian, GLCM-KNN and GLCM-Bayesian, We find these traditional methods have high sensitivity, but the low specificity. From Tables 2, 3, 4 and 5, the classification results under the confusion matrix are further investigated, and we find that a large number of mucinous cystic neoplasms are incorrectly identified as serous cystic neoplasms. There are maybe two reasons for that cases: (1) No key features are extracted, (2) Overfitting happens. Moreover, as shown in Tables 6 and 7, the results of classification

Table 2. Results of Gabor-KNN

Ground Truth	Prediction(%)	
	SCN	MCN
SCN	94.12%	5.88%
MCN	90.91%	9.09%

Table 3. Results of Gabor-Bayesian

Ground truth	Prediction(%)	
	SCN	MCN
SCN	75.00%	25.00%
MCN	69.09%	30.91%

Table 4. Results of GLCM-KNN

Ground truth	Prediction(%)	
	SCN	MCN
SCN	72.65%	27.35%
MCN	53.45%	46.55%

Table 5. Results of GLCM-Bayesian

Ground Truth	Prediction(%)	
	SCN	MCN
SCN	85.29%	14.71%
MCN	69.45%	30.55%

by using ResNet have obviously been improved. Especially in Table 7, the classification results obtained by our proposed method are the best. Therefore, the specificity of the classification in Table 1 is the highest among these methods according to the proposed MCMC method.

Table 6. Results of SC-ResNet

Ground truth	Prediction(%)	
	SCN	MCN
SCN	92.06%	7.94%
MCN	31.27%	68.73%

Table 7. Results of MCMC

Ground truth	Prediction(%)	
	SCN	MCN
SCN	92.65%	7.35%
MCN	14.55%	85.45%

4 Conclusion and Future Work

In this work, a multi-channel and multi-classifier method is proposed for the PCNs classification problem. A multi-channel image is transformed from an original CT image by adjusting the window width and window level, by using the Canny edge detection, and by calculating the gradient magnitude, respectively. A series of comparison experiments are conducted, and the results show enhancing edge features and integrating multi-classifier contribute to the classification effect. The proposed MCMC methods can obtained the best results in the comprehensive assessment index F-score and accuracy, and the performance parameters of sensitivity, specificity and precision have also a relatively high ranking among all methods. The results can help doctors to utilize the CT image to achieve reliable non-invasive disease diagnosis.

In the future, clinical information, positioning and segmentation of PCNs will be integrated to auxiliary diagnosis.

Acknowledgements. The authors would like to express their appreciation to the referees for their helpful comments and suggestions. This work was supported in part by Natural Science Foundation of Zhejiang Province (Grant No. LY18F030025), and in part by National Natural Science Foundation of China (Grant No. 61374094, U1509207, 31640053).

References

1. Hruban, R.H., et al.: Pancreatic intraepithelial neoplasia: a new nomenclature and classification system for pancreatic duct lesions. Am. J. Surg. Pathol. **25**(5), 579–586 (2001)
2. Hruban, R.H., et al.: An illustrated consensus on the classification of pancreatic intraepithelial neoplasia and intraductal papillary mucinous neoplasms. Am. J. Surg. Pathol. **28**(8), 977–987 (2004)
3. Brugge, W.R., Lauwers, G.Y., Sahani, D., Fernandez-del Castillo, C., Warshaw, A.L.: Cystic neoplasms of the pancreas. N. Engl. J. Med. **351**(12), 1218–1226 (2004)
4. Brugge, W.R., et al.: Diagnosis of pancreatic cystic neoplasms: a report of the cooperative pancreatic cyst study. Gastroenterology **126**(5), 1330–1336 (2004)
5. Li, C., Lin, X.Z., Wang, R., Hui, C., Lam, K.M., Zhang, S.: Differentiating pancreatic mucinous cystic neoplasms form serous oligocystic adenomas in spectral ct images using machine learning algorithms: a preliminary study. In: International Conference on Machine Learning and Cybernetics (ICMLC), vol. 1, pp. 271–276, Tianjin (2013)
6. Krizhevsky, A., Sutskever, I., Hinton, G.E.: Imagenet classification with deep convolutional neural networks. In: Advances in Neural Information Processing Systems, pp. 1097–1105 (2012)
7. Dmitriev, K., et al.: Classification of pancreatic cysts in computed tomography images using a random forest and convolutional neural network ensemble. In: International Conference on Medical Image Computing and Computer-Assisted Intervention, pp. 150–158, Quebec City (2017)
8. Bayramoglu, N., Heikkilä, J.: Transfer learning for cell nuclei classification in histopathology images. In: Hua, G., Jégou, H. (eds.) ECCV 2016. LNCS, vol. 9915, pp. 532–539. Springer, Cham (2016). https://doi.org/10.1007/978-3-319-49409-8_46
9. Anthimopoulos, M., Christodoulidis, S., Ebner, L., Christe, A., Mougiakakou, S.: Lung pattern classification for interstitial lung diseases using a deep convolutional neural network. IEEE Trans. Med. Imaging **35**(5), 1207–1216 (2016)
10. Hussein, S., Kandel, P., Corral, J.E., Bolan, C.W., Wallace, M.B., Bagci, U.: Deep multi-modal classification of intraductal papillary mucinous neoplasms (IPMN) with canonical correlation analysis. arXiv preprint arXiv:1710.09779 (2017)
11. Hu, H., Guan, Q., Chen, S., Ji, Z., Yao, L.: Detection and recognition for life state of cell cancer using two-stage cascade CNNs. IEEE/ACM Trans. Comput. Biol. Bioinform. (2017)
12. Esteva, A., et al.: Dermatologist-level classification of skin cancer with deep neural networks. Nature **542**, 115–118 (2017)
13. He, K., Zhang, X., Ren, S., Sun, J.: Deep residual learning for image recognition. In: Proceedings of the IEEE Conference on Computer Vision and Pattern Recognition, pp. 770–778 (2016)

14. Ioffe, S., Szegedy, C.: Batch normalization: accelerating deep network training by reducing internal covariate shift. arXiv preprint arXiv:1502.03167 (2015)
15. Glorot, X., Bordes, A., Bengio, Y.: Deep sparse rectifier neural networks. In: Proceedings of the Fourteenth International Conference on Artificial Intelligence and Statistics, pp. 315–323 (2011)
16. Chen, J., Huang, H., Tian, S., Qu, Y.: Feature selection for text classification with Naïve Bayes. Expert Syst. Appl. **36**(3), 5432–5435 (2009)
17. Ma, L., Crawford, M.M., Tian, J.: Local manifold learning-based k-nearest-neighbor for hyperspectral image classification. IEEE Trans. Geosci. Remote Sens. **48**(11), 4099–4109 (2010)
18. Gislason, P.O., Benediktsson, J.A., Sveinsson, J.R.: Random forests for land cover classification. Pattern Recogn. Lett. **27**(4), 294–300 (2006)
19. Liu, C., Wechsler, H.: Gabor feature based classification using the enhanced fisher linear discriminant model for face recognition. IEEE Trans. Image Process. **11**(4), 467–476 (2002)
20. Jain, S.: Brain cancer classification using GLCM based feature extraction in artificial neural network. Int. J. Comput. Sci. Eng. Technol. **4**(7), 966–970 (2013)

Breast Cancer Histopathological Image Classification via Deep Active Learning and Confidence Boosting

Baolin Du[1,2(✉)] 📷, Qi Qi[1,2(✉)] 📷, Han Zheng[1,2(✉)] 📷,
Yue Huang[1,2(✉)] 📷, and Xinghao Ding[1,2(✉)] 📷

[1] Fujian Key Laboratory of Sensing and Computing for Smart City,
Xiamen University, Xiamen 361005, Fujian, China
747127841@qq.com, 18150076754@163.com,
420100774@qq.com
[2] School of Information Science and Engineering, Xiamen University,
Xiamen 361005, Fujian, China
{yhuang2010, dxh}@xmu.edu.cn

Abstract. Classify image into benign and malignant is one of the basic image processing tools in digital pathology for breast cancer diagnosis. Deep learning methods have received more attention recently by training with large-scale labeled datas, but collecting and annotating clinical data is professional and time-consuming. The proposed work develops a deep active learning framework to reduce the annotation burden, where the method actively selects the valuable unlabeled samples to be annotated instead of random selecting. Besides, compared with standard query strategy in previous active learning methods, the proposed query strategy takes advantage of manual labeling and auto-labeling to emphasize the confidence boosting effect. We validate the proposed work on a public histopathological image dataset. The experimental results demonstrate that the proposed method is able to reduce up to 52% labeled data compared with random selection. It also outperforms deep active learning method with standard query strategy in the same tasks.

Keywords: Breast cancer · Histopathological image analysis
Deep active learning · Query strategy

1 Introduction

Breast cancer is ranked as the most common cancer in women worldwide, and it also featured with high morbidity and mortality among women worldwide [1]. The diagnosis by histopathological images under microscopy is one of the golden standards in clinical applications. With the development of imaging sensors, histopathological slides can be scanned and saved as digital images. As the digital image sizes increase dramatically with the magnification, it would be ideal to develop image processing and analysis tools, e.g. classification, in computer-aided diagnosis (CAD) for breast cancer.

© Springer Nature Switzerland AG 2018
V. Kůrková et al. (Eds.): ICANN 2018, LNCS 11140, pp. 109–116, 2018.
https://doi.org/10.1007/978-3-030-01421-6_11

Hand-crafted features, such as Scale invariant feature transform (SIFT), histogram of oriented gradient (HOG), gray-level co-occurrence matrix, kernel methods have been reported in the recognition or classification tasks in breast cancer histopathological image analysis. Some well-known classifiers, e.g. support vector machines (SVM), has been reported as well. Recently, deep learning methods, for example convolutional neural networks (CNN), has receive more attention and impressive performances in many tasks of histopathological image processing for breast cancer research, including recognition, classification and segmentation [2]. Chen et al. [3] detected cell mitosis in breast histology images using deep cascading CNN, which dramatically improves detection accuracy over other methods in 2014 ICPR MITOS-ATYPIA Challenge. Wang et al. [4] used CNN, which includes 27-layer breast cancer metastasis test and then won first place in Metastasis Detection Challenge of ISBI2016. Spanhol et al. [5] trained the classification of benign and malignant breast cancer pathological images by Alexnet [6], whose result is 6% higher than the traditional machine learning classification algorithm. Bayramoglu et al. [7] used deep learning to magnification independent breast pathology image classification and the recognition rate is 83%. Spanhol et al. [8] proposed an assessment of BC-recognition for caffeine-free features, increasing the accuracy to 89%. Wei et al. [9] proposed a novel breast cancer histopathological image classification method based on deep convolutional neural networks, named as BiCNN model, resulting to a higher classification accuracy (up to 97%).

The reported state-of-the-art methods strongly rely on the large-scale labeled data in training the network. However, in the view of real-world application, large-scale labeling in medical images are tedious and extremely expensive. Strong professional skills are usually required in the applications compared with annotating natural images. Very limited reports have been contributed to reduce the labeling burden in the proposed task. We proposed a deep domain adaptation method with PCAnet and a domain alignment operation to reduce the labeling cost by transferring knowledge from the source dataset to the target one [10]. We also introduced self-taught learning to PCAnet to reduce the burden of labeling [11]. However, labeled images in the training data are still randomly selected in the previous works.

In the proposed work, we want to improve the deep learning architecture for the classification task in breast cancer histopathological images by a deep active learning framework. Instead of random selection, active learning methods usually actively select samples with lowest confidence (highest entropy) as valuable samples, and they are added to query, and then the network can be fine-tuned incrementally [12]. In the proposed method, inspired by boosting, the query strategy is also improved, where samples with both high and low confidence are considered simultaneously to emphasize the confidence boosting. We consider that the network should be fine-tuned with additional supervision and its previous regularization simultaneously. The contributions of the proposed work can be summarized as: (1) the labeling cost can be reduced labeling effort with random selection; (2) The method outperforms standard active learning query strategy by the entropy boosting effect.

2   Proposed Method

As a topic in machine learning, active learning is to seek for the most informative samples in a large number of unlabeled dataset actively to annotation query, in order to reduce the labeling effort. We consider introducing the idea of active learning into our method to reduce the labeling cost required for deep learning methods in breast cancer pathological image classification. Firstly, the network is initiated with very limited random selected labeled data. Secondly, the key problem in active learning is how to define the criteria of 'valuable' samples. In the standard query strategy, 'worthness' is usually defined by the entropy calculated with deep architecture, as:

$$e_i = -\sum_{k=1}^{Y} \log\left(p_i^{j,k}\right) \cdot p_i^{j,k} \tag{1}$$

Where p_i is the confidence value of the network for a sample x_i, and Y represents the number of categories in the work. Entropy captures the uncertainty of classification system in each prediction. A larger entropy value denotes higher uncertainty of the system. In the standard query strategy, active learning methods select a certain number of high-entropy samples to the annotation query until the query size is full. Then the network is fine-tuned with the labeled samples incrementally.

In the proposed work, we believe that the evolution of the network should be fine-tuned incrementally by two factors, the additional supervision from manual labeling and the regulations from previous network. Thus in the proposed query strategy, inspired by the idea of boosting, samples with high entropy values and low entropy values are both considered for a boosting effect. It should be mentioned that the samples with high confidence or low entropy values are labeled by the previous network instead of manual annotation, so there is no additional cost of labeling with the standard active learning query strategy. The algorithm is detailed illustrated as follows.

Algorithm 1: The proposed query strategy.

    Input   : The training set for the specified dataset B_{train}; Pre trained CNN M_0; Active
                  learning times T_a; Labelled queue size n; Compare queue size m

    Output   : The final fine-tuned CNN model M_{T_a}

1    $UntagPool = B_{train}$
2   **for** $t = 1:T_a$ **do**
3   **for** $Samples \in UntagPool$ **do**
4   Entropy, EClass = ComputeEntropy (M_t,$Samples$) ;
5   **end**
6   Labelled queue, Compare queue, UntagPool = SelectSamplebyEntropy
          (Entropy, EClass, n, m);
7   Active batch = (Active batch, Labelled queue);
8   UntagPool = UpdateUntagPool (UntagPool, Active Batch) ;
9   Train batch = concatenate (Active batch, Compare queue);
10   M_t = TrainNet(Mt−1,Train batch);
11   **end**

As shown in Algorithm 1, let B represents the whole dataset with n_B images, and it is divided into training set and test set B_{train} and B_{test}. The CNN model, denoted as M_0, is initiated with n_i randomly selected samples in each category, n_i is set to be very small value, for example, two. For convenience, B_{train} is divided into labeled data B_l, and remaining unlabeled data B_u. The sizes of B_l and B_u are n_l and n_u respectively, where $n_l + n_u = n_B$. And n_l and n_u are changing during the incrementally network learning, since the main idea of active learning is to select most valuable samples from B_u to annotation queue A_t for manual annotation. In each query round, the network is fine-tuned with all the labeled samples in A_t, and then n_l turns to $n_l + n$, and B_u turns to $n_u - n$, where n is the size of A_t. A widely-used criteria is to select $n/2$ samples with highest entropy values in each category. The number of query is set to T_a, so the fine-tuned network after each query is denoted as $M_j, j = (0, \cdots, T_a)$. In the proposed work, the network in each query is fine-tuned with samples with both high entropy and low entropy. Besides n manual annotated samples, A_t contains additional m samples with lowest entropy values in each category. It should be mentioned that the labels of these m samples are auto-labeled by the previous network.

3   Experiment

3.1   Dataset Description

The proposed framework is evaluated on a public dataset of breast cancer histopathological images, BreaKHis [13]. The large-scale dataset contains 7909 images from 82 patients of breast cancer. The dataset is divided into benign and malignant tumors that are scanned with four magnification factors: 40X, 100X, 200X, and 400X. Pathological images are with size of 700×460 in RGB format. The details of the database are shown in Fig. 1.

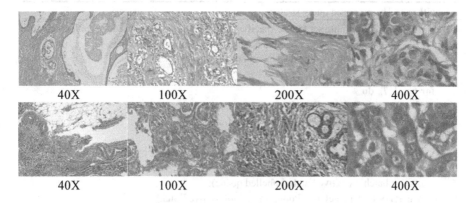

| 40X | 100X | 200X | 400X |

| 40X | 100X | 200X | 400X |

Fig. 1. Breast cancer histopathological image samples in the BreaKHis. (Top: benign. Bottom: malignant.)

3.2   Implementation Details

In this section, the proposed algorithm is implemented with TensorFlow framework. The basic CNN architecture is AlexNet pre-trained at ImageNet [14]. The basic settings of the server is intel 2.2-GHz CPU and a NVIDIA GeForce GTX 1080Ti GPU. The dataset has also been divided into training data (70%) and testing data (30%) randomly with no overlapping. In both training and testing set, the size of each category is balanced to be the same. In our work, the proposed work is evaluated on the image-level binary classification, that is, each image is predicted with benign or malignant. Since two categories have been balanced, classification accuracy is used as the metric in the validation, as follow:

$$\text{Image level accuracy} = \frac{N_c}{N_{im}} \qquad (2)$$

Where N_{im} the total number of images in the dataset, and the N_c represents the total number of images that are correctly classified.

The network is initiated with one benign sample and one malignant sample randomly selected from the training data. In each experiment, there are 5 query round, where query size for manual labeling in each round is N_m. It should be mentioned that the network is fine-tuned incrementally with 64 labeled images after each query, 48 of them are manual labeling, and the other 16 are auto-labeling.

3.3   Experiment Result

Experimental results on four magnification factors are demonstrated in Fig. 2 and Table 1. It can be observed and concluded from the figures that both standard deep active learning methods and proposed framework have consistent better performances compared with incremental learning with random selection in all the experiments. Deep active learning methods can save up to 52% of the labeling cost compared to random selection to achieve a similar accuracy. This demonstrated that in the view of real-world application, the proposed framework is a better option in recognition task with deep learning methods. It also can be concluded that our proposed method also out-performs deep active learning method with strategy of only high entropy.

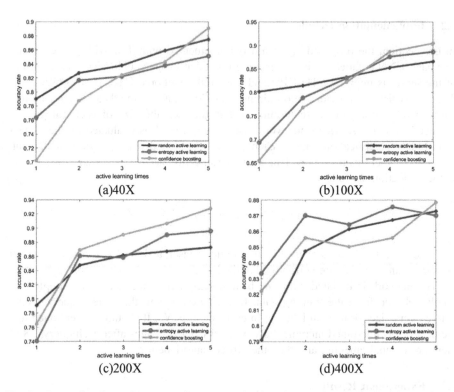

Fig. 2. Comparing the performance of entropy active learning, random active learning and our proposed method in 5 times active learning.

Table 1. Comparing to the annotation cost of our proposed method, random active learning and entropy active learning in similar accuracies. Thereinto, the cost refers to the number of labeled samples, which means the annotation cost.

Strategy	Magnification factors						
	40X		100X		200X		400X	
	Accuracy	cost	Accuracy	cost	Accuracy	cost	Accuracy	cost
Proposed	90.69%	288	90.46%	240	90.64%	192	90.96%	336
EntropyAL	90.96%	500	91.24%	400	91.98%	300	90.11%	450
RandomAL	90.96%	400	90.46%	400	90.37%	400	89.75%	400

4 Conclusions

We proposed a deep active learning framework in histopathological image analysis for breast cancer research. The main purpose of the work is to reduce the tedious labeling burden in the medical application if deep learning methods are used. Instead of randomly selecting samples for annotation as training samples, the framework actively seeking for the most valuable unlabeled data to be manual labeled, and then fine-tune the network incrementally. Besides, we also improve the query strategy with a confidence boosting operation, where both samples predicted with high confidence and low confidence are used in network training in each query round. The samples with high confidence are auto-labeled with the network, so there is no additional manual labeling cost compared with standard active learning methods. The experimental results validated on a large breast cancer histopathological images dataset have demonstrated that our proposed method significantly reduces the labeling cost compared with random selection. It also has better performances with higher accuracy when compared with standard query strategy.

References

1. Lakhani, S.R., Ellis. I.O., Schnitt, S.: WHO classification of tumours of the breast. In: International Agency for Research on Cancer, WHO Press, Lyon (2012)
2. Veta, M., Pluim, J.P.W., van Diest, P.J.: Breast cancer histopathology image analysis: a review. IEEE Trans. Biomed. Eng. 2(5), 1400–1411 (2014)
3. Chen, H., Dou, Q., Wang, X.: Mitosis detection in breast cancer histology images via deep cascaded networks. In: Thirtieth AAAI Conference on Artificial Intelligence, Phoenix, Arizona, pp. 1160–1166. AAAI Press (2016)
4. Wang, D., Khoslam, A., Gargeya, R.: Deep learning for identifying metastatic breast cancer. arXiv preprint arXiv:1606.05718 (2016)
5. Spanhol, F.A., Oliveira, L.S.: Breast cancer histopathological image classification using convolutional neural networks. In: International Joint Conference on Neural Networks, Vancouver, BC, Canada, pp. 2561–2567. IEEE (2016)
6. Krizhevsky, A., Sutskever, I., Hinton, G.E.: ImageNet classification with deep convolutional neural networks. In: International Conference on Neural Information Processing Systems, Lake Tahoe, Nevada, pp. 1097–1105. Curran Associates Inc. (2012)
7. Bayramoglu, N., Kannala, J., Heikkila, J.: Deep learning for magnification independent breast cancer histopathology image classification. In: International Conference on Pattern Recognition (ICPR), Cancun, Mexico, pp. 2440–2445. IEEE (2017)
8. Spanhol, F.A., Cavalin P.R., Oliveira, L.S.: Deep features for breast cancer histopathological image classification. In: IEEE International Conference on Systems, Los Angeles, CA, USA, pp. 1868–1873 (2017)
9. Weil, B., Han, Z., He, X.: Deep learning model based breast cancer histopathological image classification. In: 2nd IEEE International Conference on Cloud Computing and Big Data Analysis, Chengdu, China, pp. 348–353. IEEE (2017)
10. Huang, Y., Zheng, H., Liu, C.: Epithelium-stroma classification via convolutional neural networks and unsupervised domain adaptation in histopathological images. IEEE J. Biomed. Health Inform. 21(6), 1625–1632 (2017)

11. Yue Huang, Han Zheng, Chi Liu: Epithelium-stroma classification in histopathological images via convolutional neural networks and self-taught learning. In: IEEE International Conference on Acoustics, pp. 1073–1077. IEEE, New Orleans, LA, USA (2017)

12. Huang, S.-J., Jin, R., Zhou, Z.-H.: Active learning by querying informative and representative examples. In: International Conference on Neural Information Processing Systems, Vancouver, British Columbia, Canada, pp. 892–900. Curran Associates Inc. (2010)

13. Spanhol, F., Oliveira, L., Petitjean, C.: A dataset for breast cancer histopathological image classification. IEEE Trans. Biomed. Eng. **61**(7), 1455–1462 (2016)

14. Krizheevsky, A., Sutskever, I., Hinton, G.E.: ImageNet classification with deep convolutional neural networks. In: International Conference on Neural Information Processing Systems, Lake Tahoe, Nevada, pp. 1097–1105. Curran Associates Inc. (2012)

Epileptic Seizure Prediction from EEG Signals Using Unsupervised Learning and a Polling-Based Decision Process

Lucas Aparecido Silva Kitano[1], Miguel Angelo Abreu Sousa[1(✉)], Sara Dereste Santos[1], Ricardo Pires[1], Sigride Thome-Souza[2], and Alexandre Brincalepe Campo[1]

[1] Federal Institute of Education, Science and Technology of São Paulo,
Rua Pedro Vicente, 625, São Paulo, 01109-010, Brazil
angelo@ifsp.edu.br
[2] Institute of Psychiatry, Faculty of Medicine, University of São Paulo,
R. Dr. Ovídio Pires de Campos, 785, São Paulo, SP 01060-970, Brazil

Abstract. Epilepsy is a central nervous system disorder defined by spontaneous seizures and may present a risk to the physical integrity of patients due to the unpredictability of the seizures. It affects millions of people worldwide and about 30% of them do not respond to anti-epileptic drugs (AEDs) treatment. Therefore, a better seizure control with seizures prediction methods can improve their quality of life. This paper presents a patient-specific method for seizure prediction using a preprocessing wavelet transform associated to the Self-Organizing Maps (SOM) unsupervised learning algorithm and a polling-based method. Only 20 min of 23 channels scalp electroencephalogram (EEG) has been selected for the training phase for each of nine patients for EEG signals from the CHB-MIT public database. The proposed method has achieved up to 98% of sensitivity, 88% of specificity and 91% of accuracy. For each subsequence of EEG data received, the system takes less than one second to estimate the patient state, regarding the possibility of an impending seizure.

Keywords: Seizure prediction · Self-Organizing Maps
Polling-based decision process

1 Introduction

According to the World Health Organization, epilepsy is a central nervous system disorder that affects approximately 50 million people worldwide, making it one of the most common neurological diseases in the world. Epilepsy is defined as spontaneous seizures that start in the brain. Seizures are brief occurrences of involuntary movement that may involve a part of the body or the entire body, and are sometimes associated to a loss of consciousness [19]. For many patients, anti-epileptic drugs (AEDs) can be given at sufficiently high doses to prevent seizures, frequently causing side effects. For 20–40% of patients with epilepsy, AEDs are not effective [8]. Patients with epilepsy may experience anxiety due to the possibility of a seizure occurring at any time, in addition to physical integrity risk when performing some

© Springer Nature Switzerland AG 2018
V. Kůrková et al. (Eds.): ICANN 2018, LNCS 11140, pp. 117–126, 2018.
https://doi.org/10.1007/978-3-030-01421-6_12

activities like driving or swimming. In this regard, the development of reliable techniques for seizure prediction could improve the quality of epilepsy patients' life, reducing the risk of injuries and offering a better management of AEDs in individual bases, consequently reducing the side effects, improving the use of preventive-AEDs facing an imminent epileptic seizure [8].

There is evidence that the process of seizures generation (ictogenesis) is not random, originating from a brain region, and in most patients are associated to electroencephalogram (EEG) patterns. The EEG is a measure of the electrical activity captured by the cerebral cortex nerve cells. Epileptic EEG signals can be classified in four states: ictal (the epileptic seizure itself), postictal (period immediately after the seizure), interictal (period between seizures, considered a normal state of the patient) and preictal (period immediately before the seizure onset) [4]. Success in epileptic seizures prediction requires differentiating the preictal state from the other three states. Since the preictal state is the transition from the interictal to the ictal, a binary classification between the interictal and preictal states is of primary interest in seizures prediction. Patient-specific seizure onset and pre-seizure onset patterns suggest that patient-specific algorithms offer some advantage for epileptic seizure prediction, from the Machine Learning perspective [11]. Thus, supervised learning techniques are used with recorded data from each patient to discriminate characteristics between the preictal and interictal states [4].

In previous studies, patient-specific classifiers were used to separate the preictal and interictal states. In [6], binary classification with linear Bayes classifier was used in 7 patients achieving 94% of accuracy and 93% of sensitivity. In [4], SVM, KNN, LDA classifiers were compared. SVM has achieved the best results (94% of accuracy, 96% of sensitivity and 90% of specificity). SVM was also used in [13], achieving 97.5% of sensitivity. In [2], SVM and Kalman filter were combined achieving a sensitivity of 100%. These results demonstrate that the seizure prediction researches have been improving over time: a research work achieved in 2003 a sensitivity of 62.5% [3].

The goal of the seizure prediction research works, besides good performance is real-time hardware application. Therefore, reducing the dimensionality of the EEG processed data may enable neural processes with lower computational costs and/or processing time. Moreover, it can increase the results. In [4], an adaptive algorithm for EEG channel selection was proposed and compared with the use of all channels and with the Principal Components Analysis (PCA). The proposed adaptive algorithm for channel selection achieved the best results. In [6], Pearson's Correlation matrix was used as a feature selection to eliminate redundant information. Another important characteristic for developing real-time hardware applications is the number of EEG hours required for the training phase, which implies in large amounts of stored data and discomfort in patients during EEG recording. In [4], only 10 min of training data were used for each class (preictal and interictal) indicating that methods based on short time training can predict seizures.

In an attempt to find possible consistent patterns in the EEG signals, Self-Organizing Maps (SOM) [9] have been applied herein. This type of neural network, also known as Kohonen neural network, is categorized as an unsupervised learning model and allows mapping the input data into clusters. In the present proposal, SOM is used to identify the clusters corresponding to preictal and interictal states, in order to predict the seizures. More specifically, in this work, SOM integrates a patient-specific prediction method along with 4-s EEG segmentation, wavelet preprocessing and a polling-based decision process. Only 20 min of data were used in the training phase, with 10 min for each state (preictal and interictal), in contrast to many hours of EEG used in related works [1, 10, 11, 13, 14]. Moreover, the time consumed to process the EEG signals was measured to quantify the computational effort required by the proposed method.

2 Methods

The EEG signals analyzed are described in Subsect. 2.1. The initial processing step consists in segmenting each EEG channel data in 4-s windows. Then, feature extraction is performed as detailed in Subsect. 2.2. SOM is responsible to categorize the input data into preictal and interictal states, according to Subsect. 2.3. Finally, a sequence of 4-s windows is classified in a polling-based approach, as the prediction output of the system.

2.1 EEG Dataset

The dataset used in this work was recorded at the Children's Hospital Boston and is publicly available in the CHB-MIT EEG [7, 16]. This dataset comprises scalp EEG recordings from pediatric patients with intractable seizures. Due to the fact that scalp EEG is not invasive, it is advantageous compared to intracranial EEG. Pediatric EEG exhibits large variability in seizure and non-seizure activity [16]. The patients were monitored for several days following withdrawal of AEDs. All EEG signals were sampled at 256 Hz with 16-bit resolution, recorded mostly in 23 channels. The international 10–20 system [7] is used for the positioning of the EEG electrodes and for the nomenclature of the channels. In the present work, 9 of the 24 patients have been selected due to the fact that they have had, at least, 5 recorded seizures. Moreover, there was available, at least, 30 min of preictal state before seizure onset. Interictal state was defined as the period farther than 30 min from the seizure.

2.2 Feature Extraction

Methods of research in seizure predictions commonly use feature vectors built from EEG signals. In the present work, EEG data were segmented by non-overlapping 4-s windows. Then, for each window, the Discrete Wavelet Transform (DWT) is computed and the number of zero-crossings of detail coefficients of level 1 is calculated [12]. In [4] the mother Wavelet basis functions Haar, Daubechies-4 and Daubechies-8 were compared. The Haar Wavelet function allowed the highest accuracy and, in addition, it has lower computational complexity compared to the other wavelet functions. Based on those results, in the present work, the mother wavelet basis used is Haar. As in [4], the zero-crossings of the detail coefficients of the first level computed for each window results in a vector of dimension $D = 23$ channels. The total number of vectors is $n = T/4$ s, where T is the EEG period selected in seconds. In order to allow an easy visualization of the results, the vectors were represented in grayscale, with darker tones for the windows located temporally closer to the seizure (preictal state), and varying proportionality to light tones for the windows farther from the seizure (interictal state), as in Fig. 1.

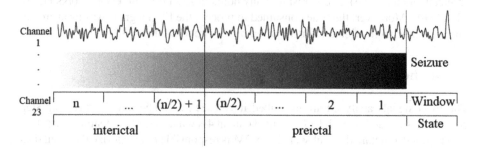

Fig. 1. Relationship between windows and grayscale attributed for n windows in training phase. Half of the data are in preictal state and the other half is in interictal state.

2.3 SOM for Unsupervised Categorization of Epileptic EEG Signals

Originally proposed by Teuvo Kohonen in 1982 [9], SOM has been widely used for multidimensional characterization and clustering tasks [15]. The network structure is composed of a set of prototypes, or neurons, represented by vectors of the same dimensionality as the input data. This neural structure is organized in one, two or three-dimensional arrays and the neurons are arranged in a topological order. The clustering occurs as a result of the comparison of the initial weights assigned to the neurons with the input data vectors. The weights are iteratively adjusted based on the distances between them, so that similar vectors in the input space are tend to be mapped onto neighboring neurons in the output array [5].

In the first step of SOM training algorithm, the distance between an input vector x_i and each neuron weight vector w_j is computed, and the neuron whose distance is closest to the input is selected as the winning neuron c, or best match unit (BMU), according to Eq. 1.

$$c = argmin_j \, dist\left(w_j, x_i\right) \tag{1}$$

In the following step, the values of the neuron vectors are adjusted. The new weights are computed by Eq. 2.

$$w_j(t + 1) = w_j(t) + \alpha(t) \cdot h_{cj}(t) \cdot \left(x_i - w_j\right) \tag{2}$$

The learning rate $\alpha(t)$ is a problem-dependent parameter. Usually, its value decreases exponentially from an initial value α_i towards a final value α_F. The neighborhood function $h_{cj}(t)$ determines the magnitude of the adjustment in the neuron vectors next to the BMU according to the distance between them $(dist_{cj})$, as shown in Eq. 3.

$$h_{cj}(t) = e^{-dist_{cj}^2/2\sigma^2(t)} \tag{3}$$

During the training phase, the magnitude of the adjustments in the neighboring neuron vectors is reduced by decreasing the width of the neighborhood function $\sigma(t)$. Hence, for stabilization of the self-organization process, $\sigma(t)$ usually decays exponentially between an initial value σ_i and a final value σ_f.

In this work, the input data comprises vectors of 23 dimensions resulting from the preprocessing of the 23 EEG channels, as described in Subsect. 2.2, and the network structure was configured as a two-dimensional array and as a one-dimensional array, both presented in Fig. 2. The aim of the initial essays using the SOM for the prediction of epileptic seizures was to verify the possible clustering effect in EEG signals that precede a seizure, according to the preprocessing described in Subsect. 2.2. In the training phase, equal amounts of preictal and interictal data were selected and presented to the network.

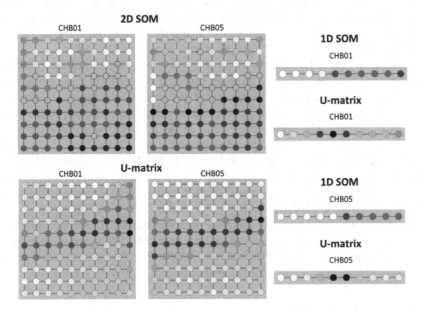

Fig. 2. Top left, 2D SOMs from patients CHB01 and CHB05, where darker neurons indicate preictal states and lighter ones indicate interictal states. Non activated neurons are represented using the background color. The corresponding U-matrices are presented at the bottom, where darker colors indicate larger distances and lighter ones, smaller distances. Top right, 1D SOM from patient CHB01 and the corresponding U-matrix. Bottom right, 1D SOM from patient CHB05 and the corresponding U-matrix.

Figure 2 shows examples of typical results obtained in the tests, for the 2D SOMs, of the mapping of EEG signals from patients 01 and 05 of the CHB-MIT dataset. It can be seen that the SOM neurons were clustered into two distinct categories. One of the categories (represented by darker tones) is associated to signals with a maximum of 30 min before seizure onset and the other category (represented by the lighter tones) is associated to signals recorded farther than 30 min before seizure onset. The mapped categories may also be seen in the U-matrix of the SOM, which denotes the vector distance among the neurons after the training process [18]. This favors the visual analysis of the grouping process which means that it is possible to distinguish different patterns in the dataset. The U-matrices associated to the SOMs of CHB01 and CHB05 patients are illustrated at the bottom of Fig. 2. It can be noticed that the SOM was able to successfully categorize the interictal and preictal states of EEG signals in an unsupervised manner.

Due to the consistent results obtained in the repetition of the initial experiments, in which the neural network succeeded in mapping EEG signals (splitting it into two clusters), the second sequence of essays aimed to explore the use of a 1D SOM architecture. The objective of using a 1D SOM architecture was to reduce the processing time of EEG categorization towards real-time hardware applications (as described in Sect. 1). Therefore, the purpose of the second sequence of experiments was to verify if the behavior of the new topology was able to achieve similar results to those obtained in the first sequence of essays, i.e., if the 1D SOM was also able to successfully categorize the interictal and preictal states of EEG signals in an unsupervised manner. Figure 2 shows the typical results obtained with 1D SOM and their respective U-matrices.

As shown in Fig. 2, 1D configurations of SOM were able to categorize the EEG signals that had been presented. In those examples, it is possible to note that the 1D SOMs identified two clusters, similarly to what had been observed in the 2D configurations: lighter neurons indicate the interictal states and darker ones, the preictal states (according to the grayscale depicted in Fig. 1). In the 1D U-matrices illustrated in the Fig. 2, it is possible to note that the two classes are located at opposite positions in the network. In both sequences of essays (1D and 2D SOMs), the training parameters employed were Euclidean distance; 10,000 epochs; $\alpha_i = 0.1$; $\alpha_f = 0.01$; $\sigma_i = 8$; and $\sigma_f = 1.1$. 2D SOMs training took approximately 207 s on an Intel Processor Dual Core i5-7200U, 3.1 GHZ, 8 GB DDR RAM, 3 MB cache, GNU/Linux operating system, Ubuntu 16.04 LTS distribution. In the same system, training 1D architectures took approximately 74 s. Besides the learning phase, decrease in processing time is also important during the inference phase. Section 3 describes the inference time results compared to the time periods of the EEG analyzed.

2.4   Classification and Evaluation

Subsections 2.2 and 2.3 presented EEG window segmentation, feature extraction and the proposed SOM model to categorize each of these windows. This subsection describes the proposal to differentiate the preictal state from the interictal state so that the seizure prediction can be performed. Moreover, this subsection presents the methods used for evaluating the quality of the prediction method results.

Figure 3 depicts the categorization method. As described in Subsect. 2.2, the 23-channel EEG signals are segmented in non-overlapping 4-s windows (Fig. 1). Then, the zero-crossings count of the DWT is computed for each one of the channels, building a vector $(d_1, d_2, ..., d_{23})$ and a previously trained SOM is used to cluster the vectors. The category of each window is thus indicated by the neuron that is activated at the output of the network. Finally, the assignment of a predicted state (interictal or preictal) is performed by counting the results in a series of windows. Hence, each sequence of SOM outputs is submitted to a polling-based decision process. In Fig. 3, the SOM neurons are identified by numbers, with neurons ranging from 0 to 4 indicating preictal states whereas neurons ranging from 5 to 9 indicate interictal states. A sequence of seven activated neurons is also represented in the figure: 9-8-8-6-2-2-5. For illustration purpose, assuming that a series of 3 windows is grouped in one polling, the sequence 9-8-8 results in the classification of the current state as interictal (I). In another example, the poll groups the sequence 2-2-5, which results in the classification of the state as preictal (P). The next section discusses seizure prediction for nine patients from the CHB-MIT dataset and the influence on the results of the number of windows in each series.

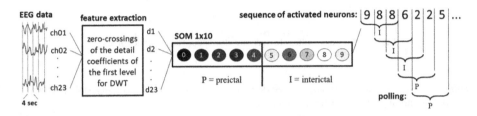

Fig. 3. Sequences of EEG data classified and evaluated by the proposed polling method.

3   Results and Discussion

To discuss the obtained results, three performance metrics are employed here: sensitivity, specificity and accuracy. These metrics are often used to evaluate seizure prediction methods [2, 4, 6, 11, 13].

The amount of data used for training was the same for all patients (20 min). For the inference, the selected time was longer due to the adopted criteria and available data, as explained in Subsect. 2.1. Table 1 shows the test time selected for each patient.

Table 1.   Amount of data test time for the patients.

Patient	chb01	chb03	chb05	chb06	chb08	chb10	chb11	chb20	chb20	Total
Data test (min)	110	212	100	150	229	279	66	166	342	1654

The experiments involved a total of 59 seizures and 24810 EEG windows were individually classified. For each of the patients, the sensitivity, specificity and accuracy were calculated with nine different numbers of windows grouped in a poll: 1, 5, 15, 45, 90, 135, 180, 225 and 270. Figure 4 shows the average over all patients for sensitivity (circles), specificity (squares) and accuracy (triangles) of the obtained results. These values and the corresponding standard deviations are presented in Table 2.

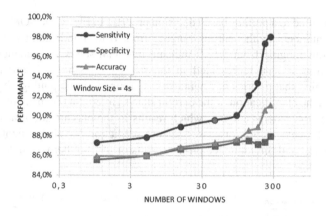

Fig. 4. Average values for sensitivity, specificity and accuracy.

Table 2. Averages (μ) and standard deviations (σ) for the accuracy, sensitivity and specificity for different numbers of windows in each poll.

		1	5	15	45	90	135	180	225	270
Accuracy	μ	85.95%	86.01%	86.85%	87.31%	87.67%	88.56%	88.93%	90.60%	91.10%
	σ	11.92%	12.71%	13.07%	14.20%	14.89%	14.92%	15.44%	15.69%	15.32%
Sensitivity	μ	87.29%	87.86%	88.95%	89.62%	90.12%	92.14%	93.36%	97.41%	98.09%
	σ	14.02%	14.22%	13.67%	13.18%	14.44%	12.44%	11.53%	6.65%	5.72%
Specificity	μ	85.58%	85.98%	86.65%	86.98%	87.38%	87.51%	87.18%	87.41%	87.99%
	σ	17.32%	17.72%	18.15%	19.11%	20.43%	20.97%	21.69%	21.44%	20.57%

According to Fig. 4, sensitivity is the metric that mostly increases with the number of the windows in a polling sequence, varying from 87% to 98%. In [4, 6, 13], the sensitivity values reported are 93%, 96% and 97.5%, respectively. The best value achieved in the present work is higher than those in related works, although no dimensionality reduction technique is applied here. This means that the evaluation by polling seems to be a reasonable tool for seizure prediction. On the other hand, specificity is less sensitive to the increase of the number of windows in a sequence (about 3% higher). This value is related to the false positives. In [4] and [11], the specificity value achieved 90% and both works has used dimensionality reduction techniques, which suggests that specificity improvement may be related to dimensionality reduction. Finally, accuracy varied from 86% to 91% while in [4] and [6], it has reached 94%. In [17], SOM was used to distinguish preictal from interictal data, achieving 89.68% of accuracy. As the accuracy can be improved through the specificity optimization, thus reducing the data dimensionality can also improve the accuracy of the method. This means that the results can be even better after a preprocessing for data dimensionality reduction.

In summary, increasing the number of windows improves the performance of the classifier. Moreover, this does not significantly affect the processing time to infer a result. This is because the system waits for the total number of windows only at the initialization. From then on, the inference happens with each new window received, that is, every

4 s. This new window simply replaces the oldest window in the sequence, and then a new polling is performed with the remaining windows.

It takes 0.912 s to process and infer a window of 4 s and a SOM inference takes 3 ms. These times were measured in a notebook, where other background tasks were being executed concurrently. Towards real-time hardware application, the time spent can be reduced by using a dedicated chip (ASIC or FPGA). Techniques for dimensionality reduction may also diminish the processing time further and improve the results, as already discussed. Moreover, reducing the number of data acquisition channels helps decreasing the computational costs, besides taking into account that a 23-channel device may be uncomfortable for a day by day wearable application.

4   Conclusion

In this paper, a patient-specific seizure prediction method was proposed involving first level of discrete wavelet transform, zero-crossings of the detail coefficients, SOM unsupervised learning algorithm and a polling-based decision process to estimate the patient state as preictal or interictal. By increasing the number of windows in the polling process, improvements have been achieved in terms of accuracy, specificity and sensitivity, up to 91%, 88% and 98%, respectively. These values are close to the best results found in related works. The main contributions of this work are the short EEG time employed in the training phase and also the low processing time, even without using any technique of dimensionality reduction. Such characteristics are relevant for future real time hardware applications. Following this work, different techniques for feature selection and data dimensionality reduction will be explored, in order to adapt a real-time monitoring system to continuous learning scenarios in which the EEG data may suffer from drift effects.

Acknowledgments. The authors acknowledge the National Council for Scientific and Technological Development (CNPq) for the undergraduate scholarship conceded to Lucas Aparecido Silva Kitano.

References

1. Alawieh, H., Hammoud, H., Haidar, M., Nassralla, M.H., El-Hajj, A.M., Dawy, Z.: Patient-aware adaptive ngram-based algorithm for epileptic seizure prediction using EEG signals. In: 2016 IEEE 18th International Conference on e-Health Networking, Applications and Services (Healthcom), pp. 1–6 (2016)
2. Chisci, L., et al.: Real-time epileptic seizure prediction using AR models and support vector machines. IEEE Trans. Biomed. Eng. **57**(5), 1124–1132 (2010)
3. D'Alessandro, M., Esteller, R., Vachtsevanos, G., Hinson, A., Echauz, J., Litt, B.: Epileptic seizure prediction using hybrid feature selection over multiple intracranial EEG electrode contacts: a report of four patients. IEEE Trans. Biomed. Eng. **50**(5), 603–615 (2003)
4. Elgohary, S., Eldawlatly, S., Khalil, M.I.: Epileptic seizure prediction using zero-crossings analysis of EEG wavelet detail coefficients. In: 2016 IEEE Conference on Computational Intelligence in Bioinformatics and Computational Biology (CIBCB), pp. 1–6 (2016)

5. Haykin, S.O.: Neural Networks and Learning Machines, vol. 3. Pearson, Upper Saddle River (2009)
6. Hoyos-Osorio, K., Castañeda-Gonzalez, J., Daza-Santacoloma, G.: Automatic epileptic seizure prediction based on scalp EEG and ECG signals. In: 2016 XXI Symposium on Signal Processing, Images and Artificial Vision (STSIVA), pp. 1–7 (2016)
7. Goldberger, A.L., et al.: PhysioBank, PhysioToolkit, and PhysioNet: components of a new research resource for complex physiologic signals. Circulation **101**, 220 (2000)
8. Kaggle: American epilepsy society seizure prediction challenge. https://www.kaggle.com/c/seizure-prediction. Accessed 25 Apr 2018
9. Kohonen, T.: The self-organizing map. Neurocomputing **21**(1–3), 1–6 (1998)
10. Li, S., Zhou, W., Yuan, Q., Liu, Y.: Seizure prediction using spike rate of intracranial EEG. IEEE Trans. Neural Syst. Rehabil. Eng. **21**(6), 880–886 (2013)
11. Liang, J., Lu, R., Zhang, C., Wang, F.: Predicting seizures from electroencephalography recordings: a knowledge transfer strategy. In: 2016 IEEE International Conference on Healthcare Informatics (ICHI), pp. 184–191 (2016)
12. Mallat, S.: A Wavelet Tour of Signal Processing. Academic Press, London (1999)
13. Park, Y., Luo, L., Parhi, K.K., Netoff, T.: Seizure prediction with spectral power of EEG using cost-sensitive support vector machines. Epilepsia **52**(10), 1761–1770 (2011)
14. Parvez, M.Z., Paul, M.: Epileptic Seizure Prediction by Exploiting Spatiotemporal Relationship of EEG Signals Using Phase Correlation. IEEE Trans. Neural Syst. Rehabil. Eng. **24**(1), 158–168 (2016)
15. Pöllä, M., Honkela, T., Kohonen, T.: Bibliography of Self-organizing Map (SOM) Papers: 2002–2005 Addendum. Neural Computing Surveys (2009)
16. Shoeb, A.H.: Application of machine learning to epileptic seizure onset detection and treatment. Ph.D. thesis, Massachusetts Institute of Technology (2009)
17. Tafreshi, A.K., Nasrabadi, A.M., Omidvarnia, A.H.: Empirical mode decomposition in epileptic seizure prediction. In: 2008 IEEE International Symposium on Signal Processing and Information Technology, pp. 275–280 (2008)
18. Ultsch, A.: Self-organizing neural networks for visualisation and classification. In: Opitz, O., Lausen, B., Klar, R. (eds.) Information and Classification, pp. 307–313. Springer, Heidelberg (1993). https://doi.org/10.1007/978-3-642-50974-2_31
19. World Health Organization: Epilepsy. http://www.who.int/en/news-room/fact-sheets/detail/epilepsy. Accessed 25 Apr 2018

Classification of Bone Tumor on CT Images Using Deep Convolutional Neural Network

Yang Li[1] , Wenyu Zhou[2], Guiwen Lv[3], Guibo Luo[1] , Yuesheng Zhu[1(✉)], and Ji Liu[1]

[1] Communication and Information Security Lab, Shenzhen Graduate School,
Peking University, Shenzhen, China
aceyli@foxmail.com, luoguibo@pkusz.edu.cn,
zhuys@pkusz.edu.cn, jiliu@pku.edu.cn
[2] Department of Spine Surgery, No. 1 Affiliated Hospital of Shenzhen University
(Shenzhen No. 2 People's Hospital), Shenzhen, China
drzhouwenyu@163.com
[3] Department of Radiology, No. 1 Affiliated Hospital of Shenzhen University
(Shenzhen No. 2 People's Hospital), Shenzhen, China
peterlgw@163.com

Abstract. Classification of bone tumor plays an important role in treatment. As artificial diagnosis is in low efficiency, an automatic classification system can help doctors analyze medical images better. However, most existing methods cannot reach high classification accuracy on clinical images because of the high similarity between images. In this paper, we propose a super label guided convolutional neural network (SG-CNN) to classify CT images of bone tumor. Images with two hierarchical labels would be fed into the network, and learned by its two sub-networks, whose tasks are learning the whole image and focusing on lesion area to learn more details respectively. To further improve classification accuracy, we also propose a multi-channel enhancement (ME) strategy for image preprocessing. Owing to the lack of suitable public dataset, we introduce a CT image dataset of bone tumor. Experimental results on this dataset show our SG-CNN and ME strategy improve the classification accuracy obviously.

Keywords: Bone tumor classification
Super label guided convolutional neural network · Multi-channel enhancement

1 Introduction

Bone tumors are tumors that occur in bones or their affiliated tissues. The incidence of bone tumors among all tumors is 2%–3% and rising in recent years [1]. In practice, bone tumor is not easy to detect accurately in the early time, and it is difficult to cure completely in the later stage, often treated with extremely surgical methods such as resection. During diagnosis, to accurately diagnose doctors often use multiple methods like imaging, observing the clinical manifestations. And CT images have been proved to be an effective imaging method [2]. To diagnose more efficiently, the introduction of effective computer-aided CT image diagnosis system is very meaningful.

© Springer Nature Switzerland AG 2018
V. Kůrková et al. (Eds.): ICANN 2018, LNCS 11140, pp. 127–136, 2018.
https://doi.org/10.1007/978-3-030-01421-6_13

However, classification of bone tumor using CT images is a challenging task. We first try SVM [3] algorithm, but it does not work well. In recent years, deep learning algorithms develop fast, and have been shown to exceed human performance in visual tasks. Deep convolutional neural networks (CNNs) show a great advantage in image classification. Many works tend to introduce deep learning methods to the field of medicine image analysis. For example, Andre Esteva et al. [4] use GoogleNet to categorize skin cancer images and reach dermatologist-level classification accuracy. Wang et al. [5] evaluate four classic CNN architectures, AlexNet [6], VGGNet [7], GoogLeNet [8], ResNet [9], on the classification of thorax diseases. Also [10–13] prove CNNs have the potential in processing clinical images. However, CNNs may perform worse on medical images compared with on natural images. For example, when to categorize skin cancer images with GoogleNet the classification accuracy is only 55% on nine-class disease partition [4] while the top-1 error rate of VGG-16 (VGG-16 has similar performance with GoogleNet, but there is only top-5 error rate of GoogleNet in [9]) is 28% on ImageNet [14] in which has 1000-class images [9].

In this paper, we apply CNNs to classification of bone tumor on CT images. To the best of our knowledge, there is no suitable public datasets. The first step is to make a CT image dataset of bone tumor. The dataset that we make contains 9 kinds of CT images of bone tumor, and every image in this dataset has a super label and a fine-grained label. Later we train CNNs with our dataset, experiments are executed on AlexNet and VGG-13 network respectively to verify the performance on classic networks. But the results do not perform well enough.

To improve classification accuracy, we propose a super label guided convolutional neural network (SG-CNN) to classify bone tumor images. The network architecture can be seen as a fine-grained image classification network with two branches. We use images and their two hierarchical labels to feed the network without image annotations, then network can automatically crop the image under the guide of super label sub-network and generate a new image which is a copy of the lesion area. After this step, background area in global image is largely cut, which makes the network more focused on lesion area. The experimental results show the classification accuracy is greatly improved by SG-CNN compared with genetic CNNs. To further improve the classification accuracy we also introduce a multi-channel enhancement (ME) strategy to preprocess the CT images of bone tumor. We utilize two morphological methods to preprocess the input image to enhance the contrast of the edges of the lesion in the image, and then we merge the original image and the processed images together into a three channel image. The experimental results show this strategy also improve the classification accuracy.

2   The Proposed Method

2.1   SG-CNN

There are many classic CNN models to choose for categorization tasks such as AlexNet, VGGNet. These networks show good performance on natural images classification like ImageNet. In natural images, the objects are usually in center position, and the difference between objects is obvious. But when it comes to fine-grained visual classification tasks like medical images categorization, classic CNNs cannot reach a high level of classification accuracy. To solve the fine-grained classification problems, scholars usually introduce new CNN structures. For example, Wei et al. [15] propose a novel end-to-end Mask-CNN model based on the part annotations of images. Zhang et al. [16] propose a part-based R-CNN model for fine-grained categorization. Huang et al. [17] propose an architecture for fine-grained visual categorization which consists of a fully convolutional network to locate multiple object parts and a two-stream classification network that encodes object-level and part-level cues simultaneously based on manually-labeled strong part annotations. However, all these methods require image annotations which means these methods can consume too much time on making datasets. To tackle this issue, we design a new CNN that can generate ROI regions automatically by the network itself without using image annotations.

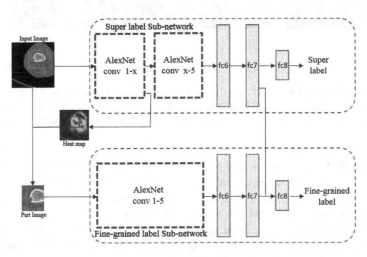

Fig. 1. The SG-CNN structure. One raw CT image and its two labels are fed into the network, without any annotations. The input image will be cropped under the guide of heat map created by one of the convolution layer and input into the other network branch. The guide layer conv x for cropping image can be any convolution layer. The output of network includes two predicted labels.

The proposed SG-CNN framework is presented in Fig. 1. It is an end-to-end network, the input includes CT image with two labels in hierarchical relationship, and the output contains two predicted labels. When making dataset, some different fine-grained labels share a same super label. And we use both super label and fine-grained label to train SG-CNN and gain their classification accuracies. In practice, we focus on classification accuracy of fine-grained label. The basic network for building sub-networks can be any CNN model, in this paper we choose AlexNet. For the architecture inside SG-CNN, basically, it has three components including super label sub-network, fine-grained label sub-network, and the connection part of them. When we train the network, images are first fed to the super label sub-network, and then all feather maps of the guide convolution layer of the sub-network would be summed up together and generate a heat map like Fig. 2. For CT images, the image background is less complex than natural images, the feature points in the heat map are distributed near lesion area. In heat map, the red part represents hot points whose value is large, the blue represents cold points whose value is small. We choose the hottest part in the heat map. The center point of hottest part is determined by formula 1, where k is the radius of the hottest part. For each $(2k + 1) \times (2k + 1)$ heat map area, we sum up all its values. Then we choose the largest one.

$$H(x, y) = \sum_{i=-k}^{k} \sum_{j=-k}^{k} X(x - i, y - i) \tag{1}$$

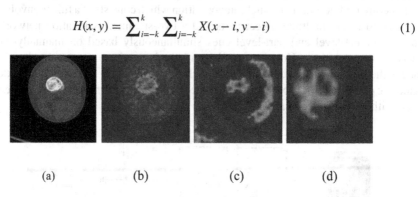

(a)   (b)   (c)   (d)

Fig. 2. Raw input image and heat maps. (a) is one input image. (b) is the heat map generated by conv1. (c) is the heat map generated by conv2. (d) is the heat map generated by conv3. The images show that with the network going deeper, heat map contains more abstract and semantic meanings. (Color figure online)

Next we find the corresponding point in the original image and select a 56×56 image whose center is the corresponding point of hottest point. After this selection, background interference can be greatly reduced. We then send the selected new image to the fine-grained label sub-network. In fine-grained label sub-network the fc8 layer is not only connected to the fc7 layer of fine-grained label sub-network, but also to the fc7 layer of super label sub-network. Also, in SG-CNN some deep learning techniques like dropout [6] and batch normalization layer [18] are applied to improve the generalization capability.

The inspiration for designing SG-CNN comes from the thinking form of human being: start with a rough sketch, and then pay more attention to details, finally do a comprehensive judgment. In a CT image of bone tumor, the lesion area takes up only a limited part of the image. After we crop the image, most of background areas can be removed. In this way the network pays more attention to the lesion area. The location accuracy of cropped area is determined by super label sub-network. When to extract the cropped image, we can select any convolutional layer as the guide layer. Finally, the network output predicted fine-grained label whose classification accuracy is determined by two network branches simultaneously.

2.2   Multi-channel Enhancement

In this paper, to further improve the classification accuracy of CNNs, we propose an image preprocessing method to make the lesion area more distinct. We conduct dilation and erosion operation on images, and combine the processed images and the original image together into a three channel image. As in CT images of bone tumor the lesion area and their surrounding areas are in high contrast, one of the new images can expend the border area between lesion area and normal area, thus CNNs can more easily locate the lesion area.

Like in Fig. 3, the lesion area is in black color, dilation operation can expand the border area and make it more palpable. For images with white lesion area, erosion operation will realize the same effect. The complete steps of multi-channel enhancement strategy are shown in Fig. 3.

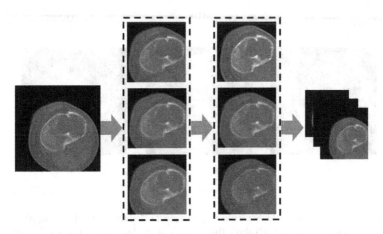

Fig. 3. Full steps of multi-channel enhancement. First, on the original 256×256 image we randomly cut a 224×224 image, then conduct dilation operation and erosion operation respectively, after these operations, we merge the processed images and original image into a three channel image.

3 Experiments

3.1 Dataset

The CT images used in this paper are obtained from Shenzhen No. 2 People's Hospital. Data is collected from patients diagnosed with bone tumors from 2014 to 2017. Original data is stored in DICOM format in which contains image data, patient information and tags. We extract the image data and resize the image to 256×256. In this paper, we use CT images in 2D form, which means we classify the bone tumor using just one layer CT image. As CT is a continuous scan, not every image in the sequence can clearly show the lesion features. The different kind of images are shown in Fig. 4. To address this issue, we pick images that clearly show the features of the lesion. After all steps above, we get proper JPG format CT images.

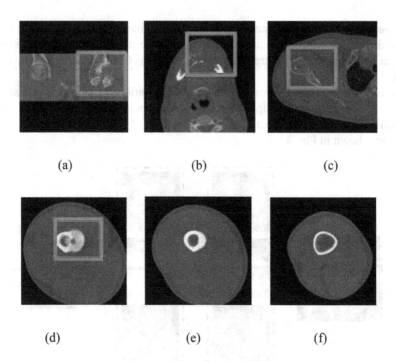

(a)   (b)   (c)

(d)   (e)   (f)

Fig. 4. (a)–(d) show the lesion features clearly, we select CT images like these, (d)–(f) are in the same CT sequence, however (e)–(f) show the features of the lesion not clearly as (d), we delete the two images. In this way, we get 2D CT images with clear lesion areas.

When training CNNs, the uniform distribution of different sorts of images is a crucial issue. Although bone tumors can occur throughout the body, the incidence between organs exists a significantly difference. It is not an easy work to collect more bone tumors CT images to balance the distribution, due, for instance, to the high costs in terms of money and time required to cooperate with other institutions. In this case, we only choose CT images of limbs to make the dataset and we finally get 6422 CT slices of bone tumor. The diagnosis results of each image is confirmed by two or more doctors (including orthopedic surgeons and imaging doctors) and finalized with clinical manifestations, we use these diagnosis results as the label of CT images.

In fact, there are over two hundred kinds of bone tumors, however, most of them are in low incidence. As it is not an easy work to get enough data of all kinds of bone tumors, thus, in this work, the bone tumors that we analyze contain only 9 class. It is noting that the similarities among the nine diseases are different. Diseases in high similarity can have a same super label. We use two super label schemes, one being benign tumor and malignant tumor, the other being cartilage tumor, osteogenic tumor, and other tumor. Based on WHO2012, we develop a two-rank classification strategy as shown in Table 1.

Table 1. The bone tumor classification strategy

	Benign tumor	Malignant tumor
Cartilage tumor	Endogenous chondroma Osteochondroma Synovial chondroma	Chondrosarcoma
Osteogenic tumor	Osteoid osteoma Osteoma	Osteosarcoma
Other tumor	Fibrous bone tumor	Giant cell tumor of bone

When training, we randomly divide the dataset, 75% images of the dataset are used for training, and the rest of image are used for test.

3.2 Experiments and Results

In this work, we use Tensorflow 1.0 as our CNN programming framework, run codes on a desktop PC equipped with a Intel i7-6700 K CPU, a NVIDIA TITAN X(Pascal) GPU and Ubuntu16.04 operating system.

In experiment, we first try traditional machine learning methods to classify CT images on our dataset. We use HOG [19] algorithm to extract image features and PCA [20] to do dimensionality reduction and the output dimensionality is 100, finally use a SVM classifier with RBF kernel to classify images.

Then we use CNN methods to do experiments. It is well-known that deep CNNs require a great deal of data for training. A small number of images can lead to over-training. Before we feed images into the network, we use data augmentation to preprocess the input images [6]. When it comes to training mode, there are currently three major techniques that successfully employ CNNs to medical image classification [21]: (1) training the CNN from scratch; (2) using off-the-shelf CNN features (without retraining the CNN) as complementary information channels to existing handcrafted image features; and (3) performing pre-training on natural or medical images and fine-tuning on medical target images. One key important factor in the choice of training strategies is the size of the dataset. In this paper, when training SG-CNN, we first use a pre-trained CNN model to initialize the network.

In practice, we first perform our experiment with AlexNet on our dataset. Next, to see the performance on deeper classification network, we use VGG-13 network to classify the images. Then we do experiment to get the performance on our proposed SG-CNN. Later we add the multi-channel enhancement method. Moreover, we do experiments using two series of super labels to test how the selection of super label schemes affect the classification accuracy. Additionally, we test how the selection of generation layer of the heat map influence classification accuracy.

We use Top-k error rate to evaluate our strategies. The results are shown in Table 2. From the table, it is obvious that all deep learning methods perform better than traditional machine learning method. For classic CNNs, with networks getting deeper, the error rate declines. But the best top-1 error rate is still 0.44 which is high. Our proposed SG-CNN significantly outperforms VGG-13 network and AlexNet.

Table 2. Comparison of five methods

Methods	Top-1 error rate (%)	Top-2 error rate (%)
HOG+PCA+SVM	76	59
Alexnet	54	43
VGG-13	44	21
SG-CNN	28	5

The comparison of two super label guided strategies is shown in Table 3. From the table we can see that the top-1 error rate of super label classification has a relative 10% increase while the top-1 error rate of fine-grained label classification has a relative 3% reduction and top-2 error rate has a relative 1% reduction, when 2-class super label strategy is replaced by 3-class super label strategy. We can suppose that the classification accuracy of fine-grained label is determined by not only classification accuracy of super label but also the number of super labels. In practice, optimizing only one factor may not improve the classification accuracy of fine-grained label.

Table 3. Comparison of two super label schemes for SG-CNN

Strategies	Top-1 error rate of super label (%)	Top-1 error rate of fine-grained label (%)	Top-2 error rate of fine-grained label (%)
2-class super label	7	28	5
3-class super label	17	25	4

The error rate comparison between different generation layers of heat map is shown in Table 4. With the network going deeper, the heat map becomes more abstract and shows less edge information like Fig. 2. From Table 4 we can see conv1 is in high error rate. The later layers show better performance than conv1. But conv3-5 do not show obviously better performance than conv2, we assume that the reason is the feather map size getting smaller as layers going deeper.

Table 4. Comparison of five cropping image generation layers

Selected layers	Top-1 error rate (%)	Top-2 error rate (%)
Conv1	35	16
Conv2	28	5
Conv3	29	6
Conv4	30	6
Conv5	28	8

Finally, we do experiments to test our ME strategy. From Table 5 we can observe that with the use of multi-channel enhancement, there are further reductions of top-1 and top-2 error rate on every networks. The results show that our ME strategy is useful for improving the performance of CNNs.

Table 5. Performance tests for ME strategy

Methods	Top-1 error rate (%)	Top-2 error rate (%)
AlexNet	54	43
AlexNet+ME	49	28
VGG-13	44	21
VGG-13+ME	37	13
SG-CNN	28	5
SG-CNN+ME	26	5

4 Conclusion and Future Work

In this paper, we have presented a novel end-to-end fine-grained classification network named SG-CNN and an image multi-channel enhancement strategy. Moreover, we produced a bone tumor CT image dataset based on the WHO2012 standard. With our dataset, we compared experimental performance of SVM, AlexNet, VGG-13 network, and our SG-CNN. Experimental results show our proposed SG-CNN can significantly outperform SVM and classic CNNs. Additionally, our multi-channel enhancement strategy proves that it can achieve higher accuracy. Among all experimental results, the lowest top-1 error rate is 0.25 and top-2 error rate is 0.04. As future work, we would focus on obtaining more image data, 3D CNN modeling, and MRI image recognition.

Acknowledgements. This work was supported in part by the Shenzhen Municipal Development and Reform Commission (Disciplinary Development Program for Data Science and Intelligent Computing), and by Shenzhen International cooperative research projects GJHZ20170313150021171.

References

1. Zhang, Y.J., Cui, X.F., Li, C.C., Li, S.J.: Efficacy of DR, CT and MRI in bone tumors. Chinese-German J Clin. Oncol. **13**(4), 181–184 (2014)
2. Keidar, Z., Israel, O., Krausz, Y.: SPECT/CT in tumor imaging: technical aspects and clinical applications. Semin. Nucl. Med. **33**(3), 205 (2003)
3. Sánchez A, V.D.: Advanced support vector machines and kernel methods. Neurocomputing. **55**(1), 5–20 (2003)
4. Esteva, A., Kuprel, B., Novoa, R.A., Ko, J., Swetter, S.M., Blau, H.M., et al.: Dermatolo gist-level classification of skin cancer with deep neural networks. Nature **542**(7639), 115–118 (2017)
5. Wang, X., Peng, Y., Lu, L., Lu, Z., Bagheri, M., Summers, R.M.: Chestx-ray8: Hospital-scale chest x-ray database and benchmarks on weakly-supervised classification and localization of common thorax diseases. arXiv:1705.02315 (2017)
6. Krizhevsky, A., Sutskever, I., Hinton, G. E.: ImageNet classification with deep convolutional neural networks. In: International Conference on Neural Information Processing Systems, pp. 1097–1105. Curran Associates Inc. (2012)
7. Simonyan, K., Zisserman, A.: Very deep convolutional networks for large-scale image recognition. arXiv:1409.1556 (2014)

8. Szegedy, C., et al.: Going deeper with convolutions. In: Proceedings of the IEEE Conference on Computer Vision and Pattern Recognition, pp. 1–9 (2015)

9. He, K., Zhang, X., Ren, S., Sun, J.: Deep residual learning for image recognition. In: Proceedings of the IEEE Conference on Computer Vision and Pattern Recognition, pp. 770–778 (2016)

10. Anthimopoulos, M., Christodoulidis, S., Ebner, L., Christe, A., Mougiakakou, S.: Lung pattern classification for interstitial lung diseases using a deep convolutional neural network. IEEE Trans. Med. Imaging **35**(5), 1207–1216 (2016)

11. Li, Q., Cai, W., Wang, X., Zhou, Y.: Medical image classification with convolutional neural network. In: International Conference on Control Automation Robotics and Vision, pp. 844–848. IEEE (2016)

12. Miki, Y., et al.: Classification of teeth in cone-beam CT using deep convolutional neural network. Comput. Biol. Med. **80**(C), 24–29 (2017)

13. Kumar, P., Grewal, M., Srivastava, M.M.: Boosted cascaded convnets for multilabel classification of thoracic diseases in chest radiographs. arXiv:1711.08760 (2017)

14. Deng, J., Dong, W., Socher, R., Li, L.J., Li, K., Li, F.F.: ImageNet: a large-scale hierarchical image database. In: Computer Vision and Pattern Recognition (CVPR), pp. 248–255. IEEE (2009)

15. Wei, X.S., Xie, C.W., Wu, J.: Mask-CNN localizing parts and selecting descriptors for fine-grained image recognition. In: Conference and Workshop on Neural Information Processing Systems (NIPS) (2016). arXiv:1605.06878

16. Zhang, N., Donahue, J., Girshick, R., Darrell, T.: Part-based R-CNNs for fine-grained category detection. In: Fleet, D., Pajdla, T., Schiele, B., Tuytelaars, T. (eds.) ECCV 2014. LNCS, vol. 8689, pp. 834–849. Springer, Cham (2014). https://doi.org/10.1007/978-3-319-10590-1_54

17. Huang, S., Xu, Z., Tao, D., Zhang, Y.: Part-stacked CNN for fine-grained visual categorization. In: Computer Vision and Pattern Recognition, pp. 1173–1182. IEEE (2016)

18. Ioffe, S., Szegedy, C.: Batch normalization: accelerating deep network training by reducing internal covariate shift. arXiv:1502.03167 (2015)

19. Dalal, N., Triggs, B.: Histograms of oriented gradients for human detection. In: IEEE Computer Society Conference on Computer Vision and Pattern Recognition, vol. 1, pp. 886–893. IEEE Computer Society (2005)

20. Abdi, H., Williams, L.J.: Principal component analysis. Wiley Interdisc. Rev. Comput. Stat. **2**(4), 433–459 (2010)

21. Hoochang, S., et al.: Deep convolutional neural networks for computer-aided detection: CNN architectures, dataset characteristics and transfer learning. IEEE Trans. Med. Imaging **35**(5), 1285 (2016)

DSL: Automatic Liver Segmentation with Faster R-CNN and DeepLab

Wei Tang, Dongsheng Zou$^{(\boxtimes)}$, Su Yang, and Jing Shi

Chongqing University, Chongqing10611, CN, No. 174 Shazheng Street,
Shapingba District, Chongqing, China
{weitang,dszou,yangsu,shijing}@cqu.edu.cn

Abstract. Liver segmentation is a crucial step in computer-assisted diagnosis and surgical planning of liver diseases. However, it is still a quite challenging task due to four reasons. First, the grayscale of the liver and its adjacent organ tissues is similar. Second, partial volume effect makes the liver contour blurred. Third, most clinical images have serious pathology such as liver tumor. Forth, each person's liver shape is discrepant. In this paper, we proposed DSL (detection and segmentation laboratory) method based on Faster R-CNN (faster regions with CNN features) and DeepLab. The DSL consists of two steps: to reduce the scope of subsequent liver segmentation, Faster R-CNN is employed to detect liver area. Next, the detection results are input to DeepLab for segmentation. This work is evaluated on two datasets: 3Dircadb and MICCAI-Sliver07. Compared with the state-of-the-art automatic methods, our approach has achieved better performance in terms of VOE, RVD, ASD and total score.

Keywords: Faster R-CNN · DeepLab · Detection · Segmentation

1 Introduction

Liver disease is largely endangering the health of men and women worldwide. As reported in 2015, the number of people suffering from liver disease worldwide reached 1.3 billion, including about 500 million in Europe and the United States. At present, non-alcoholic liver disease affects one-third of the world's adults or about one billion people [25]. Liver disease is one of the main causes of premature death, so we need liver surgery to treat patients suffering from liver disease. Liver surgery is one of the main treatment methods for common liver benign and malignant diseases of the liver. Liver segmentation is a fundamental and essential step in the diagnosis and surgical planning of computer assisted liver disease. Manual segmentation is very time consuming, boring and poorly reproducible, because of the high similarity between liver tissue and its adjacent organs, and the difference between livers and the lesion. Therefore, an automatic liver segmentation method is promising to reduce the burden of manual segmentation and avoid the subjectivity of the experts.

Medical image segmentation has attached more and more attention in the enhancement of the accuracy and efficiency of diagnosis and treatment. Automatic liver

© Springer Nature Switzerland AG 2018
V. Kůrková et al. (Eds.): ICANN 2018, LNCS 11140, pp. 137–147, 2018.
https://doi.org/10.1007/978-3-030-01421-6_14

segmentation is a key prerequisite for tasks such as living donor liver transplant, 3D reconstruction of medical images, 3D positioning in radiotherapy programs, and so on.

In general, there are four reasons why liver segmentation is completely challenging, as shown in Fig. 1. First, the liver shares the similar intensity with its surrounding organs, such as heart and stomach. Second, most clinical images have serious pathology, such as large tumors and cirrhosis of the liver, which should be part of the liver. But their intensity is significantly different from normal liver. Third, each person's liver is different in shape. Fourth, partial volume effect makes the liver contour become blurred. Up to now, many methods have been used for liver segmentation and reviewed in [2]. However, to the best of our knowledge, the existing methods are difficult to segment small and contour complex liver.

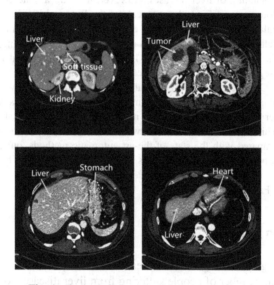

Fig. 1. Four challenges in liver segmentation.

In this paper, we proposed a fully automatic liver segmentation method using Faster R-CNN and DeepLab. This work makes three main contributions which are experimentally shown to have substantial practical merit. Firstly, Faster RCNN and DeepLab are combined for the first time and applied to liver segmentation for achieving good results. Secondly, we solve the high similarity between liver tissue and its adjacent organs by detecting liver areas. Thirdly, we can segment small and contour complex livers, which is not found in the present methods. Our DSL method has achieved a promising performance on the liver segmentation with respect to VOE, RVD, ASD and total score.

2 Related Work

In this section, we will briefly introduce previous work on liver segmentation. Considering whether human interaction is required, we simply categorize previous work as interactive segmentation method [6, 21, 22], semi-automatic segmentation method [6, 14, 27], automatic segmentation method [1, 11, 28].

The effect of interactive liver segmentation method is often superior to the effect of automatic and semi-automatic segmentation method, because it requires complete control by the researchers. But its interaction is very frequent and the workload is the largest. Dong et al. [7] raised an interactive liver segmentation method making use of random walks and narrow band threshold, which used minimal guidance to segment liver. Semi-automatic segmentation method can better segment the target contours that meet the willing of the researches, and the stability is stronger. But the workload is slightly larger. Yang et al. [29] came up with a classic hybrid semi-automatic segmentation method, which consisted of a customized fast-marching level-set method and a threshold-based level-set method. Liao [18] presented an efficient liver segmentation method based on graph cut and bottleneck detection using intensity, local context and spatial correlation of adjacent slices.

Automatic segmentation method mainly includes region growing based methods, rule based methods, graph cut based methods, statistical shape model based method, convolution neural network based method and so on. Gambino et al. [9] proposed an automatic texture based volumetric region growing method. Subsequently, Li et al. [17] used the graph cut method to effectively integrate the properties and correlations of the input image and the initialized surface. The effect of graph cut method was very well in the split larger CT images. To date, deep convolutional neural networks (DCNNs) have dominated many tasks in computer vision such as classification, detection and segmentation. In recent years, DCNNs [20, 28] has been widely used in liver segmentation. Lu et al. [20] combined the convolution neural network and graphic cutting method. Yang et al. [28] put forward an Adversarial Image-to-Image Network to comply automatic liver segmentation. Although many automatic liver segmentation methods have been used to segment liver, the metrics have yet to be improved. In this paper, our work explores a novel DSL method which greatly improves the metrics.

3 Method

3.1 Overview

An overview of the proposed DSL method is described in Fig. 2. Its framework is based on Faster R-CNN and DeepLab. We divide the procedure into two parts: training part and testing part. In the training part, we firstly need to manually annotate the proposed CT volume image using bounding box, which accurately marks the position of the liver. Then the Faster R-CNN is trained making use of annotated image of the training data. Meanwhile, DeepLab is trained using the data that the pixel value beyond the bounding box of the annotated image is set as zero. In the testing part, the testing images are input into the trained Faster R-CNN to get the detection results. Then the set images, in which the pixel value outside the bounding box of the detection results is set as zero, are input into the trained DeepLab to obtain the liver segmentation results.

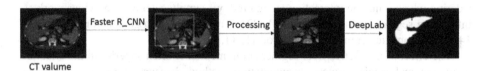

Fig. 2. Overview of the proposed framework.

3.2   Liver Detection Based on Faster R-CNN

Faster R-CNN [23] is proposed to reduce the computational burden of proposal generation. Faster R-CNN is improved by Fast R-CNN [10], which is developed from R-CNN. Faster R-CNN has evolved into a powerful framework for computer vision.

Faster R-CNN has the state-of-the-art performance in terms of accuracy in image detection. The procedure of liver detection using Faster R-CNN is introduced in Fig. 3. First of all, we input test CT volume images. Then to extract features, the entire image is entered into CNN. VGG 16, which has a more accurate valuation of the image and space saving, is adopted as the fundamental network. Thirdly, we use region proposal network (RPN) to generate three hundred region proposals for each liver image. Each region proposal has several anchors. Fourthly, region proposals are mapped to the last layer of convolution feature map on CNN. Fifthly, each region of interest (ROI) engenders a fixed size of feature map through the ROI pooling layer. Finally, classification probability and bounding box regression are jointly trained by softmax loss and smooth L1 loss. The Faster R-CNN loss function is

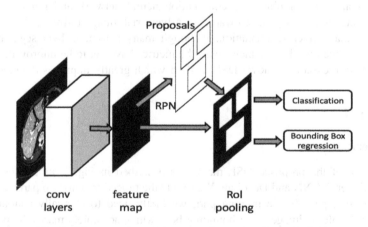

Fig. 3. The procedure of detecting liver using Faster R-CNN.

$$L(\{p_i\}, \{t_i\}) = \frac{\sum L_{cls}(p_i, p_i^*)}{N_{cls}} + \lambda \frac{\sum p_i^* L_{reg}(t_i, t_i^*)}{N_{reg}} \tag{1}$$

where i is index of an anchor and p_i denotes the probability that anchor predicts the liver. p_i^* is the ground truth label, where the label value is 0 or 1. t_i is a vector that indicates the four parameterized coordinates of the predicted bounding box, and t_i^* is the coordinate vector of the ground truth of the bounding box corresponding to the positive anchor. The classification loss $L_{cls}(p_i, p_i^*)$ is log loss on two classes (liver vs. not liver). The classification loss is computed using Eq. 2.

$$L_{cls}(p_i, p_i^*) = -log[p_i^* p_i + (1 - p_i^*)(1 - p_i)] \tag{2}$$

For regression loss $L_{reg}(t_i, t_i^*)$,

$$L_{ref}(t_i, t_i^*) = R(t_i - t_i^*) \tag{3}$$

where R represents smooth $L1$ function. $\{p_i\}$ and $\{t_i\}$ form the output of the classification layer and the regression layer. In this paper, we take advantage of Faster R-CNN to detect liver, getting good performance, as shown in Fig. 4.

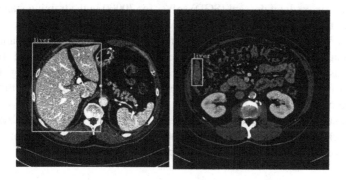

Fig. 4. Detection results by fast R-CNN.

3.3 Liver Segmentation Based on DeepLab

In this section, we will address the key aspects of DeepLab V2, which is developed by DeepLab V1 [3]. More detail technical acknowledge can be referred to the original paper [4].

To deal with reduced feature resolution, atrous convolution is introduced in the DeepLab V2. Atrous convolution has many advantages: atrous convolution magically recover full resolution feature maps, which are reduced by the repeated combination of max pooling and downsampling. Atrous convolution also can effectively enlarge the field of view of filters without increasing the number of parameters, which is employed in subsequent convolution layers. Using the atrous convolution with rate = k can get the output feature map which increases k − 1 times than traditional convolution. However, the use of atrous convolution method has some shortcomings. For example, its computational cost is relatively high, and the need to deal with a large number of high-resolution feature map will consume a lot of memory resource. Therefore, DeepLab V2 takes a compromise approach that some feature maps use the bilinear interpolation method, and the others use the atrous convolution method.

Taking into account the different scales of information, the most direct method is to input into the DCNN rescaled versions of the same image, and then these CNN feature maps are combined to generate the final results. It proved to be a good performance, but operation is too cumbersome and too time consuming.

Thus, DeepLab V2 uses atrous spatial pyramid pooling (ASPP), which can diametrically extract the multi-scale information on the basis of the input of the original image. ASPP is that we use multiple parallel atrous convolutional layers with different sampling rates. The features extracted for each sampling rate are further processed in separate branches and merged to produce the final results.

4 Experiment and Analysis

Faster R-CNN training is divided into four stages: training region proposal network (RPN), VGG-16, RPN and VGG-16. The learning rate of each stage is set as 0.001. We run the stochastic gradient descent (SGD) solver for 70000 in the training stage of RPN and 50000 in the training stage of VGG-16. We finetune the model weight of DeepLab composed of VGG-16, atrous convolution and fully connected CRF, to adapt them to the segmentation task, following the procedure of [4]. We replace the 1000-way ImageNet classifier in the VGG-16 last layer with a two-class (including the background and liver) classifier and run the SGD solver for 100000 iterations with a base of learning rate of 0.001.

We evaluate the proposed method on the 3Dircadb data set and MICCAISliver07 data set, which are well-known challenge datasets. We first report the main results on MICCAI-Sliver07, and immediately introduce the results of 3Dircadb.

4.1 MICCAI-Sliver07

Five metrics are calculated as in [13], Volumetric Overlap Error (VOE), Relative Volume Difference (RVD), Average Symmetric Surface Distance (ASD), Root Mean Square Symmetric Surface Distance (RMSD) and Maximum Symmetric Surface Distance (MSD). The score of VOE, RVD, ASD, RMSD, MSD are 80.2%, 94.1%, 80.5%, 76.4%, 71.9%, respectively. The metric comparison of the proposed methods and the other eight fully automatic liver segmentation methods [1, 12, 15, 17, 19, 20, 24, 26] based on MICCAI-Sliver07 test set, is shown in Table 1. It is obvious that the proposed method is better than DeepLab. Figure 5 presents the segmentation results of the proposed method and DeepLab. As can be seen, small and complex liver can be successfully segmented. Meanwhile, we also can observe that our proposed method performs very well. It achieves 80.6 total score, surpassing all the compared methods. The reasons why the proposed method has achieved much better performance are these:

Table 1. Compared with other state-of-the-art methods on MICCAI-Sliver07 test set

Method	VOE (%)	Score-	RVD (%)	Score -	ASD (mm)	Score -	RMSD (mm)	Score -	MSD (mm)	Score -	Total score
Li et al. [17]	6.24	–	1.18	–	1.03	–	2.11	–	18.82	–	–
Shaikhli et al. [1]	6.44	74.9	1.53	89.7	0.95	76.3	**1.58**	**78.1**	**15.92**	**79.1**	79.6
Kainmüller et al. [15]	6.09	76.2	−2.86	84.7	0.95	76.3	1.87	74	18.69	75.4	77.3
Wimmer et al. [26]	6.47	74.7	1.04	86.4	1.02	74.5	2	72.3	18.32	75.9	76.8
Linguraru et al. [19]	6.37	75.1	2.26	85	1	74.9	1.92	73.4	20.75	72.7	76.2
Heimann et al. [12]	7.73	69.8	1.66	87.9	1.39	65.2	3.25	54.9	30.07	60.4	67.6
Kinda et al. [24]	8.91	65.2	1.21	80	1.52	61.9	3.47	51.8	29.27	61.5	64.1
Fang et al. [20]	5.9	77	2.7	85.6	0.91	77.3	1.88	73.8	18.94	75.1	77.8
Only DeepLab	6.38	75.1	2.14	87.1	1.05	73.8	2.24	68.9	24.04	68.4	74.7
The proposed	**5.06**	**80.2**	**-0.09**	**94.1**	**0.78**	**80.5**	**1.7**	**76.4**	23.42	71.9	**80.6**

first, Faster R-CNN detects the liver area, which reduces the scope of follow-up liver segmentation and avoids the challenge that the grayscale of the liver and its adjacent organ tissues is similar. Second, because DeepLab is a method of semantic

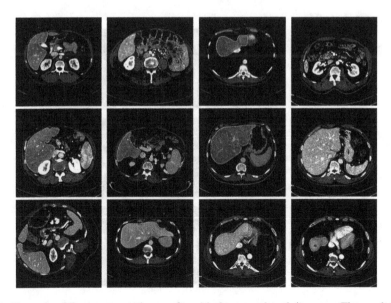

Fig. 5. Example of liver segmentation results with the ground truth in green. The result by the proposed method is in red and the result by the only DeepLab is in blue. (Color figure online)

Table 2. Compared with other state-of-the-art methods on 3Dircadb data set.

3Dircadb	VOE [%]	RVD [%]	ASD [mm]	RMSD [mm]	MSD [mm]
Chuang et al. [5]	12.99 ± 5.04	−5.66 ± 5.59	2.24 ± 1.08	–	25.74 ± 8.85
Kirscher et al. [16]	–	−3.62 ± 5.50	1.94 ± 1.10	4.47 ± 3.30	34.60 ± 17.70
Li et al. [17]	9.15 ± 1.44	−0.07 ± 3.64	1.55 ± 0.39	3.15 ± 0.98	28.22 ± 8.31
Erdt et al. [8]	10.34 ± 3.11	1.55 ± 6.49	1.74 ± 0.59	3.51 ± 1.16	26.83 ± 8.87
Lu et al. [20]	9.36 ± 3.34	0.97 ± 3.26	1.89 ± 1.08	4.15 ± 3.16	33.14 ± 16.36
The proposed	8.67 ± 0.815	0.57 ± 2.53	1.37 ± 0.41	4.15 ± 3.16	27.01 ± 7.28

segmentation, there are serious pathologies in the pathological images that will not affect the results. Third, fully connected CRF can segment the contours of liver, which can address the challenge that partial volume effect makes the liver contour blurred. All in all, the proposed method outperforms the others, especially its VOE, RVD and ASD obtained the highest score.

4.2 3Dircadb

Table 2 displays the result of other state-of-the-art automatic segmentation methods [5, 8, 16, 17, 20] with our work on 3Dircadb data set. It can be seen that our explored method achieves much better performance than all the compared methods in terms of the measure of VOE, RVD and ASD. For the RMSD and MSD metric, the results of Chuang's method and Erdt's method show slightly better performance than ours. The segmentation result is shown in Fig. 6. We can observe that small and contour complex liver can be accurately segmented and the effect of our proposed method is better than

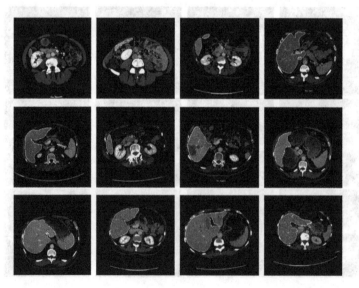

Fig. 6. Example of liver segmentation results with the ground truth in green. The result by the proposed method is in red and the result by the only DeepLab is in blue. (Color figure online)

DeepLab's, because we first use the Faster R-CNN to detect the liver area and then use DeepLab to segment. Overall, our proposed method achieves much better performance than the other compared methods.

5   Conclusion

In this paper, we proposed DSL method for automatic liver segmentation in abdominal CT images. Specifically, to handle the high similarity between liver and its adjacent tissues, Faster R-CNN is used to detect liver region. The detection results are input to DeepLab for segmenting liver. The main advantage of our approach is that small and contour complex liver can be accurately segmented. Besides, Faster R-CNN and DeepLab are combined for the first time and applied to a new scene, where no manual feature extraction or user interaction is required during the training and testing procedure.

Experimental results prove the efficiency of our method. Compared with the state-of-the-art automatic liver segmentation methods, our proposed method is ranked in the front according to the total score. Especially, the VOE, RVD and ASD metrics are much higher than the other compared method's. We plan to study new liver segmentation algorithm to boost our model's ability in future work.

References

1. Al-Shaikhli, S.D.S., Yang, M.Y., Rosenhahn, B.: Automatic 3D liver segmentation using sparse representation of global and local image information via level set formulation. Computer Science (2015)
2. Campadelli, P., Casiraghi, E.: Liver segmentation from CT scans: a survey. In: WILF, pp. 520–528 (2007)
3. Chen, L.C., Papandreou, G., Kokkinos, I., Murphy, K., Yuille, A.L.: Semantic image segmentation with deep convolutional nets and fully connected CRFs. Computer Science, pp. 357–361 (2014)
4. Chen, L.C., Papandreou, G., Kokkinos, I., Murphy, K., Yuille, A.L.: DeepLab: semantic image segmentation with deep convolutional nets, Atrous convolution, and fully connected CRFs. IEEE Trans. Pattern Anal. Mach. Intell. (2016)
5. Chung, F., Delingette, H.: Regional appearance modeling based on the clustering of intensity profiles. Comput. Vis. Image Underst. 117(6), 705–717 (2013)
6. Dawant, B.M., Li, R., Lennon, B., Li, S.: Semi-automatic segmentation of the liver and its evaluation on the MICCAI 2007 grand challenge data set. In: Workshop on 3D Segmentation in the Clinic (2007)
7. Dong, C., et al.: A knowledge-based interactive liver segmentation using random walks. In: International Conference on Fuzzy Systems and Knowledge Discovery, pp. 1731–1736 (2015)
8. Erdt, M., Steger, S., Kirschner, M., Wesarg, S.: Fast automatic liver segmentation combining learned shape priors with observed shape deviation. In: IEEE 23rd International Symposium on Computer-Based Medical Systems (CBMS), pp. 249–254 (2010)

9. Gambino, O., et al.: Automatic volumetric liver segmentation using texture based region growing. In: International Conference on Complex, Intelligent and Software Intensive Systems, pp. 146–152 (2010)
10. Girshick, R.: Fast R-CNN. In: IEEE International Conference on Computer Vision, pp. 1440–1448 (2015)
11. He, B., et al.: Fast automatic 3D liver segmentation based on a three-level AdaBoost-guided active shape model. Med. Phys. 43(5), 2421–2434 (2016)
12. Heimann, T., van Ginneken, B., Styner, M.A., et al.: Comparison and evaluation of methods for liver segmentation from CT datasets. IEEE Trans. Med. Imaging 28(8), 1251–1265 (2009)
13. Heimann, T., Meinzer, H.P., Wolf, I.: A statistical deformable model for the segmentation of liver CT volumes. In: MICCAI Workshop on 3D Segmentation in the Clinic (2010)
14. Jansen, J., Schreurs, R., Dubois, L., Maal, T.J.J., Gooris, P.J.J., Becking, A.G.: Orbital volume analysis: validation of a semi-automatic software segmentation method. Int. J. Comput. Assist. Radiol. Surg. 11(1), 11–18 (2015)
15. Kainmüller, D., Lange, T., Lamecker, H.: Shape constrained automatic segmentation of the liver based on a heuristic intensity model. In: MICCAI Workshop On 3D Segmentation in the Clinic, pp. 109–116 (2008)
16. Kirschner, M.: The probabilistic active shape model: from model construction to flexible medical image segmentation. Ph.D. thesis, Technischen Universität Darmstadt (2013)
17. Li, G., Chen, X., Shi, F., Zhu, W., Tian, J., Xiang, D.: Automatic liver segmentation based on shape constraints and deformable graph cut in CT images. IEEE Trans. Image Process. 24 (12), 5315 (2015)
18. Liao, M., et al.: Efficient liver segmentation in CT images based on graph cuts and bottleneck detection. Physica Med. 32(11), 1383 (2016)
19. Linguraru, M.G., Richbourg, W.J., Watt, J.M., Pamulapati, V., Summers, R.M.: Liver and tumor segmentation and analysis from CT of diseased patients via a generic affine invariant shape parameterization and graph cuts. In: International MICCAI Workshop on Computational and Clinical Challenges in Abdominal Imaging, pp. 198–206 (2011)
20. Lu, F., Wu, F., Hu, P., Peng, Z., Kong, D.: Automatic 3D liver location and segmentation via convolutional neural network and graph cut. Int. J. Comput. Assist. Radiol. Surg. 12(2), 171–182 (2017)
21. Lu, J., Shi, L., Deng, M., Yu, S.C.H., Heng, P.A.: An interactive approach to liver segmentation in CT based on deformable model integrated with attractor force. In: International Conference on Machine Learning and Cybernetics, pp. 1660–1665 (2011)
22. Meena, S., Palaniappan, K., Seetharaman, G.: Interactive image segmentation using elastic interpolation. In: IEEE International Symposium on Multimedia, pp. 307–310 (2016)
23. Ren, S., He, K., Girshick, R., Sun, J.: Faster R-CNN: towards real-time object detection with region proposal networks. IEEE Trans. Pattern Anal. Mach. Intell. 39(6), 1137–1149 (2017)
24. Saddi, A.K., Rousson, M., Hotel, C.C., Cheriet, F.: Global-to-local shape matching for liver segmentation in CT imaging (2007)
25. Webster, N.J.G.: Alternative RNA splicing in the pathogenesis of liver disease. Front. Endocrinol. 8 (2017)
26. Wimmer, A., Soza, G., Hornegger, J.: A generic probabilistic active shape model for organ segmentation. In: International Conference on Medical Image Computing and Computer-Assisted Intervention, pp. 26–33 (2009)
27. Yan, J., Schwartz, L.H., Zhao, B.: Semiautomatic segmentation of liver metastases on volumetric CT images. Med. Phys. 42(11), 6283–6293 (2015)

28. Yang, D., et al.: Automatic liver segmentation using an adversarial image-to-image network. In: International Conference on Medical Image Computing and Computer-Assisted Intervention, pp. 507–515 (2017)
29. Yang, X., et al.: A hybrid semi-automatic method for liver segmentation based on level-set methods using multiple seed points. Comput. Meth. Prog. Biomed. **113**(1), 69–79 (2014)

Temporal Convolution Networks for Real-Time Abdominal Fetal Aorta Analysis with Ultrasound

Nicoló Savioli[1]([✉]), Silvia Visentin[2]([✉]), Erich Cosmi[2]([✉]), Enrico Grisan[1,3]([✉]), Pablo Lamata[1]([✉]), and Giovanni Montana[1,4]([✉])

[1] Department of Biomedical Engineering, Kings College London,
London SE1 7EH, UK
{nicolo.l.savioli,enrico.grisan,pablo.lamata,giovanni.montana}@kcl.ac.uk
[2] Department of Woman and Child Health, University Hospital of Padova,
Padua, Italy
{silvia.visentin.1,erich.cosmi}@unipd.it
[3] Department of Information Engineering, University of Padova, Padua, Italy
enrigri@dei.unipd.it
[4] WMG, University of Warwick, Coventry CV4 71AL, UK
g.montana@warwick.ac.uk

Abstract. The automatic analysis of ultrasound sequences can substantially improve the efficiency of clinical diagnosis. In this work we present our attempt to automate the challenging task of measuring the vascular diameter of the fetal abdominal aorta from ultrasound images. We propose a neural network architecture consisting of three blocks: a convolutional layer for the extraction of imaging features, a Convolution Gated Recurrent Unit (C-GRU) for enforcing the temporal coherence across video frames and exploiting the temporal redundancy of a signal, and a regularized loss function, called *CyclicLoss*, to impose our prior knowledge about the periodicity of the observed signal. We present experimental evidence suggesting that the proposed architecture can reach an accuracy substantially superior to previously proposed methods, providing an average reduction of the mean squared error from $0.31\,\mathrm{mm}^2$ (state-of-art) to $0.09\,\mathrm{mm}^2$, and a relative error reduction from 8.1% to 5.3%. The mean execution speed of the proposed approach of 289 frames per second makes it suitable for real time clinical use.

Keywords: Cardiac imaging · Diameter · Ultrasound
Convolutional networks · Fetal imaging · GRU · CyclicLoss

1 Introduction

Fetal ultrasound (US) imaging plays a fundamental role in the monitoring of fetal growth during pregnancy and in the measurement of the fetus well-being. Growth monitoring is becoming increasingly important since there is an

V. Kůrková et al. (Eds.): ICANN 2018, LNCS 11140, pp. 148–157, 2018.
https://doi.org/10.1007/978-3-030-01421-6_15

epidemiological evidence that abnormal birth weight is associated with an increased predisposition to diseases related to cardiovascular risk (such as diabetes, obesity, hypertension) in young and adults [1].

Among the possible biomarkers of adverse cardiovascular remodelling in fetuses and newborns, the most promising ones are the Intima-Media Thickness (IMT) and the stiffness of the abdominal aorta by means of ultrasound examination. Obtaining reliable measurements is critically based on the accurate estimation of the diameter of the aorta over time. However, the poor signal to noise ratio of US data and the fetal movement makes the acquisition of a clear and stable US video challenging. Moreover, the measurements rely either on visual assessment at bed-side during patient examination, or on tedious, error-prone and operator-dependent review of the data and manual tracing at later time. Very few attempts towards automated assessment have been presented [2,3], all of which have computational requirements that prevent them to be used in real-time. As such, they have reduced appeal for the clinical use. In this paper we describe a method for automated measurement of the abdominal aortic diameter directly from fetal US videos. We propose a neural network architecture that is able to process US videos in real-time and leverage both the temporal redundancy of US videos and the quasi-periodicity of the aorta diameter.

The main contributions of the proposed method are as follows. First we show that a shallow CNN is able to learn imaging features and outperforms classical methods as level-set for fetal abdominal aorta diameter prediction. Second we add to the CNN a Convolution Gated Recurrent Unit (C-GRU) [15] for exploiting the temporal redundancy of the features extracted by CNN from the US video sequence. Finally, we add a new penalty term to the loss function used to train the CNN to exploit periodic variations.

2   Related Work

The interest for measuring the diameter and intima-media thickness (IMT) of major vessels has stemmed from its importance as biomarker of hypertension damage and atherosclerosis in adults. Typically, the IMT is assessed on the carotid artery by identifying its lumen and the different layers of its wall on high resolution US images. The improvements provided by the design of semi-automatic and automatic methods based mainly on the image intensity profile, distribution and gradients analysis, and more recently on active contours. For a comprehensive review of these classical methods we refer the reader to [4] and [5]. In the prenatal setting, the lower image quality, due to the need of imaging deeper in the mother's womb and by the movement of the fetus, makes the measurement of the IMT biomarker, although measured on the abdominal aorta, challenging.

Methods that proved successful for adult carotid image analysis do not perform well on such data, for which only a handful of methods (semi-automatic or automatic) have been proposed, making use of classical tracing methods and mixture of Gaussian modelling of blood-lumen and media-adventitia interfaces [2], or on level sets segmentation with additional regularizing terms linked to the specific task [3]. However, their sensitivity to the image quality and lengthy computation prevented an easy use in the clinical routine.

Deep learning approaches have outperformed classical methods in many medical tasks [8]. The first attempt in using a CNN, for the measurement of carotid IMT has been made only recently [9]. In this work, two separate CNNs are used to localize a region of interest and then segment it to obtain the lumen-intima and media-adventitia regions. Further classical post-processing steps are then used to extract the boundaries from the CNN based segmentation. The method assumes the presence of strong and stable gradients across the vessel walls, and extract from the US sequence only the frames related to the same cardiac phase, obtained by a concomitant ECG signal.

However, the exploitation of temporal redundancy on US sequences was shown to be a solution for improving overall detection results of the fetal heart [11], where the use of a CNN coupled with a recurrent neural network (RNN) is strategic. Other works, propose similar approach in order to detect the presence of standard planes from prenatal US data using CNN with Long-Short Term Memory (LSTM) [10].

3   Datasets

This study makes use of a dataset consisting of 25 ultrasound video sequences acquired during routine third-trimester pregnancy check-up at the Department of Woman and Child Health of the University Hospital of Padova (Italy). The local ethical committee approved the study and all patients gave written informed consent.

Fetal US data were acquired using a US machine (Voluson E8, GE) equipped with a 5 MHz linear array transducer, according to the guidelines in [6,7], using a 70° FOV, image dimension 720×960 pixels, a variable resolution between 0.03 and 0.1 mm and a mean frame rate of 47 fps. Gain settings were tuned to enhance the visual quality and contrast during the examination. The length of the video is between 2 s and 15 s, ensuring that at least one full cardiac cycle is imaged.

After the examination, the video of each patient was reviewed and a relevant video segment was selected for semi-automatic annotation considering its visual quality and length: all frames of the segment were processed with the algorithm described in [2] and then the diameters of all frames in the segments were manually reviewed and corrected. The length of the selected segments varied between 21 frames 0.5 s and 126 frames 2.5 s. The 25 annotated segments in the dataset were then randomly divided into training (60% of the segments), validation (20%) and testing (20%) sets. In order to keep the computational and memory requirements low, each frame was cropped to have a square aspect ratio and then resized to 128×128 pixels. The data supporting this research are [openly available].

4   Network Architecture

Our output is the predicted value $\hat{y}[t]$ of the diameter of the abdominal aorta at each time point. Our proposed deep learning solution consists of three main components (see Fig. 1): a Convolutional Neural Network (CNN) that captures the salient characteristics from ultrasound input images; a Convolution Gated Recurrent Unit (C-GRU) [15] exploits the temporal coherence through the sequence; and a regularized loss function, called *CyclicLoss*, that exploits the redundancy between adjacent cardiac cycles.

Our input consists of a set of sequences whereby each sequence $S = [s[1], ..., s[K]]$ has dimension $N \times M$ pixels at time t, with $t \in \{1, \ldots, K\}$. At each time point t, the CNN extracts the feature maps $x[t]$ of dimensions $D \times N_x \times M_x$, where D is the number of maps, and N_x and M_x are their in-plane pixel dimensions, that depend on the extent of dimensionality reduction obtained by the CNN through its pooling operators.

The feature maps are then processed by a C-GRU layer [15]. The C-GRU combines the current feature maps $x[t]$ with an encoded representation $h[t-1]$ of the feature maps $\{x[1], \ldots, x[t-1]\}$ extracted at previous time points of the sequence to obtain an updated encoded representation $h[t]$, the *current state*, at time t: this allows to exploit the temporal coherence in the data. The $h[t]$ of the C-GRU layer is obtained by two specific gates designed to control the information inside the unit: a reset gate, $r[t]$, and an update gate, $z[t]$, defined as follows:

$$r[t] = \sigma(W_{hr} * h[t-1] + W_{xr} * x[t] + b_r) \tag{1}$$

$$z[t] = \sigma(W_{hz} * h[t-1] + W_{xz} * x[t] + b_z) \tag{2}$$

Where, $\sigma()$ is the sigmoid function, $W.$ are recurrent weights matrices whose first subscript letter refers to the input of the convolution operator (either the feature maps $x[t]$ or the state $h[t-1]$), and whose second subscript letter refers to the gate (reset r or update z). All this matrices, have a dimension of $D \times 3 \times 3$ and $b.$ is a bias vector. In this notation, $*$ defines the convolution operation. The current state is then obtained as:

$$h[t] = (1 - z[t]) \odot h[t-1] + z[t] \odot \tanh(W_h * (r[t] \odot h_{t-1}) + W_x * x[t] + b). \tag{3}$$

Where $\odot$ denotes the dot product and W_h and W_x are recurrent weight matrices for $h[t-1]$ and $x[t]$, used to balance the new information represented by the feature maps $x[t]$ derived by the current input data $s[t]$ with the information obtained observing previous data $s[1], \ldots, s[t-1]$. On the one hand, $h[t]$ is then passed on for updating the state $h[t+1]$ at the next time point, and on the other is flatten and fed into the last part of the network, built by Fully Connected (FC) layers progressively reducing the input vector to a scalar output that represent the current diameter estimate $\hat{y}[t]$.

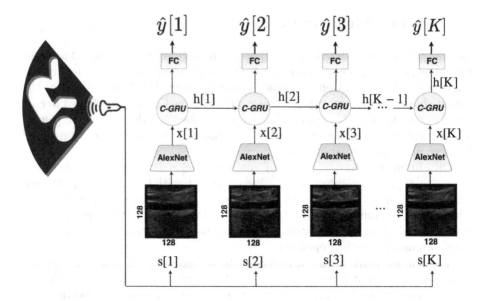

Fig. 1. The deep-learning architecture proposed for abdominal diameter aorta prediction. The blue blocks represent the features extraction through a CNN (AlexNet) which takes in input a US sequence S, and provides for each frame $s[t]$ a features map $x[t]$ that is passed to Convolution Gated Recurrent Units (C-GRU) (yellow circle) that encodes and combines the information from different time points to exploit the temporal coherence. The fully connected block (FC, in green), takes as input the current encoded state $h[t]$ as features to estimate the aorta diameter $\hat{y}[t]$. (Color figure online)

4.1   CyclicLoss

Under the assumption that the pulsatility of the aorta follows a periodic pattern with the cardiac cycle, the diameter of the vessel at corresponding instants of the cardiac cycle should ideally be equal. Assuming a known cardiac period T_{period}, we propose to add a regularization term to the loss function used to train the network as to penalize large differences of the diameter values that are estimated at time points that are one cardiac period apart.

We call this regularization term *CyclicLoss* (*CL*), computed as L_2 norm between pairs of predictions at the same point of the heart cycle and from adjacent cycles:

$$CL = \sqrt{\sum_{n=1}^{N_{cycles}} \sum_{t=0}^{T_{period}} \| \hat{y}[t + (n-1)T_{period}] - \hat{y}[t + nT_{period}] \|_2} \qquad (4)$$

The T_{period} is the period of the cardiac cycle, while N_{cycles} is the number of integer cycles present in the sequence and $\hat{y}[t]$ is the estimated diameter at time t. Notably, the T_{period} is determined through a peak detection algorithm on $y[t]$, and the average of all peak-to-peak detection distances define its value.

While the N_{cycles} is the number of cycles present, calculated as the total length of the $y[t]$ signal divided by T_{period}.

The loss to be minimized is therefore a combination of the classical mean squared error (MSE) with the CL, and the balance between the two is controlled by a constant λ:

$$Loss = MSE + \lambda \cdot CL = \frac{1}{K} \sum_{t=1}^{K} (y[t] - \hat{y}[t])^2 + \lambda \cdot CL \qquad (5)$$

where $y[t]$ is the target diameter at time point t. It is worth noting that the knowledge of the period of the cardiac cycle is needed only during training phase. Whereas, during the test phase, on unknown image sequence, the trained network provide its estimate blind of the periodicity of the specific sequence under analysis.

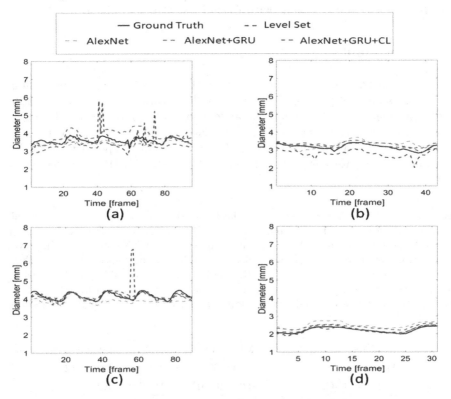

Fig. 2. Each panel (a–c) shows the estimation of the aortic diameter at each frame of fetal ultrasound videos in the test set, using the level set method (dashed purple line), the naive architecture using AlexNet (dashed orange line), the AlexNet+C-GRU (dashed red line), and AlexNet+C-GRU trained with the *CyclicLoss* (dashed blue line). The ground truth (solid black line) is reported for comparison. Panels (a, c) show the results on long sequences where more than 3 cardiac cycles are imaged, whereas panels (b, d) show the results on short sequences where only 1 or two cycles are available. (Color figure online)

4.2   Implementation Details

For our experiments, we chose AlexNet [12] as a feature extractor for its simplicity. It has five hidden layers with 11×11 kernels size in the first layer, 5×5 in the second and 3×3 in the last three layers; it is well suited to the low image contrast and diffuse edges characteristic of US sequences. Each network input for the training is a sequence of $K = 125$ ultrasound frames with $N = M = 128$ pixels, AlexNet provides feature maps of dimension $D \times N \times M = 256 \times 13 \times 13$, and the final output $\hat{y}[t]$ is the estimate abdominal aorta diameter value at each frame.

The loss function is optimised with the Adam algorithm [16] that is a first-order gradient-based technique. The learning rate used is $1e^{-4}$ with 2125 iterations (calculated as number of patients × number of ultrasound sequences) for 100 epochs. In order to improve generalization, data augmentation of the input with a vertical and horizontal random flip is used at each iteration. The λ constant used during training with *CyclicLoss* takes the value of $1e^{-6}$.

5   Experiments

The proposed architecture is compared with the currently adopted approach in Sect. 4. This method provides fully-automated measurements in lumen identification on prenatal US images of the abdominal aorta [3] based on edge-based level set. In order to understand the behaviour of different features extraction methods, we have also explored the performance of new deeper network architectures whereby AlexNet was replaced it by InceptionV4 [13] and DenseNets 121 [14].

Table 1. The table show the mean (standard deviation) of MSE and RE error for all the comparison models. The combination of C-GRU and the *CyclicLoss* with AlexNet yields the best performance. Adding recurrent units to any CNN architecture improves its performance; however deeper networks as InceptionV4 and DenseNets do not show any particular benefits with respect to the simpler AlexNet. Notably, we also consider the p-value for multiple models comparison with the propose network AlexNet+C-GRU+CL, in this case the significant level should be 0.05/7 using the Bonferroni correction [17].

Methods	MSE [mm²]	RE [%]	p-value
AlexNet	0.29(0.09)	8.67(10)	1.01e−12
AlexNet+C-GRU	0.093(0.191)	6.11(5.22)	1.21e−05
AlexNet+C-GRU+CL	**0.085(0.17)**	**5.23(4.91)**	"-"
DenseNet121	0.31(0.56)	9.55(8.52)	6.00e−13
DenseNet121+C-GRU	0.13(0.21)	7.72(5.46)	7.78e−12
InceptionV4	6.81(14)	50.4(39.5)	6.81e−12
InceptionV4+C-GRU	0.76(1.08)	16.3(9.83)	2.89e−48
Level-set	0.31(0.80)	8.13(9.39)	1.9e−04

The performance of each method was evaluated both with respect to the mean squared error (MSE) and to the mean absolute relative error (RE); all values are reported in Table 1 in terms of average and standard deviation across the test set.

In order to provide a visual assessment of the performance, representative estimations on four sequences of the test set are shown in Fig. 2. The naive architecture relying on a standard loss and its C-GRU version are incapable to capture the periodicity of the diameter estimation. The problem is mitigated by adding the *CyclicLoss* regularization on MSE. This is quantitatively shown in Table 1, where the use of this loss further decreases the MSE from $0.093 \, mm^2$ to $0.085 \, mm^2$, and the relative error of from 6.11% to 5.23%.

Strikingly, we observed that deeper networks are not able to outperform AlexNet on this dataset. Their limitation may be due to over-fitting. Nevertheless, the use of C-GRU greatly improve the performance of both networks both in terms of MSE and of RE. Further, we also performed a non-parametric test (Kolmogorov-Smirnov test) to check if the best model was statistically different compared to the others.

The results obtained with the complete model AlexNet+C-GRU+CL are indeed significantly different from all others ($p < 0.05$) also, when the significant level is adjusted for multiple comparison applying the Bonferroni correction [17,18].

6   Discussion and Conclusion

The deep learning (DL) architecture proposed shows excellent performance compared to traditional image analysis methods, both in accuracy and efficiency. This improvement is achieved through a combination of a shallow CNN and the exploitation of the temporal and cyclic coherence. Our results seem to indicate that a shallow CNNs perform better than deeper CNNs such as DenseNet 121 and InceptionV4; this might be due to the small dimension of the data set, a common issue in the medical settings when requiring manual annotations of the data.

6.1   The *CyclicLoss* Benefits

The exploitation of temporal coherence is what pushes the performance of the DL solution beyond current image analysis methods, reducing the MSE from $0.29 \, mm^2$ (naive architecture) to $0.09 \, mm^2$ with the addition of the C-GRU. The *CyclicLoss* is an efficient way to guide the training of the DL solution in case of data showing some periodicity, as in cardiovascular imaging. Please note that the knowledge of the signal period is only required by the network during training, and as such it does not bring additional requirements on the input data for real clinical application. We argue that the *CyclicLoss* is making the network learn to expect a periodic input and provide some periodicity in the output sequence.

6.2 Limitations and Future Works

A drawback of this work is that it assumes the presence of the vessel in the current field of view. Further research is thus required to evaluate how well the solution adapts to the scenario of lack of cyclic consistency, when the vessel of interest can move in and out of the field of view during the acquisition, and to investigate the possibility of a concurrent estimation of the cardiac cycle and vessel diameter. Finally, the C-GRU used in our architecture, has two particular advantages compared to previous approaches [10,11]: first, it is not subject to the vanishing gradient problem as the RNN, allowing to train from long sequences of data. Second, it has less computational cost compared to the LSTM, and that makes it suitable for real time video application.

Acknowledgement. This work was supported by the Wellcome/EPSRC Centre for Medical Engineering at Kings College London (WT 203148/Z/16/Z). Dr. Lamata holds a Wellcome Trust Senior Research Fellowship (grant n.209450/Z/17/Z).

References

1. Visentin, S., Grumolato, F., Nardelli, G.B., Di Camillo, B., Grisan, E., Cosmi, E.: Early origins of adult disease: low birth weight and vascular remodeling. Atherosclerosis **237**(2), 391–399 (2014)
2. Veronese, E., Tarroni, G., Visentin, S., Cosmi, E., Linguraru, M.G., Grisan, E.: Estimation of prenatal aorta intima-media thickness from ultrasound examination. Phys. Med. Biol. **59**(21), 6355–6371 (2014)
3. Tarroni, G., Visentin, S., Cosmi, E., Grisan, E.: Fully-automated identification and segmentation of aortic lumen from fetal ultrasound images. In: IEEE EMBC, pp. 153–156 (2015)
4. Molinari, F., Zeng, G., Suri, J.S.: A state of the art review on intimamedia thickness (IMT) measurement and wall segmentation techniques for carotid ultrasound. Comp. Meth. Prog. Biomed. **100**(3), 201–221 (2010)
5. Loizou, C.P.: A review of ultrasound common carotid artery image and video segmentation techniques. Med. Biol. Eng. Comp **52**(12), 1073–1093 (2014)
6. Cosmi, E., Visentin, S., Fanelli, T., Mautone, A.J., Zanardo, V.: Aortic intima media thickness in fetuses and children with intrauterine growth restriction. Obs. Gyn. **114**, 1109–1114 (2009)
7. Skilton, M.R., Evans, N., Griffiths, K.A., Harmer, J.A., Celermajer, D.S.: Aortic wall thickness in newborns with intrauterine growth restriction. Lancet **365**, 1484–14846 (2005)
8. Litjens, G., et al.: A survey on deep learning in medical image analysis. Med. Image Anal. **42**, 60–88 (2017)
9. Shin, J.Y., Tajbakhsh, N., Hurst, R.T., Kendall, C.B., Liang, J.: Automating carotid intima-media thickness video interpretation with convolutional neural networks. In: IEEE CVPR Conference, pp. 2526–2535 (2016)
10. Chen, H., et al.: Automatic fetal ultrasound standard plane detection using knowledge transferred recurrent neural networks. In: Navab, N., Hornegger, J., Wells, W.M., Frangi, A.F. (eds.) MICCAI 2015. LNCS, vol. 9349, pp. 507–514. Springer, Cham (2015). https://doi.org/10.1007/978-3-319-24553-9_62

11. Huang, W., Bridge, C.P., Noble, J.A., Zisserman, A.: Temporal HeartNet: towards human-level automatic analysis of fetal cardiac screening video. In: Descoteaux, M., Maier-Hein, L., Franz, A., Jannin, P., Collins, D.L., Duchesne, S. (eds.) MICCAI 2017. LNCS, vol. 10434, pp. 341–349. Springer, Cham (2017). https://doi.org/10.1007/978-3-319-66185-8_39
12. Krizhevsky, A., Sutskever, I., Hinton, G.E.: ImageNet classification with deep convolutional neural networks. In: NIPS 2012, pp. 1097–1105 (2012)
13. Szegedy, C., Ioffe, S., Vanhoucke, V.: Inception-v4, inception-ResNet and the impact of residual connections on learning. In: AAAI 2017, pp. 4278–4284 (2017)
14. Huang, G., Liu, Z., van der Maaten, L., Weinberger, K.Q.: Densely connected convolutional networks. In: IEEE CVPR Conference, pp. 2261–2269 (2017)
15. Siam, M., Valipour, A., Jägersand, M., Ray, N.: Convolutional gated recurrent networks for video segmentation. In: IEEE ICIP Conference, pp. 3090–3094 (2017)
16. Kingma, D.P., Ba, L.J.: Adam: a method for stochastic optimization. In: 3rd International Conference for Learning Representations (2015)
17. Bonferroni, C.E.: Teoria statistica delle classi e calcolo delle probabilit. Pubblicazioni del Regio Istituto Superiore di Scienze Economiche e Commerciali di Firenze (1936)
18. Dunn, O.J.: Multiple comparisons among means. J. Am. Stat. Assoc. 56(293), 52–64 (1961)

An Original Neural Network for Pulmonary Tuberculosis Diagnosis in Radiographs

Junyu Liu, Yang Liu, Cheng Wang, Anwei Li, Bowen Meng[✉],
Xiangfei Chai, and Panli Zuo

Huiying Medical Technology (Beijing) Co., Ltd., Beijing, China
liujunyu@huiyihuiying.com, liuyang@huiyihuiying.com,
wangcheng@huiyihuiying.com, mengbowen@huiyihuiying.com

Abstract. Tuberculosis (TB) is a widespread and highly contagious disease that may lead serious harm to patient health. With the development of neural network, there is increasingly attention to apply deep learning on TB diagnosis. Former works validated the feasibility of neural networks in this task, but still suffer low accuracy problem due to lack of samples and complexity of radiograph information. In this work, we proposed an end-to-end neural network system for TB diagnosis, combining preprocessing, lung segmentation, feature extraction and classification. We achieved accuracy of 0.961 in our labeled dataset, 0.923 and 0.890 on Shenzhen and Montgomery Public Dataset respectively, demonstrating our work outperformed the state-of-the-art methods in this area.

Keywords: Tuberculosis · Classification · DNN

1 Introduction

Tuberculosis is a highly contagious disease that may lead serious harm to patient health. According to the World Health Organization (WHO) [1], until the end of 2015, nearly 10 million people in the world suffered from tuberculosis and more than 1.5 million died. The WHO pointed out that early diagnosis and appropriate treatment can avoid the majority of tuberculosis deaths, and millions of people are saved each year. Nonetheless, huge number of people still suffers for high cost and lack of professional doctors. Therefore, reliable tuberculosis diagnosing system is an urgent demand.

At present, a large number of medical image data has not yet been digitized, and the level of data sharing and interoperability among hospitals is still at a low level. It is a dilemma that advanced method usually requires big data, which is impossible for medical dataset. Also, it is difficult to obtain reliable labeling data in the medical imaging field for the interdisciplinary gap. In addition, medical images contain more difficult samples and pixel-scale features, making AI image analysis in the medical field more challenging than natural image recognition. This work proposes a neural network specialized for pulmonary tuberculosis diagnosis in radiographs, to solve all above difficulties.

© Springer Nature Switzerland AG 2018
V. Kůrková et al. (Eds.): ICANN 2018, LNCS 11140, pp. 158–166, 2018.
https://doi.org/10.1007/978-3-030-01421-6_16

2 Related Works

In 2012, Hinton's team [2] first adopted convolutional neural network into the ImageNet classification challenge and achieved astonishing results, drastically reducing the Top5 error rate from 26% to 15%. This opened up a boom in deep learning. At present, deep learning has achieved remarkable results in the fields like image recognition, detection, segmentation, and so on [3, 5].

Deep learning technology was first officially applied to medical image analysis in 2015. Convolutional neural networks (CNN) soon gained increasingly popularity due to their ability to learn mid and high-level image representations. Bar Y et al. explore the ability of a CNN to identify different types of pathologies in chest x-ray images [6]. They used a pre-trained CNN on the ImageNet dataset as the first descriptor, and the second descriptor is PiCoDes, which is a compact high-level representation of popular low-level features (SIFTs [6], GIST, PHOG, and SSIM) which is optimized over a subset of the ImageNet dataset containing approximately 70,000 images. They found that the best performance was achieved using a combination of features extracted from the CNN and a set of low-level features. Of course, the capacity of system will be limited for lack of training.

U.K. Lopes et al. used a pre-trained CNN as a feature extractor, combining with traditional machine learning methods for tuberculosis detection [8]. They first used detached networks to extract features, then integrated CNN features and finally created an ensemble classifier by combining the SVMs trained using the features extracted from GoogLenet [9], ResNet [10], and VggNet [11]. The author of [12] proposed a novel method to detect pulmonary tuberculosis. The method is divided into two steps. The first step is to use pre-trained networks to make a two classification on chest X-rays. For classification, the chest X-rays are resized to respectively corresponding network, and the results of the prediction of all classification networks are averaged as the final classification result. The second step is that the sensitivity of softmax score to occlusion of a certain region in the chest X-Ray is used to find which region in the image is responsible for the classification decision. But the over-resize process will sharply reduce the accuracy of system.

Olaf Ronneberger et al. proposed a network called U-Net [13] for small-sample segmentation. The network consists of two parts, a contracted path is used to obtain contextual information and a symmetrical expansion path for precise positioning. At the same time, in order to make more efficient use of the annotation data, they also use a variety of data enhancement methods. In 2016, Milletari et al. proposed an extension to the U-Net layout that incorporates ResNet-like residual blocks and a Dice loss layer, rather than the conventional cross-entropy [14].

Inspired by all the mentioned works, we propose a combination of segmentation and classification deep neural network through the chest X-rays to detect tuberculosis. All chest X-rays were preprocessed to emphasize lung features. Main body of the network has two branches: one is a designed lung segmentation network to obtain chest masks, and the other a classification network. We achieve accuracy of 0.965 in our dataset, 0.923 and 0.890 on Shenzhen and Montgomery Public Dataset respectively, proving us the state-of-the-art in this area.

3   Proposed Methods

3.1   Method Overview

We proposed an end-to-end network for tuberculosis judgement. The whole system consists of a Lung Segmentation Network, a classification backbone and an output head. Heat maps are generated for further analysis and algorithm verification. This is the first work to combine all the steps of tuberculosis detection in a whole network, making a compromise between computational speed and preservation of image information. The whole system is demonstrated in Fig. 1.

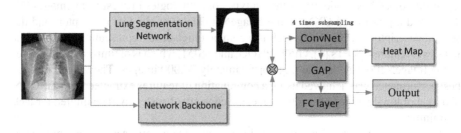

Fig. 1. The block diagram of the proposed network.

3.2   Lung Segmentation Network

According to [14], lung segmentation is necessary for automatic tuberculosis diagnosing. In this paper, we designed a simple and effective CNN with atrous convolutional layers [18] to segment the chest from X-rays referring to U-net. Basic feature extraction part has 3 conv-pooling blocks with different number of channels. Each conv-pooling block contains a pooling layer after a few convolutional blocks, while each convolutional block consists of a convolutional layer followed by a Batch-Norm layer and a ReLU activation layer. Totally 8 times subsampling was implemented and the network structure is shown in Fig. 2.

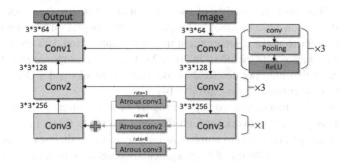

Fig. 2. ConvNet configuration for feature extraction.

Lungs in radiographs are of different sizes due to individual difference and other factors. Therefore, multi-scale segmentation was also taken into consideration. We used 3 atrous convolutional layers with different sample rates respectively. All the feature maps obtain by dilated convolution are added together and connected with the decoder of the network. Segmented results are generated by continuous up-sampling. In order to overcome the problem of low resolution after down-sampling in the FCN [17] method, we fused the feature map of each down-sampled feature with that of the corresponding up-sampling part. Chest segmentation results are shown in Fig. 3.

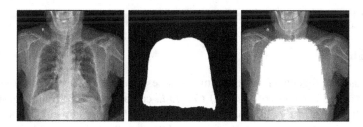

Fig. 3. Chest segmentation results. Left: original picture; Middle: segmentation result; Right: evaluation result.

3.3 Specialized Innovations

Preprocessing. Radiographs need preprocessing before checking. The grayscale of chest X-ray pixels usually range from tens to thousands, and it's impossible for human eyes to distinguish this huge change. Also, too large scales tend to cause the diagnosing network to divergent. Therefore, the original pixel values need adjustment according to WW (window width) and WP (window position). Because not all graphs are given guidance values of WW and WP, a standard set of WW and WP was generated from samples accompanied with WW and WP guidance values using cluster algorithm. We also found that histogram equalization operation can emphasize the features in lung while not significantly changing the gray level in other organs and background. Original radiographs often have as many as two thousand pixels in length, which is a huge burden for computation. But considering that some granule infections can be really small, input images are bilinear interpolated to 1024 × 1024.

Two Branches. The main body of proposed network has two branches, one for lung segmentation and the other for feature extraction with the network backbone. We choose 6 different popular and practical backbones in total for this work. To limit computation memory and time, we subsampled the feature map by 32 instead of the original picture masked by the output of segmentation branch, allowing main body of two branches to work simultaneously.

Network Head. There are two heads in the last part of network. The classification head of the network is specialized for this task. As input of our system is much larger than normal classification competitions, we need more times of subsampling than the original networks. In practical, we adopted 128 times down sampling in our network. High similarity is a dangerous character of radiographs in this task, tending to cause over-fit. Therefore, we added a heat map head to analysis if the correct feature of graphs has been learned. For heat map generation, the second to last fully connected (FC) layer is replaced by a global average pooling (GAP) [18] layer, also reducing parameters in the network. Considering the imbalance of positive and negative samples, and also false negative (FN) is much more harmful in medical area, focal loss [4] is introduced into this work, giving positive samples a higher loss during training.

4 Experiments

4.1 Database

Database used in this paper comes from 2 sources. The first dataset was provided by *Huiying Medical Technology (Beijing) Co., Ltd.*, containing 2443 frontal chest X-ray images (DICOM format), with labels marked by a reliable expert network. In the dataset, 2000 were randomly chosen as training set and the rest divided into validation and test ones. There are two public datasets [20] available on the Internet. Shenzhen Hospital dataset, which includes 662 frontal chest x-rays, was acquired from Shenzhen No. 3 People's Hospital in Shenzhen, China. Montgomery County chest X-ray set (MC) was collected in collaboration with the Department of Health and Human Services, Montgomery County, Maryland, USA, consisting of 138 frontal X-rays.

4.2 Experimental Results

To test the performance of network with different backbones, parallel comparisons were made on our test dataset. Accuracy, sensitivity, specificity, AP, and AUC results are shown in Table 1. Inception-v4 backbone without mask branch was also tested.

Table 1. Parallel comparisons of each method for our dataset

Backbone	AUC	Accuracy	AP	Sensitivity	Specificity
VGG-19	0.974	0.893	0.981	**0.988**	0.765
ResNet-50	0.983	0.875	0.992	0.979	0.892
ResNet-101	0.989	0.879	0.992	0.972	0.932
ResNet-152	0.991	0.923	**0.994**	0.960	0.945
Inception v4	**0.995**	**0.961**	**0.994**	0.966	**0.955**
ResNet-Inception v2	0.982	0.934	0.984	0.948	0.915
Inception v4 (no mask)	0.953	0.908	0.947	0.821	0.954

To be intuitive, the P-R curves and ROCs are shown in Fig. 4.

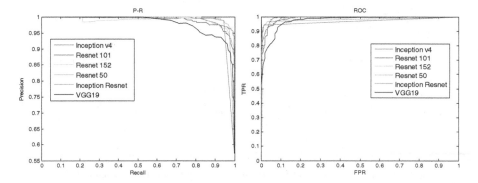

Fig. 4. P-R curves (left) and ROCs (right).

The results show that our method made a highest accuracy of over 96.1% on our test dataset, achieving by Inception v4. Mask branch contributed about 5.3% in accuracy. We also reselected training set and retrained our networks from the beginning to exclude the possibility of coincidence. We also checked the heat maps generated by our network, finding it reasonable although slight bias and blur happens due to 128 times subsampling. The visualized results are shown in Fig. 5.

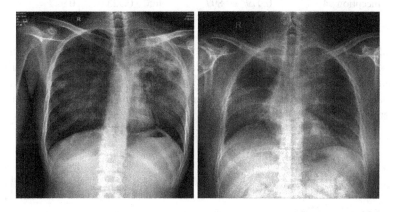

Fig. 5. The heat map acquired in our network. Although slight positioning bias happens due to totally 128 times subsampling, the red area roughly reflects position of infection. (Color figure online)

Longitudinal comparisons with former works [8, 12, 15, 16] were also accomplished. To be fair and objective, we compared the results of proposed method and the other works on two public datasets. All the data of former works cited in this paper are the best results the authors claimed. The models we used were still the ones we trained on our dataset. Figure 6 shows the visualized results of our networks on Shenzhen Dataset. Comparison with former works are shown in Table 2.

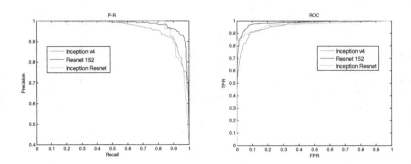

Fig. 6. P-R curves (left) and ROCs (right) of our networks on Shenzhen Dataset.

Table 2. Performance for Shenzhen Dataset. Last three are proposed methods.

Method	AUC	Accuracy	AP	Sensitivity	Specificity
U.K. Lopes et al.	0.894	0.837	-	-	-
Mohammad et al.	0.940	0.900	-	0.960	0.960
Sangheum et al.	0.926	0.837	0.940	-	-
ResNet-152	0.967	**0.923**	0.971	**0.978**	**0.986**
Inception v4	0.979	0.897	0.965	0.923	0.937
Inception-ResNet v2	**0.983**	0.917	**0.985**	0.857	0.981

Results on Montgomery Dataset are shown in Fig. 7 and Table 3. We found that many radiographs in the MC Dataset has large scale of black blocks and seriously disturbed histogram equalization, making the background of preprocessed graphs lighter than usual. We cut off the black blocks and resized the images, and saw an incredible improvement in results.

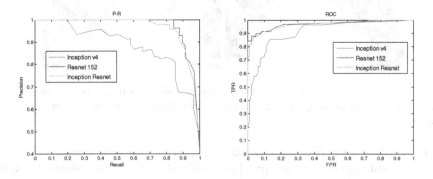

Fig. 7. P-R curves (left) and ROCs (right) of our networks on MC Dataset.

Table 3. Performance for MC Dataset. Last three are proposed methods.

Method	AUC	Accuracy	AP	Sensitivity	Specificity
U.K. Lopes et al.	0.926	0.810	-	-	-
Stefan Jaeger et al.	0.831	0.75	-	~0.5	~0.9
Sangheum et al.	0.884	0.674	0.890	-	-
ResNet-152	0.951	**0.890**	0.935	**0.711**	**0.955**
Inception v4	0.914	0.822	0.884	0.654	0.938
Inception-ResNet v2	**0.957**	0.844	**0.965**	0.618	0.913

Longitudinal and parallel experimental results show the superiority of our proposed network. The models achieved relatively good results on our own test set. It's hard to explain why ResNet 152 seems to do better than other network backbones on the public datasets. But our models undoubtedly showed adaptability to public datasets, outperforming the state-of-the-art results.

5   Conclusion and Future Work

We proposed an end-to-end network for pulmonary tuberculosis classification, including preprocessing, lung segmentation and classification. The system optimized the inference time, while guaranteeing the accuracy.

Future work will include (1) making specialized optimization on network backbones (2) optimization of preprocessing to increase adaptability of network (3) extending this system to the detection of focus of infection.

Acknowledgement. We would like to thank *Huiying Medical Technology (Beijing) Co., Ltd.* for providing essential resource and support for us.

References

1. World Health Organization (WHO): Global tuberculosis report (2017). http://www.who.int/tb/publications/global_report/en/. Accessed 26 May 2018
2. Krizhevsky, A., Sutskever, I., Hinton, G.E.: ImageNet classification with deep convolutional neural networks. In: International Conference on Neural Information Processing Systems, pp. 1097–1105. Curran Associates Inc. (2012)
3. Ren, S., He, K., Girshick, R., et al.: Faster R-CNN: towards real-time object detection with region proposal networks. IEEE Trans. Pattern Anal. Mach. Intell. **39**(6), 1137–1149 (2017)
4. Lin, T.Y., Goyal, P., Girshick, R., et al.: Focal loss for dense object detection, pp. 2999–3007. In: IEEE Computer Society (2017)
5. He, K., Gkioxari, G., Dollár, P., et al.: Mask R-CNN. In: Computer Vision and Pattern Recognition (CVPR) (2017)
6. Bar, Y., Diamant, I., Wolf, L., et al.: Deep learning with non-medical training used for chest pathology identification. In: Medical Imaging 2015: Computer-Aided Diagnosis, p. 94140V (2015)

7. Liu, C., Yuen, J., Torralba, A., Sivic, J., Freeman, W.T.: SIFT flow: dense correspondence across different scenes. In: Forsyth, D., Torr, P., Zisserman, A. (eds.) ECCV 2008. LNCS, vol. 5304, pp. 28–42. Springer, Heidelberg (2008). https://doi.org/10.1007/978-3-540-88690-7_3
8. Lopes, U.K., Valiati, J.F.: Pre-trained convolutional neural networks as feature extractors for tuberculosis detection. Comput. Biol. Med. **89**, 135–143 (2017)
9. Szegedy, C., Liu, W., Jia, Y., et al.: Going deeper with convolutions. In: IEEE Computer Society, pp. 1–9 (2014)
10. He, K., Zhang, X., Ren, S., et al.: Deep residual learning for image recognition, pp. 770–778. IEEE Computer Society (2015)
11. Simonyan, K., Zisserman, A.: Very deep convolutional networks for large-scale image recognition. Computer Science (2014)
12. Islam, M.T., Aowal, M.A., Minhaz, A.T., et al.: Abnormality detection and localization in chest x-rays using deep convolutional neural networks. arXiv (2017)
13. Ronneberger, O., Fischer, P., Brox, T.: U-Net: convolutional networks for biomedical image segmentation. In: Navab, N., Hornegger, J., Wells, W.M., Frangi, A.F. (eds.) MICCAI 2015. LNCS, vol. 9351, pp. 234–241. Springer, Cham (2015). https://doi.org/10.1007/978-3-319-24574-4_28
14. Drozdzal, M., et al.: The importance of skip connections in biomedical image segmentation. In: Carneiro, G. et al. (eds.) Deep Learning and Data Labeling for Medical Applications
15. Jaeger, S., Karargyris, A., Antani, S., et al.: Detecting tuberculosis in radiographs using combined lung masks. Conf. Proc. IEEE. Eng. Med. Biol. Soc. **2012**(4), 4978–4981 (2012)
16. Hwang, S., et al.: A novel approach for tuberculosis screening based on deep convolutional neural networks. In: Medical Imaging 2016: Computer-Aided Diagnosis, p. 97852W. International Society for Optics and Photonics (2016)
17. Shelhamer, E., Long, J., Darrell, T.: Fully convolutional networks for semantic segmentation. IEEE Trans. Pattern Anal. Mach. Intell. **39**(4), 640–651 (2014)
18. Chen, L.C., Papandreou, G., Kokkinos, I., et al.: DeepLab: semantic image segmentation with deep convolutional nets, atrous convolution, and fully connected CRFs. IEEE Trans. Pattern Anal. Mach. Intell. **40**(4), 834–848 (2018)
19. Zhou, B., et al.: Learning deep features for discriminative localization. In: Computer Vision and Pattern Recognition, pp. 2921–2929. IEEE (2016)
20. Stefan, J., et al.: Two public chest X-ray datasets for computer-aided screening of pulmonary diseases. Quant Imaging Med. Surg. **4**(6), 475–477 (2014)

Computerized Counting-Based System for Acute Lymphoblastic Leukemia Detection in Microscopic Blood Images

Karima Ben-Suliman and Adam Krzyżak[(⊠)]

Department of Computer Science and Software Engineering,
Concordia University, Montréal, Québec H3G 1M8, Canada
{k_bensul,krzyzak}@cse.concordia.ca

Abstract. Counting of white blood cells (WBCs) and detecting the morphological abnormality of these cells allow for diagnosis some blood diseases such as leukemia. This can be accomplished by automatic quantification analysis of microscope images of blood smear. This paper is oriented towards presenting a novel framework that consists of two sub-systems as indicators for detection Acute Lymphoblastic Leukemia (ALL). The first sub-system aims at counting WBCs by adapting a deep learning based approach to separate agglomerates of WBCs. After separation of WBCs, we propose the second sub-system to detect and count abnormal WBCs (lymphoblasts) required to diagnose ALL. The performance of the proposed framework is evaluated using ALL-IDB dataset. The first presented sub-system is able to count WBCs with an accuracy up to 97.38%. Furthermore, an approach using ensemble classifiers based on handcrafted features is able to detect and count the lymphoblasts with an average accuracy of 98.67%.

1 Introduction

Counting of white blood cells (WBCs) is a diagnostic procedure to detect blood malignancies. Leukemia is a blood cancer developing from the stem cells of the bone marrow, that affects the function of WBCs and their number. Leukemia can be preliminary classified based on progression of disease i.e. acute or chronic. In addition, classification can be based on the cell lineage of the stem cells i.e. lymphoid or myeloid. In this paper, we only consider Acute Lymphoblastic Leukemia (ALL) which affects a specific type of WBCs called lymphocytes.

Manual morphological observation of blood cells under the microscope and an automated haematology counting are two diagnostic procedures to diagnose ALL [1]. Observation of blood cells by the microscope requires a few drops of blood sample from a patient on a slide. Then different stains are added to the slide to assist specialists to identify different blood cells. Afterward, this blood slide is examined under the microscope with different magnifications to count WBCs and detect lymphoblasts. Detecting at least 20% of lymphoblasts in the bone marrow or peripheral blood can be an indicator for ALL diagnosis. Although

© Springer Nature Switzerland AG 2018
V. Kůrková et al. (Eds.): ICANN 2018, LNCS 11140, pp. 167–178, 2018.
https://doi.org/10.1007/978-3-030-01421-6_17

this process is very basic, the exhausting part is when a medical expert needs to observe blood samples under the microscope collected from numerous patients to count the normal and abnormal blood cells. Typically, this approach can be difficult even for the specialist because it requires experience and extensive knowledge to be able to distinguish the morphological abnormalities of the blood cells. On the other hand, an automated haematology counter, which is another way for counting WBCs, produces the output in timely manner and differentiates between blood cells by measuring cell volume and the blood cell morphology based on mechanical and electronic approaches. However, this automatic system has the ability to just count cells and cannot identify the abnormalities of these cells. For this reason, WBCs have to be analyzed manually under the microscope [2].

In this paper, we propose a computer-aided system that comprises of two sub-systems. The first one is to separate and count WBCs, including normal and abnormal cells, by adapting a deep-learning-based approach to overcome agglomerates of WBCs and comparing the results with related works. The goal of the second sub-system is to detect lymphoblasts that lead to diagnose ALL. To the best of our knowledge the presented system is the first automated system for counting lymphoblasts from microscopic images.

This paper is structured as follows: Sect. 2 presents background and related works. Section 3 describes the used dataset. Section 4 presents a detailed process of both sub-systems for counting WBCs and lymphoblasts. Section 5 reports the experimental results and discussion. Finally, Sect. 6 presents conclusions.

2   Related Work

In this section will only consider the automated systems for detection and counting WBCs and lymphoblasts. For example, Tan Le *et al.* [3] have proposed a framework for counting WBCs. To extract WBCs from the background, a threshold value has been applied on Haematoxylin-Eosin-DAB (HED) color space. Then, the edges of the segmented WBCs are detected using canny edge detector followed by separating the touching cells by using watershed segmentation algorithm. Though this approach achieved 90% of accuracy, no specific method has been mentioned to determine the threshold value. A different approach has been proposed by Putzu *et al.* [4] to count WBCs. The identification of WBCs is based on a threshold value that is determined by Zack algorithm on Y-component of CMYK color space. Then, watershed segmentation is performed to separate the adjacent cells. The performance of the proposed approach achieved an accuracy of 92%. However, it is mentioned that when the overlapping between WBCs is significant, no good results have been obtained. In [5], Bhavnani *et al.* have used Otsu's method and morphological operations on green component of RGB color space for isolating WBCs. Then, connected label component is used to count WBCs. Although the performance of the system is 94.25% for counting WBCs, a complex degree of overlapping and irregular cells toleration is limited. Moreover, Otsu's method may not be a suitable approach when the background and foreground of an image are not clearly represented. Also, this framework is partially developed because of using the morphological operations for isolation the touching cells of WBCs. This is in turn leads to change the morphological characteristics of blood cells and can't be used for fully detection system. Basima and Panicker [6] have utilized K-means algorithm on Y component of CMYK color space to segment WBCs followed by watershed segmentation to separate WBCs. However, segmentation WBCs by K-means causes losing in cytoplasm region which is an essential part needed to distinguish the lymphocytes from lymphoblasts. Also, the obtained accuracy to count WBCs by the proposed approach is not mentioned. Alomari et al. [7] have proposed another method for counting WBCs. The detection of WBCs is based on thresholding. Then, the counting of the cells is carried out by an iterative structured circle detection approach. This proposed framework exhibits an average accuracy of 98.4% for counting WBCs. However, the proposed algorithm can tolerate the overlapping cells only with a certain degree producing a noticeable amount of false positives. Moreover, selecting the optimum threshold value is very challenging. Loddo et al. [8] have introduced an approach to detect and count WBCs. Pixel based classification approach using support vector machine is performed for segmenting WBCs. Then, all the single WBCs are counted using connected label component, and the remaining of agglomerates of cells are counted by Circular Hough Transform (CHT). Although this approach exhibits an average accuracy of 99.2% for WBCs, this work is partially developed and neglects adjacent cells which limits counting and the analysis of lymphoblasts. Hence, further human visual inspection is required to detect the abnormal cells.

It can be observed from the available literature that the only work for counting the lymphoblasts for detecting the abnormality has been done by Halim et al. [9] who have proposed an automatic framework to count blasts (lymphoblasts and myeloblast) for acute leukemia in blood samples. To segment blasts from the background, thresholding based on histogram is performed on S-component in HSV color space. After that, morphological erosion is used to segregate the touching cells. While this approach is able to provide an accuracy of 97.8%, determination of the optimal threshold is not an easy task and may work successfully for some images but fails for others due to lighting condition. Moreover, the blood sample images included in this study consist of only blasts and no other WBCs are involved. There are several attempts for effective counting of WBCs, while there are few authors have proposed methods regarding the cells counting with considering adjacent cells and detecting the abnormality among them.

To tackle the issues previously mentioned, we propose an automated system for detecting the presence of ALL. This system consists of two sub-systems which can be as indicators to diagnose patients who may suffer from ALL. The first sub-system is directed to count WBCs, and the second sub-system aims to detect and count lymphoblasts.

3 Dataset

For testing the proposed approach, Acute Lymphoblastic Leukemia Image Database (ALL-IDB) has been used [10]. It is a public dataset proposed by Donida Labati. All-IDB includes microscopic images of peripheral blood samples of healthy individuals and unhealthy patients suffering from leukemia as shown in Fig. 1. The microscopic images have been collected by the M. Tettamanti Research Center-Monza, Italy, that specializes in childhood leukemia and hematological diseases. The ALL-IDB dataset is subdivided into two versions. The first version, ALL-IDB1, contains 59 healthy and 49 unhealthy images that are in full size of 1712×1368. The second version, ALL-IDB2, contains cropped subimages of 130 normal and 130 lymphoblasts of size 257×257. The images in both versions are manually labeled by expert oncologists to be used as a ground truth. In ALL-IDB1 version, each image has a related text file including the coordinates of the centroid of each lymphoblast. In this study, images belong to ALL-IDB1, which consists of 108 microscopy images of blood samples, are used. To evaluate the proposed system for counting, 50% of the images are used for training, 15% for validation set to tune a model's hyperparameters, and the remaining images are used to test our model.

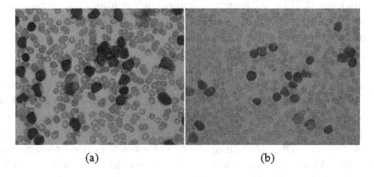

(a)   (b)

Fig. 1. Samples from ALL-IDB1 for unhealthy patients with high (a) and low magnifications (b).

4 Proposed Method

The method proposed in this work aims to count WBCs and lymphoblasts for acute lymphoblastic leukemia using blood smear images as illustrated in Fig. 2.

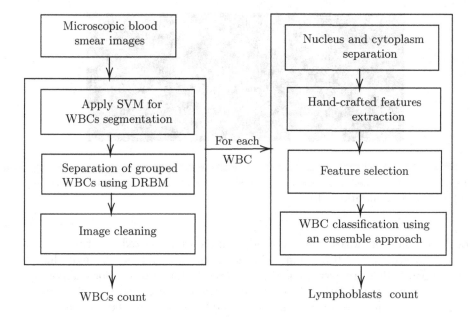

Fig. 2. Proposed approach diagram.

4.1   Counting of WBCs

WBCs Segmentation. The segmentation of WBCs, including nuclei and their cytoplasm, takes an advantage of Ruberto *et al.* [8] approach which uses support vector machine (SVM) based segmentation. This approach is characterized by its robustness against different staining procedures and illumination problems. To achieve this, three different regions represent WBCs (positive class), RBCs and background (negative classes) are selected to train binary-class SVM with a Gaussian radial basis kernel function (RBF). These regions are selected from a few images of ALL-IDB1 training set. 255 regions are selected to represent 85 and 170 regions for positive and negative classes respectively. As in the work of Ruberto *et al.* [8], from all selected regions color and statistical features are extracted from each pixel: the color features represent R, G, B intensity values of a pixel, and the statistical features represent average, entropy, uniformity and standard deviation for 3×3 neighborhood of that pixel. The obtained average accuracy of segmentation computed by means of 10 fold cross-validation is 95.21%. Figure 3 shows the results of WBCs segmentation.

Separation of Grouped WBCs. To segregate the touching cells of WBCs, we adapted deep learning approach with stacked Restricted Boltzman Machines (RBMs) followed by a discriminative fine-tuning layer as used by Duggal *et al.* [11] applying the approach to the results of SVM as a segmentation method rather than K-means algorithm. The discriminative fine-tuning layer is applied on the top of the features learned by the RBMs to identify ridge pixels of grouped WBCs, pixels that are inside WBCs, and pixels that are located on the boundary

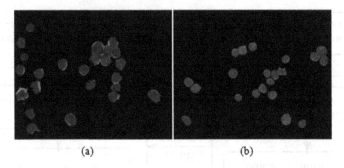

Fig. 3. WBCs segmentation for microscopic images of unhealthy patients with high (a) and low magnifications (b).

of WBCs but not ridges. Then, the ridge pixels are neglected resulting in separating the grouped WBCs. From 12 images of the training set, 12 single clusters of grouped WBCs are extracted. 80% of these clusters are used for training and 20% are used for validation. The system is trained by considering three layers of RBMs. The number of neurons in the hidden layers are 100, 300, and 1000 respectively. Figure 4 shows segregation of WBCs by considering a patch of size 31×31 as a feature vector for training.

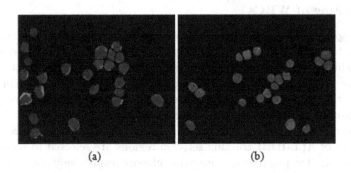

Fig. 4. Separation of grouped healthy WBCs and lymphoblasts for unhealthy patients with high (a) and low magnifications (b).

Image Cleaning and WBCs Counting. In order to avoid misidentification of WBCs for counting and mis-detection of lymphoblasts which is required for next steps, WBCs that appear partially on the edge of the microscopic images should be neglected. Discarding the partial WBCs is accomplished by suppressing the light structures that are connected to the image border using the value 8 as a connectivity value. After segmentation and separation of the agglomerates of WBCs, WBCs can be counted using connected label component with a connectivity of 8. Details related to the performance of WBCs counting are reported in the experimental results section.

4.2   Detection and Counting of Lymphoblasts

Separation of Nucleus and Cytoplasm. Once the WBCs have been separated, sub-images containing each WBC are obtained using bounding box. It is observed that WBC cytoplasm has high contrast in the green channel of RGB colour space [12]. So, to extract the cytoplasm, the green component is obtained from a sub-image of an individual cell of WBC. Afterwards, a binary image is calculated by using Otsu's algorithm [13]. To separate the WBC nucleus, the a* component of the Lab colour space is obtained. Then, a binary image is calculated by using Otsu's algorithm and this binary image is subtracted from the binary image containing only the cytoplasm.

Feature Extraction. To differentiate lymphoblasts from other healthy WBCs representing neutrophils; eosinophils; basophils; lymphocytes; and monocytes, three categories of handcrafted features including morphological, textural, and color features are computed. These features describe the nuclear, cytoplasmic, and cellular (a nucleus and its cytoplasm) changes of each sub-image containing an individual cell. The first group reflects the deformations resulting from transition to malignant case of blood cells. Therefore, 17 morphological features reflect the maturity of a cell, i.e., aspect ratio of nucleus and cytoplasm, size of a cell; nucleus; and cytoplasm, nucleus shape descriptors, and the marginal coarseness or irregularity. We compute marginal features using the fractal geometry and the variance of signature of a nucleus and cytoplasm as defined in [14]. To embody the granularity existing in some WBCs such as eosinophil and basophil, we use median robust extended local binary pattern (MRELBP) [15]. To measure the textural changes of the modifications of nuclear chromatin distribution, that indicates the malignant lymphocytes, 6 wavelet coefficients based statistical features and 21 Gray-Level Co-occurrence Matrix (GLCM) features are extracted as well [16,17]. Moreover, 6 color features are calculated for a nucleus and also for cytoplasm to reflect hyperchromatism of malignant lymphocytes. These features are computed from each color space of RGB and HSV. Finally, we add a specific measure that reflects that lymphoblasts contain variably prominent nucleoli [18]. To figure out the number of nucleoli, K-means algorithm is applied and the complement of the binary image obtained from Otsu's algorithm can reflects the elements that represent nucleoli. Grouping of all the features previously mentioned altogether we generate the set of 52 features.

Feature Selection. To identify highly predictive a subset of discriminative features among a large set of features for predicting a response, Maximum Relevance Minimum Redundancy criteria (MRMR) which is based on mutual information is applied [19]. MRMR tends to select the features having the most correlation with a class label and the least correlation between the features themselves.

Classification. In order to build a model for lymphoblast detection in microscopic blood images, we make use of different types of multiple-classifier approach (MCA). The first type consists of a single classifier with different parameters setting. In this case, we use SVM classifier with different kernels: linear, polynomial, and RBF. The second MCA consists of 3 different independent classifiers.

The used classifiers are SVM, Decision Tree (DT) and K-Nearest Neighbors (KNNs). The last MCA consists of 5 different independent classifiers: SVM, DT, Naive Bayes (NB), KNNs and Random Forest (RF)[20,21]. In all different architectures of MCA, the majority voting of class labels of independent classifiers are combined to classify WBCs of an image and count the lymphoblasts belonging to that image.

5   Experimental Results

5.1   WBCs Counting Performance

To present the results of the system performance for WBC counting with an appropriate and fair comparison, we follow the same testing strategy as in [4]. 33 images are selected from the testing set and subdivided into 11 sets. These images contains 267 WBCs and have been used for testing, then the ground truth of manual counting is compared with the results of the proposed sub-system for counting WBCs in each image.

As it can be observed from Table 1 that 260 of 267 WBCs are identified properly by the proposed approach with an accuracy of 97.38% which outperforms the results of [4]. Moreover, the proposed approach shows consistent results over sets from 6 to 11 with results of [4].

Table 1. Performance of the proposed automated WBCs counting system.

Set	Manual counting	Auto count [4]	Proposed method	Performance improvement of counting WBCs in percentage ratio by the proposed approach over [4]
1	31	26	29	10%
2	49	41	47	12%
3	31	30	31	3%
4	39	36	38	5%
5	32	27	30	9%
6	27	27	27	0%
7	17	17	17	0%
8	15	15	15	0%
9	11	11	11	0%
10	9	9	9	0%
11	6	6	6	0%

5.2   Lymphoblasts Counting Performance

For detecting lymphoblasts, the significance of the extracted features are evaluated using mutual information. Therefore, the ranked list of the top 43 features are used to represent the optimal discriminative ones and are indicated to be informative out of 52 extracted features. In all different architectures of MCA, the hyperparameters of each independent classifier are chosen experimentally on the validation set. To evaluate the effectiveness of our model, we divide the tested images into 5 sets. For each set, we determine the average test accuracy which is calculated by averaging all the accuracies resulting from each image belongs to that set. Then, we calculate the average values of True Positive Rate (TPR), True Negative Rate (TNR), and Positive Predictive Value (PPV) for that set as well.

Table 2 shows the results of majority voting of SVM classifier with different kernels: linear, polynomial, and RBF. It can be concluded that the overall average test set accuracy is 89.34%. Also, the overall performance for counting lymphoblasts (TPR) using the proposed method is 98.33%. However, the overall misclassification rate of lymphocytes classified as lymphoblast (false positive rate), which affects the correct counting of lymphoblasts, achieves 29% error rate.

Table 2. The experimental results using MCA of SVM classifier with different kernels.

Set	Manual counting of lymphoblasts	Proposed method counting	TP	FN	FP	Average test set accuracy	TPR	TNR	PPV
1	47	52	47	0	5	91.94%	100%	66.67%	90.38%
2	8	11	8	0	3	85.71%	100%	76.92%	72.73%
3	45	47	42	3	5	85.71%	93.33%	54.55%	89.36%
4	60	63	59	1	4	93.33%	98.33%	73.33%	93.65%
5	9	11	9	0	2	90%	100%	81.82%	81.82%
Total	169	184	165	4	19	89.34%	98.33%	70.66%	85.59%

The performance of our system using the majority voting of 3 different classifiers: SVM (RBF kernel), DT, and KNNs ($k = 5$) is presented in Table 3. It can be concluded that the overall average test set accuracy is 96.75%. Also, the overall performance of TPR is 97.6%. Moreover, it can be noticed that in some sets such as 3 and 5, the proposed system is able to count the lymphoblasts correctly which shows a very good influence on the overall misclassification rate of false positive rate achieving a 11% error rate.

The proposed computer-aided system for counting the lymphoblasts using the majority voting of 5 different classifiers: SVM (RBF kernel), DT, NB, KNNs ($k = 5$), and RF shows an apparent increase in the overall average test set accuracy which reaches 98.67%. Also, as it can be seen clearly from Table 4 that the proposed method for counting lymphoblasts by using our proposed approach matches the manual counting by the hematologists in most of sets. Therefore, the overall misclassification rate of false positive rate is only 7% and the overall performance of TPR is 100%.

It can be observed from the experiments that the architecture that consists of 5 different classifiers achieves the best performance for counting the lymphoblasts significantly. It achieves the lowest recorded average error rate of 1.33% while the

Table 3. The experimental results Using MCA of 3 different classifiers: SVM, DT, and KNNs.

Set	Manual counting of lymphoblasts	Proposed method counting	TP	FN	FP	Average test set accuracy	TPR	TNR	PPV
1	47	50	47	0	3	95.16%	100%	80%	94%
2	8	7	7	1	0	95.24%	88%	100%	100%
3	45	45	45	0	0	100%	100%	100%	100%
4	60	65	60	0	5	93.33%	100%	67%	92%
5	9	9	9	0	0	100%	100%	100%	100%
Total	169	176	168	1	8	96.75%	97.6%	89.4%	97.2%

Table 4. The experimental results using MCA of 5 different classifiers: SVM, DT, NB, KNNs, and RF.

Set	Manual counting of lymphoblasts	Proposed method counting	TP	FN	FP	Average test set accuracy	TPR	TNR	PPV
1	47	47	47	0	0	100%	100%	100%	100%
2	8	8	8	0	0	100%	100%	100%	100%
3	45	45	45	0	0	100%	100%	100%	100%
4	60	65	60	0	5	93.33%	100%	67%	92%
5	9	9	9	0	0	100%	100%	100%	100%
Total	169	174	169	0	5	98.67%	100%	93.4%	98.4%

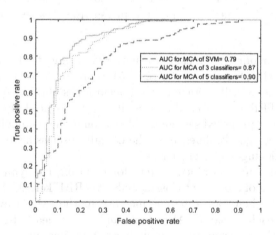

Fig. 5. AUC for all different MCA.

overall average error rates for MCA of 3 different classifiers and SVM classifier with different kernels are 3.25% and 10.66% respectively. Moreover, based on analyzing the area under the Receiver Operating Characteristic (ROC) curve

(AUC) to compare the performance of the used classification models, Fig. 5 shows that for MCA of 5 different independent classifiers the area is larger than for any other architectures of MCA taken into account in this study.

6 Conclusions

We have introduced an innovative counting-based framework consisting of two sub-systems which can be used as indicators for detection the patients who may suffer from ALL. By providing a microscopic blood image as an input to the proposed framework, it produces outputs including the number of WBCs and lymphoblasts. The first sub-system is directed to count WBCs. Therefore, medical systems such as haematology counters can be supported by the results of the first sub-system. The second sub-system aims to address the detection of the abnormalities of WBCs. An advantage of this proposed sub-system is overcoming major limitations of automated haematology counters. We would like to point out that we are proposing the first study from its kind for counting the lymphoblasts. The proposed counting-based framework seems quite promising as it can be used in the medical laboratories to aid hematologists in their diagnosis of ALL and make their decisions more precise and objective. In future work we plan to develop an automated prognostic system for subclassification of ALL based on French-American-British (FAB) and/or World Health Organization (WHO) classification systems.

Acknowledgments. This research was supported by the Natural Sciences and Engineering Research Council of Canada.

References

1. Inaba, H., Greaves, M., Mullighan, C.: Acute lymphoblastic leukaemia. Lancet **381**(9881), 1943–1955 (2013)
2. Briggs, C., Longair, I., Slavik, M., Thwaite, K., Mills, R., Thavaraja, V., Foster, A., Romannin, D., Machin, S.: Can automated blood film analysis replace the manual differential? An evaluation of the CellaVision DM96 automated image analysis system. Lab. Hematol. **31**(1), 48–60 (2009)
3. Le, D., Bui, A., Yu, Z., Bui, F.: An automated framework for counting lymphocytes from microscopic images. In. Computing and Communication (IEMCON), pp. 1–6. Vancouver (2015)
4. Putzu, L., Caocci, G., Di Ruberto, C.: Leucocyte classification for leukaemia detection using image processing techniques. Artif. Intell. Med. **62**(3), 179–191 (2014)
5. Bhavnani, L., Jaliya, U., Joshi, M.: Segmentation and counting of WBCs and RBCs from microscopic blood sample images. Image, Graph. Signal Process. **8**(11), 32 (2016)
6. Basima, C.T., Panicker, J.: Enhanced leucocyte classification for leukaemia detection. In: Information Science (ICIS), Kochi, pp. 65–71 (2016)
7. Alomari, Y., Abdullah, S., Azma, R., Omar, K.: Automatic detection and quantification of WBCs and RBCs using iterative structured circle detection algorithm. In: Computational and Mathematical Methods in Medicine 2014 (2014)

8. Di Ruberto, C., Loddo, A., Putzu, L.: A leukocytes count system from blood smear images. Mach. Vis. Appl. **27**(8), 1151–1160 (2016)
9. Abd Halim, N., Mashor, M., Hassan, R.: Automatic blasts counting for acute leukemia based on blood samples. Res. Rev. Comput. Sci. (IJRRCS) **2**(4), 971 (2011)
10. ALL-IDB Homepage. https://homes.di.unimi.it/scotti/all/. Accessed 10 May 2017
11. Duggal, R., Gupta, A., Gupta, R., Wadhwa, M., and Ahuja, C.: Overlapping cell nuclei segmentation in microscopic images using deep belief networks. In: Computer Vision Graphics and Image Processing, Guwahati, p. 82 (2016)
12. Cseke, I.: A fast segmentation scheme for white blood cell images. In: Pattern Recognition, The Hague, pp. 530–533 (1992)
13. Otsu, N.: A threshold selection method from gray-level histograms. IEEE Trans. Syst. Man Cybern. **9**(1), 62–66 (1979)
14. Mohapatra, S., Patra, D.: Automated cell nucleus segmentation and acute leukemia detection in blood microscopic images. In: Systems in Medicine and Biology (ICSMB), Kharagpur, vol. 62, no. 3, pp. 49–54 (2010)
15. Liu, L., Lao, S., Fieguth, P., Guo, Y., Wang, X., Pietikinen, M.: Median robust extended local binary pattern for texture classification. IEEE Trans. Image Process. **25**(3), 1368–1381 (2016)
16. Haralick, R., Shanmugam, K., Dinstein, I.: Textural features for image classification. IEEE Trans. Syst. Man Cybern. **6**, 610–621 (1973)
17. Busch, A., Boles, W.: Texture classification using multiple wavelet analysis. In: Digital Image Computing Techniques and Applications, pp. 341–345 (2002)
18. Smetana, K., Jirásková, I., Starỳ, J.: The number of nucleoli and main nucleolar types in lymphoblasts of children suffering from acute lymphoid leukemia. Hematol. J. **4**(3), 231–236 (1999)
19. Peng, H., Long, F., Ding, C.: Feature selection based on mutual information criteria of max-dependency, max-relevance, and min-redundancy. IEEE Trans. Pattern Anal. Mach. Intell. **27**(8), 1226–1238 (2005)
20. Bishop, C.: Mach. Learn. Pattern Recogn. Springer, Heidelberg (2006)
21. Breiman, L.: Random forests. Mach. Learn. **45**(1), 5–32 (2001)

Right Ventricle Segmentation in Cardiac MR Images Using U-Net with Partly Dilated Convolution

Gregory Borodin and Olga Senyukova$^{(\boxtimes)}$ (ID)

Faculty of Computational Mathematics and Cybernetics,
Lomonosov Moscow State University, 2nd Education Building,
GSP-1, Leninskie Gory, 119991 Moscow, Russian Federation
grihabor@mail.ru, olga.senyukova@graphics.cs.msu.ru

Abstract. Segmentation of anatomical structures in cardiac MR images is an important problem because it is necessary for evaluation of morphology of these structures for diagnostic purposes. Automatic segmentation algorithm with near-human accuracy would be extremely helpful for a medical specialist. In this paper we consider such structures as endocardium and epicardium of right ventricle. We compare the performance of the best existing neural networks such as U-Net and GridNet, and propose our own modification of U-Net which implies replacement of every second convolution layer with dilated (atrous) convolution layer. Evaluation on benchmark dataset RVSC demonstrated that the proposed algorithm allows to improve the segmentation accuracy up to 6% both for endocardium and epicardium compared to original U-Net. The algorithm also overperforms GridNet for both segmentation problems.

Keywords: Right ventricle segmentation · U-Net
Dilated convolution · Atrous convolution

1 Introduction

Morphological analysis of right ventricle (RV) on cardiac magnetic resonance images (MRI) is necessary for diagnostics of such serious diseases as coronary heart disease, congenital heart disease and others. The greatest attention is paid to myocardium, a layer located between endocardium and epicardium. Thus it is important to obtain accurate delineation of endocardial and epicardial contours. Automatic segmentation algorithm would significantly reduce the amount of routine work of a radiologist allowing him to process more cases.

There are several existing works devoted to RV segmentation. The algorithms not using deep learning, such as [1,2] provide rather good results. However, it is known that deep learning algorithms generalize better and are less prone to overfitting on a certain dataset since they learn the best features independently and do not need expert knowledge. The work [3] describes a combination of deep convolutional neural network (CNN) and regression forests for RV volume

© Springer Nature Switzerland AG 2018
V. Kůrková et al. (Eds.): ICANN 2018, LNCS 11140, pp. 179–185, 2018.
https://doi.org/10.1007/978-3-030-01421-6_18

prediction. The authors of [4] propose a two-stage solution, one deep CNN for localization of a region containing RV, and another CNN for RV segmentation. The only automatic one-stage algorithm for segmentation of right and left ventricles endocardium and epicardium that uses only one deep CNN is [5].

Among CNN architectures used for other medical image analysis problems, according to [7] the most well-known is U-Net [8]. This network is modification of fully convolutional network (FCN) [6]. It is also fully convolutional and it is constructed of a convolution (downsampling) and deconvolution (upsampling) paths. High resolution output feature maps from the convolution path are combined with the upsampled feature maps from the opposite block in order to perform better object localization. A large number of features in the upsampling part makes it almost symmetric to downsampling part and yields U-shape. This allows the network to propagate context information to higher resolution layers. U-Net and its various modifications have already been applied to plenty of medical image analysis problems, including left ventricle (LV) segmentation.

GridNet architecture [9] is inspired by U-Net. Additional convolution blocks are added between each pair of opposing convolution and deconvolution blocks. There is also a convolution block for automatic estimation of the center of mass of the object of interest. The algorithm is evaluated on the Automated Cardiac Diagnostics Challenge (ACDC) dataset [13]. The results are presented for RV, LV and myocardium.

In this work we propose a U-Net modification by including dilated convolution [12] layers in it. We neither introduce additional layers nor replace all the convolution layers by dilated convolution, we just replace every second convolution layer in each block of the contracting path.

The rest of the paper is organized as follows. In the Sect. 2, we describe the proposed CNN architecture in detail. In the Sect. 3 we provide description of experiments and results of evaluation of the proposed method and its comparison with existing state-of-the-art methods. Conclusions are drawn in the Sect. 4.

2   Method

2.1   Original U-Net

U-Net [8] consists of a contracting (convolution) path and an expansive (deconvolution) path. Each block of the contracting path consists of two convolution layers with kernel size 3×3 where each layer is followed by a rectified linear unit (ReLU). Each block is followed by 2×2 max pooling operation, after which the number of feature channels is doubled. Each block of the expansive path consists of 2×2 up-convolution that halves the number of feature channels, concatenation with the correspondingly cropped feature map from the contracting path and two 3×3 convolution layers with ReLU. At the final layer a 1×1 convolution is used to map each 64-component feature vector to the classes of the segmentation map.

2.2   Dilated Convolution

Dilated (atrous) convolution [12] is a new type of convolution that allows aggregation of multi-scale context. It was successfully applied to different tasks [11]. Dilation of the convolution kernel k of size M by the factor l means that we sample the input image with the stride l (1):

$$y[i,j] = \sum_{n=1}^{M} \sum_{m=1}^{M} x[i + l*m, j + l*n]k[m,n]. \tag{1}$$

This operation allows to enlarge the field of view of the filter without losing image resolution (Fig. 1). The receptive field grows exponentially while the filter size grows linearly.

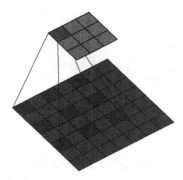

Fig. 1. Illustration of convolution kernel dilated by factor 2.

Setting dilation factor l to 1 means that traditional convolution is performed.

2.3   The Proposed Architecture

The main idea of the proposed method is to replace every second convolution layer in contracting path of U-Net by dilated convolution layer with kernel size $M = 3$ and dilation factor $l = 2$ (Fig. 2). Therefore, the receptive field is 5×5. Leaving the first 3×3 convolution layer in each block of the contracting path allows taking into account all the elements of the corresponding feature map, while introducing a dilated convolution layer after it allows capturing larger context which promotes correct inference. So only one of two convolution layers was replaced by dilated convolution layer. Kernel size 3×3 was kept the same as in the original U-Net. It was not increased in order to prevent the network from fast growth. Dilation factor with minimum value 2 was chosen in order keep as much information as possible.

The image size does not change after convolution and dilated convolution because the image is padded before the operation.

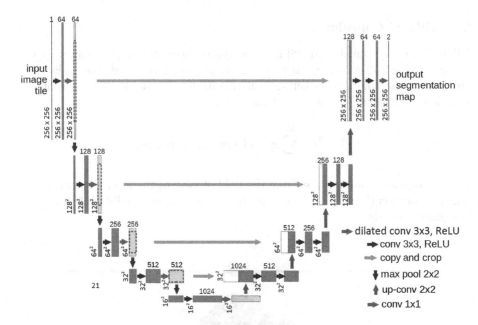

Fig. 2. The proposed CNN architecture. Convolution layers in U-Net replaced by dilated convolution layers are shown in yellow. (Color figure online)

3   Experimental Results and Discussion

3.1   Dataset

The proposed algorithm and existing algorithms were evaluated on Right Ventricle Segmentation Challenge (RVSC) dataset [10] provided as part of the MICCAI 2012 challenge on automated RV endocardium and epicardium segmentation from short-axis cine MRI. The dataset consists of images of 48 patients with various cardiac pathologies. The images are in DICOM format. The dataset is divided into three equal disjoint parts, one of which is for training, and the other two are for testing. Manual expert contours for endocardium and epicardium are provided only for the training images (16 cases).

The images were preprocessed by mean-variance normalization (MVN).

In order to artificially increase the training database we used data augmentation procedure involving image rescaling (4 scales), vertical and horizontal flipping and rotations (10 angles).

3.2   Training and Evaluation

All the networks participating in our comparison were implemented in Python 3 using Keras library [14]. They were trained with the same protocol and tested on the same datasets described below. Since the expert labeling on RVSC was provided only for 16 patients, we used 12 of them for training and the other

4 for testing. We used 4-fold cross-validation and took the segmentation result as the average between four results. Training protocol is the same as described in [5]. A learning algorithm is stochastic gradient descent with momentum of 0.9. Dropout ratio is 0.5 and L_2 weight decay regularization is 0.0005. All the networks were trained for 10 epochs. Initial learning rate is $base\_lr = 0.01$ and it is annealed according to the polynomial decay:

$$base\_lr \times (1 - \frac{iter}{max\_iter})^{power}, \tag{2}$$

where $iter$ is the current iteration, max_iter is the maximum number of iterations equal to 10 epochs, and $power = 0.5$ controls the rate of decay.

We reduced the problem of finding endocardial/epicardial contour to the problem of finding the area enclosed by this contour. This makes it possible to use Dice index [15] for evaluation of similarity (overlap) between segmentation result and manual expert labeling (ground truth):

$$D(X, Y) = 2\frac{X \cap Y}{X \cup Y}. \tag{3}$$

3.3 Results

The results for segmentation of RV endocardium and epicardium on RVSC dataset for original U-Net and the proposed algorithm (U-Net with dilated convolution layers) are provided in Table 1. Also, we compared the proposed algorithm with the other U-Net modification, GridNet [9] that was also used, in particular, for RV segmentation, but on the other dataset.

Table 1. Segmentation results (Dice index) on RVSC dataset.

Method	Endocardium	Epicardium
GridNet (Zotti et al. 2017)	0.82	0.81
U-Net (Ronneberger et al. 2015)	0.79	0.77
Our method	**0.85**	**0.83**

It can be seen that introduction of dilated convolution into U-Net increases its accuracy by 6% both for endocardium and epicardium. The proposed algorithm shows better accuracy than GridNet for both anatomical structures up to 3%. We also tried to introduce dilated convolution to GridNet but it did not help to improve the quality of segmentation.

The authors of [5] that proposed to apply fully convolutional network [6] also evaluated their algorithm on RVSC dataset, but they used all 16 cases for training, and sent predicted endocardial and epicardial contours on unlabeled test sets to challenge organizers for independent evaluation. The reported accuracy in this case is 80% for endocardium and 84% for epicardium. It seems that our method performs better for endocardium because it demonstrated 85% accuracy after training only on 12 cases, however the objective comparison could be done if there was a labeled test set.

The results example is shown in Fig. 3.

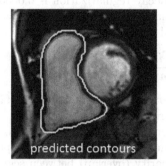 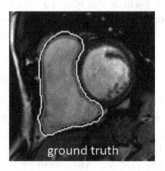

Fig. 3. Results example. Epicardial (external) contour is shown in yellow. Endocardial (internal) contour is shown in red. (Color figure online)

Further comparison with more existing methods is warranted.

In general, RV segmentation is more challenging problem than LV segmentation because of more complex shape of RV across slices and phases. Therefore the state-of-the-art accuracy of deep CNNs for this problem is still 80–85% while LV segmentation accuracy is over 90%. Also, apical slices introduce more difficulties to the segmentation process. Exploring dilated convolution for 3D networks, such as 3D U-Net [16] is a part of future work.

4   Conclusion

In this work we proposed a modification of one of the most widely used deep CNNs for medical image segmentation, U-Net, and demonstrated that it significantly overperforms the original U-Net in the context of right ventricle endocardium and epicardium segmentation problem. Moreover, it overperforms the other U-Net modification, GridNet, that contains more convolution blocks. The results are provided for real MR images from benchmark dataset which makes possible objective comparison with different algorithms. Although we managed to improve segmentation accuracy of RV, this is still an open problem and further research is warranted. The proposed CNN architecture can be used for other medical image analysis tasks.

Acknowledgments. The work was supported by the Grant of President of Russian Federation for young scientists No. MK-1896.2017.9 (contract No. 14.W01.17.1896-MK).

References

1. Ringenberg, J., Deo, M., Devabhaktuni, V., et al.: Fast, accurate, and fully automatic segmentation of the right ventricle in short-axis cardiac MRI. Comput. Med. Imag. Grap. **38**(3), 190–201 (2014)
2. Punithakumar, K., Noga, M., Ben Ayed, I., Boulanger, P.: Right ventricular segmentation in cardiac MRI with moving mesh correspondences. Comput. Med. Imag. Grap. **43**, 15–25 (2015)
3. Zhen, X., Wang, Z., Islam, A., et al.: Multiscale deep networks and regression forests for direct biventricular volume estimation. Med. Image Anal. **30**, 120–129 (2016)
4. Luo, G., An, R., Wang, K., et al.: A deep learning network for right ventricle segmentation in short-axis MRI. In: 2016 Computing in Cardiology Conference (CinC), pp. 485–488. IEEE Computer Society (2016)
5. Tran, P.V.: A fully convolutional neural network for cardiac segmentation in short-axis MRI. arXiv preprint arXiv:1604.00494 (2016)
6. Long, J., Shelhamer, E., Darrell, T.: Fully convolutional networks for semantic segmentation. In: IEEE Conference on Computer Vision and Pattern Recognition (CVPR 2015), pp. 3431–3440. IEEE Computer Society (2015)
7. Litjens, G., Kooi, T., Ehteshami, B., et al.: A survey on deep learning in medical image analysis. Med. Image Anal. **42**, 60–88 (2017)
8. Ronneberger, O., Fischer, P., Brox, T.: U-Net: convolutional networks for biomedical image segmentation. In: Navab, N., Hornegger, J., Wells, W.M., Frangi, A.F. (eds.) MICCAI 2015. LNCS, vol. 9351, pp. 234–241. Springer, Cham (2015). https://doi.org/10.1007/978-3-319-24574-4_28
9. Zotti, C., Luo, Z., Lalande, A., et al.: Novel deep convolution neural network applied to MRI cardiac segmentation. arXiv preprint arXiv:1705.08943 (2017)
10. Petitjean, C., Zuluaga, M.A., Bai, W., et al.: Right ventricle segmentation from cardiac MRI: a collation study. Med. Image Anal. **19**(1), 187–202 (2015)
11. Chen, L.-C., Papandreou, G., Kokkinos, I., et al.: DeepLab: semantic image segmentation with deep convolutional nets, atrous convolution, and fully connected CRFs. IEEE Trans. Pattern Anal. Mach. Intell. **40**(4), 834–848 (2018)
12. Yu, F., Koltun V.: Multi-scale context aggregation by dilated convolutions. In: ICLR (2016)
13. ACDC-MICCAI challenge. http://acdc.creatis.insa-lyon.fr. Accessed 10 July 2018
14. Keras: The Python Deep Learning library. https://keras.io. Accessed 10 July 2018
15. Dice, L.R.: Measures of the amount of ecologic association between species. Ecology **26**(3), 297–302 (1945)
16. Çiçek, Ö., Abdulkadir, A., Lienkamp, S.S., Brox, T., Ronneberger, O.: 3D U-Net: learning dense volumetric segmentation from sparse annotation. In: Ourselin, S., Joskowicz, L., Sabuncu, M.R., Unal, G., Wells, W. (eds.) MICCAI 2016. LNCS, vol. 9901, pp. 424–432. Springer, Cham (2016). https://doi.org/10.1007/978-3-319-46723-8_49

Model Based on Support Vector Machine for the Estimation of the Heart Rate Variability

Catalina Maria Hernández-Ruiz[1]([✉]) [iD],
Sergio Andrés Villagrán Martínez[1]([✉]),
Johan Enrique Ortiz Guzmán[2]([✉]),
and Paulo Alonso Gaona Garcia[1]([✉])

[1] Facultad de Ingeniería, Universidad Distrital Francisco José de Caldas,
Bogotá, Colombia
cmhernandezr@correo.udistrital.edu.co,
sergiovillagran92@gmail.com,
pagaonag@udistrital.edu.co
[2] Facultad de Medicina, Universidad del Rosario, Bogotá, Colombia
johan.ortiz@urosario.edu.co

Abstract. This paper shows the design, implementation and analysis of a Machine Learning (ML) model for the estimation of Heart Rate Variability (HRV). Through the integration of devices and technologies of the Internet of Things, a support tool is proposed for people in health and sports areas who need to know an individual's HRV. The cardiac signals of the subjects were captured through pectoral bands, later they were classified by a Support Vector Machine algorithm that determined if the HRV is depressed or increased. The proposed solution has an efficiency of 90.3% and it's the initial component for the development of an application oriented to physical training that suggests exercise routines based on the HRV of the individual.

Keywords: Heart Rate Variability (HRV) · Internet of Things (IOT)
Support Vector Machine (SVM) · Heart Rate Monitor (HRM)

1 Introduction

The heart rate variability (HRV) is the difference per unit of time between heartbeats in any given interval [1]. It is a useful tool to evaluate the control of the autonomic nervous system over the heart rate (HR), as it is shown by the changes given in the balance between the sympathetic and parasympathetic systems. Obtaining the HRV does not require invasive processes as it is carried out through the analysis of the electrical signals of the heart, reflecting the regularity of heartbeats [2].

Through the Internet of Things (IOT), it is possible to monitor and control a great diversity of systems through the use of sensor sets which facilitate the capture of data for further analysis and processing [3]. In order to obtain HR specifically, there are HR monitors (HRM), commonly used in medicine and sports sciences by doctors, athletes, coaches and researchers, as a reliable and robust means of recording the activity of the heart [4]. Among these HRM, there are wristbands and wireless chest straps with

© Springer Nature Switzerland AG 2018
V. Kůrková et al. (Eds.): ICANN 2018, LNCS 11140, pp. 186–194, 2018.
https://doi.org/10.1007/978-3-030-01421-6_19

electrodes connected with services and web/mobile applications so as to send the captured information. These applications also offer complementary information associated with the statistics and individual's profile, which is something beneficial for physical training purposes [5].

HRV has gained relevance in recent decades due to its association with heart diagnosis. For this reason, several authors have developed tools for their analysis and use [1]. Among the most commonly used traditional methods for calculating HRV, the frequency and time domain measurements as well as the non-linear methods can be found [6]. Song et al. [7] claim that, for the analysis of HRV, these conventional practices have some limitations to make predictions and diagnosis. Due to this fact, new techniques and mechanisms based on the usual mathematical models have emerged. These, when combined with computational systems, are more accurate in their calculation, as Matta et al. [8] who applied neural networks to obtain HRV through the recognition and categorization of patterns.

From this perspective, the work presented below is a model based on Support Vector Machine (SVM) for the classification of HRV using low cost equipment such as chest straps with HR sensors that allow monitoring and obtaining the activity of the heart. The aim of this is to generate a tool which could provide any person - an expert or not - with the value of HRV in a practical and simple way so that this can be applied afterwards in order to make decisions with regard to health areas.

The following article is organized as follows: Sect. 2 provides a context for the topic as well as related work and background information. Section 3 presents the methodology used for the work conducted. Section 4 describes the proposed model. Section 5 expresses the results obtained. Subsequently, Sect. 6 shows the analysis of results and discussions. Finally, Sect. 7 covers the conclusions and future works.

2 Related Works

The most widely used resource for the capture of HRV is the electrocardiogram (ECG), which registers the origin and propagation of electric potential through the cardiac muscle [9], and is the means by which the most information about the activity of the heart is obtained [1]. The ECG consists of waves, segments and intervals. Such waves are expressed with deflection of the electrical activity, finding either positive deflections (when the deflection is upward) or negative (when it is downward) in relation to the baseline of the heart rate. On the other hand, the segments are understood as the space lying between two consecutive waves, whereas the intervals are the period resulting from the sum of a wave and a segment. Another determining factor given by the ECG is the QRS complex, which indicates the depolarization of the ventricular muscle. In this way, the time between each heartbeat is determined by the interval between the QRS complexes, more commonly known as R-R intervals [10].

HRV is a valuable tool to examine the sympathetic and parasympathetic functions of the autonomic nervous system and is inversely proportional to the regularity of the HR; that is to say, the higher the regularity there is, the lower HRV there is and vice versa. Additionally, it serves as a measure of the balance between sympathetic and parasympathetic mediators. The former ones reflect the effect of epinephrine and norepinephrine that sympathetic nerve fibers release on the sinoatrial and atrioven-tricular nodules, which leads to an increase in the rate of cardiac contraction. The latter ones influence on the release of acetylcholine by parasympathetic nerve fibers that decrease HR [11]. Sao et al. [12] state that the combination between the electrical signals of the heart and the HRV generate a good basis for the analysis of its state. According to Giles et al. [4], from several clinical studies undertaken, it was found that the decrease in HRV is related to the diagnosis of cardiovascular diseases, diabetic neuropathy and hypertension, among others. Such authors also claim that the HRV serves as a measure in the sports environment when facing diverse conditions such as overtraining, recovery, endurance training and exercise.

Karim et al. [11] describe the calculation of heart rate variability using different methods. Time domain is among one the most known and simplest to apply, in which R-R intervals, which are necessary for the generation of statistical metrics as well as indexes for calculating HRV, are identified based on the ECG. SDNN corresponds to the standard deviation of all the R-R intervals. Besides, RMSSD and PNN50 can also be found, the former one being the square root of the mean squared difference in successive heartbeats, whereas the latter one is the number of successive intervals that differ by more than 50 ms, expressed as a percentage of the total number of heartbeats.

Some other classic measurements to determine HRV are those of the frequency domain. McCraty et al. [6] state that the heart rate oscillations are divided into 4 primary frequency bands: high frequency (HF), low frequency (LF), very low fre-quency (VLF) and ultra-low frequency (ULF). The first two will be vital for the present study since they are directly related to the HRV. The HF goes from 0.15 Hz to 0.4 Hz, which is equivalent to rhythms with periods between 2.5 and 7 s, whereas the LF lays between 0.04 Hz and 0.15 Hz, which means rhythms of 7 and 25 s respectively. The HF reflects the parasympathetic or vagal activity and is also called the respiratory band because it responds to the variations of the HR that occurs in the respiratory cycle. On the other hand, the LF shows the sympathetic activity of the system. The HR is regulated by the balance between the actions of the sympathetic and the parasympa-thetic nervous system, so it is vital to know the HF and LF bands to determine the HRV.

Among the non-linear methods, there is the Poincaré plot, which is a non-linear-visual technique that allows examining the behavior of the R-R intervals, through the classification of the forms of the ECG plot. Analysis and recognition allow to identify degrees of heart failure. This differentiation can be done through the calculation of the standard deviations SD1 and SD2 that are related to HRV [12].

To classify HRV, multiple authors have resorted to fields and techniques derived from artificial intelligence, like fuzzy logic, neural networks, ML, among others. Such as Patel et al. [13], who designed a neural network for the detection of early fatigue in people who drive for long periods of time, not only warned about the lethargy which seriously affects the performance of drivers but also claimed that this could be a very common cause of accidents. Through the classification of time domain measurements and the frequency of HRV, they were able to quantify somnolence with an accuracy of 90%, for which they distinguished the levels of sympathetic (LF) and parasympathetic (HF) activity of the organism. This technique of fatigue detection, based on HRV, was recommended as a countermeasure for fatigue.

Asl et al. [14] applied SVM for the identification of 6 different types of arrhythmias: normal sinus rhythm, premature ventricular contraction, atrial fibrillation, sick sinus syndrome, ventricular fibrillation and heart block. They did this by classifying 15 characteristics of the HRV calculated through linear and non-linear methods. The accuracy of this algorithm for each case was greater than 98%.

On the other hand, Liu et al. [15] classified the combination of cardiac variability and complexity to determine those patients who required lifesaving interventions. Such authors captured information from 104 patients through the use of wireless vital signs monitoring systems from which they obtained their heart rate data. They applied classification techniques such as neural networks and multivariable logistic regression, which were evaluated and compared by statistical analysis. The conclusions indicated that in the neural network model, the multilayer perceptron (MLP) algorithm demonstrated more efficiency and effectiveness in the classification of patients who needed a rescue measure in contrast with the logistic regression algorithm.

Considering the aforementioned reference points, the following study intends to determine the classification of HRV suggesting an algorithm based on SVM, as Song, et al. [7] did. The authors applied the same technique for the analysis and identification of patients who suffered acute myocardial infarction, based on the fact that the decrease in HRV was associated with a potential risk of ventricular arrhythmias for patients who had had such episodes. The aim of this work is to develop a tool which can support decision-making strategies for the areas of health and physical training. In view of the above, it is important to consider that classification is a problem which may be solved through ML, in which there could exist from one to two or more classifications in a sample data. The study included a process of design and implementation of the proposed algorithm, established a work methodology described in the following section.

3   Work Methodology

The working method to carry out the following study was quasi-experimental and applied. Then, in Fig. 1 a series of phases that define it and that allowed to glimpse a navigation map for the study are shown.

Fig. 1. Work phases used for study.

The first phase involved the search and analysis of literature on conventional techniques for the calculation of HRV, from them, specific methods were identified and explored in Phase 2. In stage 3, the definition of the process was carried out of capture of cardiac signals through IoT devices and the generation of a strategy for the transfer of collected data. During phase 4, a method based on SVM was implemented to classify HRV, this was applied through a case study in phase 5. The results and their analysis were performed in Phase 6, where the efficiency of the algorithm was determined.

3.1   Case Study

The case study included the capture of cardiac signals from a group of individuals through chest straps that obtained the HR value. Table 1 presents the characteristics of used strap [16].

Table 1. Characteristics of the Polar H10 chest strap.

Polar H10 heart rate sensor	
Battery type	CR 2025
Battery sealing ring	O-ring 20.0 × 0.90 Material Silicone
Battery lifetime	40 h
Operating temperature	−10 °C to +50 °C/14 °F to 122 °F
Connector material	ABS, ABS + GF, PC, Stainless steel
Strap material	38% polyamide, 29% polyurethane, 20% elastane, 13% polyester, silicone impressions

These non-invasive records were made in 33 people whose HR was obtained for 12 min. In total, 56 data constituted the training set that served as the input for the learning of ML algorithm. The average age of the individuals ranged between 25 and 35 years, mostly healthy people with few exceptions, such as thyroid dysfunctions and hypertension. Close amounts of women and men, although no data was taken on children because their nervous system has not yet fully matured as in the case of adults. During each session, the person was required to remain at rest for approximately 12 min, which included sitting without speaking and minimizing movements. In addition of HR, other information was recorded such as age, weight, height, gender, pre-existing diseases and the use of regular medications or treatments. By means of these cardiac registers the necessary information was obtained to feed the ML algorithm, its model will be described in the following section.

4   Proposed Working Model

The model that was carried out has two main components that can be observed in Fig. 2. The first is the IoT system that aims to define the capture and disposition of the information, this being the input for the following component: the HRV classification

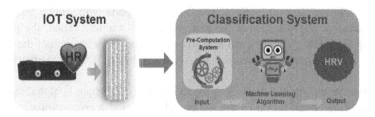

Fig. 2. Proposed working model.

system, which takes the data and processes it by classifying the HRV as depressed or increased. IoT system used pectoral bands to record the HR, its transmission was made through a mobile application that communicated with the sensor via bluetooth.

Pitale et al. [1] describe two steps for the implementation of classification algorithms: the definition of the model and the selection and application of a method to classify it. For our study, the first one included the processing of the information given by the IoT system to obtain the entries of the classification algorithm, which were diverse variables on the domains of time, frequency and non-linear methods. Among the first were the nnxx which is the number of successive R-R intervals that differ by more than xx milliseconds and pnnxx, which is its corresponding in percentage [17]. In the domain of frequency, the HF and LF were taken, due to their direct relationship with the activity of the sympathetic and parasympathetic systems of the organism [6]. Finally, variables from nonlinear methods such as SD1 and SD2 were analyzed, which are the standard deviations of the Poincaré plot perpendicular and along the identity line respectively [18]. In addition, alpha1 and alpha2 were obtained, short and long-term fluctuations of the detrended fluctuation analysis [19]. The expected results were a reduced or increased HRV as explained by Task Force et al. [20].

The classification technique chosen was SVM, due to its efficiency and reliability as described in the background section. Song et al. [7], state that SVMs are supervised learning models that are used in regression and classification problems because they are based on data analysis and pattern recognition, generating n-dimensional hyperplanes to distinguish and separate various sets of characteristics, thus finding the optimal hyperparameters. The algorithm was trained with the variables generated from the 56 records obtained with the chest strap, the results of its application are described in the following section.

5 Results Obtained

Multiple combinations of inputs were applied for the algorithm training with the purpose of obtaining the best model for the HRV classification. Zhao et al. [21] describe a multiclass classification function in Matlab fitcecoc, which was used in the present study with a linear kernel and its parameters were optimized using automatic hyperparameter optimization. The corresponding evaluation was carried out through obtaining two types of errors: the classification error in the sample, and the error generated from cross validation. He et al. [22], state that the cross-validation technique divides the training data into several non-contiguous parts with similar length. Each one is selected as test data, while the rest are used as training. Then, the prediction model is applied with these data and this process is repeated with each of the divisions obtained. All predictions are averaged to give an estimate of the performance of the algorithm.

As a first result, the most efficient inputs set was: HF, alpha1, alpha2 and nnxx. With an error of classification of the sample of 8.9% and a cross-validation error of 9.7%, the behavior of the algorithm with this configuration is presented in Fig. 3. The evaluation carried out by the optimization function to compare the expected behavior with the real one, decreasing the cross-validation error, returning 90.3% of effectiveness.

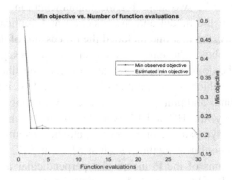

Fig. 3. Optimization of the proposed classification model.

6 Analysis of Results and Discussions

During the algorithm tests, multiple cases with negative behaviors were evidenced, such as the use of frequency domain variables only: HF and LF, because it did not grant a satisfactory classification rate for the algorithm, it presented an error of 19.6%. Likewise, the inclusion of the 8 entries in the model generated an overfitting problem, same case was perceived when modifying the algorithm's Kernel to Gaussian, presenting a perfect fit to the training set with a sample classification error of 0%, but with cross validation, the error was greater than 30%. This situation was propitiated by the amount of data for the training set being very small in contrast to a high number of features or entries, very common difficulty that is presented in the classification algorithms with few data.

The most efficient set presents a mixture between the three methods that generate variables for the HRV calculation, time and frequency domains and non-linear methods, which outlines a complementary behavior of these variables in HRV obtaining.

7 Conclusions

One of the main advantages presented in this study is the low cost in the acquisition of the cardiac registry. The use of chest straps is a non-invasive method that does not generate any secondary effects on the individual and does not present environmental requirements, it can be applicable in any person who is doing any activity. Its use is recommended in conjunction with applications that allow its consumption to be carried out, because they have shown high reliability in its evaluation.

The integration and combination of variables of time and frequency domains and nonlinear methods is a viable and effective alternative for the classification of HRV. The proposed solution is suggested as a useful and practical tool for people who need to know the HRV, since it is a health indicator and is related to various deficiencies and diseases as expressed in the section of background. As future work and continuation of this study we propose the improvement of the propounded model, increasing its efficiency through the enrichment of the training set, providing greater experience to the algorithm for its learning. Also, we want to make use of this solution as a component of an application for physical training, supporting an athlete and personal trainers suggesting exercise routines according to their physical condition, by tracking their HRV, analyzing their progress and history, making use of GPS, to know changes of altitude and length of routes.

References

1. Pitale, R., Tajane, K., Umale, J.: Heart rate variability classification and feature extraction using support vector machine and PCA: an overview. J. Eng. Res. Appl. **4**, 381–384 (2014)
2. Borchini, R., Veronesi, G., Bonzini, M., Gianfagna, F., Dashi, O., Ferrario, M.: Heart rate variability frequency domain alterations among healthy nurses exposed to prolonged work stress. Int. J. Environ. Res. Public Health **15**, 113 (2018)
3. Hernández, C., Villagrán, S., Gaona, P.: Predictive model for detecting MQ2 gases using fuzzy logic on IoT devices. In: Jayne, C., Iliadis, L. (eds.) EANN 2016. CCIS, vol. 629, pp. 176–185. Springer, Cham (2016). https://doi.org/10.1007/978-3-319-44188-7_13
4. Giles, D., Draper, N., Neil, W.: Validity of the Polar V800 heart rate monitor to measure RR intervals at rest. Eur. J. Appl. Physiol. **116**, 563–571 (2015)
5. Erkkila, M., Rae, R., Thurlin, T., Korva, T., Manninen, T.: Managing physiological exercise data. US Patent 9855463B2, 16 January 2014
6. McCraty, R., Shaffer, F.: Heart rate variability: new perspectives on physiological mechanisms, assessment of self-regulatory capacity, and health risk. Glob. Adv. Health Med. Improv. Healthc. Outcomes Worldw. **4**, 46–61 (2015)
7. Song, M., Lee, J., Cho, S., Lee, K., Yoo, S.: Support vector machine based arrhythmia classification using reduced features. Int. J. Control Autom. Syst. **3**, 571–579 (2005)
8. Matta, S., Sankari, Z., Rihana, S.: Heart rate variability analysis using neural network models for automatic detection of lifestyle activities. Biomed. Signal Process. Control **42**, 145–157 (2018)

9. Lewis, M.C., Maiya, M., Sampathila, N.: A novel method for the conversion of scanned electrocardiogram (ECG) image to digital signal. In: Dash, S.S., Das, S., Panigrahi, B.K. (eds.) International Conference on Intelligent Computing and Applications. AISC, vol. 632, pp. 363–373. Springer, Singapore (2018). https://doi.org/10.1007/978-981-10-5520-1_34

10. Barrett, K., Brooks, H., Boitano, S., Barman, S.: Ganong's Review of Medical Physiology, 23rd edn. McGraw Hill Education, New York (2016)

11. Karim, N., Hasan, J., Ali, S.: Heart rate variability - a review. J. Basic Appl. Sci. **7**, 71–77 (2011)

12. Sao, P., Hegadi, R., Karmakar, S.: ECG signal analysis using artificial neural network. Int. J. Sci. Res. (IJSR), 82–86 (2015)

13. Patel, M., Lal, S.K.L., Kavanagh, D., Rossiter, P.: Applying neural network analysis on heart rate variability data to assess driver fatigue. Expert. Syst. Appl. Int. J. **38**, 7235–7242 (2011)

14. Asl, B., Setarehdan, S., Mohebbi, M.: Support vector machine-based arrhythmia classification using reduced features of heart rate variability signal. Artif. Intell. Med. **44**, 51–64 (2008)

15. Liu, N., Holcomb, J., Wade, C., Darrah, M., Salinas, J.: Utility of vital signs, Heart rate variability and complexity, and machine learning for identifying the need for lifesaving interventions in trauma patients. Shock (Augusta, GA) **42**, 108–114 (2014)

16. Polar: Technical specifications. Polar H10 Heart Rate Sensor. https://support.polar.com/e_manuals/H10_HR_sensor/Polar_H10_user_manual_English/Content/Technical-Specifications.htm. Accessed 26 May 2018

17. Gimeno-Blanes, F.J., Rojo-Álvarez, J.L., Caamaño, A.J., Flores-Yepes, J.A., García-Alberola, A.: On the feasibility of tilt test outcome early prediction using ECG and pressure parameters. EURASIP J. Adv. Signal Process. 33 (2011)

18. Mirescu, S., Harden, S.: Nonlinear dynamics methods for assessing heart rate variability in patients with recent myocardial infarction. Rom. J. Biophys. **22**, 117–124 (2016)

19. Mazzuco, A., et al.: Relationship between linear and nonlinear dynamics of heart rate and impairment of lung function in COPD patients. Int. J. Chronic Obstr. Pulm. Dis. **10**, 1651–1661 (2015)

20. Task Force of the European Society of Cardiology and the North American Society of Pacing and Electrophysiology: Heart rate variability: standards of measurement, physiological interpretation and clinical use. Eur. Hear. J. **17**, 354–381. (1996)

21. Zhao, J., Mucaki, E., Rogan, P.: Predicting ionizing radiation exposure using biochemically-inspired genomic machine learning. F1000Research **7**, 233 (2018)

22. He, Z.: 4 - Phosphorylation site prediction. In: Data Mining for Bioinformatics Applications, pp. 29–37 (2015)

High-Resolution Generative Adversarial Neural Networks Applied to Histological Images Generation

Antoni Mauricio[1]($\boxtimes$)(iD), Jorge López[1](iD), Roger Huauya[2](iD), and Jose Diaz[2]($\boxtimes$)(iD)

[1] Research and Innovation Center in Computer Science,
Universidad Católica San Pablo, Arequipa, Peru
{manasses.mauricio,jorge.lopez.caceres}@ucsp.edu.pe
[2] Artificial Intelligence, Image Processing and Robotic Lab,
Department of Mechanical Engineering, Universidad Nacional de Ingeniería,
Bldg. A - Off. A1-221, 210 Túpac Amaru Ave., Lima, Peru
rhuauyam@uni.pe, jcdiazrosado@uni.edu.pe

Abstract. For many years, synthesizing photo-realistic images has been a highly relevant task due to its multiple applications from aesthetic or artistic [19] to medical purposes [1,6,21]. Related to the medical area, this application has had greater impact because most classification or diagnostic algorithms require a significant amount of highly specialized images for their training yet obtaining them is not easy at all. To solve this problem, many works analyze and interpret images of a specific topic in order to obtain a statistical correlation between the variables that define it. By this way, any set of variables close to the map generated in the previous analysis represents a similar image. Deep learning based methods have allowed the automatic extraction of feature maps which has helped in the design of more robust models photo-realistic image synthesis. This work focuses on obtaining the best feature maps for automatic generation of synthetic histological images. To do so, we propose a Generative Adversarial Networks (GANs) [8] to generate the new sample distribution using the feature maps obtained by an autoencoder [14,20] as latent space instead of a completely random one. To corroborate our results, we present the generated images against the real ones and their respective results using different types of autoencoder to obtain the feature maps.

Keywords: Generative Adversarial Nets · Histological images
High-resolution generated images

The present work was supported by grant 234-2015-FONDECYT (Master Program) from Cienciactiva of the National Council for Science, Technology and Technological Innovation (CONCYTEC-PERU), the Office of Research of Universidad Nacional de Ingeniería (VRI - UNI) and the research management office (OGI - UNI).

© Springer Nature Switzerland AG 2018
V. Kůrková et al. (Eds.): ICANN 2018, LNCS 11140, pp. 195–202, 2018.
https://doi.org/10.1007/978-3-030-01421-6_20

1 Introduction

Since its conception, the focus of deep learning has been to design high hierarchy architectures which extract the best feature maps to represent probability distributions over many kinds of data (images, audio, texts, etc.) [2]. This approach has been successful for applications related to discriminative models because feature maps are obtained to maximize the separation between labeled or segregated groups in high-dimensional space. Hence, feature maps extraction is associated with the discrimination process instead of prioritizing a precise representation of the data [5,15]. On the other hand, deep generative models have generated high impacts, since a few years ago, and several works [9,14,17,19,21] have overcome the most significant problems that involved them. Goodfellow et al. [8] proposed a generative model based on adversarial training, known as GAN, which overcame the approximation of intractable probabilistic computations arising in maximum likelihood strategies, and the problem of leveraging piecewise linear units in generative context.

Evidently, GANs are among the hottest topics in Deep Learning currently, but synthesizing photo-realistic images is not an easy task. Images do not have a sequential correspondence but spatial correspondence, so it is normal that edges have generation and continuity errors because GANs include a discriminator D that competes against the generator G and ideally they tie or G wins, however in practice D usually wins which implies that the feature maps obtained in the generation are more linked to D than to G. To overcome this problem, several works have proposed improvements over the original pipeline including regularization [16], re-defining cost function [17] and setting a convenient latent space [11,13].

This work is based on the improvements proposed by several authors regarding the common problems of the GAN regarding the synthesis of photo-realistic images. Our proposal is to improve the quality of the generated images using a Teacher-Network based on autoencoders to obtain a suitable latent space. Finally the results using pre-trained latent spaces are visualized in order to evaluate their relevance. We use histological images as dataset because they are used as reference for detection and diagnostic applications [1,10,12,18].

2 Proposed Approach

In the following, we describe the background techniques and methods, and provide further details on the proposed approach.

2.1 Generative Adversarial Networks

Generative adversarial networks [8] allow to model complex databases like a resampling function, to do so a generative network G is pitted against an adversary which is a discriminative network D. The discriminator model, $D(x)$, learns to determine whether a sample x came from $G(z)$ or from the original training data while the generator model, $G(z)$, maps samples z from the prior $p(z)$ to the data space and trains to maximally confuse $D(x)$ by leveraging the gradient and using that to modify its parameters, this interaction establishes a min-max adversarial game between $G(z)$ and $D(x)$. The solution to this game is expressed as following considering $V(D, G)$ as the value function:

$$min_G max_D V(D, G) = E_{x \sim P_{data}}[log(D(x))] + E_{z \sim P(z)}[log(1 - D(G(z)))] \quad (1)$$

G and D alternate the SGD training in two stages: (**1**) Train D to distinguish the true samples from the fake samples generated by G. (**2**) Train G so as to fool D with its generated samples.

In practice, Eq. 1 does not provide enough gradient for G to learn. Therefore, at the beginning of the learning process G generates poor results and D rejects z with high confidence, since z is clearly fake.

2.2 Autoencoders

An autoencoder (AE) is an unsupervised neural network that learns the probability distribution of a dataset by setting the target values equal to the inputs. In other words, it tries to learn the function $F_{W,b}(x) \sim x$ that resembles the identity function. An autoencoder has two parts: an encoder network $h = f(x)$ and a decoder network $r = g(h)$. According to Goodfellow et al. [7], autoencoders learn to generate compact representations and reconstruct their inputs well, but they are fairly limited for most of the important applications. Autoencoders latent space may not be continuous and does not allow easy interpolation, which is a big problem considering knowledge representation spaces normally have discontinuities.

Similar to GANs case, there are many variations done over the original autoencoders architecture. Doersch et al. [5] presented variational autoencoders (VAEs) as an unsupervised learning solution for complicated distributions. VAEs work well for both feature extraction and generative modeling; their latent spaces are continuous allowing easy random sampling and interpolation. Likewise, Makhzani et al. [15] proposed an adversarial autoencoder (AAEs) which is a probabilistic autoencoder improved to perform variational inference by matching the posterior encoded features, from the autoencoder, with an arbitrary prior distribution, from the GAN. AS Hitawala [9] mentions, the AAEs are trained using a dual cost function, a reconstruction error criteria and an adversarial training function that matches the aggregated posterior distribution of the latent space to an arbitrary prior distribution.

3   Related Studies

Synthesizing photo-realistic images has allowed to explore new solutions based on computer-aided diagnosis (CAD) [1,3,6,21]. Calimeri et al. [3] applies a GAN to synthesize MRI images of brain slices considering visual resolution improved by a Laplacian Pyramid in order to avoid contrast loss. Zhang et al. [21] combines GAN with wide-field light microscopy to achieve deep learning super-resolution. Finally, [21] achieved synthesize many high-quality images. Tom et al. [18] proposed a stacked GAN for the fast simulation of patho-realistic ultrasound images refining synthesized ones from an initial simulation performed with a pseudo B-model ultrasound image generator.

On the other hand, Coates et al. [4] mentions that several simple factors, such as the number of hidden nodes in the model, may be more important achieving high performance than the learning algorithm or the depth of the model. The feature learning is a high-level specialized set of algorithms that prioritizes the descriptors or feature maps over hierarchy or complexity of the learning model. Hitawala et al. [9] compares different models and improvements based on GAN, but adversarial autoencoders, in particular, lets us appreciate the impact of an adequate selection of latent space, respect to other improvements made based on the architecture. Considering feature maps as latent space, Kumar et al. [13] mentions that semi-supervised learning methods using GANs have shown promising empirical success. To do so, [13] uses the inverse mapping (the encoder) which improves semantically the reconstructed sample with the input sample and analyze the relationship between the number of fake samples and the efficiency in semi-supervised learning using GANs.

4   Experimental Analysis

4.1   Dataset Description

The dataset consists of 670 RGB segmented nuclei images and their respective masks. The images were acquired for Kaggle competition "Data Science Bowl 2018 - Find the nuclei in divergent images to advance medical discovery"[1] under a variety of conditions and cell types, magnification, and imaging modality (brightfield vs. fluorescence) (Fig. 1).

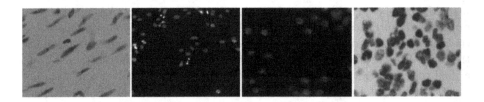

Fig. 1. Original images from Data Science Bowl 2018 - "Find the nuclei in divergent images to advance medical discovery" hosted by kaggle

---

[1] https://www.kaggle.com/c/data-science-bowl-2018/data.

In order to increase the dataset for training, we apply many classical methods of data augmentation: divide into 9 sub-images and random rotations.

4.2   Experiments

To run experiments, we used a PC with the following settings: 3,6 GHz Intel Core i7 processor, 16 GB 3000 MHz DDR4 memory and NVIDIA GTX 1070 and for the implementation we used Pytorch-0.4.0. Framework.

Our model consists on transferring the feature maps obtained from an autoencoder as the latent space of a GAN to improve its resolution in image generation. For this, it is necessary to consider a parallel training. The autoencoder trains to represent a feature map as close as possible to the dataset, while the GAN specializes in performing the generation. For a fast implementation, we used the Pytorch tutorials for autoencoders and GANs using MNIST dataset as reference[2]. To test our model and evaluate the impact of pre-trained feature maps, the synthetic images are processed in a new pre-trained discriminator specialized on nuclei detection[3].

Table 1 shows the results (acceptance ratio r_a of synthetic images) achieved by the pre-trained discriminator using a simple autoencoder (AE), a variational autoencoder (VAE) and the classic GAN model as feature maps generator. To consider that a sample meets similar standards like the original ones, it is taken into account how many nuclei it has based on the original images statistics and how good it looks considering the originals.

Table 1. Statistics of the generated groups of images respect to the originals

Dataset	μ	r_a
Original	7.20	-
GAN-AE	5.32	0.737
GAN-VAE	5.91	0.843
GAN	3.44	0.522

As Table 1 shows, the best statistical results and acceptance ratio are obtained using a VAE as the feature maps generator. Visually, Figs. 2 and 3 present the results for the classic GAN and VAE-GAN model respectively.

---

[2] https://github.com/MorvanZhou/PyTorch-Tutorial.
[3] https://github.com/aksharkkumar/nuclei-detection.

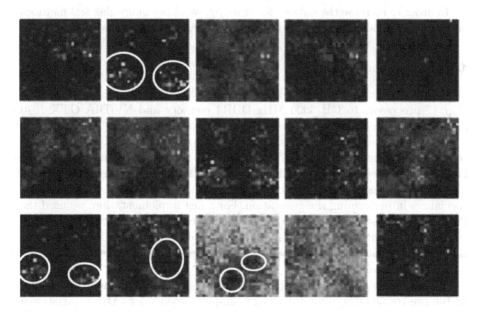

Fig. 2. Synthetic results using a simple GAN architecture. Detected nuclei in generated images are inside white circles

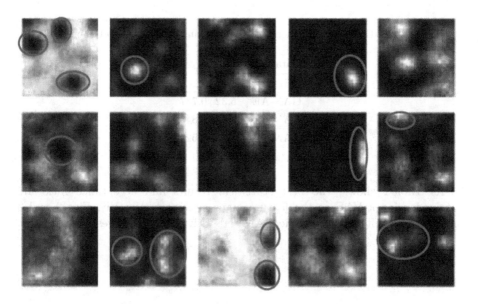

Fig. 3. Synthetic results using pre-trained feature maps from a VAE as latent space. Detected nuclei in generated images are inside red circles (Color figure online)

5   Conclusions and Future Works

After the tests we carried out, it is concluded that the feature maps are essential to adequately describe any dataset and in turn the detail of description depends on the cost functions that define the main task. To synthesize images, a considerable improvement is observed (greater than 0.2) by correctly defining the feature map which is used as a latent space in GAN model. From that point, the improvements become less and less noticeable for the VAE, but leave open two direct future jobs. First, improving the resolution of synthetic images using the RS-GAN or LAP-GAN cost function. Second, exploring more deeply the usefulness of feature maps as well as evaluate their quality inside more complex learning structures.

References

1. Asperti, A., Mastronardo, C.: The effectiveness of data augmentation for detection of gastrointestinal diseases from endoscopical images. arXiv preprint arXiv:1712.03689 (2017)
2. Bengio, Y.: Learning deep architectures for AI. Found. Trends® Mach. Learn. **2**(1), 1–127 (2009)
3. Calimeri, F., Marzullo, A., Stamile, C., Terracina, G.: Biomedical data augmentation using generative adversarial neural networks. In: Lintas, A., Rovetta, S., Verschure, P.F.M.J., Villa, A.E.P. (eds.) ICANN 2017. LNCS, vol. 10614, pp. 626–634. Springer, Cham (2017). https://doi.org/10.1007/978-3-319-68612-7_71
4. Coates, A., Ng, A., Lee, H.: An analysis of single-layer networks in unsupervised feature learning. In: Proceedings of the Fourteenth International Conference on Artificial Intelligence and Statistics, pp. 215–223 (2011)
5. Doersch, C.: Tutorial on variational autoencoders. arXiv preprint arXiv:1606.05908 (2016)
6. Eaton-Rosen, Z., Bragman, F., Ourselin, S., Cardoso, M.J.: Improving data augmentation for medical image segmentation (2018)
7. Goodfellow, I., Bengio, Y., Courville, A., Bengio, Y.: Deep Learning, vol. 1. MIT press, Cambridge (2016)
8. Goodfellow, I., et al.: Generative adversarial nets. In: Advances in Neural Information Processing Systems, pp. 2672–2680 (2014)
9. Hitawala, S.: Comparative study on generative adversarial networks. arXiv preprint arXiv:1801.04271 (2018)
10. Hou, L., et al.: Sparse autoencoder for unsupervised nucleus detection and representation in histopathology images. arXiv preprint arXiv:1704.00406 (2017)
11. Kastaniotis, D., Ntinou, I., Tsourounis, D., Economou, G., Fotopoulos, S.: Attention-aware generative adversarial networks (ATA-GANs). arXiv preprint arXiv:1802.09070 (2018)
12. Komura, D., Ishikawa, S.: Machine learning methods for histopathological image analysis. Comput. Struct. Biotechnol. J. **16**, 34–42 (2018)
13. Kumar, A., Sattigeri, P., Fletcher, T.: Semi-supervised learning with GANs: manifold invariance with improved inference. In: Advances in Neural Information Processing Systems, pp. 5534–5544 (2017)

14. Lai, W.S., Huang, J.B., Ahuja, N., Yang, M.H.: Deep Laplacian pyramid networks for fast and accurate superresolution. In: IEEE Conference on Computer Vision and Pattern Recognition, vol. 2, p. 5 (2017)
15. Makhzani, A., Shlens, J., Jaitly, N., Goodfellow, I., Frey, B.: Adversarial autoencoders. arXiv preprint arXiv:1511.05644 (2015)
16. Miyato, T., Kataoka, T., Koyama, M., Yoshida, Y.: Spectral normalization for generative adversarial networks. arXiv preprint arXiv:1802.05957 (2018)
17. Song, J., Zhao, S., Ermon, S.: A-NICE-MC: adversarial training for MCMC. In: Advances in Neural Information Processing Systems, pp. 5140–5150 (2017)
18. Tom, F., Sheet, D.: Simulating patho-realistic ultrasound images using deep generative networks with adversarial learning. In: 2018 IEEE 15th International Symposium on Biomedical Imaging (ISBI 2018), pp. 1174–1177. IEEE (2018)
19. Van Den Oord, A., Kalchbrenner, N., Espeholt, L., Vinyals, O., Graves, A., et al.: Conditional image generation with PixelCNN decoders. In: Advances in Neural Information Processing Systems, pp. 4790–4798 (2016)
20. Vincent, P., Larochelle, H., Lajoie, I., Bengio, Y., Manzagol, P.A.: Stacked denoising autoencoders: learning useful representations in a deep network with a local denoising criterion. J. Mach. Learn. Res. **11**, 3371–3408 (2010)
21. Zhang, H., Xie, X., Fang, C., Yang, Y., Jin, D., Fei, P.: High-throughput, high-resolution generated adversarial network microscopy. arXiv preprint arXiv:1801.07330 (2018)

Kernel

Tensor Learning in Multi-view Kernel PCA

Lynn Houthuys$^{(\boxtimes)}$ and Johan A. K. Suykens

Department of Electrical Engineering ESAT-STADIUS, KU Leuven, Kasteelpark,
Arenberg 10, 3001 Leuven, Belgium
{lynn.houthuys,johan.suykens}@esat.kuleuven.be

Abstract. In many real-life applications data can be described through multiple representations, or views. Multi-view learning aims at combining the information from all views, in order to obtain a better performance. Most well-known multi-view methods optimize some form of correlation between two views, while in many applications there are three or more views available. This is usually tackled by optimizing the correlations pairwise. However, this ignores the higher-order correlations that could only be discovered when exploring all views simultaneously. This paper proposes novel multi-view Kernel PCA models. By introducing a model tensor, the proposed models aim to include the higher-order correlations between all views. The paper further explores the use of these models as multi-view dimensionality reduction techniques and shows experimental results on several real-life datasets. These experiments demonstrate the merit of the proposed methods.

Keywords: Kernel PCA · Multi-view learning · Tensor learning

1 Introduction

Principal component analysis (PCA) [12] is an unsupervised learning technique that transforms the initial space to a lower dimensional subspace while maintaining as much information as possible. The technique is wildly used in applications like dimensionality reduction, denoising and pattern recognition. PCA consist of taking the eigenvectors corresponding to the n_p largest eigenvalues, also known as the *principal components*, of the covariance matrix of a dataset, which span a subspace that retains the maximum variance of the dataset. For dimensionality reduction these principal components make up the lower dimensional dataset, and thus the new dimension equals n_p.

Several nonlinear extensions to PCA were proposed. One well-known extension is kernel PCA (KPCA) [21]. Instead of working on the data directly, it first applies a, possibly nonlinear, transformation on the data that maps the input data to a high-dimensional feature space.

In multi-view learning the input data is described through multiple representations or *views*. A dataset could for example consist of images and the associated captions [14], video clips could be classified based on image as well as audio

© Springer Nature Switzerland AG 2018
V. Kůrková et al. (Eds.): ICANN 2018, LNCS 11140, pp. 205–215, 2018.
https://doi.org/10.1007/978-3-030-01421-6_21

features [13], news stories could be covered by multiple sources [7], and so on. Multi-view learning has been applied in numerous applications both as supervised [3,28] and unsupervised [2,4] learning schemes. Multi-view dimensionality reduction reduces the multi-view dataset to a lower dimensional subspace to compactly represent the heterogeneous data, where each datapoint in the newly formed subspace is associated with multiple views. Dimensionality reduction is often beneficial for the learning process, especially when the data contains some sort of noise [6,8].

Most multi-view methods optimize a certain correlation between variables of two views. For example, in CCA [10] the correlation between the score variables is maximized, and in Multi-view LS-SVM [11] the product of the error variables is minimized. In real-world applications, however, data is often described through three views or more. This is usually accounted for by optimizing the sum of the pairwise correlations between different views. Due to this approach, higher-order correlations that could only be discovered by simultaneously considering all views, are ignored. This issue was pointed out by Luo et al. [16], where the authors propose an extension to CCA, called Tensor CCA, that analyzes a covariance tensor over the data from all views. The model is formed by performing a tensor decomposition, which has a computational cost that is significantly higher than the cost of regular CCA. This idea of including tensor learning is presented in Fig. 1.

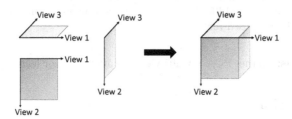

Fig. 1. An example with three views to motivate tensor learning in multi-view learning. (left) The standard coupling: only the pairwise correlations between the views are taken into account. (right) The tensor approach: the higher-order correlations between all views are modeled in a third order tensor.

Tensor learning in machine learning methods has been studied before. For example, Signoretto et al. [22] propose a tensor-based framework to perform learning when the data is multi-linear and Wimalawarne et al. [27] collect the weight vectors corresponding to separate tasks in one weight tensor to achieve multi-task learning.

This paper investigates the use of tensor learning in multi-view KPCA, in order to include the higher-order correlations. The paper proposes three multi-view KPCA methods, where the first two are special cases of the last method. Experiments, where the multi-view KPCA methods are used to reduce the dimensionality for clustering purposes, show the merit of our proposed methods.

We will denote matrices as bold uppercase letters, vectors as bold lowercase letters and higher-order tensors by calligraphic letters. The superscript $^{[v]}$ will denote the vth view for the multi-view method. Whereas the superscript $^{(j)}$ will correspond to the jth principal component.

2   Kernel PCA

Suykens et al. [26] formulated the kernel PCA problem in the primal-dual framework typical of Least Squares Support Vector Machines (LS-SVM) [25], where the dual problem is equivalent to the original kernel PCA formulation of Schölkopf et al. [21]. An advantage of the primal-dual framework is that it allows to perform estimations in the primal space, which can be used for large-scale applications when solving the dual problem becomes infeasible. The formulation further provides an out-of-sample extension to deal with new unseen test data.

Suykens [24] later formulated the kernel PCA in the Restricted Kernel Machines (RKM) framework, which preserves the advantages of the previous formulation. The primal and dual model are formed by means of conjugate feature duality, and give an expression in terms of visible and hidden layers respectively, in analogy with Restricted Boltzmann Machines (RBM) [9]. The dual problem is equivalent to the LS-SVM formulation (and hence the original formulation) up to a parameter. Furthermore it is shown how multiple RKMs can be coupled to form a Deep RKM, which combines deep learning with kernel based methods.

Given data $\{\mathbf{x}_k\}_{k=1}^N \subset \mathbb{R}^d$, the primal formulation of KPCA in the RKM framework is as follows:

$$\min_{\mathbf{w}, h_k} \quad \frac{\eta}{2}\mathbf{w}^T\mathbf{w} - \sum_{k=1}^N \varphi(\mathbf{x}_k)^T \mathbf{w}\, h_k + \frac{\lambda}{2}\sum_{k=1}^N h_k^2 \tag{1}$$

for $k = 1, \ldots, N$. The feature map $\varphi(\cdot) : \mathbb{R}^d \to \mathbb{R}^{d_h}$ maps the input data to a high-dimensional (possible infinite) feature space. λ and η are positive regularization constants and the hidden features h_k correspond to the projected values. The dual problem related to this primal formulation is:

$$\frac{1}{\eta}\boldsymbol{\Omega}\, \mathbf{h} = \lambda\, \mathbf{h} \tag{2}$$

where $\mathbf{h} = [h_1; \ldots; h_N]$ and $\boldsymbol{\Omega} \in \mathbb{R}^{N \times N}$ is a centered kernel matrix defined as

$$\Omega_{kl} = \left(\varphi(\mathbf{x}_k) - \hat{\boldsymbol{\mu}}\right)^T \left(\varphi(\mathbf{x}_l) - \hat{\boldsymbol{\mu}}\right), \quad k, l = 1, \ldots, N \tag{3}$$

with $\hat{\boldsymbol{\mu}} = (1/N)\sum_{k=1}^N \varphi(\mathbf{x}_k)$. The feature map $\varphi(\cdot)$ is usually not explicitly defined, but rather through a positive definite kernel function $K : \mathbb{R}^d \times \mathbb{R}^d \to \mathbb{R}$. Based on Mercer's condition [20] we can formulate the kernel function as $K(\mathbf{x}_k, \mathbf{x}_l) = \varphi(\mathbf{x}_k)^T\varphi(\mathbf{x}_l)$.

Every eigenvalue-eigenvector pair $(\lambda - \mathbf{h})$ can be seen as a candidate solution of Eq. (1). The first principal component, i.e. the direction of maximal variance in the feature space, is determined by the eigenvector corresponding to the highest eigenvalue of $\frac{1}{\eta}\boldsymbol{\Omega}$. The maximum number of components that can be extracted equals the number of datapoints N.

For an unseen test point $\mathbf{x}$, the projection into the subspace spanned by the jth principal component, i.e. the *score variable* $\hat{e}(\mathbf{x})^{(j)}$, can be obtained as

$$\hat{e}(\mathbf{x})^{(j)} = \frac{1}{\eta}\boldsymbol{\Omega}_{\text{test}}\mathbf{h}^{(j)} \tag{4}$$

where $\mathbf{h}^{(j)}$ is the eigenvector corresponding to the jth largest eigenvalue λ and $\boldsymbol{\Omega}_{\text{test}}$ is the centered test kernel matrix calculated through the kernel function $K(\mathbf{x}_k, \mathbf{x}) = \varphi(\mathbf{x}_k)^T\varphi(\mathbf{x})$ for all $k = 1, \ldots, N$.

If KPCA is used to perform dimensionality reduction, the new dimension of the data equals the number of selected components n_p.

3   Multi-view Kernel Principal Component Analysis

In this section we conceive a KPCA model when the data is described through different representations, or *views*. Instead of coupling the different views pairwise, we formulate an overall model so that also higher order correlations between the different views are considered.

3.1   KPCA-ADD: Adding Kernel Matrices

A first model, called KPCA-ADD, is formed by adding up the different KPCA objectives and assuming that all views share the same hidden features $\mathbf{h}$.

Let V be the number of views, given data $\{\mathbf{x}_k^{[v]}\}_{k=1}^N \subset \mathbb{R}^{d^{[v]}}$ the primal formulation is stated as follows:

$$\min_{\mathbf{w}^{[v]}, h_k} \frac{\eta}{2}\sum_{v=1}^V \mathbf{w}^{[v]^T}\mathbf{w}^{[v]} - \sum_{v=1}^V\sum_{k=1}^N \varphi^{[v]}(\mathbf{x}_k^{[v]})^T\mathbf{w}^{[v]}\, h_k + \frac{\lambda}{2}\sum_{k=1}^N h_k^2 \tag{5}$$

The stationary points of this objective function, denoted as $\mathcal{J}$, in the primal formulation are characterized by:

$$\begin{cases} \dfrac{\partial\mathcal{J}}{\partial h_k} = 0 \rightarrow \lambda h_k = \displaystyle\sum_{v=1}^V \mathbf{w}^{[v]^T}\varphi^{[v]}(\mathbf{x}_k^{[v]}), \\[2ex] \dfrac{\partial\mathcal{J}}{\partial\mathbf{w}^{[v]}} = 0 \rightarrow \mathbf{w}^{[v]} = \dfrac{1}{\eta}\displaystyle\sum_{k=1}^N \varphi^{[v]}(\mathbf{x}_k^{[v]})h_k, \\[2ex] \qquad\text{where } k = 1, \ldots, N \text{ and } v = 1, \ldots, V. \end{cases} \tag{6}$$

By eliminating the weights $\mathbf{w}^{[v]}$, the dual formulation is obtained:

$$\frac{1}{\eta}\left(\boldsymbol{\Omega}^{[1]} + \ldots + \boldsymbol{\Omega}^{[V]}\right)\mathbf{h} = \lambda\,\mathbf{h} \tag{7}$$

where $\boldsymbol{\Omega}^{[v]}$ is the centered kernel matrix corresponding to view v, defined as $\Omega_{kl}^{[v]} = \left(\varphi^{[v]}(\mathbf{x}_k^{[v]}) - \hat{\boldsymbol{\mu}}^{[v]}\right)^T \left(\varphi^{[v]}(\mathbf{x}_l^{[v]}) - \hat{\boldsymbol{\mu}}^{[v]}\right)$ for $k, l = 1, \ldots, N$.

Notice that this coupling results in adding up the kernel matrices belonging to the different views.

The score variables corresponding to a test point $\mathbf{x}$ can be calculated by:

$$\hat{e}(\mathbf{x})^{(j)} = \frac{1}{\eta} \sum_{v=1}^{V} \boldsymbol{\Omega}_{\text{test}}^{[v]} \mathbf{h}^{(j)}. \tag{8}$$

4 Including Tensor Learning in Multi-view KPCA

Even though in the KPCA-ADD formulation the views are coupled by the shared hidden features, there is still a model weight vector $\mathbf{w}^{[v]} \in \mathbb{R}^{d_h^{[v]}}$ for each view v. In order to introduce more coupling, a model tensor $\mathcal{W} \in \mathbb{R}^{d_h^{[1]} \times \ldots \times d_h^{[V]}}$ is presented. By using a tensor comprised of the weights of all views, instead of coupling them pairwise, it becomes possible to model higher order correlations.

4.1 KPCA-PROD: Product of Kernel Matrices

The introduction of a model tensor $\mathcal{W}$ leads to the KPCA-PROD model, where the primal formulation is given by:

$$\min_{\mathcal{W}, h_k} \quad \frac{\eta}{2}\langle \mathcal{W}, \mathcal{W} \rangle - \sum_{k=1}^{N}\langle \Phi_{(k)}, \mathcal{W} \rangle \, h_k + \frac{\lambda}{2}\sum_{k=1}^{N} h_k^2 \tag{9}$$

where $\langle \cdot, \cdot \rangle$ is the tensor inner product defined as

$$\langle \mathcal{A}, \mathcal{B} \rangle := \sum_{i_1=1}^{I_1} \cdots \sum_{i_M=1}^{I_M} \mathcal{A}_{i_1 \cdots i_M} \mathcal{B}_{i_1 \cdots i_M} \tag{10}$$

for two M-th order tensors $\mathcal{A}, \mathcal{B} \in \mathbb{R}^{I_1 \times \ldots \times I_M}$. The rank-1 tensor $\Phi_{(k)} \in \mathbb{R}^{d_h^{[1]} \times \ldots \times d_h^{[V]}}$ is composed by the outer product of the feature maps of all views, i.e. $\Phi_{(k)} = \varphi^{[1]}(x_k^{[1]}) \otimes \ldots \otimes \varphi^{[V]}(x_k^{[V]})$.

The stationary points of the objective function $\mathcal{J}$ in the primal formulation are characterized by:

$$\begin{cases} \dfrac{\partial \mathcal{J}}{\partial h_k} = 0 \rightarrow \lambda h_k = \langle \Phi_{(k)}, \mathcal{W} \rangle = \sum_{i_1=1}^{d_h^{[1]}} \cdots \sum_{i_V=1}^{d_h^{[V]}} \varphi^{[1]}(\mathbf{x}_k^{[1]})_{i_1} \cdots \varphi^{[V]}(\mathbf{x}_k^{[V]})_{i_V} \mathcal{W}_{i_1 \ldots i_V} \\[2ex] \dfrac{\partial \mathcal{J}}{\partial \mathcal{W}_{i_1 \ldots i_V}} = 0 \rightarrow \mathcal{W}_{i_1 \ldots i_V} = \dfrac{1}{\eta} \sum_{k=1}^{N} \varphi^{[1]}(\mathbf{x}_k^{[1]})_{i_1} \cdots \varphi^{[V]}(\mathbf{x}_k^{[V]})_{i_V} h_k, \\[2ex] \qquad \text{where } k = 1, \ldots, N \text{ and } i_v = 1, \ldots, d_h^{[v]} \text{ for } v = 1, \ldots, V. \end{cases}$$
$$\tag{11}$$

By eliminating the weights, the following dual problem is derived:

$$\frac{1}{\eta} \left(\Omega^{[1]} \odot \ldots \odot \Omega^{[V]} \right) \mathbf{h} = \lambda \, \mathbf{h} \qquad (12)$$

where $\odot$ denotes the element-wise product. Notice that the dual problem results in element-wise multiplication of the view-specific kernel matrices.

The score variable corresponding to an unseen test point $\mathbf{x}$ can hence be calculated by:

$$\hat{e}(\mathbf{x})^{(j)} = \frac{1}{\eta} \bigodot_{v=1}^{V} \Omega_{\text{test}}^{[v]} \mathbf{h}^{(j)} \qquad (13)$$

where $\bigodot$ is the element-wise multiplication operator.

4.2 KPCA-ADDPROD

Taking the element-wise product of kernel matrices can have some unwanted results. Take for example kernel matrices comprised of linear kernel functions. An element of such a linear kernel matrix could be negative, indicating a low similarity between two points. By multiplying the elements of the kernel matrices, highly negative values could result in a high positive value for a certain datapoint pair, which would indicate a very high similarity which is clearly unwanted. Even for kernel matrices comprised of RBF kernel functions, where the values lie between zero and one, a poor view indicating a certain datapoint pair as non-similar and hence assigning a value close to zero, could influence the final result to harshly.

Therefore a last model is proposed, called KPCA-ADDPROD, where the two principles of the previous models are combined. A parameter ρ is added in order to determine the influence of each part. The primal formulation is given by:

$$\min_{\mathcal{W}, \mathbf{w}^{[v]}, h_k} \quad \frac{\eta}{2} \langle \mathcal{W}, \mathcal{W} \rangle - \sqrt{\rho} \sum_{k=1}^{N} \langle \Phi_{(k)}, \mathcal{W} \rangle \, h_k + \frac{\lambda}{2} \sum_{k=1}^{N} h_k^2$$
$$+ \frac{\eta}{2} \sum_{v=1}^{V} \mathbf{w}^{[v]^T} \mathbf{w}^{[v]} - \sqrt{(1-\rho)} \sum_{v=1}^{V} \sum_{k=1}^{N} \varphi^{[v]}(\mathbf{x}_k^{[v]})^T \mathbf{w}^{[v]} h_k \qquad (14)$$

where $\rho \in [0,1] \subset \mathbb{R}$. By deriving the stationary points of the objective and eliminating the weights, the following dual problem is obtained:

$$\frac{1}{\eta} \left((1-\rho) \sum_{v=1}^{V} \Omega^{[v]} + \rho \bigodot_{v=1}^{V} \Omega^{[v]} \right) \mathbf{h} = \lambda \, \mathbf{h}. \qquad (15)$$

Note that if $\rho = 0$ the model is equivalent to KPCA-ADD, and if $\rho = 1$ it is equivalent to KPCA-PROD.

5   Experiments

This section describes the experiments performed to evaluate the multi-view KPCA models, as dimensionality reduction techniques. To assess the performance, the KPCA methods are used as a preprocessing step for clustering, and the clustering accuracy is regarded as the evaluation criterion.

Two clustering methods are considered: k-means (KM) [18], a well known linear clustering algorithm and Kernel Spectral Clustering (KSC) [1], a nonlinear clustering technique within the LS-SVM framework. To determine the clustering accuracy, the NMI [23] is reported[1]. Due to the local optima solutions found by KM, these results are averaged over 50 runs.

The performances of the proposed multi-view models are compared to the performances on the views separately. Both by clustering the views directly, and by clustering after KPCA was performed.

Model Selection. The parameter η is set to 1 in all experiments, since this parameter is of most importance when multiple RKMs are stacked to form a deep RKM. The RBF kernel function was used for all experiments, both for the KPCA methods as for KSC. The performance of the (multi-view) KPCA models depend on the (view-specific) kernel parameter and the number of principal components n_p. For KPCA-ADDPROD it will also depend on the parameter ρ. Both KSC and KM depend on the number of clusters, and KSC also on the kernel parameter. These parameters are tuned through a grid search with 5-fold crossvalidation. Since the methods are all unsupervised, the model selection criteria has to be unsupervised as well. Here the Davies-Bouldin index (DB) [5] criterion is used.

Datasets. A brief description of each dataset used is given here:

- **Image-caption dataset:** A dataset comprised of images, together with their associated captions. We thank the authors of [14] for providing the dataset. Each image-caption pair represent a figure related to sport, aviation or paintball. For each of these categories, 400 records are available. The first two views consist of different features describing the image (HSV colour and image Gabor texture). The third view describes the associated caption text by its term frequencies. Gaussian white noise is added to the first two views.
- **YouTube Video dataset:** A dataset describing YouTube videos of video gaming, was originally proposed by Madani et al. [19][2]. The videos are described through textual, visual and auditory features. For this paper we selected the textual feature LDA, the visual Motion feature through CIPD [29] and the audio feature MFCC [17] as three views. From each of the seven

---

[1] To calculate the NMI, and hence asses the performance, the labels of the dataset are used. However, notice that they are never used in the training or validation phase of KM, KSC or the proposed multi-view KPCA models.

[2] http://archive.ics.uci.edu/ml/datasets/youtube+multiview+video+games+dataset.

most occurring labels (excluding the last label, since these datapoints represent videos not belonging to any of the other 30 classes) 300 videos were randomly sampled.

- **UCI Ads dataset:** This dataset, as described by Kushmerick [15][3], was constructed for the task of predicting whether a certain hyperlink corresponds to an advertisement or not. The features are divided over three views in the same way as was done by Luo et al. [16]. The dataset consist of 2821 instances not corresponding to advertisements, and 458 instances that do.

Results. The results of the performed experiments are depicted in Table 1. The table shows the clustering accuracy found by using the clustering techniques on the views directly, and when KPCA was applied as a dimensionality reduction technique first. It further shows the accuracy when the proposed multi-view KPCA techniques are applied. For the KPCA-ADDPROD method, also the found optimal value for ρ is noted.

Table 1. NMI results, where the proposed methods function as dimensionality reduction methods for KM and KSC. The best performing methods, are indicated in bold.

Method	Image-caption			YouTube Video			Ads		
View	1	2	3	1	2	3	1	2	3
KM	0.502	0.301	0.206	**0.434**	0.200	0.052	0.068	0.028	0.071
KPCA+KM	0.516	0.328	0.412	0.375	0.207	0.065	0.016	0.021	0.047
KPCA-ADD+KM	0.596			0.273			0.016		
KPCA-PROD+KM	0.154			0.076			**0.291**		
KPCA-ADDPROD+KM	**0.643** $(\rho = 0.4)$			0.279 $(\rho = 0.2)$			**0.291** $(\rho = 1)$		
KSC	0.061	0.107	0.066	0.028	0.025	0.030	0.017	0.077	0.312
KPCA+KSC	0.474	0.330	0.295	0.243	0.167	0.037	0.013	0.094	0.046
KPCA-ADD+KSC	0.520			0.166			0.085		
KPCA-PROD+KSC	0.031			0.025			**0.147**		
KPCA-ADDPROD+KSC	**0.568** $(\rho = 0.4)$			**0.248** $(\rho = 0.2)$			**0.147** $(\rho = 1)$		

A first observation is that the performance usually improves when using KPCA as a dimensionality reduction method, when clustering the views separately. This encourages the use of dimensionality reduction in these datasets. A notable exception is the accuracy when using KM on the first view of the YouTube Video dataset.

A second observation is that the multi-view KPCA methods are able to improve the clustering accuracy in five out of the six experiments, suggesting the merit of using the multi-view techniques independently of the choice of clustering technique. Only for YouTube Video dataset, the (multi-view) dimensionality reduction is not able to improve the result of applying KM on the first

---

[3] http://archive.ics.uci.edu/ml/datasets/Internet+Advertisements.

view directly. Another interesting observation is that the found optimal ρ for each dataset is equal for both clustering methods. Since ρ determines the importance of the tensor model vector, this could be an indication of the number of relevant higher order correlations in a dataset. For the first two datasets ρ is relatively small. For these two datasets KPCA-ADD outperforms KPCA-PROD considerably, which is to be expected as it is shown that these two models are actually special cases of KPCA-ADDPROD with $\rho = 0$ and $\rho = 1$ respectively. For the Ads dataset the found optimal ρ equals 1, and hence only the tensor model vector is taken into account, suggesting a high importance of higher order correlations.

6 Conclusion

This paper introduced novel Multi-view Kernel Principal Component Analysis methods to perform KPCA when the data is represented by multiple views. Techniques from tensor learning are applied in order to account for higher order correlations between the views.

The paper starts from the primal RKM formulation of KPCA and shows three approaches for a multi-view extension. It is shown that, when assuming shared hidden features, the dual model results in kernel addition. It further shows that introducing a model tensor, containing the information of all views, results in kernel product in the dual formulation. Finally a third method is suggested combining the two techniques.

The gain of these multi-view techniques is shown by using it as a dimensionality reduction step before clustering. Experiments on multiple real-world datasets with two well known clustering techniques, show the improvement of using multiple views. The parameter controlling the importance of the model tensor seems to indicate the importance of the higher order correlations.

Acknowledgments.. Research supported by Research Council KUL: CoE PFV/10/002 (OPTEC), PhD/Postdoc grants Flemish Government; FWO: projects: G0A4917N (Deep restricted kernel machines), G.088114N (Tensor based data similarity), ERC Advanced Grant E-DUALITY (787960).

References

1. Alzate, C., Suykens, J.A.K.: Multiway spectral clustering with out-of-sample extensions through weighted kernel PCA. IEEE Trans. Pattern Anal. Mach. Intell. **32**(2), 335–347 (2010)
2. Andrew, G., Arora, R., Bilmes, J., Livescu, K.: Deep canonical correlation analysis. In: ICML, pp. 1247–1255 (2013)
3. Bekker, A., Shalhon, M., Greenspan, H., Goldberger, J.: Multi-view probabilistic classification of breast microcalcifications. IEEE Trans. Med. Imaging **35**(2), 645–653 (2016)
4. Blum, A., Mitchell, T.: Combining labeled and unlabeled data with co-training. In: COLT, pp. 92–100 (1998)

5. Davies, D.L., Bouldin, D.W.: A cluster separation measure. IEEE Trans. Pattern Anal. Mach. Intell. **1**(2), 224–227 (1979)
6. Foster, D.P., Kakade, S.M., Zhang, T.: Multi-view dimensionality reduction via canonical correlation analysis. Toyota Technical Institute-Chicago (2008)
7. Greene, D., Cunningham, P.: A matrix factorization approach for integrating multiple data views. In: Buntine, W., Grobelnik, M., Mladenić, D., Shawe-Taylor, J. (eds.) ECML PKDD 2009. LNCS (LNAI), vol. 5781, pp. 423–438. Springer, Heidelberg (2009). https://doi.org/10.1007/978-3-642-04180-8_45
8. Han, Y., Wu, F., Tao, D., Shao, J., Zhuang, Y., Jiang, J.: Sparse unsupervised dimensionality reduction for multiple view data. IEEE Trans. Circ. Syst. Video Technol. **22**(10), 1485–1496 (2012)
9. Hinton, G.E.: What kind of a graphical model is the brain? In: Proceedings of the 19th International Joint Conference on Artificial Intelligence, IJCAI 2005, pp. 1765–1775. Morgan Kaufmann Publishers Inc., San Francisco (2005)
10. Hotelling, H.: Relations between two sets of variates. Biometrica **28**, 321–377 (1936)
11. Houthuys, L., Langone, R., Suykens, J.A.K.: Multi-view least squares support vector machines classification. Neurocomputing **282**, 78–88 (2018)
12. Jolliffe, I.T.: Principal Component Analysis. Springer, New York (1986). https://doi.org/10.1007/978-1-4757-1904-8
13. Kidron, E., Schechner, Y.Y., Elad, M.: Pixels that sound. In: CVPR, vol. 1, pp. 88–95 (2005)
14. Kolenda, T., Hansen, L.K., Larsen, J., Winther, O.: Independent component analysis for understanding multimedia content. In: IEEE Workshop on Neural Networks for Signal Processing, vol. 12, pp. 757–766 (2002)
15. Kushmerick, N.: Learning to remove internet advertisements. In: AGENTS 1999, pp. 175–181 (1999)
16. Luo, Y., Tao, D., Ramamohanarao, K., Xu, C., Wen, Y.: Tensor canonical correlation analysis for multi-view dimension reduction. IEEE Trans. Knowl. Data Eng. **27**(11), 3111–3124 (2015)
17. Lyon, R.F., Rehn, M., Bengio, S., Walters, T.C., Chechik, G.: Sound retrieval and ranking using sparse auditory representations. Neural Comput. **22**(9), 2390–2416 (2010)
18. Macqueen, J.: Some methods for classification and analysis of multivariate observations. In: Berkeley Symposium on Mathematical Statistics and Probability, pp. 281–297 (1967)
19. Madani, O., Georg, M., Ross, D.A.: On using nearly-independent feature families for high precision and confidence. Mach. Learn. **92**, 457–477 (2013)
20. Mercer, J.: Functions of positive and negative type, and their connection with the theory of integral equations. Philos. Trans. R. Soc. London. Ser. A Contain. Pap. Math. Phys. Character **209**, 415–446 (1909)
21. Schölkopf, B., Smola, A., Müller, K.R.: Nonlinear component analysis as a kernel eigenvalue problem. Neural Comput. **10**(5), 1299–1319 (1998)
22. Signoretto, M., Tran Dinh, Q., De Lathauwer, L., Suykens, J.A.K.: Learning with tensors: a framework based on convex optimization and spectral regularization. Mach. Learn. **94**, 303–351 (2014)
23. Strehl, A., Ghosh, J.: Cluster ensembles - a knowledge reuse framework for combining multiple partitions. J. Mach. Learn. Res. **3**, 583–617 (2002)
24. Suykens, J.A.K.: Deep restricted kernel machines using conjugate feature duality. Neural Comput. **29**(8), 2123–2163 (2017)
25. Suykens, J.A.K., Van Gestel, T., De Brabanter, J., De Moor, B., Vandewalle, J.: Least Squares Support Vector Machines. World Scientific, Singapore (2002)

26. Suykens, J.A.K., Van Gestel, T., Vandewalle, J., De Moor, B.: A support vector machine formulation to PCA analysis and its kernel version. IEEE Trans. Neural Netw. **14**(2), 447–450 (2003)
27. Wimalawarne, K., Sugiyama, M., Tomioka, R.: Multitask learning meets tensor factorization: Task imputation via convex optimization. In: NIPS, vol. 4, pp. 2825–2833 (2014)
28. Wozniak, M., Jackowski, K.: Some remarks on chosen methods of classifier fusion based on weighted voting. In: Corchado, E., Wu, X., Oja, E., Herrero, Á., Baruque, B. (eds.) HAIS 2009. LNCS (LNAI), vol. 5572, pp. 541–548. Springer, Heidelberg (2009). https://doi.org/10.1007/978-3-642-02319-4_65
29. Yang, W., Toderici, G.: Discriminative tag learning on Youtube videos with latent sub-tags. In: CVPR, pp. 3217–3224 (2011)

Reinforcement

ACM: Learning Dynamic Multi-agent Cooperation via Attentional Communication Model

Xue Han[1], Hongping Yan[1(⊠)], Junge Zhang[2], and Lingfeng Wang[2]

[1] Department of Information Engineering, China University of Geosciences,
No. 29 College Road, Haidian District, Beijing, China
18801090174@163.com, yanhp@cugb.edu.cn
[2] Institute of Automation, Chinese Academy of Sciences,
No. 95 Zhongguancun East Road, Haidian District, Beijing, China
{jgzhang,lfwang}@nlpr.ia.ac.cn

Abstract. The collaboration of multiple agents is required in many real world applications, and yet it is a challenging task due to partial observability. Communication is a common scheme to resolve this problem. However, most of the communication protocols are manually specified and can not capture the dynamic interactions among agents. To address this problem, this paper presents a novel Attentional Communication Model (ACM) to achieve dynamic multi-agent cooperation. Firstly, we propose a new Cooperation-aware Network (CAN) to capture the dynamic interactions including both the dynamic routing and messaging among agents. Secondly, the CAN is integrated into Reinforcement Learning (RL) framework to learn the policy of multi-agent cooperation. The approach is evaluated in both discrete and continuous environments, and outperforms competing methods promisingly.

Keywords: Multi-agent · Communication · Cooperation · Attention
RL

1 Introduction

Many real-world applications, such as autonomous vehicle control, resource management systems, *etc.*, can be naturally modeled as multi-agent problems. Many solutions have been proposed to address the multi-agent problem. For example, [2] has regressively learned the strategy using a rate distortion theory-based information framework. However, it has poor adaptability to complex decentralized problems. Recently, the field of multi-agent RL has attracted massive attention [12, 13, 18], since it is one of the main methods to train the system of self-learning through interaction with environment, which is more in line with human learning model. Practically, RL can be successfully utilized to solve single agent problems [16, 19, 20]. Unfortunately, it is difficult to solve multi-agent problem via traditional RL models. One of the major challenges is the instability of the environment. The environment of multi-agent RL relies on the actions of multiple agents and involves the interactions among agents, which implies that the key problem in multi-agent environment is how to do collaboration.

© Springer Nature Switzerland AG 2018
V. Kůrková et al. (Eds.): ICANN 2018, LNCS 11140, pp. 219–229, 2018.
https://doi.org/10.1007/978-3-030-01421-6_22

Collaboration is an important manifestation of intelligence, making agents appear as a whole rather than a collection of individuals. Communication is a common scheme to achieve collaboration, of which the kernel is the construction of communication protocol, including routing and messaging. Recently, manually specified communication protocols are basically applied in the field of RL [5, 10]. Most of them adopt the action strategy of each agent as a message to stabilize the environment, which can not adapt to changing environment and strategies. In addition to Hoshen's dynamic construction of communication routing, considering the different relationships among the agents can lead to distinct influence [9]. However, except for determining the communication routing, distilling the state information into the message is important for the multi-agent problems. Because the action strategy contains a lot of useless information so that it not only consumes communication resources but also distracts the attention of agents, leading the policy to be difficult to achieve collaboration.

To address this problem, we propose an Attentional Communication Model (ACM), so as to adaptively construct the communication routing and messaging. For this purpose, we adopt the attention mechanism, which derives from the attention model of the human brain [1, 8]. To introduce ACM for multi-agent collaboration, we construct two networks, *i.e.*, the policy network of agents as well as the Cooperation-aware Network (CAN). CAN, which is a two-branch network, enables the dynamic construction of communication protocols and services to the policy network. Two networks are iteratively updated to obtain collaborating agents. ACM can effectively use the information to achieve collaboration.

The main contributions of this paper are listed as follows:

(1) We propose the CAN, which dynamically calculates the relationships among agents to ascertain the routing, and distills the state information into the message. It not only saves the communication resources but also makes better use of the action strategy so that the agents can get smart cooperation strategies and improve the stability of training. Most importantly, CAN dynamically builds the communication protocols to adapt to the changing environments and strategies.
(2) The CAN is successfully combined with the policy network built by RL algorithms to construct ACM. The ACM demonstrates the outstanding ability in collaboration with the environment after sufficient training.

2   Related Work

Early approaches of multi-agent interactions include no communication. M. Tan has experimented with Q-learning using independent agents, but does not perform well in practice [22]. This is due to the fact that each agent is partially observable and lacks the necessary information because of a limited field of view. Under the constant learning and changing of the agent's strategy, the environment is extremely unstable, resulting in the strategy of the agent being difficult to collaborate and converge. Another approach is parameter sharing, such as [7, 11]. They can sample more from training strategies, but lack the necessary information in partially observable environments, which makes the strategy poor and converge slowly. Therefore, the recent work mainly focuses on transmitting information through communications to stabilize the environment.

The core of communication is the communication protocol. Some work has passed on all the parameters of the policy [5] or simplified information about the training strategy [10]. [3, 21] have used the deep Q-network (DQN) to construct agents, except that [3] directly transmits the actions, while [21] broadcasts the communication vector which is the mean value of the states. [4, 14, 15] have used a more sophisticated actor-critic mechanism to deliver action strategies: all agents of [4] share a unique critic; [14] has studied a critic for each agent, which is applicable to both cooperative and competitive scenarios; but [15] has compared the above two settings and joined the coordinator to encode the states and actions. [6] applies to GAN which passes images to other generators. In a word, the above work has transmitted the action strategies of other agents to stabilize the environment. They adopt the manually predefined communication protocol. However, as the strategy and environment change, the necessary information is constantly changing. So in this paper, the dynamic learning of the communication protocol is adopted, and the communication messaging and routing are determined through learning. The useful information of current state is selected to prevent consuming the channel resources and distracting the attention.

Hoshen's work [9] is most similar to ours. Hoshen has proposed VAIN which uses the attention mechanism to compute the relationships among agents. This means that VAIN has constructed the routing dynamically. The most important difference between VAIN and ACM is that we dynamically build communication protocol, including routing and more sophisticated message. The benefits of our work are to save the communication resources, focus on the current useful state information, and train agents with collaboration capabilities finally.

3   Approach

Among multi-agent problems, the construction of the communication protocol is one of the most effective ways to achieve collaboration. Dynamically built the communication protocol can adapt to the changing environment. Therefore, we introduce Attentional Communication Model (ACM). In the following, we first define the model. Second, we construct the framework and explain how to determine the communication routing. Third, we elaborate how to dynamically distill the state information into the message. Finally, the routing and messaging are combined to construct the communication protocol.

3.1   Definition

The multi-agent problem is so complex, and in reality, it is usually partially observable. To address this difficulty, it is a good choice to use Shared Parameters Partial Observable Markov Decision Process (SP-POMDP) which is a classical approach among multi-agent problem. Inspired by SP-POMDP, our problem model consists of an ten-tuple $<\mathcal{A}_n, \mathcal{S}, \mathcal{O}, \mathcal{R}, \mathcal{M}, \mathcal{U}, P, R, \Omega, t>$, in which

$\mathcal{A}_n = \{a_1, a_2, \ldots, a_n\}$ is the collection of all agents. n is the number of agents.

$s_t \in \mathcal{S}$ is the state at the current time step t.

$\mathcal{O}_t^i = \{o_t^i | s_t \in \mathcal{S}, o_t^i = O(s_t, i)\}$ is the observation space of player i. The observation function $O : \mathcal{S} \times \{1, \ldots, n\} \rightarrow \mathbb{R}^d$ specifies each agent's d-dimensional view on the state space. For the sake of simplicity we will write $o_t = \{o_t^1, o_t^2, \ldots, o_t^n\}$.

$\mathcal{R}_t^i \in \mathcal{R}$, $\mathcal{R}_t^i = \{\mathcal{R}_t^{i1}, \ldots, \mathcal{R}_t^{in}\}$, $\mathcal{R}_t^i$ are the relationships among agent i and all the other agents at the current time step t.

$\mathcal{M}_t \in \mathcal{M}$, $\mathcal{M}_t$ distills the observations information for all agents into message at the current time step t.

$u_t \in \mathcal{U}$, $u_t = \{u_t^1, u_t^2, \ldots, u_t^n\}$, is the collection of actions for all agents at the current time step t. $u_t = \pi^i(o_t^i, u_{t-1}, \mathcal{R}_t^i, \mathcal{M}_t)$, and π^i is the policy of agent i.

$P(s_{t+1}|s_t, u_t)$ is the state transfer function of the agent.

$R : o_t^i \times u_t^i \times u_{t-1} \times \mathcal{R}_t^i \times \mathcal{M}_t \rightarrow R_t^i$, R_t^i is the reward function of the agent i.

$\Omega : o_t^i \times u_t^i \times u_{t-1} \times \mathcal{R}_t^i \times \mathcal{M}_t \times R_t^i \rightarrow \Omega$ stores all samples.

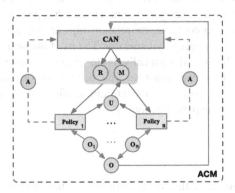

Fig. 1. The framework of ACM.

3.2   The Framework

ACM is a multi-agent communication model constructed by combining of CAN and the policy network, as shown in Fig. 1. We first train the policy until it converges and keep it fixed to train CAN. CAN uses the observations and actions of the agents to construct the communication routing and messaging which are transmitted to the policy network to get the action. Then the policy network calculates advantage values for training parameters of CAN, which only exists in training. The calculation of the advantage value is shown in Eq. 1, and $\gamma \in [0, 1)$. The trained CAN remains fixed and then integrates with the RL to obtain the final cooperative strategy.

$$Q(o_t^i, u_t^i, u_{t-1}, \mathcal{R}_t^i, \mathcal{M}_t) = \mathbb{E}_{o_{t+1}, u_{t+1}, \ldots} [\sum_{t=0}^{\infty} \gamma^t R(o_t^i, u_t^i, u_{t-1}, \mathcal{R}_t^i, \mathcal{M}_t)]$$
$$V(o_t^i, u_{t-1}, \mathcal{R}_t^i, \mathcal{M}_t) = \mathbb{E}_{u_t, o_{t+1}, \ldots} [\sum_{t=0}^{\infty} \gamma^t R(o_t^i, u_t^i, u_{t-1}, \mathcal{R}_t^i, \mathcal{M}_t)] \qquad (1)$$
$$A(o_t^i, u_t^i, u_{t-1}, \mathcal{R}_t^i, \mathcal{M}_t) = Q(o_t^i, u_t^i, u_{t-1}, \mathcal{R}_t^i, \mathcal{M}_t) - V(o_t^i, u_{t-1}, \mathcal{R}_t^i, \mathcal{M}_t)$$

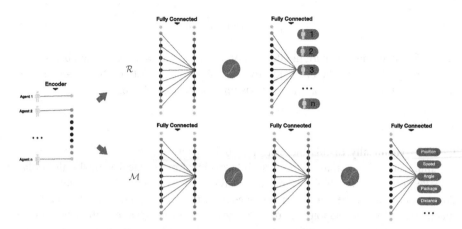

Fig. 2. Cooperation-aware Network (CAN) architecture diagram. Cooperation-aware Network Routing (CANR) consists of a fully connected layer (snaking blue line symbolizes sliding of each filter across inputs), followed by a softmax output layer, with a single output for each valid agent; Cooperation-aware Network Messaging (CANM includes two fully connected layers, followed by a softmax output layer, and each valid observation dimension has a unique output. Each hidden layer is followed by a sigmoid nonlinearity. (that is, $\frac{1}{1+e^{-x}}$) (Color figure online)

CAN is a two-branch network consisting of Cooperation-aware Network Routing (CANR) and Cooperation-aware Network Messaging (CANM). The role of CANR is to dynamically ascertain the routing, while CANM is used to dynamically distill the state information into the message. CAN originates from the attention mechanism. The architecture of the network is shown in Fig. 2.

Attention is essentially a content-based addressing mechanism, so as to followup information distillation. CAN uses the classic attention mechanism which is the additive attention [1]. Hence, the core of the network can be interpreted by the following equation,

$$f_{att}(a_i, a_j) = v^T sigmoid(W[a_i; a_j] || W[o]) \qquad (2)$$

f_{att} is the attention function of CAN. v and W are the weight matrix of CAN. CANR uses $W[a_i; a_j]$, and CANM applies $W[o]$. The use of the fully connected layers for CAN facilitates the processing and distilling of all the information. The inputs of CAN are the observations of all current agents, which are transmitted to two branches separately after dimension reduction (Encoder). Inspired by the idea of [9], we here propose CANR to determine the routing in a similar way.

CANR. CANR dynamically constructs routing. There are different relationships between agents, which make different effects. Therefore, we dynamically model the relationships between agents for determining the influence of others on the current agent.

$$\mathcal{R}_t^{ij} = softmax(a_t^i - a_t^j) \tag{3}$$

where $\mathcal{R}_t^{ij}$ represents the current attention of agent i to j. $a_t^i = E(o_t^i)$ is the observations of agent i. E indicates the encoded process. CANR can construct the real-time communication routing based on the relationships constructed above.

3.3   Message

CANM dynamically distills the state information into the message. The purpose of communication is to transfer the state information for the agent to make the policy achieve collaboration, thus the message plays a crucial role. When the information dimension is large, the agent can not handle all the information well. Accepting too much redundant information may distract agents and make agent not effectively utilize the state information. Therefore, we propose to distill the message based on the attention mechanism in a dynamic manner. As agents have different information requirements in different periods, we distill the message before each iteration of the agent's policy.

CANM learns from the Trust Region Policy Optimization (TRPO) algorithm of RL. TRPO [17] is a deterministic strategy gradient algorithm, which is characterized by guaranteeing a monotonous increase of policies and is effective for optimizing large-scale nonlinear strategies. At each time step, the goal of TRPO algorithm is to optimize the policy under constraints:

$$\underset{\theta}{\text{maximize}}\, \mathbb{E}_{s \sim \rho_{\theta_{old}}, u \sim q}[\frac{\pi_\theta(u|s)}{q(u|s)}A_{\theta_{old}}(s, u)]$$
$$s.t.\mathbb{E}_{s \sim \rho_{\theta_{old}}}[D_{KL}(\pi_{\theta_{old}}(\cdot|s)||\pi_\theta(\cdot|s))] \le \delta \tag{4}$$

where $q(u|s) = \pi_{\theta_{old}}(u|s)$ indicates using existing $\pi_{\theta_{old}}$ for importance sampling. $\rho_{\theta_{old}} = \rho_{\pi_{\theta_{old}}}$ is the state-access frequency defined by $\pi_{\theta_{old}}$. D_{KL} shows the KL variance between the two strategy distributions, and δ controls the maximum change between two strategies at each time step. A is the advantage value likes Eq. (1).

CANM updates the network parameters as in Eq. (5) according to the advantage value passed by the policy network.

$$\underset{\omega}{\text{maximize}}\, \mathbb{E}_{o \sim \rho_{\pi_\theta}, u \sim \pi_\theta}[\frac{\Delta}{\Delta_t}A_\theta(o_t^i, u_t^i, u_{t-1}, \varphi_t^i, \Delta_t)]$$
$$s.t.\mathbb{E}_{o \sim \rho_{\pi_\theta}}[D_{KL}(\Delta_t||\Delta) \le \delta \tag{5}$$

where $\Delta = \mathcal{M}_\omega$ is the CANM network distribution. i is the index of agent. $\varphi_t^i = \mathcal{R}_t^i$ indicates the relationships among agent i to others at current time step. The advantage value is still calculated by the policy network, but the parameters of the policy network are currently fixed (θ), with the only variable being the parameters of CANM. For the policy network, we add an input that dynamically distills message for the current step to measure the impact of the currently selected message on the agent's reward value. The goal is to update the parameters of CANM in a direction that increases the reward. Eventually, the optimization problem of CANM is shown in Eq. (6):

$$\text{maximize}_{\omega} \mathbb{E}_{o \sim \rho_{\pi_\theta}, u \sim \pi_\theta} \left[\frac{M_\omega(E(o_t))}{M_{\omega_t}(E(o_t))} A_\theta(o_t^i, u_t^i, u_{t-1}, \mathcal{R}_t^i, \mathcal{M}_{\omega_t}) \right]$$
$$s.t. \mathbb{E}_{o \sim \rho_{\pi_\theta}} \left[D_{KL}(\mathcal{M}_{\omega_t}(\cdot | E(o_t)) || \mathcal{M}_\omega(\cdot | E(o_t))) \right] \leq \delta \tag{6}$$

where $E(o_t)$ is the input to the CANM network, which is the encoded value of the observations for all current agents. We propose using TRPO to update the CANM as it ensures monotonically increasing.

The CANM iteration algorithm, as shown in Algorithm 1, iterates the parameters until convergence under the fixed policy network.

Algorithm 1 CANM Iteration Algorithms

Initialize $\mathcal{M}_0$

Obtain π_θ

for t=0,1,2,... until convergence **do**

    Compute all advantage values $A_\theta(o_t^i, u_t^i, u_{t-1}, \mathcal{R}_t^i, \mathcal{M}_t)$ by π_θ

    Solve the constrained optimization problem

$$\eta(\mathcal{M}_{t+1}) = \text{maximize}_{\mathcal{M}} L_{\mathcal{M}_t}(\mathcal{M}) - CD_{KL}^{\max}(\mathcal{M}_t, \mathcal{M})$$

$$where C = \frac{4\varepsilon\gamma}{(1-\gamma)^2}$$

and

$$L_{M_t}(M) = \eta(M_t) + \sum_{o_t} \rho_{M_t} \sum_{u_t^i} \pi_\theta(u_t^i | o_t^i, u_{t-1}, \mathcal{R}_t^i, \mathcal{M}_t) A_\theta(o_t^i, u_t^i, u_{t-1}, \mathcal{R}_t^i, \mathcal{M}_t)$$

end for

Algorithm 2 Attentional Communication Model

Obtain o_t, u_{t-1}, n // o_t is the observations of all agents at time step t

$M_t \leftarrow CANM(E(o_t))$

for i=1 to n **do**

    for j=1 to n **do**

        $R_t^{ij} \leftarrow CANR(E(o_t))$

        $c_i \leftarrow [c_i; [\mathcal{R}_t^{ij} \cdot \mathcal{M}_t(E(o_t)) \cdot o_t^j]; [\mathcal{R}_t^{ij} \cdot u_{t-1}]]$

    end for

    $u_t \leftarrow Policy(c_i, o_t^j)$

end for

3.4   Attentional Communication Model

The final communication is:

$$c_i = [[[\mathcal{R}_{i1}\mathcal{M}_\omega(E(o_t)) \cdot o_t^1]; [\mathcal{R}_{i1} \cdot u_{t-1}]], \ldots, [[\mathcal{R}_{in}\mathcal{M}_\omega(E(o_t)) \cdot o_t^n]; [\mathcal{R}_{in} \cdot u_{t-1}]]] \quad (7)$$

where c_i represents the communication of agent i.

The ACM algorithm is illustrated in Algorithm 2. Firstly, the observations of the agents are distilled into the communication message by CANM. Secondly, the communication routing is determined by CANR. Thirdly, the communication routing and messaging are combined to construct the communication protocol. And finally, communication is passed to the policy for selecting the action.

4   Experiment

In this section, we compare the performance of our algorithm ACM with benchmark experiments to demonstrate that our model achieves better results than competing approaches. We test two tasks covering discrete and continuous environment. In all experiments, we apply TRPO algorithm for learning the policy. The number of agents is 10.

4.1   Environment

Pursuit. The state action space of pursuit is discrete. The environment contains two types of agents - pursuer and evader. We train pursuer, and the goal is to catch the evaders as soon as possible. In the experiment, evader takes a random policy. The agent receives a reward (+5) when pursuers catch an evader. We also set a shaping reward of 0.01 for encountering an evader to ease exploration. Agents' observations include the information of surroundings, such as the locations of their nearest pursuer and evader.

Coordinating Bipedal Walkers. Multi-walker is a continuous environment. Each walker, consists of a pair of legs, with the goal of multiple agents coordinated delivery of a box. When the box drops, the reward minus 100, and with the reward 1 when moving forward. They also receive an action penalty defined as the square norm of the force applied. Each walker observes the terrain, adjacent walker location information and package.

4.2   Experimental Settings

- Shared Parameters-TRPO (SP-TRPO): Shared parameters among all agents is the basic form of TRPO algorithm applied in the field of multi-agent.
- Communication All-TRPO (CA-TRPO): The current observations and the last move of all agents are taken as message. All agents use the same communications.

- CANR-TRPO[1]: The current observations and previous actions of all agents are used as the communication contents. CANR dynamically calculates the relationships among agents to determine the routing.
- ACM: The messaging and routing of the agent are constructed dynamically based on the environment using ACM.

4.3 Experimental Results Evaluation

In Fig. 3 we compare the performance of our method ACM with SP-TRPO, CA-TRPO and CANR-TRPO in different environments. We can clearly contrast ACM of which the average reward is higher than several other benchmark experiments in both discrete and continuous environments. As expected, this indicates that ACM is effective in multi-agent collaboration.

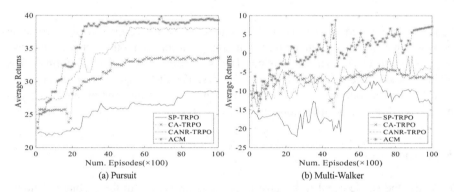

(a) Pursuit   (b) Multi-Walker

Fig. 3. Average returns for multi-agent policies.

It can be seen in Fig. 3(a) that for the discrete problem, the final results of ACM and CANR-TRPO are not significantly different. Because the dimension of the action state space is small, the agent can handle it well. On the contrary, in Fig. 3(b) the results of ACM are much higher than CANR-TRPO which are slightly higher than CA-TRPO, indicating that distilling for information has a significant impact on experimental results. Therefore, the proposed ACM is more suitable for continuous problems with complex state space.

The message distillation results are visualized in Fig. 4. It can be seen that the importance of information changes with the update of the strategy. Compared with pursuit, the difference between final message distillation of multi-walker is greater. In Fig. 4(b), the overall velocity of the agent, that is the 2,3,4-dimensional values, compared with the velocity of each joint in each leg of each agent, which is values of 5 to 12-dimension, can be defined as abstract information. The values of 2,3,4-dimensional information show an upward trend, indicating that more attention is paid

---

[1] CANR-TRPO is built using the idea of [9], except that the TRPO algorithm is used here to build the strategy.

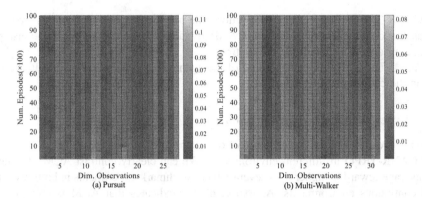

Fig. 4. Message distillation diagram. The horizontal coordinate represents the information dimension. We use different colors to represent the message distillation results.

to the overall speed of the agent. The values of 5 to 12-dimensional information decrease, indicating the attention on the turning point for each joint decreased, and pay more attention to abstract information. This shows that the need for information is different among agents with different mentalities. The junior agents may require more specific information; advanced agents may require more emphasis on abstract information and less on specific information.

5   Conclusions

Recently, the single agent tasks have made great progress, but the problem of multi-agent is still beset with difficulties. We develop a new ACM for multi-agent collaboration within the SP-POMDP framework. ACM is a multi-agent attentional communication model used to dynamically build the communication protocol. The experimental results show that the proposed ACM can promote the agent to collaborate as well as accelerate the learning of the agent.

References

1. Chorowski, J.K., Bahdanau, D., Serdyuk, D., Cho, K., Bengio, Y.: Attention-based models for speech recognition. In: Advances in Neural Information Processing Systems, pp. 577–585 (2015)
2. Dobbe, R., Fridovich-Keil, D., Tomlin, C.: Fully decentralized policies for multi-agent systems: an information theoretic approach. In: Advances in Neural Information Processing Systems, pp. 2945–2954 (2017)
3. Foerster, J., Assael, Y., de Freitas, N., Whiteson, S.: Learning to communicate with deep multi-agent reinforcement learning. In: Advances in Neural Information Processing Systems, pp. 2137–2145 (2016)
4. Foerster, J., Farquhar, G., Afouras, T., Nardelli, N., Whiteson, S.: Counterfactual multi-agent policy gradients. arXiv preprint arXiv:1705.08926 (2017)

5. Foerster, J.N., Chen, R.Y., Al-Shedivat, M., Whiteson, S., Abbeel, P., Mordatch, I.: Learning with opponent-learning awareness. arXiv preprint arXiv:1709.04326 (2017)
6. Ghosh, A., Kulharia, V., Namboodiri, V.: Message passing multi-agent gans. arXiv preprint arXiv:1612.01294 (2016)
7. Gupta, J.K., Egorov, M., Kochenderfer, M.: Cooperative multi-agent control using deep reinforcement learning. In: Sukthankar, G., Rodriguez-Aguilar, J.A. (eds.) AAMAS 2017. LNCS (LNAI), vol. 10642, pp. 66–83. Springer, Cham (2017). https://doi.org/10.1007/978-3-319-71682-4_5
8. Hermann, K.M., et al.: Teaching machines to read and comprehend. In: Advances in Neural Information Processing Systems, pp. 1693–1701 (2015)
9. Hoshen, Y.: Vain: attentional multi-agent predictive modeling. In: Advances in Neural Information Processing Systems, pp. 2698–2708 (2017)
10. Hüttenrauch, M., Šošić, A., Neumann, G.: Learning complex swarm behaviors by exploiting local communication protocols with deep reinforcement learning. arXiv preprint arXiv:1709.07224 (2017)
11. Kurek, M., Jaśkowski, W.: Heterogeneous team deep q-learning in low-dimensional multi-agent environments. In: 2016 IEEE Conference on Computational Intelligence and Games (CIG), pp. 1–8. IEEE (2016)
12. Lanctot, M., et al.: A unified game-theoretic approach to multiagent reinforcement learning. In: Advances in Neural Information Processing Systems, pp. 4191–4204 (2017)
13. Leibo, J.Z., Zambaldi, V., Lanctot, M., Marecki, J., Graepel, T.: Multi-agent reinforcement learning in sequential social dilemmas. In: Proceedings of the 16th Conference on Autonomous Agents and Multi-agent Systems. pp. 464–473. International Foundation for Autonomous Agents and Multiagent Systems (2017)
14. Lowe, R., Wu, Y., Tamar, A., Harb, J., Abbeel, P., Mordatch, I.: Multi-agent actor-critic for mixed cooperative-competitive environments. arXiv preprint arXiv:1706.02275 (2017)
15. Mao, H., et al.: ACCNet: Actor-coordinator-critic net for "learning-to-communicate" with deep multi-agent reinforcement learning. arXiv preprint arXiv:1706.03235 (2017)
16. Mnih, V., et al.: Human-level control through deep reinforcement learning. Nature 518 (7540), 529–533 (2015)
17. Schulman, J., Levine, S., Abbeel, P., Jordan, M., Moritz, P.: Trust region policy optimization. In: Proceedings of the 32nd International Conference on Machine Learning (ICML-15), pp. 1889–1897 (2015)
18. da Silva, F.L., Glatt, R., Costa, A.H.R.: Simultaneously learning and advising in multi-agent reinforcement learning. In: Proceedings of the 16th Conference on Autonomous Agents and MultiAgent Systems. pp. 1100–1108. International Foundation for Autonomous Agents and Multiagent Systems (2017)
19. Silver, D., et al.: Mastering the game of go with deep neural networks and tree search. Nature 529(7587), 484–489 (2016)
20. Silver, D., et al.: Mastering the game of go without human knowledge. Nature 550(7676), 354 (2017)
21. Sukhbaatar, S., Fergus, R., et al.: Learning multiagent communication with back propagation. In: Advances in Neural Information Processing Systems, pp. 2244–2252 (2016)
22. Tan, M.: Multi-agent reinforcement learning: independent vs. cooperative agents. In: Proceedings of the Tenth International Conference on Machine Learning, pp. 330–337 (1993)

Improving Fuel Economy with LSTM Networks and Reinforcement Learning

Andreas Bougiouklis[✉], Antonis Korkofigkas, and Giorgos Stamou

National Technical University of Athens, Athens, Greece
andreasbougiouklis@gmail.com

Abstract. This paper presents a system for calculating the optimum velocities and trajectories of an electric vehicle for a specific route. Our objective is to minimize the consumption over a trip without impacting the overall trip time. The system uses a particular segmentation of the route and involves a three-step procedure. In the first step, a neural network is trained on telemetry data to model the consumption of the vehicle based on its velocity and the surface gradient. In the second step, two Q-learning algorithms compute the optimum velocities and the racing line in order to minimize the consumption. In the final step, the computed data is presented to the driver through an interactive application. This system was installed on a light electric vehicle (LEV) and by adopting the suggested driving strategy we reduced its consumption by 24.03% with respect to the classic constant-speed control technique.

Keywords: Trajectory optimization · Velocity profile · Racing line
Topographical data · Electric vehicle · LEV · Neural network · LSTM
Reinforcement learning · Q-Learning

1 Introduction

Over the last decade there has been a great effort to reduce fuel consumption and dependence on fossil fuels. Electric cars have limited autonomy due to the poor energy density of current batteries. The need for ever improving autonomy has stimulated research aiming at developing control strategies that exploit the characteristics of a particular terrain [1,2]. These strategies regard the best overall velocities and trajectory that a vehicle has to maintain in order to minimize energy consumption. We will refer to these strategies as trajectory optimization.

A plethora of research has been conducted on vehicle trajectory optimization [3–7]. Most of the publications use theoretical analysis and Newtonian physics in order to model the consumption characteristics of a vehicle. In this paper, we present an architecture based on Long Short Temp Memory Networks (LSTM) [8] that model the consumption of a light electric vehicle (LEV). The Neural Network (NN) has been trained with data acquired from the vehicle during the European Shell Eco Marathon.

© Springer Nature Switzerland AG 2018
V. Kůrková et al. (Eds.): ICANN 2018, LNCS 11140, pp. 230–239, 2018.
https://doi.org/10.1007/978-3-030-01421-6_23

Researchers have identified that real time speed guidance decreases long-term fuel consumption up to 47% [6]. For the purpose of this paper we conducted a parametrical analysis of a Q-Learning algorithm [9] to approximate the optimum velocity profile for a LEV. The optimum velocity profile is a sequence of elements which correspond to the velocities that a vehicle has to maintain on every part of a specific route and leads to consumption minimization. A second Q-Learning algorithm approximates the racing line [10,11], which is the optimum trajectory the driver has to follow on the track.

The driver has to remain focused on the road. The calculated data has to be presented to the driver in a simple and intuitive way. For that reason, we propose an interactive system which can be mounted on the steering wheel of a vehicle and guide the driver through a simple graphical interface.

The completed system was installed on a LEV and was tested in a closed test track during the European Shell Eco Marathon 2017.

2   Onboard Systems

2.1   Vehicle Characteristics

The vehicle under study is a three-wheel light electric vehicle (LEV) equipped with an In-wheel Surface Mounted Permanent Magnet (SMPM) motor with Fractional Slot Concentrated Windings (FSCW) and unequal stator teeth, comprising of 16 poles and 18 slots, which is mounted in the back wheel [7]. The electric motor is driven by a three phase, two-level-bridge voltage source inverter. The system is fed by lithium batteries.

2.2   Data Gathering System

The vehicle is equipped with a telemetry system, which takes measurements of the phase current of the motor and a Global Positioning System (GPS) which calculates elevation, velocity, latitude and longitude of the vehicle. The sampling rate of the system is 50 Hz. The gathered data is used to train the NN consumption model and the Q-Learning algorithms offline.

2.3   Online Monitoring System

The online monitoring system uses sensors to oversee the dynamics of the vehicle and present the guiding application to the driver. The exact position of the vehicle is calculated by two Lidar V3 sensors, which measure the distance of it from the boundaries of the testing track, and one GPS sensor. The vehicle current speed is measured with a speedometer and the exact position of the steering wheel is captured by a linear potentiometer mounted on the steering wheel column. As a computational unit we use a Raspberry pi 3 with a monitor.

3   Neural Network Consumption Model

The LSTM NN [8] consumption model uses elevation, E(n), and velocity, V(n), sequences as inputs. The output is the consumed phase current of the electric motor, I(n). For the hidden layers we chose LSTM units with a sigmoid activation function. Finally, the output layer is a fully connected node.

The selected architecture has 50 LSTM nodes in the first layer and 35 LSTM nodes in the second. We concluded to this particular layout by examining all the combinations of nodes between 0 and 100 for a two layer NN. This architecture minimizes the mean square error of the training process.

The data acquired from the telemetry system is first passed through a cleaning process. In this stage, we remove data corresponding to negative phase current values. These are invalid elements as the vehicle does not have regenerative braking and the phase current is always positive. Also, zero latitude and longitude measurements are removed. The zero values correspond to loss of signal on the GPS sensor. At a 50 Hz sampling rate the percentage of the removed values is significantly smaller than the size of the training set and therefore we did not alter the sequence of the data.

The inputs fed into the network are sequences of 300 elements each and the output is the sum of the consumed phase current from these measurements.

The training process was conducted with a training data set of 658.500 measurements which correspond to 13 laps from the eco-marathon 2016 and 9 rounds from the eco-marathon 2017. The validation set consisted of 36.000 elements from 1 lap on the 2017 track.

The neural network was implemented with the KERAS library. We used the RMSprop optimizer and early stopping with the patience parameter set to 13 epochs. Finally, the learning rate was set to 0.001. After training, the mean squared error was 0.3972 (Figs. 1 and 2).

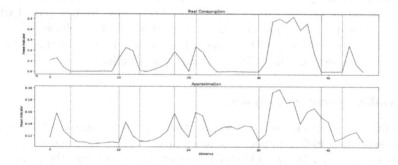

Fig. 1. The real consumption of the vehicle and the approximation of the NN for an unknown dataset are shown in this figure. The vertical lines represent the changes of monotony on the consumption curve. The network is able to identify the areas of the track in which the vehicles consumption monotony differs. The difference between the consumed current of the test round and the approximation of the network is 17.48%.

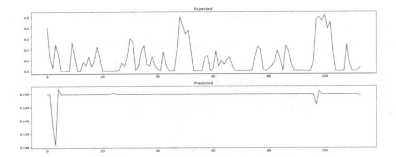

Fig. 2. As a baseline we designed a Multilayer Perceptron (MLP) network [13] with the same architecture as the LSTM NN described above. The approximation of the MLP is presented here.

4 Velocity Optimization

4.1 Q-Learning Algorithm Design

The grade of the driving surface is the most important factor when deciding the fuel optimum velocity profile [1]. Therefore to set the states of the environment we examined the elevation data from the GPS system. We made a segmentation in accordance with the monotony of the elevation. Every time the monotony changes we set a different state. The results of this segmentation are presented in Fig. 3b. According to our research a larger set of track slots does not lead to better results.

The second step of the algorithm design involves the appropriate values of action, which correspond to the appropriate values of speed. All velocities that the agent is able to choose from have been described as follows:

$$v\_min \leq v \leq v\_max \tag{1}$$

Where $v\_min = 10\,km/h$ (2.778 m/s) and $v\_max = 45\,km/h$ (12.5 m/s)

The policy has been initialized with the desirable average velocity for every state. The other constants of the algorithm have been set to the following values. The discount factor has been set to 0, as the reward from the next state is not affected from the taken action. Moreover, the learning rate has been set to 0.7. Finally we assume that the policy has converged when it does not change for 2000 epochs.

4.2 Reward Function

The Reward function has the greatest impact on successfully training the agent. It consists of two important factors. Firstly, it evaluates if the desirable average speed is being maintained. Secondly, it evaluates whether the policy of the agent

is an improvement on the consumption of the previous strategy. These are the
two criteria that the algorithm has to meet.

The time reward concerning the average velocity of the vehicle has been set to
a constant. Specifically, if the average speed is within the desirable margin then
the reward is set to 0.5, otherwise it has the value of −0.5. To approximate the
average velocity, the algorithm computes the weighted average from the length
of each state (w_i) and the corresponding velocity (v_i).

$$\mu = \frac{\sum w_i \times v_i}{\sum w_i} \tag{2}$$

The desirable margin is $(m-1, m+1)$, where m is the desirable average
speed.

To approximate the consumption of the vehicle for every velocity profile the
NN described above has been used. Every time the agent makes the choice to
maintain a specific speed into the boundaries of a state, the NN calculates the
consumed energy for the entire trip. Then, this approximation is being subtracted from the policy's consumption. Finally, the result from the subtraction
is multiplied by a discount factor k. We used this discount factor to keep the
balance between the two rewards. To set the optimum value for the parameter
k we conducted a statistical analysis of the used data. We discovered that the
expected value of the subtraction between the policy consumption and the new
approximation (d) was:

$$E[d] = 32.369 \tag{3}$$

Thus, in order to balance these two amounts we set the value of k as 0.02.
With this specific setting the expected value of the consumption reward is:

$$k \times E[d] = 0.647 \tag{4}$$

That means there is balance between the two rewards. The final reward is
equal to the sum of the time reward and the consumption reward.

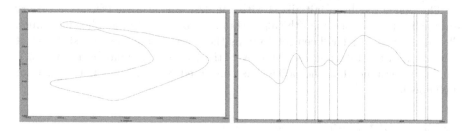

Fig. 3. (a) The testing track map. (b) Track segmentation based on the elevation data.

4.3   Action Selection Strategy

The primary challenge is choosing the agent's action. We used the ϵ-greedy strategy to balance the exploitation and the exploration by behaving most of the time greedily, while choosing a uniform random action with a small probability p.

$$selection strategy = \begin{cases} \text{random choise of action with probability p} \\ \text{argmax } a \in A \ \ Q(s,a) \ \text{ with propability } 1-p \end{cases} \quad (5)$$

The probability that we used is:

$$p = e^{-n \times \epsilon} \quad (6)$$

An initial analysis has been conducted to establish the most suitable exploration rate. To test the decaying setting, the value of ϵ as in Eq. 6 had been set to have a varying rate at 0.001, 0.0001, and 0.00001. For the gradually decreasing exploration method the value of $\epsilon = 0.0001$ has been selected for this study as it provides the best performance over other values (Table 1).

Table 1. Experimentation with ϵ-Value

$\epsilon - Value$	Convergence Speed	Consumption Approximation
0.001	3870	4.449
0.0001	4970	4.408
0.00001	8620	4.428

5   The Racing Line

5.1   Introduction

The racing line is the trajectory that a driver should follow to achieve the best lap-time on a given track with a given car. The racing line depends on several factors [10, 11] including the track shape, the tire grip and the mass of the vehicle. Besides engine dynamics, the maximum velocity of a vehicle depends on the following parameters:

$$v_{max} = \sqrt{\frac{F \times r}{m}} \quad (7)$$

F is the gripping force from the tires, m is the mass of the vehicle and r is the radius of the circle which is tangent to the trajectory of the vehicle. To approximate the racing line we calculate the trajectory that maximizes the radius of the tangent circle.

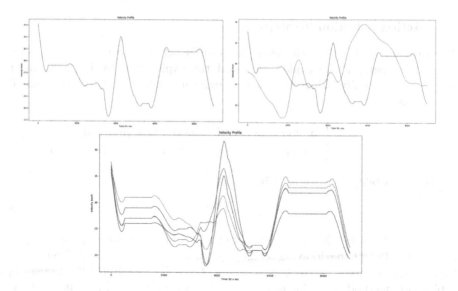

Fig. 4. (a) The chosen optimum velocity profile for the track of Fig. 3a with a desirable average speed of 25 km/h. The actual average velocity of the profile is 25.975 km/h. (b) In orange we distinguish the elevation profile of the test track and in blue the velocity profile. (c) Velocity profiles with different average speeds of 24.8, 25.9, 27.1, 28.7, 29.8 km/h, the same strategy is being used for various trip times. (Color figure online)

5.2   Algorithm Design

The trajectory has been represented by points of the track. Each element of the trajectory is a state of the environment.

The agent is able to move each point across the width of the track. The average width of this specific route is 6 m and we have set the movement step to 1 m. All the calculations were conducted with the latitude and longitude coordinates.

The policy has been initialized with the trajectory which corresponds to the middle of the track. We set the discount factor to 0, the learning rate to 0.001 and we assumed that the policy has converged when it does not change for 10000 epochs.

5.3   Reward Function

As Eq. 7 shows, the goal of the agent is to approximate the trajectory of the vehicle which maximizes the radius of the tangent circle. For the purpose of this study every circle is tangent to three elements of the trajectory (A, B and C). In order to calculate the radius, firstly, we approximate the two lines which connect these elements. Secondly, we approximate the common point of their mediators (M). Finally, we measure the distance between A and M, this measurement is the radius of the tangent circle of the trajectory.

In every iteration one point P_i of the trajectory is moved and the radii of three tangent circles is calculated. Every circle is tangent to three successive points. The first circle (a) is tangent to the point being moved and the two previous points on the trajectory (P_{i-1}, P_{i-2}), the second one (b) to P_i and two points ahead (P_{i+1}, P_{i+2}) and the third one (c) to P_{i-1}, P_i, P_{i+1}. The reward is equal to the sum of the radial differences from the policy of the agent and the new action.

$$r = (r_a - r_{policy_a}) \times i + (r_b + r_{policy_b}) \times j + (r_c + r_{policy_c}) \times k \qquad (8)$$

Where r_a, r_b, r_c correspond to the radiuses of the new trajectory and the r_{policy_a}, r_{policy_b}, r_{policy_c} to the policy's trajectory. Furthermore, the i, j, k are constant parameters the value of which has been set to i =1, j = 0.1 and k = 0.1. These values have been optimized for this particular track and they were the result of experimentation in the range [0, 1].

5.4   Action Selection Strategy

An initial analysis has been conducted to establish the most suitable exploration rate for the ϵ in ϵ-greedy strategy. The value of ϵ as in Eq. 6 has been set to have a varying rate at 0.01, 0.001, 0.0001, and 0.00001.

For the gradually decreasing exploration method the value of $\epsilon = 0.001$ has been selected for this study as it provides the best performance over other values (Table 2 and Fig. 5).

Table 2. Experimentation with ϵ-Value

$\epsilon - Value$	$Convergence\ Speed$	$\%Total\ State\ Action\ Pair\ Visited$
0.01	1800	84.877
0.001	9600	85.34
0.0001	68000	85.031
0.00001	999996	94.256

Fig. 5. The red points indicate the racing line approximation of the algorithm and the green points the middle line of the track. As it is shown the tangent circles of the racing line always have bigger radii, thus the racing line approximation is a better solution than the middle line. (Color figure online)

6   Interface

We developed an application which can be mounted on the steering wheel of a vehicle and present in real time the optimum trajectory and the velocity profile. The interface includes a red ball which moves up or down if the vehicle's cruising speed is too fast or too slow and tends to go right or left if the vehicle does not follow the racing line. The driver can make the appropriate corrections by moving the steering wheel or pushing the throttle. The behavior of the driver is always monitored by the system described in Sect. 2.

The completed system is simple and its minimalistic design leaves the concentration of the driver unaffected.

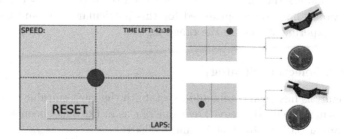

Fig. 6. (a) The implementation of the graphical interface into the raspberry pi. (b) Illustration of a game scenario.

7   Testing and Results

The presented system has been installed on the LEV described in Sect. 2. To test the results of the system and the behavior of the driver when the system is running we conducted the following experiment during the Europe Shell Eco Marathon event 2017. First, we asked the driver to maintain a constant velocity on the closed track mentioned above, which is 1.7 km in length, as a regular

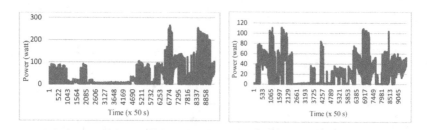

Fig. 7. Graph 7a shows the generated power from the engine of the LEV when the driver maintains a constant velocity of 25 km/h in the testing track. Graph 7b shows the generated power when the driver uses our system with the velocity profile of Fig. 4a and the racing line of Fig. 6a.

cruise control system would do. Second, we used the suggested system and the driver tried to follow the optimum trajectory while driving with the same desired average velocity. The experiment showed that the driver was able to follow the instructions of the system and by adopting the suggested driving strategy the total consumption was reduced by 24.03% (Fig. 7).

Acknowledgements. We would like to thank Prometheus research team of National Technical University of Athens for providing the LEV for the research.

References

1. Kamal, M.A.S., Mukai, M., Murata, J., Kawabe, T.: Ecological vehicle control on roads with up-down slopes. IEEE Trans. Intell. Transp. Syst. **12**(3), 783–794 (2011)
2. Lin, Y.-C., Nguyen, H.L.T.: Development of an eco-cruise control system based on digital topographical data. Inventions **1**(3), 19 (2016)
3. Gilbert, E.G.: Vehicle cruise: improved fuel economy by periodic control. Automatica **12**(2), 159–166 (1976)
4. Yi, Z., Bauer, P.H.: Optimal speed profiles for sustainable driving of electric vehicles. In: IEEE Vehicle Power and Propulsion Conference (VPPC), pp. 1–6, 19–22 (2015)
5. Chang, D.J., Morlok, E.K.: Vehicle speed profiles to minimize work and fuel consumption. J. Transp. Engrg. **131**(3), 173–182 (2005)
6. Wu, X., He, X., Yu, G., Harmandayan, A., Wang, Y.: Energy-optimal speed control for electric vehicles on signalized arterials. IEEE Trans. Intell. Transp. Syst. **16**(5) (2015)
7. Sivak, M., Schoettle, B.: Eco-driving: Strategic, Tactical, and Operational Decisions of the Driver that Influence Vehicle Fuel Economy. Elsevier Ltd. (2012)
8. Hochreiter, S., Schmidhuber, J.: Long short-term memory. Neural Comput. **9**(8), 1735–1780 (1997)
9. Gamage, H.D., (Brian) Lee, J.: Machine learning approach for self-learning eco-speed control. In: Australasian Transport Research Forum (2016)
10. Sharp, R.S., Casanova, D.: On minimum time vehicle manoeuvring: the theoretical optimal time. Ph.D. thesis, Cranfield University (2000)
11. Braghin, F., Cheli, F., Melzi, S., Sabbioni, E.: Race driver model. Comput. Struct. **86**(13–14), 1503–1516 (2008)
12. Medsker, L.R., Jain, L.C.: Recurrent Neural Networks Design and Applications. CRC Press, New York (2001)
13. Mazroua, A.A., Salama, M.M.A., Bartnikas, R.: PD pattern recognition with neural networks using the multilayer perceptron technique. IEEE Trans. Electr. Insulation (1993)

Action Markets in Deep Multi-Agent Reinforcement Learning

Kyrill Schmid[✉], Lenz Belzner, Thomas Gabor, and Thomy Phan

Mobile and Distributed Systems Group, LMU Munich, Munich, Germany
{kyrill.schmid,belzner,thomy.phan,thomas.gabor}@ifi.lmu.de
http://www.mobile.ifi.lmu.de

Abstract. Recent work on learning in multi-agent systems (MAS) is concerned with the ability of self-interested agents to learn cooperative behavior. In many settings such as resource allocation tasks the lack of cooperative behavior can be seen as a consequence of wrong incentives. I.e., when agents can not freely exchange their resources then greediness is not uncooperative but only a consequence of reward maximization. In this work, we show how the introduction of markets helps to reduce the negative effects of individual reward maximization. To study the emergence of trading behavior in MAS we use Deep Reinforcement Learning (RL) where agents are self-interested, independent learners represented through Deep Q-Networks (DQNs). Specifically, we propose *Action Traders*, referring to agents that can trade their atomic actions in exchange for environmental reward. For empirical evaluation we implemented action trading in the Coin Game – and find that trading significantly increases social efficiency in terms of overall reward compared to agents without action trading.

1 Introduction

The success of combining reinforcement learning (RL) and artificial neural networks (ANNs) in single agent settings has also respawned interest in multi agent reinforcement learning (MARL) [8,9,16,20]. In so called independent learning each agent is represented by a neural network which is trained according to a specific learning rule such as Q-learning [12]. When agents are self-interested the emergent behavior is often suboptimal as agents learn behavior w.r.t. their individual reward signal. In tasks such as resource allocation problems this leads to first-come, first-served strategies. The resulting allocations from such strategies are in general inefficient. An allocation is said to be inefficient, if there is another allocation under which at least one agent has higher reward and all other agents have at least equally high rewards compared to the former allocation.

While some work tries to mitigate greedy behavior based on game theoretic strategies such as Tit-for-Tat [9] we argue that inefficiency can also be seen as a consequence of market failure. Specifically, many settings provide no incentives for agents to increase efficiency. I.e., as long as an agent's best alternative in terms of utility is being greedy then the learned behavior is rational rather than

© Springer Nature Switzerland AG 2018
V. Kůrková et al. (Eds.): ICANN 2018, LNCS 11140, pp. 240–249, 2018.
https://doi.org/10.1007/978-3-030-01421-6_24

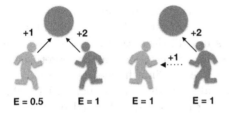

Fig. 1. Two agents competing for a coin: while pure self-interested behavior without trading incentivizes agents to act greedily the introduction of a market can help to increase both agents' expected value. (Color figure online)

uncooperative. However, individual utility maximization can originate efficiency when agents are enabled to incentivize other agents. We call such a mechanism a market for behavior as it enables agents to trade behavior in exchange for other resources e.g. environmental reward. In the presence of a behavior market a utility maximizing agent can invest to stimulate behavior.

Figure 1 illustrates how the introduction of a behavior market helps to overcome inefficiency in a stylized scenario. Suppose two agents are competing for a coin where agent 1 (yellow) gains a reward of +1 while agent 2 (blue) gains a reward of +2 from gathering the coin. When there is a probability of 0.5 for both agents to get it when they step forward then they will have an expected value of 0.5 (agent 1) and 1 for agent 2. As each agent only considers it's own reward there will be no incentive for agent 1 to dedicate the coin to agent 2 while this would maximize the overall outcome. This changes when agents are enabled to exchange reward for behavior. When being able to trade, agent 2 could propose agent 1 a reward +1 when agent 1 steps back. In this case, expected values are both 1 which increases overall reward.

The main contributions of this paper are:

- A definition of action trading as a realization of a behavior market.
- Empirical evidence that the introduction of markets is sufficient in order to increase efficiency in MAS.

The rest of this paper is organized as follows: Sect. 2 gives an overview about related work. Section 3 describes the learning methods. Section 4 introduces action trading. Finally, in Sect. 5 we evaluate action trading in two experiments comparing self-interested agents with and without action trading in a matrix game and the Coin Game.

2   Related Work

Independent and cooperative RL in multi-agent systems has been researched for decades [10,14,21]. Recent successes of both model-free and model-based deep RL extending classical approaches with learned abstractions of state and action spaces [12,17,19] motivated the use of deep RL also in multi-agent domains [1,3].

The tensions of cooperation, competitiveness, self-interest and social welfare have traditionally been researched in the framework of game theory [13]. Game theory has also been a central theoretic tool for studying multi-agent systems [18]. A recent line of research investigates game-theoretic considerations in multi-agent (deep) RL settings, extending the idea of classical games into the setting of sequential decision making under uncertainty [8,9,16,20].

In particular, to bring the concept of social dilemmas closer towards real-world problems the authors of [8] propose sequential social dilemmas (SSDs) where cooperation and competition cannot be seen as an atomic action but are represented through complex policies. In different experiments the authors show how learned behavior depends on the choice of environmental factors such as resource abundance. Through variation of these external properties the authors train different policies and classify these as cooperative or competitive respectively. In this work we adopt the idea of SSDs with multiple independent agents each represented through deep Q-networks. Still, in our analysis we do not focus on the emergence of cooperative policies through variation of environmental factors. Instead we were interested in answering the question whether in a system of autonomous, self-interested agents the chance to make economical decisions leads to efficient allocation of resources and hence increases social welfare.

In [20] the authors demonstrated how cooperative behavior emerges as a function of the rewarding scheme in the classic video game Pong. Agents, represented by autonomous Deep Q-Networks, learned strategies representing cooperation and competition respectively through modification of the reward function. In our approach we do not specify the rewarding scheme as a static property of the environment but rather as a changing structure through which agents can express their willingness to cooperate.

To deal with resource allocation in MARL the authors in [11] propose resource abstraction where each available resource is assigned to an abstract group. Abstract groups build the basis for new reward functions from which learning agents receive a more informative learning signal. Whereas the building of abstract resource groups and hence the shaping of rewards is done at design time, in this work the transformation of reward schemes is part of the learning process.

An approach to carry the successful Prisoner's Dilemma strategy tit-for-tat into complex environments has been recently made by Lerer and Peysakhovich [9]. In their work they construct tit-for-tat agents and show through experiments and theoretically their ability to maintain cooperation while purely reactive training techniques are more likely to result in socially inefficient outcomes. The analysis of reward trading agents is more interested in emergent properties than in implementing a fixed strategy. We therefore make no other assumption than agents maximizing their own returns.

3   Reinforcement Learning

For the purpose of this work we follow the line of descriptive approaches similar to [8]. Rather than asking what learning rule agents should use we model each agent as a specific learner and observe the emergent system behavior. In this sense we model agents as independent learners, i.e., agents cannot observe each other but only recognize a changing environment which is the result of the learning of other agents. We apply methods from the framework of reinforcement learning where it is known that indepenent learning results in non-stationarity as well as to the violation of the Markov property [4,7]. However, as [8] points out in the descriptive approach this can be considered as a feature rather than a bug as it is an aspect of the real environment that the model captures.

Reinforcement learning (RL) are methods where an agent learns a policy π from repeated interaction with an environment. If multiple agents are involved the problem can be described with a so called Stochastic Game (SG). Formally, a SG is a tuple $(\mathcal{S}, \mathcal{N}, \mathcal{A}, \mathcal{T}, \mathcal{R})$ where: $\mathcal{S}$ is a finite set of states, $\mathcal{N}$ is a finite set of $\mathcal{I}$ players, $\mathcal{A} = \mathcal{A}_1 \times ... \times \mathcal{A}_\mathcal{I}$ describes the joint-action space where $\mathcal{A}_i$ is the finite action set of player i, $\mathcal{T} : \mathcal{S} \times \mathcal{A} \times \mathcal{S} \to \mathbb{R}$ is the transition function and $\mathcal{R} = r_1, ..., r_\mathcal{I}$ where $r_i : \mathcal{S} \times \mathcal{A} \to \mathbb{R}$ is the reward function for player i [4].

An agent's goal is to maximize its expected return which is $\mathcal{R}_t := \sum_{t=1}^{\infty} \gamma^{t-1} R_t$. An agent decides which actions to take in a certain state according to a policy π which is a function $\pi : \mathcal{S} \to \mathcal{P}(\mathcal{A})$ from states to probability distributions over $\mathcal{A}$. Over the course of training the agent is supposed to learn a policy that maximizes the expected return. One way to obtain a policy is to learn the action value function $Q : \mathcal{S} \times \mathcal{A} \to \mathbb{R}$ that gives the value of an action in a certain state. A popular way to learn the action value function is Q-learning where an agent i updates its values according to: $Q_i(s, a) \leftarrow Q_i(s, a) + \alpha \left[r_i + \gamma \max_{a' \in \mathcal{A}^i} Q_i(s', a') - Q_i(s, a) \right]$ where α is the learning rate and γ is a discount factor. From Q a policy π can be derived by using e.g. ϵ-greedy action selection where with probability $1 - \epsilon$ the agent selects an action with $argmax_{a \in \mathcal{A}} Q(s, a)$ and with probability ϵ the agent selects an action random uniform from the available actions.

In this work, we model agents as independent Q-Learners. Deep RL refers to methods that use deep neural networks as function approximators. In deep multi-agent RL each agent can be represented by a deep Q-network (DQN) [12]. For independent learners, each agent stores a function $Q_i : \mathcal{S} \times \mathcal{A}_i \to \mathbb{R}$ that approximates the state-action values.

4   Action Trading

This section formally introduces action trading which is realized through extending agents' action spaces. The idea of action trading is to let agents exchange environmental reward for atomic actions. Learning then comprises two parts: policies for the original action space of the stochastic game and a trading policy that represents an agent's trading behavior. To keep notation simple we define action trading for the two agent case i.e., $\mathcal{N} = \{1, 2\}$.

For a given stochastic game $(\mathcal{S}, \mathcal{N}, \mathcal{A}, \mathcal{T}, \mathcal{R})$, action trading is realized through extending action spaces $\mathcal{A}_1$ and $\mathcal{A}_2$ in the following way: $\mathcal{A}_1' = \mathcal{A}_1 \times (\mathcal{A}_2 \times [0, .., N])$ and $\mathcal{A}_2' = \mathcal{A}_2 \times (\mathcal{A}_1 \times [0, .., N])$. I.e., action spaces $\mathcal{A}_i'$ comprise

244   K. Schmid et al.

the original actions $a_{orig} \in \mathcal{A}_i$ and also trading actions $a_{trade} \in \mathcal{A}_j \times [0, .., N]$.
A trading action a_{trade} is a tuple (a_{ij}, p) that defines the amount of reward
$p \in [0, ..., N]$ that agent i is offering agent j for an action a_{ij}. p therefore is
the price an agent pays and is transferred from agent i to agent j if a trade is
established.

In this work we require a successful trade to satisfy two conditions. Firstly,
agent i made an offer to agent j at time-step t for action a written as a_{ij}.
Secondly, also at time-step t agent j actually chose action a, written as a_j. Thus,
a trade will only be established if offer and supply match at the same time step.
The resulting rewards at time-step t in the two agents scenario for agent 1 are
$r_t^1 = \mathcal{R}^1 + p_2 * \delta_{21} - p_1 * \delta_{12}$ and for agent 2 $r_t^2 = \mathcal{R}^2 + p_1 * \delta_{12} - p_2 * \delta_{21}$ where
$\mathcal{R}^i$ represents the original environmental reward and δ_{ij} are boolean values to
define successful trades i.e., $\delta_{ij} = \begin{cases} 1, & \text{if } a_{ij} = a_j, \\ 0, & \text{otherwise} \end{cases}$.

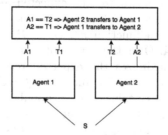

Fig. 2. Action trading describes a mechanism to offer other agents environmental
reward in exchange for specific actions. Agents therefore choose in addition to their
original actions also trading actions. A trade is realized when an offer matches an actual
action.

Figure 2 visualizes how action trading is realized. Agents select actions from
their original action space and from the trading action space. Trading actions
describe agents' offers towards other agents for specific actions. Whenever an
offer matches an actual performed action a trade is realized i.e., a fixed amount
of reward is transferred between the two involved agents.

5   Experiments

In this section, we describe two experiments. The first experiment is an iterated
matrix game that has been extended to enable agents to trade actions. The
second experiment is the Coin Game, which is used for studying sequential social
dilemmas in the recent literature for multi-agent learning [2,9]. In all experiments
we compared action traders with self-interested agents.

To measure the social outcomes of multi-agent learning, it is necessary to
define a metric as the value function cannot be used as a performance metric
like in single agent RL. To measure efficiency, we use the total sum of rewards

obtained by all agents over an episode of duration T, also called the Utilitarian metric (U), which is defined by [15]: $U = \mathbb{E}[\frac{\sum_{i=1}^{N} R^i}{T}]$ where $R^i = \sum_{i=1}^{T} r_i^t$ is the return for agent i for a sequence of rewards $\{r_t^i | t = 1, ..., T\}$ over an episode of duration T. For the Coin Game the Utilitarian is complemented by the total number of collected coins, and the share of correctly collected coins within one episode.

5.1 Iterated Matrix Game

To study the effects of action trading in a simple matrix game, we used a game with pay-offs as given in Fig. 3a. Action trading in the matrix game was realized by extending action spaces $\mathcal{A}_i = \{1, 2\}$ to $\mathcal{A}_i = \{(1, 0), (1, 1), (1, 2), (2, 0), (2, 1), (2, 2)\}$, i.e., each agent decides what action to take from the original action space in combination with a trading action. The price in terms of reward is fixed with $p = 1$ for all actions. As learning rule we used tabular Q-learning with learning rate $\alpha = 0.001$. For action selection we used the ϵ-greedy Q-Function with ϵ decaying from 1.0 to 0.1 over 2500 steps.

The results from 100 runs each comprising 2500 steps are shown in Fig. 3. Independent learners without trading (blue) start to select the dominating action $(1, 1)$ with high probability which is reasonable as agent 2 only ever receives reward when choosing action 1. Likewise, agent 1 learns to choose action 1 as a best response to the selection of agent 2. In contrast, independent learners with action trading (green) have decreasing reward for around 1000 steps. Afterwards overall reward constantly increases.

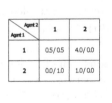

(a) Payoffs   (b) Overall reward

Fig. 3. 100 runs of the iterated matrix game with payoffs as given in the table (left). Whereas non-trading agents (blue) fail to find a global optimum agents with action trading (green) eventually learn to maximize overall and individual reward (Color figure online)

5.2 The Coin Game

To study the effects of action trading in a problem with sequential decision making we adopt the Coin Game first proposed in [9]. The Coin Game is a 2-dimensional grid world that includes 2 agents (blue and yellow) and their respective coins. The task is to collect the coins and agents get a reward of +1 for collecting coins of any color. However, whenever an agent collects a coin that is different from its own color the other agent loses two points. To evaluate the performance of action trading for $n > 2$ we also tested an extended version of the Coin Game comprising 4 agents. The 4 agents Coin Game works in the same way, i.e., agents have their associated coins and impose costs on a fellow agent whenever they collect a differently colored coin.

From the perspective of this work, the Coin Game can be seen as a task where resources (coins) need to be allocated to agents. When efficiency is measured as overall reward then it would be best if agents only collected their own coins to prevent imposing costs on the other agent. As a consequence agents have an incentive to pay the other agent for not collecting their own coins. Consider the situation, when agent 1 (yellow) is about to collect the blue coin. This will bring agent 1 a reward of $+1$ and -2 for agent 2 (blue). Consequently, agent 2 would be willing to pay a price $p \leq 3$ to agent 1 in exchange for the coin.

Action spaces A^i in the Coin Game have four actions: $A^i = \{North, South, East, West\}$. To reduce the trading options for agents at any step, we decided to define a single tradeable action $StepBack$ which is any action that increases the distance between an agent and the current coin. The trading decision an agent has to make is whether to offer another agent the fixed price p in exchange for a $StepBack$ action. I.e., each agent i chooses actions from: $A^i \times \prod_{j \neq i} s^j$ where A^i describes the original action space of agent i and $s^j = \{0, 1\}$ describes the binary choice to trade with any other agent j.

Learning. Agents in the Coin Game were represented as deep Q-Networks (DQNs). During learning, exploration was encouraged by using a linear Boltzman policy, defined by: $\pi(s) = \text{argmax}_a(V_a)$, where V_a is sampled from $V_a \sim \frac{\exp(q_t(a)/\tau)}{\sum_{i=1}^n \exp(q_t(i)/\tau)}$ for each $a \in A$. All agents updated their policies from a stored batch of transitions $\{(s, a, r_i, s')_t : t = 1, ..., T\}$ [6]. For the Coin Game experiments, the batch size was limited to $50k$ transitions, where older transitions are discarded after inserting new transitions. The network was trained with the Adam optimization algorithm with a learning rate of $1e^{-3}$ [5]. Coin Game episodes lasted for 100 steps and after 25 episodes we logged 50 test episodes. The discount rate γ was 0.99.

Modeling trade in the Coin Game required to set a couple of trading related parameters. Firstly, the price p for an action a. In our experiments, we set $p = 1.25$ as it exceeds an agents profit from collecting a coin and is less than the designated owner of the coin would lose if the other agent collected the coin.

The second parameter of interest is the trading budget m i.e., the available budget until the current coin is collected. We experimented with different budgets and chose m to be 2.5 which allowed for a maximum of 2 trades when $p = 1.25$. A third critical question was whether agents should be allowed to accumulate wealth over steps or even episodes. Although this seems an interesting aspect we decided not to let agents gather their earnings and leave the analysis of such a setting for future work.

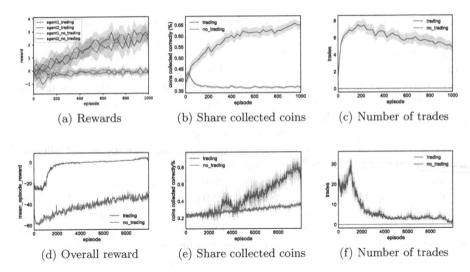

Fig. 4. Coin Game results for 2 agents (upper row) and 4 agents (lower row). Results comprise 1000 (2 agents) and 10000 (4 agents) episodes and show mean values and confidence intervals from 80 runs for 2 agents and 10 runs for 4 agents. Each plot shows results for agents with action trading (green) and without trading (blue). Action traders show increasing individual and overall rewards (left column) along with an increasing share of correctly collected coins (middle column). The number of trades (third column) decreases after a steep rise during the early learning period (best viewed in color). (Color figure online)

Results. Figure 4 shows Coin Game results for 2 agents (upper row) and 4 agents (lower row) respectively. Experiments involve agents without trading (blue) and trading (green) for 80 runs (2 agents) and 10 runs (4 agents) where runs last for 1000 episodes (2 agents) and 10000 episodes (4 agents). Shaded areas show .95 confidence intervals. The left column shows the overall reward and the individual rewards in the 2 agents setting. While non-trading agents' reward never increases, action traders manage to increase individual and overall reward. This comes from an increasing share of correctly collected coins (middle column). The number of trades sharply increase during the first 200 episodes and continuously decrease afterwards.

6 Discussion

Action trading in the iterated matrix game outperformed pure self-fish agents. Nevertheless, prices for actions were given at design time which renders the question on the ability of agents to find prices on their own.

The results from the Coin Game clearly confirm that action trading effectively increases social welfare, measured through overall increase of reward for all agents. It also shows that a given number of available resources (coins) are allocated more efficiently as the proportion of correctly collected coins also constantly increases. This is the consequence of agents' trading activity that increases sharply at early learning phases and is kept at a high level afterwards. In learning to trade, agents realize Pareto improvements and empirically confirm the first fundamental theorem of welfare economics according to which competitive markets will tend towards Pareto efficiency. From the experiments we realized that the trading budget is a critical parameter with respect to the problem of interest which will be left for future work.

An interesting point seems the slow decrease in the number of trades. This might be caused by an agent speculating for short-term profits by not offering a trade in the hope that the other agent might be doing the expected action anyway. This could cause distrust which threatens future trades.

We recognize that trading actions in MARL presumes that a trade can be controlled, i.e., agents cannot cheat on each other by making offers which they do not hold afterwards. While this seems like a strong assumption, it appears less restrictive from a practical point of view. The only extension with respect to the environment is that agents' rewards need to include the net earnings that where realized by their trading activity. I.e., the environment adopts the role of an neutral auctioneer that matches supply and offer and returns the resulting rewards for each agent.

References

1. Foerster, J., Assael, Y.M., de Freitas, N., Whiteson, S.: Learning to communicate with deep multi-agent reinforcement learning. In: Advances in Neural Information Processing Systems, pp. 2137–2145 (2016)
2. Foerster, J.N., Chen, R.Y., Al-Shedivat, M., Whiteson, S., Abbeel, P., Mordatch, I.: Learning with opponent-learning awareness. arXiv preprint arXiv:1709.04326 (2017)
3. Gupta, J.K., Egorov, M., Kochenderfer, M.: Cooperative multiagent control using deep reinforcement learning. In: Proceedings of the Adaptive and Learning Agents Workshop (AAMAS 2017) (2017)
4. Hernandez-Leal, P., Kaisers, M., Baarslag, T., de Cote, E.M.: A survey of learning in multiagent environments: Dealing with non-stationarity. arXiv preprint arXiv:1707.09183 (2017)
5. Kingma, D., Ba, J.: Adam: a method for stochastic optimization. arXiv preprint arXiv:1412.6980 (2014)
6. Lange, S., Gabel, T., Riedmiller, M.: Batch reinforcement learning. In: Wiering, M., van Otterlo, M. (eds.) Reinforcement Learning, pp. 45–73. Springer, Heidelberg (2012). https://doi.org/10.1007/978-3-642-27645-3_2
7. Laurent, G.J., Matignon, L., Fort-Piat, L., et al.: The world of independent learners is not Markovian. Int. J. Knowl. Based Intell. Eng. Syst. 15(1), 55–64 (2011)
8. Leibo, J.Z., Zambaldi, V., Lanctot, M., Marecki, J., Graepel, T.: Multi-agent reinforcement learning in sequential social dilemmas. In: Proceedings of the 16th Conference on Autonomous Agents and MultiAgent Systems, pp. 464–473. International Foundation for Autonomous Agents and Multiagent Systems (2017)
9. Lerer, A., Peysakhovich, A.: Maintaining cooperation in complex social dilemmas using deep reinforcement learning. arXiv preprint arXiv:1707.01068 (2017)

10. Littman, M.L.: Markov games as a framework for multi-agent reinforcement learning. In: Proceedings of the Eleventh International Conference on Machine Learning, vol. 157, pp. 157–163 (1994)
11. Malialis, K., Devlin, S., Kudenko, D.: Resource abstraction for reinforcement learning in multiagent congestion problems. In: Proceedings of the 2016 International Conference on Autonomous Agents and Multiagent Systems, pp. 503–511. International Foundation for Autonomous Agents and Multiagent Systems (2016)
12. Mnih, V., et al.: Human-level control through deep reinforcement learning. Nature **518**(7540), 529–533 (2015)
13. Osborne, M.J., Rubinstein, A.: A Course in Game Theory. MIT Press, Cambridge (1994)
14. Panait, L., Luke, S.: Cooperative multi-agent learning: the state of the art. Auton. Agents Multi Agent Syst. **11**(3), 387–434 (2005)
15. Perolat, J., Leibo, J.Z., Zambaldi, V., Beattie, C., Tuyls, K., Graepel, T.: A multi-agent reinforcement learning model of common-pool resource appropriation. arXiv preprint arXiv:1707.06600 (2017)
16. Peysakhovich, A., Lerer, A.: Prosocial learning agents solve generalized stag hunts better than selfish ones. arXiv preprint arXiv:1709.02865 (2017)
17. Schulman, J., Wolski, F., Dhariwal, P., Radford, A., Klimov, O.: Proximal policy optimization algorithms. arXiv preprint arXiv:1707.06347 (2017)
18. Shoham, Y., Leyton-Brown, K.: Multiagent Systems: Algorithmic, Game-Theoretic, and Logical Foundations. Cambridge University Press, Cambridge (2008)
19. Silver, D., et al.: Mastering the game of Go without human knowledge. Nature **550**(7676), 354–359 (2017)
20. Tampuu, A., et al.: Multiagent cooperation and competition with deep reinforcement learning. PloS One **12**(4), e0172395 (2017)
21. Tan, M.: Multi-agent reinforcement learning: independent vs. cooperative agents. In: Proceedings of the Tenth International Conference on Machine Learning, pp. 330–337 (1993)

Continuous-Time Spike-Based Reinforcement Learning for Working Memory Tasks

Marios Karamanis, Davide Zambrano, and Sander Bohté[(✉)]

CWI, Machine Learning Group, Amsterdam, The Netherlands
{marios,davide,sbohte}@cwi.nl

Abstract. As the brain purportedly employs on-policy reinforcement learning compatible with SARSA learning, and most interesting cognitive tasks require some form of memory while taking place in continuous-time, recent work has developed plausible reinforcement learning schemes that are compatible with these requirements. Lacking is a formulation of both computation and learning in terms of spiking neurons. Such a formulation creates both a closer mapping to biology, and also expresses such learning in terms of asynchronous and sparse neural computation. We present a spiking neural network with memory that learns cognitive tasks in continuous time. Learning is biologically plausibly implemented using the AuGMeNT framework, and we show how separate spiking forward and feedback networks suffice for learning the tasks just as fast the analog CT-AuGMeNT counterpart, while computing efficiently using very few spikes: 1–20 Hz on average.

Keywords: Reinforcement learning · Working memory
Spiking neurons

1 Introduction

Reinforcement Learning [17] describes how animals can learn to act effectively given sparse and possibly delayed rewards from their environment. For many tasks, optimal action selection requires some form of memory: the shortest path to a parked car relies on remembering where the car was parked, and understanding text requires the integration of information over the length of the sentence, if not from earlier paragraphs. For event-based and discrete-time optimization problems, Reinforcement Learning has been used to successfully train deep [11,16] and recurrent neural networks [1]. For working memory tasks, [1] demonstrated that LSTMs can be trained with the RL Advantage Learning algorithm, but this type of "off-policy" RL based on error-backpropagation is considered biologically implausible given the preponderance for "on-policy" RL like SARSA [12]. How animals can learn such tasks with SARSA-like RL and neural network models has been the topic of much research in neuroscience, with implications also in fields like deep learning and neuromorphics.

© Springer Nature Switzerland AG 2018
V. Kůrková et al. (Eds.): ICANN 2018, LNCS 11140, pp. 250–262, 2018.
https://doi.org/10.1007/978-3-030-01421-6_25

Recent work [15,20] has suggested how working memory tasks can be learned in neural network models equipped with memory neurons, where memory neurons learn which stimuli need to be remembered for later use; learning is then made local and plausible using feedback connections [13]. While standard RL is formulated in an event-based manner, that is, framed in terms of state-changes, animals operate in a continuous-time setting and Zambrano et al. showed in [20] that a continuous-time version of AuGMEnT (CT-AuGMEnT) can be realized using an action selection mechanism that integrates evidence - drawing inspiration from the brain's basal ganglia structures - combined with a separate feedback network for learning. Missing so far is a model of biologically plausible RL based on spiking neurons: here we present such a model, and we show how learning can in fact be based on the (sparse) relative timing of spikes.

We show how the CT-AuGMEnT framework can be extended to asynchronous and sparsely active spiking neural networks. Recent work has shown how spiking neurons can be used to computed convolutional neural networks [5,18] and compute control [7]; RL versions are lacking. We turn to adaptive spiking neurons [2] and develop two spike-based approaches: the first where spikes carry approximations of both forward and feedback signals, and the CT-AuGMEnT-derived learning mechanism uses these signal approximations. In the second, we develop spike-triggered learning by exploiting the fact that the dynamics of the tasks are much slower than the timescale of timesteps in the simulation, and CT-AuGMEnT weights-updates can be approximated by sparse sampling of the learning components – spike-triggered learning then uses the asynchronous nature of adaptive spike-coding where changes in signals elicit more spikes in the network, and hence higher precision sampling.

We show how these approaches can be applied to two standard RL working memory tasks (T-Maze and Saccade-anti-Saccade), and find that networks trained with both spike-based learning methods successfully and efficiently learn the tasks. When using spike-based learning, we find that very low firing rates in the network suffice, where the spike-triggered learning approach requires only slightly higher firing rates, as can be expected since so very learning events take place. Together, we demonstrate spiking neural networks to learn cognitive tasks, capable of online-learning using sparse spike-triggered learning.

2   CT-AuGMEnT

In [14,15], AuGMEnT was developed as an artificial neural network (ANN) implementation of the on-policy SARSA reinforcement learning algorithm for solving Markov Decision Processes (MDPs) that require learnable working memory to construct Markov states in the hidden layer of the neural network model. AuGMEnT implements a biologically plausible local learning rule based on four factors: attentional feedback, forward activation, the local derivative of the transfer function, and a global neuromodulatory scalar value that signals the temporal difference error (TD-error) δ (Fig. 1a). This learning rule is local and enables the learning of XOR-like non-linear function mappings in multi-layer networks [15].

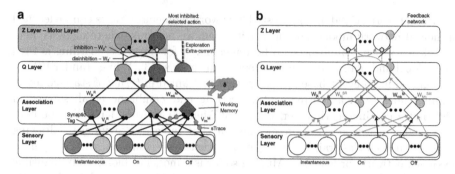

Fig. 1. (a) The CT-AuGMEnT architecture. The feedforward layers include memory units in the association layer (diamonds) to compute Q-values in the Q-layer. The Q-values are integrated in the action-selecting Z-layer, where the most inhibited action is selected at any point in time. Feedback from the (sole) selected action induces tags and traces on the synapses, which in combination with TD-error (δ) determines changes in synaptic weights. (b) In continuous-time, the feedback activity from the selected action is carried by a separate feedback network with its own weights (orange network). (Color figure online)

In [19,20] the CT-AuGMEnT framework was developed as an extension of AuGMEnT to include a realistic notion of continuous-time, introducing a dynamic action selection system and demonstrating an explicit feedback network with layer-wise delays and separately learned feedforward and feedback weights. The inclusion of an action selection system decouples the typical timescale of actions from the time resolution of the simulation, allowing for continuous-time on-policy SARSA learning. The resulting network is depicted in Fig. 1b.

As described in [20], the CT-AuGMENT network comprises of four layers (Fig. 1a, b): a sensory input layer, a hidden "association" layer, a Q-layer, and an action layer Z. In the sensory layer, instantaneous units directly represent the stimulus intensity $x(t)$, and transient "on/off" units represent positive and negative changes in stimulus intensity, $x^+(t)$ ("on") and $x^-(t)$ ("off"):

$$x^+(t) = \frac{1}{dt}[x(t) - x(t - dt)]_+, \qquad x^-(t) = \frac{1}{dt}[x(t - dt) - x(t)]_+, \qquad (1)$$

where $[.]_+$ is a thresholding operation returning 0 for negating inputs. The hidden layer is comprised of regular units and memory units, where the instantaneous units i connect to the regular units j via connections v_{ij}^R and the transient units l connect to the memory units m via connections v_{lm}^M. Activations are then computed as:

$$a_j^R(t) = \sum_i v_{ij}^R x_i(t) \qquad y_j^R(t) = f(a_j^R(t)) \qquad (2)$$

$$a_m^M(t) = a_m^M(t - dt) + \sum_l v_{lm}^M x_l'(t) \qquad y_m^M(t) = f(a_m^M(t)). \qquad (3)$$

where $f(.)$ denotes the neuron's transfer function, here the standard sigmoid transfer function; for brevity of notation, $x_l'(t) = [x^+(t) \quad x^-(t)]$. The third layer is connected to the association layer via connections w_{mk}^M and w_{jk}^R, computing Q-values for every possible action k in the current state s, $q_k(t)$:

$$q_k(t) = \sum_m w_{mk}^M y_m^M(t) + \sum_j w_{jk}^R y_j^R(t). \tag{4}$$

The Z-layer, modeled after action selection in the basal ganglia [8], implements an action-selection model based on competition between possible actions by connecting the Z-layer to the Q-layer with off-center on-surround connectivity: each q-unit inhibits its corresponding Z-unit and excites all other Z-neurons (Fig. 1a, top). The input to a Z-layer unit u_i is thus:

$$u_i(t) = -w^- q_i(t) + w^+ \sum_{j \neq i}^n q_j(t), \tag{5}$$

where we set $w^-/w^+ = \nu$, with ν the number of possible actions in the task; the activation of the Z units can then be modeled as a leaky integrator:

$$\dot{a}_i(t) = -\rho(a_i(t) - u_i(t)), \tag{6}$$

where ρ is a rate constant that determines how fast equilibrium is reached. The Z-layer output $y_i(t)$ is bounded using the sigmoid activation function:

$$y_i(t) = \sigma(a_i(t)). \tag{7}$$

The Q-layer thus determines the degree of inhibition in the Z-layer, where, somewhat counterintuitive, the selected action is the one that receives the most inhibition. Exploration is implemented as the addition of an external current to the explorative action unit in Eq. (5) [20].

Learning: In the CT-AuGMEnT network, network plasticity is modulated by two factors: a global neuromodulatory signal and an attentional feedback signal. At every time-step, the Z-unit corresponding to the winning action a creates synaptic tags (equivalent to eligibility traces) by sending feedback activity to earlier processing levels. Tags in the Q-layer decay and are updated as:

$$Tag_{jk}(t + dt) = -\frac{1}{\phi} Tag_{jk}(t) + dt[y_j(t)z_k(t)], \tag{8}$$

with $z_k = 1$ for the selected action and $z_k = 0$ for the other actions. The association units that provided strong input to the winning action a thus also receive the strongest feedback. Tags - mimicking eligibility trace - on connections between regular units and instantaneous units are equivalently computed as:

$$Tag_{ij}(t + dt) = -\frac{1}{\phi} Tag_{ij}(t) + dt[x_i(t)f'(a_j^R(t))w_{kj}^R], \tag{9}$$

where $f'(\cdot)$ denotes the local derivative of the transfer function f, and the feedforward connections w_{jk}^R and the feedback connections w_{kj}^R may have different

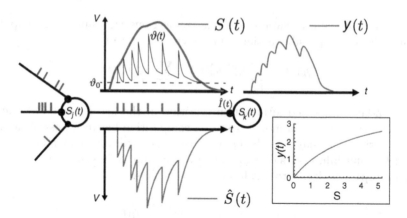

Fig. 2. ASN-based neural coding. Input spikes (red ticks), induce a smoothed activation $S(t)$ in the post-synaptic neurons. The neuron emits spikes (blue ticks) when the input activation exceeds a variable threshold $\vartheta(t)$, and a refractory response scaled by the momentary adaptation is subtracted from the activation at the time of spiking. The resulting total refractory response $\hat{S}(t)$ approximates the rectified activation $S(t)^+$. At the next target neuron, the emitted spike-train induces an (unweighted) activation $y(t)$; the transfer function (inset) describes the average relationship between the activation $S(t)$ and the target activation $y(t)$. (Color figure online)

strength [13]. Synaptic traces between sensory units l and memory cells m enable the proper learning of working memory:

$$sTrace_{lm}(t + dt) = sTrace_{lm}(t) + dt[x'_l(t)]$$

$$Tag_{lm}(t + dt) = -\tfrac{1}{\phi}Tag_{lm}(t) + dt[sTrace_{lm}(t)f'(a_m^M(t))w_{km}^M]. \tag{10}$$

To implement on-policy SARSA temporal difference (TD) learning [17], the predicted outcome $q_a(T - 1)$ is compared to the sum of the reward $r(t)$ and the discounted action-value $q_{a'}(T)$ of the unit a' that wins the competition at time T, resulting in a TD error $\delta(T) = r + \gamma q_{a'}(T) - q_a(T - 1)$. For continuous-time TD learning, [20] gives the following TD error:

$$\delta(t) = r(t) + \frac{1}{dt}\left[\left(1 - \frac{dt}{\tau}\right)q_{a'}(t) - q_a(t - dt)\right], \tag{11}$$

with learning rate β, weight updates are then defined as:

$$v_{ij}(t + dt) = v_{ij}(t) + dt[\beta\delta(t)Tag_{ij}(t)],$$

$$v_{lm}(t + dt) = v_{lm}(t) + dt[\beta\delta(t)Tag_{lm}(t)], \tag{12}$$

$$w_{jk}(t + dt) = w_{ja}(t) + dt[\beta\delta(t)Tag_{jk}(t)].$$

3   Adaptive Spiking Neurons

Adaptive Spiking Neurons (ASNs) [2] are a variant of standard Leaky-Integrate-and-Fire spiking neurons incorporating a fast multiplicative adaptation mechanism, where the fast adaptation limits the neuron's asymptotic firing rate. The ASN includes spike-triggered adaptation and a dynamical threshold that allows it to match neural responses while maintaining a high coding efficiency.

Illustrated in Fig. 2, adaptive spike-based neural coding is described as a Spike Response Model (SRM) [6], where the input to a neuron j is computed as a sum of spike-triggered post-synaptic currents (PSCs) from pre-synaptic input neurons i. The total PSC, $I(t)$, is computed as a sum over spike-triggered (normalized) kernels $\kappa(t_s^i - t)$ each weighted by synaptic efficacies w_{ij}:

$$I(t) = \sum_i \sum_{t_s^i} w_{ij}\, \kappa(t_s - t), \tag{13}$$

where t_s^i denotes the timing of spikes from input neuron i. A normalized exponential filter $\phi(t)$ is applied to $I(t)$ to obtain the neuron's activation $S(t)$:

$$S(t) = (\phi * I)(t). \tag{14}$$

In the SRM formulation [2], the membrane potential of the neuron is obtained as the neuron's activation $S(t)$ from which the total refractory response $\hat{S}(t)$ is subtracted, where $\hat{S}(t)$ is computed as the sum of spike-triggered refractory response kernels $\eta(t)$ each scaled by the (variable) value of the neuron's threshold at the time of spiking ($\vartheta(t_j)$); $\hat{S}(t)$ then approximates the rectified $S(t)$: $S(t)_+$.

A spike is emitted by neuron j at time t whenever $S - \hat{S}(t) > \theta(t)$ and the membrane potential is reset by subtracting a scaled refractory kernel $\eta(t)$ which is then added to the total refractory response $\hat{S}(t)$. Spike-triggered adaptation is incorporated into the model by multiplicatively increasing the variable threshold $\theta(t)$ with a decaying kernel $\gamma(t)$ at the time of spiking, and by controlling the speed of the firing rate adaptation using the multiplicative parameter m_f:

$$\theta(t) = \theta_0 + \sum_{t_s} m_f \theta(t_s)\gamma(t_s - t), \qquad \hat{S}(t) = \sum_{t_s} \theta(t_s)\eta(t_s - t). \tag{15}$$

We set the PSC kernel as equal to the refractory response kernel $\eta(t)$, and model this kernel and the threshold kernel $\gamma(t)$ as decaying exponentials with corresponding time-constants τ_η, τ_γ; as is the membrane filter $\phi(t)$ (τ_ϕ):

$$\kappa(t) = \eta(t) = \exp\left(\frac{t_s - t}{\tau_\eta}\right), \tag{16}$$

$$\gamma(t) = \exp\left(\frac{t_s - t}{\tau_\gamma}\right), \qquad \phi(t) = \phi_0 \exp\left(\frac{t_s - t}{\tau_\phi}\right), \tag{17}$$

where the timing of outgoing spikes is denoted by t_s, θ_0 is the resting threshold.

Given a fixed input current $I(t)$ resulting in a fixed activation $S(t)$, the emitted spike-train from the post-synaptic neuron has an (unweighted) fixed size impact $y(t)$ on the next target neuron. We characterize the relationship between activation $S(t)$ and target impact $y(t)$ as the effective ASN transfer-function (inset); this function has a half-sigmoid like shape and can be either computed analytically for particular parameter choices (i.e. [18]) or approximated. For the analog spike-like network in Sect. 4, we approximate the shape of this transfer-function with the positive rectified $tanh()$ function: $tanhP()$.

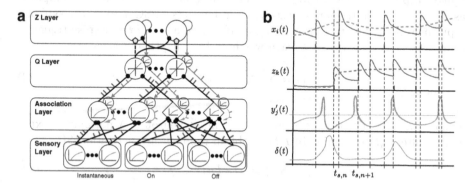

Fig. 3. (a) Spiking CT-AuGMent. Indicated by the half-sigmoid graphs are the neurons that are set to have $tanhP()$ as transfer functions (in the analog rectified network), which are substituted by ASN neurons in the spiking network versions. Ticks along network connections indicate which part of the network "spikes". (b) Spike-based and spike-triggered learning: spike-based learning uses the analog global δ and local $y'(t)$ signals and those derived from feedforward spikes, $x(t)$ and feedback spikes, $z(t)$; spike-triggered learning considers those signals only at spike times $t_{s,n}$.

4   Spike-Based CT-AuGMenT

Analog Rectified CT-AuGMenT. To convert the CT-AuGMenT network to a spiking neural network, we replace the analog neurons by ASN models. The main obstacle here is that ASNs effectively have a rectified half-sigmoid-like transfer function, as illustrated in Fig. 2. The CT-AuGMenT network uses sigmoidal transfer-functions for the feedforward stage, and linear neurons for Q-layer and the feedback network [20]. While for instance [10,13] suggest that there is some flexibility with regard to the feedback network, we create an analog network where the neurons in the feedforward Sensory and Association layer use the $tanhP()$ transfer-function, as well as the feedback network from the Q-layer projecting to the Association layer (illustrated in Fig. 3a). We train this network on the tasks to ascertain the feasibility of training spike-based networks with rectified half-sigmoid-like transfer functions.

Spike-Based Learning. Spiking-AuGMenT incorporates ASNs in the feedback-learning network to include spike-based learning. Inspecting the learning rules (8)–(12) we see that four terms are involved in updating a synapse between a neuron i and j: the feedforward activation $x_i(t)$, the TD-error $\delta(t)$, the gradient of the transfer function $f'(a_i(t))$, and, for the hidden layer neurons j, the feedback activity from the winning action k, $z_k(t)$.

In the spiking-AuGMenT formulation, we use ASNs in both the forward and the feedback network, also while training the network. The feedforward and feedback activations $x_i(t)$ and $z_k(t)$ are both computed as a sum of spike-triggered kernels, corresponding to $S(t)$ in the ASN model. Reformulating CT-AuGMeNT, we denote the spiking neurons of spiking-AuGMenT with s and we use the same subscripts with the analog CT-AuGMenT. Instantaneous and transient units emit spikes to the regular and memory spiking neurons, respectively:

$$a_{\phi j}^R(t_s) = \sum_{t_s} \sum_i v_{ij}^R x_i(t_s) * \phi(t_s), \quad s_j^R(t_s) = f(a_{\phi j}^R(t_s)), \qquad (18)$$

$$a_{\phi m}^M(t_s) = a_m^M(t_s - dt) + \sum_{t_s} \sum_l v_{lm}^M x_l'(t_s) * \phi(t_s), \quad s_m^M(t_s) = f(a_{\phi m}^M(t_s)), \qquad (19)$$

where t_s is the time of outgoing spikes, f is the effective transfer function and $\phi(t)$ an exponential decay filter. As before, the Q-layer is fully connected to the association layer and the values are updated when there are input spikes:

$$q_k(t_s) = \sum_{t_s} \left(\sum_m w_{mk}^M \sigma_m^M(t_s) + \sum_j w_{jk}^R \sigma_j^R(t_s) \right). \qquad (20)$$

Equivalently to the analog network, the Z-layer involves the action mechanism and determines the amount of inhibition an action receives. Note that now the transfer-function is implicit. The spiking neurons in the feedback network are defined as:

$$a_{\phi k}^Z(t_s) = \sum_{t_s} \sum_k z_k(t_s) * \phi(t_s), \qquad (21)$$

$$s_{kj}^R(t_s) = f\left(\sum_{t_s} \sum_k w_{kj}^R(t_s) a_{\phi k}^Z(t_s) \right), \quad s_{kj}^M(t_s) = f\left(\sum_{t_s} \sum_k w_{kj}^M(t_s) a_{\phi k}^Z(t_s) \right). \qquad (22)$$

Equations (8)–(10) and (12) are reformulated accordingly, where we approximate the local gradient of the transfer-function as the derivative of the positive part of the $tanh$-function: $tanhP' = \max(0, 1 - \tanh^2)$ - while a rough approximation, we find this works well in practice. Tags between the association layer and the Q-layer are then defined as:

$$Tag_{jk}(t + dt) = -\frac{1}{\phi} Tag_{jk}(t) + dt[y_j(t) a_{\phi k}^Z(t_s))]. \qquad (23)$$

For tags that are formed between the sensory layer and the association layer:

$$Tag_{ij}(t+dt) = -\frac{1}{\phi}Tag_{ij}(t) + dt[x_i(t_s)tanhP'(a_{\phi j}^R(t_s))s_{kj}^R(t_s)].\quad (24)$$

$$sTrace_{lm}(t+dt) = sTrace_{lm}(t) + dt[x_l'(t_s)],$$

$$(25)$$

$$Tag_{lm}(t+dt) = -\frac{1}{\phi}Tag_{lm}(t) + dt[sTrace_{lm}(t)tanhP'(a_{\phi m}^M(t_s))s_{kj}^M(t)].$$

In the spike-based learning process the weights are updated again by (12), where the TD-error $\delta(t)$ is still an analog broadcasted signal.

In both tasks the initial weights are positive uniformly distributed, motivated by the rectified-positive nature of the spike-based feedback network (22) (Fig. 3a).

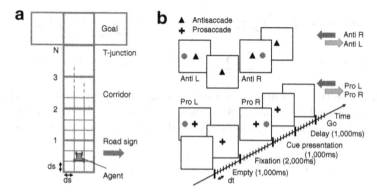

Fig. 4. Tasks. (a) T-Maze task, (b) Saccade-anti-Saccade task. See text for explanation.

Spike-Triggered Learning. In the spiking-AuGMenT formulation, each weight is updated every dt, even though the typical dynamics of the tasks have substantially longer temporal dynamics - milliseconds versus hundreds of milliseconds: a more sparse sampling approach to learning should suffice. Rather than fixed interval learning, we here propose to exploit the asynchronous nature of adaptive spike-coding: we only update the weights when a neuron receives or emits a spike (illustrated in Fig. 3b). The benefit of this sampling scheme is that with adaptive neural coding, the spike-rate increases there is a large change in signal, thus allowing for more and more precise sampling when needed. In more detail, whenever a neuron emits a spike we update the weights, otherwise the learning process pauses. Here, we denote with n the number of the current learning update. Hence, the rule for the update of the weights is:

$$v_{ij}(t_{s,n+1}) = v_{ij}(t_{s,n}) + \delta t[\beta\delta(t)Tag_{ij}(t_{s,n})],$$

$$v_{lm}(t_{s,n+1}) = v_{lm}(t_{s,n}) + \delta t[\beta\delta(t)Tag_{lm}(t_{s,n})],\quad (26)$$

$$w_{jk}(t_{s,n+1}) = w_{jk}(t_{s,n}) + \delta t[\beta\delta(t)Tag_{jk}(t_{s,n})],$$

where δt equals the time between two successive spikes: $\delta t = t_{s,n+1} - t_{s,n}$ (note that here each neuron updates only for its "own" spikes $t_{s,n}$).

5   Results

We demonstrate the spike-based CT-AuGMenT model of Fig. 1 on two working memory tasks: the T-Maze task from the machine learning literature [1,14] and the Saccade/Antisaccade task from the neuroscience literature (both as in [20]).

The **T-Maze** task is a working memory task where information that is presented at the start of the maze has to be maintained to make optimal decisions at the end of the corridor. The agent can choose actions to move in directions N, E, S, W; the corridor length N scales the task difficulty. The same details for corridor representation, reward and time-out conditions as in [20] were applied. For the simulations, we gave each network at most 10,000 trials to learn the task. Convergence was determined by checking at 90% optimal choices as in [20] for each condition. The parameters of the network for the T-Maze task are: $\beta = 0.02$, $\lambda = 0.3$, $\gamma = 0.9$, $\epsilon = 0.025$, $\tau = 0.5$ and corridor length $N = 10$. The ASNs use fixed values for $\theta_0 = 0.1$ and $\tau_\phi = 2.5$ ms. The network is updated at time increments of $dt = 0.01$, equivalent to 10 ms. The network consists of 24 neurons: a sensory layer with 9 input neurons (3 instantaneous and 6 transient units), an Association layer with 7 neurons (4 memory neurons and 3 regular neurons), and, matching the number of possible actions, both the output and the action layer have 4 neurons. Weights between the Sensory and Association and Q-layer are randomly initialized from the uniform distribution $U[0, 0.25]$.

In the **Saccade/Antisaccade (SaS)** task, the agent has to learn that the color of the fixation mark determines the strategy. Every trial started with an empty screen, shown for one second. Then a fixation mark was shown, either black or white, indicating that a pro- or anti-saccade was required. The model had to fixate within ten seconds, otherwise the trial was terminated without reward. If the model fixated for two consecutive seconds, we presented a cue on the left or the right side of the screen for one second and gave the fixation reward r_{fix}. This was followed by a memory delay of two seconds during which only the fixation point was visible. At the end of the memory delay the fixation mark turned off. To collect the final reward r_{fin} in the pro-saccade condition, the model had to make an eye-movement to the remembered location of the cue and to the opposite location on anti-saccade trials. The trial was aborted if the model failed to respond within eight seconds. The maximum number of trials the model is allowed to learn the task is set to 35,000. As to the implementation in [20], we kept the same temporal sequence of the events, and we updated the network at an increased rate of $dt = 0.01$ (corresponding to 10 ms per time step). The chosen parameters for the simulation are: $\beta = 0.01$, $\lambda = 0.2$, $\gamma = 0.9$, $\epsilon = 0.025$, $\tau = 0.5$, $\theta_0 = 0.1$ and $\tau_\phi = 2.5$ ms. The initialization of the weights is also uniformly distributed $U[0, 0.25]$. In this task the network is comprised of 26 neurons, with 12 neurons in the sensory layer (4 instantaneous and 8 transient units), 8 neurons in the Association layer (4 memory and 4 regular units) and both output and action layers have 3 neurons.

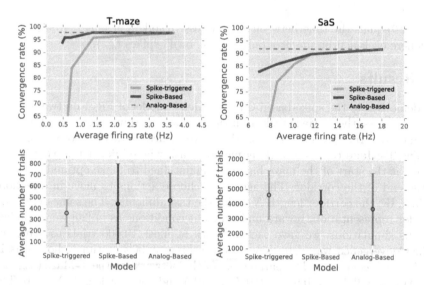

Fig. 5. *First row:* the convergence rate over the average firing rate (Hz) for the two tasks. In the T-Maze task we used $\tau_\gamma = [50, 150, 450, 1000, 1750]$ ms and $\tau_\eta = [150, 450, 1000, 1750, 2500]$ ms. In the SaS task we have $\tau_\gamma = 50$ ms fixed and $\tau_\eta = [100, 150, 200, 250, 300]$ ms. *Bottom row:* The average number of trials for each model and task for spiking network that match the analog network's convergence rate.

In both tasks, the spiking neuron time-constants τ_γ, τ_η are varied to generate spiking neurons that have varying asymptotic activation rates. We tested 50 randomly initialized networks for each set of τ_η and τ_γ. At the end of each learning phase we set $\beta = \epsilon = 0$ to validate the convergence.

We plot the results for both tasks in Fig. 5, both in terms of convergence rate of the networks (top row) and the number of trials required for learning the tasks. We find that both spiking methods, spike-based and spike-triggered CT-AuGMenT, are able to learn the tasks with convergence rates similar to that of CT-AuGMenT [19,20] and the analog rectified version (dashed line) for sufficiently high firing rates. We also compare the average number of trial needed for those spiking networks where the convergence rate matches the analog network (bottom row): we find that for all three learning models, the networks need a similar number of trials to converge. We note also that for both tasks, a majority of networks still converge even for very low average firing rates (<1 Hz for the T-Maze, <8 Hz for SaS).

6   Conclusion

We demonstrated how a continuous-time spiking neural network with working memory can be constructed with plausible spiking neuron models and plausible learning rules that uses on-policy reinforcement learning to learn hard cognitive tasks, a first such network to the best of our knowledge. These spiking neural networks learn the tasks equally fast as their analog counterparts, while needing very few spikes to both learn and carry out the neural computations. As such, this work can be considered an important milestone for creating efficient, sparsely-active and always-on neural networks, with promise for emerging neuromorphic paradigms like the Intel Loihi architecture [4].

Here, we focused on creating a spiking network to learn and compute Q-values, while using an analog action-selection system as we chose to focus here on the learning aspect of the tasks; we see no principled problem to create a spike-based version of this system. The spike-based transmission of potentially negative Q-values represents the greatest challenge, as we found that replacing the linear transfer functions in the Q-layer with half-sigmoid-like rectified functions - or the spiking equivalent, did not work; this is a challenge we presently tackling.

Compared to LSTM networks [9], the presented architecture lacks gating mechanisms and recurrence; LSTM-like gating however is notoriously hard to implement with spiking neurons in continuous time, and we find that for many tasks these structures however are not necessary. We will consider this in future research, incorporating for instance subtractive gating [3].

Acknowledgments. DZ is supported by NWO NAI project 656.000.005.

References

1. Bakker, B.: Reinforcement learning with long short-term memory. In: Dietterich, T., Becker, S., Ghahramani, Z. (eds.) NIPS 14, pp. 1475–1482 (2002)
2. Bohte, S.M.: Efficient spike-coding with multiplicative adaptation in a spike response model. In: NIPS 25, pp. 1844–1852 (2012)
3. Costa, R., Assael, I.A., Shillingford, B., de Freitas, N., Vogels, T.: Cortical micro-circuits as gated-recurrent neural networks. In: NIPS 29, pp. 272–283 (2017)
4. Davies, M., Srinivasa, N., Lin, T.H., Chinya, G., Micro, Y.C.I.: Loihi: a neuromor-phic manycore processor with on-chip learning. ieeexplore.ieee.org (2018)
5. Diehl, P., Neil, D., Binas, J., Cook, M., Liu, S.C., Pfeiffer, M.: Fast-classifying, high-accuracy spiking deep networks through weight and threshold balancing. In: IJCNN, pp. 1–8 (2015)
6. Gerstner, W., Kistler, W.: Spiking Neuron Models: Single Neurons, Populations, Plasticity. Cambridge University Press, Cambridge (2002)
7. Gilra, A., Gerstner, W.: Predicting non-linear dynamics by stable local learning in a recurrent spiking neural network. Elife **6**, e28295 (2017)
8. Gurney, K.N., Prescott, T.J., Redgrave, P.: A computational model of action selec-tion in the basal ganglia. I. A new functional anatomy. Biol. Cybern. **84**, 401–410 (2001)
9. Hochreiter, S., Schmidhuber, J.: Long short-term memory. Neural Comput. **9**(8), 1735–1780 (1997)
10. Lillicrap, T.P., Cownden, D., Tweed, D.B., Akerman, C.J.: Random synaptic feed-back weights support error backpropagation for deep learning. Nat. Commun. **7**, 13276 (2016)
11. Mnih, V., Kavukcuoglu, K., Silver, D., Rusu, A.A., Veness, J.: Human-level control through deep reinforcement learning. Nature **518**, 529–533 (2015)

12. Niv, Y., Daw, N.D., Dayan, P.: Choice values. Nat. Neurosci. **9**(8), 987–988 (2006)
13. Roelfsema, P.R., van Ooyen, A.: Attention-gated reinforcement learning of internal representations for classification. Neural Comput. **17**(10), 2176–2214 (2005)
14. Rombouts, J., Bohte, S.M., Roelfsema, P.R.: Neurally plausible reinforcement learning of working memory tasks. In: NIPS 25, pp. 1880–1888 (2012)
15. Rombouts, J.O., Bohte, S.M., Roelfsema, P.R.: How attention can create synaptic tags for the learning of working memories in sequential tasks. PLoS Computat. Biol. **11**(3), e1004060 (2015)
16. Silver, D., Huang, A., Maddison, C.J., Guez, A., Sifre, L.: Mastering the game of Go with deep neural networks and tree search. Nature **529**(7587), 484–489 (2016)
17. Sutton, R.S., Barto, A.G.: Reinforcement Learning: An Introduction. MIT Press, Cambridge (1998)
18. Zambrano, D., Nusselder, R., Scholte, H.S., Bohte, S.: Efficient computation in adaptive artificial spiking neural networks. arXiv preprint arXiv:1710.04838 (2017)
19. Zambrano, D., Roelfsema, P., Bohté, S.: Learning continuous-time working memory tasks with on-policy neural reinforcement learning (2018, in preparation)
20. Zambrano, D., Roelfsema, P.R., Bohte, S.M.: Continuous-time on-policy neural reinforcement learning of working memory tasks. In: IJCNN 2015, April 2015

Reinforcement Learning for Joint Extraction of Entities and Relations

Wenpeng Liu[1,2], Yanan Cao[1(✉)], Yanbing Liu[1], Yue Hu[1], and Jianlong Tan[1]

[1] Institute of Information Engineering, Chinese Academy of Sciences, Beijing, China
{liuwenpeng,caoyanan,liuyanbing,huyue,tanjianlong}@iie.ac.cn
[2] School of Cyber Security, University of Chinese Academy of Sciences, Beijing, China

Abstract. Entity and relation extraction is an important task in natural language processing (NLP). Most existing researches handle this issue in a pipelined work or joint learning methods relied on human-annotated corpora, which are vulnerable to errors cascading. On the other side, in order to obtain large training data for methods of supervised learning, distant supervision are used in previous work whereas largely suffer from noisy labeling problem. To solve these problems, we propose a reinforcement learning framework for joint extraction of entities and relations. First, we construct a relation extractor based on a tagging scheme to extract entities and relations jointly. Meanwhile, a data cleaner is designed to select high-quality sentences and feed them into relation extractor, by means of cleaning noisy sentences generated by distant supervision hypothesis. Afterwards, the two modules are trained jointly with reinforcement learning to optimize models. In experiments, our model achieved better performance than comparative methods on the public dataset.

Keywords: Relation extraction · Reinforcement learning
End-to-end model · Deep learning · Distant supervision

1 Introduction

Joint extraction of entity and relation is aiming to detect entity mentions and recognize their semantic relations simultaneously from unstructured text. It is an important problem in natural language processing, especially for knowledge graph completion and question answering systems.

Traditional methods treat this task as a pipeline of two separated tasks, i.e., named entity recognition (NER) [13] first and then relation classification (RC) [4]. This separated processing method makes the mission more manageable and flexible, while it neglects the connection between these two sub-tasks. Furthermore, it leads to errors cascading due to that the results of entity recognition will affect the performance of relation classification. Different from the pipelined methods, recent studies focus on joint extraction methods to resolve error propagation.

© Springer Nature Switzerland AG 2018
V. Kůrková et al. (Eds.): ICANN 2018, LNCS 11140, pp. 263–272, 2018.
https://doi.org/10.1007/978-3-030-01421-6_26

Joint learning framework is to extract entities and relation together using a single model. It can effectively capture the inherent linguistic dependencies between relations and entity arguments, which could also avoid cascading of errors. However, most existing joint learning framework are feature-based structural systems [7,12,18]. They need complicated feature engineering and heavily rely on the supervised NLP toolkits, which might also lead to error propagation. In order to reduce the manual work in feature extraction, recently, [11,23] present neural network-based method for entity and relation extraction. Nevertheless, they also extract the entities and relations separately, even if entities and relations are jointly represented with shared parameters in a single model. In our work, we solve this problem use an end-to-end model.

The task we deal with is a classification problem and the method we proposed is a supervised learning algorithm requiring a large amount of labeled data. Due to the high cost of manually tagging samples, existing relation extraction methods obtained data rely on distant supervision proposed by [10], assuming that if two entities have a relation in a given knowledge base, all sentences that contain the two entities will mention that relation, result to largely suffer from the noisy labeling problem. To address the issue of noisy labeling problem, multi-instance learning are adopted to relieve the noisy of instances [5,8,16,20]. Unfortunately, these methods performing classification at the bag level, cannot identity the mapping between a relation and a sentence, also suffer from the noisy sentences in each bag.

To handle the above two limitations, we propose a novel end-to-end model to extract entities and relations simultaneously, which consists of two modules: a relation extractor based on a tagging scheme, and a data cleaner with reinforcement learning. The relation extractor takes advantage of a tagging scheme [24] that devise some tags which contain the information of entities and relationships they carry. In this way, the task can be transformed into a tagging problem without use of complicated features engineering. For another, the data cleaner is used to select high quality sentences from noisy data for better relation extraction. Under the guidance of reinforcement learning, two modules are trained jointly to optimize the relation extractor and data cleaner processes.

The major contribution of our work are:

- We apply reinforcement learning method to learn data cleaner module, which enables selecting clean instances at the sentence level and feed them into another module for better relation extraction.
- We conduct our experiments on a widely used dataset and outperform the comparative baselines significantly.

2   Related Work

Entity and relation extraction is a common and important task in natural language processing used for complete knowledge graph and improve question answering systems. In summary, there are two main frameworks to address this problem, one is pipelined method and another is joint learning method.

The pipelined method mostly are utilized on those traditional systems that treat entity and relation extraction as a pipeline of two separated tasks, extract named entity first and then classify relation. Some early models for named entity recognition are linear statistical models, such as Hidden Markov Models and Conditional Random Fields [9,14]. Recent researches focus on utilizing neural network architecture [1,6] for NER and have achieved big improvements, which regarded it as a sequential token tagging task. As for relation classification, existing methods can also be divided into handcrafted feature based methods [17] and neural network based methods [19,21,22]. With this method, the results of entity recognition may affect the performance of relation classification and lead to errors cascading.

The joint learning models extract entities and relations simultaneously by means of using a single model. Most of previous studies belong in this method are feature based structured systems [7,12,15] such as prior knowledge get from knowledge map and dependency parsing. Recently, neural network architectures are used to jointly extract entities and relations. For example, [11] use a LSTM-based model to extract entities and relations, which contribute to reduce the manual work. [23] construct a hybrid neural model consists a CNN and a RNN to tackle this joint learning task. However, they also extract the entities and relations separately through two submodels.

In general, a large amount of labeled data are required for training neural network models. To address this issue, distant supervision [10] are proposed to generate mass data while largely suffers from noisy labeling problem. In order to solve the problems we mentioned above, we propose a new framework of reinforcement learning inspired by [2] which consists two modules, an end-to-end model for relation extraction and a data cleaner for cleaning noisy data, to jointly extract entities and relations.

3   Methodology

We propose an end-to-end model based on a reinforcement learning framework to jointly extract entities and their relations. Figure 1 gives an illustration of how the proposed framework works. The model is trained based on a reinforcement learning framework which consists of two modules: the *relation extractor* and the *data cleaner*. The relation extractor we construct adopts a bi-directional Long Short Term Memory (Bi-LSTM) layer and a LSTM-based layer to automatically determine the entity and relation tag in a sentence. As for the data cleaner, each sentence x_i has a corresponding *action* a_i to indicate whether or not x_i will be selected as a training instance for relation extractor according to the current state of x_i, represented as s_i. And then, the data cleaner distills the training data to the relation extractor to train the LSTM network. Meanwhile, the relation extractor gives feedback to the data cleaner to refine its policy function.

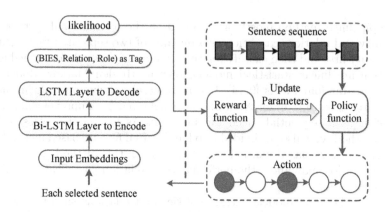

Fig. 1. Overall architecture for LSTM-LSTM-RL

3.1 Relation Extractor

In this module, we cast relation extractor as a sequence labeling problem and construct an end-to-end model to solve this task.

The Tagging Scheme. In our tagging scheme, each word in a sentence is assigned a label that contribute to extract the results. Tag "O" represents the "Other" tag, means that the word is excluded as the entity we want. The other tags consists of three parts: the word position in the entity, the relation type, and the relation role. "BIES" is used to represent the position of a word in the entity. The relation type is acquired from a predefined set of relations. As for the third part of the tag, we use "1" to express that the word belongs to the first entity in a triplet (a triplet like "$Entity_1$, $RelationType$, $Entity_2$"), and "2" to express the second. Figure 2 gives an example of how the results are tagged based on the tagging scheme.

It should be noted that, if two or more triplets with the same relation type appeared in a sentence, we combine every two entities into a triplet based on the nearest principle.

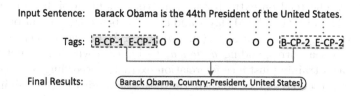

Fig. 2. A standard annotation for an example sentence based on the tagging scheme, where "CP" is short for "Country-President".

The End-to-End Model. End-to-end model based on neural network has been widely used in sequence tagging task and have shown promising results. In this paper, we adopt an end-to-end model to train the tags sequence as Fig. 1 shows.

The Bi-LSTM Encoding Layer. The Bi-LSTM encoding layer has been shown their superiority to capture the semantic information of each word in sequence tagging problems. In our model, it contains forward lstm layer, backward lstm layer and the concatenate layer. The detail operations are defined as follows:

$$i_t = \delta(W_{wi}w_t + W_{hi}h_{t-1} + W_{ci}c_{t-1} + b_i) \tag{1}$$

$$f_t = \delta(W_{wf}w_t + W_{hf}h_{t-1} + W_{cf}c_{t-1} + b_f) \tag{2}$$

$$z_t = tanh(W_{wc}w_t + W_{hc}h_{t-1} + W_{cf}c_{t-1} + b_c) \tag{3}$$

$$o_t = \delta(W_{wo}w_t + W_{ho}h_{t-1} + W_{co}c_{t-1} + b_o) \tag{4}$$

$$c_t = f_t c_{t-1} + i_t z_t \qquad h_t = o_t tanh(c_t) \tag{5}$$

The LSTM Decoding Layer. A layer of LSTM structure is adopted to produce the tag sequence. The inputs of decoding layer are: h_t obtained from Bi-LSTM encoding layer, former predicted tag embedding T_{t-1}, former cell value $c_{t-1}^{(2)}$, and the former hidden vector in decoding layer $h_{t-1}^{(2)}$. The detail operations are defined as follows:

$$i_t^{(2)} = \delta(W_{wi}^{(2)}h_t + W_{hi}^{(2)}h_{t-1}^{(2)} + W_{ti}T_{t-1} + b_i^{(2)}) \tag{6}$$

$$f_t^{(2)} = \delta(W_{wf}^{(2)}h_t + W_{hf}^{(2)}h_{t-1}^{(2)} + W_{tf}T_{t-1} + b_f^{(2)}) \tag{7}$$

$$z_t^{(2)} = tanh(W_{wc}^{(2)}h_t + W_{hc}^{(2)}h_{t-1}^{(2)} + W_{tc}T_{t-1} + b_c^{(2)}) \tag{8}$$

$$o_t^{(2)} = \delta(W_{wo}^{(2)}h_t + W_{ho}^{(2)}h_{t-1}^{(2)} + W_{co}^{(2)}c_t^{(2)} + b_o^{(2)}) \tag{9}$$

$$c_t^{(2)} = f_t^{(2)}c_{t-1}^{(2)} + i_t^{(2)}z_t^{(2)} \qquad h_t^{(2)} = o_t^{(2)}tanh(c_t^{(2)}) \tag{10}$$

$$T_t = W_{ts}h_t^{(2)} + b_{ts} \tag{11}$$

Loss Function. We train our model to maximize the log-likelihood of the data and the optimization method we used is RM-Sprop. The objection function can be defined as:

$$L = \max \sum_{j=1}^{|\hat{X}|} \sum_{t=1}^{L_j} (\log(p_t^{(j)} = r_t^{(j)}|x_j, \theta) \cdot I(O) + \alpha \cdot \log(p_t^{(j)} = r_t^{(j)}|x_j, \theta) \cdot (1 - I(O)))$$

$$\tag{12}$$

in which $|\hat{X}|$ is the size of training set, L_j is the length of sentence x_j, $r_t^{(j)}$ indicate the label of word t in sentence x_j and $p_t^{(j)}$ denote the normalized probabilities of tags. Besides, $I(O)$ is a switching function defined as follows:

$$I(O) = \begin{cases} 1, & if\ tag = 'O' \\ 0, & if\ tag \neq 'O' \end{cases} \tag{13}$$

3.2   Data Cleaner

With the help of data cleaner, our model could directly filters out noisy sentences. The data cleaner is a agent, which interacts with the environment that consists of data and the relation extractor [2]. The agent is to decide which action at each state, and then receive a delayed reward from the relation extraction when the selection on all the training instances are finished.

To make the training process more efficiently, we divide the training sentences into N bags, and compute a reward when we finish samples selection in a bag. When all selections on all the training data completed, we merge all the selected sentences in each bag to obtain a cleansed dataset $\widehat{X}$. Then, the cleaned data will be used to train the relation classifier at the sentence level.

State. When making decision on the i-th sentences of the bag B, we use state s_i to represent the state that we need to consider: (1) The vector representation of the current sentence, which is obtained from the relation extraction; (2) The representation of the chosen sentence set, which are the average of the vector representations of all chosen sentences; (3) The vector representations of the two entities in a sentence.

Action. We define the action $a_i \in \{0, 1\}$ to indicate whether the i-th sentence of the bag B will be selected or not. In our work, we adopt a logistic function as the policy function of a_i, where Θ is the parameters to be learned and $F(s_i)$ is the state feature vector:

$$
\begin{aligned}
\pi_\Theta(s_i, a_i) &= P_\Theta(a_i|s_i) \\
&= a_i\sigma(W * F(s_i) + b) + (1 - a_i)(1 - \sigma(W * F(s_i) + b))
\end{aligned}
\tag{14}
$$

Reward. The reward function is an indicator of the worth of the chosen sentences. We only receive a delayed reward at the terminal state $s_{|B|+1}$ owing that the model has a terminal reward only when it finished all the selection. In consequence, the reward is defined as follows:

$$
r(s_i|B) =
\begin{cases}
0 & i < |B| + 1 \\
\frac{1}{|\widehat{B}|} \sum\limits_{x_j \in \widehat{B}} \log p(r|x_j) & i = |B| + 1
\end{cases}
\tag{15}
$$

where $\widehat{B}$ is the set of selected sentences, which is a subset of B, and r is the relation label of bag B. $p(r|x_j)$ is calculated by the relation extractor.

Optimization. For a bag B, we aim to maximize the expected total reward. Our objective function is defined as:

$$
\begin{aligned}
J(\Theta) &= V_\Theta(s_0|B) \\
&= E_{s_0, a_0, s_1, \ldots, s_i, a_i, s_{i+1}\ldots} [\sum_{i=0}^{|B|+1} r(s_i|B)]
\end{aligned}
\tag{16}
$$

We compute the gradient int following way: For each bag B, we sample an action for each state sequentially according to the current policy. We then get a sampled trajectory and a corresponding terminal reward.

3.3 Model Training

In order to make two modules correlated mutually, we train them jointly. Algorithm 1 demonstrate the complete process of joint learning.

Algorithm 1. Overall Training Procedure

---

1. Initialize the parameters of the RE model of relation extraction with random weights
2. Initialize the parameters of policy network of data cleaner with random weights
3. Pre-train the RE model to predict relation r_i given the sentence x_i by maximizing $logp(r_i|x_i)$
4. Pre-train the policy network with the RE model fixed.
5. Jointly train the RE model and the policy network until convergence.

In step 5 of jointly training process, the relation extractor provides a mechanism that computing the rewards of the cleansed sentences to refine the data cleaner. Correspondly, the data cleaner provides high-quality sentences by means of dispose of wrongly labeled sentences to better train the relation extractor. We update the parameters in the policy network and relation extractor network respectively by linear interpolation: $\Theta' \leftarrow (1 - \tau)\Theta' + \tau\Theta$, $\phi' \leftarrow (1 - \tau)\phi' + \tau\phi$, where $\tau \ll 1$ is a hyper-parameter.

4 Experiments and Results

4.1 Experimental Setting

Dataset. We conduct experiments on a widely used public dataset[1] generated by the sentences in NYT[2]. There are total 522,611 sentences, 281,270 entity pairs, and 18,252 relational facts in the training data; and 172,448 sentences, 96,678 entity pairs and 1,950 relational facts in the test data. Besides, the size of relation set is 26. We adopt the official evaluation metric to evaluate our systems, which is based on macro-averaged F1-score for the nine actual relations.

Hyperparameters. For the parameters of the relation extractor, we utilize the word embeddings with 300 dimensions initialed by running word2vec[3] on NYT training corpus. We leverage dropout method to training the neural network with

---

[1] http://iesl.cs.umass.edu/riedel/ecml.

[2] New York Times, a widely used text corpus.

[3] https://code.google.com/archieve/word2vec.

Table 1. Experimental results of our model and comparative methods

Methods	Prec.	Rec.	F1
DS-logistic	0.306	0.397	0.320
FCM	0.553	0.154	0.240
DS-Joint	0.574	0.256	0.354
CoType	0.423	**0.511**	0.463
LSTM-CRF	**0.693 ± 0.007**	0.310 ± 0.007	0.428 ± 0.008
LSTM-LSTM-Bias	0.615 ± 0.008	0.414 ± 0.005	0.495 ± 0.006
LSTM-LSTM-RL	0.684 ± 0.008	0.387 ± 0.005	**0.529 ± 0.006**

0.5 dropout ratio. The bias parameter α corresponding to the results in Table 1 is 10. We use 300 lstm units in encoding layer and 600 lstm units in decoding layer. As for the parameters in data cleaner, the delay coefficient is 0.001. An initial learning rate of 0.001 and a 0.99 learning rate exponential decay factor at each training step.

Baselines. To evaluate the effectiveness of our model, we compare its performance with notable pipelined methods, jointly extracting methods and classical end-to-end tagging models. The comparative methods are introduced in the following.

The Pipelined Methods. DS-logistic [10]: a distant supervised and feature-based method, combines the advantages of supervised IE and unsupervised IE features. FCM [3] is a compositional model utilize lexicalized linguistic context for relation extraction.

The Jointly Extracting Methods. DS-Joint [7]: using structured perceptron on human annotated dataset. CoType [15]: a domain independent framework by jointly embedding several wonderful features like entity mentions, relation mentions and type labels.

Classical Tagging Models. LSTM-CRF [6]: using a bidirectional LSTM to recognize entity and a conditional random fields to predict the tag sequence. LSTM-LSTM-Bias [24]: convert the task as a sequence to sequence problem, jointly extracting based on a novel tagging scheme.

4.2   Results Analysis

Table 2 presents the best F1 score achieved by our reinforcement learning based model (LSTM-LSTM-RL) and comparative methods. It shows that the effectiveness of our proposed method. Furthermore, we also could summarize that the jointly extracting methods are better than traditional methods of pipelined framework.

We also find that the LSTM-CRF have better effect than our model on precision. Because, CRF is good at capturing the joint probability of the entire sequence of labels. While LSTM-LSTM models can be better to balance the precision and recall. Maybe it's just because that these end-to-end models use a LSTM layer to encoding input and another LSTM layer to decode the results which could better learning deep linguistic features and well fit the data.

It should be noted that our model is better than LSTM-LSTM-Bias on all indicators, attributed to that the reinforcement learning frame we employed could help to distill the training data and feed cleansed samples into relation extractors. Therefore, in this task, our method perform better than the competitive methods.

5   Conclusions and Outlook

In this paper, we proposed a reinforcement learning framework for joint extraction of entities and relations, named LSTM-LSTM-RL, to improve the performance and noise immunity of relation extraction. Experimental results demonstrate that, training with reinforcement learning outperformed the method of pipelined framework and other joint learning methods. Besides, our model based on a tagging scheme transformed the task into a sequence to sequence problem without use of NLP toolkits or human-annotated corpora. In the future work, we will construct various relation classifier models and apply the reinforcement learning framework on other tasks.

Acknowledgement. This work was supported by the National Key Research and Development program of China (No. 2018YFB1004703).

References

1. Chiu, J.P.C., Nichols, E.: Named entity recognition with bidirectional LSTM-CNNs. Computer Science (2015)
2. Feng, J., Huang, M., Zhao, L., Yang, Y., Zhu, X.: Reinforcement learning for relation classification from noisy data (2018)
3. Gormley, M.R., Yu, M., Dredze, M.: Improved relation extraction with feature-rich compositional embedding models. Computer Science (2015)
4. Zhou, G.D., Su, J., Zhang, J., Zhang, M.: Exploring various knowledge in relation extraction. In: Proceedings of the 43rd Annual Meeting on Association for Computational Linguistics, pp. 427–434. Association for Computational Linguistics (2005)
5. Ji, G., Liu, K., He, S., Zhao, J., et al.: Distant supervision for relation extraction with sentence-level attention and entity descriptions. In: AAAI, pp. 3060–3066 (2017)
6. Lample, G., Ballesteros, M., Subramanian, S., Kawakami, K., Dyer, C.: Neural architectures for named entity recognition, pp. 260–270 (2016)
7. Li, Q., Ji, H.: Incremental joint extraction of entity mentions and relations. In: Proceedings of the 52nd Annual Meeting of the Association for Computational Linguistics (Volume 1: Long Papers), vol. 1, pp. 402–412 (2014)
8. Lin, Y., Shen, S., Liu, Z., Luan, H., Sun, M.: Neural relation extraction with selective attention over instances. In: Proceedings of the 54th Annual Meeting of the Association for Computational Linguistics (Volume 1: Long Papers), vol. 1, pp. 2124–2133 (2016)

9. Luo, G., Huang, X., Lin, C.Y., Nie, Z.: Joint entity recognition and disambiguation. In: Conference on Empirical Methods in Natural Language Processing, pp. 879–888 (2016)

10. Mintz, M., Bills, S., Snow, R. Jurafsky, D.: Distant supervision for relation extraction without labeled data. In: Joint Conference of the Meeting of the ACL and the International Joint Conference on Natural Language Processing of the AFNLP: Volume, pp. 1003–1011 (2009)

11. Miwa, M., Bansal, M.: End-to-end relation extraction using LSTMs on sequences and tree structures. arXiv preprint arXiv:1601.00770 (2016)

12. Miwa, M., Sasaki, Y.: Modeling joint entity and relation extraction with table representation. In: Proceedings of the 2014 Conference on Empirical Methods in Natural Language Processing (EMNLP), pp. 1858–1869 (2014)

13. Nadeau, D., Sekine, S.: A survey of named entity recognition and classification. Lingvisticae Investigationes **30**(1), 3–26 (2007)

14. Passos, A., Kumar, V., Mccallum, A.: Lexicon infused phrase embeddings for named entity resolution. Computer Science (2014)

15. Ren, X., et al.: CoType: joint extraction of typed entities and relations with knowledge bases. In: Proceedings of the 26th International Conference on World Wide Web, pp. 1015–1024. International World Wide Web Conferences Steering Committee (2017)

16. Riedel, S., Yao, L., McCallum, A.: Modeling relations and their mentions without labeled text. In: Balcázar, J.L., Bonchi, F., Gionis, A., Sebag, M. (eds.) ECML PKDD 2010. LNCS (LNAI), vol. 6323, pp. 148–163. Springer, Heidelberg (2010). https://doi.org/10.1007/978-3-642-15939-8_10

17. Rink, B., Harabagiu, S.: UTD: classifying semantic relations by combining lexical and semantic resources. In: International Workshop on Semantic Evaluation, pp. 256–259 (2010)

18. Roth, D., Yih, W.: Global inference for entity and relation identification via a linear programming formulation. In: Getoor, L., Taskar, B. (eds.) Introduction to Statistical Relational Learning, pp. 553–580. MIT Press, Cambridge (2007)

19. Xu, Y., Mou, L., Li, G., Chen, Y., Peng, H., Jin, Z.: Classifying relations via long short term memory networks along shortest dependency paths. In: Proceedings of the 2015 Conference on Empirical Methods in Natural Language Processing, pp. 1785–1794 (2015)

20. Zeng, D., Liu, K., Chen, Y., Zhao, J.: Distant supervision for relation extraction via piecewise convolutional neural networks. In: Proceedings of the 2015 Conference on Empirical Methods in Natural Language Processing, pp. 1753–1762 (2015)

21. Zeng, D., Liu, K., Lai, S., Zhou, G., Zhao, J.: Relation classification via convolutional deep neural network. In: Proceedings of COLING 2014, the 25th International Conference on Computational Linguistics: Technical Papers, pp. 2335–2344 (2014)

22. Zheng, H., Li, Z., Wang, S., Yan, Z., Zhou, J.: Aggregating inter-sentence information to enhance relation extraction. In: AAAI, pp. 3108–3115 (2016)

23. Zheng, S., et al.: Joint entity and relation extraction based on a hybrid neural network. Neurocomputing **257**, 59–66 (2017)

24. Zheng, S., Wang, F., Bao, H., Hao, Y., Zhou, P., Xu, B.: Joint extraction of entities and relations based on a novel tagging scheme. arXiv preprint arXiv:1706.05075 (2017)

Pattern Recognition/Text Mining/Clustering

TextNet for Text-Related Image Quality Assessment

Hongyu Li[✉], Junhua Qiu, and Fan Zhu

AI Lab., ZhongAn Information Technology Service Co., Ltd., Shanghai, China
{lihongyu,qiujunhua,zhufan}@zhongan.io

Abstract. With the rapid increase of consumer photos, annotating and retrieving such images with text are becoming more significant, which requires optical character recognition (OCR) techniques. However, to predict OCR accuracy, text-related image quality assessment (TIQA) is necessary and of great value, especially in online business processes. With more interests in text, TIQA aims to compute the quality score of an image through predicting the degree of degradation at textual regions.

To assess text-related quality on detected textlines, this paper proposes a deep neural network, *TextNet*, which mainly includes three layers: encoder, decoder, and prediction. The decoder layer combines the encoded feature map with the decoded map through deconvolution and concatenation. The prediction layer is designed for textline detection and quality assessment with a new loss function. Under the TIQA framework, the overall text-related image quality is computed through pooling the quality of all detected textlines by way of weighted averaging. Experimental results show that the proposed framework can work well in jointly assessing text related image quality and detecting textlines, even for unknown scene images.

Keywords: Text-related image quality
Document image quality assessment · Textline detection · TextNet

1 Introduction

With the pervasive use of smart devices in our daily life, mobile captured document images are often required to be submitted in business processes of Internet companies. For the purpose of intelligent analysis of such document images, three sequential processing steps are generally needed: document image quality assessment, text detection and text recognition, each of which is active as an independent research topic in most cases.

The success of text recognition, however, is highly dependent on the quality of acquired document images. The text recognition performance of mobile captured document images is often decreased with the low document image quality due to artifacts introduced during image acquisition [18], which probably hinders the following business process severely.

© Springer Nature Switzerland AG 2018
V. Kůrková et al. (Eds.): ICANN 2018, LNCS 11140, pp. 275–285, 2018.
https://doi.org/10.1007/978-3-030-01421-6_27

Document image quality is closely related to text, where the major concern is word/text. Moreover, text is frequently scattered throughout natural scene or web images. Obviously, text-related image quality assessment (TIQA) is of great value in scene understanding and document image analysis.

The judgement on image quality is often biased by interest. Traditional image quality assessment methods are not suitable in the TIQA case since they pay more attention to striking objects in scene images. Inspired by the fact that textual areas can be found with textline detection methods, this paper proposes a neural network, *TextNet*, to achieve TIQA while detecting textlines.

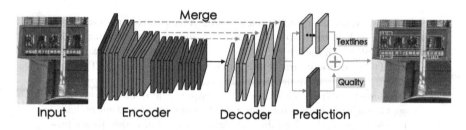

Fig. 1. Architecture of the proposed network composed of encoder, decoder and prediction layers.

The proposed network can be divided into three parts: encoder, decoder, and prediction layers, as shown in Fig. 1. The encoder layer is a light weight network to extract implicit features of input images at varied levels. The decoder layer aims to merge feature maps gradually. The prediction layer will produce a score map for text quality as well as rotated boxes for textlines. To estimate the overall text quality of an image, textline quality scores are pooled by way of weighted averaging.

According to the point of view in [18], blur seems the most common issue in text-related images, which suggests that detecting the blur degradation is more attractive and useful in practical applications. To train the proposed network, we synthesize a set of training images with both labels involving text quality and textline position. The proposed method has been tested on three benchmarks and our collected web image dataset. Experimental results demonstrate that the proposed method is feasible and promising in TIQA and textline detection.

2   Related Work

This study is closely related to two active, but disjoint, research topics, document image quality assessment (DIQA) and text detection. This section will briefly introduce the current progress in both fields.

Many no-reference quality assessment algorithms have been developed to estimate the quality of document images. According to the difference of feature extraction, these methods can be categorized as two groups: metric-based assessment and learning-based assessment. The metric-based methods are usually based on hand-crafted features that have shown to correlate with the OCR accuracy. Around 30 degradation-specific quality metrics have been proposed to measure noise and character shape preservation [10]. Although much progress has been made in metric-based assessment, the performance of such features is relatively poor and sensitive to surrounding noise. The learning-based DIQA methods take advantage of learning techniques, such as [4,12], to extract discriminant features for different types of document degradations. In [4], the authors proposed a deep learning approach for document image quality assessment, which crops an image into patches and then uses the CNN to estimate quality scores for selected patches. However, the strategy of selecting text patches is based upon the simple technique, Otsu's binarization, which often can not work well for consumer photos.

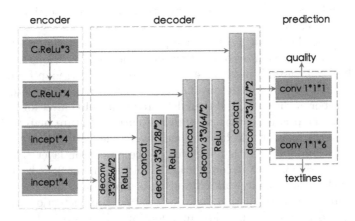

Fig. 2. Details of the proposed network

Comprehensive reviews about text detection can be found in survey papers [19,22]. The core of text detection is the design of features to distinguish text from backgrounds. Previous text detection approaches [2,16] have already obtained promising performances on various benchmarks and deep neural network based algorithms [16,20,21] are becoming the mainstream in this field. [20] proposes to utilize fully convolutional networks (FCN) for heatmap generation and to use component projection for orientation estimation. [21] presents a scene textline detector that directly predicts word/text with a FCN based network. Deep features have been shown to be effective for both textline detection and document quality assessment [4], which motivates us to jointly achieve textline detection and quality assessment in a deep neural network.

3   Methodology

3.1   Network Design

To take advantage of valid textlines to assess text-related image quality, this paper designs a deep neural network, *TextNet*, which simultaneously achieves text quality assessment and detection.

Text quality assessment needs high-level information in late stages of a neural network, and textline detection would require features from both early and late stages due to the various size of text. Therefore the network must use features from different levels to fulfill these requirements. To meet these conditions on features maps, we designed a network that can be decomposed into three parts: encoder, decoder, and prediction layers, as illustrated in Fig. 1.

The encoder layer can be a convolutional network pretrained on the ImageNet dataset [3], with interleaving convolution and pooling layers. Since PVANET [7] is a light weight network for feature extraction in object detection, we adopt PVANET as the encoder.

In the decoder layer, we gradually merge the encoded feature map with the decoded base map through deconvolution and concatenation along the channel axis level by level. In each merging stage, the decoded base map from the last stage is first fed to a 3×3 deconvolutional layer to double its size and cut down the number of channels, and then delivered to a ReLU layer for activation. Next, the base map is concatenated with the current feature map to fuse the information in the following deconvolutional layer. The feature map produced in the last deconvolutional layer is finally fed to the prediction layer. The number of output channels for each deconvolution, depicted in Fig. 2, is kept small in decoder, which makes the network efficient in computation.

We designed a new prediction layer for joint textline detection and quality assessment, and proposed a new loss function for this network. The prediction layer contains several 1×1 operations to project 16 channels of feature maps into two branches: a quality score map Q_s with 1 channel, and textlines with 6 channels. In the quality score map, pixel values are in the range $[0, 1]$. The geometry shape for textlines is described with rotated boxes. In the textline branch, 4 channels are for bounding boxes, 1 channel for rotation angle and the other 1 channel for text confidence. For bounding boxes, each channel represents a distance from the pixel location to the top, right, bottom, or left boundary of the rectangle.

In summary, the proposed network can not only predict textline quality but also simultaneously detect textlines that are applicable in following text recognition.

3.2   Loss Functions

In order to complete both tasks of textline detection and quality assessment in the prediction layer, the total loss L in the network should include two components: one for the quality loss L_q and the other for the textline detection loss L_t.

The quality loss L_q represents the difference between the predicted quality p_q and the ground truth g_q in the textline, and can be measured in the L_2 norm,

$$L_q = \sqrt{(p_q - g_q)^2}. \tag{1}$$

The textline detection loss L_t is composed of three parts: rotation loss L_r, text confidence loss L_c, and bounding box loss L_b. For simplicity, we use the cosine loss as the rotation loss L_r to measure the difference between the predicted and ground truth angles.

In [21], the cross-entropy loss is used to describe text confidence. However, this loss is not essentially good at binary clustering. To make text confidence loss L_c more beneficial to evaluating the performance of binary clustering, we utilize dice score coefficient [15] to define L_c as follows,

$$L_c = 1 - \frac{\sum_i g_i p_i + \epsilon}{\sum_i (g_i + p_i) + \epsilon} - \frac{\sum_i (1 - g_i)(1 - p_i) + \epsilon}{\sum_i (2 - g_i - p_i) + \epsilon}, \tag{2}$$

where p_i is text confidence prediction and g_i is ground truth. The ϵ term is used to ensure the stability of the loss function by avoiding the numerical issue of dividing by 0.

To predict accurate geometry for both large and small textlines, the bounding box loss L_b should be scale-invariant, and can be described as,

$$L_b = -log \frac{P_b \cap G_b}{P_b \cup G_b}, \tag{3}$$

where P_b represents the predicted bounding box and G_b is its corresponding ground truth.

The textline detection loss L_t can be finally expressed as the weighted sum of these three parts, $L_t = \alpha L_c + \beta L_r + \gamma L_b$. In this case, α, β and γ are the weighted cofficients to balance the importance among three losses. α and γ are set to 1, and β is 10 in our experiments.

Through combining the quality loss and the textline detection loss, the total loss L used in the network is formulated as:

$$L = L_t + cL_q, \tag{4}$$

where c weighs the importance between two losses. Parameter c is set to 0.5 in our experiments.

3.3 Framework for Text-Related Image Quality Assessment

A high-level overview of the proposed framework for text-related image quality assessment is illustrated in Fig. 3. In this framework, an image is first fed into the proposed network TextNet and the network outputs 1 channel for pixel-level text quality and 6 channels for textlines. Valid textline are extracted through thresholding the text confidence channel and running non-maximum-suppression (NMS).

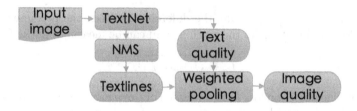

Fig. 3. Framework for text-related image quality assessment.

The overall text-related image quality is predicted with a weighted pooling strategy on the basis of textline areas and text quality. To compute the overall image quality, textline quality is required to be worked out. The textline quality q_t can be computed through averaging the pixel-level text quality on the textline areas: $q_t = \frac{1}{N}\sum_{i \in R_t} p_q(i)$. Here $p_q(i)$ represents the text quality at pixel i outputed by TextNet, and N is the total number of pixels in the textline region R_t.

The overall quality $\hat{q}$ with regard to text is defined as the weighted pooling of the quality of all textlines in the image. It can be computed in the following form, $\hat{q} = \sum_j w_j q_t(j)$, where w_j is a weight on the j-th textline of the image. The weight is linearly proportional to the textline area, $w_j = \frac{R_t(j)}{\sum_k R_t(k)}$, where $R_t(j)$ represents the area of the j-th textline in the image.

4   Experiments

To train the proposed network, it is required that the training samples must contain two types of labels, quality scores and rotated boxes of textlines. This section introduces a new way of generating training data with both types of labels.

To compare the proposed framework with existing methods, we conducted experiments of text-related image quality assessment on two public benchmarks: DIQA and SmartDoc-QA. In addition, we evaluated the proposed method on our collected web image dataset.

4.1   Data Generation for Training

For now, the publicly available datasets have only a type of ground truth labels, for example, ICDAR2013 [6] with bounding boxes for textline detection, and DIQA [8] with OCR accuracies as the quality metric. As a result, we need to collect data with both labels to train the proposed network model. The whole process is briefly introduced as follows:

Step1: label textlines manually from images;
Step2: pick some high-quality textlines and blur them using a Gaussian function with a random kernel size s;

Step3: put the blurred textlines back into the original images to replace the corresponding textlines.

Since blur seems the most common issue in text-related images, we model the Gaussian blur to smooth textual regions and produce images with blurry text. In the above process, the ground truth quality for each textline is computed as $q_t = 1 - s/2.5$, in terms of the kernel size s with a range $[0,2.5]$. In this case, the originally labeled textlines are assumed to be of high quality, $q_t = 1$.

4.2   Datasets and Protocols

The DIQA dataset [8] contains a total of 175 color images with resolution 1840×3264. These images are captured from 25 documents containing machine-printed English characters using a smartphone. 6–8 photos were taken for each document to generate different levels of blur degradations.

In SmartDoc-QA [11], there are 30 different documents used to capture 4260 images, where 142 different images are captured per document. Those captures are taken using representative values of different distortions. For each image, the information about the document and capture conditions is stored as ground truth for evaluation purposes.

One traditional quality indicator for document images is the OCR accuracy [17]. We define the OCR accuracy as ground truth for each document image in our quality assessment task. To compute the correlation between the predicted quality scores and ground truth OCR accuracies, we use the Linear Correlation Coefficient (LCC) and the Spearman Rank Order Correlation Coefficient (SROCC) to evaluate the performance of the proposed method.

ICDAR2013 and ICDAR2015 were used in ICDAR Robust Reading Competition [5,6]. In our experiments, 229 pictures were selected from ICDAR2013 and 1000 from ICDAR2015 for training. The textual regions are originally annotated by 4 vertices of the quadrangle, and the rotation angle is assumed to be zero in ICDAR2013. In addition, a web image dataset[1] was collected with high-quality textlines from Internet. This dataset includes 600 posters, where 500 posters were selected for training.

4.3   Implementation Details

To produce both types of lables, we run the above data generation process on the selected pictures. The obtained training samples, composed of total 1729 images, were used to train a base model. In our experiments for comparative analysis, we randomly sampled 60% from the DIQA and SmartDoc-QA datasets to finetune the base model. The remaining data were averagely separated into a validation set and a test set. The random split in the DIQA dataset was conducted at the group level, where each group corresponds to a document. We repeated the random split tests 100 times to compute 100 LCCs and SROCCs, and reported the median LCC and SROCC.

---

[1] https://pan.baidu.com/s/1sRPuedHEwdvUYVcGh86uqg.

We implemented the proposed network in the Tensorflow framework. The encoder layer is pretrained on the ImageNet dataset [3]. The network was trained end-to-end using ADAM optimizer, with learning rate starting from 1e-4, decaying to one-tenth every 30000 minibatches, and stoping at 1e-6. To speed up learning, we resized images to a fixed size and formed the minibatch size of 12. Meanwhile, the ground truth labels about textlines are also resized.

After the network inference, the obtained results need to be resized back to the original size. On average, the whole process spends about 100ms in computation for each image on a server using a single Nvidia 1080 Ti graphic card with an Intel i7-6800k @3.40 GHz CPU.

4.4   Comparative Analysis

We conducted experiments of text-related image quality assessment with the fintuned models on two datasets, DIQA and SmartDoc-QA. Three state-of-the-art approaches, a deep learning approach (DLA) [4], the Focus [13], the BRISQUE [1], the Sharpness [8], and the CG-DIQA [9], are selected for comparative analysis. The DLA approach uses a convolutional neural network to predict quality scores for a document image, and the other four approaches adopts hand-crafted features to compute the quality prediction.

Table 1 presents the quantitative results with LCC and SROCC on both DIQA and SmartDoc-QA datasets. It is observed that, for DIQA over the FinerReader OCR accuracy, the proposed method obtains a higher median LCC (0.960) than the other five approaches. With the median SROCC indicator, however, our method performs only better than the DLA and BRISQUE approaches, and a little worse than the other three hand-crafted methods (Focus, Sharpness and CG-DIQA). The cause is probably that the ground truth text quality is labelled as the value linear to the Gaussian kernel size s. In essence, the degree of blur degradation of textlines is not linearly in accordance with the change of s, thus the current ground truth can not reflect the degree of degradation in training samples well enough.

Table 1. Comparison on DIQA and SmartDoc-QA datasets

		DLA	Focus	BRISQUE	Sharpness	CG-DIQA	Proposed
DIQA	Median LCC	0.950	0.9378	−0.0097	0.8488	0.9523	**0.960**
	Median SROCC	0.898	**0.9643**	0.0574	0.9524	0.9429	0.9286
SmartDoc-QA	Median LCC	N/A	N/A	0.1851	0.6242	0.6250	**0.6841**
	Median SROCC	N/A	N/A	0.0753	0.5964	0.6305	**0.6729**

In [4] and [13], the authors did not conduct experiments on SmartDoc-QA, and the original codes are unavailable, so these two methods are not compared on the SmartDoc-QA dataset. Our method outperforms the other three methods in the median LCC (0.6841) and SROCC (0.6729) over the Tesseract accuracy. It is worth noting that the SmartDoc-QA dataset is greatly complicated compared to the DIQA dataset. That is why the overall evaluation indicators seem lower in general.

From the comparative tests, it is observed that the proposed framework for TIQA is better than or comparable to the state-of-the-art. In addition, this framework is characterized by the ability of better embodying the linear correlation than the monotonicity between the predicted and ground truth.

4.5   Other Results

With the base model, we have tested the proposed framework on the remaining 100 web images and the ICDAR2017 [14]. Some results are shown in Fig. 4, where the top row is originally from our collected test set and the bottom from the ICDAR2017. In the results, each textline is bounded with yellow boxes and the quality prediction score is added beside the textline. It is easily observed that the clear textlines have higher quality scores, and the textline is generally quite blurry if its predicted quality score is below 0.80.

Under the proposed framework, the overall text quality score for images is computed in a weighted pooling way. For these images, the corresponding scores

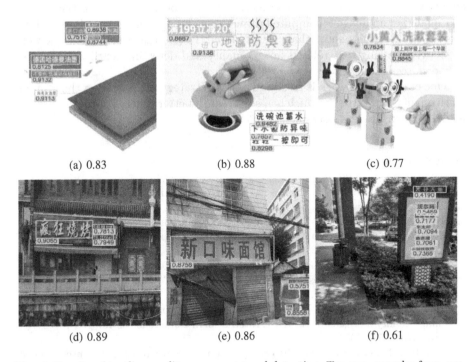

(a) 0.83   (b) 0.88   (c) 0.77

(d) 0.89   (e) 0.86   (f) 0.61

Fig. 4. Results of textline quality assessment and detection. Top row: samples from our collected dataset, bottom row: samples from the ICDAR2017. Each sample is overlaid with quality scores and rotated boxes for textlines. The overall text quality prediction score is shown in the corresponding caption.

are respectively, 0.83, 0.88, 0.77, 0.89, 0.86, and 0.88, where the higher quality score means the better image quality with respect to text. With the generated ground truth, the overall LCC and SROCC for these 100 web images are respectively, 0.6649 and 0.6134. Due to unavailability of the ground truth involving text quality in the ICDAR2017, we cannot compute the LCC or SROCC indicators. But the perceptual judgement is basically consistent with the overall text quality score. For example, the image in Fig. 4(e), assessed with the text quality of 0.86, is perceptually a lot clearer than the one in Fig. 4(f) with the text quality prediction 0.61. Moreover, the ICDAR2017 images never appeared in the training set of the base model, which proves that the proposed approach has the good scalability to new real scene images.

5   Conclusion and Future Work

This paper proposes a new deep neural network, *TextNet*, to estimate text-related image quality while detecting textlines. The proposed network mainly includes three parts: encoder, decoder, and prediction layers. The decoder layer combines the encoded feature map with the decoded map through deconvolution and concatenation. The prediction layer is designed for textline detection and quality assessment with a new loss function. For the purpose of TIQA, the overall text quality of an image is computed through weighted pooling of textline quality. Experimental results show that the proposed TIQA framework can work well in jointly assessing text related image quality and detecting textlines, even for unknown scene images.

One of our future work is to design a novel strategy of generating the ground truth quality for textlines, which helps to create a better general-purpose network model for text quality assessment and detection.

References

1. BRISQUE   software   release.   http://live.ece.utexas.edu/research/quality/BRISQUE_release.zip
2. Buta, M., Neumann, L., Matas, J.: FASText: efficient unconstrained scene text detector. In: IEEE International Conference on Computer Vision, pp. 1206–1214 (2015)
3. Deng, J., Dong, W., Socher, R., Li, L.J., Li, K., Li, F.F.: ImageNet: a large-scale hierarchical image database. In: IEEE Conference on Computer Vision and Pattern Recognition, CVPR 2009, pp. 248–255 (2009)
4. Kang, L., Ye, P., Li, Y., Doermann, D.: A deep learning approach to document image quality assessment. In: IEEE International Conference on Image Processing, pp. 2570–2574 (2014)
5. Karatzas, D., et al.: ICDAR 2015 competition on robust reading. In: International Conference on Document Analysis and Recognition, pp. 1156–1160 (2015)
6. Karatzas, D., et al.: ICDAR 2013 robust reading competition. In: International Conference on Document Analysis and Recognition, pp. 1484–1493 (2013)

7. Kim, K.H., Hong, S., Roh, B., Cheon, Y., Park, M.: PVANET: deep but lightweight neural networks for real-time object detection (2016)
8. Kumar, J., Chen, F., Doermann, D.: Sharpness estimation for document and scene images. In: International Conference on Pattern Recognition, pp. 3292–3295 (2013)
9. Li, H., Zhu, F., Qiu, J.: CG-DIQA: no-reference document image quality assessment based on character gradient (2018). https://arxiv.org/abs/1807.04047
10. Nayef, N.: Metric-based no-reference quality assessment of heterogeneous document images. In: SPIE Electronic Imaging, p. 94020L-12 (2015)
11. Nayef, N., Luqman, M.M., Prum, S., Eskenazi, S., Chazalon, J., Ogier, J.M.: SmartDoc-QA: a dataset for quality assessment of smartphone captured document images - single and multiple distortions. In: International Conference on Document Analysis and Recognition, pp. 1231–1235 (2015)
12. Peng, X., Cao, H., Natarajan, P.: Document image quality assessment using discriminative sparse representation. In: Document Analysis Systems, pp. 227–232 (2016)
13. Rusinol, M., Chazalon, J., Ogier, J.M.: Combining focus measure operators to predict OCR accuracy in mobile-captured document images. In: IAPR International Workshop on Document Analysis Systems, pp. 181–185 (2014)
14. Shi, B., Yao, C., Liao, M., Yang, M., Xu, P., Cui, L., Belongie, S., Lu, S., Bai, X.: ICDAR 2017 competition on reading Chinese text in the wild (RCTW-17). In: 2017 14th IAPR International Conference on Document Analysis and Recognition (ICDAR), vol. 01, pp. 1429–1434 (2017)
15. Sudre, C.H., Li, W., Vercauteren, T., Ourselin, S., Cardoso, M.J.: Generalised dice overlap as a deep learning loss function for highly unbalanced segmentations (2017)
16. Tian, Z., Huang, W., He, T., He, P., Qiao, Y.: Detecting text in natural image with connectionist text proposal network. In: European Conference on Computer Vision, pp. 56–72 (2016)
17. Xu, J., Ye, P., Li, Q., Liu, Y., Doermann, D.: No-reference document image quality assessment based on high order image statistics. In: IEEE International Conference on Image Processing, pp. 3289–3293 (2016)
18. Ye, P., Doermann, D.: Document image quality assessment: a brief survey. In: International Conference on Document Analysis and Recognition, pp. 723–727 (2013)
19. Ye, Q., Doermann, D.: Text detection and recognition in imagery: a survey. IEEE Trans. Pattern Anal. Mach. Intell. **37**(7), 1480–1500 (2015)
20. Zhang, Z., Zhang, C., Shen, W., Yao, C., Liu, W., Bai, X.: Multi-oriented text detection with fully convolutional networks, pp. 4159–4167 (2016)
21. Zhou, X., et al.: EAST: an efficient and accurate scene text detector. In: IEEE Conference on Computer Vision and Pattern Recognition, CVPR 2017, Honolulu, HI, USA, 21–26 July 2017, pp. 2642–2651 (2017)
22. Zhu, Y., Yao, C., Bai, X.: Scene text detection and recognition: recent advances and future trends. Front. Comput. Sci. **10**(1), 19–36 (2016)

A Target Dominant Sets Clustering Algorithm

Jian Hou[1]([✉]), Chengcong Lv[1], Aihua Zhang[1], and Xu E.[2,3]

[1] College of Engineering, Bohai University, Jinzhou 121013, China
dr.houjian@gmail.com
[2] College of Information Science, Bohai University, Jinzhou 121013, China
[3] College of Food Science, Bohai University, Jinzhou 121013, China

Abstract. The dominant sets clustering algorithm has some interesting properties and has achieved impressive results in experiments. However, with the data represented as feature vectors, we need to estimate data similarity and the regularization parameter influences the clustering results and number of clusters significantly. To obtain a specified number of clusters efficiently with the dominant sets algorithm, we present a target dominant set clustering algorithm. Our algorithm detects clusters in the first step, and then extracts dominant sets around the cluster centers based on a specially designed game dynamics. In addition, we show that this game dynamics can be utilized to reduce the computation and memory load significantly. Experiments show that our algorithm performs favorably to the original dominant sets algorithm in clustering quality with much smaller computation load than the latter.

Keywords: Clustering · Dominant set · Cluster center

1 Introduction

The commonly used clustering algorithms include k-means, EM, DBSCAN [6]), mean shift [5], normalized cuts (NCuts) [17] and their variants. In general, the problems afflicting existing algorithms include inability to generate clusters of arbitrary shapes, low clustering accuracy, parameter dependence and large computation load. In order to solve one or more of the aforementioned problems, in recent developments the robust spectral clustering [21], affinity propagation (AP) [1], density peak (DP) [16] algorithms are proposed and they reported impressive clustering results in certain applications.

While the majority of existing clustering algorithms work in the partitioning mode, i.e., all clusters are obtained from a partitioning process simultaneously, the dominant sets (DSets) algorithm [15] is a notable exception. This algorithm presents dominant set as a formal definition of a cluster, and detects the clusters sequentially. Compared with existing approaches, the DSets algorithm has some special properties. First, the clusters are detected following a certain order. In contrast, the obtained clusters from DBSCAN do not follow any specific order.

© Springer Nature Switzerland AG 2018
V. Kůrková et al. (Eds.): ICANN 2018, LNCS 11140, pp. 286–295, 2018.
https://doi.org/10.1007/978-3-030-01421-6_28

In contrast, the DSets algorithm tends to extract large-density clusters firstly, and large-size clusters are also given priority in the clustering process [3]. Second, this algorithm assigns a weight to each data in a cluster, which reflects the relationship of the data with others in the cluster. Third, with the data represented as a pairwise similarity matrix, this algorithm has no dependence on any parameters. These nice properties enable the DSets algorithm to be applied in various fields including image segmentation [11], object classification [12,13], object detection [19] and human activity analysis [9].

Although the DSets algorithm is shown to be effective in many applications, we have found that it has its own problems. If the data for clustering are represented as pairwise similarity matrix, this algorithm involves on parameters. However, with data represented as feature vectors, it is necessary to estimate the data similarity and construct the pairwise similarity matrix firstly. With the common similarity measure $s(x, y) = exp(-d(x, y)/\sigma)$ where $d(x, y)$ denotes the Euclidean distance between data x and y, the parameter σ is introduced. We have found that this parameter influences the number of clusters and clustering results significantly. If we intend to obtain a specified number of clusters with the DSets algorithm so that the nice properties can be utilized, a tuning of the parameter σ is necessary, which often means a large computation load. To solve this problem, we present a target dominant sets clustering algorithm in this paper. We firstly detect the cluster centers following the method proposed in [16]. With the cluster centers available, we then extract clusters around the cluster centers with a specially designed dynamics [10] motivated by the one proposed in [2]. This algorithm also allows us to reduce the computation load significantly without degrading the clustering results. Experiments are provided to compare our algorithm with the original DSets algorithm with parameter tuning.

2   Dominant Sets Algorithm

The majority of clustering algorithms generate the clusters from the partitioning process, and no definition is provided as to what subset of data form a cluster. In contrast, the DSets clustering algorithm defines a cluster formally and then detects the clusters one by one. Specifically, this algorithm defines a non-parametric measure of internal coherency, and it extracts a cluster by maximizing the subset which is internally coherent. Based only on the pairwise similarity matrix, the DSets algorithm requires no input parameters. A brief introduction is provided below.

We denote n data to be clustered by V, and $A = (a_{ij})$ stands for the pairwise $n \times n$ similarity matrix. As the data similarities are used to group data into clusters, we force the similarity of one data with itself to be zero, namely $a_{ii} = 0$ for $i \in V$.

To define a cluster formally, the DSets algorithm designs a non-parametric measure of internal coherency on the basis of the pairwise similarity, and treats a maximal, internally coherent subset as a cluster. With $D \subseteq V$ denoting a non-empty subset, $i \in D$ and $j \notin D$, it is defined that

$$\phi_D(i,j) = a_{ij} - \frac{1}{|D|} \sum_{k \in D} a_{ik}, \tag{1}$$

where $|D|$ denotes the size of D, and

$$w_D(i) = \begin{cases} 1, & \text{if } |D| = 1, \\ \sum_{j \in D \setminus \{i\}} \phi_{D \setminus \{i\}}(j,i) w_{D \setminus \{i\}}(j), & \text{otherwise.} \end{cases} \tag{2}$$

The $w_D(i)$ is a key in defining the internal coherency, and can be interpreted approximately as follows. With one data p and a subset $H \subseteq V$, we define

$$\Phi(p, H) = \frac{1}{|H|} \sum_{k \in H} a_{pk}, \tag{3}$$

$$\Phi(H) = \Phi(H, H) = \frac{1}{|H|(|H| - 1)} \sum_{p \in H, k \in H} a_{pk}. \tag{4}$$

Evidently, $\Phi(p, H)$ measures the average similarity between p and the data in H, and $\Phi(H)$ evaluates the overall average similarity inside H. Furthermore, $w_D(i)$ can be regarded as the difference between $\Phi(i, D \setminus \{i\})$ and $\Phi(D \setminus \{i\})$ approximately, with $D \setminus \{i\}$ denoting the subset D excluding i. Therefore $w_D(i) > 0$ means that i has a large similarity with the other data in D, and $w_D(i) < 0$ implies that i is loosely connected to the other data in D.

With $W(D) = \sum_{i \in D} w_D(i)$, we call the subset D a dominant set if

1. $W(T) > 0$, for all non-empty $T \subseteq D$.
2. $w_D(i) > 0$, for all $i \in D$.
3. $w_{D \cup \{i\}}(i) < 0$, for all $i \notin D$.

Here we observe that a dominant set is a maximal, internally coherent subset. The three conditions guarantee that a dominant set has large internal similarities and small external similarities, and enable a dominant to be regarded as a cluster.

The work in [15] detects a dominant set with the replicator dynamics. Specifically, with $x \in R^n$ denoting the weight vector of the n data, the weights are updated iteratively by

$$x_i^{[k+1]} = \frac{x_i^{[k]} (Ax^{[k]})_i}{x^{[k]'} Ax^{[k]}}. \tag{5}$$

At convergence, the data whose weights are larger than a threshold form a dominant set. In addition, it is shown that the weight of data i equals to $\frac{w_D(i)}{W(D)}$, reflecting the relationship of i with the other data in D. Specifically, a large weight indicates that the data has a large similarity with the other data. Furthermore, [2] proposes the infection and immunization dynamics (InImDyn) to improve the computation efficiency. The InImDyn calculates data weights by

$$x^{(t+1)} = \delta_{F(x^{(t)})}(x^{(t)})[F(x^{(t)}) - x^{(t)}] + x^{(t)}, \tag{6}$$

where F is used to calculate the most infective strategy y for x, and θ represents the minimum share of y to make $(1 - \theta)x + \theta y$ immune to y. For space reason, the details of this dynamics are skipped in this paper.

After one dominant set (cluster) is obtained, the included data are removed. Then the next cluster is detected in the remaining unclustered data. By repeating this process we are able to accomplish the clustering.

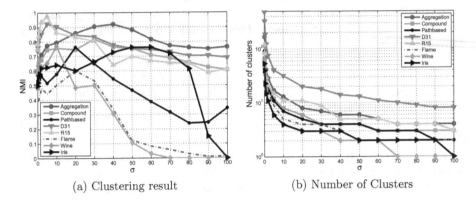

(a) Clustering result   (b) Number of Clusters

Fig. 1. DSets clustering results and obtained number of clusters with different σ's.

3 Our Approach

The DSets algorithm has some interesting properties and has been applied in diverse tasks. However, with data represented as feature vectors, the parameter σ impacts on the clustering results significantly. In this section we discuss this problem and present target dominant sets clustering as a solution.

3.1 Problems

The DSets algorithm detect clusters based only on the pairwise similarity matrix. With data represented as feature vectors, we use $s(x, y) = exp(-d(x, y)/\sigma)$ to estimate data similarity and introduce the parameter σ. We study the impact of σ on clustering results below.

The eight datasets used in experiments are Aggregation [8], Compound [20], Pathbased [4], D31 [18], R15 [18], Flame [7] and the Wine and Iris datasets from UCI machine learning repository. The parameter σ is tested with the values $\sigma = \alpha \bar{d}$, where $\bar{d}$ denotes the mean of pairwise distances and α takes values from 0.1, 0.2, 0.5, 1, 2, 5, 10, 20, 30, $\cdots$, 100. We use NMI (Normalized Mutual Information) to evaluate the clustering results, which are reported in Fig. 1(a). Evidently the clustering results on all the eight datasets are influenced by σ significantly. To find out the reason of this influence, we further have a look at the obtained numbers of clusters with different σ's. As shown in Fig. 1(b), the numbers of clusters decrease or remain unchanged with the increase of σ.

This means that σ influences the number of clusters, cluster sizes and then the clustering results.

We discuss the observations from Fig. 1 as follows. By definition, a dominant set is a maximal, internally coherent subset, and only the data with large internal similarities can be grouped into one dominant set. With a small σ, $s(x,y) = exp(-d(x,y)/\sigma)$ generates small similarity values, and one data has large similarities with only a limited number of nearest neighbors, resulting in many small clusters. With a large σ, the similarity values are large and we obtain large clusters correspondingly. This explains why the numbers of clusters decrease or keep unchanged with the increase of σ in Fig. 1(b). As the cluster sizes increase with the increase of σ, the clusters are smaller than the real ones at first, and become larger than the real ones gradually. Consequently, σ improves the clustering results at first, and then results in a degradation when σ is too large, as shown in Fig. 1(a).

The experiments above imply that a tuning process of σ is need to obtain the desired clustering result and number of clusters. In the case that the number of clusters is specified beforehand, and we also intend to make use of the special properties of dominant set, we have to try different σ's to obtain the specified number of clusters. In general, this means a large computation load.

3.2   Target Dominant Set Extraction

In order to generate a specified number of clusters with the DSets algorithm efficiently, we present a target dominant sets algorithm. We detect cluster centers and treat them as seeds in the first step, and then extract clusters containing the seeds. As the extracted cluster contain a specified data, i.e., the seed, we call the obtained cluster (dominant set) as target cluster (dominant set). These two steps are described in details below.

The first step is to detect cluster centers. While there are different methods for this task, in our implementation we adopt the one proposed in [16]. Each data is represented by local density ρ and the distance δ to the nearest data of larger local density. By regarding local density peaks as cluster centers, it is found that both ρ's and δ's of cluster centers are large, whereas either ρ's or δ's of the other data are small. Based on this difference, we sort the data according to their $\gamma = \rho\delta$, and those with the largest γ's are selected as the cluster centers.

While the original DSets algorithm detects clusters sequentially, we don't know which data will be included in extracting each cluster. In order to extract a target cluster containing a specified data, the game dynamics must be modified to serve this purpose [10]. With InImDyn, the weights of data are updated iteratively according to Eq. (6). Even if we assign the initial weight of the seed to be 1, it is still possible that the seed data is assigned a zero weight, which means it is not in the obtained cluster. Therefore we need a different weight updating method. In the iteration, each state $x^{(t)}$ can be regarded as an approximation of the final weight vector, and the final weights are shown to be equal to

$$x_i^D = \begin{cases} \frac{w_D(i)}{W(D)}, & \text{if} \quad i \in D, \\ 0, & \text{otherwise.} \end{cases} \tag{7}$$

Consequently, each time the most infective strategy y is selected with the F function in Eq. (6), we can use Eq. (7) to update the weights, instead of Eq. (6). In this way, once one data is selected, it will never be assigned a zero weight, and it will stay in the obtained cluster. This guarantees that the obtained cluster contains the seed, since the seed is the first selected data.

However, the recursive form of $w_D(i)$ in Eq. (2) means a large computation load, especially if the cluster size is large. We therefore explore an approximation of $w_D(i)$ to improve the computation efficiency. As discussed in Sect. 2, $w_D(i)$ measures the relationship between $\Phi(i, D \setminus \{i\})$ and $\Phi(D \setminus \{i\})$. We make use of this relationship to estimate $w_D(i)$ as

$$w_D(i) = \begin{cases} 1, & \text{if} \quad |D| = 1, \\ \sum\limits_{j \in D \setminus \{i\}} a_{ij}, & \text{if} \quad |D| = 2, \\ \frac{\Phi(i, D \setminus \{i\})}{\Phi(D \setminus \{i\})}, & \text{otherwise.} \end{cases} \tag{8}$$

Given a dataset, we firstly detect the cluster centers. For each cluster center, we then extract the target cluster containing the cluster center. In this process, it is possible that some data are grouped into more than one clusters. We make use of the data weights to solve this problem and obtain the final result. As a large data weight means a large probability of one data in one cluster, we compare the weights of one data assigned by each cluster, and group the data into the cluster where it is assigned the largest weight.

As a special type of dominant sets clustering, our approach is proposed to eliminate the impact of σ and generate a specified number of clusters with the DSets algorithm. While non-parametric similarity measures, e.g., cosine, can also be used to estimate data similarity, the work in [14] indicates that non-parametric measures usually generate unsatisfactory results. In addition, with non-parametric similarity measures we are not guaranteed to obtain the specified number of clusters.

3.3 Improvement Measure

The DSets algorithm is computationally expensive in comparison with some other algorithms, e.g., k-means, DBSCAN and NCuts. The running time comparison of these four algorithms is shown in Table 1, where $\sigma = 30\bar{d}$ is adopted for the best average result for the DSets algorithm. It is evident that on all the datasets except for Iris, the running times of DSets algorithm are much more longer than those of the other algorithms. Even on the Iris dataset, only the DBSCAN algorithm consumes more running time than the DSets algorithm.

Table 1. Running time (ms) comparison of different clustering algorithms.

	Aggregation	Compound	Pathbased	D31	R15	Flame	Wine	Iris
DSets	473.9	132.5	66.9	12377.9	1275.0	51.3	52.9	19.7
k-means	4.5	2.2	1.8	100.2	9.3	1.2	2.0	1.5
NCuts	193.0	56.6	29.5	3701.5	113.8	19.3	12.6	10.5
DBSCAN	46.4	25.3	16.2	487.0	108.4	8.9	10.3	42.5

As our approach is based on dominant set extraction, it is also afflicted by the large computation load.

In our opinion, the reason of the large computation load of the DSets algorithm is two folds. First, the clusters are obtained sequentially and each cluster is extracted by updating the data weights iteratively. This means a large number of iterations and leads to a large computation load, especially if there are a large amount of clusters. Second, each cluster is detected in all the unclustered data, although the data in a cluster usually correspond to a small subset of unclustered data. Considering it is inherited in the DSets algorithm to extract clusters by updating the data weights, we choose to explore measures to reduce the computation load based on the second reason. Since one cluster usually corresponds to a subset of the unclustered data, one natural solution is to extract a cluster within a part, instead of all, of the unclustered data. However, with the original DSets algorithm it is not clear which data will be included into one cluster before the cluster is obtained. In this case, it is not possible to reduce the computation load by extracting a cluster in a subset of unclustered data.

Fortunately, in our algorithm the cluster centers are detected in the first step, and the clusters are then extracted to include these cluster centers. As one cluster center and the farthest data are unlikely to be in the same cluster, it is not necessary to extract the target cluster in all the unclustered data. Instead, we can safely discard the farthest data and work with only the nearest neighbors of the cluster centers. As the data used in calculation is reduced, the computation load is expected to decrease correspondingly. Furthermore, since the major memory load is caused by the pairwise data similarity matrix, and the matric size is square of data amount, the memory load can be reduced significantly.

4   Experiments

In this part, we firstly illustrate the effect of the improvement measure in reducing computation load presented in Sect. 3. Then we compare the running time and clustering results of our approach with the original DSets algorithm based on tuning of the parameter σ.

4.1   Effect in Reducing Computation Load

In Sect. 3 we show that it is possible to reduce computation load by discarding the farthest data to the cluster centers. In order to test to which degree the farthest data can be discarded without degrading the clustering results, the data are sorted based on to their distances to the cluster center. Then different percentages of data in the farthest part are discarded and the corresponding clustering results are recorded in Fig. 2(a).

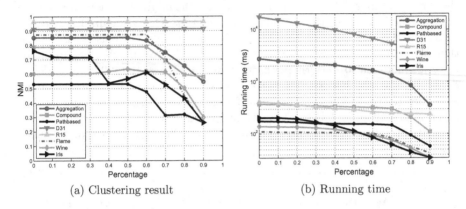

(a) Clustering result   (b) Running time

Fig. 2. Clustering results and running time with respect to different percentage of discarded data.

It can be observed from Fig. 2(a) that on all the datasets except for Iris, at least 50% of the farthest data can be discarded without degrading the clustering results. Especially with the D31 and R15 datasets, we can discard up to 90% of the farthest data safely. In our opinion, the reason for this observation is that these two datasets contain 31 and 15 clusters respectively, and all the clusters in one dataset have the same amount of data. In this case, in extracting one cluster, the contained data are often less than 10% of the data. Therefore we can remove up to 90% of data without influencing the clustering results. In contrast, with the Iris dataset, discarding even 10 percent of data results in an evident decrease in the clustering accuracy. One possible reason is that on this dataset the features are extracted from iris flowers and it is not suitable to measure the difference with Euclidean distance. On the other datasets, the number of clusters ranges from 2 to 7, and we can discard 50 to 60 percent of farthest data safely in extracting target clusters. This means that the new matrix size is about 25% or smaller of the original one, indicating a significant reduction in memory load.

Intuitively, the reduction of data in computation will result in the reduction of computation load. Similar to the last experiment, we show the running time with respect to different percentage of discarded data in Fig. 2(b). With all the datasets the computation load is reduced evidently with the reduction of data in computation.

It is worth noticing that in our implement we discard the farthest data to the cluster centers in all the data, instead of the unclustered data. This is helpful to determine a fixed ratio to discard the farthest data. Otherwise, with the extraction of clusters, the amount of unclustered data becomes smaller and smaller, and it is difficult to find out such a fixed ratio.

4.2 Comparison

To obtain a specified number of clusters with the DSets algorithm, we present the target dominant sets algorithm. Since Fig. 1(b) indicates that we can also achieve this purpose by selecting a proper σ, we compare the running time of these two methods. With our approach, we use the original version and no data are discarded to reduce the computation load. With DSets, we firstly use $\sigma = \bar{d}$ to obtain the clustering results. If the obtained number of clusters is smaller than the real one, we find the σ which generates the real number of clusters by bisection between $[0, \bar{d}]$. Otherwise, we continue to test $10\bar{d}$, $20\bar{d}$, $\cdots$ and also determine the σ by bisection. Here we call this algorithm with parameter tuning as parameter-tuned DSets (PT-DSets) for ease of expression. The running time of our approach and PT DSets is shown in Table 2, where it is evident that on the majority of datasets our approach is much more efficient than parameter-tuned DSets.

Table 2. Running time (seconds) comparison between our algorithm and PT-DSets.

	Aggregation	Compound	Pathbased	D31	R15	Flame	Wine	Iris
PT-DSets	4.80	1.05	1.01	128.39	2.44	0.64	0.28	0.24
Ours	2.75	0.37	0.17	17.39	0.41	0.11	0.14	0.20

Table 3. Clustering results comparison between our algorithm and PT-DSets.

	Aggregation	Compound	Pathbased	D31	R15	Flame	Wine	Iris
PT-DSets	0.90	0.75	0.39	0.87	0.97	0.12	0.49	0.60
Ours·	0.85	0.79	0.53	0.91	0.96	0.87	0.60	0.76

Finally, we compare the clustering accuracy of our approach and PT-DSets in Table 3. Our algorithm outperforms PT-DSets on 6 out of the 8 datasets, is outperformed by the latter slightly on the other two datasets. This observation indicates that our approach performs better than PT-DSets in both clustering accuracy and computation efficiency.

5 Conclusions

We present a target dominant sets algorithm to obtain a specified number of clusters with the dominant sets algorithm efficiently. In the first step cluster centers are determined based on the local density relationship among the data. Then we extract the target clusters around the cluster centers, which is based on a revised infection and immunization dynamics. We further show that the computation and memory load of our approach can be reduced significantly without degrading the clustering results by discarding the farthest data to the cluster centers. Experiments on some datasets indicate that our algorithm outperforms the dominant sets algorithm with parameter tuning in both clustering accuracy and computation efficiency.

Acknowledgement. This work is supported by the National Natural Science Foundation of China under Grant No. 61473045, and the Natural Science Foundation of Liaoning Province under Grant No. 20170540013 and No. 20170540005.

References

1. Brendan, J.F., Delbert, D.: Clustering by passing messages between data points. Science **315**, 972–976 (2007)
2. Bulo, S.R., Pelillo, M., Bomze, I.M.: Graph-based quadratic optimization: a fast evolutionary approach. Comput. Vis. Image Underst. **115**(7), 984–995 (2011)
3. Bulo, S.R., Torsello, A., Pelillo, M.: A game-theoretic approach to partial clique enumeration. Image Vis. Comput. **27**(7), 911–922 (2009)
4. Chang, H., Yeung, D.Y.: Robust path-based spectral clustering. Pattern Recogn. **41**(1), 191–203 (2008)
5. Cheng, Y.: Mean shift, mode seeking, and clustering. IEEE Trans. Pattern Anal. Mach. Intell. **17**(8), 790–799 (1995)
6. Ester, M., Kriegel, H.P., Sander, J., Xu, X.W.: A density-based algorithm for discovering clusters in large spatial databases with noise. In: International Conference on Knowledge Discovery and Data Mining, pp. 226–231 (1996)
7. Fu, L., Medico, E.: Flame, a novel fuzzy clustering method for the analysis of DNA microarray data. BMC Bioinform. **8**(1), 1–17 (2007)
8. Gionis, A., Mannila, H., Tsaparas, P.: Clustering aggregation. ACM Trans. Knowl. Discov. Data **1**(1), 1–30 (2007)
9. Hamid, R., Maddi, S., Johnson, A.Y., Bobick, A.F., Essa, I.A., Isbell, C.: A novel sequence representation for unsupervised analysis of human activities. Artif. Intell. **173**, 1221–1244 (2009)
10. Hou, J., Xu, E., Chi, L., Xia, Q., Qi, N.: Dominant sets and target clique extraction. In: International Conference on Pattern Recognition, pp. 1831–1834 (2012)
11. Hou, J., Gao, H., Li, X.: DSets-DBSCAN: a parameter-free clustering algorithm. IEEE Trans. Image Process. **25**(7), 3182–3193 (2016)
12. Hou, J., Gao, H., Li, X.: Feature combination via clustering. IEEE Trans. Neural Netw. Learn. Syst. **29**(4), 896–907 (2018)
13. Hou, J., Pelillo, M.: A simple feature combination method based on dominant sets. Pattern Recogn. **46**(11), 3129–3139 (2013)
14. Hou, J., Xia, Q., Qi, N.: Experimental study on dominant sets clustering. IET Comput. Vis. **9**(2), 208–215 (2015)
15. Pavan, M., Pelillo, M.: Dominant sets and pairwise clustering. IEEE Trans. Pattern Anal. Mach. Intell. **29**(1), 167–172 (2007)
16. Rodriguez, A., Laio, A.: Clustering by fast search and find of density peaks. Science **344**, 1492–1496 (2014)
17. Shi, J., Malik, J.: Normalized cuts and image segmentation. IEEE Trans. Pattern Anal. Mach. Intell. **22**(8), 167–172 (2000)
18. Veenman, C.J., Reinders, M., Backer, E.: A maximum variance cluster algorithm. IEEE Trans. Pattern Anal. Mach. Intell. **24**(9), 1273–1280 (2002)
19. Yang, X.W., Liu, H.R., Laecki, L.J.: Contour-based object detection as dominant set computation. Pattern Recogn. **45**, 1927–1936 (2012)
20. Zahn, C.T.: Graph-theoretical methods for detecting and describing gestalt clusters. IEEE Trans. Comput. **20**(1), 68–86 (1971)
21. Zhu, X., Loy, C.C., Gong, S.: Constructing robust affinity graphs for spectral clustering. In: IEEE International Conference on Computer Vision and Pattern Recognition, pp. 1450–1457 (2014)

Input Pattern Complexity Determines Specialist and Generalist Populations in Drosophila Neural Network

Aaron Montero[✉], Jessica Lopez-Hazas, and Francisco B. Rodriguez

Grupo de Neurocomputación Biológica, Dpto. de Ingeniería Informática,
Escuela Politécnica Superior, Universidad Autónoma de Madrid,
28049 Madrid, Spain
aaron.montero.m@gmail.com, jessicalopezhazas@gmail.com,
f.rodriguez@uam.es

Abstract. Neural heterogeneity has been reported as beneficial for information processing in neural networks. An example of this heterogeneity can be observed in the neural responses to stimuli, which divide the neurons into two populations: specialists and generalists. Being observed in the neural network of the locust olfactory system that a balance of these two neural populations is crucial for achieving a correct pattern recognition. However, these results may not be generalizable to other biological neural networks. Therefore, we took advantage of a recent biological study about the Drosophila connectome to study the balance of these two neural populations in its neural network. We conclude that the balance between specialists and generalists also occurs in the Drosophila. This balancing process does not affect the neural network connectivity, since specialist and generalist neurons are not differentiable by the number of incoming connections.

Keywords: Pattern recognition · Bio-inspired neural networks
Neural computation · Supervised learning · Connectivity
Specialist neuron · Generalist neuron · Neural variability
Olfactory system

1 Introduction

In a recently published study [7], we observed that in a neural network that simulated the locust olfactory system, pattern recognition was influenced by the balance of specialist and generalist neurons. These neurons are defined in this way based on their neural responses to different stimuli, for which the specialists respond to few of them and the generalists to a wide number of them. Because of this, it is suggested that specialists are essential for discrimination, while generalists extract common features [15]. However, these results may not be generalizable to other insects, so we have taken advantage of a recent and extensive study on Drosophila [3] to test our results using a computational model

© Springer Nature Switzerland AG 2018
V. Kůrková et al. (Eds.): ICANN 2018, LNCS 11140, pp. 296–303, 2018.
https://doi.org/10.1007/978-3-030-01421-6_29

that simulates its olfactory system. Some of the differences between the locust neural network and the Drosophila one are the number of neurons in the antennal lobe (AL) (~1,000 [8] vs ~250 [3]), the number of Kenyon cells (KCs) in the mushroom body (MB) (~50,000 [8] vs ~2,500 [3]) and the connection probability between the AL and the KCs (~0.2 [6,8] vs ~0.01 [3]), see Fig. 1. The study of specialism/generalism on Drosophila will not only serve to strengthen our results, since we will also use the data of Drosophila to analyze the connectome obtained by the balance of these two types of neurons.

The computational model to perform this study on Drosophila is a single-hidden-layer neural network (Fig. 1) which represents in its input layer the AL, in the hidden layer the KCs and in the output layer the MB output neurons (MBONs). AL and KCs are connected by a non-specific connectivity matrix [5] that increases the separability between different encoded stimuli. On the other hand, the connectivity matrix that links KCs with MBONs is subjected to a learning process that can be emulated by using Hebbian rules [2]. Finally, the information received by the MBONs is subject to a process of lateral inhibition, which is similar to the winner-take-all principle [9].

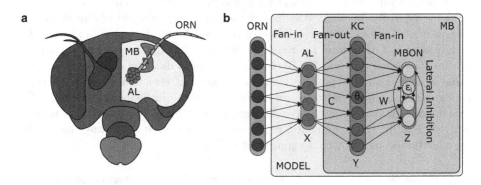

Fig. 1. Neural network model. Panel (a) shows the biological structure of the olfactory system of the Drosophila. When the olfactory receptors react to odor plumes the olfactory receptor neurons (ORNs) send the odor information using a fan-in connectivity network to the AL. AL codifies this information and relays it via fan-out connections to the MB. Inside MB, the odor information is received by KCs, which are responsible for increasing its separability. Finally, the KC send the stimulus signal to the MBONs, which are responsible for its final classification process by means of convergent synaptic connections. Panel (b) shows the computational model used, which is a single-hidden-layer neural network with the AL layers as input (X), the KCs as hidden layer (Y) and the MBONs as output (Z). The connectivity matrices C and W link AL to KCs and KCs to MBONs respectively. The thresholds or biases for the hidden and output layer are θ_j and ε_l respectively.

In this computational model, we introduced Gaussian patterns for analyzing input data of different complexities, since this complexity can be easily controlled through overlap between classes of these patterns. On the other hand, to analyze the role of specialist and generalist neurons in the KC layer, we calculated the classification success for different combinations of these neurons. We started with a network with only generalists neurons moving to a network with only specialists, going through several intermediate states. The results obtained by this process are consistent with those previously obtained for locust [7]. Furthermore, we noted that the number of incoming connections to specialist and generalist neurons is similar. This suggests that the neural sensitivity of KCs seems to be due only to the spatial distribution of stimuli in the AL layer.

2   Methods

2.1   Gaussian Patterns

The AL encodes the olfactory stimuli so that a specific odorant stimulates specific glomeruli of it [10]. This activity can be propagated to the rest of the glomeruli according to the intensity of the stimulus [10]. This behavior has led us to simulate the odor patterns as Gaussians. The specific glomeruli are represented by the expected value of the Gaussians and the propagated activity because of the stimulus intensity by their standard deviation. The variation of the standard deviation of these Gaussians will determine the degree of overlap between pattern classes and, therefore, their complexity level. In Fig. 2 we can see examples of these Gaussian patterns for 10 classes used and 3 different complexity levels, these examples show a pattern example for each of their classes and different configurations. These patterns are defined in a two-dimensional space: the X-axis defines the spatial location of AL neurons and the Y-axis shows their neural activity. Finally, since the neural response to a stimulus is not always identical, we added noise to the activity generated by stimuli.

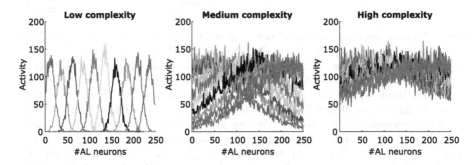

Fig. 2. Gaussian patterns. This figure shows an example of Gaussian pattern for each of the 10 classes used and 3 different complexities. The Gaussian patterns represent the AL neurons by the X-axis and their activity by the Y-axis. The variation of the standard deviation of these Gaussians determines the overlap degree and, therefore, their complexity level. Furthermore, we added noise to the activity generated by stimuli, since the neural response to them can change.

2.2 Neural Network and Neuron Model

The network model is a single-hidden-layer neural network that retains the most relevant structural properties of the insect olfactory system [4,6,7] (see Fig. 1). The input layer represents the AL, the hidden one is the KCs and the output layer is composed of MBON populations, between which there is lateral inhibition. The dimensions of this network are based on the Drosophila ones, 250 input neurons [13], 2500 hidden neurons [14] and 100 output neurons (which are divided into populations of 10 neurons, one for each of the 10 pattern classes).

These three layers are connected by the matrices C and W, which are initialized at the beginning of each learning process. The connectivity matrix C is established randomly by independent Bernoulli processes with probability $p_c = 0.01$ in the Drosophila [3] for each existing connection and $1 - p_c$ for each lack of it [4]. The reason for this non-specific connectivity matrix is due to the individual connection variability of insects of the same species [5]. On the other hand, the matrix W is initialized by a random matrix N_0, because its weights will be gradually strengthened or weakened using a supervised Hebbian learning [7]. According to the learning rules, if the hidden layer neuron y_j has fired and the output neuron z_l should fire due to the output target, then the connection between these neurons (w_{lj}) is reinforced with a probability p_+. In case of the output neuron should not fire, the connection is weakened with the same probability. Instead, If the hidden layer neuron y_j has not fired and the output neuron z_l should fire, then the connection between these neurons is weakened with a probability p_-. The value chosen for these Hebbian probabilities were $p_+ = 1$ and $p_- = 0.05$ because of their good learning performance [4,7].

In terms of the neuron model, and taking into account the simple dynamics of KCs (mostly silent, a single spike followed by a reset and its response is produced by the coincidence of concurrent spikes) [8], we choose the McCulloch-Pitts model. This neuron model changes slightly for the MBONs given the lateral inhibition present in them [12]. Hence, the equations for the KCs and MBONs are as follows:

$$y_j = \varphi(\sum_{i=1}^{N_{AL}} c_{ji}x_i - \theta_j), \quad j = 1, \ldots, N_{KC}, \tag{1}$$

$$z_l = \varphi\left(\sum_{j=1}^{N_{KC}} w_{lj}y_j - \frac{1}{N_{class}} \sum_{k=1}^{N_{class}} \sum_{j=1}^{N_{KC}} w_{kj}y_j - \varepsilon_l\right), \quad l = 1, \ldots, N_{class}, \tag{2}$$

where x_i, y_j and z_l are activation states for an input neuron, a hidden neuron and a group of MBONs specialized in a certain pattern class, respectively. The input and hidden layer are linked by c_{ji} weights, and the hidden and output layer by w_{lj} ones. On the other hand, the neural thresholds (bias) for the hidden and output layer are θ_j and ε_l. Finally, the Heaviside activation function φ is 0 when its argument is negative or 0 and 1 otherwise. In the case of MBONs, where we used the winner-take-all concept [9], the activation function φ is only 1 for the winner MBON group.

Finally, we used different thresholds for KCs (heterogeneous thresholds) and the same threshold for all MBONs (homogeneous threshold). The reasons for using heterogeneous thresholds in KCs is their existence in this kind of neurons [8] and their use in neural networks can improve pattern recognition [6]. To select different threshold values for KCs, we used the concept of limit threshold in the training phase [6,7]. Limit threshold is the neural activity of a neuron generated by a given stimulus and, therefore, the minimum value for which the neuron will not react to it. We extracted the distribution of limit thresholds for each KC and used these values to made the KCs react randomly to a percentage of patterns in order to introduce a greater differentiation between specialists and generalists in KC layer [7]. However, this variability was not needed in MBON layer, since a homogeneous threshold for all neurons is enough because of the learning process in the matrix W and, furthermore, there are no records in biology about their presence in these neurons.

2.3   Selection Criteria of Specialist and Generalist Neuron

Specialist neurons are selective responding to stimuli, while generalists code for multiple stimuli [1]. Based on this definition, we can assume the extreme case that specialists respond only to one odorant class and generalists respond to all of them (10 pattern classes in our case). However, in a previous study [7], we observed that the computational model worked better when we did not exclude intermediate sensitivities (number of neural responses of a neuron to different stimuli). Therefore, we decided to divide neural sensitivities equally between specialist and generalist neurons. Specialists will be those with a neural sensitivity from 1 to 5 and generalists the ones with neural sensitivity from 6 to 10.

Once specialists and generalists had been defined, we made two sets of each type of neurons. These sets will be used to create a new KC layer with the same dimensions than the original but with the percentages of these two types of neurons that we choose. To observe their impact on the classification success, the KC layer starts with all generalist neurons and they are gradually replaced by specialist neurons. This balancing process will allow us to estimate which combination is the most suitable for pattern recognition.

3   Results

The following results are the average of 10 simulations with 5-cross-validation and supervised Hebbian learning for a total of 1000 Gaussian patterns (100 for each of the 10 pattern classes).

3.1   Balance of Specialists and Generalists

In Fig. 3, we can see that when the overlap is less than 28%, the maximum success is achieved for all combinations of specialist and generalist neurons in the KCs. Once this percentage of overlap has been overcome, the maximum classification success rate is only achieved for a specific balance of these neurons. This balance initially requires a small number of specialists (10 − 20%), but for overlaps greater than 70% this number increases quickly. This growth causes the neural network of the Drosophila finally only needs specialists to achieve the highest classification success, for input patterns with extremely high overlap (~90%) and, therefore, high complexity.

These results are consistent with those observed for locust [7]. The only remarkable difference between both results is that the region of balance between specialists and generalists is greater in Drosophila, as well as the percentage of specialist neurons required on it is usually lower. A variation that may be due to the fact that the connection probability between AL and MB in Drosophila ($p_c \sim 0.01$) [3] is much lower than the one estimated for the locust ($p_c \sim 0.2$) [6,8]. Therefore, the amount of odor information transmitted by this lower connectivity will be also lower and the Drosophila system requires initially a larger number of generalists to offset this loss.

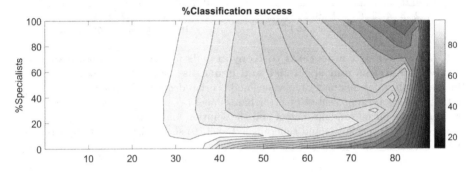

Fig. 3. Relationship between overlap, the required percentage of specialist neurons and classification success. This picture shows the evolution of the classification success and the percentage of specialists required to achieve this success based on the overlap between patterns. When the overlap is less than 28%, the maximum success is achieved for all combinations of specialists and generalists in KCs. For an overlap from 28% to 90%, the system requires a balance between these two types of neurons to classify correctly. During this period, the number of specialists required by the system increases quickly. Finally, for overlaps higher than 90%, the classification gets worse and the system only needs specialists for improving its performance.

3.2 Neural Sensitivity Independent of the Number of Connections

As we mentioned previously, we have based on a recent and extensive study on Drosophila [3] to analyze the role of specialist and generalist neurons in its olfactory system. This study differentiates KCs according to their incoming connections, which led us to wonder if the randomness of the network that connects AL to KCs, matrix C (see Fig. 1), disappears after the balance between specialists and generalists.

As shown in panel (a) of Fig. 4, the connectivity distributions between the initial matrix C and the solution matrix C' (after the balancing process) are similar. The reason for not losing the random structure of connectivity by the balancing process could be due to the similarity between the connectivity distributions of specialists and generalists, panel (b) of Fig. 4. Therefore, when we modify the specialist and generalist populations in the KC layer, Subsect. 2.3, we do not affect the number of connections between AL and KCs and how they are distributed. This leads us to think that the neural sensitivity of a neuron is not directly proportional to the number of incoming connections, if not mainly is due to the spatial distribution of stimuli in the input layer of AL.

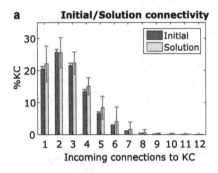 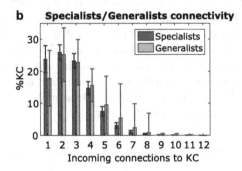

Fig. 4. Number of connections to Kenyon cells for initial and solution connectivity matrices and specialist and generalist neurons. These panels show the mean values for different simulations and overlap degrees, the standard deviations of these values are represented by error bars. Panel (a) shows the connectivity distributions of the initial random matrix and the solution matrix obtained by the optimal balance between specialists and generalists. Panel (b) shows the connectivity distributions of specialist and generalist neurons.

4   Discussion and Conclusions

In a previous study [7], we analyzed computationally what proportion of specialist and generalist neurons was suitable to improve the neural network learning of the olfactory system. We noted that when the complexity of the patterns was low, the system could reach the maximum classification success with almost any ratio of specialists and generalists and, therefore, their roles in pattern recognition was unspecific. For intermediate complexities, the system required a balance between these types of neurons (both were relevant). Finally, when the input complexity was high, the pattern recognition problem was such that only specialist neurons could improve the classification success. However, it was not clear that these results in the locust olfactory system would be generalized to other insects. So we decided to also study it for Drosophila and analyze the resulting connectome from the balance between specialists and generalists.

We observed by using Gaussian patterns with different levels of overlap (complexity) and a Drosophila-inspired neural network that the results obtained are consistent with the ones obtained for the locust. Furthermore, the balance between specialist and generalists neurons does not affect the randomness of the connections between AL and MB in agreement with the biological facts. This fact is due to the similar number of incoming connections of these two types of neurons, which means that the neural sensitivity of KCs seems to be related only to the spatial distribution of stimuli in the AL. Therefore, the regularization of the ratio of specialists and generalists could be applied in randomized neural networks [11] to improve their classification without removing its randomness.

Acknowledgments. This research was supported by MINECO/FEDER projects TIN2014-54580-R and TIN2017-84452-R (http://www.mineco.gob.es/). We also thank Ramon Huerta for his useful discussions.

References

1. Christensen, T.A.: Making scents out of spatial and temporal codes in specialist and generalist olfactory networks. Chem. Senses **30**, 283–284 (2005)
2. Dubnau, J., Grady, L., Kitamoto, T., Tully, T.: Disruption of neurotransmission in drosophila mushroom body blocks retrieval but not acquisition of memory. Nature **411**(6836), 476–480 (2001)
3. Eichler, K., et al.: The complete connectome of a learning and memory centre in an insect brain. Nature **548**(7666), 175 (2017)
4. Huerta, R., Nowotny, T., Garcia-Sanchez, M., Abarbanel, H.D.I., Rabinovich, M.I.: Learning classification in the olfactory system of insects. Neural Comput. **16**, 1601–1640 (2004)
5. Masuda-Nakagawa, L.M., Tanaka, N.K., O'Kane, C.J.: Stereotypic and random patterns of connectivity in the larval mushroom body calyx of Drosophila. Proc. Natl. Acad. Sci. USA **102**, 19027–19032 (2005)
6. Montero, A., Huerta, R., Rodriguez, F.B.: Regulation of specialists and generalists by neural variability improves pattern recognition performance. Neurocomputing **151**, 69–77 (2015)
7. Montero, A., Huerta, R., Rodriguez, F.B.: Stimulus space complexity determines the ratio of specialist and generalist neurons during pattern recognition. J. Frankl. Inst. **355**(5), 2951–2977 (2018)
8. Perez-Orive, J., Mazor, O., Turner, G.C., Cassenaer, S., Wilson, R.I., Laurent, G.: Oscillations and sparsening of odor representations in the mushroom body. Science **297**(5580), 359–365 (2002)
9. Rabinovich, M.I., Huerta, R., Volkovskii, A., Abarbanel, H.D., Stopfer, M., Laurent, G.: Dynamical coding of sensory information with competitive networks. J. Physiol. Paris **94**(5–6), 465–471 (2000)
10. Rubin, J.E., Katz, L.C.: Optical imaging of odorant representations in the mammalian olfactory bulb. J. Neurophysiol. **23**, 449–511 (1999)
11. Scardapane, S., Wang, D.: Randomness in neural networks: an overview. Wiley Interdiscip. Rev. Data Min. Knowl. Discov. **7**(2), e1200 (2017)
12. Schürmann, F.W., Frambach, I., Elekes, K.: Gabaergic synaptic connections in mushroom bodies of insect brains. Acta Biol. Hung. **59**, 173–181 (2008)
13. Shen, H.-C., Wei, J.-Y., Chu, S.-Y., Chung, P.-C., Hsu, T.-C., Hung-Hsiang, Y.: Morphogenetic studies of the drosophila DA1 ventral olfactory projection neuron. PloS One **11**(5), e0155384 (2016)
14. Turner, G.C., Bazhenov, M., Laurent, G.: Olfactory representations by drosophila mushroom body neurons. J. Neurophysiol. **99**, 734–746 (2008)
15. Wilson, R.I., Turner, G.C., Laurent, G.: Transformation of olfactory representations in the drosophila antennal lobe. Science **303**(5656), 366–370 (2004)

A Hybrid Planning Strategy Through Learning from Vision for Target-Directed Navigation

Xiaomao Zhou[1,2]([✉]), Cornelius Weber[2], Chandrakant Bothe[2], and Stefan Wermter[2]

[1] College of Automation, Harbin Engineering University,
Nantong Street 145, Harbin 150001, China
[2] Department of Informatics, University of Hamburg,
Vogt-Kölln-Strasse 30, 22527 Hamburg, Germany
{zhou,weber,bothe,wermter}@informatik.uni-hamburg.de
http://www.informatik.uni-hamburg.de/WTM

Abstract. In this paper, we propose a goal-directed navigation system consisting of two planning strategies that both rely on vision but work on different scales. The first one works on a global scale and is responsible for generating spatial trajectories leading to the neighboring area of the target. It is a biologically inspired neural planning and navigation model involving learned representations of place and head-direction (HD) cells, where a planning network is trained to predict the neural activities of these cell representations given selected action signals. Recursive prediction and optimization of the continuous action signals generates goal-directed activation sequences, in which states and action spaces are represented by the population of place-, HD- and motor neuron activities. To compensate the remaining error from this look-ahead model-based planning, a second planning strategy relies on visual recognition and performs target-driven reaching on a local scale so that the robot can reach the target with a finer accuracy. Experimental results show that through combining these two planning strategies the robot can precisely navigate to a distant target.

Keywords: Navigation · Place cell · Head-direction cell
Vision-recognition

1 Introduction

Studies in neuroscience have revealed that animals' spatial cognition and planning behaviors during navigation involve certain types of location- and direction-sensitive cells in the hippocampus, which support an animal's sense of place and direction [1,2]. More recent studies suggest that these spatially related firing activities also underlie animals' behavioral decisions [3].

© Springer Nature Switzerland AG 2018
V. Kůrková et al. (Eds.): ICANN 2018, LNCS 11140, pp. 304–311, 2018.
https://doi.org/10.1007/978-3-030-01421-6_30

Considering existing approaches for modeling hippocampal cells, most of them just focus on how to develop the location- or direction-related firing patterns while only few care about the computational principle underlying the formation of these firing activities [4]. Slow feature analysis (SFA) [5] tries to explain this problem by an unsupervised learning algorithm that extracts slowly varying features from fast-changing source signals based on the slowness principle. In our previous work, place- and HD cells were simultaneously learned from visual inputs using a modified SFA learning algorithm which can develop separated populations of place and HD cell types by restricting their learning to separate phases of spatial exploration [6]. However there remains a question of how to use the metric information hidden in these cell activities, which are obtained by unsupervised learning, to support a navigation task.

In this paper, based on the learned cell representations, we propose a navigation model that performs forward look-ahead planning and predicts a sequence of neural activities encoding intermediate waypoints from a starting position to a goal position, where the spatial positional state and directional state are represented by the learned place and HD cell representations, respectively. Furthermore, inspired by the biological finding that place cells are able to generate future sequences encoding spatial trajectories towards remembered goals, which demonstrates their predictive role in navigation [7], we propose a model of their functional role in directing spatial behaviors. Here, we mainly introduce the look-ahead planning whose architecture is shown in Fig. 1. The front part (visual processing part) consists of two parallel image-processing channels with a different network for the emergence of place and HD cells, respectively. For the unsupervised training and network parameters please refer to our previous work [6]. The latter (route planning part) is a world model that supports the imaginary planning in goal-directed navigation, where the world state is represented by the ensemble activity of place and HD cells.

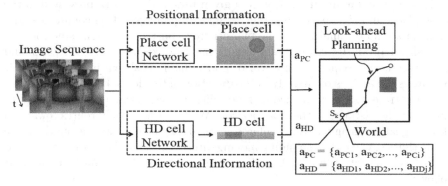

Fig. 1. An overview of the system architecture. The immediate response of the trained place or HD cell network to an image resembles the firing activity of place and HD cells at a certain position or to a certain direction where the image is captured. The world model trained based on the learned cell representations is used to support look-ahead planning.

However such model-based forward planning suffers from significant accumulation errors when dealing with long-range predictions. Furthermore, it takes into account only the place cell representations of the target, irrespective of specific visual properties of a target. In many cases, this planning can only lead the robot to the neighboring areas of a target, instead of to the precise target position. To solve this problem, we propose a second planning strategy that starts to perform after the look-ahead planning. Its aim is to recognize the target based on vision and to move directly towards it after recognizing it.

2 Hybrid Planning Strategy

Based on information learned from vision, the proposed hybrid planning strategy uses two different coordinate systems. The first one is based on space representations which are obtained in an unsupervised way. The second one is based directly on visual representations of the goal. The concept of switching between different planning strategies during navigation can be found in similar work [8,9].

2.1 Model-Based Look-Ahead Planning

For look-ahead planning, we first train a predictive world model network which predicts the subsequent state given the current state and action. The continuous spatial state is represented by the ensemble activity of place and HD cells and the continuous action determines the change of moving direction during a transition, assuming a forward movement of constant speed. The world model is represented by a multi-layer perceptron (MLP) with 81 inputs (30 place cells + 50 HD cells + 1 rotation angle) and 80 outputs (30 place cells + 50 HD cells).

The planning process is based on the recursive use of the fully trained world model which generates a sequence of neural activations encoding the spatial trajectory from an initial location to a given target location (represented in the same place- and HD space), together with corresponding action commands [10]. To generate an optimal route, the planner first constructs a multi-step forward look-ahead probe by sequentially simulating the execution of each command in a given action sequence on a world model chain, as shown in Fig. 2. Then it optimizes the actions recursively in the direction of the desired goal location. The planning trajectory is optimized by modifying the actions via gradient descent to minimize the distance to the goal location. With this approach, routes towards a desired goal are imaginatively explored prior to execution by activating the place cell activities, while corresponding moving directions along the route are encoded by HD cell activities. For each optimization iteration, the action is updated as follows:

$$\Delta a(t) = -\eta \frac{\partial E_{plan}}{\partial a(t)}, \text{ where } E_{plan} = \sum_{k}^{K} \frac{1}{2}(S_k^{goal} - S_k^{pred})^2 \qquad (1)$$

The state vector S consists of an ensemble firing activity of place and HD cells (K in total), η is a constant learning rate. The training objective is to optimize the action sequence $a(t)$ such that the predicted ending state S^{pred} is close to the goal state S^{goal}, which is calculated by the SFA network given the image taken at the target position.

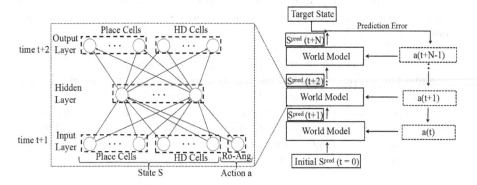

Fig. 2. An overview of the planning architecture. The world model which has been trained based on the learned cell representations is used to support look-ahead planning. Left (inset), the MLP used for one-step prediction. Right, multi-step prediction in the planning phase with feedback of the prediction error.

Note that planning assumes a predefined prediction depth according to the distance to a goal location, while prior information about the optimal depth is not always available. To overcome this assumption of the existing model [10], we propose an adaptive-depth approach where the planning starts with a 1-step prediction and incrementally increases the depth until adding one more prediction step would let the ending position of the current plan go beyond the goal location. During depth increase, the previous plan naturally provides a good proposal for the initialization of the next plan whose prediction increases in depth. Since the previous plan is already optimized but fails due to its small prediction depth, this enables the planner to find the best prediction depth towards a goal without any prior information to efficiently optimize the trajectory.

2.2 Vision-Directed Reaching Based on Target Recognition

While the look-ahead planning can approximately navigate the robot towards the target position, the robot will either overstep or stop short of the target by about one step size and will rarely stop precisely on the target. To solve this problem, we adopt a second planning strategy that is based on object/scene recognition. The goal-directed planning will be activated after the robot has executed the plans optimized by the look-ahead planning, in which case the robot is supposed to be close to the target and will be able to see the target. Since a target always refers to particular objects (like chair, computer...) or specific scenes (like kitchen, corridor...), the robot can recognize the target. After perceiving the target, the robot will adjust its head direction to keep the target in the center of its view and move towards it.

3   Experiments and Results

3.1   Simulation Experiment for Look-Ahead Planning

To test the look-ahead planning, we first used a simulated robot moving in a RatLab virtual-reality environment which also generated the visual data for training place- and HD cell networks [11]. RatLab is designed to simulate a virtual rat doing random explorations and allows to modify the environmental parameters and movement patterns according to the user's purposes.

We first trained place- and HD cell networks by learning from the visual input with SFA, where the images generated during turning movements are used to train the place cell network, while the HD cell network is mainly trained using images from forwarding movements [6]. We trained 30 place cells and 50 HD cells whose ensemble activity encodes the spatial position and direction, respectively. Training results are partly shown in Fig. 3.

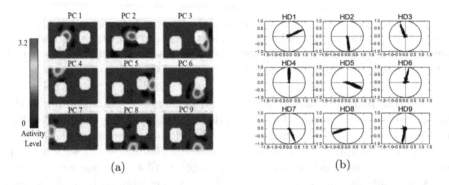

Fig. 3. Firing patterns of learned place and HD cells to different positions or directions. (a) Firing patterns of 9 representative place cells. (b) Polar plots showing the firing patterns of 9 representative HD cells.

For the planning result, Fig. 4(a) and (b) show separately plans with a fixed depth of 10 and adaptive-depth plans, where the planning in the place cell space is mapped to the 2D space through finding the position that yields the most similar firing pattern. The prediction depth of 10 for Fig. 4(a) is obtained empirically and the initial route 0 is gradually optimized towards the desired goal location. The given example shows plans with a quite good initialization, while if given a starting route 0 that extends into a very different direction from the desired one, the planning may not be successful. This is because a long prediction makes the planning optimization based on back-propagating through a long chain of world models very difficult. Due to a vanishing gradient, initial segments receive too little correction. While the adaptive-depth planning could start with a bad initialization, as route 0 shown in Fig. 4(b), the planning starts with a 1-step prediction and is optimized immediately to a better direction through the world model chain which currently contains only one model step. This optimized plan then works as a good basis for initializing the next plan with one step more.

This explains why the initial part of each route in Fig. 4(b) clusters in a narrow area. The planning depth increases incrementally until finding an appropriate plan (route 8) to the goal location.

To evaluate the look-ahead planning performance over the global area, we fixed the starting position and uniformly sampled 120 positions from the environment as the target. As shown in Fig. 5, the planning performance deteriorates as the distance between the target and the starting position increases. Especially when the target lies in the areas behind the second obstacle, which is far away, planning becomes very difficult and may fail. This might be due to the accumulation error in the long world model chain and also the optimization based on backpropagation is difficult for a long-step planning.

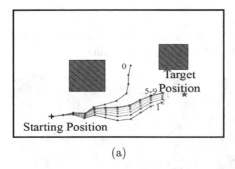
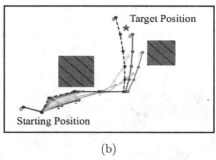

(a)   (b)

Fig. 4. The proposed look-ahead trajectories with (a) a fixed depth of 10 steps and (b) an adaptive depth. The solid dots represent the intermediate locations from the starting position to the target position (red star). The dashed line (route 9) represents a route that exceeds the goal. Planning is performed in place- and HD cell representation space and the trajectory based on actions of the plan is shown in x, y- space for visualisation. (Color figure online)

3.2 Real-World Experiment for Target Object Approaching

As a second step in our hybrid model, we test the vision-based target approaching in a real-world environment with a Turtlebot3 robot in a simple goal reaching task. The robot is placed at a position where the target is in the range of its vision (which refers to the state after executing the look-ahead planning) and its goal is to find the target object and move close to it. For detecting and recognizing the target, we used the YOLO network which is fast and can accurately recognize, classify and localize objects [12]. If the robot cannot see the target object at the initial state, it will rotate locally with a constant speed until perceiving and recognizing the object with a certain probability. While trying to keep the target object in the center of the view, the robot moves directly towards it until reaching the threshold distance to the target (Fig. 6).

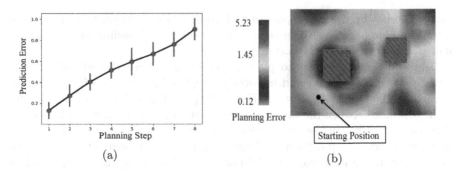

(a)   (b)

Fig. 5. (a) The prediction error of the world model increases with the number of the planning steps. (b) The planning error over the whole environment, where the starting position is fixed (the black dot) and the target is sampled uniformly from the rectangular environment which has a size of 14×10 units and 120 positions are sampled from it. The error value is represented by the color. (Color figure online)

Fig. 6. Test of the object recognition and target approaching. The robot starts from a neighboring area and needs to reach the target orange. Left: The robot starts without the target in the current view (shown in the red box) and starts rotating. Middle: The robot perceives and recognizes the target and starts moving towards it. Right: The robot reaches the orange and stops just next to it. (Color figure online)

4   Conclusion and Future Work

We have proposed a navigation system that relies on a hybrid navigation strategy in order to precisely reach a target location, which consists of two planning strategies that work on different distance scales but both rely on vision. The first one is look-ahead planning that works on a global coordinate system and proposes a spatial trajectory close to the desired goal location. The spatial state is represented by the ensemble activity of place and HD cells, which are modeled by learning directly from visual input based on an unsupervised SFA learning algorithm. The planning network allows looking into the future based on a chain of world model predictions and adaptively proposes optimized prediction steps to the goal location. The second part is a target approaching strategy working on a local scale, which enables object recognition and goal-directed reaching. Through combining these two complementary strategies, the robot can move from a random position to a target position with a high accuracy using just its vision system. As future work, we will extend the simulated scenario to a physical world where place and HD cells are modeled on a real robot using its vision sensor and the planning is validated in a challenging dynamic environment.

Acknowledgments. We acknowledge support from the German Research Foundation DFG, project CML (TRR 169) and the EU, project SECURE (No. 642667).

References

1. O'Keefe, J., Nadel, L.: The Hippocampus as a Cognitive Map. Clarendon Press, Oxford (1978)
2. Taube, J.S., Muller, R.U., Ranck, J.B.: Head-direction cells recorded from the postsubiculum in freely moving rats. I. Description and quantitative analysis. J. Neurosci. **10**(2), 420–435 (1990)
3. Wills, T.J., Muessig, L., Cacucci, F.: The development of spatial behaviour and the hippocampal neural representation of space. Phil. Trans. R. Soc. B (2014). https://doi.org/10.1098/rstb.2013.0409
4. Zeno, P.J., Patel, S., Sobh, T.M.: Review of neurobiologically based mobile robot navigation system research performed since 2000. J. Robot. (2016). https://doi.org/10.1155/2016/8637251
5. Franzius, M., Sprekeler, H., Wiskott, L.: Slowness and sparseness lead to place, head-direction, and spatial-view cells. PLoS Comput. Biol. **3**(8), e166 (2007)
6. Zhou, X., Weber, C., Wermter, S.: Robot localization and orientation detection based on place cells and head-direction cells. In: Lintas, A., Rovetta, S., Verschure, P.F.M.J., Villa, A.E.P. (eds.) ICANN 2017. LNCS, vol. 10613, pp. 137–145. Springer, Cham (2017). https://doi.org/10.1007/978-3-319-68600-4_17
7. Pfeiffer, B.E., Foster, D.J.: Hippocampal place-cell sequences depict future paths to remembered goals. Nature **497**(7447), 74–79 (2013)
8. Dollé, L., Sheynikhovich, D., Girard, B., Chavarriaga, R., Guillot, A.: Path planning versus cue responding: a bio-inspired model of switching between navigation strategies. Biol. Cybern. **103**(4), 299–317 (2010)
9. Oess, T., Krichmar, J.L., Röhrbein, F.: A computational model for spatial navigation based on reference frames in the hippocampus, retrosplenial cortex, and posterior parietal cortex. Front. Neurorobotics (2017). https://doi.org/10.3389/fnbot.2017.00004
10. Thrun, S., Möller, K., Linden, A.: Planning with an adaptive world model. In: Advances in Neural Information Processing Systems, pp. 450–456 (1991)
11. Schönfeld, F., Wiskott, L.: RatLab: an easy to use tool for place code simulations. Front. Comput. Neurosci. (2013). https://doi.org/10.3389/fncom.2013.00104
12. Redmon, J., Divvala, S., Girshick, R., Farhadi, A.: You only look once: unified, real-time object detection. In: Proceedings of the IEEE Conference on Computer Vision and Pattern Recognition, pp. 779–788 (2016)

Optimization/Recommendation

Check Regularization: Combining Modularity and Elasticity for Memory Consolidation

Taisuke Kobayashi[(✉)] [iD]

Division of Information Science, Graduate School of Science and Technology,
Nara Institute of Science and Technology, Nara, Japan
kobayashi@is.naist.jp
https://kbys_t.gitlab.io/en/

Abstract. Catastrophic forgetting, which means that old tasks are forgotten mostly when new tasks are learned, is a crucial problem of neural networks for autonomous robots. This problem is due to backpropagation overwrites all network parameters, and therefore, can be solved by not overwriting important parameters for the old tasks. Hence, regularization methods, represented by elastic weight consolidation, give the globally stable equilibrium points to the optimal parameters for the old tasks. They unfortunately aim to hold all parameters, even if the regularization is weak. This paper therefore proposes a regularization method, named Check regularization, to consolidate only the important parameters for the tasks and to initialize the other parameters preparing for the future tasks. Simulations with two tasks to be learned sequentially show that the proposed method outperforms the previous method under a condition where the interference between the tasks is severe.

Keywords: Continual learning · Locally stable equilibrium point
Reinforcement learning

1 Introduction

Highly versatile robots, such as humanoid robots, gain a high demand to perform various tasks on behalf of human [3,8]. It is however difficult to preliminarily design all kinds of the various tasks, hence the versatile robots are desired to learn new tasks through their daily activities in the real world like human does. Development of such "autonomous robots" is the final goal of this research.

Reinforcement learning (RL) is a methodology to let an agent learn the optimal policy, which maximizes accumulation of rewards (i.e., return) from the environment by sampling the optimal action, through trial and error of interactions between the agent and the environment [19]. RL is absolutely suitable to control the autonomous robots described above.

Recently, the state-of-the-art RL algorithms have outperformed human as video and board games players [18]. Even in applications of real autonomous

© Springer Nature Switzerland AG 2018
V. Kůrková et al. (Eds.): ICANN 2018, LNCS 11140, pp. 315–325, 2018.
https://doi.org/10.1007/978-3-030-01421-6_31

robots, they have acquired complicated tasks that could not be learned to date, such as manipulating deformable clothes [20]; and picking from bulked objects [12]. What is essential behind these successes is a function approximator by (deep) neural networks (NN or DNN) [9]. Specifically, the policy and value functions in RL are precisely approximated by NN, even when state space is extremely large like raw images. Note that, in general, the methods to stably learn them have been employed since the convergence of parameters in NN is not guaranteed.

However, backpropagation of gradients of loss (or objective) functions would cause a crucial problem, so called "catastrophic forgetting," which means that old tasks are mostly forgotten when new tasks are learned [2,13]. This problem must be solved to let the autonomous robots continuously learn the new tasks in the real world as human does, although it can easily be ignored by preparing huge data sets including all the tasks in fields where offline learning is allowable such as image recognition. Storing all of data is of course intractable since it ultimately requires infinite storage and memory. This problem can also be ignored when different networks are prepared corresponding to respective tasks, however the cost of switching networks is not allowable in the autonomous robots, which require to switch tasks seamlessly.

To solve such catastrophic forgetting, three approaches have mainly been studied as follows (their details are in the next section): (i) data for the old tasks are augmented by a generative model [5,17]; (ii) network is modularized to avoid interferences in the new tasks [1,10,22,23]; and (iii) parameters are given elasticity to the optimal values for the old tasks [7,11,14,24]. In the approach (i), it would be possible to reliably mitigate the catastrophic forgetting by using a sophisticated generative model by DNN in recent years [6,15], while the generative model also requires to mitigate its catastrophic forgetting. The approach (ii) tackles the cause of the catastrophic forgetting, while it basically has no function to keep the parameters in the optimal values. The approach (iii) has recently been established as a powerful method by designing the elasticity according to the importance of parameters for the old tasks, while it has no function to select only the minimum necessary parameters from all of them.

To compensate respective functions of the approaches (ii) and (iii), this paper proposes a new regularization method, named Check regularization, which combines the modularization of network and the elasticization of parameters. These two, however, give different globally stable equilibrium points, and therefore, they cannot be combined without any consideration. Hence, a log regularization term is heuristically introduced to derive two locally stable equilibrium points corresponding to the approach (ii) and (iii). All parameters are regularized toward either the two depending on the importance of parameters for the old tasks. That is, the necessary/unnecessary parameters for the tasks are regularized for the elasticization/initialization, respectively. Check regularization was evaluated through RL for two types of tasks in three kinds of simulations for each. As a result, its effectiveness was verified in the simulations where there was strong interference between the tasks. To the best of my knowledge, this is the first study for combining the modularization of network and the elasticization of parameters, i.e., the approaches (ii) and (iii), as regularization.

2   Related Work

2.1   Data Augmentation

The most straightforward approach to mitigate the catastrophic forgetting is to learn the generative model of input (and output) data, instead of storing all data. The costs for storage and memory would be constant when the generative model is obtained as NN, such as variational autoencoder [6] and generative adversarial network [15] (or their relatives). The pseudo data related to the old tasks can be generated from the generative model, and mini batch, which includes the generated and observed data, is used for learning the parameters [5,17]. In that case, NN would maintain the performance of the old tasks without being biased to the new tasks. However, the generative model is not desired to be prepared for each tasks from the viewpoint of cost, but if a single NN is used to explain the multiple tasks, the catastrophic forgetting would be caused.

2.2   Modular Network

Switching perfectly different networks for respective tasks is inappropriate from the viewpoint of control. It is however effective to divide a single NN implicitly and modularize the area of NN (i.e., the parameters) used for respective tasks. Ellefsen et al. [1] employed evolutionary algorithm to promote such the modularization, which certainly mitigated the catastrophic forgetting although the task performance just after switching was somewhat deteriorated. Since it is a waste of resources that can be shared among tasks when NN is completely modularized, Velez and Clune [22] developed a diffusion-based neuromodulation, which not only induced task-specific learning but also produced functional parameters for each subtask. Yu et al. [23] also proposed the way to select whether the parameters should be shared/specialized among tasks/for single task depending on the gradients of loss function.

Alternatively, NN can easily be modularized by L1 regularization, in particular, its truncated version [10] would have a capability to keep the parameters for the old tasks. Here, the gradient of the truncated L1 regularization is defined as following equation and is illustrated in Fig. 1(a).

$$\mathcal{L}_{L1} = \lambda_{L1} \|\boldsymbol{\theta}\|_1 \tag{1}$$

$$\therefore g_{L1} = \begin{cases} \lambda_{L1}\text{sign}(\boldsymbol{\theta}) & |\boldsymbol{\theta}| > \text{Threshold} \\ 0 & \text{Otherwise} \end{cases} \tag{2}$$

where λ_{L1} is the magnitude of regularization and $\boldsymbol{\theta}$ are the parameters in NN. The threshold is given as a half of maximum value among all parameters in this paper. $\boldsymbol{\theta}$ is updated as $\boldsymbol{\theta} \leftarrow \boldsymbol{\theta} - g_{L1}$. L1 regularization can be interpreted that

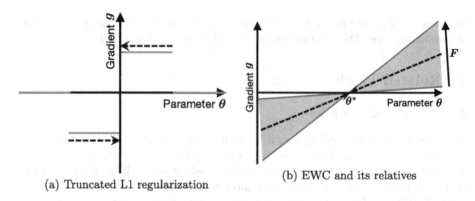

(a) Truncated L1 regularization

(b) EWC and its relatives

Fig. 1. Gradients of regularization to mitigate the catastrophic forgetting: (a) the parameters smaller than a threshold converge to 0 for modularization, and the other parameters are no longer regularized for keeping their values although they easily move by the gradients of loss function; (b) all parameters converge to $\boldsymbol{\theta}^*$, while the convergence speed and strength depend on $\boldsymbol{F}$.

it has a globally (locally if the truncated version) stable equilibrium point to $\theta = 0$. Even when the truncated version, however, the catastrophic forgetting would be caused because the parameters are never fixed.

2.3   Elastic Parameters

If the important parameters for the old tasks are discriminated, letting their values be invariant would avoid to overwrite them. The methods, represented by elastic weight consolidation (EWC) [7], regularize the parameters toward the optimal values for the old tasks, $\boldsymbol{\theta}^*$, by a following gradient (see Fig. 1(b)).

$$\mathcal{L}_{\mathrm{EWC}} = \frac{\lambda_{\mathrm{EWC}}}{2} \boldsymbol{F}^\top (\boldsymbol{\theta} - \boldsymbol{\theta}^*)^2 \tag{3}$$

$$\therefore \boldsymbol{g}_{\mathrm{EWC}} = \lambda_{\mathrm{EWC}} \boldsymbol{F} \odot (\boldsymbol{\theta} - \boldsymbol{\theta}^*) \tag{4}$$

where λ_{EWC} is the magnitude of regularization and $\boldsymbol{F}$ is the importance of the parameters, which have been defined as the diagonal of Fisher information matrix in the paper of EWC. Specifically, $\boldsymbol{\theta}^*$ and $\boldsymbol{F}$ correspond to the mean and the precision of diagonal multivariate Gaussian distribution of $\boldsymbol{\theta}$, respectively. Note that several types of relatives have been proposed: incremental moment matching is employed to approximate $\boldsymbol{\theta}^*$ and $\boldsymbol{F}$ [11]; $\boldsymbol{F}$ is defined in a biologically plausible manner [24]; and $\mathcal{L}_{\mathrm{EWC}}$ is converted from sum squared error to Kullback-Leibler divergence through variational inference [14]. Due to a non-verification target, this paper employs a moving average to estimate $\boldsymbol{\theta}^*$ and $\boldsymbol{F}$ for simplicity.

This design means that the parameters with high precision (small variance) are forced to converge to $\boldsymbol{\theta}^*$, and the other parameters have room to learn the new tasks. Even with the room to learn the new tasks, however, it would not fully be utilized because this approach set globally stable equilibrium points to $\boldsymbol{\theta}^*$. That is, all parameters aim to converge to $\boldsymbol{\theta}^*$ regardless of the magnitude of regularization (i.e., $\boldsymbol{F}$), thereby not minimizing the number of parameters that are used for the old tasks.

3   Check Regularization

3.1   Formulation

As mentioned in the above section, the modularization of network and the elasticization of parameter let the parameters converge to respective globally (to be exact, locally in the truncated L1 regularization) stable equilibrium points. To achieve both properties, the globally stable equilibrium points should be converted into locally stable ones with an appropriate boundary, although it cannot be decided easily (see the left side of Fig. 2).

Our proposal, named Check regularization, gives the appropriate boundary automatically depending on the mean and the precision of the parameters, as shown in the right side of Fig. 2. Here, the name "Check" comes from the shape of this gradient like a check mark. Its formulation is given as follows:

$$
\mathcal{L}_{\text{Check}} = \begin{cases} \lambda_{\text{L1}}\|\boldsymbol{\theta}\|_1 & \boldsymbol{\theta} \odot \boldsymbol{\theta}^* < 0 \\ \frac{\lambda_{\text{EWC}}}{2}\boldsymbol{F}^\top(\boldsymbol{\theta}-\boldsymbol{\theta}^*)^2 & |\boldsymbol{\theta}| > \boldsymbol{\theta}^* \\ \left(\frac{\lambda_0}{\kappa}\right)^\top \ln(1 + \boldsymbol{\kappa}\odot|\boldsymbol{\theta}|) + \boldsymbol{\lambda}_1^\top|\boldsymbol{\theta}| + \frac{1}{2}\boldsymbol{\lambda}_2^\top\boldsymbol{\theta}^2 & \text{Otherwise} \end{cases}
\tag{5}
$$

where $\boldsymbol{\lambda}_{0,1,2}$ and $\boldsymbol{\kappa}$ are design parameters, which are analytically derived in the next subsection. λ_{L1} and λ_{EWC} are given as hyperparameters with almost the same values as the original ones. The boundary whether the parameter is assigned to the modularization or elasticization is given in the third equation.

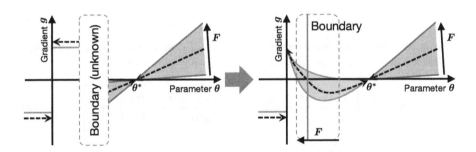

Fig. 2. Concept of Check regularization: to combine the modularization of network and the elasticization of parameters, a boundary between them is difficult to be determined; by adding a log regularization term, the boundary can be determined automatically depending on the precision of parameter.

The gradient of Check regularization is derived as follows:

$$
g_{\text{Check}} = \begin{cases} \lambda_{\text{L1}} \text{sign}(\boldsymbol{\theta}) & \boldsymbol{\theta} \odot \boldsymbol{\theta}^* < 0 \\ \lambda_{\text{EWC}} \boldsymbol{F} \odot (\boldsymbol{\theta} - \boldsymbol{\theta}^*) & |\boldsymbol{\theta}| > \boldsymbol{\theta}^* \\ \left(\frac{\lambda_0}{1 + \kappa \odot |\boldsymbol{\theta}|} + \lambda_1 \right) \odot \text{sign}(\boldsymbol{\theta}) + \lambda_2 \odot \boldsymbol{\theta} & \text{Otherwise} \end{cases} \tag{6}
$$

The gradients of the first and second equations in Check regularization are almost the same as Eqs. (2) and (4), respectively (difference is whether there is the threshold or not).

3.2 Derivation of Design Parameters

Now, $\lambda_{0,1,2}$ and κ are uniquely designed to give the appropriate boundary to separate the two locally stable equilibrium points. Note that $\boldsymbol{\theta}^*$ is limited to be positive in this subsection without losing generality. In addition, only $\lambda_{0,1,2}$ and κ for a single parameter θ (with θ^* and F) are derived as below since all parameters are independent.

First, to make it branch naturally, the following three conditions are given.

$$
\lim_{\theta \to +0} g_{\text{Check}} = \lambda_{\text{L1}}, \quad \left. \frac{\partial g_{\text{Check}}}{\partial \theta} \right|_{\theta = \theta^*} = \lambda_{\text{EWC}} F, \quad g_{\text{Check}}|_{\theta = \theta^*} = 0 \tag{7}
$$

Next, an additional design parameter, η, which corresponds to the boundary explicitly, are given so that the boundary exists in $[0, \theta^*]$.

$$
g_{\text{Check}}|_{\theta = (1 - \eta)\theta^*} = 0 \tag{8}
$$

The conditional equations are still insufficient and this derivation becomes an ill-posed problem, and therefore, a constraint, where κ that gives two intersections of the gradient and θ axis is uniquely determined, is additionally given as follows:

$$
\kappa = 4\lambda_2 / \lambda_0 \tag{9}
$$

From the above five conditional equations, $\lambda_{0,1,2}$, κ, and η are uniquely solved as follows (their derivations are omitted due to page limitation).

$$
\kappa = \frac{1}{\theta^*} \left\{ \frac{\lambda_{\text{EWC}} F \theta^* - \lambda_{\text{L1}}}{\lambda_{\text{EWC}} F \theta^* + \lambda_{\text{L1}}} + \sqrt{\left(\frac{\lambda_{\text{EWC}} F \theta^* - \lambda_{\text{L1}}}{\lambda_{\text{EWC}} F \theta^* + \lambda_{\text{L1}}} \right)^2 + 3} \right\} \tag{10}
$$

$$
\beta = \frac{(\kappa \theta^* - 1)(\kappa \theta^* + 3)}{\kappa \theta^* (\kappa \theta^* + 1)} \tag{11}
$$

$$
\lambda_2 = \begin{cases} \frac{\lambda_{\text{L1}}}{\theta^*} & \kappa \theta^* = 1 \\ \frac{\lambda_{\text{EWC}} F \theta^* (\kappa \theta^* + 1)}{(\kappa \theta^* - 1)(\kappa \theta^* + 3)} & \text{Otherwise} \end{cases} \tag{12}
$$

$$
\lambda_0 = 4\lambda_2 / \kappa \tag{13}
$$

$$
\lambda_1 = \lambda_{\text{L1}} - \lambda_0 \tag{14}
$$

As for λ_2, two cases are prepared to obtain a numerically stable solution. In addition, a very small amount ϵ is added to θ^* since θ^* is desired not to be 0 for stable calculation.

Let us confirm that the gradient formed by the derived design parameters changes depending on the precision F. Note that the mean θ^* is fixed to be 0.1 since it would not change the property of the gradient. The gradients g_{Check} with low, middle, and high precisions are depicted in Figs. 3(a)–(c), respectively. As shown in Fig. 3(a), we found that the boundary (the intersection with lower value) is very close to θ^*, thereby prioritizing the modularization of network. The boundary becomes close to 0 continuously, and finally, e.g., Fig. 3(c), the elasticization of parameters becomes dominant. In this way, Check regularization decides the boundary between the initialization/elasticization of parameters automatically without any additional hyperparameters.

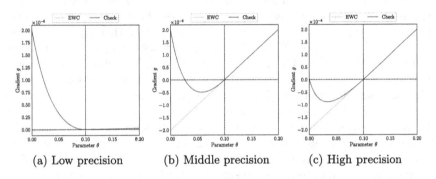

(a) Low precision   (b) Middle precision   (c) High precision

Fig. 3. Examples of the gradients of Check regularization formed by the design parameters: the intersection of the gradient and θ axis (not $\theta^* = 0.1$), i.e., the boundary between the modularization of network and the elasticization of parameters, is automatically determined depending on the precision of the parameter, F.

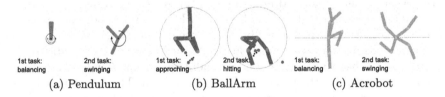

1st task: balancing   2nd task: swinging   1st task: approching   2nd task: hitting   1st task: balancing   2nd task: swinging

(a) Pendulum   (b) BallArm   (c) Acrobot

Fig. 4. RL simulation environments: (a) Pendulum aims (i) to keep balance on the top and (ii) to maximize its angular velocity; (b) BallArm aims (i) to be close to the tip of arm and the ball and (ii) to maximize velocity of the ball; (c) Acrobot aims (i) to keep balance from swinging up and (ii) to maximize angular velocity of the root axis.

4   Simulations

4.1   Conditions

The performance of Check regularization is verified in three kinds of RL simulations, i.e., (a) Pendulum, (b) BallArm, and (c) Acrobot in Fig. 4. Respective environments have two different tasks, which tend to interfere with each other. As a learning procedure, the target task to be learned is switched every 300 episodes by turns, and after third switching, the remaining two are used for evaluation. A score is defined as a weighted mean with inversely proportional to the number of episodes of average rewards normalized by the maximum one, and is mainly affected by up to 50 episodes. This procedure is conducted 20 times.

To clarify the adverse effect of the interference between the tasks, a reservoir computing [4] is used as one of the NN. It updates only readout parameters, namely it is regarded to be a linear regression model, which has an advantage that the parameters used for the task are in clear. Here, the number of parameters is roughly given as product of the number of neuron (500 in this paper) and action space ((a) 1, (b) 3, and (c) 2). In addition, experience replay is not applied not to reuse the observations for the old tasks. Instead, an actor-critic algorithm combining eligibility trace [16,21] enables to learn the current tasks efficiently.

As baselines, the truncated L1 regularization [10] in Eq. (2) and EWC [7] in Eq. (4) are evaluated in the same manner. Learning rate is set as $0.01/500$ so as to avoid local optima, and other hyperparameters for RL are set as typical values (e.g., discount rate is 0.99). λ_{EWC} is given as 10^{-14} since F is large when the learning rate is small. λ_{L1} is heuristically given as 10^{-3}, but only for Check regularization, it is multiplied by 10 since the gradient is small near θ^*.

4.2   Results

Learning curves and scores were summarized in Figs. 5(a)–(c). Note that, in legends, the means and standard deviations of the scores for respective methods were additionally described. As can be seen in Fig. 5, in Acrobot and BallArm, Check regularization outperformed both the baselines, although all methods succeeded in avoiding the catastrophic forgetting in Pendulum. The catastrophic forgetting was observed in Acrobot and BallArm, except Pendulum, with all methods, in particular, the truncated L1 regularization. This is due to subtasks in the tasks, e.g., a swing-up motion in Acrobot and a motion approaching to ball in BallArm, which would cause the interference between the tasks.

Although the catastrophic forgetting could be mitigated to a certain extent by EWC, the performance in the second task was sluggish. Check regularization, in contrast, succeeded in acquiring both tasks. This difference implies the importance of the modularization of network. Note that the elasticity in EWC and Check regularization would be too strong as can be deduced from the higher average rewards at the last episodes in the truncated L1 regularization.

Nevertheless, significant differences between Check regularization and the other methods could not be observed due to the fixed random network in the

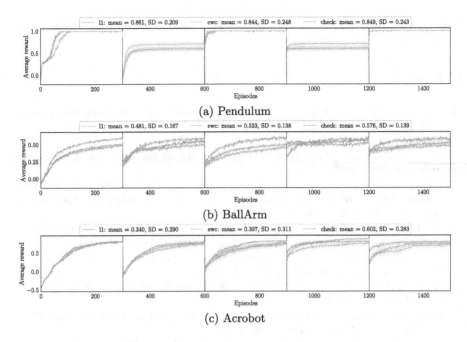

Fig. 5. Learning curves and scores for respective environments: before and after dashed lines, the target task was changed; (a) all methods could avoid the catastrophic forgetting since the tasks hardly interfered with each other in practice; (b) EWC and Check regularization could keep the performances of both tasks in comparison with the truncated L1 regularization, although the performance of the first task seemed to be deteriorated by their elasticity; (c) Check regularization could immediately recover the performances of both tasks from the catastrophic forgetting.

reservoir computing. Depending on the network structure, the number of parameters required to learn the task was increased, and the parameters that memorize multiple tasks were insufficient. More trials with fixed random seeds may show the validity of Check regularization statistically.

5 Conclusion

This paper proposed the regularization method, named Check regularization, to combine the two important functions for mitigating the catastrophic forgetting: the modularization of network and the elasticization of parameters. In Check regularization, two locally stable equilibrium points corresponding to respective functions are given each parameter. Their boundary is automatically determined according to the precision (and mean) of each parameter. As a result, the necessary/unnecessary parameters to the tasks are initialized/fixed. Indeed, Check regularization outperformed the state-of-the-art method, i.e., EWC, in the three kinds of RL simulations. Future work in this study is to apply the proposed method to curriculum learning in real autonomous robots.

Acknowledgement. This research has been supported by the Kayamori Foundation of Information Science Advancement.

References

1. Ellefsen, K.O., Mouret, J.B., Clune, J.: Neural modularity helps organisms evolve to learn new skills without forgetting old skills. PLoS Comput. Biol. **11**(4), e1004128 (2015)
2. French, R.M.: Catastrophic forgetting in connectionist networks. Trends Cogn. Sci. **3**(4), 128–135 (1999)
3. Hirai, K., Hirose, M., Haikawa, Y., Takenaka, T.: The development of Honda humanoid robot. In: IEEE International Conference on Robotics and Automation, vol. 2, pp. 1321–1326. IEEE (1998)
4. Jaeger, H., Haas, H.: Harnessing nonlinearity: predicting chaotic systems and saving energy in wireless communication. Science **304**(5667), 78–80 (2004)
5. Kamra, N., Gupta, U., Liu, Y.: Deep generative dual memory network for continual learning. arXiv preprint arXiv:1710.10368 (2017)
6. Kingma, D.P., Welling, M.: Auto-encoding variational bayes. arXiv preprint arXiv:1312.6114 (2013)
7. Kirkpatrick, J., et al.: Overcoming catastrophic forgetting in neural networks. Proc. Natl. Acad. Sci. **114**(13), 3521–3526 (2017)
8. Kobayashi, T., Aoyama, T., Sekiyama, K., Fukuda, T.: Selection algorithm for locomotion based on the evaluation of falling risk. IEEE Trans. Robot. **31**(3), 750–765 (2015)
9. Krizhevsky, A., Sutskever, I., Hinton, G.E.: ImageNet classification with deep convolutional neural networks. In: Advances in Neural Information Processing System, pp. 1097–1105 (2012)
10. Langford, J., Li, L., Zhang, T.: Sparse online learning via truncated gradient. J. Mach. Learn. Res. **10**, 777–801 (2009)
11. Lee, S.W., Kim, J.H., Jun, J., Ha, J.W., Zhang, B.T.: Overcoming catastrophic forgetting by incremental moment matching. In: Advances in Neural Information Processing Systems, pp. 4655–4665 (2017)
12. Levine, S., Pastor, P., Krizhevsky, A., Quillen, D.: Learning hand-eye coordination for robotic grasping with large-scale data collection. In: Kulić, D., Nakamura, Y., Khatib, O., Venture, G. (eds.) ISER 2016. SPAR, vol. 1, pp. 173–184. Springer, Cham (2017). https://doi.org/10.1007/978-3-319-50115-4_16
13. McCloskey, M., Cohen, N.J.: Catastrophic interference in connectionist networks: the sequential learning problem. In: Psychology of Learning and Motivation, vol. 24, pp. 109–165. Elsevier (1989)
14. Nguyen, C.V., Li, Y., Bui, T.D., Turner, R.E.: Variational continual learning. In: International Conference on Learning Representations (2018). https://openreview. net/forum?id=BkQqq0gRb
15. Radford, A., Metz, L., Chintala, S.: Unsupervised representation learning with deep convolutional generative adversarial networks. arXiv preprint arXiv:1511.06434 (2015)
16. Schulman, J., Moritz, P., Levine, S., Jordan, M., Abbeel, P.: High-dimensional continuous control using generalized advantage estimation. In: International Conference for Learning Representations, pp. 1–14 (2016)

17. Shin, H., Lee, J.K., Kim, J., Kim, J.: Continual learning with deep generative replay. In: Advances in Neural Information Processing Systems, pp. 2994–3003 (2017)
18. Silver, D., et al.: Mastering the game of go without human knowledge. Nature **550**(7676), 354 (2017)
19. Sutton, R.S., Barto, A.G.: Reinforcement Learning: An Introduction. MIT press, Cambridge (1998)
20. Tsurumine, Y., Cui, Y., Uchibe, E., Matsubara, T.: Deep dynamic policy programming for robot control with raw images. In: IEEE/RSJ International Conference on Intelligent Robots and Systems, pp. 1545–1550 (2017)
21. Van Seijen, H., Mahmood, A.R., Pilarski, P.M., Machado, M.C., Sutton, R.S.: True online temporal-difference learning. J. Mach. Learn. Res. **17**(145), 1–40 (2016)
22. Velez, R., Clune, J.: Diffusion-based neuromodulation can eliminate catastrophic forgetting in simple neural networks. PloS one **12**(11), e0187736 (2017)
23. Yu, W., Turk, G., Liu, C.K.: Multi-task learning with gradient guided policy specialization. arXiv preprint arXiv:1709.07979 (2017)
24. Zenke, F., Poole, B., Ganguli, S.: Continual learning through synaptic intelligence. In: International Conference on Machine Learning, pp. 3987–3995 (2017)

Con-CNAME: A Contextual Multi-armed Bandit Algorithm for Personalized Recommendations

Xiaofang Zhang[1,2]([⊠]), Qian Zhou[2], Tieke He[1], and Bin Liang[2]

[1] State Key Lab for Novel Software Technology,
Nanjing University, Nanjing, China
[2] School of Computer Science and Technology,
Soochow University, Suzhou, China
xfzhang@suda.edu.cn

Abstract. Reinforcement learning algorithms play an important role in modern day and have been applied to many domains. For example, personalized recommendations problem can be modelled as a contextual multi-armed bandit problem in reinforcement learning. In this paper, we propose a contextual bandit algorithm which is based on Contexts and the Chosen Number of Arm with Minimal Estimation, namely Con-CNAME in short. The continuous exploration and context used in our algorithm can address the cold start problem in recommender systems. Furthermore, the Con-CNAME algorithm can still make recommendations under the emergency circumstances where contexts are unavailable suddenly. In the experimental evaluation, the reference range of key parameters and the stability of Con-CNAME are discussed in detail. In addition, the performance of Con-CNAME is compared with some classic algorithms. Experimental results show that our algorithm outperforms several bandit algorithms.

Keywords: Recommender systems · Reinforcement learning
Multi-armed bandit · Context-aware

This work is supported in part by the National Key Research and Development Program of China (2016YFC0800805).

1 Introduction

Reinforcement learning (RL) is an important part in machine learning [1]. RL has gained much attention in last decade which can be used in combination with collaborative filtering, Bayesian networks etc. for recommendations [2, 3]. In this work, a RL based contextual Multi-Armed Bandit (MAB) algorithm named Con-CNAME is discussed to implement a personalized recommendation.

The primary target of recommender systems is to propose one or several items which users might be interested in. The books, articles or music provided by the recommender systems are items [4, 5]. Recommender systems need to focus on items that raise users' interest and explore new items to improve users' satisfaction at the

V. Kůrková et al. (Eds.): ICANN 2018, LNCS 11140, pp. 326–336, 2018.
https://doi.org/10.1007/978-3-030-01421-6_32

same time. That creates an exploration-exploitation dilemma, which is the core point of Multi-Armed Bandit (MAB) problems [6]. The payoff of a recommendation is widely measured by Click-Though Rate (CTR) [7]. Then the goal of recommendations is to maximize the CTR over all users. Personalized recommendation services identify the preferences of users and appropriately show the web content to suit to their preferences [8]. The classic collaborative recommender systems may not retain high CTR if large number of users or items are new to the system. Such an issue is referred to as a cold-start problem [9] and in such situations the recommendation task can be modelled as a contextual Multi-armed bandit problem [10].

Contextual bandit approaches are already studied in many fields of recommender systems [11]. We propose a context-aware bandit algorithm which tries to further improve the obtained CTR in personalized recommendations. The recommendation is made based on the user feedback and priori information of contexts. The cold start issue is addressed by continuously exploration and contexts. Exploration means learning new items' payoff for a particular user by recommending new items. Exploitation means recommending the optimal items based on the payoffs observed so far. Experiments are made on the user click log dataset of Yahoo! Front Page Today Module. The aim of our algorithm is to achieve higher CTRs than some existed bandit approaches.

The rest of the paper is organized as follows. Section 2 describes some related works. In Sect. 3, we introduce our algorithm and discuss the influence of key parameters. Section 4 discusses experimental results. Conclusion is made in Sect. 5.

2 Related Work

Filtering-based and reinforcement learning methods are two main categories of recommendation algorithms [12]. In this paper, we focus on reinforcement learning methods. Reinforcement learning methods, such as MAB and Markov Decision Processes (MDPs) [13], are widely used in recommender systems. MDP-based approaches model the last k choices of a user as the state and the available items as the action set to maximize the long-run payoff. [14]. MAB-based approaches make recommendations by balancing exploration and exploitation, such as ε-greedy [15], softmax [16], EXP3 [17] and UCB1 [6]. The ε-greedy is the simplest approach among these context-free approaches, which always has competitive performance and is easy to be extended to various applications. Softmax makes recommendations according to a probability distribution based on user feedbacks. As a complicated variant of softmax, the main idea of EXP3 is to divide the payoff of an item by its chosen probability. UCB1 always recommends the item with the highest upper confidence index. However, UCB1 needs to sweep all items during the initial period, it may be inappropriate for recommender systems whose items are huge.

Contexts are considered, aiming at improving the effectiveness of recommendations. In a contextual MAB setting, there is a set of arms available to the algorithm at a time step which is associated with the contextual information vector. Generally, contexts represent the situations of the user when a recommendation is made, such as time, gender and age [18, 19]. Using the previously acquired knowledge and the context at the current time step, the algorithm chooses to show an arm and obtains a reward.

This reward is dependent on the contextual features and the chosen arm. The LinUCB algorithm is proposed to solve news article recommendation problems [20]. The Naive III and Linear Bayes approaches define a user-group via a set of features that individual users may have in common, but not that must have in common [21]. A MAB-based clustering approach constructs an item-cluster tree for recommender systems [22]. The CNAME and Asy-CNAME algorithms are based on the chosen number of minimal estimation, which are applied to recommender systems where the prior information is unavailable [23]. Specifically, the CNAME algorithm choses an arm according to exploration probability which is based on the chosen number of arm with minimal estimation. The exploration probability changes with the practical environment since the chosen number of minimal estimation can make full use of user feedback. To further improve the efficiency of the CNAME algorithm, the Asy-CNAME algorithm is updated in an asynchronous manner.

3 Our Approach

In this section, we present a context-aware bandit approaches for personalized recommendations. This approach is based on Contexts and the Chosen Number of Action with Minimal Estimation, namely Con-CNAME.

Almost all the multi-armed bandit algorithms use the average rewards of actions as an estimation method. Inspired by the prior probability of contexts, we put forward another kind of estimation method: the chosen probability. There is initial probability distribution for actions, we adjust the chosen probability of every selected action according to the actual user feedback. Specifically, when the reward is 1 after choosing an action, i.e. the recommended article is clicked by users, the chosen probability of this action will be improved; when the reward is 0 after choosing an action, i.e. the recommended article is not clicked by users, and the chosen probability of this action will not be updated. Combining chosen probability of actions and prior probability of contexts, this paper proposes the Con-CNAME algorithm, which introduces weight β to control the influences of chosen probability and prior probability. The framework of Con-CNAME algorithm is shown in Fig. 1:

Here, the prior probability is based on Naïve III algorithm, which defines a user-group by a set of features that individual users may have in common [21]. Then, we define that $clicks[a][i] = \sum_t \mathbf{x}_t(i)g_t$ and $selections[a][i] = \sum_t \mathbf{x}_t(i)$ for $a_t = a$, where each context $\mathbf{x}_t$ contains some binary vectors indicating user's contextual features, such as gender, age, language and so on. g_t is user click status (i.e. 1 if article obtained click and 0 otherwise). The article a_t recommended by Naive III algorithm at trial t is $a_t = \arg\max_a \left(\sum_{i \neq 0} P_t(a, i) \right)$, where $P(a, i) = clicks[a][i]/selections[a][i]$.

Different from Naive III algorithm, our Con-CNAME combines prior probability $\sum_{i \neq 0} P_t(a, i)$ and chosen probability $S_t(a)$ by weight β. The article a_t recommended by Con-CNAME at trial t is $a_t = \arg\max_a \left(\beta S_t(a) + (1 - \beta) \sum_{i \neq 0} P_t(a, i) \right)$ during exploitation. Besides, different from most contextual bandit algorithm, Con-CNAME

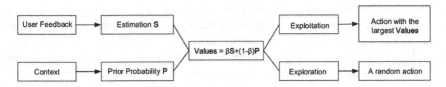

Fig. 1. The framework of Con-CNAME algorithm

explores randomly according to exploration probability, and the exploration probability is updated based on user feedbacks (the classic estimation $Q_t(a)$) which has been proposed in our context-free algorithm named CNAME [23]. The full Con-CNAME algorithm is as follows:

Algorithm 1: Con-CNAME

---

1) **Input**: w , α and β
2) **for** *each action a* **do**
3) $Q_0(a) = 0$
4) $N_0(a) = 0$
5) $S_0(a) = 0$
6) **end**
7) **if** a not in **possibleActions**
8)   Initialize click vector **clicksFeature**[a] to all 1 vector
9)   Initialize select vector **selectionsFeature**[a] to all 1 vector
10) **end**
11) **for** a in **possibleActions**
12) $P(a) = \sum_{i \neq 0} \dfrac{clicksFeature[a][i]}{selectionsFeature[a][i]}$
13) $Values(a) = (1-\beta) P(a) + \beta S_t(a)$
14) **end**
15) **for** *time step* t **do**
16) $m_t = N_t(\arg\min_a Q_t(a))$
17)   Generate a random number x in open interval (0,1)
18) $a_t \leftarrow \begin{cases} \arg\max_a Values(a) & \text{if } x > \dfrac{w}{w + m_t^2} \\ \text{a random action in } \textbf{possibleActions} & \text{otherwise} \end{cases}$
19)   Observe a reward $X_{a_t,t}$
20)   **if** $X_{a_t,t} > 0$
21) $S_t(a_t) = S_{t-1}(a_t) + \alpha (1 - S_{t-1}(a_t))$
22)   **end**
23) $N_t(a_t) = N_{t-1}(a_t) + 1$
24) $Q_t(a_t) = Q_{t-1}(a_t) + \dfrac{1}{N_{t-1}(a_t)}[X_{a_t,t} - Q_{t-1}(a_t)]$
25) **end**

The Con-CNAME starts by setting the parameters w, α and β(Line 1), where $w \in (0,1)$ affects the speed at which the exploration probability is changed, the learning rate $\alpha \in (0,1)$ affects the update of chosen probability and the weight β controls the proportion of chosen probability and prior probability in **Values**. After initializing the estimations (the classic estimation $Q(a)$ and our proposed chosen probability $S(a)$) and the chosen number $N(a)$ of each action a (Line 2–6), it initializes the click vector and selection vector for a not in **possibleActions** (Line 7–10). Here, **possibleActions** is the list of actions (articles) that are available to user during that particular visit. Elements *clicksFeature*$[a][i]$ and *selectionsFeature*$[a][i]$ of **clicksFeature**$[a]$ and **selectionsFeature**$[a]$ represent *clicks*$[a][i]$ and *selections*$[a][i]$ respectively. Then calculate the prior probability and *Values*(a) for every action a in **possibleActions** (Line 11–14). The Con-CNAME iteratively chooses an action to play (referred to recommend an item in recommender systems) based on the exploration probability (Line 15–18), and receives a reward $X_{a_t,t}$ (Line 19). The exploration probability $w/(w + m_t^2)$ is adjusted according to the chosen number of action with minimal estimated payoff, defined by m_t. The chosen probability $S_t(a_t)$ is improved only when $X_{a_t,t} > 0$ (Line 20–22). Finally, updates the chosen number and classic estimation at time step t (Line 23–24).

There are three key points of Con-CNAME algorithm. Firstly, **Values** includes chosen probability (based on user feedback) and prior probability (based on contexts). Secondly, different from most contextual algorithm, the Con-CNAME algorithm keeps the exploration process, which can also help address cold start problem. Besides, exploration may bring surprise to users and help to learn users' interest. Thirdly, there are a lot of emergency in practical process, the Con-CNAME algorithm can still work as CNAME algorithm normally if the contextual information is unobtainable suddenly.

Similar to our proposed context-free Asy-CNAME algorithm, the Con-CNAME algorithm can be updated in an asynchronous manner. Asynchronous manner weakens the impact of the user's short-term behavior to a certain extent, which plays a role in improving the CTR. On the other hand, the implementation complexity is reduced in an asynchronous manner, which can help decrease the calculation time.

4   Experimental Evaluation

Evaluating a contextual multi-armed bandit algorithm by online evaluation has always been a challenging task mainly due to limited availability of data. The evaluator ideally desires for datasets that explicitly contain the data which forms the basis of evaluation, such as the changes in users' preferences, demographics etc. In this section, the user clicks log dataset of Yahoo! Front Page Today Module, which has been widely used, is applied to evaluate the Con-CNAME algorithm. We discuss the influence of key parameters α and β, then provide the reference ranges of these two parameters through simulation on Yahoo! dataset. Furthermore, we compare the performance of our algorithm with other bandit algorithms.

4.1   Yahoo! Front Page Today Module User Click Log Dataset (R6B)

This dataset contains a fraction of user click log for news articles displayed in the Featured Tab of the Today Module on Yahoo! Front Page[1]. This dataset includes 15 days of data from October 2 to 16, 2011 and some raw features. There are 28,041,015 user visits to the Today Module on Yahoo!'s Front Page. Each of these user visits is a single line in the data file. For example, the structure of the data line is like tuples as follows:

"1317513293 id-563643 0 |user 1 8 12 13 22 16 18 54 24 26 17 42 19 25 15 61 14 21 |id-552077 |id-555224 |id-555528 |id-559744 |id-559855 |id-560290 |id-560518 |id-560620 |id-563115 |id-563582 |id-563643 |id-563787 |id-563846 |id-563938 |id-564335 |id-564418 |id-564604 |id-565364 |id-565479 |id-565515 |id-565533 |id-565561 |id-565589 |id-565648 |id-565747 |id-565822"

Table 1. Meanings of tuples in the data line of Yahoo! R6B dataset

Tuple of data line	Tuple's meaning
1317513293	Timestamp
id-563643	Article ID
0	Click Status
user	Start of user's contexts
1 8 12 13 22 16 18 54 24 26 17 42 19 25 15 61 14 21	User's contexts
|id-552077 |id-555224 ...|id-565822	List of recommended articles

Table 1 shows the meaning of each tuple in data line. Timestamp is considered as a unique user. Article ID corresponds to the arms or actions in multi-armed bandit problem. Click status has two values: 1 if the article is clicked by a user and 0 otherwise. User's contexts start from string "user" which is followed by binary vectors. Binary vectors indicate user's contextual features, such as user's age and gender. The list of recommended articles contains articles that are available to users during this particular visit.

4.2   Influence of Key Parameters

In this part, we study the influence of two parameters in Con-CNAME algorithm. We design learning rate α to affect the update of chosen probability and weight β to control the proportion of chosen probability and prior probability in **Values**. The performance of different parameter values evaluated through CTR are shown in Table 2. We make recommendations over the first 200000 lines and 1200000 lines respectively. In the experimental setting, we adopt a step of 0.1, through 0.1 to 0.9, only to find the variations of the results are not that obvious, so we choose to demonstrate the final results with 0.2 and 0.8. The corresponding results are shown in Table 2. Two values of α and β are experimented with 0.5 as a benchmark. In detail, $\alpha = 0.2$ represents that

---

[1] https://webscope.sandbox.yahoo.com

Table 2. Obtained CTR with different parameter values

Lines = 200000				Lines = 12200000		
α \\ β	0.2	0.8		α \\ β	0.2	0.8
0.2	**0.0499**	0.0461		0.2	0.0718	0.0719
0.8	0.0489	0.0469		0.8	0.0719	**0.0721**

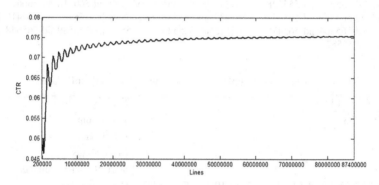

Fig. 2. CTR obtained over the first 87400000 lines of Yahoo! R6B dataset

chosen probability increases slightly each time while $\alpha = 0.8$ represents that chosen probability increases greatly each time. $\beta = 0.2$ means the context has a larger impact than chosen probability on recommendations while $\beta = 0.8$ means the context has a smaller impact. In Table 2, the best results are highlighted respectively in boldface.

We can see that the values of learning rate α does not have obvious impact on CTRs. That's easy to explain, no matter how fast chosen probability is updated each time, each updated chosen probability increases in same degree. From the results in Table 2, we can figure out that when the number of lines is small, there is little context information obtained through parameter α, the CTR is most influenced by β. As for weight β, it has an important influence on obtained CTRs: larger value of β brings lower CTR over the first 200000 lines. When processed lines increase to 12200000, larger value of β is more likely to obtain higher CTR, but the influence of β is relatively weaken. In detail, when $\beta = 0.2$, it means the context information contributes significantly, the results of smaller number of lines implies that context information are fully exploited, and when the number of lines increases, it leads to the local optimum.

In order to confirm the stability of Con-CNAME algorithm, we make recommendations over the first 87400000 lines of Yahoo! R6B dataset with $\alpha = 0.8$ and $\beta = 0.8$. Figure 2 shows the CTR obtained by Con-CNAME. At the beginning, the CTRs grow fast. Then the speed of CTRs increasing slow down with the increasing lines, but it still keeps increasing. Hence, it is indicated that the Con-CNAME algorithm can be applied to personalized recommendations.

4.3   Performance Comparison

In this section, performance comparison of various MAB-based approaches on recommendations for large-scale recommender systems is conducted. The Random approach randomly chooses an item each time. This can be seen as the benchmark for other approaches. The Most click approach always recommends the article which obtained the most clicks. The Click rate approach recommends article with the highest CTR. The Contextual click approach makes a recommendation according to the contextual information of the clicked article. Naïve III algorithm and Linear Bayes algorithm are also based on the context information. In addition to context-aware approaches, we compare Con-CNAME with our context-free approaches CNAME and Asy-CNAME. The CTR performance of these 9 approaches are summarized in Table 3, and Table 4 shows the relative variance of Con-CNAME over other comparison approaches, where the best results are highlighted respectively in boldface.

Table 3. Performance in CTR on the Yahoo! R6B dataset

Algorithm	Lines				
	2.0×10^5	3.6×10^6	7.2×10^6	1.06×10^7	1.4×10^7
Random	0.036	0.034	0.034	0.034	0.034
Most click	**0.047**	0.043	0.043	0.043	0.042
Click rate	0.046	0.068	0.068	0.069	0.070
Contextual click	0.040	0.068	0.070	0.071	0.072
Linear Bayes	0.033	0.034	0.034	0.034	0.034
Naive III	**0.047**	0.066	0.067	0.068	0.069
CNAME	0.043	0.067	0.069	0.070	0.071
Asy-CNAME	0.044	0.068	0.069	0.070	0.072
Con-CNAME	**0.047**	**0.069**	**0.071**	**0.072**	**0.073**

Table 4. Relative variance of Con-CNAME over other comparison approaches in CTR on the Yahoo! R6B dataset

Algorithm difference	Lines				
	2.0×10^5	3.6×10^6	7.2×10^6	1.06×10^7	1.4×10^7
Con-CNAME over Random	31%	103%	109%	112%	**115%**
Con-CNAME over Most click	0%	60%	65%	67%	**74%**
Con-CNAME over Click rate	2%	1%	**4%**	**4%**	**4%**
Con-CNAME over Contextual click	**18%**	1%	1%	1%	1%

(*continued*)

Table 4. (*continued*)

Algorithm difference	Lines				
	2.0×10^5	3.6×10^6	7.2×10^6	1.06×10^7	1.4×10^7
Con-CNAME over Linear Bayes	42%	103%	109%	112%	**115%**
Con-CNAME over Naïve III	0%	5%	**6%**	**6%**	**6%**
Con-CNAME over CNAME	**9%**	3%	3%	3%	3%
Con-CNAME over Asy-CNAME	**7%**	1%	3%	3%	1%

As shown in Tables 3 and 4, the Con-CNAME algorithm can get the highest CTRs over the first 200000 to 14000000 lines with $\alpha = 0.8$ and $\beta = 0.8$. The CTRs obtained by Con-CNAME is significantly higher than those of Random, most click and Linear Bayes algorithm, and slightly higher than those of Click rate, Contextual click and Naïve III algorithm. Besides, compared with CNAME and Asy-CNAME, Con-CNAME algorithm further improves CTR by using contextual information.

With the increase of processed data, the CTR obtained by Most click approach does not continue to increase, but has a downward trend. Most click algorithm makes a recommendation only based on clicks, which may cause the recommended article is always popular article. Thus the articles recommended are stultifying or repeated in terms of the content. The Click rate approach makes use of user feedback, and obtains higher CTRs than Most click approach. On the other hand, the Click rate approach can get higher CTR than Contextual Click approach and Naïve III algorithm at the beginning of experiment. With the increase of lines, Contextual Click approach and Naïve III algorithm can learn more about users' interests, the recommended articles are more likely to meet users' interests. So the CTRs of Contextual Click approach and Naïve III algorithm catch up with and surpass the CTRs of Click rate approach in the later stages of the experimental process.

To sum up, user feedback and contextual information are both helpful to improve the CTRs with various emphasis. Making a recommendation based on user feedback always prefers to maximize the short-term reward, which is easy to fall into local optimum. Based on the contextual information, the users' interest can be better learned in the long run with the increase of contexts. The Con-CNAME algorithm combines user feedback and contextual information, and finally contributes to the highest CTRs.

5   Conclusion

In this paper, we study recommender systems based on contextual MAB problems. The Con-CNAME algorithm makes good recommendations combining user feedback and contextual information. The cold start problem is addressed by continuous exploration and contexts in our approach.

Different from the classic contextual MAB algorithms, our algorithm keeps the exploration. And the Con-CNAME algorithm can still work as CNAME algorithm normally if the contexts are unobtainable during some sudden emergencies. The influences of key parameters of our algorithm are discussed, besides, the performance of our algorithm and other MAB-based recommendation approaches are compared on Yahoo! Front Page Today Module user click log dataset. Experimental results show that our algorithm outperforms other algorithms in terms of CTR. The Con-CNAME algorithm is effective and steady for personalized recommender systems. Although our algorithm achieves significant result, a possible improvement can be made by updating it in an asynchronous manner.

References

1. Sutton, R.S., Barto, A.G.: Introduction to reinforcement learning. Mach. Learn. **16**(1), 285–286 (2005)
2. Li, S., Karatzoglou, A., Gentile, C.: Collaborative filtering bandits. In: International ACM SIGIR Conference on Research and Development in Information Retrieval, pp. 539–548 (2016)
3. Eghbali, S., Ashtiani, M.H.Z., Ahmadabadi, M.N., et al.: Bandit-based structure learning for bayesian network classifiers. In: International Conference on Neural Information Processing, pp. 349–356 (2012)
4. Resnick, P., Varian, H.R.: Recommender systems. Commun. ACM **40**(3), 56–58 (1997)
5. Balabanović, M., Shoham, Y.: Fab: content-based, collaborative recommendation. Commun. ACM **40**(3), 66–72 (1997)
6. Auer, P., Cesa-Bianchi, N., Fischer, P.: Finite-time analysis of the multiarmed bandit problem. Mach. Learn. **47**(2), 235–256 (2002)
7. Liu, J., Dolan, P., Pedersen, E.R.: Personalized news recommendation based on click behavior. In: International Conference on Intelligent User Interfaces, pp. 31–40 (2010)
8. Dhanda, M., Verma, V.: Personalized recommendation approach for academic literature using high-utility itemset mining technique. Progress in Intelligent Computing Techniques: Theory, Practice, and Applications (2018)
9. Schein, A.I., Popescul, A., Ungar, L.H., et al.: Methods and metrics for cold-start recommendations. In: Proceedings of ACM SIGIR Conference on Research & Development in Information Retrieval, vol. 39(5), 253–260 (2002)
10. Mary, J., Gaudel, R., Philippe, P.: Bandits warm-up cold recommender systems. Computer Science (2014)
11. Tang, L., Jiang, Y., Li, L., Li, T.: Ensemble contextual bandits for personalized recommendation. In: RecSys, pp. 73–80 (2014)
12. Adomavicius, G., Tuzhilin, A.: Toward the next generation of recommender systems: a survey of the state-of-the-art and possible extensions. IEEE Trans. Knowl. Data Eng. **17**(6), 734–749 (2005)
13. Shani, G., Heckerman, D., Brafman, R.I.: An MDP-based recommender system. J. Mach. Learn. Res. **6**(1), 1265–1295 (2005)
14. Ren, Z., Krogh, B.H.: State aggregation in markov decision processes. In: IEEE Conference on Decision and Control, pp. 3819–3824 (2002)
15. Cesa-Bianchi, N., Lugosi, G.: Prediction, Learning, and Games. Cambridge University Press, Cambridge (2006)

16. Cesa-Bianchi, N., Fischer, P.: Finite-time regret bounds for the multi-armed bandit problem. In: ICML, pp. 100–108 (1998)
17. Bubeck, S., Slivkins, A.: The best of both worlds: stochastic and adversarial bandits. J. Mach. Learn. Res. **23**(42), 1–23 (2012)
18. Adomavicius, G., Tuzhilin, A.: Context-aware recommender systems. In: Recommender Systems Handbook, pp. 191–226 (2015)
19. Adomavicius, G., Sankaranarayanan, R., Sen, S., Tuzhilin, A.: Incorporating contextual information in recommender systems using a multidimensional approach. ACM Trans. Inf. Syst. **23**(1), 103–145 (2005)
20. Li, L., Chu, W., Langford, J., Schapire, R. E.: A contextual-bandit approach to personalized news article recommendation. In: World Wide Web, pp. 661–670 (2010)
21. Song, L., Tekin, C., Schaar, M.V.D.: Online learning in large-scale contextual recommender systems. IEEE Trans. Serv. Comput. **9**(3), 433–445 (2016)
22. Jośe, A.M.H., Vargas, A.M.: Linear bayes policy for learning in contextual-bandits. Expert Syst. Appl. **40**(18), 7400–7406 (2013)
23. Zhou, Q., Zhang, X.F, Xu, J., et al.: Large-scale bandit approaches for recommender systems. In: International Conference on Neural Information Processing, pp. 811–821 (2017)

Real-Time Session-Based Recommendations Using LSTM with Neural Embeddings

David Lenz[1]($\boxtimes$), Christian Schulze[2], and Michael Guckert[2]

[1] Fachbereich Wirtschaftswissenschaften, Justus-Liebig-Universität Gießen,
Giessen, Germany
`david.lenz@wirtschaft.uni-giessen.de`
[2] KITE - Kompetenzzentrum für Informationstechnologie, Technische Hochschule
Mittelhessen, Friedberg, Germany
`{christian.schulze,michael.guckert}@mnd.thm.de`

Abstract. Recurrent neural networks have successfully been used as core elements of intelligent recommendation engines in e-commerce platforms. We demonstrate how LSTM networks can be applied to recommend products of interest for a customer, based on the events of the current session only. Inspired by recent advances in natural language processing, our network computes vector space representations (VSR) of available products and uses these representations to derive predictions of user behaviour based on the clickstream of the current session. The experimental results suggest that the Embedding-LSTM is well suited for session-based recommendations, thus offering a promising method for attacking the user cold start problem. A live test gives proof that our LSTM model outperforms a recommendation model created with traditional methods. We also show that providing the learned VSR as features to neighbourhood-based methods leads to improved performance as compared to standard nearest neighbour methods.

Keywords: LSTM · Neural embeddings
Session-based recommendations · Real-time recommendations

1 Introduction

Real-time session based recommendations become increasingly important for state of the art e-commerce platforms. Recommendation systems predict useful items for users, providing them with a richer experience and increasing the success of the website in consequence [10]. Conventional approaches for recommendation systems typically use collaborative (CF) or content-based filtering (CBF).

This work was partially funded by LOEWE HA project PAROT (no. 509/16-21, State Offensive for the Development of Scientific and Economic Excellence).

V. Kůrková et al. (Eds.): ICANN 2018, LNCS 11140, pp. 337–348, 2018.
https://doi.org/10.1007/978-3-030-01421-6_33

Whenever a user rejects cookies or has not visited the website before, only information of the current session can be exploited. No historic data about previous purchases is available and therefore the challenge of creating recommendations is then referred to as the (user) cold-start problem [13]. Session based recommendations (SBR) view the user as being anonymous and algorithms can only make use of implicit user feedback, since no explicit ratings are available. However, SBR plays an increasingly important role for modern e-commerce websites. As collaborative filtering methods heavily rely on historic data they are not applicable in session-based recommendation settings. The alternative of item-to-item recommendations often only has myopic access to items clicked and can't exploit context-dependent preferences of the user.

Other than most of the previously published research in SBR we focus on deep learning techniques to predict products of interest based on the current browsing session. We use vector space representations (VSR) of the items as input to the network, as it has been recently done with words in the context of NLP [9]. Different from typical VSRs implementations which use an additional network for learning, our approach does not require pre-training of product features and can be learned in an end-to-end fashion, i.e. the product embeddings and network weights are learned simultaneously.

We show that the Embedding-LSTM model provides more accurate and more diverse recommendations than other frequently used SBR approaches when applied to real-world datasets. In a case-study we demonstrate this by deploying an Embedding-LSTM into a production environment to capture live feedback from users.

The ability to test models online gives access to new metrics beyond those mostly used in literature, e.g. we can evaluate our model performance based on how much revenue is generated by the recommendations. From an economic and business point of view this seems to be of higher relevance compared to merely counting the products an algorithm can correctly recommend. We demonstrate the applicability of the proposed approach with an LSTM generating higher click counts from a higher number of overall users, selling more products and creating a higher overall revenue compared to the currently implemented association rule model.

2   Related Work

The idea to use RNNs for session-based recommendations has gained much attention recently. [5] demonstrated the general applicability of RNNs in SBR and the improved performance of RNNs in comparison to widely used approaches. [6] showed how additional information can significantly improve the performance of RNN based recommendation systems. We improve these approaches with an extended architecture using product embeddings as done by Barkan and Koenigstein [1], who propose a collaborative filtering method based on neural network embeddings which they call *item2vec*. The authors use the Word2Vec algorithm to learn product embeddings similar to our approach. However, they follow the original shallow architecture. This means they discard the sequential information since they represent the history of events as a vector with only a single time step. They predict the most similar items to the current item based on the cosine similarity between the calculated VSRs. Their results were better than the baseline model used, which was item-based collaborative filtering using singular value decomposition. [12] show that increasing the amount of training data through data augmentation techniques improves the performance of RNNs in SBR. [2] uses the item dwell time as an additional indicator of interest for specific items. The authors show that this leads to an increased performance as compared to the pure sequence based approach.

3 Session Based Recommendations with Embedding-LSTM

In order to achieve reasonable recommendations every information contained in a given sequence of events must be processed. Using recurrent neural networks allows us to easily frame the recommendation problem as a sequence prediction problem. Not only do we take into account the set of previously clicked items, but we also consider the order in which the items appeared, thus explicitly capturing how the preference of a user evolved over time.

In Long Short-Term Memory (LSTM) [7] networks the hidden layer activation is split into multiple interacting computations. Using an elaborate architecture of gated cells LSTMs can keep information over a series of input steps. LSTMs have successfully been applied to model temporal and sequential aspects of data e.g. machine translation [11] and are an adequate tool for analysing sequential user activity.

Learning vector space representations of products allows to capture fine-grained relationships and regularities between products. We use an embedding method to represent products in a continuous high-dimensional vector space in which multiple relations for a single product can be represented. We therefore expect to capture the sequential relationships between items in such *item vectors*. The VSRs replace the extremely sparse one-hot encoding by a dense vector representation. The reduction of computational complexity as compared to a one-hot encoding scheme is one of the benefits of this approach. Additionally, the learned embeddings can be reused as meaningful representations of input data for other machine learning models, e.g. we experimentally demonstrate how the learned VSR can be used as input to nearest neighbour recommendation methods to improve the recommendation performance. Investigation of the learned embeddings allows to learn more about relationships between products and the reasoning of the model.

4 Experiments

4.1 Datasets

Our dataset contains data collected in three different web-shops, which we denote by A, B, C covering a period of roughly 9 months (November 2016 to

August 2017). Table 1 details descriptive statistics of the datasets. *Users* is the number of unique users, *Items* the number of unique products and *Observations* is the number of recorded events per web-shop. *Avg observations per item* shows the average number of interactions between users and items and *Avg daily events* is the mean number of events recorded per day.

Table 1. Descriptive statistics

Data set	A	B	C
User Sessions	701,773	1,296,748	4,396,280
Items	5,937	7,829	8,999
Observations	1,679,144	3,820,461	13,837,585
Avg observations per item	283	488	1537
Avg daily events	6261	14,250	51,623
Max date	2017/07/25	2017/07/25	2017/07/25
Min date	2016/10/31	2016/10/31	2016/10/31

We evaluate the performance of our model for three different dictionary sizes $D \in \{500, 2000, 5000\}$. For each D the most popular items are identified. Popularity based pre-filtering is common in practical RS, since discarding unpopular products has negligible effects on the evaluations [6]. The network then has D output nodes in a softmax layer that applies a cross-entropy loss function.

4.2 Baseline Algorithms

The following algorithms are commonly used baselines for session-based recommendations [5,6].

- **POP:** Popularity predictor always recommends the most popular items in the training set.
- **Item-KNN (I-KNN):** This approach is inspired by traditional content-based filtering methods for session-based recommendations and recommends items similar to the item currently viewed. Similarity is measured based on the co-occurrence of items within sessions and calculated for each pair of products. See [5] for details. During inference, the top k items with the highest similarity to the current item are selected for recommendation. Item-KNN is one of the most commonly used item-to-item solutions in real world systems [5].
- **Embedding-KNN (E-KNN):** E-KNN also recommends products based on their similarity. The content-based filtering approach uses learned vector space representations (VSR) extracted from an Embedding-LSTM and re-uses them as features. Cosine similarity of two VSRs is used as similarity measure for the corresponding products.

4.3   Metrics

The top-k metric is similar to the sps metric described in [4]. The top-k metric for a single example is one, if the next click of a user appears in the top-k recommendations provided by the model, otherwise zero. Formally, this can be written as shown in Eq. 1.

$$\text{top-k} = \frac{1}{n} \sum_{i=1}^{n} \begin{cases} 1, & \text{if } y_i \in \hat{y}_{k,i} \\ 0, & \text{else} \end{cases} \tag{1}$$

For a given example i, $\hat{y}_{k,i}$ denotes the top k items with the highest predicted probability. Let y_i be the actual target item and n the number of examples. We measure the top-k for $k \in \{1, 10, 20, 30\}$. For $k = 1$ the top-k metric equals the accuracy, i.e. the recommendation with the highest probability is indeed the correct label.

The *reciprocal rank* metric measures the position of the relevant item in the list of recommended items. This is important in cases where the order of recommendations is relevant, for example if the lower ranked items are only visible after scrolling. The mean reciprocal rank (MRR) is the average of the reciprocal ranks for all examples and is calculated as

$$MRR = \frac{1}{n} \sum_{i=0}^{n} \frac{1}{rank_i} \tag{2}$$

with n denoting the number of training instances and $rank_i$ the position in the recommendation list in which the correct item occurred.

5   Results

5.1   Embedding Visualization

Dimensionality reduction techniques convert high-dimensional embeddings into lower dimensional data vectors while preserving local and global structures using t-SNE [8]. Figure 1 shows the two dimensional representation of the learned item embeddings for web-shop C with a dictionary size $D = 2000$ using the t-SNE algorithm in which points are coloured and annotated according to their product category. HOUSEKEEPING, GARDENING & RECREATION and LIVING are located closely together in the representation, TEXTILE, UNDERWEAR and SHOES are interconnected with each other and BABY & TODDLERS products while WELLBEING is close to SHOES and HOUSEKEEPING. This shows that the learned embeddings align with intuition. Moreover, items that are intuitively considered to be similar from a perspective of taste are close in the embedding space from what we can conclude that the network is able to learn meaningful representations of items that can be used to produce valuable recommendations.

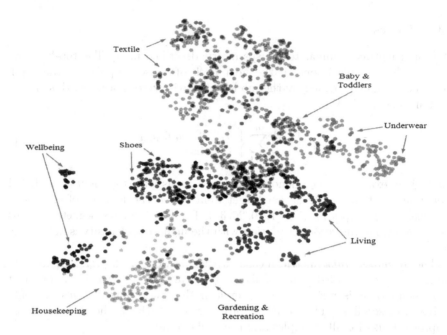

Fig. 1. 2D Item Embeddings from t-SNE for web-shop C (D = 2000) Two dimensional representation of the embeddings from web-shop C (D = 2000) with the t-SNE algorithm (perplexity = 12). Items are coloured according to their affinity to a product category.

5.2   Top-K

Table 2 provides the top-k and MRR metrics for our experiments. Results which we discuss in detail are printed in bold type.

The table contains the results of the tested algorithms and the difference between LSTM and the second best competitor (column *DIFF*) for different shops, dictionary sizes D and values of k.

LSTM outperforms the baseline algorithms in all data sets, with the POP algorithm being the weakest model throughout. As expected, results deteriorate with increasing dictionary size. Interestingly, I-KNN outperforms E-KNN in terms of plain accuracy ($k = 1$) in all data sets. However E-KNN has an edge over the I-KNN for all other $k \in \{10, 20, 30\}$ except in data sets $(A, 500)$ and $(A, 5000)$, where the I-KNN is higher for $k = 10$. A possible interpretation for this effect is that I-KNN learned a more problem specific solution (high $k = 1$) compared to E-KNN, in which the VSR captured the structure of the problem on a more general level (better performance for all other k). The mean value of the differences between E-KNN and I-KNN is 2.39 pp. which can be interpreted such that using VSR as features in the nearest-neighbour approach improved the recommendations. Therefore, an LSTM does not have to be implemented in a

Table 2. Metrics: Top-k and MRR

Shop	D	K	LSTM	E-KNN	I-KNN	POP	DIFF
A	500	1	11.18	4.75	7.69	0.62	3.48
		10	**38.51**	24.59	**26.03**	6.01	12.48
		20	48.84	33.32	32.93	9.99	15.53
		30	54.96	38.75	38.49	13.80	**16.22**
		MRR	0.20	0.18	0.08	0.01	0.02
	2000	1	8.74	2.42	6.52	0.42	2.21
		10	31.91	22.62	21.87	2.96	9.28
		20	40.50	30.39	27.34	4.92	10.11
		30	45.94	35.22	31.79	6.74	10.72
		MRR	0.16	0.12	0.07	0.00	0.04
	5000	1	6.54	3.55	6.10	0.24	**0.44**
		10	26.10	19.25	20.21	2.25	5.89
		20	35.31	26.26	25.48	3.87	9.06
		30	40.84	30.40	29.91	5.35	10.44
		MRR	0.13	0.12	0.06	0.00	0.01
B	500	1	6.21	4.13	5.02	0.85	1.19
		10	28.54	22.94	17.74	6.71	5.6
		20	39.54	32.57	23.98	11.71	6.98
		30	46.96	38.64	29.41	16.19	8.32
		MRR	0.14	0.11	0.05	0.01	0.03
	2000	1	5.60	2.92	4.48	0.46	1.11
		10	23.78	16.67	14.71	3.38	7.11
		20	32.88	23.64	19.90	5.88	9.24
		30	38.46	27.80	24.36	8.06	10.66
		MRR	0.12	0.10	0.05	0.01	0.02
	5000	1	5.01	2.63	4.40	0.29	0.61
		10	22.11	15.36	13.49	2.54	6.75
		20	30.97	21.85	18.14	4.49	9.12
		30	36.35	25.97	22.28	6.54	10.38
		MRR	0.11	0.10	0.04	0.00	0.01
C	500	1	10.79	4.46	7.40	0.89	3.39
		10	**38.33**	**30.22**	25.41	6.44	8.11
		20	48.59	39.88	31.65	11.51	8.7
		30	**54.69**	45.43	38.02	15.95	9.26
		MRR	0.20	0.14	0.08	0.01	0.05
	2000	1	8.47	4.14	5.90	0.68	2.57
		10	31.12	23.07	19.53	3.15	8.05
		20	40.83	31.82	25.11	5.39	9.01
		30	46.73	36.80	30.08	7.11	9.94
		MRR	0.16	0.13	0.06	0.01	0.03
	5000	1	7.03	3.83	5.41	0.43	1.62
		10	27.82	22.12	17.36	2.23	5.7
		20	36.92	30.17	22.35	3.74	6.75
		30	42.34	34.98	27.15	5.13	7.37
		MRR	0.14	0.13	0.05	0.00	0.01

production environment to benefit from its sequential knowledge, simply replacing the features in existing implementations with learned embeddings already improves the results instead.

5.3 MRR

The MRR can be translated back to the average position in the list of recommendations by taking $\frac{1}{MRR}$. The result is detailed in the boxplot in Fig. 2. In the upper figure all algorithms are shown, while the lower figure leaves out POP to allow for a better comparison between the remaining algorithms. The inner line represents the median value, the edges of the box indicate the upper and lower quartile and the whiskers detail the extreme values. For the LSTM, the median position of the correct recommendation is 7.31, the E-KNN at position 8.25, the I-KNN at position 16.81 and the POP at position 198.11. During the live-test of the model (next section), the number of recommendations shown at once is eight[1], so theoretically the LSTM would be the only algorithm where users would (given the median value) see the correct recommendation without using the slider. The LSTM also has the lowest uncertainty involved in the recommendation quality, indicated by the smaller overall range of the box plot (4.350 for the LSTM compared to 4.595 for the E-KNN), so the results are the most stable over all datasets.

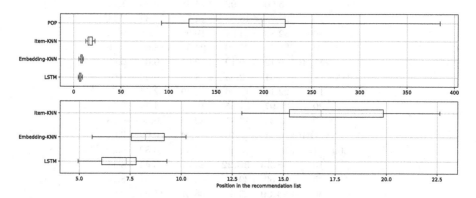

Fig. 2. Average position of the correct recommendation over all datasets. The upper image displays all algorithms. In the lower image the POP predictor is not shown. Whiskers represent minimum and maximum values.

To see whether the predictions align with intuition it is useful to visualize some example predictions. Here we only provide the recommendations from the LSTM model, as this is the model of interest. Results are visualized in Table 3.

Each row holds a single example of inputs and predictions. Column *Input* on the left contains the inputs to the model with the currently viewed item

---

[1] This is dependent on the display size. Here we assume a 24 in. monitor.

in column (x_t) and the previously viewed item in (x_{t-1}). Column *Predictions* contains the predictions, sorted from left to right in descending order of their probabilities, so that the item for which is most likely to be clicked. In the first row we assume a user has only clicked on the product 'cabinet' before. Without sequential information and only a single input this is simply an item-to-item recommendation. The big cabinet that is on the top position is quite similar to the currently viewed cabinet. In line with intuition more cabinets and commodes follow. In the second row a another piece of furniture is clicked and sequential information is now available. The model accounts for this by adjusting the importance of different products. The big cabinet that has already been the top prediction in row 1 again is on top, now with a commode which has not been in the top 8 recommendations before as second best recommendation. Obviously, the model found evidence that the commode is an important recommendation given the sequence of previous inputs. In the third row the currently viewed article is again the cabinet, however this time another product has been viewed before. Again the top prediction has not changed but the previous article influences the order of the recommendations. This is seen in row 3 in which the list of top recommendations changes, e.g. rank 8 has not been in the recommendation list before at all and rank 4 was not listed in row 2.

Table 3. LSTM example predictions from (C, 5000)

In row 4 the previously viewed product is identical to row 3, but the one currently viewed is now a shoe. The model completely ignores the previous item and only recommends items that are similar to the currently viewed product which might be explained by the fact that shoes 'score' on other shoes significantly, so the importance of other shoes regarding the current session is greater than the importance of more furniture.

5.4 Model Deployment

The best performing model for web shop C with $D = 5000$ has been deployed into production giving us the opportunity to capture metrics, which are typically not available without user interaction.

The model was benchmarked with an A/B test for one week against the currently deployed prediction model which uses association rule mining (see [3] for details). The model creates predictions exploiting user history (if available) combined with short-term predictions based on the current browsing session to come up with the final set of recommendations. Intuitively, this should give the model an advantage whenever the system can identify a user and access the explicit purchasing history of this user. Rather than predicting the next item to be clicked, the benchmark model has been optimized to generate high revenue by increasing the importance of more expensive articles.

Table 4 provides an overview of the metrics for both models as well as the sum or average of the metric. The recorded metrics are the number of users who clicked on a recommendation (Users), the number of clicks on recommendations (Clicks), the ratio of clicks per user (Clicks/Users), the average price of the clicked items (Clicked Avg price), the total value of the clicked items (Clicked Price), the number of different products sold (Unique Products), the number of total sold products (Sold Quantity), the total revenue generated by the recommendations (Sold Value) and the average price of sold products (Sold Avg Value). 27.290 users saw the LSTM recommendations and 27,836 users saw the baseline recommendations. The LSTM attracted nearly twice as many users $(2,508$ vs $4,390)$, who more than doubled the number of overall clicks $(4,495$ vs $9,924)$. Additionally the users also spent more time clicking through the recommendations as can be seen by the higher Clicks/User metric (1.81 vs 2.31). The LSTM clicked price is 486,222 € higher and the average clicked price is 15.24 € above the baseline model. 95 additional unique products and 131 additional total products were sold by the recommendations generated by the LSTM model. This results in 18,131.4 € revenue generated by the model in one week, which is 2,238.7 € extra revenue compared to the currently deployed model. Over the course of a year, the LSTM would generate 826,420.4 € in revenues, which is an increase of 116,412.4€ compared to the baseline[2].

---

[2] From a marketing perspective, an interesting metric is the revenue/click. However, this neglects the cost of running the systems which is indeed high so that only looking at the revenue/click does not incorporate all relevant costs and is therefore only a skewed metric. Unfortunately, we cannot publish details about the associated cost structures.

Table 4. Live-test results

Model	Baseline	LSTM
Users	2,508	4,390
Clicks	4,495	9,924
Clicks/User	1.81	2.31
Clicked Price	€ 274,350	€ 760,572
Clicked Avg price	€ 70.26	€ 85.50
Unique Products	298	393
Sold Quantity	339	470
Sold Value	€ 15,892.7	€ 18,131.4
Sold Avg price	€ 52.52	€ 42.42
Sold Avg Value	€ 55.10	€ 46.09

Interestingly, the average price of each unique product sold is over 10 € higher in the baseline model, while the average purchase value (users can buy several products at once) is 9.01 € higher in the benchmark. This stands in contrast to the average click price which has been around 15 € higher for the LSTM. A possible explanation might be the explicit usage of user histories by the baseline model. Since known users already interacted with the company, the initial interaction hurdle might be gone, so providing these users with improved recommendations can lead to a multiplying effect. Furthermore, the baseline model has been optimized to maximize revenue, while the LSTM was optimized to predict the next click. Another interpretation of the differences is that users enjoy the recommendations from the LSTM and curiously click on the products to learn more about them without the intention to actually buy something. As users signal interest through clicking on recommendations, the high click rate leads to the suggestion that the LSTM architecture learned useful dependencies from the data to provide interesting recommendations.

6   Conclusion

We have demonstrated that recurrent neural networks can successfully be applied as real-time session-based recommendation engines. Our deep learning architecture outperformed standard algorithms in all metrics when applied to practice-relevant datasets. A live test provided proof for the superiority of Embedding-LSTMs compared to the baseline model. Its recommendations lead to a significantly higher number of users with higher clickrates and in consequence to an increase of products sold thus generating a higher overall revenue. Furthermore, we showed the emergence of meaningful vector space representations for the products using an efficient end-to-end training approach. Our architecture enables smart marketing based on machine learning algorithms for a variety of customer orientated businesses in a scalable way. Future research will focus on further improving the proposed architecture.

References

1. Barkan, O., Koenigstein, N.: Item2Vec: neural item embedding for collaborative filtering. CoRR abs/1603.04259 (2016). http://arxiv.org/abs/1603.04259
2. Dallmann, A., Grimm, A., Pölitz, C., Zoller, D., Hotho, A.: Improving session recommendation with recurrent neural networks by exploiting dwell time. ArXiv e-prints, June 2017
3. Davahri, M.: Kollaborative empfehlungssysteme im e-commerce. Technical report, Technische Hochschule Mittelhessen in cooperation with Dastani Consulting (2016)
4. Devooght, R., Bersini, H.: Collaborative filtering with recurrent neural networks. CoRR abs/1608.07400 (2016). http://arxiv.org/abs/1608.07400
5. Hidasi, B., Karatzoglou, A., Baltrunas, L., Tikk, D.: Session-based recommendations with recurrent neural networks. CoRR abs/1511.06939 (2015). http://arxiv.org/abs/1511.06939
6. Hidasi, B., Quadrana, M., Karatzoglou, A., Tikk, D.: Parallel recurrent neural network architectures for feature-rich session-based recommendations. In: Proceedings of the 10th ACM Conference on Recommender Systems, RecSys 2016, pp. 241–248. ACM, New York (2016). https://doi.org/10.1145/2959100.2959167. http://doi.acm.org/10.1145/2959100.2959167
7. Hochreiter, S., Schmidhuber, J.: Long short-term memory. Neural Comput. 9(8), 1735–1780 (1997). https://doi.org/10.1162/neco.1997.9.8.1735
8. van der Maaten, L., Hinton, G.: Visualizing high-dimensional data using t-SNE (2008)
9. Mikolov, T., Sutskever, I., Chen, K., Corrado, G., Dean, J.: Distributed representations of words and phrases and their compositionality. CoRR abs/1310.4546 (2013). http://arxiv.org/abs/1310.4546
10. Ricci, F., Rokach, L., Shapira, B., Kantor, P.B. (eds.): Recommender Systems Handbook, 1st edn. Springer, Boston (2011). https://doi.org/10.1007/978-0-387-85820-3
11. Sutskever, I., Vinyals, O., Le, Q.V.: Sequence to sequence learning with neural networks. Technical report arXiv:1409.3215 [cs.CL], Google (2014). NIPS 2014
12. Tan, Y.K., Xu, X., Liu, Y.: Improved recurrent neural networks for session-based recommendations. In: Proceedings of the 1st Workshop on Deep Learning for Recommender Systems, DLRS 2016, pp. 17–22. ACM, New York (2016). https://doi.org/10.1145/2988450.2988452. http://doi.acm.org/10.1145/2988450.2988452
13. Yuan, J., Shalaby, W., Korayem, M., Lin, D., AlJadda, K., Luo, J.: Solving cold-start problem in large-scale recommendation engines: a deep learning approach. CoRR abs/1611.05480 (2016). http://arxiv.org/abs/1611.05480

Imbalanced Data Classification Based on MBCDK-means Undersampling and GA-ANN

Anping Song and Quanhua Xu[⊠]

School of Computer Engineering and Science,
Shanghai University, Shanghai 200444, China
{apsong, beth0330}@shu.edu.cn

Abstract. The imbalanced classification problem is often a problem in classification tasks where one class contains a few samples while the other contains a great deal of samples. When the traditional machine learning classification method is applied to the imbalanced data set, the classification performance is bad and the time cost is high. As a result, mini batch with cluster distribution K-means (MBCDK-means) undersampling method and GA-ANN model is proposed in this paper to solve these two problems. MBCDK-means chooses the samples according to the clusters distribution and the distance from the majority class clusters to the minority class cluster center. This technology can keep the original distribution of cluster and increase the sampling rate of boundary samples. It is helpful to improve the final classification performance. At the same time, compared with the classic K-means clustering undersampling method, the presented MBCDK-means undersampling method has lower time complexity. Artificial neural network (ANN) is widely used in data classification but it is easily trapped in a local minimum. Genetic algorithm artificial neural network (GA-ANN), which uses genetic algorithm to optimize the weight and bias of neural network, is raised because of this. GA-ANN achieves better performance than ANN. Experimental results on 8 data sets show the effectiveness of the proposed algorithm.

Keywords: Imbalanced classification · Clustering sampling
Artificial neural network · Genetic algorithm

1 Introduction

Imbalanced classification problem refers to the pattern classification problem in which the number of training samples is distributed unevenly among classes [1]. When traditional classification methods are applied to imbalanced data, in order to improve the overall accuracy of the classification, the classifier will reduce the attention of minority classes and thus tend to favor the majority class. It makes that the minority class samples are difficult to be identified and leads to a bad classification performance. The literature [2] shows that in some applications, it is difficult to build a correct classifier when the class distribution imbalance ratio exceeds 1:35. Furthermore, Some

© Springer Nature Switzerland AG 2018
V. Kůrková et al. (Eds.): ICANN 2018, LNCS 11140, pp. 349–358, 2018.
https://doi.org/10.1007/978-3-030-01421-6_34

applications make it difficult to establish a correct classifier when the imbalance ratio reaches 1:10.

Data resampling is an effective way to solve data imbalance problem. Resampling mainly contains two methods: over sampling [3–5] and under sampling [6–8]. Over-sampling technique increases samples of minority class artificially. However, this will introduce redundant information. Under sampling technique balances the data set by reducing the number of majority class samples. Random under sampling (RUS) randomly reduces samples which will probably lose important information. Recently, some resampling methods based on clustering technology have been discussed. After clustering, the data in the same cluster is similar while the data in different cluster is unlike. Because of this, clustering technology is appropriate to be applied in resampling. Lin et al. [9] applied K-means to under sampling approaches. However, the time complexity of K-means undersampling algorithm is huge especially on big data. Besides, the distribution of clusters is not considered in this approach. Based on that, MBCDK-means is proposed in order to solve these two problems. At the same time, artificial neural network is prevailing in classification task. Unfortunately, it is easy to be trapped in local minimum. That's why we propose GA-ANN. Genetic algorithm is used here to optimize the weight and bias of neural network.

The rest of this paper is organized as follows. Section 2 presents the proposed method including the construction of model and the algorithm flow. Results, discussions and comparative analysis are made in Sect. 3. Final conclusion is drawn in Sect. 4.

2 Methodology

2.1 MBCDK-means Undersampling

MBCDK-means undersampling divides the majority class samples into k clusters while the minority into a separate class. Assuming that M is the number of majority class and m_i is the number of the ith cluster, then $M = \sum_{i=1}^{k} m_i$. Supposing that the distance between the ith majority class cluster center and the minority class cluster centers is d_i. d_i is denoted as follows:

$$d_i = \sqrt{(X_i - X_N)^2} \tag{1}$$

where X_i represents the ith majority class cluster center and X_N is the minority class cluster center. Then the average distance from the majority class clusters to the minority class cluster d_{avg} can be defined as follows.

$$d_{avg} = \frac{1}{k} \sum_{i=1}^{k} d_i \tag{2}$$

The calculation formula of the sample number n_i that needs to be extracted in the ith cluster is as follows:

$$n_i = \frac{N}{M} * m_i + \frac{d_{avg}}{d_i} \tag{3}$$

The number that needs to be extracted from each cluster is determined by the number of samples in the cluster and the distance between the majority class cluster centers and the minority class cluster center. The original distribution of the majority class samples can be retained. At the same time, it can increase the sampling number of boundary samples of the majority class. This contributes to the identification of boundary samples.

Moreover, mini batch K-means uses Mini Batch to calculate the distance. The advantage of Mini Batch is that it is not necessary to use all the data samples in the calculation process. Instead, some samples are taken from different types of samples to compute on behalf of each type.

For each small batch, updated centroid is created by calculating the average value. Data in the small batch are assigned to the centroid. With the iteration, the changes in these centroids gradually decrease until the centers of clusters are stable or the specified number of iterations are reached. Then the calculation will be stopped. Assuming that the size of a batch is b, the number of cluster is k, sample number is m, feature number is n and the iteration number is t. As the number of clusters in the K-means under-sampling algorithm is set to a small number of N, the time complexity is $O(tNmn)$. However, the time complexity of MBCDK-means algorithm becomes $O(tbkn)$. Obviously, the under-sampling algorithm proposed in this paper has faster convergence rate than the K-means under-sampling algorithm.

2.2 GA-ANN

ANN is widely used in data classification but it is easily trapped in a local minimum. Fortunately, genetic algorithm can solve this problem. Because of this, GA-ANN is put forward which uses genetic algorithm to optimize the weight and bias of neural network.

GA-ANN mainly deals with two key problems, namely, the encoding mapping from weights to chromosome bit strings and fitness function of genetic algorithm.

1. The encoding mapping from weights to chromosome bit strings.

Considering a simple artificial neural network that has a input layer nodes, b hidden layer nodes and c output layer nodes, the neural network will generate 4 matrices.

The weight matrix of input layer and hidden layer: $W = \begin{bmatrix} W_{11} & \cdots & W_{1b} \\ \cdots & \cdots & \cdots \\ W_{a1} & \cdots & W_{ab} \end{bmatrix}$

The threshold value matrix of hidden layer: $\alpha = \begin{bmatrix} \alpha_1 \\ \cdots \\ \alpha_b \end{bmatrix}$

The weight matrix of hidden layer and output layer: $V = \begin{bmatrix} V_{11} & \cdots & V_{1c} \\ \cdots & \cdots & \cdots \\ V_{b1} & \cdots & V_{bc} \end{bmatrix}$

The threshold value matrix of output layer: $\beta = \begin{bmatrix} \beta_1 \\ \cdots \\ \beta_c \end{bmatrix}$

Using GA to optimize the weights of ANN, and the above four matrices are optimized. The four matrices are converted to the chromosome strings in GA operation.

A binary string is used as the chromosome encoding. x chromosome bits represent a coefficient value, and the range of x values is determined according to the range and accuracy of the weight range. The mapping relationship between chromosome bit strings and weight values is shown in Fig. 1.

2. The fitness function.

The fitness function f of GA-ANN used to evaluate the chromosome is the area under ROC curve (AUC). AUC is based on the concept of confusion matrix, and a matrix used to represent the situation of sample identification in binary classification case. In this situation, the minority class is positive and the majority class is negative. TP indicates the prediction of positive samples is still positive; FN indicates the prediction of positive samples is negative; FP indicates negative samples' prediction is positive, and TN indicates negative samples' prediction is still negative. Each sample in the classification has a corresponding probability value that belongs to a different category. The final category prediction changes according to the set threshold on different probabilities. Each threshold corresponds to a set of metrics $(FPrate, TPrate)$. $FPrate$ is the false positive rate and $TPrate$ is true positive rate. $FPrate$ and $TPrate$ are defined as follows:

$$FPrate = \frac{FP}{FP + TN} \tag{4}$$

$$TPrate = \frac{TP}{TP + FN} \tag{5}$$

Then the fitness function f of GA-ANN is defined as follows:

$$f = AUC = \int_0^1 TPrate \, d\, FPrate \tag{6}$$

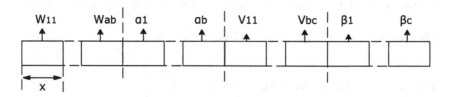

Fig. 1. Mapping relationship between chromosome bit strings and weight values

2.3 Imbalanced Classification Based on MBCDK-means Undersampling and GA-ANN

The flow of Imbalanced classification based on MBCDK-means undersampling and GA-ANN is given by Fig. 2. The imbalanced dataset is split into training data and testing data. MBCDK-means is applied to training data and then gains balanced training data. GP-ANN is used to train balanced data and then test testing data.

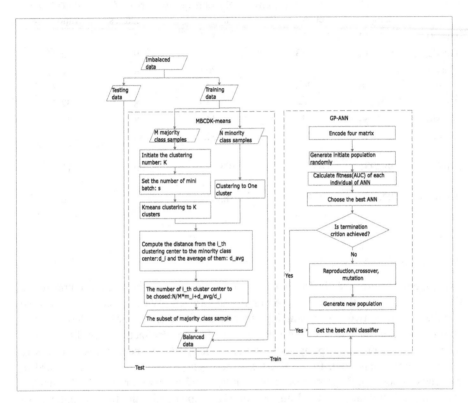

Fig. 2. Flow of Imbalanced classification based on MBCDK-means undersampling and GA-ANN

3 Computer Experiment Results

3.1 Datasets

This article discusses three experimental studies. 8 datasets are used in these experiments. 6 data sets with small scale are from UCI machine learning repository. Imbalanced ratio of these datasets is between 3.23 to 32.78, and the amount of sample is between 214 to 1484. A European credit card transaction record data set is used in our experiments. There are 284,807 records in this dataset, which only includes 492 fraud records. Feature number is 30, and the imbalanced ratio of data reaches up to 578.

The last dataset is KKBox's Churn Prediction Challenge dataset in 2017. It includes more than 400 million data and feature number is 30, which includes 12 features extracted on our own. Training dataset's imbalanced ratio is 14.58. The description of dataset is in Table 1.

Table 1. Description of datasets

Dataset	No. of samples	No. of minority class	No. of majority class	No. of features	Imbalance ratio
Glass0	214	51	163	9	3.19
Glass2	214	13	201	9	15.47
Glass4	214	9	205	9	22.81
Vehicle0	846	200	646	18	3.23
Yeast5	1484	44	1440	8	32.78
Yeast6	1484	37	1447	8	39.15
Credit card	284807	492	284315	30	577.88
KKBOX-train	992931	63741	929490	30	14.58
KKBOX-test	970960	87330	883630	30	10.12

3.2   Results

Experiment 1: Since the six UCI data sets are small, there is no need to compare the time complexity of the two under-sampling algorithms. We only compare the time complexity of the two under-sampling algorithms on the credit card and KKBox user churn prediction data sets. In the European credit card transaction recording experiment, K-means under-sampling took 801 s, while MBCDK-means took only 1 s to complete under-sampling. In the KKBox experiment, memory overflow happened in K-means under-sampling process after running for 7 h. In contrast, MBCDK-means took only 3 h to complete the sampling process. Apparently, the time complexity of MBCDK-means is much lower than that of K-means under-sampling.

At the same time, we used C4.5 decision tree as a classifier on 8 data sets to compare the difference in classification performance after using MBCDK-means under-sampling and K-means under-sampling respectively. Figure 3 shows the results of this comparative experiment. Obviously, on these 8 data sets, the under-sampling algorithm proposed in this paper achieves better classification performance than K-means under-sampling algorithm in classification performance. It can be seen that the algorithm proposed in this paper can deal with the imbalanced dataset more effectively than K-means under-sampling algorithm.

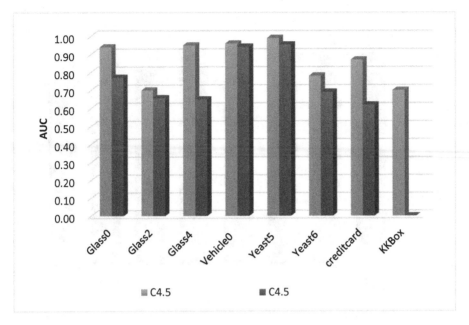

Fig. 3. Comparison of classification performance of MBCDK-means and K-means undersampling

Experiment 2: After the MBCDK-means under-sampling on 8 datasets, GA-ANN model and ANN model were sequentially used to compare the classification performance of the two models. The experimental results are shown in Fig. 4. It can be seen that GA-ANN achieves better classification performance than ANN. It shows that the genetic algorithm is effective for the improvement of ANN.

Experiment 3: the classification performance is compared between traditional machine learning methods and the classifier based on MBCDK-means under-sampling and GA-ANN model. The traditional machine learning models used in this experiment are C4.5 classification tree, bagging, random forest, and ANN and gradient boosting. The experimental results are shown in Fig. 5. Obviously, on small datasets, the classification performances of the proposed algorithm, bagging, boosting and random forest are similar while ANN and C4.5 decision tree achieve bad results. On big datasets such as European credit card and KKBox user churn prediction, the proposed algorithm achieves better performance than traditional machine learning algorithm.

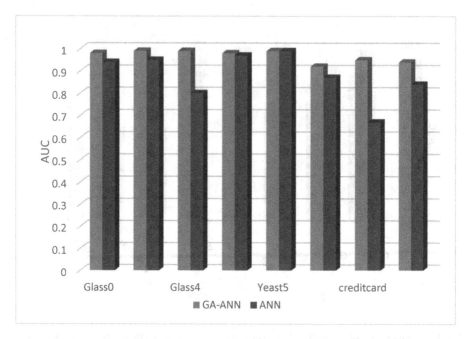

Fig. 4. Comparison of classification performance of GA-ANN and ANN

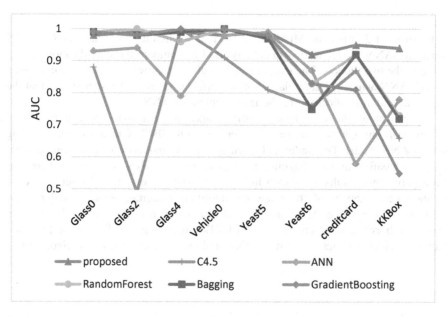

Fig. 5. Comparison of classification performance between traditional classifiers and the classifier based on MBCDK-means undersampling and GA-ANN

4 Conclusion

This article proposes a new sampling method called MBCDK-means undersampling and a classification model named GA-ANN. MBCDK-means undersampling fuses mini batch into K-means resampling. Meanwhile, this resampling method chooses samples according to the distribution of cluster samples and the distance between the cluster centers of majority class samples and that of the minority class samples. It remains the information of original data distribution. Besides, it increases the sampling rate of boundary samples. It is effective to improve final classification performance. After acquiring balanced data, these data should be classified. ANN is a common classifier but it is easy to be trapped in a local minimum. That's why GA-ANN is presented. Genetic algorithm is a method to find the optimal solution. Introducing GA to ANN helps ANN to find the optimal weights and biases. In 8 datasets, compared with K-means undersampling algorithm, MBCDK-means achieves better classification performance on the AUC. In the meantime, the time and space complexity of MBCDK-means is much lower than K-means undersampling in the experiments of credit card and KKBox churn prediction. In addition, GA-ANN gains better classification performance in contrast to ANN. In the end, the classification performance based on MBCDK-means and GA-ANN is competitive in 6 small UCI datasets and is better than traditional machine learning methods in big datasets. Experiment results show that our method is efficient in imbalanced data classification.

References

1. Krawczyk, B.: Learning from imbalanced data: open challenges and future directions. Prog. Artif. Intell. **5**(4), 1–12 (2016)
2. Batista, G.E., Prati, R.C., Monard, M.C.: A study of the behavior of several methods for balancing machine learning training data. ACM SIGKDD Explor. Newsl. **6**(1), 20–29 (2004)
3. Chawla, N.V., Bowyer, K.W., Hall, L.O., Kegelmeyer, W.P.: SMOTE: synthetic minority over-sampling technique. J. Artif. Intell. Res. **16**(1), 321–357 (2002)
4. Dong, Y., Wang, X.: A new over-sampling approach: random-SMOTE for learning from imbalanced data sets. In: Xiong, H., Lee, W.B. (eds.) KSEM 2011. LNCS (LNAI), vol. 7091, pp. 343–352. Springer, Heidelberg (2011). https://doi.org/10.1007/978-3-642-25975-3_30
5. Han, H., Wang, W.-Y., Mao, B.-H.: Borderline-SMOTE: a new over-sampling method in imbalanced data sets learning. In: Huang, D.-S., Zhang, X.-P., Huang, G.-B. (eds.) ICIC 2005, Part I. LNCS, vol. 3644, pp. 878–887. Springer, Heidelberg (2005). https://doi.org/10.1007/11538059_91
6. Tomek, I.: Two modifications of CNN. IEEE Trans. Syst. Man Cybern. **SMC-6**(11), 769–772 (1976)
7. Laurikkala, J.: Improving identification of difficult small classes by balancing class distribution. In: Quaglini, S., Barahona, P., Andreassen, S. (eds.) AIME 2001. LNCS (LNAI), vol. 2101, pp. 63–66. Springer, Heidelberg (2001). https://doi.org/10.1007/3-540-48229-6_9

8. Lin, W.C., Tsai, C.F., Hu, Y.H., Jhang, J.S.: Clustering-based undersampling in class-imbalanced data. Inf. Sci. **5**(8), 17–26 (2017)
9. Idris, A., Iftikhar, A., Rehman, Z.U.: Intelligent churn prediction for telecom using GP-AdaBoost learning and PSO undersampling. Cluster Comput. 1–15 (2017)

Evolutionary Tuning of a Pulse Mormyrid Electromotor Model to Generate Stereotyped Sequences of Electrical Pulse Intervals

Angel Lareo[(✉)], Pablo Varona, and F. B. Rodriguez

Grupo de Neurocomputación Biológica, Departamento de Ingeniería Informática,
Escuela Politécnica Superior, Universidad Autónoma de Madrid, Madrid, Spain
{angel.lareo,pablo.varona,f.rodriguez}@uam.es

Abstract. Adjusting parameters of a neural network model to reproduce complete sets of biologically plausible behaviors is a complex task, even in a well-described neural system. We show here a method for evolving a model of the mormyrid electromotor command chain to reproduce highly realistic temporal firing patterns as described by neuroethological studies in this system. Our method uses genetic algorithms for tuning unknown parameters in the synapses of the network. The developed fitting function simulates each evolved model under different network inputs and compare its output with the target patterns from the living animal. The obtained synaptic configuration can reveal new information about the functioning of electromotor systems.

Keywords: Genetic algorithms · Complex firing patterns
Neural models · Network parameter optimization
Information sequences · Pulse intervals · Electroreception

1 Introduction

To accomplish the robustness and flexibility that shape characteristic temporal patterns in neural activations is a complex task that networks in the nervous system seem to perform in a robust manner. However, mimicking these temporal patterns in models is not an easy task, particularly taking into account that the same network has to generate different patterns without changes in its structure. This is so even in simplified models with a reduced number of parameters.

The main objective of this paper is to present an evolutionary method to adjust the parameters of a model in order to reflect the different temporal structures of neural activations that occur in its biological counterpart. Genetic algorithms (GAs) are a convenient tool for computing global optimization, including temporal matching, inspired by biological evolution [14]. GAs have been extensively applied to parameter adjusting in neuron models [8,20] and modeled neural networks [19]. It has enable improvements in robot locomotion [15,23]

© Springer Nature Switzerland AG 2018
V. Kůrková et al. (Eds.): ICANN 2018, LNCS 11140, pp. 359–368, 2018.
https://doi.org/10.1007/978-3-030-01421-6_35

and in the development of biomimetic neuroprosthesis [11]. Also, regarding temporal patterns of electrical activity, GAs have been applied, for instance, to design sequences of neural stimulation that improve clinically-standard patterns in biophysically-based models [6]. It is worth noting that multi-objective optimization for constraining a model by experimental data using GAs allows more flexible and realistic models [10]. In this paper a method for adjusting the parameters of a neural network model to reproduce a set of different temporal patterns of activity using the same topology is presented.

The electromotor command network in pulse mormyrids, a family of weakly electric fish, is a well-known system [1] commonly used for studying information processing in the nervous system [12,16,17]. The rapid voltage transients (pulses) produced by the electric organ of these fishes (known as electric organ discharges, or EODs) can be detected in the fish surroundings. This EODs are 1:1 correlated with pulses of a neural ensemble known as the command nucleus (CN - Fig. 1). As a result, pulse mormyrids constitute a well suited system for non-invasively monitoring a living nervous system during long-time periods.

This system has other advantages. First, ethological studies have described stereotyped sequences of pulse intervals (SPI) in these animals (see Sect. 1.2). Furthermore, temporal patterns produced in the EOD are related with overall fish behavior, for example aggression of courtship [5]. Finally, physiological studies have described the network topology of the electromotor system [3]. The neural ensembles responsible for the generation of different SPI patterns have also been described [2,4].

Information from these studies have been used to develop an initial model of this system (see Sect. 1.1). The topology of the network was composed as four neurons and five synapses [4,18]. The preliminary hand-tuned model was able to show some of the characteristics of the real system, but it was not able to reproduce the temporal structure of all the target SPIs with the described connectivity.

Due to the intrinsic complexity of the network, hand-fitting to experimental data is a hard and time-consuming process [24], which in most cases fails to achieve the expected results. Even though several studies have successfully hand-tuned neural models [21], an automatic approach for model optimization has many advantages. In particular, it allows for searches that meet several requirements in shaping specific temporal patterns using modern high performance computing systems.

Two different GAs were used to improve the initial electromotor model and reproduce the temporal structure of all the target SPIs patterns (see Sect. 2). These GAs are described in Sect. 2.1 and both use the same evaluation function, which is described in Sect. 2.2. The development of an adequate evaluation function is crucial. This function will guide the evolutionary process scoring the individuals. Here, a function based on the mean square error between the model output sequences and the target SPIs is presented. The convergence results of both GAs is showed in Sect. 3, aside with a simulation of the best individual. These results are analyzed and discussed in Sect. 4.

1.1 Electromotor Command Network

The electromotor system commands the activity of the electric organ [2]. Each EOD is initiated by a pulse of the medullary command nucleus (CN) [4]. CN integrates influences mainly from two sources: the mesencephalic precommand nucleus (PCN) and the adjacent thalamic dorsal posterior nucleus (DP). After an EOD, motor outputs return to the command network through a corollary discharge pathway that activate the dorsal region of the ventroposterior nucleus (VPd). Finally, VPd provides inhibition feedback to DP and PCN, regulating the resting electromotor rhythm. Figure 1 shows a simplified representation of this network.

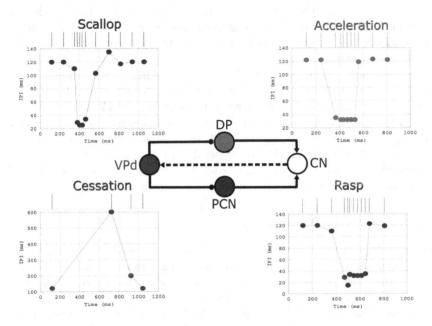

Fig. 1. Stereotyped sequences of pulse intervals (Scallop, acceleration, rasp and cessation) and simplified representation of the electromotor command network (center), based in [2,4]. Each SPI chart represents inter-pulse intervals (or IPIs, Y axis) along time (X axis). In the schematic, the neurons (VPd, DP, PCN, CN) are connected by five synapses, three of them are excitatory (those ended by arrows) and two of them inhibitory (those ended by circles). The dashed line represents the corollary discharge pathway. CN is the output of the network. Colors relate each SPI pattern with the neuron ensemble: DP activation is related with accelerations, PCN activation is related with scallops, VPd activation is related with cessations and activation of both DP and PCN is related with rasps.

1.2   Stereotyped Sequences of Pulse Intervals (SPIs)

Sequences of EODs are not random. They are grouped composing stereotyped patterns of pulse intervals [2,5]. Four SPI patterns have been well-described: accelerations, scallops, rasps and cessations.

Accelerations are prolonged decreases of electrical inter-pulse intervals (IPIs) to a series of nearly regular shorter intervals, as a result of activation in the DP nucleus. This kind of pattern is variable both in the final duration and in the minimum IPI reached. They are related to aggressive behaviors.

Scallops are sudden drops to very short IPIs followed by an immediate recovery, where IPIs rapidly increase to regular values. PCN activation is related to this electrical signalling. It may function as an advertisement signal.

Rasps have an initial sudden decrease to very short IPIs, similar to the ones observed in scallops, followed by a sustained slow increase like in accelerations. Both DP/PCN nuclei activations lead to this EOD pattern, which is used by male fish for courtship.

Cessations are a stop in the EOD generation during long time periods of around one second. It has been related with both aggressive and submissive behavior. This firing modality is triggered by activation of VPd.

The model was built to reproduce the temporal structure of these patterns as a function of the network inputs, without changing the network topology. Inputs were different stimuli that corresponded to the neuron ensemble activations described by the experimental studies. Due to the complexity of the task, an automatic method for synaptic parameter adjusting was developed.

2   Evolving the Network

We started from a previously developed electromotor model ([18] and unpublished work). Both the neuron and synapse models were initially hand-tuned to mimic the main characteristics of the real system. We improved the model through a trial-and-error process. Manual fitting of individual parameters was followed by an analysis of the results obtained, which iteratively leads to new changes in the parameters. Nevertheless, hand-fitting the synaptic parameters became almost impossible, as little is known about synaptic conductances in the system. As a result, a GA method was developed to refine the synaptic parameters.

The method selected for modeling the synapses describes receptor bindings to describe the dynamics of synaptic conductances [9]. The synaptic current received by the post-synaptic neuron is calculated as follows:

$$I(t) = g \cdot r(t) \cdot (V_{\text{post}}(t) - E_{\text{syn}})$$

where g is the synaptic conductance, $V_{\text{post}}(t)$ the postsynaptic potential, E_{syn} the synaptic reversal potential and $r(t)$, the ratio of bound chemical neurotransmitter receptors, which is given by:

$$\dot{r} = \begin{cases} \alpha[T](1-r) - \beta r, & \text{if } t \leq t_{max} \\ -\beta r, & \text{otherwise} \end{cases}$$

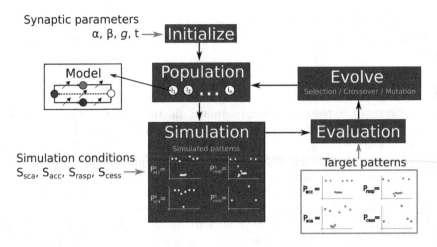

Fig. 2. Schematic representation of the GA fitting process. Iterations continue until 100 generations are reached.

where α and β are the forward and backward rate constants for transmitter binding and $[T]$ is the neurotransmitter concentration. As $[T]$ is described as a pulse in this model, it is maximum while $t \leq t_{max}$ and, when $t > t_{max}$, $[T] = 0$.

According to the insight gained from the manual fitting process, a set of synaptic parameters controlling the time evolution of the conductance were selected for being evolved. Four parameters of each of the synapses were modified: (i) α, forward rate constant (chemical neurotransmitter binding); (ii) β, backward rate constant (chemical neurotransmitter unbinding); (iii) g, synaptic conductance; (iv) t_{max}, maximum release time. Validity ranges for each parameter were limited by different percentages (5%, 20% and 50%) relative to its initial value, set from the hand-tuned model.

2.1   Genetic Algorithms

Different kind of GAs and operators were tested: a simple GA (SGA) [13] and a steady-state GA (SSGA) [7]. Individuals in both GAs were different sets of parameters and each parameter was represented by a real value. In both SGA and SSGA, the initial population was formed by clones of the initial hand-tuned model, provided as an input.

In SGA, each generation created an entirely new population of individuals. First, it selected individuals from the previous population, by elitism (best fitting individual remained unchanged between generations) and roulette wheel selection (the fitness value of each individual determined its probability for being selected). Selected individuals were crossed to produce individuals for the new population. This process continued for 100 generations.

In SSGA, the initial population was created in the same way. Nevertheless, in each generation, a temporary population was created and added to the previous

population. Then, individuals were ranked and the worst of them were removed
to return the population to its original size, with a 10% overlap between generations.

2.2   Evaluation Function

Each individual I in the population contained different synaptic parameter values for the model. I was formed by a set of 20 parameter values, the ones
indicated above $(\alpha, \beta, g, t_{max})$ for each synapse (Fig. 1). On each generation,
parameters of all individuals were used for building a model. Then, it was evaluated with a set of simulations (Fig. 2).

Four different simulations (S) were defined, each one corresponding to a
target SPI: acceleration (S_{acc}), scallop (S_{sca}), rasp (S_{rasp}), cessation (S_{cess}).
Each simulation S established the inputs to the network. Each I was simulated under all four simulation cases. The fitness function $(F(I))$ of the overall
individual was defined as the sum of the evaluation results under each case
$(F(I_i) = f_{acc}(I) + f_{sca}(I) + f_{rasp}(I) + f_{cess}(I))$.

The four target patterns P (acceleration, scallop, rasp and cessation) were
defined in terms of an ordered sequence of IPIs $(P = p_0, ..., p_n)$ where p_i is each
interval. For evaluating a pattern $(f_S(I)$, where S was one of the four simulations
$S_{acc}, S_{sca}, S_{rasp}, S_{cess})$, the individual I was simulated and the output of CN was
obtained in term of IPIs: $P^S(I) = p^S(I)_0, ..., p^S(I)_m$. The evaluation searched in
the output for the best fitting sequence with the target pattern. Mean squared
error (MSE) was used for the evaluation. If $m < n$ (i.e. the number of IPIs in
the simulation was smaller than those in the target pattern) the fit value was 0.
Otherwise, the fitting value was calculated as follows:

$$MSE = min_l \left(\frac{\sum_{i=0}^{n}(p_i - p^S(I)_{l+i})^2}{n} \right)$$

where $0 <= l < n - m$, is an index to search for the best fitting SPI in the
output. Then,

$$f_P(I) = \frac{100}{1 + MSE}$$

Finally, several examples of the same pattern were provided. The fitness
function compared the output of the network with all of them and selected the
optimal one (i.e. the one that minimized MSE).

2.3   Implementation

The implementation of the GA was done in C++ using the MIT library GAlib[1].
The primary goal of the implementation was efficiency. The random search performed by the GA is computationally expensive, as it generates a wide range
of individuals. Simulation of the neural model in each individual under different simulation conditions also implies a huge execution cost. Finally, an extra
computational cost is added by the evaluation function.

---

[1] http://lancet.mit.edu/ga/.

3 Results

The best hand-fitted model obtained a fitness score of 0.019 according to the evaluation function. It could not reproduce all four target patterns, so it did not meet the goal. All results of the GA largely improved this result. The best fitting model was obtained by the SSGA algorithm after 61 generations (see Table 1 and Fig. 3). The fitness score of this final model was 61.11 and reproduced all the target patterns. Both the target patterns and the simulated patterns which were obtained using the best fitting model are represented in Fig. 4. The results of the best fitting model were not equally good. While the scallop incremented the overall error, all other patterns were accurately reproduced. This constitutes a paradigmatic case, as in most examples the scallop was the pattern that contributed more to increase the MSE.

SGA and SSGA (the GAs used in the evolutionary process) produced quite different results (as it can be seen in Fig. 3). Even though SGA improved the fitness results from the initial hand-fitted model (from 1.19 to 2.28, see Table 1), SSGA lead to significantly better fitting results (up to 61.11). In addition, it produced the best fitting results in a smaller number of generations. In their best cases, SSGA obtained the best fit individual after 60 generations, while SGA did not obtain its best individual until generation 98.

According to the change percentage allowed for each parameter, results showed better fitting when a wider range of changes was allowed (see Table 1).

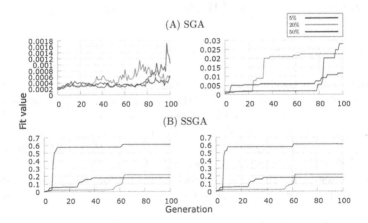

Fig. 3. (A) SGA and (B) SSGA evaluation results per generation: Average fitting value per generation (left) and best individual results per generation (right). In (B), once an individual improved the previous BFV, all generations reached that score in a few generations.

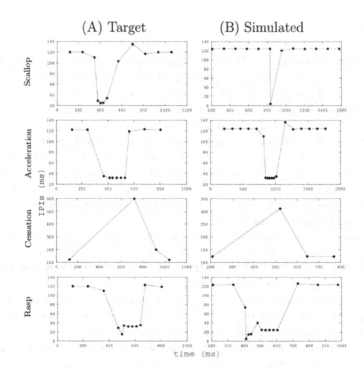

Fig. 4. Target patterns and simulation results from the best fitting individual. The fitting result for this simulation is 61.11, obtained using SSGA.

4   Discussion and Conclusions

Replicating the flexibility and adaptability of the nervous system with models is a difficult problem, especially regarding the temporal structure of the wide diversity of sequential activity observed in living systems. Hand-fitting the parameters of a neural model to produce this sequential information is difficult and time-consuming, but in some cases it is possible to manually tune the model to a specific behavior [21]. Nevertheless, when a model aims to reproduce a wider set of characteristics under the same network configuration, the problem becomes almost impossible to address manually. Genetic algorithms, as a powerful method

Table 1. Best fitting values (BFV) for each GA, and number of generations required to reach BFV (100 individuals per generation).

GA	change %	BFV	Generation	GA	change %	BFV	Generation
SGA	5%	1.19	96	SSGA	5%	17.74	37
	20%	2.23	63		20%	21.57	62
	50%	2.80	98		50%	61.11	61

for a wide variety of optimization problems, can help in the parameter adjusting process [6,22].

This work presents a GA-based approach for parameter optimization in a computational model of a biological neural network. It has been applied to develop of a model of the electromotor system of *mormyrids*, a family of pulse type weakly electric fish which constitutes a remarkable example of temporal coding in sensory-motor systems [1,16]. In our case, an initial hand-fitting gave insight about how changes in the parameter space affected the entire network. However, as the hand-fitted model failed to reproduce the target temporal patterns, the automatic adjustment method described in this paper was developed and the resulting network could effectively reproduce all targets. The resulting best fitting model largely improves the results obtained by hand-tuning and accurately reproduces the temporal structure of the patterns.

The electromotor command chain is a well-described neural network. However, most of the underlying signaling mechanisms are yet unknown. In spite of vast experimental work on electric fish, there have been very few attempts to model the networks that generate electrical signaling [21]. In part, this is because of the difficulty to reproduce the temporal patterns of neural activations observed experimentally. The network configurations produced by our evolutionary approach can be used to address the study of encoding of behavioral signals in a widely used animal model.

Acknowledgments. This work has been supported by Spanish grants MINECO (http://www.mineco.gob.es/) TIN2014-54580-R, TIN2017-84452-R, DPI2015-65833-P. Also by project PEJD-2016/TIC-2633 of the CAM (http://www.madrid.org/).

References

1. Baker, C.A., Kohashi, T., Lyons-Warren, A.M., Ma, X., Carlson, B.A.: Multiplexed temporal coding of electric communication signals in mormyrid fishes. J. Exp. Biol. **216**(Pt 13), 2365–2379 (2013)
2. Caputi, A.A., Carlson, B.A., Macadar, O.: Electric organs and their control. In: Bullock, T.H., Hopkins, C.D., Popper, A.N., Fay, R.R. (eds.) Electroreception. Springer Handbook of Auditory Research, pp. 410–451. Springer, New York (2005). https://doi.org/10.1007/0-387-28275-0_14
3. Carlson, B.A.: Neuroanatomy of the mormyrid electromotor control system. J. Comp. Neurol. **454**(4), 440–455 (2002)
4. Carlson, B.A.: Single-unit activity patterns in nuclei that control the electromotor command nucleus during spontaneous electric signal production in the mormyrid Brienomyrus brachyistius. J. Neurosci. **23**(31), 10128–10136 (2003)
5. Carlson, B.A., Hopkins, C.D.: Stereotyped temporal patterns in electrical communication. Anim. Behav. **68**(4), 867–878 (2004)
6. Cassar, I.R., Titus, N.D., Grill, W.M.: An improved genetic algorithm for designing optimal temporal patterns of neural stimulation. J. Neural Eng. **14**(6), 066013 (2017)
7. De Jong, K.A.: Analysis of the behavior of a class of genetic adaptive systems (1975)

8. Deka, R., Dutta, J.C.: Estimation of parameters using evolutionary algorithm in Hodgkin-Huxley model. In: 2016 2nd International Conference on Advances in Electrical, Electronics, Information, Communication and Bio-Informatics (AEE-ICB), pp. 219–223. IEEE (2016)
9. Destexhe, A., Mainen, Z.F., Sejnowski, T.J.: An efficient method for computing synaptic conductances based on a kinetic model of receptor binding. Neural Comput. **6**(1), 14–18 (1994)
10. Druckmann, S., Banitt, Y., Gidon, A.A., Schürmann, F., Markram, H., Segev, I.: A novel multiple objective optimization framework for constraining conductance-based neuron models by experimental data. Front. Neuroscience **1**, 1 (2007)
11. Dura-Bernal, S., Neymotin, S., Kerr, C., Sivagnanam, S., Majumdar, A., Francis, J., Lytton, W.: Evolutionary algorithm optimization of biological learning parameters in a biomimetic neuroprosthesis. IBM J. Res. Dev. **61**(2/3), 6-1 (2017)
12. Forlim, C.G., Pinto, R.D., Varona, P., Rodriguez, F.B.: Delay-dependent response in weakly electric fish under closed-loop pulse stimulation, **10**(10) (2015)
13. Goldberg, D.E.: Genetic Algorithms in Search, Optimization and Machine Learning, 1st edn. Addison-Wesley Longman Publishing Co., Inc., Boston (1989)
14. Holland, J.H.: Adaptation in Natural and Artificial Systems: An Introductory Analysis with Applications to Biology, Control, and Artificial Intelligence. MIT press (1992)
15. Kamimura, A., Kurokawa, H., Yoshida, E., Murata, S., Tomita, K., Kokaji, S.: Automatic locomotion design and experiments for a modular robotic system. IEEE/ASME Trans. Mechatron. **10**(3), 314–325 (2005)
16. Lareo, A., Forlim, C.G., Pinto, R.D., Varona, P., Rodriguez, F.: Temporal code-driven stimulation: definition and application to electric fish signaling. Front. Neuroinformatics **10**, 41 (2016)
17. Lareo, Á., Forlim, C.G., Pinto, R.D., Varona, P., Rodríguez, F.B.: Analysis of electroreception with temporal code-driven stimulation. In: Rojas, I., Joya, G., Catala, A. (eds.) IWANN 2017. LNCS, vol. 10305, pp. 101–111. Springer, Cham (2017). https://doi.org/10.1007/978-3-319-59153-7_9
18. Lareo, A., Rodriguez, F.B.: Sequential information processing in electroreception: a modelling approach. In: Dynamic Days in Latin America and the Caribbean, Puebla, México (2016)
19. Leung, F.H.F., Lam, H.K., Ling, S.H., Tam, P.K.S.: Tuning of the structure and parameters of a neural network using an improved genetic algorithm. IEEE Trans. Neural Netw. **14**(1), 79–88 (2003)
20. Menon, V., Spruston, N., Kath, W.L.: A state-mutating genetic algorithm to design ion-channel models. Proc. Natl. Acad. Sci. **106**(39), 16829–16834 (2009)
21. Moortgat, K.T., Bullock, T.H., Sejnowski, T.J.: Gap junction effects on precision and frequency of a model pacemaker network. J. Neurophysiol. **83**(2), 984–997 (2000)
22. Russell, A., Orchard, G., Etienne-Cummings, R.: Configuring of spiking central pattern generator networks for bipedal walking using genetic algorithms. In: IEEE International Symposium on Circuits and Systems, ISCAS 2007, pp. 1525–1528. IEEE (2007)
23. Silva, P., Santos, C.P., Matos, V., Costa, L.: Automatic generation of biped locomotion controllers using genetic programming. Robot. Auton. Syst. **62**(10), 1531–1548 (2014)
24. Van Geit, W., De Schutter, E., Achard, P.: Automated neuron model optimization techniques: a review. Biol. Cybern. **99**(4–5), 241–251 (2008)

An Overview of Frank-Wolfe Optimization for Stochasticity Constrained Interpretable Matrix and Tensor Factorization

Rafet Sifa[1,2,3]([envelope])

[1] Fraunhofer Center for Machine Learning, Sankt Augustin, Germany
[2] Fraunhofer IAIS, Sankt Augustin, Germany
Rafet.Sifa@iais.fraunhofer.de
[3] University of Bonn, Bonn, Germany

Abstract. In this paper we give an overview about utilizing Frank Wolfe optimization to find interpretable constrained matrix and tensor factorizations. We will particularly concentrate on imposing stochasticity constraints and show how factors of Archetypal Analysis as well as Decomposition Into Directed Components can be found using Frank Wolfe optimization to respectively decompose bipartite matrices and asymmetric similarity tensors. We will show how the derived algorithms perform by presenting case studies from behavioral profiling in digital games.

1 Introduction

As popular representation learning tools, matrix and tensor factorization methods have been widely used for variety of descriptive, predictive and prescriptive machine learning applications including user profiling [1,12,13], behavior prediction [15], natural language processing [4,11] and recommender systems [10,16,17]. The main idea behind matrix and tensor factorization methods is to decompose data matrices or tensors into combinations of low-rank matrices that are usually found by minimizing a predefined objective function for assessing the reconstruction quality.

When they are used as descriptive features, the resulting factors are usually expected to be interpretable to human experts. A popular choice of assuring interpretability of the resulting factors is to constrain them to possess a certain set of characteristics [11,14,15,17]. Among the numerous possibilities for such constraints, enforcing stochasticity not only allows for interpreting the factors as probabilities but also, due to particular mathematical properties of the solution space, provides a way to find optimal factors without requiring any projections [2,14]. Our main focus in this paper is to review Frank-Wolfe Optimization algorithm [6,8] to come up with stochasticity constrained matrix and tensor factorizations. To this end, we will give an overview of the optimization procedure and show its applicability to find factors of Archetypal Analysis [5],

© Springer Nature Switzerland AG 2018
V. Kůrková et al. (Eds.): ICANN 2018, LNCS 11140, pp. 369–379, 2018.
https://doi.org/10.1007/978-3-030-01421-6_36

which is a two factor matrix factorization model to represent the factorized data-points as convex combinations of artificially created extremal datapoints (called *archetypes*) that are as well defined to be convex combinations of selected data-points. In addition, we extend our previous work in [14] to factorize asymmetric similarity tensors by deriving a new algorithm to find stochasticity constrained Decomposition into Directed Components (DEDICOM) factors [7]. So as to better understand the outcomes of the studied algorithms, we will present two case studies covering behavioral profiling [13] from a digital game, where our focus will be mainly on the interpretability of the resulting factors.

2   Frank Wolfe Optimization on Standard Simplices

For matrix and tensor factorization, imposing stochasticity constraints to factors is usually tantamount to obtaining column (and/or row) stochastic matrices. Formally, an arbitrary factor vector $\mathbf{h} \in \mathbb{R}^p$ is stochastic (or stochasticity constrained) when all of its elements are nonnegative and its $l1$-norm is 1, which is equivalent to state that $h_i \geq 0 \; \forall \, i \in [1, 2, \ldots, p]$ and $\mathbf{h}^T \mathbf{1} = 1$. Following these properties, we note that stochastic vectors in $\mathbb{R}^p$ reside in the standard simplex Δ^{p-1}, which is the convex hull of the standard basis vectors of $\mathbb{R}^p$. That is, we define the standard simplex Δ^{p-1} as

$$\Delta^{p-1} = \Big\{ \sum_{i=1}^{p} \beta_i \mathbf{v}_i \mid \sum_{i=1}^{p} \beta_i = 1 \wedge \beta_j \geq 0 \; \forall \, j \in [1, 2, \ldots, p] \Big\}, \tag{1}$$

where $\mathcal{V} = \{ \mathbf{v}_1, \mathbf{v}_2, \ldots, \mathbf{v}_p | \mathbf{v}_i = [\delta_{i1}, \delta_{i2}, \ldots, \delta_{ip}]^T \}$ is the set of standard basis vectors and δ_{ij} represents the Kronocker delta. Considering that we assess the quality of the data representation through the resulting factors using a differentiable and continuous convex function, Frank-Wolfe optimization allows us to efficiently find proper factors minimizing our objective function by performing the optimization process in the standard simplex [2,3,14]. As an iterative optimization method, Frank-Wolfe algorithm aims to minimize differentiable convex functions by linear approximation over their predefined compact convex domains till achieving provable ϵ-convergence [6,8] (for its neural network implementation we refer to [3]). Namely, Frank-Wolfe algorithm aims to solve

$$\min_{\mathbf{x} \in \mathcal{S}} \; f(\mathbf{x}) \tag{2}$$

for a differentiable convex function $f : \mathcal{S} \to \mathbb{R}$ and a compact convex set $\mathcal{S}$, by iteratively solving for

$$\mathbf{s}_t = \min_{\mathbf{s} \in \mathcal{S}} \; \mathbf{s}^T \nabla f(\mathbf{x}_t), \tag{3}$$

where $\nabla f(\mathbf{x}_t)$ is the gradient of the optimized function f evaluated at the current solution $\mathbf{x}_t$. We then consider the subgradient updates with a monotonically decreasing learning rate $\alpha_t \in [0, \ldots, 1]$ as

$$\mathbf{x}_{t+1} = \mathbf{x}_t + \alpha_t(\mathbf{s}_t - \mathbf{x}_t). \tag{4}$$

It is worth mentioning that, the update in (4) for the case of stochasticity constraints amounts to choosing a standard basis vector minimizing (3) due to the
equivalence $\mathcal{S} = \mathcal{V}$ [2,14].

3   Archetypal Analysis: Representing Data with Extremes

As our first application of this work, we will now present a Frank-Wolfe algorithm
from [2] to find factors of Archetypal Analysis [5] and show a case study on
user profiling from game analytics [12,13]. The main idea behind archetypal
data representations is to first find a set of prototypical extreme data points,
called *archetypes*, that encapsulate the entire dataset as well as possible to later
represent every data point as a convex combination of the archetypes [2,5,13].
Such data representations have numerous advantages when used for descriptive
analytics applications such as behavior profiling, as they not only allow us to
compare extreme behavior in terms of variety but also allow us to obtain compact
data representations that are easily interpretable and can also be used as features
in more advanced applications such as behavior prediction [12,13,16]. Formally,
given a column data matrix $\boldsymbol{X} \in \mathbb{R}^{m \times n}$, Archetypal Analysis factorizes it as
$\boldsymbol{X} \approx \boldsymbol{Z}\boldsymbol{H}^T = \boldsymbol{X}\boldsymbol{B}\boldsymbol{H}^T$, where the column matrix $\boldsymbol{Z} \in \mathbb{R}^{m \times k}$ contains the k
archetypes, $\boldsymbol{H} \in \mathbb{R}^{n \times k}$ contains the *row stochastic* coefficient vectors and finally
$\boldsymbol{B} \in \mathbb{R}^{n \times k}$ contains *column stochastic* data mixing coefficients to *construct* the
archetypes as convex mixtures of data points in $\boldsymbol{X}$.

Finding appropriate archetypes can be formulated as solving a constrained
optimization problem to minimize the residual sum of squares as

$$\min_{\boldsymbol{B},\boldsymbol{H}} E(\boldsymbol{B},\boldsymbol{H}) = \left\| \boldsymbol{X} - \boldsymbol{X}\boldsymbol{B}\boldsymbol{H}^T \right\|^2 \tag{5}$$

with the following constraints

$$b_{ij} \geq 0 \ \wedge \ \sum_{i=1}^{n} b_{ij} = 1 \ \wedge \ h_{ij} \geq 0 \ \wedge \ \sum_{j=1}^{k} h_{ij} = 1. \tag{6}$$

Due to not being convex on the optimized factors, algorithms to optimize (5)
usually follow an alternating least squares (ALS) scheme, where the objective
function is iteratively optimized while updating each factor independently and
keeping the other factors fixed (see [2,14,17] for examples).

Taking a look at the optimization setting for finding archetypal representations, note that the minimized objective in (5) is a convex function and owing
to the stochasticity constraints imposed in (6), columns of $\boldsymbol{B}$ and rows of $\boldsymbol{H}$
live in the standard simplices Δ^{n-1} and Δ^{k-1} respectively. In the light of this,
we can now derive a Frank-Wolfe based *projection-free* ALS algorithm to find
respectively optimal row and column stochastic archetypal factor matrices $\boldsymbol{H}$
and $\boldsymbol{B}$. Starting with feasible random solutions or with one of the vertices of
the corresponding simplices for $\boldsymbol{H}$ and $\boldsymbol{B}$, we iteratively update the rows and
columns of $\boldsymbol{H}$ and $\boldsymbol{B}$ as in (4), where at each iteration the Frank-Wolfe updates

Randomly initialize $\boldsymbol{H}$ and $\boldsymbol{B}$ to be respectively row and column stochastic
Let $\mathcal{V}^q = \{\mathbf{v}_1^q, \mathbf{v}_2^q, \ldots, \mathbf{v}_n^q | \mathbf{v}_i^q = [\delta_{i1}, \delta_{i2}, \ldots, \delta_{iq}]^T\}$
Let T_H and T_B be the maximum number of local iterations for resp. $\boldsymbol{H}$ and $\boldsymbol{B}$
while *Stopping condition is not satisfied* **do**
    while $t_H \neq T_H$ *and updates of* $\boldsymbol{H}$ *are not small* **do**
        $G = \frac{\partial E(H)}{\partial H} = 2\left(HB^T X^T X B - X^T X B\right)$
        $\alpha_H \leftarrow 2/(t_H + 2)$
        for $b \in \{1, \ldots, n\}$ **do**
            $j = \underset{l}{\operatorname{argmin}}\, g_{bl}$
            $\mathbf{h}_{b:} \leftarrow \mathbf{h}_{b:} + \alpha_H\left(\mathbf{v}_j^k - \mathbf{h}_{b:}\right)$
        $t_H \leftarrow t_H + 1$
    while $t_B \neq T_B$ *and updates of* $\boldsymbol{B}$ *are not small* **do**
        $O = \frac{\partial E(B)}{\partial B} = 2\left(X^T X B H^T H - X^T X H\right)$
        $\alpha_B \leftarrow 2/(t_B + 2)$
        for $c \in \{1, \ldots, k\}$ **do**
            $i = \underset{l}{\operatorname{argmin}}\, o_{lc}$
            $\mathbf{b}_c \leftarrow \mathbf{b}_c + \alpha_B\left(\mathbf{v}_i^n - \mathbf{b}_c\right)$
        $t_B \leftarrow t_B + 1$

Algorithm 1. A Frank-Wolfe based *projection-free* ALS algorithm with monotonically decreasing learning rates for Archetypal Analysis. The algorithm iteratively update to find respectively the row and column stochastic archetypal factor matrices $\boldsymbol{H}$ and $\boldsymbol{B}$.

move the considered factors into the direction of selected standard basis vectors till convergence is achieved. To this end, we calculate the gradient matrix $G = \frac{\partial E(H)}{\partial H} = 2\left(HB^T X^T X B - X^T X B\right)$ and define updates for each bth row of $\boldsymbol{H}$ (denoted as $\mathbf{h}_{b:}$) by first finding the minimizer simplex vertex j as $j = \underset{l}{\operatorname{argmin}}\, g_{bl}$, where g_{bl} corresponds to the lth element of the bth row of $\boldsymbol{G}$. After that we move the current solution $\mathbf{h}_{b:}$ in the direction of the corresponding jth standard basis as $\mathbf{h}_{b:} \leftarrow \mathbf{h}_{b:} + \alpha_H\left(\mathbf{v}_j^k - \mathbf{h}_{b:}\right)$, where α_H is the learning rate for updating the rows of $\boldsymbol{H}$ and $\mathbf{v}_i^q = [\delta_{i1}, \delta_{i2}, \ldots, \delta_{iq}]^T$ is the corresponding basis vector defined as $\mathbf{v}_j^k$. These are repeated until the number of iterations hit the maximum number of iterations T_H or updates of rows of $\boldsymbol{H}$ become relatively small. Similarly, an update rule for columns of $\boldsymbol{B}$ can be defined by first calculating the gradient matrix $O = \frac{\partial E(B)}{\partial B} = 2\left(X^T X B H^T H - X^T X H\right)$ and then finding the minimizer simplex vertex $i = \underset{l}{\operatorname{argmin}}\, o_{lc}$ and defining an update for each cth column of $\boldsymbol{B}$ as $\mathbf{b}_c \leftarrow \mathbf{b}_c + \alpha_B\left(\mathbf{v}_i^n - \mathbf{b}_c\right)$, where $\mathbf{v}_i^n$ ith is the basis vector in $\mathbb{R}^n$ and α_B is the learning rate to assure convexity and convergence. In Algorithm 1 we summarize the steps for finding optimal $\boldsymbol{H}$ and $\boldsymbol{B}$ with a Frank-Wolfe algorithm.

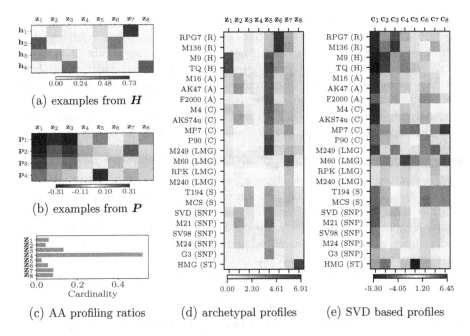

(a) examples from H

(b) examples from P

(c) AA profiling ratios

(d) archetypal profiles

(e) SVD based profiles

Fig. 1. Profiling players with respect to their weapon proficiency by means of Archetypal Analysis using Frank Wolfe algorithm and unconstrained matrix factorization for $k = 8$. (a, b) illustrate mixing coefficients from (the same) example players, that are resp. extracted from Archetypal Analysis and SVD. (c) shows the hard clustering assignments as a result of maximizing the probability of the archetypal coefficients. Turning our attention to the basis matrices, (d) illustrates the basis matrix that is calculated as the convex combination of selected data points (i.e. $Z = XB$), whereas (e) shows the profiles generated by factorizing the data matrix without constraints.

To illustrate the use of Archetypal Analysis for user profiling in games, we used the item-proficiency dataset from [13], which contains score-per-minute (SpM) values of 23 weapons of a first person shooter game for more than 23,000 players. The analyzed game offers its player three different solider roles: special ops, rifleman and sniper, whereas, eight different weapon categories which include (with their abbreviations) rocket launchers (R), handguns (H), assault (A) and carbine (C) rifles, light machine guns (LMG), shotguns (S), snipers (SNP) and a stationary weapon (ST). In Fig. 1 we illustrate how Archetypal Analysis can be used for profiling by decomposing the weapon-player matrix using our Frank-Wolfe based algorithm from Algorithm 1 for $k = 8$ and compare the profiles to the ones obtained from factorizing the data matrix without constrains as $X = CP^T$. To this end we considered the popular refactorization of Singular Value Decomposition (SVD) factors to obtain two factor decompositions [9,16,17] by considering the SVD of the data matrix as $X = U\Sigma V^T = U\Sigma^{\frac{1}{2}}\Sigma^{\frac{1}{2}}V^T$ to obtain $C = U\Sigma^{\frac{1}{2}}$ and $P = V\Sigma^{\frac{1}{2}}$, where U and V are the basis matrices whereas the diagonal Σ contains the sorted nonnegative singular values. Compared to the archetypal factors in Fig. 1(a, d), the unconstrained factors in Fig. 1(b, e) contain negative values (although the factorized data is nonnegative) and hence the results are very difficult to interpret. Whereas, the resulting profiles extracted from archetypal factors show extreme (w.r.t behavior) yet interpretable player like profiles summarizing the main behavior of the analyzed dataset (see also examples from [13]).

Analyzing the resulting profiles from Fig. 1(d), represented by z_5 and z_7, we note the presence of the typical *elite* behavior [13] with high SpM values overall except the light machine guns and, for the latter, the stationary gun. This is followed by the *newbie* behavior with very low weapon performance values that is represented by the archetype z_4. Dissecting the rest of the profiles, we observe *specialized* players that perform well with one or a group of weapons, which (similar to the results from [13]) are primarily based on expertise in particular weapon types. That is, z_1 represents players with very high hand gun performance, z_2 represents specialized players with the basic character weapons, z_3 represents shotgun experts, z_6 represents players with extremely high rocket launcher performance and z_8 has overall good results with very high stationary weapon performance.

Another key advantage of Archetypal Analysis for such descriptive analytics tasks is soft clustering [5,11–13], which can be performed by analyzing the stochastic mixing coefficients in H and turned into hard clustering by probability maximization or sampling (see results from the former in Fig. 1(c)). To illustrate this, we compare the mixing coefficients from Archetypal Analysis and SVD for four different players respectively in Fig. 1(a) and (b). Dissecting the results from Fig. 1(a), we note that the stochastic coefficients for the first player (represented by $h_{1:}$) show that they belong to the elite class due to the high belongingness values to z_5 and z_7. Following that, the second and the third players share common characteristics with respect to having high belongingness values for profiles z_1 and z_6 indicating proficiency in hand guns and rocket launchers. In addition, with high belongingness value to z_2, the third player is good at using the assault and carbine weapons. Finally, with high belongingness values to z_3 and z_8, the fourth player is proficient in using shotguns and the stationary weapon HMG. As for the profiles, coefficients from SVD are difficult to interpret since they contain negative entries.

4   DEDICOM: Factorizing Similarity Tensors

In some analytics applications the analyzed data matrices might inherently have special structures such as for the case of similarity matrices, where each entry in such a matrix encodes pairwise similarities between a predefined set of entities. Additionally, considering the involvement of another dimension into the analysis such as time [1] or predefined categories [15], a collection of matrices, that share the same characteristics with respect to the entities they are representing, is known to form a tensor [1,9,15]. In this section, we will study how we can factorize similarity tensors that are asymmetric by nature. Since asymmetric square tensors cover their symmetric counterparts, the method we propose here can be used to analyze symmetric similarity tensors as well. We will base our method on factorizing similarity tensors into combinations of low rank matrices by means of Decomposition into Directed Components (DEDICOM) [7] and extend the Frank Wolfe algorithm introduced in [14] to factorize tensors in an interpretable fashion.

Formally, we group a set of d asymmetric similarity matrices (a.k.a *slices*) $\{S_1, S_2, ..., S_d\}$ in a three dimensional array (or a *third order tensor*) $\mathcal{S} \in \mathbb{R}^{n \times n \times d}$ where s_{ijp} defines the directional relation between ith and jth entity in the pth slice (which we denote as $S_p \in \mathbb{R}^{n \times n}$). Namely given a tensor $\mathcal{S}$, Tensor-DEDICOM partitioning is defined as $S_p \approx A R_p A^T \ \forall \ p \in [1, 2, \ldots, d]$, where $A \in \mathbb{R}^{n \times k}$ is the global loading matrix containing the latent factors and $R_p \in \mathbb{R}^{k \times k}$(the pth slice of $\mathcal{R} \in \mathbb{R}^{k \times k \times d}$) is an affinity matrix describing the asymmetric relationships between the structures in columns of A. In this work we will consider the stochasticity constrained nonnegative (STNN) DEDICOM factorization from [14] by incorporating stochasticity constraints to the columns of A, while having nonnegative affinities in R. This becomes especially useful when we are dealing with data sets with only non-negative values for which the resulting affinity matrices will be equivalent to their compressed versions encoding the importance of relations between structures defined in the columns of A. In this case an arbitrary loading value a_{ij} encodes how much element i contributes to (or belongs to) structure j.

Turning our attention to finding proper factors, we note that similar to Archetypal Analysis, finding a three way DEDICOM partitioning can be cast as a norm minimization problem for the loading matrix A and tensor of affinities $\mathcal{R}$ as

$$\min_{A, \mathcal{R}} G(A, \mathcal{R}) = \sum_{p=1}^{d} \left\| S_p - A R_p A^T \right\|^2. \tag{7}$$

Following an alternating least squares scheme we can minimize (7) for A and each slice of $\mathcal{R}$ by keeping the rest of the factors constant. It is important to note that, yet unlike (5), our loss function in (7) is convex in any slice of $\mathcal{R}$ but not in A, which typically requires approximate solutions for A [1, 14, 15] while keeping ALS updates for each slice of $\mathcal{R}$.

Since each affinity matrix is updated independently from each other, at each ALS step, we find optimal non-negative slices of $\mathcal{R}$ by solving a nonnegative least squares problem for $G(R_p) = \left\| \text{vec}(S_p) - (A \otimes A) \text{vec}(R_p) \right\|^2$ [14, 15], such that $r_{ijp} \geq 0 \ \forall \ p \in [1, 2, ..., d] \wedge i, j \in [1, 2, ..., k]$.

Similar to our previous derivation, we can generalize the STNN algorithm for DEDICOM [14] to find stochasticity constrained basis matrix A by evaluating the partial derivative of the objective function $\frac{\partial G(A)}{\partial A}$ in (7). To this end, we start by considering the trace representation of the error function in (7) and

Randomly initialize A with stochastic columns and R with nonnegative entries
Let $\mathcal{V} = \{\mathbf{v}_1, \mathbf{v}_2, \ldots, \mathbf{v}_n | \mathbf{v}_i = [\delta_{i1}, \delta_{i2}, \ldots, \delta_{in}]^T\}$
while *Stopping condition is not satisfied* **do**
    while $t \neq t_{max}$ *and updates of A are not small* **do**

$$W = \frac{\partial G(A)}{\partial A} = 2\sum_{p=1}^{d} \left(AR_p^T A^T AR_p + AR_p A^T AR_p^T - S_p^T AR_p - SAR_p^T\right)$$

        $\alpha \leftarrow 2/(t+2)$
        for $b \in \{1, \ldots, k\}$ **do**
            $i = \underset{l}{\text{argmin}}\ w_{lb}$
            $\mathbf{a}_b \leftarrow \mathbf{a}_b + \alpha(\mathbf{v}_i - \mathbf{a}_b)$
        $t \leftarrow t + 1$

    for $p \in [1, 2, ..., d]$ **do**
        $R_p \leftarrow \underset{R_p}{\text{argmin}}\ \left\|\text{vec}(S_p) - (A \otimes A)\text{vec}(R_p)\right\|^2$ for $r_{ijp} \geq 0\ \forall\ i, j, p$

Algorithm 2. A Frank-Wolfe based ALS algorithm to find Tensor DEDI-COM factorizations constraining the columns of the loading matrix A to be column stochastic and the affinity tensor $\mathcal{R}$ to be nonnegative.

eliminating the factors that are independent of A to obtain the gradient matrix for the tensor representation [14,15] as

$$\frac{\partial G(A)}{\partial A} = 2\sum_{p=1}^{d} \left(AR_p^T A^T AR_p + AR_p A^T AR_p^T - S_p^T AR_p - SAR_p^T\right), \quad (8)$$

which, can be used to define a set of Frank Wolfe updates for each column of A to come up with Tensor DEDICOM partitioning with column stochastic A. In Algorithm 2 we summarize the necessary steps to find Stochastic Nonnegative DEDICOM factors.

In order to understand how Tensor DEDICOM partitioning works in practice, we will now present a new case study on analyzing asymmetric relationships between weapons of the same dataset as above based on grouping the players with respect to the total playtime they spent in the game. To this end, we first split the players based on whether they have played more or less than the average playtime (133 hours). This split has created two groups forming a 76.5% to 23.5% split of the analyzed players, whose playtime was respectively below and above the average. We will refer to these groups as regular and long-term players respectively. After splitting the players into two groups, using the method from [14], we constructed a bipartite indicator matrix and created a directional square weapon similarity matrix S for each group. In this case, s_{ij} indicates the empirical conditional probability value of proficiency in weapon j given the proficiency in weapon i. Following that, we constructed a tensor $\mathcal{S}$ with two *slices* containing the weapon similarities for the regular and long-term players and factorized it using our tensor DEDICOM algorithm with $k = 3$.

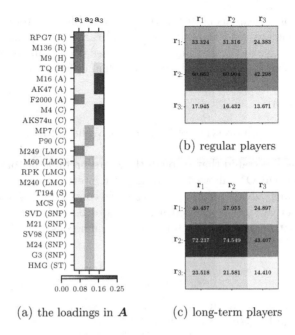

(a) the loadings in A

(b) regular players

(c) long-term players

Fig. 2. The resulting Tensor DEDICOM factors from factorizing the asymmetric weapon association tensor by means of our stochasticity constrained nonnegative (STNN) DEDICOM. (a) shows the loading matrix A that is column stochastic and (b) and (c) show the resulting nonnegative affinity matrices for respectively the regular and long-term players.

Analyzing the resulting factors in Fig. 2, we observe three different weapon-type based separations. Loading matrix of our STNN DEDICOM partitioning in Fig. 2(a) shows that the active weapons for the first mode are primarily the secondary weapons, elite assault weapons and the light machine gun M249, the third mode's active weapons are the *basic* assault and carbine weapons and finally the second mode covers the remaining ones (the elite carbine weapons, light machine guns, snipers, T194 and the stationary weapon HMG).

Comparing the affinities of our regular and long-term players (see respectively Fig. 2(b) and (c)), we note similarities between relative relationships of particular affinities. For instance the self affinities of the first and the second mode are the highest, whereas, the third mode has the lowest self affinity for both of the player groups. Yet the higher self affinity in the first mode indicates that long-term players, for instance, that handle rocket launchers or handguns are also better at using the elite assault weapon F2000 and the light machine gun M249. Relationships among elite carbine weapons, light machine guns, the T194, snipers and the stationary weapons is the highest affinity for both of the player groups, yet, the affinity towards the first mode is higher for long-term players. Analyzing the affinities corresponding to the third mode (i.e. values of $r_{3:}$ in Fig. 2(b) and (c)), we note that with higher self affinity the long-term players handle basic assault and carbine weapons better than the regular players. Additionally, long-term players that are good at basic assault and carbine weapons are better at using weapons active in the first and second modes (we usually observe 30–40% difference in probability when analyzing individual differences).

5 Conclusion

In this work we gave an overview of using Frank Wolfe optimization to come up with stochasticity constrained matrix and tensor factorizations. Our case studies on user profiling illustrated that through their interpretable factors, Archetypal Analysis and DEDICOM allowed us to discover interesting insights about the behavior of the analyzed population. With a given convex differentiable objective function, the derivations we showed here can also be easily utilized to obtain interpretable matrix and tensor factorizations of numerous kinds, such as, CUR, PARAFAC, and INDSCAL [9,15].

References

1. Bader, B., Harshman, R., Kolda, T.: Temporal analysis of semantic graphs using ASALSAN. In: Proceedings of IEEE ICDM (2007)
2. Bauckhage, C., Kersting, K., Hoppe, F., Thurau, C.: Archetypal analysis as an Autoencoder. In: Proceedings of Workshop New Challenges in Neural Computation (2015)
3. Bauckhage, C.: A neural network implementation of Frank-Wolfe optimization. In: Lintas, A., Rovetta, S., Verschure, P.F.M.J., Villa, A.E.P. (eds.) ICANN 2017. LNCS, vol. 10613, pp. 219–226. Springer, Cham (2017). https://doi.org/10.1007/978-3-319-68600-4_26
4. Chew, P.A., Bader, B.W., Rozovskaya, A.: Using DEDICOM for completely unsupervised part-of-speech tagging. In: Proceedings of Workshop on Unsupervised and Minimally Supervised Learning of Lexical Semantics (2009)
5. Cutler, A., Breiman, L.: Archetypal analysis. Technometrics 36(4), 338–347 (1994)
6. Frank, M., Wolfe, P.: An algorithm for quadratic programming. Nav. Res. Logist. Q. 3(1–2), 95–110 (1956)
7. Harshman, R.: Models for analysis of asymmetrical relationships among N objects or stimuli. In: Proceedings of Joint Meeting of the Psychometric Society and the Society for Mathematical Psychology (1978)
8. Jaggi, M.: Revisiting Frank-Wolfe: projection-free sparse convex optimization. In: Proceedings of ACM ICML (2013)
9. Kolda, T.G., Bader, B.W.: Tensor decompositions and applications. SIAM Rev. 51(3), 455–500 (2009)
10. Koren, Y., Bell, R., Volinsky, C.: Matrix factorization techniques for recommender systems. Computer 42(8), 30–37 (2009)
11. Morup, M., Hansen, L.: Archetypal analysis for machine learning and data mining. Neurocomputing 80, 54–63 (2012)
12. Rattinger, A., Wallner, G., Drachen, A., Pirker, J., Sifa, R.: Integrating and inspecting combined behavioral profiling and social network models in *Destiny*. In: Wallner, G., Kriglstein, S., Hlavacs, H., Malaka, R., Lugmayr, A., Yang, H.-S. (eds.) ICEC 2016. LNCS, vol. 9926, pp. 77–89. Springer, Cham (2016). https://doi.org/10.1007/978-3-319-46100-7_7

13. Sifa, R., Bauckhage, C.: Online k-maxoids clustering. In: Proceedings of IEEE DSAA (2017)
14. Sifa, R., Ojeda, C., Cvejoski, K., Bauckhage, C.: Interpretable matrix factorization with stochasticity constrained nonnegative DEDICOM. In: Proceedings of KDML-LWDA (2017)
15. Sifa, R., Srikanth, S., Drachen, A., Ojeda, C., Bauckhage, C.: Predicting retention in sandbox games with tensor factorization-based representation learning. In: Proceedings of IEEE CIG (2016)
16. Sifa, R., Bauckhage, C., Drachen, A.: Archetypal game recommender systems. In: Proceedings of KDML-LWA (2014)
17. Takács, G., Piltászy, I., Németh, B., Tikk, D.: Scalable collaborative filtering approaches for large recommender systems. JMLR **10**, 623–656 (2009)

Computational Neuroscience

A Bio-Feasible Computational Circuit for Neural Activities Persisting and Decaying

Dai Dawei, Weihui$^{(\boxtimes)}$, and Su Zihao

Laboratory of Cognitive Model and Algorithms,
Department of Computer Science, Shanghai Key Laboratory of Data Science,
Fudan University, Shanghai, China
weihui@fudan.edu.cn

Abstract. The neurophysiological view considers the working memory (WM) as a persistence of neural information in the cerebral cortex [1], that external stimulation will activate some pyramidal cells and their continuous activation after stimulus being removed indicates the memory of stimulus, but with the fading of activities, memory will be gradually decaying. More and more studies [2] have shown that the mechanism of neural activities persisting and decaying is not only related to the structure of neural circuits, but also closely related to the synaptic mechanisms. In this paper, we design the neural computational circuit of persistence of neural activities by combining the synaptic mechanism and the structure of neural circuit. Firstly, in the aspect of circuit structure, the recurrent circuit of pyramidal neurons was used as the main circuit to achieve the persistence, and then an auxiliary circuit was designed to regulate the firing rate of main circuit to achieve the "decaying" of neural activities; Secondly, in the computational circuit, we consider the mechanism of synaptic depression and slow synapse. From the structure of neural circuits and synaptic mechanism, we try to explore the neural computational mechanism of neural information persisting and decaying over the time, which is beneficial to explore the true neural mechanism of WM.

Keywords: Synaptic depression · Slow synapse · Neural circuit

1 Introduction

In cognitive behavior, WM is considered instantaneous processing and storage of finite information. The previous studies [3] have shown that WM plays an important role in advanced cognitive behaviors. The neurophysiological view considers WM a persistence of the neural information in the brain. External stimulation can activate some pyramidal cells. Their continued activation of pyramidal cells after the stimulus being revoked indicates the memory of the stimulus. Understanding the working mechanism of the persisting and decaying of neural activities is crucial to interpret the WM. At present, two main types of neural structure have been used widely to achieve the persistence function: (1) recurrent connections [4, 5], and (2) random connections

© Springer Nature Switzerland AG 2018
V. Kůrková et al. (Eds.): ICANN 2018, LNCS 11140, pp. 383–392, 2018.
https://doi.org/10.1007/978-3-030-01421-6_37

(a type of loop structure) [1]. The advantage of the first structure is that only a small number of neurons (dozens, hundreds) are needed to achieve persistence of neural information and it has an anatomical basis [6]. For the second, which uses random connections between pyramidal neurons, the basic principle for maintaining information is that there must be many loops. Since, activation of one neuron requires synchronous and continuous stimulation by multiple neurons. Therefore, each neuron must participate in formation of multiple loop circuits. Thus, this type of circuit requires a large number of neurons to achieve persistent function.

The ability of a neural circuit to achieve a specific function depends not only on its structure, but also on complex electrophysiological functions. Neural circuits are the basic functional units of the nervous system, and a neuron is the smallest component of a neural circuit, and neurons form different neural circuits by establishing different synaptic connections with each other. A synapse is a functional connection between neurons and a key part of information transmission. Therefore, properties of synapses inevitably affect functional performance of neural circuits [2, 7].

In this paper, first, we used recurrent connections as the main circuit to achieve persistence of neural information based on the spike neuron model, and an auxiliary neural circuit was designed to regulate firing rate of the main circuit. Second, we considered the computational mechanisms of synaptic depression and slow synapses in the model. Results show that the neural computational model can achieve the functional of persisting and decaying of neural activities.

2   Biological Neuron and Synapse

2.1   Neuron Model

Artificial neural network models had achieved great success in both numerical optimization and behavior modeling. Although, ANN model can replicate the macro behavior, which is not suite to model and interpret the neural mechanism of behaviors [8, 9]. A simple spiking neuron model [10] that reduces the HH model to a 2-D system was used in this paper, which has good biological plausibility and high computational efficiency. Ordinary differential equations were of the form (1). Interpretation of parameters refers to [10]. In this paper, typical values of parameters for an excitatory neuron were: $a = 0.02$, $b = 0.2$, $c = -65$, and $d = 8$. Typical values of parameters for an inhibitory neuron were: $a = 0.1$, $b = 0.25$, $c = -60$, and $d = 2$. Typical firing mode of excitatory and inhibitory neuron is shown in Fig. 1.

$$\frac{dv}{dt} = 0.04v^2 + 5v + 140 - u + I$$
$$\frac{du}{dt} = a(bv - u)$$
$$\text{If } v \geq 30, \text{Then} \begin{cases} v \leftarrow c; \\ u \leftarrow u + d; \end{cases} \tag{1}$$

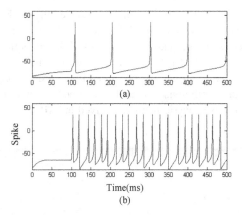

Fig. 1. Two typical firing modes of neuron. (a) Regular spiking for Excitatory neurons; (b) Fast spiking for Inhibitory neurons.

2.2 Time Delays in Action Potential Transmission and Neuron's Asynchronous Working

As we know, the delays exist in the process of action potential transmission (action potential transmission delay, ATD) [11]. The difference of ATD may be one of the reasons to the asynchrony working of neurons, which plays an important role in neural encoding [12]. Two of the reasons are considered in this paper: (1) Due to different positions of synapses that are distributed on axons or different positions of dendrites that receive AP, there are different delays when AP propagates from presynaptic neurons to postsynaptic neurons in the nervous system. In particular, the transmission of the action potential from the receptor to the nerve center along hundreds or even thousands of millimeters of nerve fiber, and there must be a time delay of more than a few hundred milliseconds; (2) APs propagate from upstream neurons to downstream neurons, which were regulated by neural circuit and delayed a specific time. A wide range of time delays (up to hundred ms) could occur [13]. Thus, ATD may be one of factors to produce the asynchrony working of the neurons. In this paper, we do not try to explore the specific electrophysiological and neural circuit mechanism of ATD, but only uses such mechanism in the circuit.

The current view is that time is involved in advanced cognitive processes such as memory, learning and reasoning [14]. The firing rate of neurons is considered to be involved in information encoding, and the firing of neurons has the property of "all or nothing". From a single neuron's perspective, the duration from when the AP is generated to its arrival at the postsynaptic neuron is time-critical or time-sensitive, which should not be ignored. In this paper, the different delays of APs may be similar to "time multiplexing" in signal processing, which may play an important role in behavioral decision logic.

From a computational view, the different neurons in the neuron group naturally have different delays. In computational simulation, by setting the transmission delay (ATD) parameter. Action potential transmission delay and simulation were shown in

Fig. 2. We simulated the ATD by using different queue lengths. For example, using 4 different queue lengths, as shown in Fig. 2(d, Queue 1–4). If the length of a queue is n, then the AP is delayed n milliseconds. Four queues with sequential increases in length indicated that as the location of the synapse on the axon moved away from the cell body, the delays increased. If an AP was generated in the presynaptic neuron, we added 1 to the head of the queue; otherwise, we added 0. When the end of queue element was 1, it indicated that the postsynaptic neuron received an AP.

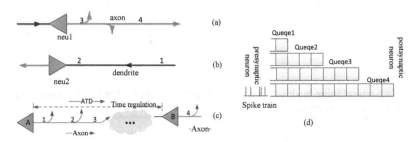

Fig. 2. AP transmission delay and simulation. (a) ATD of presynaptic neurons as shown by points 3 and 4. (b) Delays of postsynaptic neurons as shown by 1 and 2. (c) A specific ATD was controlled by a circuit, when APs propagate from upstream neurons to downstream neurons. (d) Simulation of the delays in AP transmission along an axon using queues.

2.3   Synaptic Depression

Synapse is the key component in transmission of information. When an AP is generated and propagated to the presynaptic axon terminal. Neurotransmitters then diffuse through the synaptic gap and bind to receptors in the postsynaptic membrane, which generate the excitatory postsynaptic potentials (EPSPs) or inhibitory postsynaptic potentials (IPSPs).

When a presynaptic neuron releases neurotransmitters to generate EPSPs or IPSPs in a postsynaptic neuron, the amount of neurotransmitters in presynaptic vesicles will decrease in a short time and then gradually recover in a long time. However, how large is the postsynaptic potential generated by a single AP? Since, the conduction of an AP along the axon is attenuated. Therefore, range of a postsynaptic potential depends on at least two factors: how much neurotransmitter is released once time and how many receptors are activated in the postsynaptic neuron? When only the first factor is considered, which involves storage of neurotransmitters in synapses, we regard the neurotransmitters as a kind of "resource" as shown in Fig. 3. Two cases as follows. Case 1: When a neuron fires at a high rate, the rate of resource depletion can be faster than that of recovery, which means that the "resource" is reduced for subsequent APs. In this case, subsequent APs produce smaller postsynaptic potentials. Case 2: When a neuron fires at a low rate, the rate of resource depletion is slower than that of recovery, which means that the "resource" is constant for each AP. In this case, subsequent APs produce the same size of postsynaptic potential. Consider the second factor, when the number of postsynaptic receptors is much enough for the neurotransmitters receiving from

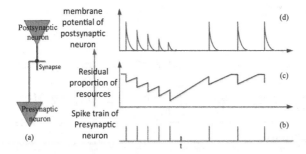

Fig. 3. (a) Presynaptic and postsynaptic neurons; (b) Spike sequence generated by the presynaptic neuron, which fires at a high rate before time t and at a low rate after time t; (c) Surplus of "resource" of the presynaptic neuron depends on the rate of release and the rate of recovery; (d) Membrane potential of the postsynaptic neuron raises (EPSPs) following APs in the presynaptic neuron (excitatory neuron).

presynaptic neurons, then EPSP or IPSP size depends primarily on the amount of neurotransmitter received. However, when the number of postsynaptic receptors is not enough for the coming neurotransmitters, then EPSP or IPSP size depends on the number of available receptors in the postsynaptic neuron.

The above description is a complex electrochemical process, which may differ among organisms or even different brain regions of the same organism. However, we can describe the above process from the function approximately. Based on a study by research [7], we formalized the above process as shown in Table 1. $C1$ is the attenuation coefficient of resources, and $C2$ is the recovery coefficient of resources. R is the residual proportion of resources, and W_i_0 is the synaptic connection strength of the ith neuron at initial time. T is time (milliseconds). When neuron i generates an AP, the amount of its "resources" is reduced once by constant $C1$, and the amount of resources gradually recovers in between APs. The second factor can be described simply in that the postsynaptic current produced by the presynaptic neuron cannot be larger than a given value. The influence of synaptic depression mechanism on the firing of neuron was shown in Fig. 4.

Table 1. Algorithm of synaptic depression

```
0 < c1 < 1
1 < c2 < 2
R = 1
W_i_0 = w_k;
For k = 1: T
    If Neuron_i is Active:
        R = R * c1;
    Else:
        R = R * c2;
    If R > 1: R = 1;
    W_i_k = W_i_(k-1) * R;
End For
```

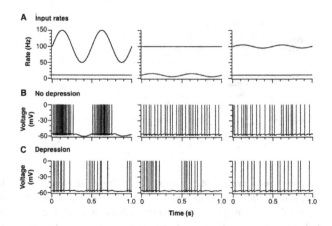

Fig. 4. The influence of synaptic depression mechanism on the firing of neuron (from [7]).

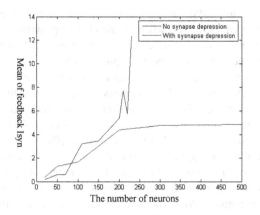

Fig. 5. Effects of synaptic depression on feedback intensity in recurrent circuit.

In a recurrent neural circuit, as the firing rate increases with an increase in the number of neurons in both the presence and absence of synaptic depression, but firing rate saturates with synaptic depression, as shown in Fig. 5. It is because of the depression mechanism of synapses (i.e. "resource limitation") that although neurons may receive connections from thousands of presynaptic neurons in the nervous system, neurons do not fire at high rate.

2.4   Slow and Fast Synapse

Fast and slow postsynaptic potentials can be observed by recording membrane potentials of sympathetic ganglionic neurons and cerebral cortex neurons. The duration of fast postsynaptic potentials is within milliseconds, and the duration of slow postsynaptic potentials can range from hundreds of milliseconds to several seconds. Slow EPSPs are generally attributed to a decrease in membrane permeability to K^+, and slow

IPSPs are due to an increase in membrane permeability to K$^+$. Generation of slow postsynaptic potentials is a complex electrochemical process involving different neurotransmitters, different receptors, and various ions.

In a previous neuron model, the input is current stimulation (external stimulus current and synaptic current), and APs of presynaptic neurons generate postsynaptic potentials by generating postsynaptic currents. Therefore, fast and slow postsynaptic potentials can be understood as a continuous postsynaptic current (positive and negative ion flow) generated by one AP. It is assumed that a neuron generates an AP at time k and generates a postsynaptic current of $I_{syn}(k)$. At time t (after time k), the AP can also generate synaptic current, which results from gradual attenuation of synaptic current $I_{syn}(k)$, as shown in Eq. (2). Fast and slow postsynaptic potentials are shown in Fig. 6. Since, single AP only can generate small EPSP, to generate a AP in postsynaptic neuron, many of presynaptic Aps are required during a very short time. Therefore, the slow synapse makes the persistence of neural activities easy to be achieved in nervous system and simulation.

$$I_{syn}(t) = I_{syn}(k) * \prod_{i=k}^{i=t} e^{-ci} \qquad (2)$$

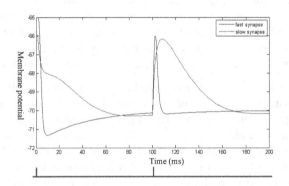

Fig. 6. Fast and slow postsynaptic potentials.

3   Neural Circuit

A neural circuit with recurrent connections of pyramidal neurons (excitatory neurons) was used as the basic neural circuit for persistence of neural activity. Using a recurrent neural circuit, it is very easy to achieve a steady state firing rate with addition of synaptic depression. Thus, how can the circuit produce gradual fading of neuronal activity? The answer is the inhibitory neurons, which can regulate the firing rate of pyramidal neuron and stronger inhibitory effect causes a greater decrease in firing rate [9]. However, this inhibitory process is too fast (milliseconds). Information in WM shows a process of "continuous" fading over time that lasts for several seconds, which mean that the inhibitory effect was not added once time. Therefore, we introduced a "continuous" (at the set intervals) negative feedback effect to the positive feedback

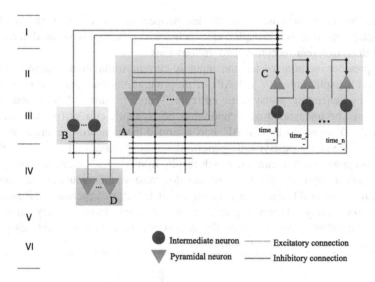

Fig. 7. Neural circuit for persistence and fading of neural information.

neural circuit. As shown in Fig. 7 (Maintenance and fading of neural activity are also information processes. The neurons are distributed in the second and third layers of the cerebral cortex, and the input neurons are distributed in the fourth layer [15]). Neuron cluster A is the memory module, and B is an inhibitory neuron cluster. Neural circuit C continuously introduces negative feedback, and D is an input neuron cluster.

(1) *Neuron cluster A* is the memory module, which receives APs from multiple sources, including the input neuron cluster D, which can be regarded as the external stimuli, self-positive feedback input, and inhibitory input from cluster C.

(2) *Inhibitory neuron cluster B* receives APs from the input neuron cluster, which acts as a switch. The negative feedback input of neural circuit C to A is closed before external input from D removed. When neuron cluster A receives external stimuli, the memory mechanism has not started yet. If negative feedback is introduced during this period, it will greatly reduce normal activity of A. After the external input being removed, and establishing self-maintenance of A (memory begins), B begins to be used to open the "gradual" inhibition of C to A.

(3) *Circuit C* is a chain neural circuit that receives APs from neuron cluster A. Each node of the chain is a pyramidal neuron cluster including 30 excitatory neurons, which is connected to an inhibitory neuron cluster (including 5 inhibitory neurons) and the next pyramidal neuron cluster. Each inhibitory neuron cluster connected to neuron cluster A.

ATD between each node ranged from 20–50 ms randomly; Neuron cluster A contains 100 pyramidal neurons and 20 inhibitory neurons, $W_a = 0.2$ (*Connection weight in A*); B contain 120 inhibitory neurons, $W_b = 0.4$; C contain 150 pyramidal neuron nodes (each node contain 30 neurons) and 100 inhibitory neuron node (each node contain 5 neurons), $W_{c\_a} = 0.4$. The principle of designing parameters is to ensure

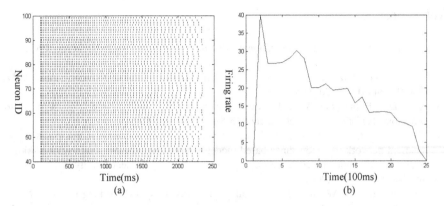

Fig. 8. The persistence of neural activities of neuron cluster A, external stimuli from neuron cluster D was removed after 500 ms. (a) Neural activities of neuron cluster A; (b) Firing rate of neuron cluster A in the self-maintenance process.

that upstream neurons are able to activate downstream neurons at least, *and then fine tune*. Neural circuit C continuously introduces negative feedback to A so that firing activity of neuron cluster A gradually fades over time.

Neural activities of neuron cluster A are shown in Fig. 8. Following gradual introduction of negative feedback, the intensity of negative feedback (postsynaptic current) for neuron cluster A is gradually enhanced, which lead to the firing rate of A gradually decreasing, as shown in Fig. 8(a), (b). Fine tune the parameters (Connection strength of negative feedback, W_{c_a}) of circuit, we can obtain the different duration of persistence. For example, the larger the W_{c_a} is, the shorter the duration of persistence is; the smaller the W_{c_a} is, the longer the duration of persistence is.

4   Discussion

How do microscopic activities of neurons in circuits support achievement of cognitive ability? However, the gap between circuits and behavior is too wide, neural computation that occurs in neurons is an intermediate level [16]. Since we cannot get the details of circuit in the brain, design a biologically feasible circuit for a specific neural computation maybe an efficient method to understand the brain.

In this paper, we integrated known neurophysiological principles as much as possible to design the computational neural circuit. We designed a neural circuit for the persistence of neural information by combining synaptic mechanisms and structure of the neural circuit. We try to explore the neural computational mechanism of neural information persistence and gradual degradation over time, which may help in exploring neural mechanisms that underlie the WM.

Acknowledgments. This work was supported by the NSFC project (Project Nos. 61771146 and 61375122), and (in part) by Shanghai Science and Technology Development Funds (13dz2260200, 13511504300).

References

1. Chaudhuri, R., Fiete, I.: Computational principles of memory. Nat. Neurosci. **19**(3), 394 (2016)
2. Mongillo, G., Barak, O., Tsodyks, M.: Synaptic theory of working memory. Science **319** (5869), 1543–1546 (2008)
3. Amit, D.J., Bernacchia, A., Yakovlev, V.: Multiple-object working memory—a model for behavioral performance. Cereb. Cortex **13**(5), 435–443 (2003)
4. Seung, H.S., Lee, D.D., Reis, B.Y., et al.: Stability of the memory of eye position in a recurrent network of conductance-based model neurons. Neuron **26**(1), 259–271 (2000)
5. Wang, X.J.: Synaptic reverberation underlying mnemonic persistent activity. Trends Neuro-Sci. **24**(8), 455–463 (2001)
6. Constantinidis, C., Wang, X.J.: A neural circuit basis for spatial working memory. Neuro-Sci. **10**(6), 553–565 (2004)
7. Abbott, L.F., Varela, J.A., Sen, K., et al.: Synaptic depression and cortical gain control. Science **275**(5297), 221–224 (1997)
8. Wei, H., Bu, Y., Dai, D.: A decision-making model based on a spiking neural circuit and synaptic plasticity. Cogn. Neurodyn. **11**(5), 415–431 (2017)
9. Wei, H., Dai, D., Bu, Y.: A plausible neural circuit for decision making and its formation based on reinforcement learning. Cogn. Neurodyn. **11**(3), 259–281 (2017)
10. Izhikevich, E.M., et al.: Simple model of spiking neurons. IEEE Trans. Neural Netw. **14**(6), 1569–1572 (2003)
11. Tolnai, S., Englitz, B., Scholbach, J., et al.: Spike transmission delay at the calyx of Held in vivo: rate dependence, phenomenological modeling, and relevance for sound localization. J. Neurophysiol. **102**(2), 1206–1217 (2009)
12. Wang, R., Zhang, Z., Qu, J., et al.: Phase synchronization motion and neural coding in dynamic transmission of neural information. IJM **1000**, 1 (2011)
13. Haberly, L.B.: Neuronal circuitry in olfactory cortex: anatomy and functional implications. Chem. Senses **10**(2), 219–238 (1985)
14. Wilson, M.: Six views of embodied cognition. Psychon. Bull. Rev. **9**(4), 625 (2002)
15. Le Bé, J.V.: Structure and dynamics of the neocortical microcircuit connectivity. EPFL (2007)
16. Carandini, M.: From circuits to behavior: a bridge too far? Nat. Neurosci. **15**(4), 507–509 (2012)

Granger Causality to Reveal Functional Connectivity in the Mouse Basal Ganglia-Thalamocortical Circuit

Alessandra Lintas[1(✉)], Takeshi Abe[2], Alessandro E. P. Villa[1], and Yoshiyuki Asai[2]

[1] NeuroHeuristic Research Group, University of Lausanne,
Quartier UNIL-Chamberonne, 1015 Lausanne, Switzerland
alessandra.lintas@unil.ch

[2] AI Systems Medicine Research and Training Center (AISMEC),
Yamaguchi University Graduate School of Medicine, Yamaguchi University Hospital,
1-1-1 Minami-Kogushi, Ube, Yamaguchi 755-8505, Japan
http://www.neuroheuristic.org

Abstract. In this study we analyze simultaneously recorded spike trains at several levels of the basal ganglia-thalamocortical circuit in freely moving parvalbumin (PV)-deficient and wildtype (WT) (i.e., expressing PV at normal levels) mice. Parvalbumin is a Calcium-binding protein, mainly expressed in GABAergic inhibitory neurons, that affects the dynamics of the Excitatory/Inhibitory balance at the network level. We apply Granger causality analysis in order to measure the functional connectivity of different selected brain areas and their possible alterations due to PV depletion. Our results show that connections between ventromedial prefrontal cortex and Nucleus Accumbens are not affected by PV depletion.

Keywords: Basal ganglia-thalamocortical circuit
Nucleus accumbens · Spike train analysis · Granger causality

1 Introduction

The basal ganglia-thalamocortical network is formed by several parallel and segregated circuits involving different areas of the cerebral cortex, striatum, pallidum, thalamus, subthalamic nucleus and midbrain [3,4]. This network is characterized by a combination of "open" and "closed" loops with ascending sensory afferences reaching the thalamus and the midbrain, as well as with descending motor efferences from the midbrain (the tectospinal tract) and the cortex (the corticospinal tract). Brain imaging studies in human patients have emphasized that learning impairment in Parkinson's disease was directly related to gray matter loss in the ventromedial prefrontal cortex, inferior frontal gyrus and nucleus accumbens [19]. The reticular nucleus of the thalamus (RTN), formed by a thin

© Springer Nature Switzerland AG 2018
V. Kůrková et al. (Eds.): ICANN 2018, LNCS 11140, pp. 393–402, 2018.
https://doi.org/10.1007/978-3-030-01421-6_38

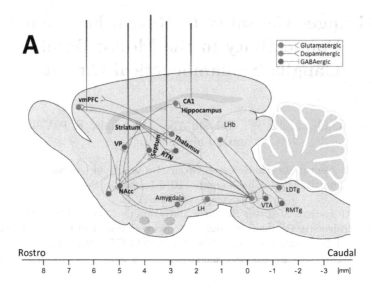

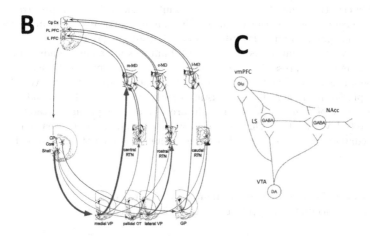

Fig. 1. A. Simplified schematic of the targeted areas of this experiment alongside with major dopaminergic, glutamatergic and GABAergic connections to and from the ventral tegmental area (VTA) and nucleus accumbens (NAcc) in the rodent brain, modified from [23]. B. Parallel circuits link the caudate-putamen (CPu), nucleus accumbens core and shell with pallidal and thalamo-cortical systems, adapted from [20]. C. Model by which the lateral septum (LS) contributes to regulation of NAcc function [26].

sheet of neurons whose majority are GABAergic cells expressing PV, plays a pivotal role in the basal ganglia-thalamocortical network (Fig. 1).

The RTN is a unique gateway in filtering and sorting sensory information that passes through the thalamocortical and corticothalamic axis and its activity is strongly regulated by the basal ganglia via the dopaminergic (DA) afferences from the substantia nigra compacta and by the GABAergic inhibitory projections from the pallidum and from the substantia nigra pars reticulata. In particular, the DA-mediated effect on the GABAergic inhibitory neurons expressing PV affects the balance between Excitatory/Inhibitory (E/I) balance at the level of the basal ganglia-thalamocortical system and dysfunction of RTN is likely to be involved in several behavioural or psychiatric conditions [27]. PV is a Calcium-binding protein, mainly expressed in GABAergic inhibitory neurons, that affects the dynamics of the Excitatory/Inhibitory balance at the network level [2,16,24]. Therefore, it is essential to reappraise the model of the basal ganglia-thalamocortical network in the light of what we can experimentally study in the absence of PV.

Multivariate time series analyses of point processes have been recently aimed to identify causal relationships between the recorded neurons and analysis of multiple spike trains by Granger causality (GC) has proven its potential to provide insights in determining functional neural connectivity [10,14,15]. This approach allows to extract the directed information flow pattern in neuronal networks and has between used to study functional connectivity between brain areas in neuroimaging [25] and electroencephalographic recordings [22]. In this study we analyze simultaneously recorded spike trains at several levels of the basal ganglia-thalamocortical circuit in freely moving WT and PV-deficient mice (PVKO). We extend our previous work [13] with the application of GC analysis in order to measure the functional connectivity of different selected brain areas and their possible alterations due to PV depletion. This method has never been applied in studying changes in causal interactions due to protein depletions in mutant mice and it is used here as a complementary tool to crosscorrelation analysis previously applied to PVKO mice [16] and mutual information [5] and partial coherence analysis [8].

2   Materials and Methods

2.1   Experimental Data

WT and PVKO of approximately 3 months of age weighing 15–21 g were anesthetized with 0.8–1.5% isoflurane and implanted with multiple electrodes (50 μm, Teflon-coated, tungsten wires) aimed at ventromedial prefrontal cortex (vmPFC), thalamus (Thal), Nucleus Accumbens (Nacc), lateral septum (LS) and hippocampus (CA1) for chronic recordings (as show in Fig. 1A). A bare silver wire was affixed to the bone as ground and all the implanted wires were soldered to a six-pin socket that was fixed to the skull with two small bone screws and dental cement [12].

Electrophysiological signals sampled at 20 kHz were band-pass filtered and recorded simultaneously from multiple electrodes in WAV format for computerized offline analysis with template matching spike sorting algorithm at a time resolution of 1 ms [6]. The recording sessions were performed during 20 min while the animals were roaming freely in the cage before the operant behavioral training session was started. We analyzed the discrete time series derived from spike trains by means of time-domain [1], frequency-domain [7] and Granger causality analysis [11,21] to study the fine dynamic relationships within different elements of the circuit and study differences between PVKO and WT.

2.2 Granger Causality

Estimating Granger causality (GC) for the frequency domain between two time series consists of two steps [11]. The first step is to fit a two-variable autoregressive model to these time series, i.e., to find coefficient matrix $(a, b, c,$ and $d)$ of the equations

$$
\begin{aligned}
X_t &= \sum_{i=1}^{n}(a_i X_{t-i} + b_i Y_{t-i}) + \epsilon_t \\
Y_t &= \sum_{i=1}^{n}(c_i Y_{t-i} + d_i X_{t-i}) + \eta_t
\end{aligned}
\tag{1}
$$

so as to minimize regression error terms ϵ_t and η_t. The second step is obtaining both the transfer function of the frequency domain and the noise covariance from the fitted model. These procedures were performed using the `nitime.analysis.granger` module of Nitime v0.7 [28]. Notice that it is necessary to determine the order n of autoregressive equations, which is shown in Eq. (1), in advance. While it is conventional to estimate it by minimizing a well-known information criterion such as the Bayesian Information Criterion, in this study we varied several values of n in the range 10–100 to confirm the consistency of the Granger causality with different orders of the autoregressive model. Numerical integration of Granger causality was approximated by the trapezoidal rule.

3 Results

We have analyzed spike trains from 18 recording sites along 3 tracks for the WT and 3 tracks for PVKO mice. An example of raster analysis from a WT mouse display four cells recorded simultaneously in the vmPFC (cell #294), NAcc (cells #227, #178) and LS (cell #394) of a freely-moving WT mouse (Fig. 2A). All cells are characterized by a firing rate in the range 3.2–4.6 spikes/s. We have computed the bidirectional Granger causality (GC) among all these cells and the results obtained with an autoregressive model of order 20 are shown in Fig. 2B.

This result illustrates two kind of aspects. Firstly, notice that mutual causal connectivity strengths may be very asymmetrical. For instance, the projection $394 \rightarrow 227$ is about twice stronger than in the opposite direction #227 $\rightarrow$ #394. Secondly, the overall causal connectivity strength is also very different from region to region. In particular, we observed a rather strong and similar ($GC \approx$ 0.5) causal connectivity between cells #394 and #209. The weakest values in this group ($GC \approx 0.2$) were observed between cells #178 and #209. Hence, it is

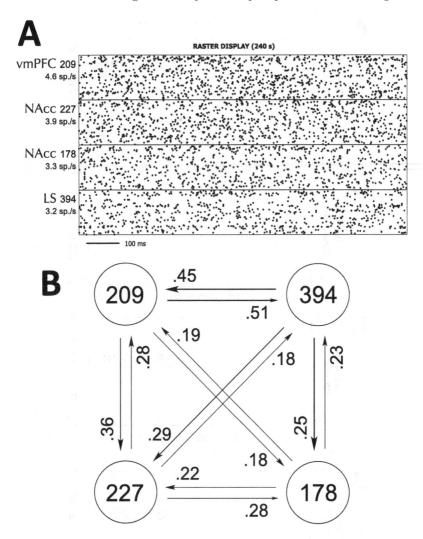

Fig. 2. A. Raster display of four cells recorded simultaneously in the ventromedial prefrontal cortex (vmPFC), nucleus accumbens (NAcc) and lateral septum (LS) of a freely-moving WT mouse. The horizontal time scale corresponds to 1000 ms. B. Connectivity diagram as determined following the Granger causality analysis using autoregressive model of order 20.

possible to estimate whether a direct causality may be assumed as a composition of indirect projections. For example consider #209 ⤳ #178 ($GC = 0.18$) as a composition of #209 → #227 → #178 ($GC_1 = 0.36 \times 0.28 = 0.10$) with #209 → #394 → #178 ($GC_2 = 0.51 \times 0.25 = 0.13$). The sum $GC_1 + GC_2 = 0.23$ is similar or less than the direct value ($GC = 0.18$), thus suggesting that the direct causal interaction is marginal and that causality from cell #209 to #178 is mainly due to the other connections.

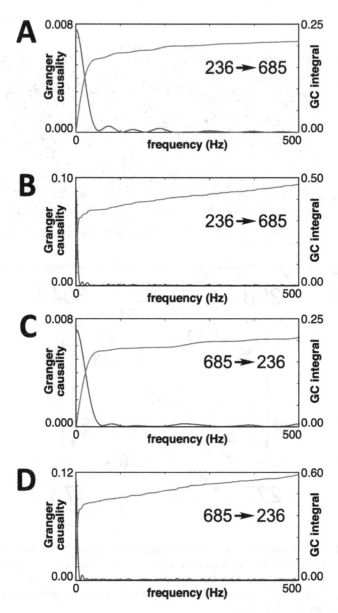

Fig. 3. Granger causality (GC) is a measure of causal or directional influence from one time series to another and is based on linear predictions of time series by higher orders of autoregressive models. A. GC with autoregressive model of order 20. B. Same GC with autoregressive model of order 100.

To evaluate the influence of different orders used in autoregressive models over our analysis, we compared resulting GC values. Figure 3 has shown a typical line graph of frequency-domain GC with two distinct orders.

In principle, larger order n in Eq. (1) allows the model to recognize the linear effect of a wider time window to current spiking status. However, calculating numeric GC values with larger order accumulates more computational demands as well as more numerical errors. In the preliminary analysis performed in this paper, we refrained from drawing any conclusion from the case when the GC values depends too much on the choice of orders and consider an order $n = 20$ as a convenient value for spike train analysis (Fig. 3).

We have extended the previous approach by grouping and averaging all causal interactions between brain areas of the basal ganglia-thalamocortical circuit recorded in freely moving WT and PVKO mice (Fig. 4). We would like to illustrate the principle of this analysis, but more data are presently collected from new experiments and the neurophysiological significance of the results presented here should be considered carefully. The values of GC strength between vmPFC and NAcc were not affected by depletion of PV as illustrated in Fig. 4. In the data sample analyzed here it was not possible to find comparable recording sites in the thalamus (Thal) and in the lateral septum (LS) of WT and PVKO mice, unfortunately. However, these areas have a similar pattern of projections with the prefrontal cortex and the Nucleus Accumbens (NAcc). To this respect, it is interesting to notice that in PVKO the strengths of GC between LS/Thal cells with NAcc and vmPFC were decreased to about half of the values observed in WT mice.

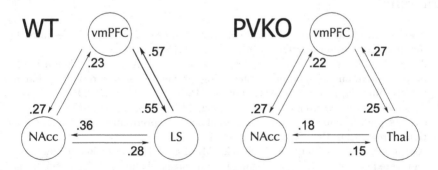

Fig. 4. Granger causality analysis of the connectivity diagram, based on autoregressive models of order 20 between different nodes of the basal ganglia thalamocortical network in freely moving WT and PVKO mice. Results are obtained by pooling and averaging four pairs of spike trains GC analysis for each arrow.

4   Discussion

This paper presents for the first time, to our knowledge, an analysis of causal interactions between neural spike trains and brain areas of the basal ganglia-thalamocortical circuit of PVKO freely-moving mice. We have applied Granger analysis and confirmed the potential of this analytical tool for the understanding of functional neural interactions [14,18]. It has been reported that Granger causality cannot detect inhibitory connections with the same accuracy as excitatory ones [9], which could be a serious hindrance in our study because Calcium-binding protein expressed in GABAergic inhibitory neurons of the thalamic reticular nucleus, a brain structure playing a key role in controlling the dynamics of the E/I balance at the network level [2,16,24]. The results presented here concern only a limited data sample, but they represent an exemplar application of this analysis. We have observed that an important pathway, such as the projections between the ventromedial prefrontal cortex and the Nucleus Accumbens, which is an area involved in decision-making processes and cognitive processing of reward and aversion, is not affected by PV depletion. Our preliminary results suggest also that other circuits, such as those involving the thalamus and the lateral septum are responsible of the disruption of the E/I balance leading to schizophrenia, autisme and other neural dynamic psychiatric disorders [17]. Additional data currently analyzed in our laboratory are expected to provide further results and shed new insights in the functional connectivity of the basal ganglia thalamo-cortical network.

Acknowledgments. The authors wish to thank B. Schwaller for providing the PV-deficient mice, J.M. Delgado-García for his scientific supervision and J.M. González Martin, M. Sánchez Enciso, R. Sánchez-Campusano, J.A. Santos Naharro, and M. Kaczorowski for their technical assistance.

References

1. Abeles, M.: Quantification, smoothing, and confidence limits for single-units' histograms. J. Neurosci. Methods **5**(4), 317–325 (1982)
2. Albéri, L., Lintas, A., Kretz, R., Schwaller, B., Villa, A.E.: The calcium-binding protein parvalbumin modulates the firing properties of the reticular thalamic nucleus bursting neurons. J. Neurophysiol. **109**(11), 2827–2841 (2013)
3. Alexander, G.E., Crutcher, M.D., DeLong, M.R.: Basal ganglia-thalamocortical circuits: parallel substrates for motor, oculomotor, "prefrontal" and "limbic" functions. Prog. Brain Res. **85**, 119–46 (1990)
4. Alexander, G.E., DeLong, M.R., Strick, P.L.: Parallel organization of functionally segregated circuits linking basal ganglia and cortex. Annu. Rev. Neurosci. **9**, 357–81 (1986)
5. Asai, Y., Guha, A., Villa, A.E.P.: Deterministic neural dynamics transmitted through neural networks. Neural Netw. **21**(6), 799–809 (2008)
6. Asai, Y., Aksenova, T.I., Villa, A.E.P.: On-line real-time oriented application for neuronal spike sorting with unsupervised learning. In: Duch, W., Kacprzyk, J., Oja, E., Zadrożny, S. (eds.) ICANN 2005. LNCS, vol. 3696, pp. 109–114. Springer, Heidelberg (2005). https://doi.org/10.1007/11550822_18
7. Brillinger, D.R.: Nerve cell spike train data analysis: a progression of technique. J. Am. Stat. Assoc. **87**(418), 260–271 (1992)

8. Brillinger, D.R., Villa, A.E.P.: Assessing connections in networks of biological neurons. In: Brillinger, D.R., Fernholz, L.T., Morgenthaler, S. (eds.) The Practice of Data Analysis: Essays in Honor of John W. Tukey, pp. 77–92. Princeton University Press, Princeton (1997)

9. Cadotte, A.J., DeMarse, T.B., He, P., Ding, M.: Causal measures of structure and plasticity in simulated and living neural networks. PLoS One **3**(10), e3355 (2008)

10. Chen, Y., Rangarajan, G., Feng, J., Ding, M.: Analyzing multiple nonlinear time series with extended granger causality. Phys. Lett. A **324**(1), 26–35 (2004)

11. Ding, M., Chen, Y., Bressler, S.L.: Granger causality: basic theory and application to neuroscience. In: Schelter, B., Winterhalder, M., Timmer, J. (eds.) Handbook of Time Series Analysis, Chap. 17, pp. 437–460. Wiley-Blackwell, Weinheim (2006)

12. Gruart, A., Muñoz, M.D., Delgado-García, J.M.: Involvement of the CA3-CA1 synapse in the acquisition of associative learning in behaving mice. J. Neurosci. **26**(4), 1077–1087 (2006)

13. Gruart, A., Delgado-García, J.M., Lintas, A.: Effect of parvalbumin deficiency on distributed activity and interactions in neural circuits activated by instrumental learning. In: Wang, R., Pan, X. (eds.) Advances in Cognitive Neurodynamics (V), pp. 111–117. Springer, Singapore (2016). https://doi.org/10.1007/978-981-10-0207-6_17

14. Kim, S., Putrino, D., Ghosh, S., Brown, E.N.: A Granger causality measure for point process models of ensemble neural spiking activity. PLoS Comput. Biol. **7**(3), e1001110 (2011)

15. Krumin, M., Shoham, S.: Multivariate autoregressive modeling and granger causality analysis of multiple spike trains. Comput. Intell. Neurosci. **2010**, 9 (2010). https://doi.org/10.1155/2010/752428. Article ID 752428

16. Lintas, A., Schwaller, B., Villa, A.E.P.: Visual thalamocortical circuits in parvalbumin-deficient mice. Brain Res. **1536**, 107–118 (2013)

17. Marín, O.: Interneuron dysfunction in psychiatric disorders. Nat. Rev. Neurosci. **13**(2), 107–20 (2012)

18. Nedungadi, A.G., Rangarajan, G., Jain, N., Ding, M.: Analyzing multiple spike trains with nonparametric Granger causality. J. Comput. Neurosci. **27**(1), 55–64 (2009)

19. O'Callaghan, C., et al.: Fronto-striatal gray matter contributions to discrimination learning in Parkinson's disease. Front. Comput. Neurosci. **7**, 180 (2013)

20. O'Donnell, P., Lavín, A., Enquist, L.W., Grace, A.A., Card, J.P.: Interconnected parallel circuits between rat nucleus accumbens and thalamus revealed by retrograde transsynaptic transport of pseudorabies virus. J. Neurosci. **17**(6), 2143–2167 (1997)

21. Pearl, J.: Causal inference in statistics: an overview. Stat. Surv. **3**, 96–146 (2009)

22. Protopapa, F., Siettos, C.I., Evdokimidis, I., Smyrnis, N.: Granger causality analysis reveals distinct spatio-temporal connectivity patterns in motor and perceptual visuo-spatial working memory. Front. Comput. Neurosci. **8**, 146 (2014)

23. Russo, S.J., Nestler, E.J.: The brain reward circuitry in mood disorders. Nat. Rev. Neurosci. **14**(9), 609–625 (2013)

24. Schwaller, B.: The use of transgenic mouse models to reveal the functions of Ca2+ buffer proteins in excitable cells. Biochim. Biophys. Acta **1820**(8), 1294–1303 (2012)

25. Seth, A.K., Barrett, A.B., Barnett, L.: Granger causality analysis in neuroscience and neuroimaging. J. Neurosci. **35**(8), 3293–7 (2015)

26. Sheehan, T.P., Chambers, R.A., Russell, D.S.: Regulation of affect by the lateral septum: implications for neuropsychiatry. Brain Res. Brain Res. Rev. **46**(1), 71–117 (2004)
27. Steullet, P., et al.: The thalamic reticular nucleus in schizophrenia and bipolar disorder: role of parvalbumin-expressing neuron networks and oxidative stress. Mol. Psychiatry 1–9 (2017). (PMID: 29180672)
28. The NIPY community: Nitime: time-series analysis for neuroscience (2017). http://nipy.org/nitime/. Accessed 27 Apr 2018

A Temporal Estimate of Integrated Information for Intracranial Functional Connectivity

Xerxes D. Arsiwalla[1,2,4(✉)], Daniel Pacheco[1,2,4], Alessandro Principe[3],
Rodrigo Rocamora[3], and Paul Verschure[2,4,5]

[1] Universitat Pompeu Fabra, Barcelona, Spain
`x.d.arsiwalla@gmail.com`
[2] Institute for BioEngineering of Catalonia, Barcelona, Spain
[3] Hospital del Mar, Barcelona, Spain
[4] Barcelona Institue of Science and Technology, Barcelona, Spain
[5] Institució Catalana de Recerca i Estudis Avançats (ICREA), Barcelona, Spain

Abstract. A major challenge in computational and systems neuroscience concerns the quantification of information processing at various scales of the brain's anatomy. In particular, using human intracranial recordings, the question we ask in this paper is: How can we estimate the informational complexity of the brain given the complex temporal nature of its dynamics? To address this we work with a recent formulation of network integrated information that is based on the Kullback-Leibler divergence between the multivariate distribution on the set of network states versus the corresponding factorized distribution over its parts. In this work, we extend this formulation for temporal networks and then apply it to human brain data obtained from intracranial recordings in epilepsy patients. Our findings show that compared to random re-wirings of the data, functional connectivity networks, constructed from human brain data, score consistently higher in the above measure of integrated information. This work suggests that temporal integrated information may indeed be a good starting point as a future measure of cognitive complexity.

Keywords: Computational neuroscience · Brain networks
Complexity measures · Functional connectivity

1 Introduction

The human brain is an extremely complex non-linear dynamical system that processes information from the external world, coming in through sensory channels, in order to determine the sequence of actions necessary for goal-oriented behavior, given the agent's internal drives and emotional states. Investigating the mechanisms of information integration, flow and distribution provide a vital ingredient in advancing our understanding of brain function and cognition.

© Springer Nature Switzerland AG 2018
V. Kůrková et al. (Eds.): ICANN 2018, LNCS 11140, pp. 403–412, 2018.
https://doi.org/10.1007/978-3-030-01421-6_39

This is point at which information theory meets neuroscience. The former provides rigorous theoretical tools that can effectively be employed to quantify biophysical processes that encode and assimilate knowledge from the world, which is then used to generate goal-oriented action. In this paper, we focus on quantifying the amount of information integrated by functional connectivity networks constructed from local field potentials (LFPs) obtained using intracranial recordings from human epilepsy patients. The underlying non-linearities in neural processing are reflected in the fact that these functional connectivity (FC) networks are not static, but dynamic. For our purposes, this can be analyzed as a stack of temporal networks, signifying the multitude of functional states the brain can occupy. This also calls for new dynamical measures of information processing to investigate these temporal networks.

Such measures are part of a larger class of complexity measures that seek to quantify information generated by all causal sub-processes in such a network. One candidate measure for global information processing is integrated information, usually denoted as Φ. It was introduced as a complexity measure for neural networks, and by extension, as a possible correlate of consciousness itself [30]. It is defined as the quantity of information generated by a network as a whole, due to its causal dynamical interactions, and one that is over and above the information generated independently by the disjoint sum of its parts. As a complexity measure, Φ seeks to operationalize the intuition that complexity arises from simultaneous integration and differentiation of the network's structural and dynamical properties. The earliest proposals defining integrated information were made in the pioneering work of [27,29,30]. Since then, considerable progress has been made towards development of a normative theory of consciousness as well as applications of integrated information [1,4–11,15,17,23,28]. In fact, there are now several candidate measures of integrated information such as neural complexity [30], causal density [25], Φ from integrated information theory: IIT 1.0, 2.0 & 3.0 [27], [15], [23], stochastic interaction [14,31], empirical Φ [17] and synergistic Φ [22], plus several variations of these (see [26] for an overview).

We will work with a recent formulation of network integrated information that is based on the Kullback-Leibler divergence between the multivariate distribution on the set of network states versus the corresponding factorized distribution over its parts [12]. This formulation is particularly suited for large networks with stochastic dynamics. In this paper, we extend this formulation for temporal networks. Note that in an ideal setting, to use the measure in [12] one would need the realistic anatomical connectivity of neural populations generating LFPs as well as details of the non-linear model generating those dynamics. In the absence of both these pieces of information, we rely on temporal FC networks as proxy to the realistic non-linear processes in the brain and compute the temporal integrated information of these networks.

2   Mathematical Formulation of Integrated Information

Let us begin this discussion considering networks endowed with linear stochastic dynamics. The state of each node is given by a random variable pertaining to a given probability distribution. These variables may either be discrete-valued or continuous. However, for many biological applications, Gaussian distributed, continuous-valued state variables are fairly reasonable abstractions (for example, aggregate neural population firing rate, EEG or fMRI signals). The state of the network $\mathbf{X_t}$ at time t is taken as a multivariate Gaussian variable with distribution $\mathbf{P_{X_t}}(\mathbf{x_t})$. $\mathbf{x_t}$ denotes an instantiation of $\mathbf{X_t}$ with components x_t^i (i going from 1 to n, n being the number of nodes). When the network makes a transition from an initial state $\mathbf{X_0}$ to a state $\mathbf{X_1}$ at time $t = 1$, observing the final state generates information about the system's initial state. The information generated equals the reduction in uncertainty regarding the initial state $\mathbf{X_0}$. This is given by the conditional entropy $\mathbf{H(X_0|X_1)}$. In order to extract that part of the information generated by the system as a whole, over and above that generated individually by its parts, one computes the relative conditional entropy given by the Kullback-Leibler divergence of the conditional distribution $\mathbf{P_{X_0|X_1=x'}}(\mathbf{x})$ of the system with respect to the joint conditional distributions $\prod_{k=1}^{r}\mathbf{P_{M_0^k|M_1^k=m'}}$ of its non-overlapping sub-systems demarcated with respect to a partition $\mathcal{P}_r$ of the system into r distinct sub-systems. Denoting this as $\varPhi_{\mathcal{P}_r}$, we have

$$\varPhi_{\mathcal{P}_r}(\mathbf{X_0} \rightarrow \mathbf{X_1} = \mathbf{x'}) = D_{KL}\left(\mathbf{P_{X_0|X_1=x'}}\,\Big|\Big|\,\prod_{k=1}^{r}\mathbf{P_{M_0^k|M_1^k=m'}}\right) \tag{1}$$

where for an r partitioned system, the state variable $\mathbf{X_0}$ can be decomposed as a direct sum of state variables of the sub-systems

$$\mathbf{X_0} = \mathbf{M_0^1} \oplus \mathbf{M_0^2} \oplus \cdots \oplus \mathbf{M_0^r} = \bigoplus_{k=1}^{r}\mathbf{M_0^k} \tag{2}$$

and similarly, $\mathbf{X_1}$ decomposes as

$$\mathbf{X_1} = \mathbf{M_1^1} \oplus \mathbf{M_1^2} \oplus \cdots \oplus \mathbf{M_1^r} = \bigoplus_{k=1}^{r}\mathbf{M_1^k} \tag{3}$$

For stochastic systems, it is useful to work with a measure that is independent of any specific instantiation of the final state $\mathbf{x'}$. So we average with respect to final states to obtain an expectation value from Eq. (1). After some algebra, we get

$$\langle\varPhi\rangle_{\mathcal{P}_r}(\mathbf{X_0} \rightarrow \mathbf{X_1}) = -\mathbf{H(X_0|X_1)} + \sum_{k=1}^{r}\mathbf{H(M_0^k|M_1^k)} \tag{4}$$

This is our definition of integrated information, which we use in the rest of this paper. Note that the measure described in [15] is not applicable to networks with stochastic dynamics. They do use Eq. (1) as their definition but endow their nodes with discrete states. On the other hand, [17] uses a different definition of integrated information, where conditional entropies as in Eq. (4) are replaced by conditional mutual information. This definition only matches the definition of

Eq. (1) in special cases but not in general for any distribution. From an information theory perspective, the Kullback-Leibler divergence offers a principled way of comparing probability distributions, hence we follow that approach in formulating our measure in Eq. (4).

The state variable at each time $t = 0$ and $t = 1$ follows a multivariate Gaussian distribution

$$\mathbf{X_0} \sim \mathcal{N}\left(\bar{\mathbf{x}}_0, \Sigma(\mathbf{X_0})\right) \qquad \mathbf{X_1} \sim \mathcal{N}\left(\bar{\mathbf{x}}_1, \Sigma(\mathbf{X_1})\right) \tag{5}$$

The generative model for this system is equivalent to a multi-variate autoregressive process

$$\mathbf{X_1} = \mathcal{A}\, \mathbf{X_0} + \mathbf{E_1} \tag{6}$$

where $\mathcal{A}$ is the weighted adjacency matrix of the network and E_1 is Gaussian noise. Next, taking the mean and covariance respectively on both sides of this equation, while holding the residual independent of the regression variables, yields

$$\bar{\mathbf{x}}_1 = \mathcal{A}\, \bar{\mathbf{x}}_0 \qquad \Sigma(\mathbf{X_1}) = \mathcal{A}\, \Sigma(\mathbf{X_0})\, \mathcal{A}^{\mathbf{T}} + \Sigma(\mathbf{E}) \tag{7}$$

In the absence of any external inputs, stationary solutions of a stochastic linear dynamical system as in Eq. (6) are fluctuations about the origin. Therefore, we can shift coordinates to set the means $\bar{\mathbf{x}}_0$ and consequently $\bar{\mathbf{x}}_1$ to the zero. The second equality in Eq. (7) is the discrete-time Lyapunov equation and its solution will give us the covariance matrix of the state variables.

The conditional entropy of a multivariate Gaussian variable is computed to be

$$\mathbf{H}(\mathbf{X_0}|\mathbf{X_1}) = \frac{1}{2} n \log(2\pi e) - \frac{1}{2} \log\left[\det \Sigma(\mathbf{X_0}|\mathbf{X_1})\right] \tag{8}$$

which is fully specified by the conditional covariance matrix. Inserting this in Eq. (4) yields

$$\langle \Phi \rangle_{\mathcal{P}_r}(\mathbf{X_0} \to \mathbf{X_1}) = \frac{1}{2} \log \left[\frac{\prod_{k=1}^{r} \det \Sigma(\mathbf{M_0^k}|\mathbf{M_1^k})}{\det \Sigma(\mathbf{X_0}|\mathbf{X_1})} \right] \tag{9}$$

To compute the conditional covariance matrix we use the following identity (the proof for the Gaussian case can be found in [16])

$$\Sigma(\mathbf{X}|\mathbf{Y}) = \Sigma(\mathbf{X}) - \Sigma(\mathbf{X}, \mathbf{Y})\Sigma(\mathbf{Y})^{-1}\Sigma(\mathbf{X}, \mathbf{Y})^{\mathbf{T}} \tag{10}$$

The appropriate covariance we will need to insert in this expression is

$$\Sigma(\mathbf{X_0}, \mathbf{X_1}) \equiv \left\langle (\mathbf{X_0} - \bar{\mathbf{x}}_0)(\mathbf{X_1} - \bar{\mathbf{x}}_1)^{\mathbf{T}} \right\rangle = \Sigma(\mathbf{X_0})\, \mathcal{A}^{\mathbf{T}} \tag{11}$$

which gives for the conditional covariance

$$\Sigma(\mathbf{X_0}|\mathbf{X_1}) = \Sigma(\mathbf{X_0}) - \Sigma(\mathbf{X_0})\, \mathcal{A}^{\mathbf{T}}\, \Sigma(\mathbf{X_1})^{-1} \mathcal{A}\, \Sigma(\mathbf{X_0})^{\mathbf{T}} \tag{12}$$

And similarly for the sub-systems

$$\Sigma(\mathbf{M_0^k}|\mathbf{M_1^k}) = \Sigma(\mathbf{M_0^k}) - \Sigma(\mathbf{M_0^k})\,\mathcal{A}^\mathbf{T}\big|_\mathbf{k}\,\Sigma(\mathbf{M_1^k})^{-1}\mathcal{A}\big|_\mathbf{k}\,\Sigma(\mathbf{M_0^k})^\mathbf{T} \tag{13}$$

where k indexes the partition such that $\mathbf{M_0^k}$ denotes the kth sub-system at $t = 0$ and $\mathcal{A}\big|_k$ denotes the restriction of the adjacency matrix to the kth sub-network.

Further, for linear multi-variate systems, a unique fixed point always exists. We try to find stable stationary solutions of the dynamical system. In that regime, the multi-variate probability distribution of states approaches stationarity and the covariance matrix converges, such that

$$\Sigma(\mathbf{X_1}) = \Sigma(\mathbf{X_0}) \tag{14}$$

$t = 0$ and $t = 1$ refer to time-points taken after the system converges to the fixed point. Then the discrete-time Lyapunov equations can be solved iteratively for the stable covariance matrix $\Sigma(\mathbf{X_t})$. For networks with symmetric adjacency matrix and independent Gaussian noise, the solution takes a particularly simple form

$$\Sigma(\mathbf{X_t}) = \left(1 - \mathcal{A}^2\right)^{-1}\Sigma(\mathbf{E}) \tag{15}$$

and for the parts, we have

$$\Sigma(\mathbf{M_0^k}) = \Sigma(\mathbf{X_0})\big|_\mathbf{k} \tag{16}$$

given by the restriction of the full covariance matrix on the kth sub-network. Note that Eq. (16) is not the same as Eq. (15) on the restricted adjacency matrix as that would mean that the sub-network has been explicitly severed from the rest of the system. Indeed, Eq. (16) is precisely the covariance of the sub-network while it is still part of the network and $\langle\Phi\rangle$ yields the integrated and differentiated information of the whole network that is greater than the sum of these connected parts. Inserting Eqs. (12), (13), (15) and (16) into Eq. (9) yields $\langle\Phi\rangle$ as a function of network weights for symmetric and correlated networks. For the case of asymmetric weights, the entries of the covariance matrix cannot be explicitly expressed as a matrix equation. However, they may still be solved by Jordan decomposition of both sides of the Lyapunov equation.

For partitioning the network, we will use the Maximum Information Partition (MaxIP). Following [21] and [1], the MaxIP is defined as the partition of the system into its irreducible parts. This is the finest partition and is unique as there is only one way to combinatorially reduce a system into all of its sub-units. $\langle\Phi\rangle$ computed using this partition was shown to accounts for the maximum amount of information that the network can integrate compared to any other partitioning of the system and is therefore a natural choice for quantifying whole versus parts [12].

3   Experimental Protocol

Intracranial EEG data for a single subject performing a navigation task was collected as part of a pre-surgical procedure in an epileptic patient. The participant provided written informed consent to participate in the study. The protocol of the experiment was approved by the local Ethical Committee "Clinical Research Ethical Committee (CEIC) Parc de Salut Mar" (Barcelona, Spain). Recordings were performed using a standard clinical EEG system (XLTEK, subsidiary of Natus Medical) with 500 Hz sampling rate. A unilateral implantation was performed, using 10 intra-cerebral electrodes (Dixi Medical, Besancon, France; diameter: 0.8 mm; 5 to 15 contact points, 2 mm long, 1.5 mm apart) that were stereotactically inserted using robotic guidance (ROSA, Medtech Surgical, Inc).

The subject navigated a squared virtual environment in which discrete visual stimuli were presented at specific locations in a 5×5 grid formed by red boxes located on the ground. Navigation was performed with a joystick. Boxes remained visible during the whole navigation period. When subjects were close to one of the boxes, the item pertaining to that specific location was presented through a small inset in the top-right of the user interface. Participants were instructed to visit all boxes. The subject completed six blocks of three minutes each. Navigation data (i.e., positions and orientations) of the subject during the active condition was recorded at 1000 Hz. We band-pass filtered the signal for the selected electrodes from 1 to 200 Hz using EEGLAB [20] before building the FCs. Functional correlation matrices were constructed by binning the activity of all electrodes in sliding windows of 500 ms. We calculated the Spearman's correlation of the activity of all pairs of electrodes over time. Electrode localization included frontal, parietal and temporal lobes, including brain structures such as the hippocampus and the amygdala (these locations were checked using the BrainX^3 system [2,3,13,18,19,24]). After filtering the data for removal of artifacts, we were left with a stack of 1797 FC networks of size 60×60.

4   Results

As described above, the data extraction process gives us a stack of 1797 temporal networks. We apply the mathematical machinery of integrated information to this stack. The measure being defined at each time-point yields a profile of $\langle \Phi \rangle$ values reflecting variations in informational complexity across time. As mentioned earlier, we use the structure of these temporal FC networks as proxy to the underlying complex neural connectivity and dynamics. Equation (9) is computed at each time-point using the corresponding FC network as the connectivity matrix $\mathcal{A}$. We use all positive correlations for this analysis. Furthermore, network weights are normalized by an overall scaling factor of 19.2 for all networks in order to ensure that all eigenvalues of all networks are bounded by 1 for reasons of stability. This yields the temporal $\langle \Phi \rangle$ profile for the FC networks, shown in red in Fig. 1. As a possible null model, we randomize the data by shuffling the edges of each FC network while preserving the total network degree at each point of time. Computing $\langle \Phi \rangle$ for these randomized networks yields the green profile in Fig. 1. Figure 2 shows the corresponding histograms of these $\langle \Phi \rangle$ profiles.

Given these profiles, we can now perform test statistics on $\langle \Phi \rangle$ itself in order to compare the temporal FC with their randomized counterparts. More, generally this method may also be used for making statistical statements for $\langle \Phi \rangle$ under

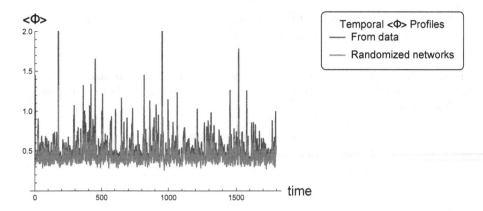

Fig. 1. Temporal ⟨Φ⟩ for data (red profile) versus randomized networks (green profile) Here ⟨Φ⟩ is computed as bits of information, while time runs in steps of 100 ms. (Color figure online)

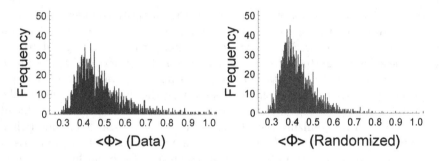

Fig. 2. Histograms of ⟨Φ⟩ for data (left) and randomized networks (right)

different experimental conditions. We compute the mean, median and variance of the ⟨Φ⟩ profiles for both the data and the randomized case. Since the ⟨Φ⟩ profiles do not follow a normal distribution, we use then use the Mann-Whitney-Wilcoxon test to compare the medians between the two ⟨Φ⟩ profiles and we find a significant difference in favor of the brain FCs. For comparing the variances we employ the Brown-Forsythe test (for non-parametric and non-symmetric distributions) and again find significant difference in favor of the data. Our results are shown in Table 1 below. What these results show is that integrated information is a useful measure for quantifying the plethora of patterns observed in temporal FC networks corresponding to various brain states. Compared to random rewirings, the original FC networks scored consistently higher values of ⟨Φ⟩ with a greater mean and median (statistically significant). Additionally, the data networks show a much greater variance (statistically significant) in ⟨Φ⟩ than their random counterparts. This suggests that realistic temporal FC networks of the brain explore a greater region of state space than random configurations. For future work, it might be interesting to look closer at the occasional strong peaks in $\langle \Phi \rangle$ that we observe in the FC networks, which may be driven either by task complexity or by spontaneous neural activity.

Table 1. Test statistics on $\langle \Phi \rangle$ profiles showing the median, mean and variance in values of $\langle \Phi \rangle$ for brain data versus the randomized network. The last column shows p-values for each test.

	$\langle \Phi \rangle$ (FC)	$\langle \Phi \rangle$ (Randomized)	p-value
Median	0.45	0.41	$< 10^{-40}$
Mean	0.51	0.43	N.A.
Variance	0.28	0.01	$< 10^{-20}$

5   Discussion

Information-based methods offer a useful way to quantify complexity of brain functions. Integrated information is interesting as a global measure of a system's collective behavior. In this work, we extend the computational framework of network integrated information for temporal networks and applied it to local field potential (LFP) data obtained from human intracranial recordings. This generates a time-series profile of Φ reflecting the dynamical nature of the brain's informational complexity. As a null model we generate another profile of Φ obtained from randomizing the FC networks at each instance of time (while preserving total degree for each network). This enables a statistical comparison of complexity under two conditions. More specifically, for brain functional networks we find that compared to random re-wirings, the original FC networks scored consistently higher values of $\langle \Phi \rangle$ with a greater mean and median (statistically significant). Additionally, the data networks show a much greater variance (statistically significant) in $\langle \Phi \rangle$ than their random counterparts, thus suggesting that realistic temporal FC networks of the brain explore a greater region of state space than random configurations. This work demonstrates that temporal integrated information may be a good starting point as a future measure of cognitive complexity. This can have potential impact in the clinic for identifying information-based differences between healthy subjects and patients of neurodegenerative diseases.

Acknowledgments. This work is supported by the European Research Council's CDAC project: "The Role of Consciousness in Adaptive Behavior: A Combined Empirical, Computational and Robot based Approach", (ERC-2013- ADG 341196).

References

1. Arsiwalla, X.D., Verschure, P.F.M.J.: Integrated information for large complex networks. In: The 2013 International Joint Conference on Neural Networks (IJCNN), pp. 1–7, August 2013
2. Arsiwalla, X.D., Betella, A., Bueno, E.M., Omedas, P., Zucca, R., Verschure, P.F.: The dynamic connectome: A tool for large-scale 3d reconstruction of brain activity in real-time. In: ECMS, pp. 865–869 (2013)
3. Arsiwalla, X.D., et al.: Connectomics to semantomics: addressing the brain's big data challenge. Procedia Comput. Sci. **53**, 48–55 (2015)
4. Arsiwalla, X.D., Herreros, I., Moulin-Frier, C., Sanchez, M., Verschure, P.F.: Is Consciousness a Control Process? pp. 233–238. IOS Press, Amsterdam (2016)
5. Arsiwalla, X.D., Herreros, I., Verschure, P.: On three categories of conscious machines. In: Lepora, N.F.F., Mura, A., Mangan, M., Verschure, P.F.M.J., Desmulliez, M., Prescott, T.J.J. (eds.) Living Machines 2016. LNCS (LNAI), vol. 9793, pp. 389–392. Springer, Cham (2016). https://doi.org/10.1007/978-3-319-42417-0_35
6. Arsiwalla, X.D., Mediano, P.A., Verschure, P.F.: Spectral modes of network dynamics reveal increased informational complexity near criticality. Procedia Comput. Sci. **108**, 119–128 (2017)
7. Arsiwalla, X.D., Moulin-Frier, C., Herreros, I., Sanchez-Fibla, M., Verschure, P.F.: The morphospace of consciousness. arXiv preprint arXiv:1705.11190 (2017)
8. Arsiwalla, X.D., Verschure, P.: Computing information integration in brain networks. In: Wierzbicki, A., Brandes, U., Schweitzer, F., Pedreschi, D. (eds.) NetSci-X 2016. LNCS, vol. 9564, pp. 136–146. Springer, Cham (2016). https://doi.org/10.1007/978-3-319-28361-6_11
9. Arsiwalla, X.D., Verschure, P.: Why the brain might operate near the edge of criticality. In: Lintas, A., Rovetta, S., Verschure, P.F.M.J., Villa, A.E.P. (eds.) ICANN 2017. LNCS, vol. 10613, pp. 326–333. Springer, Cham (2017). https://doi.org/10.1007/978-3-319-68600-4_38
10. Arsiwalla, X.D., Verschure, P.: Measuring the complexity of consciousness. Front. Neurosci. **12**, 424 (2018)
11. Arsiwalla, X.D., Verschure, P.F.M.J.: High integrated information in complex networks near criticality. In: Villa, A.E.P., Masulli, P., Pons Rivero, A.J. (eds.) ICANN 2016. LNCS, vol. 9886, pp. 184–191. Springer, Cham (2016). https://doi.org/10.1007/978-3-319-44778-0_22
12. Arsiwalla, X.D., Verschure, P.F.: The global dynamical complexity of the human brain network. Appl. Netw. Sci. **1**(1), 16 (2016)
13. Arsiwalla, X.D.: Network dynamics with BrainX3: a large-scale simulation of the human brain network with real-time interaction. Front. Neuroinformatics **9**, 2 (2015)
14. Ay, N.: Information geometry on complexity and stochastic interaction. Entropy **17**(4), 2432–2458 (2015)
15. Balduzzi, D., Tononi, G.: Integrated information in discrete dynamical systems: motivation and theoretical framework. PLoS Comput. Biol. **4**(6), e1000091 (2008)
16. Barrett, A.B., Barnett, L., Seth, A.K.: Multivariate granger causality and generalized variance. Phys. Rev. E **81**(4), 041907 (2010)
17. Barrett, A.B., Seth, A.K.: Practical measures of integrated information for time-series data. PLoS Comput. Biol. **7**(1), e1001052 (2011)
18. Betella, A., et al.: Understanding large network datasets through embodied interaction in virtual reality. In: Proceedings of the 2014 Virtual Reality International Conference, VRIC 2014, pp. 23:1–23:7. ACM, New York (2014)

19. Betella, A., et al.: Brainx3: embodied exploration of neural data. In: Proceedings of the 2014 Virtual Reality International Conference, VRIC 2014, pp. 37:1–37:4. ACM, New York (2014)

20. Delorme, A., Makeig, S.: EEGLAB: an open source toolbox for analysis of single-trial EEG dynamics including independent component analysis. J. Neurosci. Methods **134**(1), 9–21 (2004)

21. Edlund, J.A., Chaumont, N., Hintze, A., Koch, C., Tononi, G., Adami, C.: Integrated information increases with fitness in the evolution of animats. PLoS Comput. Biol. **7**(10), e1002236 (2011)

22. Griffith, V., Koch, C.: Quantifying synergistic mutual information. In: Prokopenko, M. (ed.) Guided Self-Organization: Inception. ECC, vol. 9, pp. 159–190. Springer, Heidelberg (2014). https://doi.org/10.1007/978-3-642-53734-9_6

23. Oizumi, M., Albantakis, L., Tononi, G.: From the phenomenology to the mechanisms of consciousness: integrated information theory 3.0. PLoS Comput. Biol. **10**(5), e1003588 (2014)

24. Omedas, P., et al.: XIM-engine: a software framework to support the development of interactive applications that uses conscious and unconscious reactions in immersive mixed reality. In: Proceedings of the 2014 Virtual Reality International Conference, VRIC 2014, pp. 26:1–26:4. ACM, New York (2014)

25. Seth, A.K.: Causal connectivity of evolved neural networks during behavior. Netw. Comput. Neural Syst. **16**(1), 35–54 (2005)

26. Tegmark, M.: Improved measures of integrated information. arXiv preprint arXiv:1601.02626 (2016)

27. Tononi, G.: An information integration theory of consciousness. BMC Neuroscience **5**(1), 42 (2004)

28. Tononi, G.: Integrated information theory of consciousness: an updated account. Arch. Ital. Biol. **150**(2–3), 56–90 (2012)

29. Tononi, G., Sporns, O.: Measuring information integration. BMC Neuroscience **4**(1), 31 (2003)

30. Tononi, G., Sporns, O., Edelman, G.M.: A measure for brain complexity: relating functional segregation and integration in the nervous system. Proc. Natl. Acad. Sci. **91**(11), 5033–5037 (1994)

31. Wennekers, T., Ay, N.: Stochastic interaction in associative nets. Neurocomputing **65**, 387–392 (2005)

SOM/SVM

Randomization vs Optimization
in SVM Ensembles

Maryam Sabzevari$^{(\boxtimes)}$, Gonzalo Martínez-Muñoz, and Alberto Suárez

Escuela Politécnica Superior, Universidad Autónoma de Madrid,
C/ Francisco Tomás y Valiente, 11, 28049 Madrid, Spain
maryam.sabzevari@uam.es

Abstract. Ensembles of SVMs are notoriously difficult to build because of the stability of the model provided by a single SVM. The application of standard bagging or boosting algorithms generally leads to small accuracy improvements at a computational cost that increases with the size of the ensemble. In this work, we leverage on subsampling and the diversification of hyperparameters through optimization and randomization to build SVM ensembles at a much lower computational cost than training a single SVM on the same data. Furthermore, the accuracy of these ensembles is comparable to a single SVM and to a fully optimized SVM ensemble.

Keywords: Ensemble learning · Support vector machines
Randomization

1 Introduction

The SVM algorithm has received much attention in the machine learning community because of its strong theoretical foundations and its state-of-the-art performance in a wide range of applications [1,2]. In a binary classification problem, an SVM is built by finding the maximum-margin hyperplane that separates the two classes. The parameters of the hyperplane are determined by solving a convex optimization problem that can be formulated in terms of scalar products. To allow for the possibility of class overlap, a regularization term that penalizes errors in the training set and preserves the convexity of the optimization problem is included in the objective function. The strength of this regularization is quantified by a non-negative constant C whose value needs to be carefully adjusted. Finally, a non-linear classifier that maximizes the margin can be built by replacing the scalar products that appear in the objective function of the optimization problem by the corresponding inner products in a Reproducing Hilbert Space associated to a kernel. Linear, polynomial, or RBF kernels are typically used for this embedding. In practice, SVMs built with an RBF kernel have good generalization capacity provided that the value of the kernel width $(1/\gamma)$ is properly adjusted [3].

© Springer Nature Switzerland AG 2018
V. Kůrková et al. (Eds.): ICANN 2018, LNCS 11140, pp. 415–421, 2018.
https://doi.org/10.1007/978-3-030-01421-6_40

In spite of their success, there are some difficulties in the practical application of SVMs. The main one is the high computational cost of training. This disadvantage is exacerbated by their sensitivity to the values of the hyperparameters (C, γ), which are commonly selected by grid search using a costly cross-validation procedure. A possible way to improve the performance of a single SVM is to build ensembles [4–9]. If subsampling is used to train the individual SVMs, building an ensemble can be faster than training a single SVM [7] on the same data. In general, the improvements of an ensemble over a single SVMs are generally small. The reason is that SVM are strong and stable classifiers. In consequence, they are difficult to diversify without introducing large distortions that reduce their accuracy. The goal of this work is to design ensembles of SVMs that are at least as accurate as a single SVM at a reduced computational cost. To this end, we leverage on subsampling and explore the interplay between optimization and randomization methods in the determination of the hyperparameters of the individual SVMs in the ensemble.

2   SVM Ensembles

In this work we analyze three strategies to build bootstrapped ensembles of SVMs: The completely-optimized SVM ensemble (COSE), the partially-optimized SVM ensemble (POSE), and the randomized-optimized SVM ensemble (ROSE). The individual SVMs in all these ensembles are built using independent bootstrap samples drawn from the original training data. The strategies differ in the way that the hyperparameters for the individual SVMs are chosen. In the completely-optimized SVM ensemble (COSE), optimal values of C and γ are selected for each individual SVM in the ensemble. In the partially-optimized SVM ensemble (POSE), optimal combinations of the SVM hyperparameters $\{(C_b, \gamma_b)\}_{b=1}^{B}$ are determined for $B = T/M \ll T$ different bootstrap samples of the original training data, where T is the desired size of the complete ensemble. The final ensemble is built in B batches. For each of these batches ($b = 1, \ldots, B$), we fix the hyperparamters (C_b, γ_b) and build M different SVMs on independent bootstrap samples of the training data. Finally, in the randomized-optimized SVM ensemble (ROSE), T SVM's are built on independent bootstrap samples using randomized values of the hyperparamters C and γ. From these, we select the best $\{(C_b, \gamma_b)\}_{b=1}^{B}$, for $B = T/M \ll T$. The final ensemble is built in B batches, in the same way as the POSE ensemble.

3   Experimental Evaluation

We now present the results of an empirical evaluation of the strategies to build SVM ensembles introduced in the previous section. Specifically, the accuracy and training costs of the proposed methods are compared with those of SVM in 8 binary classification problems from the UCI repository [10] and two synthetic ones (*Threenorm* and *Twonorm*). For the UCI problems, stratified random train/test partitions are used. The training set is composed of 2/3 of the labeled instances available for learning. The remaining 1/3 are set aside for testing. In the synthetic classification problems we generate 300 examples for training and 2000 for testing. The attributes of the instances are normalized so that they have zero mean and unit variance in the training set. The results reported are averages over 10 realizations of the classification problems: either random partitions for real-world data, or independent generations of the training/test sets for synthetic data. The methods are implemented in Python using Scikit-learn library [11].

We have considered the use of bootstrap samples built either with replacement, as in standard bagging, or without replacement, as in subbagging [12,13]. The size of the bootstrap samples with replacement coincides with the original training data. The size of the bootstrap samples without replacement is 50 % of the original one. Subbagging using this ratio is expected to yield similar results as standard bagging [13,14]. In the classification problems considered, the overall accuracy of subbagging is slightly better than bagging. Even though the differences in accuracy are not statistical significant, there is a marked computational advantage of using subbaging. For this reason, only the results of subbagging are reported.

In all three ensemble methods considered and in the single SVMs, an RBF kernel is used. The values of the hyperparameters are selected from a grid in which $C = 2^q$ with $q = -5, \ldots, 15$ and $\gamma = 2^p$ with $p = -15, \ldots, 3$. C is the regularization parameter that controls the complexity of the learning model. A smaller C corresponds to a model with higher margin in which more errors are allowed to occur during the fitting phase. Larger values of C promote more complex models that fit the training data with more precision. The second tuned hyperparameter is γ, which is the inverse of the width of the gaussian RBF kernel. This parameter controls the local influence of the support vectors. For very small values of γ, all support vectors influence the classification of most training examples, which means that the data complexity cannot be captured by the model. Choosing a large γ can potentially over-fit the data as each support vector influences only its vicinity.

For the single SVM and for the individual SVMs in COSE, 10-fold crossvalidation within the corresponding training sets is used to select the optimal values of these hyperparameters. In POSE and ROSE, $B = 10$ different pairs of hyperparameter values, $\{(C_b, \gamma_b)\}_{b=1}^{10}$, are selected using out-of-bag data. According to the empirical investigation carried out, the behavior of POSE and ROSE ensembles is not particularly sensitive to this parameter: ensembles built using values of B between 5 and 50 exhibit similar accuracies in the problems considered. The size of the ensembles generated is $T = 501$, which is sufficiently large for convergence of the classification errors to their asymptotic (optimal) limit [15].

A summary of the results of the experiments performed is given in Table 1. For each dataset the errors rate of a single SVM, the completely-optimized (COSE), the partially-optimized (POSE), and the randomized-optimized (ROSE) SVM ensemble are shown. The values displayed are averages

Table 1. Generalization error for a single SVM and for SVM ensembles

Dataset	SVM	COSE	POSE	ROSE
Australian	15.70 ± 2.32	$\mathbf{14.09 \pm 1.62}$	$\underline{14.17 \pm 0.97}$	14.22 ± 2.62
Boston	13.85 ± 2.93	$\underline{13.73 \pm 1.93}$	$\mathbf{13.43 \pm 2.14}$	14.26 ± 1.56
Colic	20.74 ± 1.64	$\underline{20.57 \pm 2.55}$	20.66 ± 2.07	$\mathbf{20.41 \pm 2.43}$
German	23.96 ± 1.56	$\underline{23.51 \pm 1.54}$	23.75 ± 1.46	$\mathbf{23.48 \pm 1.63}$
Heart	17.78 ± 3.78	$\underline{17.22 \pm 2.58}$	$\mathbf{16.78 \pm 2.69}$	19.44 ± 3.24
Parkinsons	$\underline{8.62 \pm 2.73}$	9.85 ± 3.26	10.77 ± 3.40	$\mathbf{8.31 \pm 3.18}$
Pima	23.28 ± 2.24	$\underline{22.15 \pm 2.16}$	$\mathbf{21.95 \pm 2.60}$	22.23 ± 2.74
Spambase	$\mathbf{6.30 \pm 0.65}$	6.38 ± 0.28	$\underline{6.36 \pm 0.34}$	6.51 ± 0.24
Threenorm	14.01 ± 0.63	$\mathbf{13.51 \pm 0.56}$	$\underline{13.74 \pm 0.64}$	13.90 ± 0.73
Twonorm	2.73 ± 0.64	$\mathbf{2.46 \pm 0.15}$	$\underline{2.53 \pm 0.17}$	2.63 ± 0.21

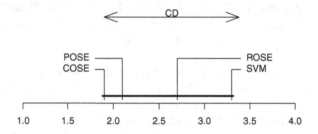

Fig. 1. Average ranks for SVM, COSE, POSE and ROSE (more details in the text)

over 10 realizations of the classification problems considered, followed by the corresponding standard deviations after the $\pm$ sign. For each dataset, the most accurate method is highlighted in boldface. The second best is underlined. In addition, we have used the methodology proposed in [16] to perform an overall comparison of the classifiers' performance across the different datasets. Following this methodology, in Fig. 1 the average ranks of the different methods are displayed. The ranks of the investigated methods are determined in terms of their test errors. For each dataset the best model is ranked first, the second best is ranked second and so on. The figure shows, for each method, its average rank over all dataset. In this diagram, the differences in accuracy of methods that are connected by a horizontal solid line, are not statistically significant according to a Nemenyi test (p-value < 0.05). From this figure, it can be observed that the proposed strategies have an average rank better than the average rank of SVMs, although the differences are not statistically significant according to the Nemenyi test. Finally, in Table 2 we report the training time in seconds to build a single SVM with grid search (second column) and speed-up obtained in training for each method relative to the SVM training time (last three columns). These times were measured on a single core of a CPU Intel Core i5, 64 bits, 2.30 GHz with 8 GB of memory.

From Table 1 one observes that the single SVM is the most accurate predictor only in one dataset (*Spambase*). By contrast, each of the ensemble methods considered achieves the highest accuracy in three problems. The best overall accuracy, in terms of average ranks, correspond to COSE. However, the computational cost of COSE is enormous: around 50–100 times slower to train than a single SVM. Even though the differences are not statistically significant, the average rank of POSE and ROSE ensembles are higher than single SVMs. As shown by the speedup factors displayed in Table 2, these improvements in accuracy are achieved with much lower training costs: POSE ensembles are between 2 and 3 times faster to build than a single SVM. More impressively, the speedup factors for ROSE are between 5 and 20. Furthermore, the differences between the average ranks between each of these and COSE, which is the best ensemble according to this measure, are not statistically significant.

Table 2. Training times in seconds for a single SVM and speedup factors for COSE, POSE and ROSE with respect to SVM

Dataset	SVM (s)	COSE	POSE	ROSE
Australian	63.9	1.8e−02	2.7	15.4
Boston	23.8	9.7e−03	2.3	9.6
Colic	23.2	9.7e−03	2.3	9.6
German	186.9	2.7e−02	2.8	18.4
Heart	10.8	5.6e−03	2.2	6.9
Parkinsons	7.3	4.1e−03	2.2	5.4
Pima	127.8	2.7e−02	3.3	19.6
Spambase	2892.4	2.7e−02	2.0	14.4
Threenorm	30.2	1.1e−02	2.4	10.6
Twonorm	18.8	8.4e−03	2.1	8.5
Average		1.5e−02	2.4	11.8
Stdev		9.1e−03	0.4	4.8

4 Conclusions

In this work, we have proposed and analyzed three types of fast and accurate SVM ensembles built using subagging. Each individual SVM is induced from a bootstrap sample that includes 50% of the original instances, without repetitions. The behavior of a subagging ensemble with this sample size is expected to be similar to the corresponding standard bagging ensemble. Different combinations of optimization and randomization are used to determine the hyperparameters of the individual SVMs in the ensemble: In COSE, the strength of the regularization term (C) and the inverse width of the RBF kernel (γ) are fully optimized. In POSE and ROSE, a small number of different values of these parameters

$\{(C_b, \gamma_b)\}_{b=1}^{B}$ is used repeatedly to build individual SVMs. Specifically, each of these combinations of values is used $M = T/B$ times to build an ensemble of size T. In POSE the combinations of values are determined by optimization in B independent bootstrap samples. In ROSE, the best B out of T randomly generated combinations is selected. For ensembles of size $T = 501$, values of B between 5 and 50 lead to very accurate POSE and ROSE ensembles whose accuracy is comparable to the completely optimized ensemble (COSE) and slightly better than a single SVM. In addition, the training speed of POSE and ROSE is over 2 and 10 times faster than the training time of a SVM optimized using a standard grid search procedure. This training speed improvement can be specially beneficial in the context of large datasets.

Acknowledgments. The research has been supported by the Spanish *Ministry of Economy, Industry, and Competitiveness*, project TIN2016-76406-P, and *Comunidad de Madrid*, project CASI-CAM-CM (S2013/ICE-2845).

References

1. Cortes, C., Vapnik, V.: Support-vector networks. Mach. Learn. **20**(3), 273–297 (1995)
2. Burges, C.J.C.: A tutorial on support vector machines for pattern recognition. Data Min. Knowl. Discov. **2**(2), 121–167 (1998)
3. Cherkassky, V., Ma, Y.: Practical selection of SVM parameters and noise estimation for SVM regression. Neural Netw. **17**(1), 113–126 (2004)
4. Vapnik, V.N.: The Nature of Statistical Learning Theory, 2nd edn. Springer, New York (1999). https://doi.org/10.1007/978-1-4757-3264-1
5. Kim, H.-C., Pang, S., Je, H.-M., Kim, D., Bang, S.Y.: Constructing support vector machine ensemble. Pattern Recognit. **36**(12), 2757–2767 (2003)
6. Valentini, G., Dietterich, T.G.: Bias-variance analysis of support vector machines for the development of SVM-based ensemble methods. J. Mach. Learn. Res. **5**, 725–775 (2004)
7. Claesen, M., De Smet, F., Suykens, J.A.K., De Moor, B.: EnsembleSVM: a library for ensemble learning using support vector machines. J. Mach. Learn. Res. **15**, 141–145 (2014)
8. Stork, J., Ramos, R., Koch, P., Konen, W.: SVM ensembles are better when different kernel types are combined. In: Lausen, B., Krolak-Schwerdt, S., Böhmer, M. (eds.) Data Science, Learning by Latent Structures, and Knowledge Discovery, pp. 191–201. Springer, Heidelberg (2015). https://doi.org/10.1007/978-3-662-44983-7_17
9. Mayhua-López, E., Gómez-Verdejo, V., Figueiras-Vidal, A.R.: A new boosting design of support vector machine classifiers. Inf. Fusion **25**(Suppl. C), 63–71 (2015)
10. Lichman, M.: UCI machine learning repository (2013)
11. Pedregosa, F., et al.: Scikit-learn: machine learning in Python. J. Mach. Learn. Res. **12**, 2825–2830 (2011)
12. Bühlmann, P., Bin, Y.: Analyzing bagging. Ann. Stat. **30**(4), 927–961 (2002)
13. Friedman, J.H., Hall, P.: On bagging and nonlinear estimation. J. Stat. Plan. Inference **137**(3), 669–683 (2007)

14. Martínez-Muñoz, G., Suárez, A.: Out-of-bag estimation of the optimal sample size in bagging. Pattern Recognit. **43**(1), 143–152 (2010)
15. Hernández-Lobato, D., Martínez-Muñoz, G., Suárez, A.: Inference on the prediction of ensembles of infinite size. Pattern Recognit. **44**(7), 1426–1434 (2011)
16. Demšar, J.: Statistical comparisons of classifiers over multiple data sets. J. Mach. Learn. Res. **7**, 1–30 (2006)

An Energy-Based Convolutional SOM Model with Self-adaptation Capabilities

Alexander Gepperth[1](✉), Ayanava Sarkar[1], and Thomas Kopinski[2]

[1] University of Applied Sciences Fulda, Leipzigerstr. 123, 36037 Fulda, Germany
alexander.gepperth@cs.hs-fulda.de
[2] South Westphalia University of Applied Sciences,
Lindenstrae 53, 59872 Meschede, Germany

Abstract. We present a new self-organized neural model that we term ReST (**R**esilient **S**elf-organizing **T**issue). ReST can be run as a convolutional neural network (CNN), possesses a C^∞ energy function as well as a probabilistic interpretation of neural activities, which arises from the constraint of log-normal activity distribution over time that is enforced during learning. We discuss the advantages of a C^∞ energy function and present experiments demonstrating the self-organization and self-adaptation capabilities of ReST. In addition, we provide a performance benchmark for the publicly available TensorFlow-implementation.

Keywords: SOM · Convolutional neural networks · Self-adaption

1 Introduction

This article is in the context of self-organized map (SOM) models that have a continuous energy function. The lack of such an energy function for the original SOM model [7] has been the subject of many articles [2,10]. As it was shown that the original SOM learning rule cannot be derived from a continuous energy function [2], several proposals were made to remedy this problem [4,6]. In general, one may cite the following advantages of energy-based SOM models:

- **Estimation of learning success and parameter selection** A big issue for SOMs is to know whether the model has converged to a "desirable" state. For problems that do not allow a visual quality inspection, there is no universal criterion to determine optimal values for the model parameters (final neighbourhood radius, final learning rate etc.), whereas an energy function provides a simple quality measure.
- **Proof of stability** If a continuous energy function exists and is bounded from below, this automatically guarantees the eventual convergence of SOM learning.
- **Use of advanced stochastic gradient descent methods** With a continuous energy function, many widely-used methods for performing stochastic gradient descent (SGD) in the domain of deep learning can be transferred to SOM learning.

© Springer Nature Switzerland AG 2018
V. Kůrková et al. (Eds.): ICANN 2018, LNCS 11140, pp. 422–433, 2018.
https://doi.org/10.1007/978-3-030-01421-6_41

– **Outlier detection** A sudden increase of energy (which is supposed to be minimized by learning) is a strong indication for a change in data statistics and can thus be used for outlier or concept drift detection. The latter property is especially relevant for our own ongoing work on incremental learning methods [3].

1.1 Related Work on Energy-Based SOM Models

There has been a huge amount of primarily mathematical literature about It was shown conclusively in [2] that the original Kohonen learning rule cannot be exactly derived from the minimization of *any* error function. In the same article, it is mentioned that the Kohonen learning rule follows instead from the individual minimization of per-neuron energy functions [10], but these functions are very complex, non-unique and do not lend themselves to a simple interpretation (e.g., minimization of a distortion measure or similar). Another approach was proposed by Kohonen [7] and taken further by Heskes [6]: instead of finding error functions whose minimization would lead to the Kohonen learning rule, these authors attempted to very slightly modify the Kohonen rule itself. Obviously, the modification should in no way impair the self-organization capabilities of the model while allowing an intuitive interpretation through a (preferably simple) energy function. An modification satisfying these requirements was proposed in [5,6], offering a continuous energy function for discrete as well as continuous data distributions. While this was an important theoretical result, there was no real follow-up in terms of applications in data visualization and/or clustering. It may be supposed that this lack of interest was due to the added computational complexity (an additional convolution needs to be calculated), as well as the problems that convolutions encounter at boundaries. Similar SOM variants having an energy function were proposed in [4] but they suffer from the same "convolution problem".

2 Methods and Data

We rely on the well-known MNIST benchmark [8] for handwritten digit recognition that is a standard problem in machine learning. For our purposes, it is ideal for testing our implementations as it allows a visual inspection of the learned prototypes, facilitating the detection of implementation errors through obviously corrupted prototypes. The MNIST dataset contains 60.000 training samples in 10 classes that are approximately equiprobable, as well as 10.000 samples in the test set.

2.1 The ReST Model

We assume a dataset (or a mini-batch) of input vectors $x_n \in \mathbb{R}^k$ and a two-dimensional set of $K \times K$ neurons with non-negative activities $a_i \geq 0, i = 1 \ldots, K^2$. It is convenient to express activities computed for an input x_n as a one-dimensional vector $a_n \in \mathbb{R}^{K^2}$. A neuron with (linear) index i and coordinates x_i, y_i has an associated prototype $p_i \in \mathbb{R}^k, i = 1, \ldots, K^2$, as well as an $K \times K$ neighbourhood matrix that we write as a one-dimensional vector $g_i \in \mathbb{R}^{K^2}$ in analogy to the vector of activities. Differing from the SOM model, each neuron possesses two internal variables o_i and s_i that play a role in enforcing log-normal statistics for the activities a_n which are computed as:

$$d_{ni} = \sqrt{(p_i - x_n)^2} \tag{1}$$

$$\tilde{a}_{ni} = o_i - s_i d_{ni} \tag{2}$$

$$a_{ni} = \exp(\tilde{a}_{ni}). \tag{3}$$

The adaptation of the prototypes p_i is now achieved by minimizing the energy function

$$c_{ni} = \langle g_i, \log a_n \rangle = \langle g_i, \tilde{a}_n \rangle \tag{4}$$

$$\mathcal{E} = \frac{1}{N} \sum_n \langle c_n, S(c_n) \rangle. \tag{5}$$

The first equation essentially represents a convolution operation as the per-neuron vectors g_i are (for self-organized models) represented by Gaussians centered on neuron i. Generally, one assumes such Gaussians to be periodic where they exceed the map boundaries (for neurons that are close to these boundaries). In this article, we investigate the possibility to simply cut off the Gaussians at map boundaries but to re-weigh them according to the part that is "lost". The logarithm and the vector-valued softmax function $S(v)$ in Eq. (4) are applied in a component-wise fashion as

$$e_i = \exp(\beta v_i) \tag{6}$$

$$S(v)_i = \frac{e_i}{\sum_j e_j} \equiv S_i, \tag{7}$$

β being a parameter that controls the selectivity of the softmax: for higher β values, the output $S(v)$ will tend to be more strongly peaked, the maximal value closer to 1.0 and the rest to 0.0. For lower β values, this relationship is inversed. The minimization of the energy function is performed as a constrained optimization problem, the constraint being that the temporal distribution of activities a_n is log-normal with parameters μ and σ. This implies that $\log a_n$ (with logarithm applied component-wise!) is normally distributed, with the empirical mean and standard deviation $\hat{\mu}$, $\hat{\sigma}$ coinciding with μ, σ:

$$\hat{\mu} \equiv \frac{1}{N} \sum_n \log a_{ni} = \frac{1}{N} \sum_n \tilde{a}_{ni} \stackrel{!}{=} \mu \tag{8}$$

$$\hat{\sigma} \equiv \sqrt{\frac{1}{N} \sum_n (\log a_i - \hat{\mu})^2} = \sqrt{\frac{1}{N} \sum_n (\tilde{a}_i - \hat{\mu})^2} \stackrel{!}{=} \sigma \tag{9}$$

From these requirements, the per-neuron parameters o_i and s_i can be determined unambiguously from the first two moments of the input-prototype distances

$$s_i = \sqrt{\frac{\sigma^2}{\overline{d_i^2} - \overline{d_i}^2}} \tag{10}$$

$$o_i = \mu + s_i \overline{d_i}, \tag{11}$$

which can be computed empirically over a dataset of N samples:

$$\overline{d_i} = \frac{1}{N} \sum_n d_{ni}$$

$$\overline{d_i^2} = \frac{1}{N} \sum_n d_{ni}^2 \tag{12}$$

In a mini-batch setting, we instead take averages over the current mini-batch of N samples (the extreme case being fully online learning where $N = 1$). If we wish to compute the averages $\overline{d_i}$ and $\overline{d_i^2}$ over periods longer than the mini-batch size N, we replace Eq. (12) by exponential smoothing of mini-batches averages:

$$\overline{d_i}(\nu) = (1 - \alpha_d N)\overline{d_i}(\nu - 1) + \alpha_d \sum_n d_{ni} \tag{13}$$

$$\overline{d_i^2}(\nu) = (1 - \alpha_d N)\overline{d_i^2}(\nu - 1) + \alpha_d \sum_n d_{ni}^2 \tag{14}$$

where variable ν expresses the number of the current mini-batch. We scale the adaptation rate $\alpha_d < 1$ with the mini-batch size N since a larger N implies that more samples are used per step in Eq. (13), and thus adaptation can proceed more quickly. Please note that by setting $\alpha_d = 0$ we can turn off the moving average mechanism. In this case only the current mini-batch is considered, as it is the case in Eq. (12).

ReST Learning Rule. For performing gradient descent for the energy function of Eq. (4), we take its derivative w.r.t. to the k-th element of prototype i:

$$\frac{\partial E}{\partial p_{ik}} = \frac{\partial}{\partial p_{ik}} \frac{1}{N} \sum_{nj} c_{nj} S(\mathbf{c})_{nj} = \tag{15}$$

$$= \frac{1}{N} \sum_{nj} \left(S(\mathbf{c}_n)_j \frac{\partial c_{nj}}{\partial p_{ik}} + \beta S(\mathbf{c}_n)_i (\delta_{ij} - S(\mathbf{c}_n)_j) \right) \tag{16}$$

$$\approx \frac{1}{N} \sum_n \frac{\partial c_{n*}}{\partial p_{ik}} \tag{17}$$

where we have used the expression $\partial_j S_i = \beta S_i(\delta_{ij} - S_j)$ for the derivative of the softmax function. If we assume that the softmax function puts 1.0 at the position of the maximal value (whose index is expressed by *), and 0 everywhere else, we obtain the approximation result of Eq. (17) and arrive at the update rule

$$p_i \leftarrow p_i + \frac{\epsilon s_i g_{*i}}{2N} \sum_n \frac{p_i - x_n}{||p_i - x_n||} \qquad (18)$$

where we have one more time designed the index of the best-matching unit (BMU) by a star: $* = \arg\max_i c_i$. If we had omitted the square root in the definition of input-prototype distances in Eq. (1), we would have arrived at the equivalent rule

$$p_i \leftarrow p_i + \frac{\epsilon s_i g_{*i}}{N} \sum_n (p_i - x_n) \qquad (19)$$

which differs (for the online case of $N = 1$) from the energy-based SOM model proposed in [6] only by a factor of s_i for each neuron, an additional difference to [7] being that BMU is not determined from input-prototype distances but from the convolution c of activities with the neighbourhood matrix, see Eq. (4). We observe that the learning rules (18, 19) scale each neuron's prototype adaptation by a factor which is, by Eq. (10), inversely proportional to the activity variance of that neuron. Thus, neurons whose prototypes are either too unspecific or too generic (resulting in uniformly low or high activations with low variance) receive a competitive advantage. This mechanism is self-limiting: increased prototype adaptation usually increases the variance of a neuron's activities, thus eventually annulling the competitive advantage and leading to stable competitive learning dynamics.

Implementation of Constrained Optimization. Minimizing the energy function (4) is performed by performing repeated gradient descent steps using learning rule (18) on the whole available training data set or mini-batch, each step followed by an explicit enforcement of the constraints by applying Eq. (10), this again being followed by an update of the averages using Eq. (12). For speeding up convergence, the neighbourhood matrix g_i of neuron i is modelled as a Gaussian whose standard deviation $S(\nu)$ is decayed exponentially over time, as it is usual with SOMs:

$$g_{ij} = \exp\left(-\frac{(x_j - x_i)^2 + (y_j - y_i)^2}{2S(\nu)^2}\right) \qquad (20)$$

In contrast to normal SOM learning, we do not decay the ReST learning rate α over time, since this complicates advanced gradient descent strategies and introduces unnecessary parameters. Additionally, we impose an initial period without prototype adaptation where only neural statistics are adapted. This allows "adiabatic" prototype updates, causing only small corrections to the already converged o_i and s_i, which avoids potentially problematic feedback loops between the two adaptation processes. The training procedure, as well as all relevant parameters, is detailed in Algorithm 1.

Algorithm: Constrained ReST optimization

Parameters :

- nr of iterations T
- mini-batch size N
- initial and final neigh. radius S_0, S_∞
- learning rate α
- self-adaptation rate α_d
- time parameters t_A, t_0 and t_∞
- target values σ, μ for self-adaptation

Result: trained prototypes p_i
begin
    Initialize all prototypes p_i to small random values ;
    Initialize moving averages $\overline{d_i}(0) = 0$ and $\overline{d_i^2} = 0$;
    Initialize per-neuron parameters $s_i = 0.5$, $o_i = 0$;
    Compute decay time constant $\lambda = -\frac{\log(-S_\infty/S_0)}{t_\infty - t_0}$;
    for *mini-batch* $\nu < T$ **do**
        compute nb.radius $S(\nu)$ and learning rate $\alpha(\nu)$: **begin**
            if $\nu < t_A$ **then** $\alpha(\nu) = 0$, $S(\nu) = S_0$;
            else if $\nu < t_0$ **then** $\alpha(\nu) = \alpha$, $S(\nu) = S_0$;
            else if $\nu < t_\infty$ **then** $\alpha(\nu) = \alpha$, $S(\nu) = S_0 e^{-\lambda\nu}$;
            else $\alpha(\nu) = \alpha$, $S(\nu) = S_\infty$;
        end
        recompute nb. matr. g_i based on $S(\nu)$;
        select a random mini-batch x_n, $0 < n < N$;
        update prototypes p_i according to Eq. (18) ;
        enforce constraint using Eq. (10) ;
        adapt averages $\overline{d_i}(\nu)$ and $\overline{d_i^2}(\nu)$ using Eq. (13) ;
    end
    return p_i
end

Algorithm 1. Mini-batch based learning with the ReST model.

Choice of ReST Parameters. The self-adaptation process is governed by the parameters μ and σ of the log-normal distribution that the activities a_i are required to obey, which raises the question of what their intrinsic significance could be, especially within the context of self-organizing maps and incremental learning. First of all, from the properties of log-normal distributions we know that the quantity e^μ represents both the geometric mean and at the same time the median of a log-normally distributed variable, so essentially we could just fix a median value M and compute $\mu = \log M$ from it. The median for this distribution is smaller but usually close to the arithmetic mean as well so we can also see M as a rough indicator for the arithmetic time average of a neuron's activity. The quantity e^σ is sometimes termed the geometric standard deviation and can be expressed as

$$e^{\sigma} = \exp\left(\sqrt{\frac{1}{N}\sum_n \left(\log \frac{a_{ni}}{e^{\hat{\mu}}}\right)^2}\right) =$$

$$= \sqrt[N]{\Pi_n \exp\left(\left(\log \frac{a_{ni}}{e^{\hat{\mu}}}\right)^2\right)} = E_n^g \sqrt{\exp\left(\left(\log \frac{a_{ni}}{e^{\hat{\mu}}}\right)^2\right)} \qquad (21)$$

and is thus related to the geometric mean of the expression $\sqrt{\exp\left(\left(\log \frac{a_{ni}}{e^{\hat{\mu}}}\right)^2\right)}$.

This expresses the multiplicative spread of values around their empirical geometric mean $e^{\hat{\mu}}$, regardless of the direction. Higher values of e^{σ} will push the activities further away from their geometric mean, forcing them to be more specific, either close to 0 or far away from it. We can thus think of σ as a parameter controlling the sparsity of neural responses, which previous studies on transfer functions for self-organized maps [9] found to be an important factor for performing classification based on SOM activities.

In order to guarantee identical functioning of the WTM mechanism for variable map sizes, the softmax function needs to be parameterized correctly, and more specifically as a function of the number of neurons in the SOM. We therefore need to set the parameter β such that qualitatively identical behavior ensues for any map size. We measure identical behavior by demanding that the maximal response of the softmax function be ξ when given a vector $\boldsymbol{x} \in \mathbb{R}^n$ that consists of $n-1$ times value B and 1 time value λB. Solving this for β gives us the expression

$$\beta = \frac{\ln(\xi^{-1} - 1) - \ln(n - 1)}{B(1 - \lambda)} \qquad (22)$$

The softmax function is a very useful tool for obtaining a "hard" yet differentiable winner selection, in addition to allowing a steady transition between "hard" and "soft" winner selection. In some cases, problems can occur: first of all, sensible choices for B and λ may be hard to obtain because they depend on the learning dynamics. Furthermore, when $\beta > 700$, numerical issues arise due to the exponentials involved. Fortunately there is a simple rule-of-thumb solution for both problems that consists of applying a softmax function with "best guess" parameters *several times* in Eq. (4). This complicates the gradient, but as long as the final softmax function gives a sufficiently hard winner assignment, the learning rule (18) remains valid. Software frameworks like TensorFlow can compute the gradient symbolically, so even the exact gradient can be used regardless of how often softmax was applied. We found that a three-fold application was always sufficient to guarantee a unique winner selection.

The parameter S_0 is usually made to depend on the map size. A rule of thumb that always worked well is to choose it proportional to the diagonal of the quadratic $K \times K$ map, i.e., $S_0 = \frac{K}{4}$. In contrast, classification experiments always give best results the smaller S_∞ is, so this is always fixed at small values like $S_\infty = 0.01$. The values of t_0, t_A and t_∞ can be determined empirically be requiring that (i) self-adaptation has occurred before t_A (ii) the energy function has converged to a stable value before t_0 and (iii) that the energy function is as low as possible while still satisfying all constraints at t_∞. Here, we see the value of an energy function as it can be used to determine convergence, so these parameters which for SOMs have to be obtained by visual inspection, can be determined by cross-validation. By a similar reasoning, a good value for the learning rate can be obtained, where smaller values are always acceptable but lead to increased training time. The mini-batch size is generally assumed to be $N = 1$ in this article. The self-adaptation rate, $\alpha_d N$, should be chosen such that the constraints are approximately upheld during prototype adaptation, meaning it will depend on the choice of α and is thus not a free parameter but can be indirectly obtained by cross-validation.

3   Experiments

The ReST model used in all experiments is implemented in Python using Tensor-Flow 1.5 [1]. The gradients (18, 15) are computed automatically by the software. Energy minimization is done by plain stochastic gradient descent, although more advanced optimizers minimize the ReST energy function equally well.

3.1   Self-organization and Self-adaptation in the ReST Model

In this section we will demonstrate that the ReST model, while differing from both the original SOM model [7] and the energy-based "Heskes model" [6], achieves the same basic type of prototype self-organization. At the same time, we will demonstrate the effectiveness of ReST's self-adaptation process as described in Sect. 2.1 and comment on its beneficial effects. To this end, we will conduct simulations with the dataset described in Sect. 2. ReST parameters are chosen as follows (in the terms of Sect. 2.1): $K = 10$, $T = 40000$, $t_A = 5000$, $t_0 = 10000$, $t_\infty = 30000$, $S_0 = K/4$, $S_\infty = 0.1$, $\alpha_d = 0.01$, $\alpha = 0.05$, $e^\sigma = 3$ and $e^\mu = 0.1$. After ReST convergence at t_∞, statistics is collected for 5000 iterations and subsequently evaluated. Histograms of all neural activities during these 5000 iterations are computed and compared to the theoretical log-normal distribution determined by μ and σ. From Fig. 1, it can be observed that self-organization proceeds exactly in the same manner as in a SOM, starting with a coarse "global ordering" of prototypes followed by refinement as $S(\nu)$ is decreased, showing that ReST performs essentially the same function as a SOM, only with convergence in 2D guaranteed and a self-adaptation process that give a probabilistic interpretation to the computed activities. As can be seen in Fig. 2, the fit between theoretical and measured distribution is generally acceptable for all datasets, although of course a perfect fit is not to be expected. This is because we only fit the first two moments of the log activities to defined values. For a better fit, at least the third moment of the log activities should be controlled, which would however result in a more complex constrained optimization scheme. Figure 1 shows this homogeneity is achieved by quite heterogeneous settings of the per-neuron parameters o_i and s_i, see Eq. (1).

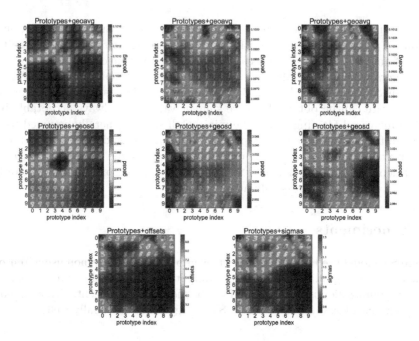

Fig. 1. Upper two rows: Different stages of ReST training on the MNIST dataset. Upper row, from left to right: ReST prototypes with long-term geometric activity averages superimposed on them for times $t = 7000, 12000, 24000$. Middle row, from left to right: ReST prototypes with long-term geometric standard deviation averages superimposed on them for times $t = 7000, 12000, 24000$. We observe that activity averages and deviations are strictly adhered to, as well as the SOM-like topological organization of prototypes. Lower row: distribution of per-neuron parameters o_i and s_i after convergence of the ReST layer at iteration 24000.

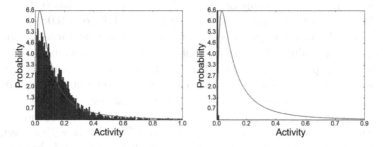

Fig. 2. Activity histograms for neuron $(4, 4)$ in a ReST layer trained on MNIST both for the case of enabled (left) and disabled (right) self-adaptation. The theoretical lognormal density is superimposed onto the histograms as a solid green line, showing a very good match.

3.2   Convolutional ReST Experiments

As with CNNs, convolutional ReST layers have a great number of possible configurations for the filter sizes (f_x^H, f_y^H) and step sizes (Δ_x^H, Δ_y^H), of which we can test only a few. Experimental outcomes are the learned filters for each configuration as shown in Fig. 3, where we see that ReST performs both topological organization (as in a SOM) as well as feature extraction (as in a CNN layer).

Fig. 3. Prototypes for convolutional/independent ReST architectures (left to right), defined by f_x^H, Δ_x^H, y, x: ind-14-7-0-0, ind-14-7-1-1, ind-14-7-2-2, conv-14-7, ind-7-3-3-3, ind-7-3-6-6.

3.3   Intuitive Interpretation of the Self-adaptation Process

To better understand what the self-adaptation mechanism in ReST actually does, we create a set of 10.000 two-dimensional data points $x_i \in \mathbb{R}^2$ which are drawn from a normal distribution with mean $\mu = (0.5, 0.5)^T$ and standard deviation $\Sigma = 0.15$. We subsequently train a non-convolutional ReST layer of size $K = 10$ using the parameters of Sect. 3.1. The final prototype positions and values of the per-neuron parameters s_i and o_i are shown in Fig. 4 and show the following things:

- where data points are more dense(sparse), overall offsets o_i are lower(higher). This is intuitive since prototypes that react to less frequently occurring samples need to have a higher offset to maintain a constant average activity.
- where data points are more dense(sparse), selectivities s_i are higher(lower), meaning that a neuron will react less(more) strongly to nearby samples.

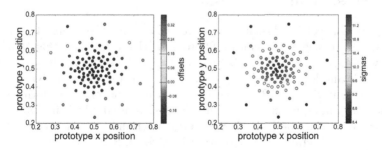

Fig. 4. Prototype positions overlaid in color with per-neuron parameters o_i (left) and s_i (right) when training a ReST layer on a 2D normal distribution.

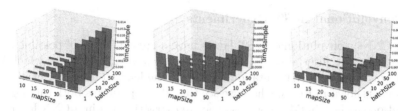

Fig. 5. ReST execution speed depending on batch size and map size, measured on: CPU without updating(left), GPU without updating (middle), GPU with updating (right).

This is intuitive as well, since a higher number of nearby samples would mean a near-constant activity, with low variance, if neurons could not become more selective in their reactions.

These results show that ReST neurons can adapt to the sample density in their Voronoi cell, a behavior that closely mimics self-adaptation mechanisms in biological neurons.

3.4 Implementation and GPU Speed-Up

Unless otherwise stated, benchmark experiments always use the following parameters: Map size $H^H = W^H = 10$, $\Sigma_0 = 2$, $\epsilon_0 = 0.1$, $\epsilon_\infty = 0.0001$, $\Sigma_\infty = 0.01$, $T_{\mathrm{conv}} = 3000$, $T_{\mathrm{conv}} = 10000$. We compare the execution time per sample by feeding the ReST model 2000 randomly selected samples, either running it on CPU or GPU (NVIDIA GeForce 1080), and vary the map size $W^H = H^H \in \{10, 15, 20, 30, 50\}$ and the input batch size $N^I \in \{1, 5, 10, 20, 50, 100\}$ independently. The results of Fig. 5 show that, first of all, GPU acceleration is most effective at high batch sizes and amounts to a factor of roughly 10–20 w.r.t. CPU speed. Secondly, as expected, for high batch and map sizes the GPU is saturated, resulting in no more speed improvements from parallelization. And lastly, updating the ReST layer incurs a heavy speed penalty even on GPU, probably because of the convolution in Eq. (4).

4 Discussion and Conclusion

The experiments of the last section have shown that the energy-based ReST model is both efficient and can profit from GPU acceleration, that it behaves as one would expect a SOM to behave, and that the self-adaptation process is both feasible and leads to a clear probabilistic interpretation of ReST activities. We believe that the new ReST model (in its non-convolutional form) can be used as a drop-in replacement anywhere SOMs are used, albeit in a much more intuitive way because both the ReST energy function as well as ReST activities have a clear interpretation. In its convolutional form, ReST layers can be stacked in deep hierarchies, which we believe can be a very interesting approach when creating "deep" versions of incremental learning methods as proposed, e.g., in [3].

References

1. Abadi, M., et al.: TensorFlow: a system for large-scale machine learning. In: OSDI, vol. 16, pp. 265–283 (2016)
2. Erwin, E., Obermayer, K., Schulten, K.: Self-organizing maps: ordering, convergence properties and energy functions. Biol. Cybern. **67**(1), 47–55 (1992)
3. Gepperth, A., Karaoguz, C.: A bio-inspired incremental learning architecture for applied perceptual problems. Cogn. Comput. **8**(5), 924–934 (2016)
4. Graepel, T., Burger, M., Obermayer, K.: Self-organizing maps: generalizations and new optimization techniques. Neurocomputing **21**(1–3), 173–190 (1998)
5. Heskes, T.: Energy functions for self-organizing maps. In: Kohonen Maps, pp. 303–315. Elsevier (1999)
6. Heskes, T.M., Kappen, B.: Error potentials for self-organization. In: 1993 IEEE International Conference on Neural Networks, pp. 1219–1223. IEEE (1993)
7. Kohonen, T.: Self-organized formation of topologically correct feature maps. Biol. Cybern. **43**, 59–69 (1982)
8. LeCun, Y., Bottou, L., Bengio, Y., Haffner, P.: Gradient-based learning applied to document recognition. In: Haykin, S., Kosko, B. (eds.) Intelligent Signal Processing, pp. 306–351. IEEE Press
9. Lefort, M., Hecht, T., Gepperth, A.: Using self-organizing maps for regression: the importance of the output function. In: European Symposium on Artificial Neural Networks (ESANN) (2015)
10. Tolat, V.: An analysis of kohonen's self-organizing maps using a system of energy functions. Biol. Cybern. **64**(2), 155–164 (1990)

A Hierarchy Based Influence Maximization Algorithm in Social Networks

Lingling Li, Kan Li$^{(\boxtimes)}$, and Chao Xiang

Beijing Institute of Technology,
5 South Zhongguancun Street, Haidian District, Beijing, China
{2120161008, likan}@bit.edu.cn, bit_xiangchao@163.com

Abstract. Influence maximization refers to mining top-K most influential nodes from a social network to maximize the final propagation of influence in the network, which is one of the key issues in social network analysis. It is a discrete optimization problem and is also NP-hard under both independent cascade and linear threshold models. The existing researches show that although the greedy algorithm can achieve an approximate ratio of $(1 - 1/e)$, its time cost is expensive. Heuristic algorithms can improve the efficiency, but they sacrifice a certain degree of accuracy. In order to improve efficiency without sacrificing much accuracy, in this paper, we propose a new approach called Hierarchy based Influence Maximization algorithm (HBIM in short) to mine top-K influential nodes. It is a two-phase method: (1) an algorithm for detecting information diffusion levels based on the first-order and second-order proximity between social nodes. (2) a dynamic programming algorithm for selecting levels to find influential nodes. Experiments show that our algorithm outperforms the benchmarks.

Keywords: Social networks · Influence maximization · Hierarchy

1 Introduction

Influence maximization is to find K nodes (called the seeds) in a social network, so that the expected spread of the influence can be maximized by activating these nodes. Kempe et al. [9] first formulated influence maximization as a discrete optimization problem. Besides, they proposed a greedy algorithm that can approximate the optimal solution within a factor of $(1 - 1/e)$, which is the best approximation guarantee one can hope for according to Feige's approximation threshold for max k-cover [5]. However, due to the large scale of social network data, greedy algorithms have poor efficiency although their accuracy is high. Despite the fact that many more efficient algorithms [2, 3, 8, 10, 11, 13] have been proposed, most methods still spend a lot of time calculating the expected spread of influence.

In this paper, we propose a new approach called Hierarchy based Influence Maximization algorithm, the basic idea is that nodes rely on social groups to spread information and nodes with similar social attributes are more likely to influence each other. We describe a group of nodes by a hierarchical structure which is segmented into levels according to the belonging coefficients of nodes. The belonging coefficients [1]

© Springer Nature Switzerland AG 2018
V. Kůrková et al. (Eds.): ICANN 2018, LNCS 11140, pp. 434–443, 2018.
https://doi.org/10.1007/978-3-030-01421-6_42

reflect the strength of relation between a node and its social group. Nodes with similar belonging coefficients are in the same level. Intuitively, a level is a densely connected subset of nodes that are only sparsely linked to the remaining network [1, 6]. If we find influential node in these levels instead of the whole network, then the prohibitive cost of mining K seeds will be greatly reduced. The method we propose is two-phase. Firstly, we assume that the information publisher is known, then we calculate belonging coefficients by random walk according to the first-order proximity and the second-order proximity between nodes, and then the nodes are segmented into levels by linear regression and dynamic programming. The first-order proximity [14] describes whether the two nodes have an edge, that is, pairwise proximity. The second-order proximity [14] describes whether two nodes have common neighbors, that is, the similarity degree of the neighbor structure of a pair of nodes. Secondly, we use dynamic programming to find the level where influential nodes lie in, then in order to find the influential nodes in the level, we exploit the expected spread value of nodes instead of the traditional Monte-Carlo simulation to calculate the optimization function which significantly improves the efficiency of our algorithm. Our method achieves a good performance compared with benchmark algorithms on three real world datasets.

In summary, the contributions of the paper are given as follows.

1. we propose a new approach called Hierarchy based Influence Maximization.
   The method exploits the first-order and second-order proximity between nodes to detect information diffusion levels, and then mines the influential nodes from these levels by dynamic programming. To the best of our knowledge, we are among the first to use both the first-order and second-order proximity to divide the levels, which is robust to sparse network.
2. we conduct experiments on three real world datasets, compared to benchmark algorithms, our algorithm outperforms in mining influential nodes in social networks.

2 Related Work

The influence maximization problem is first proposed by Domingos and Richardson [4]. Later, Kempe et al. [9] formulated it as a discrete optimization problem, besides, they proposed a greedy climbing approximation algorithm to approximate the optimal solution. Leskovec et al. [11] proposed the CELF (Cost- Effective Lazy Forward) schema, an optimized greedy algorithm to reduce the running time. However, since the greedy algorithms use Monte-Carlo simulation to accurately calculate the influence of candidate nodes, when the network size increases, the running time will increase sharply. As a result, some researchers began to consider using heuristics. Chen et al. [3] presented the DegreeDiscount heuristic which assumes that influence propagation is related to the degree of nodes, and it cut reduces the running time while not sacrificing too much accuracy. In recent years, there are some other heuristics, such as SIMPATH [7], IRIE (Influence Rank Influence Estimation) [8], TIM [13]. Although these heuristics improve the efficiency to some extent, the accuracy is more or less affected. Given that nodes disseminate information and influence each other in the form of social groups, some researchers began to study the influence maximization problem from the perspective of community structure. Wang et al. [15] proposed the CGA (Community-based Greedy Algorithm) for mining top-K influential nodes. Unlike other community detection, CGA takes into account information diffusion between nodes when detecting community. Zhu et al. [16] put forward the hierarchical community structure based algorithm (HCSA) for influence maximization, which gains a wider range of influence spread and less running time compared with heuristic algorithms. The aforementioned approaches handle the efficiency or accuracy issues by improving greedy or heuristic algorithms or by leveraging the community structure of social networks, but, none of them take into consideration the hierarchical structure of nodes according to the first-order and second-order proximity.

3 Method

3.1 Problem Definition

In order to clarify the main idea, we list the major notations used in the paper in Table 1.

Table 1. Major notations used in the paper.

Notations	Descriptions
$G(V, E)$	A social network graph
V	The set of nodes, $|V| = N$
E	The set of edges
pp	The propagation probability
K	The seed set size
I_k	The set of influential nodes obtained in the previous k steps
M	The number of levels
$level_m$	The mth level
$R(I_k)$	The influence degree in G of set I_k
$R_m(I_k)$	The influence degree, in $level_m$ of set I_k

In the paper, we use Independent Cascade (IC) model as information diffusion model. The principle of IC model can be stated as:

Given a social network graph $G(V, E)$, V represents the set of nodes ($|V| = N$), E represents the set of edges ($E = (u, v)|u, v \in V$), and pp represents the propagation probability. For each edge $(u, v) \in E$, $pp_{uv} \in [0, 1]$. In IC model, if a node changes from an inactive state to an active state at the moment t, it only has once opportunity to try to activate its inactive neighbor nodes. Moreover, once the node is activated, it will remain active in the whole process. This process terminates until there are no more new nodes are activated.

3.2   The Hierarchy Based Influence Maximization

The Hierarchy based Influence Maximization algorithm proposed in this paper is divided into two stages. The first stage is to divide the information diffusion into levels, and the second stage is to find influential nodes in each level.

Detection of Information Diffusion Levels. To better measure the closeness of other nodes with respect to the information publisher, we use random walk to calculate the belonging coefficient of other nodes relative to the source node (publisher) to ensure the comparability and continuity of results when detecting the information diffusion levels. The main idea of random walk is: at each step, a walker standing at a node selects one node from its neighbors to move according to a transition probability. As the walking proceeds, the probability of reaching a node gradually decreases, this process ensures that every node has a path to the source node, thus ensuring the continuity of information diffusion.

The measurement of the belonging coefficient consists of the first-order proximity and the second-order proximity between the nodes. $S1_{ij}$ and $S2_{ij}$ are used to represent the first-order proximity and second-order proximity between node v_i and v_j, respectively, then their definitions are as follows:

$$S1_{ij} = \frac{A_{ij}}{d_i} \tag{1}$$

$$S2_{ij} = \frac{|N(i) \cap N(j)|}{|N(i) \cup N(j)|} \tag{2}$$

Where, A_{ij} indicates whether there is an edge between node v_i and node v_j, if it exists, $A_{ij} = 1$, otherwise, $A_{ij} = 0$. d_i indicates the degrees of node v_i. $N(i)$ and $N(j)$ represent the neighbor node set of node v_i and v_j, respectively. And then we give the definition of transition probability p_{ij} between two nodes v_i and v_j:

$$p_{ij} = \alpha S1_{ij} + (1 - \alpha)S2_{ij} \tag{3}$$

Where, the corresponding matrix P is called the transition matrix, the adjustment factor $\alpha \in [0, 1]$. Given a information publisher s, the probability of walking from node v_i to node s within T steps is the belonging coefficient:

$$C_s^T = \sum_{t=1}^{T} q_s^t(i) \tag{4}$$

Where $q_s^t(i) = \sum_{j=1}^{N} q_s^{t-1}(j)Q_{ij}$ is equals to the transition matrix except $Q_{si} = 0, i = 1, \cdots, N$.

The belonging coefficient measures the closeness degree of the node v_i relatives to the source node s. Nodes with more paths and fewer steps from the source node have a higher belonging coefficient. We sort the nodes according to the belonging coefficient and use L to represent the result sequence. Nodes at the same level tend to form a line segment, and the combination of multiple line segments constitutes the entire sequence. We use linear regression to fit the line segment of each level. Because there are more connections within the information hierarchy than that in the outside, the gaps of the ranked belonging coefficient can represent the boundaries of the information diffusion levels. For a given M (representing the number of levels to be detected), we choose $(M - 1)$ breakpoints to minimize the inconsistency. To solve this problem, we design an algorithm based on dynamic programming. We define the state f_{ij} using the minimum value of inconsistency of the first j nodes within i levels. Assuming that $f_{i-1,j'}(j' = 1, 2, \ldots, j)$ is known, we can calculate f_{ij} by enumerating the last breakpoint. The definition of the transition function f_{ij} is as follows:

$$f_{ij} = \min\{f_{i-1,\omega} + cost(\omega + 1, j)\}, \omega = i - 1, \cdots, j - 1 \tag{5}$$

Where, $cost(p, q)$ represents the minimum residual error to fit the part of order from the p th node to the q th node, which is defined as follows:

$$cost(p, q) = \sum_{i=p}^{q} (y(i) - L_i)^2 \tag{6}$$

$$y(i) = \omega i + b \tag{7}$$

$$\omega = \frac{n \sum_i iL(i) - \sum_i i \sum_i L(i)}{n \sum_i i^2 - \sum_i i \sum_i i} \tag{8}$$

$$b = \frac{\sum_i i^2 \sum_i L(i) - \sum_i i \sum_i iL(i)}{n \sum_i i^2 - \sum_i i \sum_i i} \tag{9}$$

Where, $i = p, \cdots, q, n = q - p + 1$. Then we use g_{ij} to record the breakpoint selected by f_{ij}. The definition of g_{ij} is as follows:

$$g_{ij} = \underset{\omega}{argmax}\{f_{i-1,\omega} + cost(\omega + 1, j)\}, \omega = i - 1, \cdots, j - 1 \tag{10}$$

By iteratively computing, we can obtain the division of the information diffusion levels by the breakpoints stored in g. For the number of the final levels, we set it according to the stability of the hierarchical structure. The stability of the hierarchical structure is determined by the fitting function $FL_m = Fitness(C_m) = \frac{d_{in}}{d_{in} + d_{out}} (C_m = \bigcup_{m'}^{m} level_{m'})$, where, C_m consists of top-m levels, d_{in} and d_{out} represent the internal and external degrees of the nodes in these levels, respectively. A hierarchical structure with a local maximum quality is considered stable, as M increases, although more segments can better match the order of the nodes' belonging coefficients, the structure's inconsistency is also increasing. Therefore, we use as few lines as possible to obtain a good hierarchical structure.

Finding the Influential Nodes. In stage one, we have divided social networks into levels. The remaining challenge is to choose which level to find top-K influential nodes. We use a dynamic programming algorithm to select the level of the k th ($k \in [1, K]$) influential node lies in. Let I_{k-1} denote the set of influential nodes obtained in the previous $(k-1)$ steps, if the k th node is mined in $level_m$, the maximal increase ΔR_m of the influence degree of $level_m$ is calculated as follows:

$$\Delta R_m = \max\{R_m(I_{k-1} \cup \{j\}) - R_m(I_{k-1})|j \in level_m\} \tag{11}$$

$$R(I_k) = \frac{\sigma(I_k)}{N} \tag{12}$$

Where, $\sigma(I_k)$ represents the number of nodes influenced by the set I_k in the process of information dissemination. N indicates the number of network nodes.

In order to find the k th influential node, we need to select the level that produces the largest increment of influence among all levels. Let $R[m, k]$ ($m \in [1, M]$ and $k \in [1, K]$) expresses the influence degree of mining the k th influential node in the first m levels, we have:

$$R[m, k] = \max\{R[m-1, k], R[M, k-1] + \Delta R_m\}, (R_m[m, 0], R[0, k] = 0) \tag{14}$$

We select one of the first m levels to mine the k th influential node. We use a sign function $s[m, k]$ to record the selected level, and the sign function is defined as follows:

$$s[m, k] = \begin{cases} s[m-1, k], & |R[m-1, k] \geq R[M, k-1] + \Delta R_m \\ m, & |R[m-1, k] < R[M, k-1] + \Delta R_m \end{cases} \quad s[0, k] = 0 \tag{14}$$

After finding the level $s[m, k]$ where the k th influential node locates, we need to find this influential node in the level and add it to the seed set.

When calculating $\sigma(I_k)$, the existing influence maximization algorithm mostly uses Monte Carlo simulation to calculate the average influence of a solution set, resulting in a time consuming operation. In this paper, we use the expected spread value of I_k instead of the Monte Carlo simulation when calculating $\sigma(I_k)$ to reduce the computational cost. Let $NB(I_k)$ denote the one-hop area of the set I_k, and E denote the set of edges of the social network, then $NB(I_k)$ is defined as follows:

$$NB(I_k) = \{u|u \in I_k\} \cup \{v|\exists u \in I_k, \overrightarrow{uv} \in E\} \tag{15}$$

$$r(v) = |\{u|u \in I_k, \overrightarrow{uv} \in E\}| \tag{16}$$

We extract the edges between the nodes in $NB(I_k)$ and $NB(I_k)$ to form a subgraph of graph G. Then given a small propagation probability pp in the IC model, we use the expected number of nodes activated by I_k in the one-hop area as the fitting function $\sigma(I_k)$ which is given as follows:

$$\sigma(I_k) = |I_k| + \sum_{v \in NB(I_k)-I_k} \left(1 - (1-pp)^{r(v)}\right) \tag{17}$$

To sum up, we use dynamic programming to find out the level that the influential node lies in firstly, then we find the influential node in the level and add it to the seed set. The aforementioned process is repeated until the size of the seed set reaches the target K.

4 Experiments

4.1 Datasets

We adopt the three datasets: Facebook, Twitter and Epinions downloaded from the Stanford Large Network Dataset Collection http://snap.stanford.edu/data/index.html as experimental datasets. Table 2 lists the statistical properties of these three datasets.

Table 2. Statistical properties of datasets.

Dataset	Nodes	Edges	Average degree	Directed
Facebook	4,039	88,234	43.7	False
Twitter	81,306	1,768,149	43.5	True
Epinions	75,879	508,837	6.71	True

4.2 Baseline Algorithms

We compare the performance of the proposed HBIM algorithm with several existing algorithms as follows:

Greedy: a greedy algorithm [11] that makes use of 20,000 Monte-Carlo simulations to evaluate the influence spread.

Degree-Discount: a single degree discount heuristic algorithm [3] that based on nodes' out-degree. The node's out-degree decreases by 1 if its neighbor is selected as a seed node.

CGA: a community-based greedy algorithm [15], which first detects communities by considering into information diffusion, then exploits dynamic programming algorithm to find influential nodes in these communities.

TIM: an influence maximization algorithm [13] based on the-state-of-the-art random sampling with theoretical support.

4.3 Parameter Settings

In order to obtain the influence spread of the seed set, we run 20000 Monte Carlo simulations on the network, and then take the average of the results as the final influence spread. As for the benchmark algorithms, we use the parameter settings mentioned in their papers [3, 11, 13, 15].

As for the HBIM algorithm proposed in this paper, We implement the algorithm under the IC model, besides, we assign the propagation probability pp_{uv} of the link (u, v) in the following way.

$$pp_{uv} = \min\{p_{uv}, 0.01\} \tag{18}$$

Where, p_{uv} denotes the transition probability from node u to node v, which is calculated by the first-order proximity and the second-order proximity between u and v, and its calculation method was mentioned as Eq. (3).

4.4 Experiment Results

Influence Spread. In order to estimate the influence spread of the HBIM algorithm and the benchmark algorithms, we run a Monte-Carlo simulation with 20000 times and take the average of all the simulation results as the final influence spread of the selected seed sets returned from the experiments. We run the five algorithms to be compared on the three datasets to obtain influence spread results with regards to the seed set size K which increases from 5 to 50 with a spacing of 5. We list the results in Fig. 1(a)–(c).

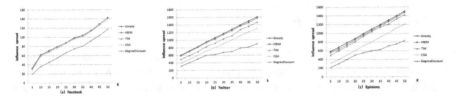

Fig. 1. (a)–(c). Influence spread results varying from seed set size K on the three datasets.

According to Fig. 1(a)–(c), the influence spread results increase with the increment of K, and HBIM gains significant performance on three datasets. An important observation result is that in the three figures, the influence spread of HBIM is comparable to that of Greedy which indicates that the accuracy of the HBIM algorithm is guaranteed. The idea of nodes segments can divide nodes with similar social attributes into the same level, which avoids the overlapping problem of influence in the process of finding seed set, and that results in a higher accuracy of the influence spread. Although the influence spread of TIM algorithm is comparable to that of HBIM, the TIM algorithm has a technical flaw in that it will run again to obtain a smaller set than the one it gets for the first time, that is, it does not guarantee the sequence of the seed set is the order of the influential nodes. The CGA detects communities based on label propagation, the main principle of label propagation is that the community to which the node belongs is a community that contains the maximum number of its influenced neighbors. The algorithm neglects the influence of common neighbors on the detection of communities, therefore, the accuracy of CGA is not as high as that of HBIM. The influence spread of DegreeDiscount is relatively small on three datasets, this is because it reduces time cost at the expense of accuracy. Furthermore, as the scale of the datasets increase, the gap between DegreeDiscount and the other algorithms is gradually increased, that is, the scalablity of DegreeDiscount is not as good as other algorithms.

Running Time. Figure 2 shows the time cost of the four algorithms on the three datasets. Particularly, compared to other algorithms, Greedy has a much more orders of magnitude of running time, especially when the dataset is large-scale, so we did not show it in the figure. From Fig. 2, we can see that the order of the magnitude of running time of HBIM proposed in this paper is equivalent with that of DegreeDiscount and CGA, which shows that HBIM guarantees the accuracy while improving the efficiency.

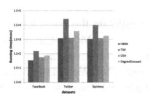

Fig. 2. Running time of different algorithms with seed size K = 50.

5   Conclusions and Future Work

In this paper, we propose HBIM, an influence maximization method based on the hierarchical structure of social network nodes, to mine the top-K influential nodes. HBIM has two main contents. One is to detect information diffusion levels by considering into nodes' first-order and second-order proximity, and the other is to use dynamic programming to select levels to discover seed nodes. Empirical studies on three real-world social network datasets show that our algorithm outperforms in both accuracy and efficiency. In addition, it scales well to big networks. In the future, we can take into account the semantic mechanisms [12] in the process of detecting of information diffusion levels at the first phase of the HBIM algorithm.

Acknowledgments. The research was supported in part by National Basic Research Program of China (973 Program, No. 2013CB329605).

References

1. Chen, F., Li, K.: Detecting hierarchical structure of community members in social networks. Knowl.-Based Syst. **87**, 3–15 (2015)
2. Chen, W., Wang, C., Wang, Y.: Scalable influence maximization for prevalent viral marketing in large-scale social networks. In: Proceedings of the 16th ACM SIGKDD International Conference on Knowledge Discovery and Data Mining, pp. 1029–1038. ACM (2010)
3. Chen, W., Wang, Y., Yang, S.: Efficient influence maximization in social networks. In: Proceedings of the 15th ACM SIGKDD International Conference on Knowledge Discovery and Data Mining, pp. 199–208. ACM (2009)
4. Domingos, P., Richardson, M.: Mining the network value of customers. In: Proceedings of the Seventh ACM SIGKDD International Conference on Knowledge Discovery and Data Mining, pp. 57–66. ACM (2001)

5. Feige, U.: A threshold of ln n for approximating set cover. J. ACM (JACM) **45**(4), 634–652 (1998)
6. Girvan, M., Newman, M.E.: Community structure in social and biological networks. Proc. Natl. Acad. Sci. **99**(12), 7821–7826 (2002)
7. Goyal, A., Lu, W., Lakshmanan, L.V.: Simpath: an efficient algorithm for influence maximization under the linear threshold model. In: 2011 IEEE 11th International Conference on Data Mining (ICDM), pp. 211–220. IEEE (2011)
8. Jung, K., Heo, W., Chen, W.: IRIE: scalable and robust influence maximization in social networks. In: 2012 IEEE 12th International Conference on Data Mining (ICDM), pp. 918–923. IEEE (2012)
9. Kempe, D., Kleinberg, J., Tardos, É.: Maximizing the spread of influence through a social network. In: Proceedings of the Ninth ACM SIGKDD International Conference on Knowledge Discovery and Data Mining, pp. 137–146. ACM (2003)
10. Kim, J., Kim, S.K., Yu, H.: Scalable and parallelizable processing of influence maximization for large-scale social networks? In: 2013 IEEE 29th International Conference on Data Engineering (ICDE), pp. 266–277. IEEE (2013)
11. Leskovec, J., Krause, A., Guestrin, C., Faloutsos, C., VanBriesen, J., Glance, N.: Cost-effective outbreak detection in networks. In: Proceedings of the 13th ACM SIGKDD International Conference on Knowledge Discovery and Data Mining, pp. 420–429. ACM (2007)
12. Razis, G., Anagnostopoulos, I.: Semantifying twitter: the influence tracker ontology. In: International Workshop on Semantic and Social Media Adaptation and Personalization, pp. 98–103 (2014)
13. Tang, Y., Xiao, X., Shi, Y.: Influence maximization: near-optimal time complexity meets practical efficiency. In: Proceedings of the 2014 ACM SIGMOD International Conference on Management of Data, pp. 75–86. ACM (2014)
14. Wang, D., Cui, P., Zhu, W.: Structural deep network embedding. In: Proceedings of the 22nd ACM SIGKDD International Conference on Knowledge Discovery and Data Mining, pp. 1225–1234. ACM (2016)
15. Wang, Y., Cong, G., Song, G., Xie, K.: Community-based greedy algorithm for mining top-k influential nodes in mobile social networks. In: Proceedings of the 16th ACM SIGKDD International Conference on Knowledge Discovery and Data Mining, pp. 1039–1048. ACM (2010)
16. Zhu, C.S., Zhu, F.X., Yang, X.L., School, C., University, W.: Hierarchical community structure based algorithm for influence maximization. Computer Engineering & Design (2017)

Convolutional Neural Networks in Combination with Support Vector Machines for Complex Sequential Data Classification

Antreas Dionysiou[1], Michalis Agathocleous[1], Chris Christodoulou[1(✉)], and Vasilis Promponas[2]

[1] Department of Computer Science, University of Cyprus, P.O. Box 20537, 1678 Nicosia, Cyprus
{adiony01,magath06,cchrist}@cs.ucy.ac.cy
[2] Department of Biological Sciences, University of Cyprus, P.O. Box 20537, 1678 Nicosia, Cyprus
vprobon@ucy.ac.cy

Abstract. Trying to extract features from complex sequential data for classification and prediction problems is an extremely difficult task. Deep Machine Learning techniques, such as Convolutional Neural Networks (CNNs), have been exclusively designed to face this class of problems. Support Vector Machines (SVMs) are a powerful technique for general classification problems, regression, and outlier detection. In this paper we present the development and implementation of an innovative by design combination of CNNs with SVMs as a solution to the Protein Secondary Structure Prediction problem, with a novel two dimensional (2D) input representation method, where Multiple Sequence Alignment profile vectors are placed one under another. This 2D input is used to train the CNNs achieving preliminary results of 80.40% per residue accuracy (Q3), which are expected to increase with the use of larger training datasets and more sophisticated ensemble methods.

Keywords: Convolutional Neural Networks
Support Vector Machines · Deep learning · Machine learning
Bioinformatics · Protein Secondary Structure Prediction

1 Introduction

Learning, is a many-faceted phenomenon. The learning process includes the acquisition of new declarative knowledge, the development of cognitive skills through instructions and practice, the organizing of new knowledge into general, the effective representation of data and finally, the discovery of new theories and facts through practice and experimentation. Analysis of sequential data, feature extraction and prediction through Machine Learning (ML) algorithms/techniques, has been excessively studied. Nevertheless, the complexity

© Springer Nature Switzerland AG 2018
V. Kůrková et al. (Eds.): ICANN 2018, LNCS 11140, pp. 444–455, 2018.
https://doi.org/10.1007/978-3-030-01421-6_43

and divergence of the big data that exist nowadays keep this field of research open. When designing ML techniques for complex sequential data prediction, one must take into account, (a) how to capture both short- and long-range sequence correlations [1], and (b) how to focus on the most relevant information in large quantities of data [2].

A Convolutional Neural Network (CNN) is a class of deep, feedforward artificial neural networks (NN) that has successfully been applied to analyzing visual imagery [3,4]. CNNs were inspired by the human visual system, where individual cortical neurons respond to stimuli, only in a restricted region of the visual field, known as the receptive field. The receptive fields of different neurons partially overlap such that they cover the entire visual field. CNNs have enjoyed a great success in large-scale image and video recognition [5]. This has become possible due to the large public image repositories, such as ImageNet [3], and high-performance computing systems, such as GPUs or large-scale distributed clusters [6]. Overall, CNNs are in general a good option for feature extraction, immense complexity sequence and pattern recognition problems [3–10].

Support Vector Machines (SVMs) were introduced by Cortes and Vapnik [11], initially for binary classification problems. SVMs are a powerful technique for linearly and non-linearly separable classification problems, regression, and outlier detection, with an intuitive model representation [11].

A challenging task for ML techniques is to make predictions on sequential data that encode high complexity of interdependencies and correlations. Application examples include problems from Bioinformatics such as Protein Secondary Structure Prediction (PSSP) [12–15]; even though the three dimensional (3D) structure of a protein molecule is determined largely by its amino acid sequence, yet, the understanding of the complex sequence-structure relationship is one of the greatest challenges in computational biology. A ML model designed for such data has to be in position to extract relevant features, and at the same time reveal any long/short range interdependencies in the sequence of data given. The major key point that needs to be considered when trying to solve the PSSP problem is the complex sequence correlations and interactions between the amino acid residues of a protein molecule. In order to maximize the prediction accuracy of a proposed NN technique for a specific amino acid in a protein molecule, the adjacent amino acids have to be considered by the proposed NN architecture.

In this paper we present a hybrid machine learning method based on the application of CNNs in combination with SVMs, for complex sequential data classification and prediction. The implemented model is then tested on the PSSP problem for 3-state secondary structure (SS) prediction.

2   Methodology

2.1   The CNN Architecture

CNNs are biologically-inspired variants of Multi-Layer Perceptrons (MLPs). The CNN architecture consists of an input layer (inactive), multiple hidden layers and an output layer. Generally speaking, CNNs combine three architectural ideas to ensure some degree of shift, scale, and distortion invariance: local receptive fields, shared weights, and spatial subsampling/pooling [7]. The hidden layers of a CNN typically consist of convolutional layers, pooling layers and fully connected layers. There are four main operations performed by a CNN: (a) convolution, (b) non linearity (Rectifier Linear Unit - ReLU), (c) pooling or sub sampling, and (d) classification. One of the major characteristics of CNNs is that they take advantage of the fact that the input would be like an "image", so they constrain the architecture in a more sensible way. Every layer of a CNN transforms one volume of activations to another through a differential function. The arrangement of a CNN's neurons, unlike a regular NN, is in 3 dimensions: width, height and depth. The Convolutional Layer (CL) is the core building block of a CNN that basically performs the feature extraction process. The key hyperparameter of a CL is the kernel. The kernel is basically a 2D array initialized with random values, and it is used to compute dot products between the entries of the filter and the input volume at any position. The stride is another important hyperparameter that defines the amount of sliding of the kernel across the width and height of the input volume. The result of the kernel sliding over the width and height of the input volume is the feature map, a 2D array holding the responses/activations of the kernel at any spatial position. Moreover, the CNNs' ability to handle complex sequential data relies in part to the sparse connections of neurons. More specifically, each neuron is connected to only a local region of the input volume (i.e., receptive field), and as a result CNNs are capable of encoding complex sequential data correlations in their structure. The Pooling Layer (PL) is another critical block, for building a CNN. Generally speaking, a common technique for constructing a CNN is to insert a pooling layer in-between successive CLs. The main purpose of a pooling layer is to (a) reduce the representation size, (b) reduce the amount of computation in the NN, and (c) control overfitting. The PL uses a filter of a certain dimension and resizes the input given spatially, by striding the filter across the input volume and performing usually the MAX operation. The last layer of a CNN is usually a fully-connected Softmax output layer. Nevertheless, this final step can be practically realized with any suitable classifier. In particular, a small advantage was reported when the softmax output layer of a CNN was replaced by a linear SVM [16].

In this work, the libraries used for CNN and SVM implementations are Deeplearning4j (https://deeplearning4j.org) and LibSVM [17] with Scikit-learn front-end (http://scikit-learn.org), respectively.

2.2   Data Representation

As mentioned above, CNNs are capable of analyzing image-like inputs. The major obstacle on trying to solve a complex sequential data classification problem with CNNs is the representation of the data, in such a way that the network is able not only to understand the shape of the input volume, but also to track the complex sequence correlations among the input volume. Transforming the sequential data shape so as to make it look like an "image", allows CNNs to capture the complex sequence-structure relationship, including to model the SS interactions among adjacent or distant amino acid residues in the PSSP problem. Along these lines, we reorganised the input data shape so that the vectors of each sample in the sequential data are placed one under another, and in such a way create an "image-like" input that will be effectively read correctly and understood by the CNN. In particular, for PSSP we have created a new input volume by placing Multiple Sequence Alignment (MSA) [18] profile vectors of each amino acid one under another to construct a 2D representation of the MSA profiles of a certain number of neighbouring amino acid residues (Fig. 1). By sliding the kernel over the newly constructed input volume, CNNs are able to perform feature extraction for each record data, but also consider neighboring correlations and interactions, if any exist. Note that unlike other techniques, the attention given to any neighboring record correlations is equally weighted across all the input volume, for each sample given. This lets the CNN discover and capture any short, mid- and long range correlations among the input records and consider them all equally in terms of the output volume created. One of the major contributions of this paper is this innovative input data representation, especially designed for the complex sequential data of the PSSP problem.

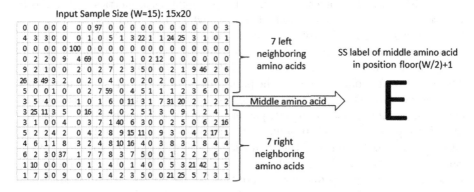

Fig. 1. Example of Data Representation Method: An example of data representation of an input sample using a window size of 15 amino acids. Each line represents the MSA profile vector for the specific amino acid. The SS label for the example input sample showed in this figure, is the SS label for the middle amino acid.

2.3   Application Domain and Data

High quality datasets for training and validation purposes are a prerequisite when trying to construct useful prediction models [2]. Therefore, we have chosen PSSP a well known bioinformatics problem, which is characterized by the complexity of the correlations between the data records due to the existence of combinations of short, mid and long range interactions.

The PSSP, which is based on the Primary Structure (PS) of a protein molecule is considered to be an important problem, since the SS can be seen as a low-resolution snapshot of a protein's 3D structure, and can thus shed light on its functional properties and assist in many other applications like drug and enzyme design. As mentioned above, the understanding of the complex sequence-structure relationship is one of the greatest challenges for the PSSP problem. Since the currently known experimental methods for determining the 3D structure of a protein molecule are expensive, time consuming and frequently inefficient [12], different methods and algorithms for predicting the secondary structure of a protein molecule have been developed [8,12,14,15,19,20]. In particular, Recurrent Neural Networks (RNNs) were successful in the PSSP problem [20], as their architecture may capture both short- and long-range interactions needed for PSSP. CNNs though can detect and extract high complexity features from an input sequence and at the same time track any short-, mid- or long-range interactions depending on the window size. Thus we decided to use CNNs in combination with our novel data representation method for the PSSP problem.

A protein is typically composed by 20 different amino acid types which are chemically connected to form a polypeptide chain, folding into a 3D structure by forming any-range interactions. There are eight main SS states that each amino acid can be assigned to, when a protein 3D structure is available, which are typically grouped in three classes, namely: Helix (H), Extended (E) and Coil/Loop (C/L) with different geometrical and hydrogen-bonding properties. In this work, we use CB513 [19], a non-redundant dataset which has been heavily used as a benchmark for the PSSP problem that contains 513 proteins excluding eight proteins with names: 1coiA_1-29, 1mctI_1-28, 1tiiC_195-230, 2erlA_1-40, 1ceoA_202-254, 1mrtA_31-61, 1wfbB_1-37 and 6rlxC_-2-20 due to corrupted MSA profiles. The use of MSA profiles enhanced the performance of PSSP ML algorithms, since they incorporate information of homologous sequences, which may facilitate the detection of subtle, yet important, patterns along the sequences [14]. In particular, for representing each protein sequence position, we use a 20-dimensional vector, which corresponds to the frequencies of 20 different amino acid types as calculated from a PSI-BLAST [21] search against the NCBI-NR (NCBI: https://www.ncbi.nlm.nih.gov/) database. Note that we have also performed an experiment on a much larger dataset, namely PISCES [22] which shows promising results.

2.4   Support Vector Machines (SVMs)

The main idea behind SVMs is that the input vectors are non-linearly mapped to a higher dimensional feature space using an appropriate kernel function with the hope that a linearly inseparable problem in the input space becomes linearly separable in the new feature space, i.e., a linear decision surface can constructed [23]. An important advantage of SVMs is that the search for the decision surface that maximizes the margin among the target class instances ensures high generalization ability of the learning machine [24]. Their robust performance with respect to sparse and noisy data makes them a good choice in a number of applications from text categorization to protein function prediction [25]. Moreover, SVMs were shown to be the best technique for filtering on the PSSP problem [13]. Given this, we decided to test the filtering capabilities of SVMs on the CNNs' SS prediction results, to see whether the accuracy is improved, and correct the predicted SS of a protein molecule gathered from an ensemble of CNNs.

3 Results and Discussion

3.1 Optimising the Parameters

The CNN implementation using the innovative input data representation described in Sect. 2.2 has been used and tested on the PSSP problem. To train the CNN, we have used the already mentioned CB513 dataset. More specifically, the model's input was a combination of a certain number of neighboring amino acids MSA profile record vectors, one under another, forming a 2D array. The target output label was the SS class for the middle point amino acid that had been examined.

A single CNN has been trained each time. We have decided to track the optimal hyperparameter values using a specific fold after dividing CB513 dataset into ten (10) folds. The main reason for optimizing the hyperparameters on a specific fold is the small size of CB513 dataset. Accuracy results using different hyperparameter values on the other folds are not expected to vary considerably. During this phase, multiple experiments were performed in order to tune up our model and finally achieve the highest results using the CNN. These were Q3 of 75.155% and Segment OVerlap (SOV [30]) of 0.713. CNNs with different numbers of CLs, PLs, kernel sizes, strides, number of parallel filters in each CL, and Gradient Descent (GD) optimization algorithms (Fig. 2) have been tested for optimising the parameter values. The optimization algorithms used are: Gradient Descent (GD), Gradient Descent with momentum (GD with momentum), Adaptive Gradient Algorithm (AdaGrad) [26], RMSprop [27], AdaDelta [28], Adaptive Moment Estimation (Adam) [29]. The two most critical hyperparameters that showed a big impact on the results are: (a) the optimization method used and (b) the number of neighboring amino acids to be considered in each sample (window size). More specifically, the parameter W is the number of total amino acids to be considered by the CNN when trying to predict the SS of the floor(W/2) + 1 amino acid. Then, according to the W parameter we reconstruct the input sample so as to become a 2D array with shape $W \times 20$. The results are shown in Fig. 3. Unlike Wang's et al. [8] method, where they use 42 input features for each residue in an one dimensional input vector format, we use $20 \times W$ (20 input features for each amino acid × window size) input features for each residue in a two dimensional input vector format where each line represents the MSA profile of an amino acid at any specific position. Generally speaking Wang's et al. [8] 42 input features used include our 20 input features (MSA profile for each amino acid) plus extra 22 input features for each amino acid. In this way, our method reduces the dimensionality of the problem without losing too much important information. Moving forward, we had to tune up the parameters that determine the network's architecture.

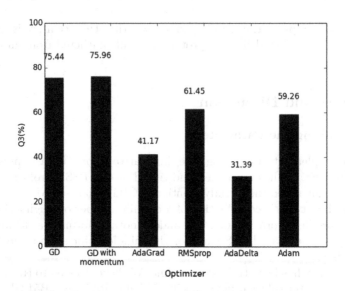

Fig. 2. Optimizers: CNNs Q3 accuracy results using different Gradient Descent (GD) optimization algorithms.

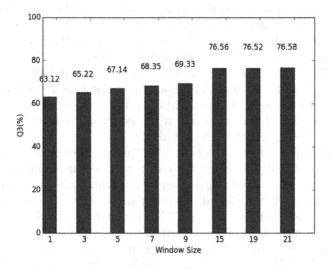

Fig. 3. Window Size: CNNs Q3 accuracy results with different window (W) sizes.

To get a general idea about the CNN performance we have trained it using the CB513 dataset. After tuning up the network architecture, the following optimal CNN parameter values resulted: (a) Number of convolutional layers: 3, (b) Number of Pooling Layers: 0, (c) Kernel/Filter size: 2×2, (d) Stride: 1, (e) Number of Parallel Filters per Layer: 5, (f) Neurons Activation Function: Leaky ReLU, and (g) Optimization method: Gradient Descent with momentum $= 0.85$.

The number of neighboring amino acids (W) that leads to some among the highest Q3 results and at the same time limiting the complexity of information been used (i.e., minimizing the window) was 15. Moreover, no significant change on Q3 accuracy results was noticed using larger window (W) sizes (Fig. 3). Based on the results, we realized that (i) smaller W values do not provide enough information to the network regarding the adjacent interactions between amino acids, and (ii) larger W values contain way too much (unnecessary in some way) information for the network to be handled and decoded properly.

We did not use pooling layers for our CNN architecture due to the fact that subsampling the features gathered from CNN is not relevant in the PSSP problem. Getting only the maximum value of a spatial domain does not work in PSSP as every value extracted from CLs may represent interactions of amino acids in a certain region. These are the most important factors that lead to low Q3 and SOV results using PLs.

3.2   10-Fold Cross-Validation on CB513

In order to validate the robustness of the model as well as to prove its efficiency to the exposure of various training and testing data, we had to complete the evaluation of the PSSP problem on the CB513 dataset, using a 10-fold cross-validation test. All the experiments made are with the optimal parameters of the model as described in Sect. 3.1. As shown in Table 1, the Q3 and SOV accuracy results of CNN with 10-fold cross-validation are 75.15% and 0.713 respectively.

Table 1. Summary of the results for all methods.

Method	$Q_3(\%)$	$Q_H(\%)$	$Q_E(\%)$	$Q_L(\%)$	SOV	SOV_H	SOV_E	SOV_L
CNN	75.155	69.474	67.339	84.566	0.713	0.696	0.669	0.734
CNN Ensembles	78.914	72.748	68.854	85.385	0.744	0.738	0.722	0.737
CNN Ens. + ER Filt.	78.692	70.147	66.921	87.053	**0.756**	0.669	0.713	0.731
CNN Ens. + SVM Filt.	**80.40**	80.911	70.578	85.165	0.736	0.724	0.716	0.743

3.3   Ensembles and External Rules Filtering

After tracking the optimal parameters for the CNN, we have performed six (6) experiments for each fold. Then, in an attempt to maximize the quality of the results gathered as well as to increase the Q3 and SOV accuracy, we proceeded with using the winner-take-all ensembles technique [31,32] on every single fold separately. This technique obtains the predictions of a number of same ML model experiments, and applies the winner takes all method on each amino acid residue SS class predicted. The dramatically improved results are shown in Table 1.

Filtering the SS prediction using external empirical rules is usually the last step made, as a final attempt to improve the quality of the results. This is accomplished by removing conformations that are physicochemically unlikely to happen [15]. Applying the external rules filtering on the CNN's SS prediction, interestingly, does not improve the Q3 score, but it improves the SOV. The results are shown in Table 1.

3.4   Filtering Using Support Vector Machines (SVMs)

CNNs showed very good results on the PSSP (Figs. 2, 3 and Table 1). Nevertheless, as mentioned above, we tried to use SVMs to perform the filtering task. More specifically, after gathering the predictions from the CNN we have trained a SVM using a window of SS states predicted by the CNN. After performing several experiments using different kernels, misclassification penalty parameters (C) [11], Gamma values (G) [11] and window sizes (WIN), we have decided for the optimal SVM parameters that lead to the highest Q3 and SOV accuracy on the PSSP problem and which are: (a) Kernel: Radial Basis Function, (b) $C = 1$, (c) $G = 0.001$ and (d) $WIN = 7$. The results are shown in Tables 2 and 3.

3.5   Summary of the Results

The results shown in Table 1 summarize the Q3 accuracy and SOV results gathered, with all the methods discussed in this paper, using 10-fold cross-validation. It is shown that the CNN can achieve relatively high Q3 and SOV results (75.155% and 0.713 respectively) by its own. Nevertheless, the CNN using ensembles improved the Q3 accuracy results by approximately 3% and SOV score by 0.031. Moving on, filtering the results using External Rules mentioned above, decreases the overall Q3 accuracy results to 78.692%, but dramatically increases the SOV score from 0.744 to 0.756. This was expected as filtering with External Rules has previously been reported to improve SOV scores, but at the same time decrease the overall Q3 accuracy [12]. Finally, using the combination of CNN ensembles and SVM as a filtering technique, achieves the highest Q3 accuracy results (80.40%). The Q3 values for different folds vary from 78.96% to 83.91% and the SOV from 0.71 to 0.78 (Table 2). This indicates that the results for different folds are of comparable quality. Moreover, the accuracies for the three classes, H, E, L, are calculated separately (see Q_H, Q_E, Q_L and SOV_H, SOV_E, SOV_L in Table 2) for getting deeper insight on the quality of the classifier, and mispredictions are quantified in a confusion matrix, graphically represented in Fig. 4. As we can see from Table 2, Q3 accuracy results gathered using CNN Ensembles and SVM filtering are just over **80%**, which is considered to be a high enough percentage when it comes to PSSP, and which also makes this combination of NN techniques a good option when it comes to complex sequential data classification and prediction problems. Heffernan's et al. [20] method achieves 84.16% Q3 accuracy using Bidirectional Recurrent Neural Networks without using a window, but these results are not directly comparable with our results, as they make use of a much larger dataset that contains 5789 proteins, compared to CB513 which contains 513 proteins.

As a conclusion to all the results presented in this paper, we can see that the CNNs can effectively detect and extract features from complex sequential data,

Table 2. CNN Ensembles and SVM Filtering: Q3 and SOV Results for each Fold.

Fold	$Q_3(\%)$	$Q_H(\%)$	$Q_E(\%)$	$Q_L(\%)$	SOV	SOV_H	SOV_E	SOV_L
0	79.69	79.77	70.05	84.75	0.74	0.73	0.71	0.75
1	79.74	78.69	68.06	86.77	0.73	0.73	0.71	0.74
2	78.96	78.64	68.27	84.94	0.72	0.71	0.71	0.73
3	79.55	79.09	67.89	86.12	0.71	0.72	0.70	0.73
4	79.26	78.55	70.00	84.79	0.73	0.72	0.73	0.72
5	79.70	80.27	70.18	84.31	0.73	0.71	0.72	0.73
6	79.64	79.85	68.87	85.26	0.73	0.73	0.71	0.74
7	83.70	87.68	76.86	83.91	0.76	0.73	0.71	0.77
8	83.91	87.53	76.33	84.62	0.78	0.75	0.74	0.79
9	79.85	79.04	69.27	86.18	0.73	0.71	0.72	0.73
Avg.	**80.40**	**80.91**	**70.57**	**85.16**	**0.736**	**0.724**	**0.716**	**0.743**

Table 3. CNN Ensembles and SVM Filtering: Statistical Analysis

	Q3	SOV
Sample standard deviation (s)	1.8140	0.0141
Variance (Sample standard) (s^2)	3.2906	0.0002
Mean (Average)	80.4	0.736
Standard error of the mean $(SE_{\bar{x}})$	0.5736	0.0044

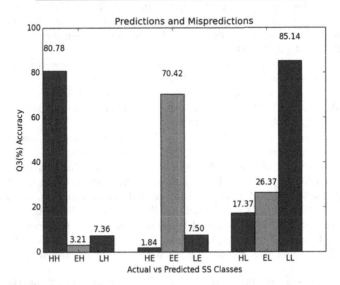

Fig. 4. Confusion Matrix: Predictions and mispredictions of the secondary structure classes H, E and C/L after applying ensembles on each fold using CB513 dataset. Q3 accuracy scores are shown for each class.

by utilizing our proposed "image" like data representation method used to train the CNNs for the PSSP problem. This is due to the fact that our CNN architecture was exclusively designed to face such problems. In addition, SVMs seem to be a good technique to be used for filtering the CNN output. The combination though, of these two ML algorithms seem to be a great option for complex feature extraction and prediction on sequential data, as we take advantage of the benefits of both techniques. Finally, by observing the results from the confusion matrix of Fig. 4, we can conclude that the combination of CNNs with SVMs filtering is a robust and high quality methodology and architecture, as it maximizes the correct predictions for each SS class. Results are expected to be improved by collecting more experiments for each fold, using larger datasets (e.g., PISCES) and deploying more sophisticated ensemble techniques.

References

1. Graves, A.: Generating sequences with recurrent neural networks. arXiv preprint arXiv:1308.0850 (2013)
2. Blum, A.L., Langley, P.: Selection of relevant features and examples in machine learning. Artif. Intell. **97**(1–2), 245–271 (1997)
3. Krizhevsky, A., Sutskever, I., Hinton, G. E.: ImageNet classication with deep convolutional neural networks. In: Pereira, F., Burges, C.J.C., Bottou, L., Weinberger, K.Q. (eds.) Advances in Neural Information Processing Systems 25: Proceedings of the 26th International Conference on Neural Information Processing Systems, pp. 1097–1105. Curran Associates, Lake Tahoe, Nevada, Red Hook, NY (2012)
4. Rawat, W., Wang, Z.: Deep convolutional neural networks for image classification: a comprehensive review. Neural Comput. **29**(9), 2352–2449 (2017)
5. Srinivas, S., Sarvadevabhatla, R.K., Mopuri, K.R., Prabhu, N., Kruthiventi, S.S., Babu, R.V.: A taxonomy of deep convolutional neural nets for computer vision. Front. Robot. AI **2**, 36 (2016)
6. Simonyan, K., Zisserman, A.: Very deep convolutional networks for large-scale image recognition. arXiv preprint arXiv:1409.1556 (2014)
7. LeCun, Y., Bengio, Y.: Convolutional networks for images, speech, and time series. In: Arbib, M.A. (ed.) The Handbook of Brain Theory and Neural Networks, pp. 255–258. MIT Press, Cambridge (1998)
8. Wang, S., Peng, J., Ma, J., Xu, J.: Protein secondary structure prediction using deep convolutional neural fields. Sci. Rep. **6**, 18962 (2016)
9. Bluche, T., Ney, H., Kermorvant, C.: Feature extraction with convolutional neural networks for handwritten word recognition. In: Proceedings of the 12th IEEE International Conference on Document Analysis and Recognition, pp. 285–289 (2013)
10. Graves, A., Mohamed, A.R., Hinton, G.: Speech recognition with deep recurrent neural networks. In: Proceedings of IEEE International Conference on Acoustics, Speech and Signal Processing, Vancouver, BC, Canada, pp. 6645–6649 (2013)
11. Cortes, C., Vapnik, V.: Support-vector networks. Mach. Learn. **20**(3), 273–297 (1995)
12. Baldi, P., Brunak, S., Frasconi, P., Soda, G., Pollastri, G.: Exploiting the past and the future in protein secondary structure prediction. Bioinformatics **15**(11), 937–946 (1999)

13. Kountouris, P., Agathocleous, M., Promponas, V.J., Christodoulou, G., Hadji-costas, S., Vassiliades, V., Christodoulou, C.: A comparative study on filtering protein secondary structure prediction. IEEE/ACM Trans. Comput. Biol. Bioinform. **9**(3), 731–739 (2012)

14. Rost, B., Sander, C.: Combining evolutionary information and neural networks to predict protein secondary structure. Proteins: Struct. Funct. Bioinform. **19**(1), 55–72 (1994)

15. Salamov, A.A., Solovyev, V.V.: Prediction of protein secondary structure by combining nearest-neighbor algorithms and multiple sequence alignments. J. Mol. Biol. **247**(1), 11–15 (1995)

16. Tang, Y.: Deep learning using linear support vector machines. arXiv preprint arXiv:1306.0239 (2013)

17. Chang, C.C., Lin, C.J.: LIBSVM: a library for support vector machines. ACM Trans. Intell. Syst. Technol. **2**(3), 27 (2011)

18. Wallace, I.M., Blackshields, G., Higgins, D.: Multiple sequence alignment. Curr. Opin. Struct. Biol. **15**(3), 261–266 (2005)

19. Cuff, J.A., Barton, G.J.: Evaluation and improvement of multiple sequence methods for protein secondary structure prediction. Proteins: Struct. Funct. Bioinform. **34**(4), 508–519 (1999)

20. Heffernan, R., Yang, Y., Paliwal, K., Zhou, Y.: Capturing non-local interactions by long short-term memory bidirectional recurrent neural networks for improving prediction of protein secondary structure, backbone angles, contact numbers and solvent accessibility. Bioinformatics **33**(18), 2842–2849 (2017)

21. Schaffer, A.A., et al.: Nucl. Acids Res. **25**, 3389–3402 (1997)

22. Wang, G., Dunbrack Jr., R.L.: PISCES: a protein sequence culling server. Bioinformatics **19**(12), 1589–1591 (2003)

23. Vapnik, V.N.: An overview of statistical learning theory. IEEE Trans. Neural Netw. **10**(5), 988–999 (1999)

24. Meyer, D., Wien, F.T.: Support vector machines. R News **1**(3), 23–26 (2001)

25. Furey, T.S., Cristianini, N., Duffy, N., Bednarski, D.W., Schummer, M., Haussler, D.: Support vector machine classification and validation of cancer tissue samples using microarray expression data. Bioinformatics **16**(10), 906–914 (2000)

26. Duchi, J., Hazan, E., Singer, Y.: Adaptive subgradient methods for online learning and stochastic optimization. J. Mach. Learn. Res. **12**, 2121–2159 (2011)

27. Tieleman, T., Hinton, G.: Lecture 6.5 - RMSProp, Divide the gradient by a running average of its recent magnitude. COURSERA: Neural Netw. Mach. **4**(2), 26–31 (2012)

28. Zeiler, M. D.: ADADELTA: An Adaptive Learning Rate Method. arXiv preprint arXiv:1212.5701 (2012)

29. Kingma, D. P., Ba, J. L.: Adam: a method for stochastic optimization. In: Suthers, D., Verbert, K., Duval, E., Ochoa, X. (Eds.) Proceedings of the 3rd International Conference on Learning Representations (ICLR 2015), Leuven, Belgium, pp. 1–13. ACM, New York, NY, USA (2015)

30. Rost, B., Sander, C., Schneider, R.: Redefining the goals of protein secondary structure prediction. J. Mol. Biol. **235**(1), 13–26 (1994)

31. Granitto, P.M., Verdes, P.F., Ceccatto, H.A.: Neural network ensembles: evaluation of aggregation algorithms. Artif. Intell. **163**(2), 139–162 (2005)

32. Fukai, T., Tanaka, S.: A simple neural network exhibiting selective activation of neuronal ensembles: from winner-take-all to winners-share-all. Neural Comput. **9**(1), 77–97 (1997)

Classification of SIP Attack Variants with a Hybrid Self-enforcing Network

Waldemar Hartwig[1]([⊠]), Christina Klüver[1], Adnan Aziz[2],
and Dirk Hoffstadt[2]

[1] Computer Based Analysis of Social Complexity,
University of Duisburg-Essen, 45117 Essen, Germany
Waldemar.Hartwig@mail.de,
Christina.Kluever@uni-due.de
[2] Computer Networking Technology Group, University of Duisburg-Essen,
45141 Essen, Germany
{Adnan.Aziz,Dirk.Hoffstadt}@uni-due.de

Abstract. The Self-Enforcing Network (SEN), a self-organized learning neural network, is used to analyze SIP attack traffic to obtain classifications for attack variants that use one of four widely used User Agents. These classifications can be used to categorize SIP messages regardless of User-Agent field. For this, we combined SEN with clustering methods to increase the amount of traffic that can be handled and analyzed; the attack traffic was observed at a honeynet system over a month. The results were multiple categories for each User Agent with a low rate of overlap between the User Agents.

Keywords: Self-Enforcing Network · SEN · VoIP · Session initiation protocol SIP · Misuse · Fraud · Reference type · Clustering

1 Introduction

Voice over IP (VoIP) systems enable advanced communication (such as voice or video) over the Internet and other data networks and therefore are replacing the traditional phone infrastructures. Nowadays, VoIP is widely used in organizations, companies, and private environments, as it has the advantage of the flexibility and low costs. Many existing devices and applications use standardized VoIP protocols (e.g. SIP for signaling [1] or Real-Time Transport Protocol (RTP) for media transmission [2]). SIP is a text-based application layer protocol similar to File Transfer Protocol (FTP) used to establish, maintain and terminate multimedia sessions between User Agents (UA). The SIP communication uses a request-response protocol, i.e., the source sends a SIP *request message* and receives a SIP *response message*. SIP is an inherently stateful protocol and uses the HyperText Transfer Protocol (HTTP) Digest Authentication for user authentication [3]. In its simplest form SIP uses the transport protocol User Datagram Protocol (UDP), but others can also be used, e.g., Transmission Control Protocol (TCP) or Stream Control Transmission Protocol (SCTP).

This high availability of SIP-based VoIP systems has lured attackers to misuse the VoIP systems. The SIP servers, particularly if they are accessible from external

© Springer Nature Switzerland AG 2018
V. Kůrková et al. (Eds.): ICANN 2018, LNCS 11140, pp. 456–466, 2018.
https://doi.org/10.1007/978-3-030-01421-6_44

networks, are subject to fraudulent registration attempts as a prerequisite for calls via compromised SIP accounts. This is extremely attractive for attackers because they can gain immediate financial benefit by making toll calls (international, cellular, premium services) via third-party accounts. This attack is called *Toll Fraud* and can cause the account owner substantial financial damage in a very short time.

Accordingly, several anti-fraud and anti-phishing techniques were applied, consisting of rule-based approaches, supervised and unsupervised methods, as well as hybrid techniques (for an overview [4]).

It has also become very prevalent to perform denial-of-service (DoS) attacks at application level due to increased code complexity and modular nature of the Internet. Elsabagh et al. [5] have proposed a practical system, Cogo, for early detection and mitigation of software DoS attacks. Cogo recognizes the future exhaustion of resources by employing the Probabilistic Finite Automata (PFA) on the network I/O events, modeled in linear time fashion.

Manunza et al. [6] have presented a rule-based real-time fraud detection system for VoIP networks, Kerberos, that is highly dependent on an Online Charging System, which generates events associated with setup, evolution, and termination of calls in the VoIP network. Kerberos uses these events to identify patterns associated with the malicious use of the resources. Vennila et al. [7] have proposed a 2-tier model to protect users from spam over Internet telephony (SPIT) calls. This 2-tier model is based on stochastic models, Markov Chain (MC) and incremental support vector machine (ISVM).

Aziz et al. [8, 9] have used a Honeynet System to capture the SIP attack traffic to analyze the attacker behavior. This approach is useful in scenarios where it is not possible to access the user's data due to security policies of the country.

In this paper, the goal is to identify an unknown amount of attack patterns for four User Agents. For this purpose, a hybridization of the self-organized learning neural network, namely the *Self-Enforcing Network,* and a *modified Single Linkage* (MSL) clustering algorithm is used to analyze attack traffic at honeynet systems.

The remainder of this paper is organized as follows: Sect. 2 gives a brief overview of SIP, Toll Fraud attack and four dominant attack tools recorded at the honeynet systems. An overview of the artificial neural network, Self-Enforcing Network (SEN), is given in Sect. 3 followed by the presentation of the sequential clustering in Sect. 4 where the organization of the data with SEN is augmented with other clustering algorithms. In Sect. 5 the analysis of the SIP attack data is covered. Finally, Sect. 6 concludes the paper.

2   SIP and Attack-Tools

SIP is a signaling protocol used to establish, modify and terminate multimedia sessions in IP-based networks. It supports a number of messages for different purposes. For this paper, the following SIP messages are relevant: The User Agent (UA) (i.e., SIP device) uses REGISTER method to register its location to the SIP server. During this process, the UA sends credentials (username and password) to the SIP server. After successful registration, the UA can initiate calls using INVITE messages. The OPTIONS messages allow a UA to query a server's capabilities and to discover information about the supported SIP methods, extensions, codecs, etc. without establishing a session.

The Toll Fraud attack comprises of the following four stages

1. *SIP Server & Device Scan.* An attacker can use OPTIONS packets to "ping" any single IP address or whole subnets in order to identify SIP devices, because of the fact that the SIP protocol requires every SIP device to answer OPTIONS packets. Even if a UA's SIP stack implementation is not standard compliant, the attacker can instead use REGISTER requests to identify SIP devices.
2. *Extension Scan.* To identify active extensions (user accounts) of known SIP servers, the attacker tries to register at several extensions, typically without using a password. An extension identifier consists of digit sequences and/or strings. If the extension exists, the server normally answers with a 401 UNAUTHORIZED, because no password is given. If it does not exist, a 404 NOT FOUND is returned. The result of this attack stage is a complete list of existing extensions (provider accounts).
3. *Registration Hijacking.* To register for a given extension, the attacker tries to guess the password sending – possibly many – REGISTER messages with different passwords to a specific extension. If a valid password is found, the information is stored by the attacker and used later on the credentials to register at this extension.
4. *Toll Fraud.* The term multi-stage "toll fraud" is used if a person generates costs (toll) by misusing a hijacked extension using the VoIP functionality to make calls, specifically international calls or calls to premium numbers. Another motivation to use a hijacked account is to obfuscate the caller identity. In terms of SIP messages, the attacker first sends a REGISTER message with the correct password. After the "200 OK" message from the server, the attacker can initiate calls by using INVITE messages.

The first three stages (1–3) of multi-stage Toll Fraud can be executed, either completely or partially, by using paid/freely available tool suites. Some commonly used tools are SIPVicious, SIPCli, VAXSIPUserAgent, and Random user agent (RUA). *SIPVicious* contains several small programs: The first one is a SIP scanner called "svmap". It scans an IP address range for SIP devices, either sequentially or in random order, typically with OPTIONS packets. SIPVicious also provides tools to find active SIP accounts with REGISTER messages ("svwar") and to crack passwords ("svcrack"). If not modified, SIPVicious identifies itself as UA "friendly-scanner". *SIPCli* is a Windows-based command line tool, which usually sends only the INVITE packets and is capable to perform all four stages of the multi-staged Toll Fraud attack. *VaxSIPUserAgent* [9] is another tool used to perform the Toll Fraud attacks. It sends REGISTER and INVITE packets. *RUA* tool [10] sends OPTIONS packets only; therefore, it performs Server Scans only.

To analyze the behavior of different attackers and attack tools – used to perform the Toll Fraud attacks – it is necessary to inspect the attack traffic. Due to data protection laws in Germany, it is not possible to access the user data from VoIP service providers. The Computer Network and Technology Group (TdR) of the University of Duisburg-Essen have implemented a honeynet system [11] to capture the SIP traffic. The traffic destined to this honeynet system is by default attack traffic, as it does not contain any legitimate user in it. The attack traffic is stored in MySQL database using a tool, SIP Trace recorder (STR) [12]. The STR then performs some statistical analysis on the captured attack traffic, e.g., number of requests per day, number of requests per attack tool, clustering the requests with respect to different stages of multi-staged Toll Fraud attack, etc. The clustering of SIP requests performed by STR is based on MySQL queries. No machine learning techniques or clustering algorithms were used to group the SIP requests into different stages of multi-staged Toll Fraud attacks.

3   The Self-enforcing Network

The Self-Enforcing Network (SEN) is a self-organized learning neural network, developed by the Research Group "Computer-Based Analysis of Social Complexity" (CoBASC). In this section, the functionalities that are relevant to the study are briefly presented. More in-depth descriptions of the SEN are found in e.g. [13–15].

The data (objects and attributes) are represented in a "semantical matrix" where the rows represent the objects o and the columns represent the attributes a. A value of the matrix w_{ao} represents the degree of affiliation of an attribute to an object. In this case, the values of the semantical matrix are the encoded fields of the SIP request messages monitored by the honeynet system. The encoding is explained in Sect. 5 below.

The training of the network is done by transforming the min-max normalized values of the semantical matrix (interval $[-1.0 - 1.0]$ or $[0.0 - 1.0]$ depending on the attribute) into the weight matrix of the network with the following learning rule:

$$w(t+1) = w(t) + \Delta w, \text{ and}$$
$$\Delta w = c * w_{ao} \tag{1}$$

where c is a constant usually defined as $0 \leq c \leq 1$ with the same purpose as the learning rate in standard neural networks.

For the analysis of real data, the "cue validity factor" (cvf) is introduced, which is a measure of how important an attribute is for the membership in each category [16]. The cvf allows to exclude (cvf = 0.0) or to dampen (0.0 < cvf < 1.0) certain attributes to steer the formation of clusters. Equation (1) then becomes

$$\Delta w = c * w_{ao} * cvf_a \tag{2}$$

For the activation function the Enforcing Activation Function (EAF) was used:

$$a_j = \sum_{i=1}^{n} \frac{w_{ij} * a_i}{1 + |w_{ij} * a_i|} \tag{3}$$

a_j is the activation value of the receiving neuron j, a_i is the activation values of the sending neurons i and w_{ij} is the respective weight value ($= w_{ao}$). In this study, the topology of SEN can be seen as a two-layered network with a feed-forward topology with the attributes as input neurons and the objects as output neurons.

After the learning process is finished, new input vectors (*new* SIP request messages) with the same attribute names can be inserted and classified. These input vectors are computed in two different ways: the computed similarities according to the highest activated neuron (*ranking*), and the smallest difference (*distance*) between the input vectors and the learned vectors from the semantical matrix.

SEN offers several methods to visualize the results allowing for a fast interpretation. For the analysis primary the "map visualization" was used. It maps the objects to a 2D plane according to the Euclidean distance between two objects. Similar objects are moved closer to one another while dissimilar objects are moved further apart.

4 Sequential Clustering

Self-organized learning neural networks along with clustering methods excel in situations where unlabeled data have to be organized into a probably unknown number of groups of objects [17]. The conditions are that objects in a group should be as similar to one another as possible, and objects in different groups as dissimilar as possible. For an overview [18–20] describe different frameworks and methods.

Note that the goal of this study is to identify an unknown amount of attack variants from the data with a focus on attack variants related to the four known ATs (see Sect. 2). Therefore, an unsupervised method is considered more suitable than a supervised or semi-supervised one.

For that reason, the self-organized learning Self-Enforcing Network (SEN) was chosen for the analysis of the attack traffic. In addition, the visualization components of SEN allow a fast interpretation of the results.

To increase the amount that can be processed with SEN the data is split into fragments, which are read sequentially into the SEN as objects. The SEN then organizes these fragments and clusters are calculated based on the highest *activation* values *and* the smallest *distance* between the inserted objects as input vectors and the learned objects. The centroids or geometric centers of the clusters are extracted with a clustering algorithm and used as "reference types" [14] of their clusters and all centroids from all fragments are read into a single SEN.

The clustering algorithm used is called MSL. It is a *modification of a Single-Linkage* [21] *algorithm* (MSL) with two distance metrics and thresholds instead of one, namely the previous mentioned calculations. Both thresholds have to be met for two clusters to be merged into a single one. Meaning that

- the activation of at least one object o_1 in the first cluster for an object o_2 in the other cluster has to be higher than the activation-threshold and
- the distance between these objects o_1 and o_2 has to be smaller than the distance-threshold.

Instead of a fixed threshold MSL introduces a *dynamic definition of the thresholds* through a single parameter r. The parameter r dictates that the activation between two objects o_1 and o_2 must be at least the rth highest and the distance at max the rth lowest compared all other activation- and distance-pairs with o_1.

Previous, other clustering algorithms that were tested with smaller sized data from the honeynet system were a variation of Lloyd's k-means algorithm [22], a Single Linkage algorithm using only one distance metric and a combined algorithm using evidence accumulation. The variation of k-means uses multiple k-means runs and selects the k-means run with the least mean square error as the result of the algorithm [23]. The combined algorithm using evidence accumulation uses multiple k-means runs to generate multiple clusterings. The co-occurrences of a pair of patterns in a cluster are mapped to a co-association matrix. An MST-based clustering algorithm (minimum spanning tree [21]) is then applied to this matrix to calculate the final clustering [23, 24].

While most algorithms were able to successfully detect all known attack variants (see [8] for the variants) in the preliminary test data the **MSL** algorithm stood out with its low time complexity and its ease of use. It performed significantly faster than Multiple k-Means and Evidence Accumulation and the lack of parameters meant less parameter exploration to discover successful parameter combinations.

5   SIP-Data Analysis and Results

The data used for the analysis contains SIP requests, for the month of January 2016, recorded at the Honeynet system (cf. Sect. 2), consisting of around 4.2 million SIP packets. For the analysis purposes, the following SIP header fields we used: SourceIP, SourcePort, DestinationIP, DestinationPort, Method, CallID, UserAgent, ContactUser, ContactHost, ToUser, ToHost, FromUser, FromHost, Via and Time.

Aside from numerical fields like *SourcePort* most other fields had to be encoded into real values before they could be inserted into a SEN. e.g. the IP addresses were split into three attributes: the first 8 and the last 24 bits as decimals and the IP address class as an integer (1 to 5 where 1 represents A and 5 represents E). Other non-numerical fields were encoded as the arithmetic mean of the ASCII decimal values of all characters rounded to an integer value with values above 130 were changed to -130. Additionally, 12 comparison attributes were added, which contain $+1.0$ if the fields of the compared attributes are equal and -1.0 otherwise.

In this analysis, 17 attributes were considered, which have a cvf equal to 1. Figure 1 shows these attributes along with their lower and upper limits, which are needed for the min-max normalization.

For the analysis and the sequential clustering, the Enforcing Activation Function with c = 0.1 and one learning step was used. The dataset was split into fragments of 2000 objects each and the clustering algorithm parameter r was set to 1 (r = 1) with a precision of two decimal places.

The 4.2 million SIP requests were compressed to 3400 elements through the sequential clustering, which is organized into 15 groups by SEN (see Fig. 2). For visibility only four attack tools (ATs) SIPVicious, SIPCli, VAXSIPUserAgent and RUA (with UserAgents names *"friendly-scanner"* (FS), *"SIPCli"* (CLI), *"VaxSIPUserAgent"* (VAX) and a random String consisting of 8 alphabetical characters (RND)) are shown in red, blue, green and purple respectively.

Name	Default	Minimum	Maximum	Encoding
SourceIP-8	50.00	-255.00	255.00	[-1; 1]
SourceIP-24	1,975,095.00	-16,777,216.00	16,777,216.00	[-1; 1]
ContactUser	-1.00	-130.00	130.00	[-1; 1]
SourceIP-Class	0.00	-5.00	5.00	[-1; 1]
SourcePort	0.00	-65,535.00	65,535.00	[-1; 1]
ToUser	-1.00	-130.00	130.00	[-1; 1]
FromUser	-1.00	-130.00	130.00	[-1; 1]
ContactUser==ToUser	0.00	-1.00	1.00	[-1; 1]
ContactUser==FromUser	0.00	-1.00	1.00	[-1; 1]
ToUser==FromUser	0.00	-1.00	1.00	[-1; 1]
ContactHost==SourceIP	0.00	-1.00	1.00	[-1; 1]
ContactHost==DestinationIP	0.00	-1.00	1.00	[-1; 1]
ContactHost==ToHost	0.00	-1.00	1.00	[-1; 1]
ContactHost==FromHost	0.00	-1.00	1.00	[-1; 1]
ToHost==SourceIP	0.00	-1.00	1.00	[-1; 1]
ToHost==DestinationIP	0.00	-1.00	1.00	[-1; 1]
ToHost==FromHost	0.00	-1.00	1.00	[-1; 1]
FromHost==SourceIP	0.00	-1.00	1.00	[-1; 1]
FromHost==DestinationIP	0.00	-1.00	1.00	[-1; 1]

Fig. 1. Selected attributes with the cvf = 1 for all attributes

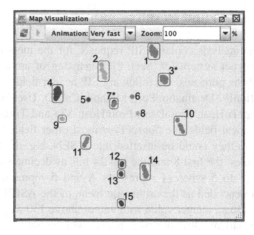

Fig. 2. Visualization of AT categories (15 identified groups) after sequential clustering (Color figure online)

13 out of 15 groups contain elements of a single Attack Tool only, while group 3 contains FS and VAX-elements and group 7 contains FS-, CLI- and VAX-elements. Messages from RND can be distinguished in 100% of all cases; CLI in 4 out of 5, FS in 5 out of 7 and VAX in 3 out of 5.

Considering that the groups 3 and 7 contain more elements than a single Attack Tool (AT), 18 reference types were derived from the groups to identify all elements.

The correlation of all reference types for *Friendly Scanner* (FS) with the attack variants is shown in Table 1.

The first seven FS reference types correlate to an attack variant presented by [8]. For example, reference type 1 correlates with variant SS-b or SS-f just from the shown characteristics.

Table 1. Correlation of Reference Types (1–7) to Attack Variants from [8] with new additional characteristics of the reference types

Ref. type	Attack variant	Additional characteristics
1	SS-b	CU/TU/FU = 100; TH/FH = 1.1.1.1
2	SS-d	CU/TU/FU = 100; TH/FH = 1.1.1.1
3	SS-f	CU/TU/FU = 100; TH/FH = invalid;
4	RH-a	CU/TU/FU = 123; CH = 1.1.1.1
5	SS-d	CU/TU/FU = "" and others mixed; CH/TH/FH = invalid; Method, 50% REG
6	ES-a	CH = 1.1.1.1
7	ES-b1	Method: 75% REG, 20% INV
8	–	Method: 99.9% INV
9	–	CU/FU = 100; TU = ""; TH = invalid
10	–	CU/TU/FU = 123
11	–	CU/FU = ""; CH/FH = invalid
12	–	CU/FU = ""; CH/FH = invalid
13	–	–
14	–	TH/FH = 1.1.1.1
15	–	–
16	–	CU = 1 or multiple 1 s; TU/FU = 100; CH = 127.0.0.1; TH/FH = 1.1.1.1
17	–	Method: 40% INV
18	–	CU/TU/FU = alphabetical Strings

The characteristics of the other 11 reference types (to the best knowledge of the authors) are not presented in any other publication. Reference types 11 and 12, for example, have invalid IP-addresses and empty ContactUser and FromUser fields, while reference type 16 contains "1.1.1.1" for ToHost and FromHost and "127.0.0.1" for ContactHost.

Moreover, the reference types were tested with random data samples, i.e. new input vectors, from August 2016 and December 2016 where multiple new reference types were discovered. These reference types are shown in Fig. 3 together with the reference types from January 2016.

The 18 previously found reference types are confirmed by the new data, and additional 7 attack variations for the four dominant attack tools are detected and defined as reference types. The obtained 25 reference types are identified and organized in 17 groups out of which 12 contain only reference types of a single Attack Tool. Out of six attack tool-pairs, VAX/RND can be distinguished for all reference types.

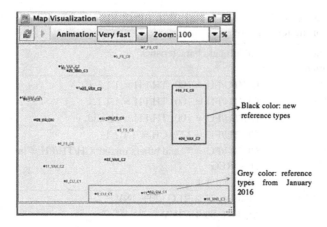

Fig. 3. 18 reference types from January 2016 with additional 7 reference types from test data.

6   Conclusion and Further Work

The self-organized learning neural network Self-Enforcing Network (SEN) was used to analyze received SIP request messages from a honeynet system at the University of Duisburg-Essen. The goal was to identify categories for four dominant User Agents and the attack tools behind them. For that purpose, the SEN was extended with clustering capabilities to increase the amount of data that can be analyzed.

The SIP attack traffic for January 2016 was analyzed and 18 different categories were identified for four User Agents including "*friendly-scanner*" (FS), "*SIPCli*" (CLI), "*VaxSIPUserAgent*" (VAX) and a string of eight *random alphabetical characters* (RND). The 7 out of 18 categories were correlated to attack variants discovered by [8] while SEN discovered the previously unknown other 11. The 18 categories are organized into 15 groups. Most contain categories of a single Attack Tool meaning that input messages classified into those categories could be mapped to a specific AT without conflict.

A test with messages from two other months discovered seven new categories for three out of four User Agents: three FS attack variations, three VAX variations, and an additional RND variation.

As part of future work, the importance and consideration of certain attributes could be adjusted to create more diverse categories for the User Agents. Another part of future work is the analysis of other user agents that were not considered in this study. The final part of future work includes the analysis of traffic from users in regular VoIP Systems and the comparison to the identified categories for the purpose of distinguishing attacks from regular usage in a live system.

References

1. Rosenberg, J., et al.: SIP – Session Initiation Protocol. No. RFC 3261 (2002)
2. Jacobson, V., Frederick, R., Casner, S., Schulzrinne, H.: RTP – A transport protocol for real-time applications. No. RFC 3550 (2003)
3. Franks, J., Hallam-Baker, P., Hostetler, J., Lawrence, S., Leach, P., Luotonen, A., Stewart, L.: HTTP authentication – Basic and Digest Access Authentication. No. RFC 2617 (1999)
4. Aleroud, A., Zhou, L.: L.: Phishing environments, techniques, and countermeasures: a survey. Comput. Secur. **68**, 160–196 (2017)
5. Elsabagh, M., Fleck, D., Stavrou, A., Kaplan, M., Bowen, T.: Revisiting difficulty notions for client puzzles and DoS resilience. In: Dacier, M., Bailey, M., Polychronakis, M., Antonakakis, M. (eds.) ISC 2012. LNCS, vol. 10453, pp. 39–54. Springer, Heidelberg (2012). https://doi.org/10.1007/978-3-319-66332-6_20
6. Manunza, L., Marseglia, S., Romano, S.P.: Kerberos: a real-time fraud detection system for IMS-enabled VoIP networks. J. Netw. Comput. Appl. **80**, 22–34 (2017)
7. Vennila, G., Manikandan, M.S.K., Suresh, M.N.: Detection and prevention of spam over Internet telephony in Voice over Internet Protocol networks using Markov chain with incremental SVM. Int. J. Commun. Syst. **30**(11), e3255 (2017)
8. Aziz, A., Hoffstadt, D., Ganz, S., Rathgeb, E.: Development and analysis of generic VoIP attack sequences based on analysis of real attack traffic. In: 2013 12th IEEE International Conference on Trust, Security and Privacy in Computing and Communications (TrustCom 2013), pp. 675–682. IEEE, Melbourne (2013)
9. Aziz, A., Hoffstadt, D., Rathgeb, E., Dreibholz, T.: A distributed infrastructure to analyse SIP attacks in the internet. In: IFIP Networking Conference 2014 (IFIP Networking), pp. 1–9 (2014)
10. Gruber, M., Hoffstadt, D., Aziz, A., Fankhauser, F., Schanes, C., Rathgeb, E., Grechenig, T.: Global VoIP security threats – large scale validation based on independent honeynets. In: IFIP Networking Conference (IFIP Networking) 2015, pp. 1–9 (2015)
11. Hoffstadt, D., Marold, A., Rathgeb, E.P.: Analysis of SIP-based threats using a VoIP honeynet system. In: Conference proceedings of the 11th IEEE International Conference on Trust, Security and Privacy in Computing and Communications (TrustCom). Liverpool, UK (2012)
12. Hoffstadt, D., Monhof, S., Rathgeb, E.: SIP trace recorder: monitor and analysis tool for threats in SIP-based networks. In: 2012 8th International on Wireless Communications and Mobile Computing Conference (IWCMC), August 2012
13. Klüver, C.: Steering clustering of medical data in a self-enforcing network (SEN) with a cue validity factor. In: 2016 IEEE Symposium Series on Computational Intelligence (SSCI), pp. 1–8 (2016)
14. Klüver, C.: A self-enforcing network as a tool for clustering and analyzing complex data. Procedia Comput. Sci. **108**, 2496–2500 (2017)
15. Klüver, C., Klüver, J., Zinkhan, D.: A self-enforcing neural network as decision support system for air traffic control based on probabilistic weather forecasts. In: Proceedings of the IEEE International Joint Conference on Neural Networks (IJCNN), Anchorage, Alaska, USA, pp. 729–736 (2017)
16. Rosch, E., Mervis, C.B.: Family resemblances: studies in the internal structure of categories. Cognit. Psychol. **7**(4), 573–605 (1975)
17. Liu, H., Ban, X.J.: Clustering by growing incremental self-organizing neural network. Expert Syst. Appl. **42**(11), 4965–4981 (2015)

18. Xu, R., Wunsch, D.: Survey of clustering algorithms. IEEE Trans. Neural Netw. **16**(3), 645–678 (2005)
19. Fahad, A., et al.: A survey of clustering algorithms for big data: taxonomy and empirical analysis. IEEE Trans. Emerg. Top. Comput. **2**(3), 267–279 (2014)
20. Aggarwal, C.C., Reddy, C.K. (eds.): Data clustering: algorithms and applications. CRC Press, Boca Raton (2013)
21. Gower, J.C., Ross, G.J.: Minimum spanning tree and single linkage cluster analysis. Appl. Stat. **18**, 54–64 (1969)
22. Lloyd, S.: Least squares quantization in PCM. IEEE Trans. Inf. Theory **28**(2), 129–137 (1982)
23. Jain, A.K.: Data clustering: 50 years beyond K-means. Pattern Recognit. Lett. **31**(8), 651–666 (2010)
24. Fred, A.L., Jain, A.K.: Data clustering using evidence accumulation. In: 16th International Conference on Pattern Recognition Proceedings, vol. 4, pp. 276–280. IEEE (2002)

Anomaly Detection/Feature Selection/Autonomous Learning

Generalized Multi-view Unsupervised Feature Selection

Yue Liu, Changqing Zhang$^{(\boxtimes)}$, Pengfei Zhu, and Qinghua Hu

School of Computer Science and Technology, Tianjin University,
Tianjin 300350, China
{liuyue76,zhangchangqing,zhupengfei,huqinghua}@tju.edu.cn

Abstract. Although many unsupervised feature selection (UFS) methods have been proposed, most of them still suffer from the following limitations: (1) these methods are usually just applicable to single-view data, thus cannot well exploit the ubiquitous complementarity among multiple views; (2) most existing UFS methods model the correlation between cluster structure and data distribution in linear ways, thus more general correlations are difficult to explore. Therefore, we propose a novel unsupervised feature selection method, termed as generalized Multi-View Unsupervised Feature Selection (gMUFS), to simultaneously explore the complementarity of multiple views, and complex correlation between cluster structure and selected features as well. Specifically, a multi-view consensus pseudo label matrix is learned and, the most valuable features are selected by maximizing the dependence between the consensus cluster structure and selected features in kernel spaces with Hilbert Schmidt independence criterion (HSIC).

Keywords: Unsupervised · Multi-view · Feature selection

1 Introduction

For many real-world applications, such as image understanding [15], bioinformatics [20] and text mining [19], data are usually represented as high dimensional feature vectors. However, direct utilization of these high-dimensional data usually suffers from high computation cost, heavy storage burden and, performance degradation. Feature selection can reduce time and space requirements, alleviate the over-fitting problem due to the "curse of dimensionality" and address the poor performance resulting from irrelevant and redundant features [8].

According to whether labels are available, feature selection approaches are basically categorized into supervised and unsupervised ones. Supervised feature selection methods usually jointly evaluate the importance of different features via the correlation between features and class labels [8, 25]. Unfortunately, labeled data are usually scarce and manually labeling is rather expensive, while unlabeled data are much more abundant. Therefore, unsupervised feature selection (UFS) [3, 14, 17, 24] is practically important and has attracted close attention.

© Springer Nature Switzerland AG 2018
V. Kůrková et al. (Eds.): ICANN 2018, LNCS 11140, pp. 469–478, 2018.
https://doi.org/10.1007/978-3-030-01421-6_45

Early methods [10,24] usually evaluate the importance of each feature individually and select features in the one by one manner, which could not well explore the correlation among features. Then, some methods [3,25] address this issue in two steps. Recently, researchers have proposed methods [9,14,17,23,26] to simultaneously exploit discriminative information and feature correlation in a unified framework. In this manner, it avoids the separation of structure identification and feature selection, and thus better performance could be expected. Generally, there are two key factors for the success of unsupervised feature selection, i.e., ***identification of underlying data structure and, exploration of correlation between underlying data structure and selected features***. For the first one, due to the lack of label information, the underlying data structure is difficult to accurately identified. Therefore, we attempt to borrow other information from the data to guide the process of feature selection. These multi-view representations can capture rich information from multiple cues to benefit the underlying structure identification. For the second one, most existing methods [14,17,26] hold the underlying assumption that there exists linear correlation between the selected features and data structure. However, correlation in practice is usually much more complex than linear correlation in most existing approaches.

To address the above limitations, we propose a novel unsupervised feature selection approach for multi-view data, termed as *generalized Multi-View Unsupervised Feature Selection* (**gMUFS**). Specifically, there are two contributions in gMUFS. First, our method identifies cluster structure of data with the help of complementarity among multiple views. Second, to explore more general correlation between the consensus data structure and the selected features, Hilbert Schmidt independence criterion (HSIC) is introduced to capture feature-label dependence in kernel spaces. To solve our problem, an efficient alternating optimization algorithm is developed. Experimental results on benchmark datasets validate the effectiveness of the proposed approach over other state-of-the-arts.

2   gMUFS: Our Feature Selection Model

2.1   Preliminaries

Throughout this paper, we use bolded lower-case letters to denote vectors in column form, bolded upper-case letters to denote matrices and upper-case letters to denote constants. We denote the data collection with N samples and V views as $\mathcal{D} = \{\mathbf{X}^{(v)} \in \mathbb{R}^{D_v \times N}\}_{v=1}^{V}$, where $\mathbf{X}^{(v)}$ is the feature matrix of the vth view. By concatenating these views, the feature matrix corresponding to all views can be denoted as $\mathbf{X} = [\mathbf{X}^{(1)}; \cdots ; \mathbf{X}^{(V)}] \in \mathbb{R}^{D \times N}$, where $D = \sum_{v=1}^{V} D_v$.

Considering the effectiveness of spectral clustering technique [2,18], it is utilized to learn pseudo cluster labels to guide the process of feature selection in our approach. Specifically, for the affinity matrix used in spectral clustering, a k-nearest-neighbor graph is introduced since local structure of the data generally reflects both important discriminative and cluster information, and its effectiveness has been empirically proved by many feature selection methods

[3,14]. Moreover, it usually works better than other ones constructed according to global geometry structures. The affinity matrix $\mathbf{S}$ is defined as:

$$S_{ij} = \begin{cases} \exp(-\frac{\|\mathbf{x}_i - \mathbf{x}_j\|^2}{\sigma^2}), \mathcal{N}_k(\mathbf{x}_i, \mathbf{x}_j) = 1 \\ 0, \text{otherwise}, \end{cases} \tag{1}$$

where $\mathcal{N}_k(\mathbf{x}_i, \mathbf{x}_j)$ indicates the k-nearest neighboring relationship. Specifically, $\mathcal{N}_k(\mathbf{x}_i, \mathbf{x}_j) = 1$ if $\mathbf{x}_i$ (or $\mathbf{x}_j$) belongs to the set of k-nearest neighbors of $\mathbf{x}_j$ (or $\mathbf{x}_i$), otherwise, $\mathcal{N}_k(\mathbf{x}_i, \mathbf{x}_j) = 0$. Accordingly, the objective function of spectral clustering with local geometric structure is defined as follows:

$$\min_{\mathbf{U}} \sum_{i,j=1}^{N} S_{ij} \| \frac{\mathbf{u}_i}{\sqrt{D_{ii}}} - \frac{\mathbf{u}_j}{\sqrt{D_{jj}}} \|^2 = \min_{\mathbf{U}} \text{Tr}(\mathbf{U}^T \mathbf{L} \mathbf{U}), \ s.t. \ \mathbf{U}^{(v)^T} \mathbf{U}^{(v)} = \mathbf{I}, \tag{2}$$

where $\mathbf{D}$ is a diagonal matrix with $D_{ii} = \sum_{j=1}^{n} S_{ij}$, and $\mathbf{L}$ is the normalized graph Laplacian matrix constructed with $\mathbf{L} = \mathbf{D}^{-1/2}(\mathbf{D} - \mathbf{S})\mathbf{D}^{-1/2}$.

2.2 Generalized Correlation

For unsupervised feature selection [6,14,17], to ensure the quality of the selected features, many approaches try to maximize the correlation between the selected features and the pseudo label matrix. Typically, the loss function is usually defined as $\|\mathbf{X}^T \mathbf{W} - \mathbf{U}\|_F^2$ or $\|\mathbf{X}^T \mathbf{W} - \mathbf{U}\|_{2,1}$ for robust issue, where $\mathbf{W} \in \mathbb{R}^{D \times C}$ is the feature selection matrix. Clearly, the underlying assumption is that the pseudo label matrix could be linearly reconstructed by the selected features, which is limited for the cases of complex dependence in practice. Therefore, we propose to measure the dependence in kernel space, which maps variables into a reproducing kernel Hilbert space such that the correlations measured in that space corresponds to high-order joint moments between the original distributions [1,7,16].

Supposing that $\mathcal{Z} = \{\mathbf{x}_i, \mathbf{y}_i\}_{i=1}^{N}$ are jointly drawn from two domains $\mathcal{X}$ ($\mathbf{x}_i \in \mathcal{X}$) and $\mathcal{Y}$ ($\mathbf{y}_i \in \mathcal{Y}$), with $\mathcal{F}$ and $\mathcal{G}$ being kernel spaces on $\mathcal{X}$ and $\mathcal{Y}$ respectively, then, the dependence of the two random variables is measured as:

$$\text{HSIC}(\mathcal{Z}, \mathcal{F}, \mathcal{G}) = (N - 1)^{-2} \text{Tr}(\mathbf{K}_1 \mathbf{H} \mathbf{K}_2 \mathbf{H}), \tag{3}$$

where $\mathbf{K}_1$ and $\mathbf{K}_2$ are the Gram matrices corresponding to different variables. For a constant N, $\mathbf{1}_N \in \mathbb{R}^N$ is a column vector with all elements being 1 and $\mathbf{H} = \mathbf{I} - \frac{1}{N}\mathbf{1}_N \mathbf{1}_N^T \in \mathbb{R}^{N \times N}$ centers the matrix to have zero mean.

For our approach, we aim to select the features with high correlation with pseudo labels. Therefore, we should maximize the dependence between selected features and pseudo labels. By ignoring the constant scaling factor $(N - 1)^{-2}$, we should select features that could maximize the following objective:

$$\text{HSIC}(\mathbf{X}^T \mathbf{W}, \mathbf{U}) = \text{Tr}(\mathbf{K}_F \mathbf{H} \mathbf{K}_L \mathbf{H}), \tag{4}$$

where $\mathbf{K}_F$ and $\mathbf{K}_L$ are the Gram matrices corresponding to the selected features and pseudo labels, respectively.

2.3   Generalized Multi-view UFS

For our multi-view feature selection model, the goal is to jointly select features from different views, thus, we will explore the complementarity across these views. To ensure the consistency of multi-view data, we introduce a consensus pseudo label matrix and enforce each view-specific pseudo label matrix $\mathbf{U}^{(v)}$ towards consensus pseudo label matrix $\mathbf{U}^{(*)}$ that will be more reasonable and robust, accordingly, well guides the feature selection. Specifically, we introduce the disagreement measure [12] between the consensus pseudo cluster label matrix and that of each view as follows:

$$\mathrm{DA}(\mathbf{U}^{(v)}, \mathbf{U}^{(*)}) = \left\| \frac{\mathbf{K}_{\mathbf{U}^{(v)}}}{||\mathbf{K}_{\mathbf{U}^{(v)}}||_F^2} - \frac{\mathbf{K}_{\mathbf{U}^{(*)}}}{||\mathbf{K}_{\mathbf{U}^{(*)}}||_F^2} \right\|_F^2, \tag{5}$$

where $\mathbf{K}_{\mathbf{U}^{(\cdot)}}$ is the affinity matrix for $\mathbf{U}^{(\cdot)}$ and $||\cdot||_F$ denotes the Frobenius norm of a matrix.

Under the condition $\mathbf{U}^{(v)^T}\mathbf{U}^{(v)} = \mathbf{I}$ and with using inner product kernel, i.e., $\mathbf{K}_{\mathbf{U}^{(v)}} = \mathbf{U}^{(v)}\mathbf{U}^{(v)^T}$, we have $||\mathbf{K}_{\mathbf{U}^{(v)}}||_F^2 = C$, where C is the number of clusters. By ignoring the constant additive and scaling terms, Eq. (5) turns out to be:

$$\mathrm{DA}(\mathbf{U}^{(v)}, \mathbf{U}^{(*)}) = -\mathrm{Tr}(\mathbf{U}^{(v)}\mathbf{U}^{(v)^T}\mathbf{U}^{(*)}\mathbf{U}^{(*)^T}). \tag{6}$$

Accordingly, the proposed generalized multi-view unsupervised feature selection model is induced as:

$$\min_{\substack{\mathbf{U}^{(1)},\dots,\mathbf{U}^{(V)} \\ \mathbf{U}^{(*)},\mathbf{W}}} \sum_{v=1}^{V} \mathrm{Tr}(\mathbf{U}^{(v)^T}\mathbf{L}^{(v)}\mathbf{U}^{(v)}) + \gamma\|\mathbf{W}\|_{2,1}$$

$$+ \alpha \sum_{v=1}^{V} \mathrm{DA}(\mathbf{U}^{(v)}, \mathbf{U}^{(*)}) + \beta \mathrm{IND}(\mathbf{X}^T\mathbf{W}, \mathbf{U}^{(*)})$$

$$s.t. \ \ \mathbf{U}^{(v)^T}\mathbf{U}^{(v)} = \mathbf{I}, \ \mathbf{U}^{(*)^T}\mathbf{U}^{(*)} = \mathbf{I}, \ \mathbf{U}^{(v)} \geq 0, \mathbf{U}^{(*)} \geq 0. \tag{7}$$

Note that, under the nonnegative and orthogonal constraints, there is only one element in each row of $\mathbf{U}$ which is greater than zero and all of the others are zeros. The structure-sparsity regularization on $\mathbf{W}$ is realized by $\ell_{2,1}$-norm. For the consistence of signs for different terms, we define the independence measure as $\mathrm{IND}(\cdot, \cdot) = -\mathrm{HSIC}(\cdot, \cdot)$. The nonnegative scalars α, β and γ are tradeoff parameters. The nonnegative constrains are imposed on pseudo labels matrices to agree with label definition and interpretability [14]. $\ell_{2,1}$-norm imposed on the feature selection matrix $\mathbf{W}$ ensures the sparseness in rows, making it particularly suitable for feature selection. According to the objective function, our method simultaneously promotes the quality of pseudo labels by exploiting the complementarity of different views and explores the complex correlation between the selected features and the multi-view consensus cluster structure.

3   Optimization

In this section, we propose an iterative updating algorithm to solve the optimization problem of gMUFS. The objective function in Eq. (7) is difficult to resolve with respect to $\{\mathbf{U}^{(v)}\}_{v=1}^{V}$, $\mathbf{U}^{(*)}$ and $\mathbf{W}$, therefore, the alternating optimization is introduced. Firstly, the objective function is rewritten as:

$$
\min_{\substack{\mathbf{U}^{(1)},\cdots,\mathbf{U}^{(V)} \\ \mathbf{U}^{(*)},\mathbf{w}}} \sum_{v=1}^{V} \mathrm{Tr}(\mathbf{U}^{(v)T}\mathbf{L}^{(v)}\mathbf{U}^{(v)}) + \gamma\|\mathbf{W}\|_{2,1} + \alpha\sum_{v=1}^{V}\mathrm{DA}(\mathbf{U}^{(v)},\mathbf{U}^{(*)})
$$

$$
+ \beta\mathrm{IND}(\mathbf{X}^T\mathbf{W},\mathbf{U}^{(*)}) + \frac{\eta}{2}(\left\|\mathbf{U}^{(*)T}\mathbf{U}^{(*)} - \mathbf{I}\right\|_F^2 + \sum_{v=1}^{V}\left\|\mathbf{U}^{(v)T}\mathbf{U}^{(v)} - \mathbf{I}\right\|_F^2), \quad (8)
$$

where $\eta > 0$ is the parameter for orthogonality condition. In practice, η should be large enough to ensure the orthogonality satisfied. For convenience, we define

$$
\mathcal{L}(\mathbf{U}^{(1)},\cdots,\mathbf{U}^{(V)},\mathbf{U}^{(*)},\mathbf{W}) = \sum_{v=1}^{V}\mathrm{Tr}(\mathbf{U}^{(v)T}\mathbf{L}^{(v)}\mathbf{U}^{(v)}) + \alpha\sum_{v=1}^{V}\mathrm{DA}(\mathbf{U}^{(v)},\mathbf{U}^{(*)})
$$

$$
+ \beta\mathrm{IND}(\mathbf{X}^T\mathbf{W},\mathbf{U}^{(*)}) + \gamma\|\mathbf{W}\|_{2,1} + \frac{\eta}{2}(\left\|\mathbf{U}^{(*)T}\mathbf{U}^{(*)} - \mathbf{I}\right\|_F^2 + \sum_{v=1}^{V}\left\|\mathbf{U}^{(v)T}\mathbf{U}^{(v)} - \mathbf{I}\right\|_F^2).
$$
$$
(9)
$$

- **Update $\mathbf{W}$ by fixing $\mathbf{U}^{(1)},\cdots,\mathbf{U}^{(V)}$ and $\mathbf{U}^{(*)}$**: Similarly to existing method [4] and for optimization convenience, we employ inner product kernel for HSIC. Accordingly, the subproblem should minimize the following function:

$$
\mathcal{L}(\mathbf{W}) = \mathrm{Tr}(\mathbf{W}^T(\gamma\mathbf{G} - \beta\mathbf{M})\mathbf{W}), \quad (10)
$$

where $\mathbf{G}$ is a diagonal matrix with elements defined as $G_{ii} = \frac{1}{2\|\mathbf{w}_i\|_2}$ and $\mathbf{M} = \mathbf{X}\mathbf{H}\mathbf{U}^{(*)}\mathbf{U}^{(*)T}\mathbf{H}\mathbf{X}^T$. To avoid trivial solution, we constrain $\mathbf{W}$ with $\mathbf{W}^T\mathbf{W} = \mathbf{I}$. Then the above problem is actually similar to the objective of spectral clustering. Therefore, the solution for $\mathbf{W}$ is the first P eigenvectors (corresponding to smallest P eigenvalues) of the matrix $\gamma\mathbf{G} - \beta\mathbf{M}$. It is noteworthy that, since the dependence is measured in kernel space, the dimensionalities of $\mathbf{U}^{(*)}$ and $\mathbf{X}^T\mathbf{W}$ need not to be the same, i.e., $P \neq C$. Therefore, our method is more flexible than others [14,17].
- **Update $\mathbf{U}^{(v)}$ by fixing $\mathbf{W}$ and $\mathbf{U}^{(*)}$**: We introduce the multiplicative updating rules [13]. Specifically, since $\mathbf{U}^{(v)} \geqslant 0$, we can solve the problem by introducing Lagrange multiplier matrix $\mathbf{\Phi} = [\phi_{ij}]$ with ϕ_{ij} corresponding $U_{ij}^{(v)}$. Then, the Lagrange function is as follows:

$$
\mathrm{Tr}\left(\mathbf{U}^{(v)T}\mathbf{L}^{(v)}\mathbf{U}^{(v)}\right) + \alpha\mathrm{DA}(\mathbf{U}^{(v)},\mathbf{U}^{(*)}) + \frac{\eta}{2}\left\|\mathbf{U}^{(v)T}\mathbf{U}^{(v)} - \mathbf{I}\right\|_F^2 + \mathrm{Tr}(\mathbf{\Phi}\mathbf{U}^{(v)T}).
$$
$$
(11)
$$

474   Y. Liu et al.

Setting the derivative of Lagrange function with respect to $\mathbf{U}^{(v)}$ to be zero, we can get

$$2\mathbf{N}\mathbf{U}^{(v)} - 2\eta\mathbf{U}^{(v)} + \mathbf{\Phi} = 0, \tag{12}$$

where $\mathbf{N} = \mathbf{L}^{(v)} - \alpha\mathbf{U}^{(*)}\mathbf{U}^{(*)T} + \eta\mathbf{U}^{(v)}\mathbf{U}^{(v)T}$. According to the Karush-Kuhn-Tucker (KKT) condition, i.e., $\phi_{ij}U_{ij}^{(v)} = 0$, we can get the updating rule as follows:

$$U_{ij}^{(v)} \leftarrow U_{ij}^{(v)} \frac{(\eta\mathbf{U}^{(v)})_{ij}}{(\mathbf{N}\mathbf{U}^{(v)})_{ij}}. \tag{13}$$

- **Update $\mathbf{U}^{(*)}$ by fixing $\mathbf{U}^{(1)}, \cdots, \mathbf{U}^{(V)}$ and $\mathbf{W}$:** Similarly, we obtain the following update rule:

$$U_{ij}^{(*)} \leftarrow U_{ij}^{(*)} \frac{(\eta\mathbf{U}^{(*)})_{ij}}{(\mathbf{Q}\mathbf{U}^{(*)})_{ij}}, \tag{14}$$

where $\mathbf{Q} = \eta\mathbf{U}^{(*)}\mathbf{U}^{(*)T} - \alpha\sum_{v=1}^{V}\mathbf{U}^{(v)}\mathbf{U}^{(v)T} - \beta\mathbf{H}\mathbf{X}^T\mathbf{W}\mathbf{W}^T\mathbf{X}\mathbf{H}$. Similarly to the work [14], we normalize $\mathbf{U}^{(v)}$ and $\mathbf{U}^{(*)}$ to ensure $(\mathbf{U}^{(v)T}\mathbf{U}^{(v)})_{ii} = 1$ and $(\mathbf{U}^{(*)T}\mathbf{U}^{(*)})_{ii} = 1$ after the above steps in Eqs. (13) and (14). We initialize each $\mathbf{U}^{(v)}$ with standard spectral clustering corresponding to the vth view and $\mathbf{U}^{(*)}$ is initialized by averaging these $\mathbf{U}^{(v)}$s.

4   Experiments

In this section, we conducted extensive experiments to evaluate the proposed *gMUFS*. Following previous unsupervised feature selection approaches [3,23], we also report performances of different methods in terms of clustering.

The experiments are conducted on 7 real-world datasets. For WIDE[1], we extract 5 types of features, i.e., color histogram (64), color autocorrelogram (144), edge direction histogram (73), wavelet texture (128) and block-wise color moments (225), where the numbers in parentheses indicate the dimensionality of each view. For MSRCv1 [22] and Caltech101-7 [5], 5 types of features are as follows: HOG (100), GIST (521), LBP (256), SIFT (210/441), and CENT (1302). For Flickr[2] and Oxford[3], 4 types of features are extracted, i.e., SIFT(200), GIST(512), LBP(59) and PHOG(680). For action recognition datasets Still DB [11] and Willow[4], 3 types of features are used, i.e., Sift Bow (200), Color Sift Bow (200) and Shape Context Bow (200).

4.1   Experiment Setup

We compare our method with several state-of-the-art unsupervised feature selection methods on clustering task. **AllFeatures** concatenates all types of features

---

[1]   http://lms.comp.nus.edu.sg/research/NUS-WIDE.htm.
[2]   https://www.flickr.com/.
[3]   http://www.robots.ox.ac.uk/~vgg/data/oxbuildings/.
[4]   http://www.di.ens.fr/willow/research/stillactions/.

for clustering. **NDFS** [14] performs feature selection within a joint framework of nonnegative spectral analysis and $\ell_{2,1}$-norm regularized regression. **UDFS** [23] exploits local discriminative information and feature correlation simultaneously. **SPEC** [24] selects features with spectral regression. **MCFS** [3] utilizes spectral regression with ℓ_1-norm to select features. **AUMFS** [6] and **MSSFL** [21] exploit both intra-view and inter-view information to jointly select features. Specifically, beyond comparing with multi-view feature selection methods AUMFS and MSSFL, to comprehensively compare different algorithms, we perform feature selection for each view by using NDFS, UDFS, SPEC and MCFS with the performance of best view reported. Furthermore, we conduct multi-view feature selection by concatenating all types of features for these methods: AllFeatures, NDFS, UDFS, SPEC, and MCFS. Following previous work, we set $k = 5$ for all the datasets to specify the size of neighborhoods and construct the affinity graph. We tune the parameters for all methods with the grid search strategy from $\{10^{-6}, 10^{-4}, ..., 10^4, 10^6\}$. For gMUFS, NDFS, we set $\eta = 10^8$ to insure the orthogonality satisfied [14]. The number of the selected features is set as the value from $\{10, 20, ..., 100\}$, while from $\{10, 20, \cdots, 50\}$ when the dimensionality of is smaller than 100, reporting the best results. Due to the randomness of K-means clustering employed, we repeat each experiment 20 times with random initialization and, the average results with standard deviations are reported.

4.2 Experiment Results and Analysis

As shown in Tables 1 and 2, we report the quantitative results in terms of Accuracy (ACC) and Normalized Mutual Information (NMI) for different methods. SV and MV indicate single-view and multi-view methods, respectively. First, it is observed that the results by directly concatenating all views are significantly better than the performance of using each single view. This confirms the importance of integrating multiple views. Second, although using all views, the performances of the traditional single-view methods are obviously worse than AUMFS,

Table 1. Clustering results (ACC% $\pm$ std) of different algorithms.

	Method	WIDE	MSRCv1	Caltech101	Flickr	Oxford	Willow	Still DB
SV	NDFS	25.2±1.0	59.7±4.8	62.1±3.6	25.7±0.9	24.9±1.1	26.2±1.0	31.5±1.5
	UDFS	24.4±1.0	53.5±4.5	60.6±3.1	25.4±1.0	24.3±1.1	26.4±0.7	31.0±1.2
	SPEC	24.6±1.3	46.2±4.7	56.5±3.6	24.4±0.9	23.4±1.1	24.5±0.9	30.0±1.9
	MCFS	24.3±1.2	51.5±5.0	56.1±3.1	25.3±0.9	24.1±0.9	25.2±1.0	30.4±1.3
MV	All-Feat	26.0±1.1	42.0±1.3	69.3±4.0	27.5±1.1	23.2±0.8	23.4±0.8	30.4±1.6
	NDFS	28.2±1.3	57.2±5.1	65.5±5.7	28.0±1.4	27.9±1.9	28.7±1.0	32.4±1.6
	UDFS	25.6±1.4	62.6±3.0	58.2±5.0	26.8±1.0	22.5±1.1	**29.1±2.0**	30.3±1.6
	SPEC	23.4±0.8	57.6±4.8	45.9±4.4	23.7±1.3	21.1±1.3	26.8±1.5	29.7±0.8
	MCFS	24.2±1.3	67.9±5.0	58.2±4.2	23.2±0.8	24.4±0.6	25.9±1.3	31.0±1.5
	MSSFL	28.4±1.7	56.8±5.8	72.0±5.0	29.3±1.5	28.0±1.2	27.4±1.0	31.7±1.3
	AUMFS	28.5±1.3	53.7±0.3	58.0±3.5	27.4±0.9	26.8±1.4	28.8±1.1	31.4±2.3
	Ours	**29.7±1.4**	**78.9±3.8**	**75.6±3.5**	**30.0±1.3**	**29.1±0.8**	28.4±1.0	**33.0±1.7**

Table 2. Clustering results (NMI% ± std) of different algorithms.

	Method	WIDE	MSRCv1	Caltech101	Flickr	Oxford	Willow	Still DB
SV	NDFS	14.6±0.8	51.3±3.6	54.7±2.8	14.9±0.6	12.7±1.0	7.6±0.6	10.7±0.8
	UDFS	13.9±0.7	45.8±3.4	52.8±2.7	13.9±0.5	11.5±0.6	6.5±0.6	10.4±0.8
	SPEC	12.9±0.7	38.7±4.0	46.9±2.6	12.7±0.6	10.5±0.7	6.0±0.5	9.6±1.1
	MCFS	13.5±0.7	43.7±3.4	48.9±2.9	14.5±0.5	11.3±0.6	6.5±0.6	9.7±1.1
MV	AllFeat	18.0±1.1	40.0±1.6	67.4±2.6	15.5±0.6	14.7±0.5	4.0±0.4	10.9±1.5
	NDFS	16.7±1.5	50.1±5.5	62.5±4.9	16.5±0.8	15.2±0.6	9.2±0.5	13.1±0.9
	UDFS	15.0±0.7	55.3±3.0	55.0±3.3	15.6±0.5	11.6±0.5	8.6±0.8	12.5±0.5
	SPEC	11.4±0.7	49.8±3.6	34.6±4.0	12.1±0.7	7.9±0.8	8.0±0.6	11.5±0.7
	MCFS	12.8±1.1	62.8±2.4	50.5±4.1	12.9±0.4	14.3±1.1	7.6±0.6	12.7±1.2
	MSSFL	18.4±0.8	48.7±5.5	60.5±2.4	18.8±0.6	16.1±1.0	8.3± 0.5	13.8±1.0
	AUMFS	16.0±1.1	47.8±1.3	52.9±2.8	16.2±0.5	15.6±1.1	**9.9±0.6**	12.0±1.0
	Ours	**19.8±1.0**	**69.1±3.7**	**67.7±1.8**	**19.3±0.5**	**16.2±1.0**	8.7±0.4	**14.4±1.0**

MSSFL and ours. This is principally because these approaches could not explore the complementarity among multiple views by simply feature concatenation. Third, the proposed method, gMUFS, achieves the best performance on 6 out of 7 datasets, which empirically proves the effectiveness of jointly exploiting multi-view representations and exploring the complex correlation between the selected features and cluster structure. We provide the parameter sensitiveness analysis in Fig. 1. By fixing the value of one parameter (with 1 in our experiments), we tune the other two parameters. The results demonstrate that our method is relatively robust to the three parameters, α, β and γ, since promising results could be expected with wide ranges. It is noteworthy that, compared with single-view unsupervised feature selection methods [14,23], although our multi-view method introduces one more parameter α for handling multi-view correlation, it is very robust and easy to tune in practice. We empirically study the property of convergence of our optimization algorithm. According to Fig. 2, our algorithm could converge within 10 iterations, which validates the effectiveness of the proposed optimization algorithm.

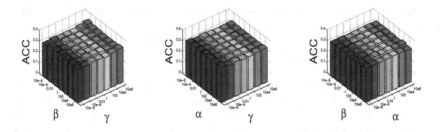

Fig. 1. Parameter sensitivity evaluation on Still DB.

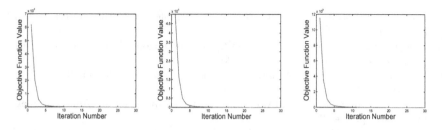

Fig. 2. Convergence curves on Oxford, Caltech and Still DB.

5 Conclusion

In this work, we have developed a novel multi-view unsupervised feature selection approach, which jointly exploits complementarity of multiple views and explores general correlation between the selected features and underlying cluster structure. Benefiting from the complementarity of different views, underlying cluster structure can be well identified and, subsequently, Hilbert-Schmidt independence criterion (HSIC) is employed to address more general dependencies between the selected features and the pseudo cluster labels. Extensive experimental results on real-world datasets demonstrate the effectiveness of our model. For simplicity and efficiency, we adopted inner product kernel for HSIC and, in the future we will take more kernels into account for better performance.

Acknowledgments. This work was supported in part by National Natural Science Foundation of China (Grand No:61602337, 61732011, 61702358, 61402323).

References

1. Bach, F.R., Jordan, M.I.: Kernel independent component analysis. JMLR **3**, 1–48 (2002)
2. Belkin, M., Niyogi, P.: Laplacian eigenmaps and spectral techniques for embedding and clustering. In: NIPS, pp. 585–591 (2002)
3. Cai, D., Zhang, C., He, X.: Unsupervised feature selection for multi-cluster data. In: SIGKDD, pp. 333–342 (2010)
4. Cao, X., Zhang, C., Fu, H., et al.: Diversity-induced multi-view subspace clustering. In: CVPR, pp. 586–594 (2015)
5. Fei-Fei, L., Fergus, R., Perona, P.: Learning generative visual models from few training examples: an incremental Bayesian approach tested on 101 object categories. Comput. Vis. Image Underst. **106**(1), 59–70 (2007)
6. Feng, Y., Xiao, J., Zhuang, Y., Liu, X.: Adaptive unsupervised multi-view feature selection for visual concept recognition. In: Lee, K.M., Matsushita, Y., Rehg, J.M., Hu, Z. (eds.) ACCV 2012. LNCS, vol. 7724, pp. 343–357. Springer, Heidelberg (2013). https://doi.org/10.1007/978-3-642-37331-2_26
7. Gretton, A., Bousquet, O., Smola, A., Schölkopf, B.: Measuring statistical dependence with Hilbert-Schmidt norms. In: Jain, S., Simon, H.U., Tomita, E. (eds.) ALT 2005. LNCS (LNAI), vol. 3734, pp. 63–77. Springer, Heidelberg (2005). https://doi.org/10.1007/11564089_7

8. Guyon, I., Elisseeff, A.: An introduction to variable and feature selection. JMLR **3**, 1157–1182 (2003)
9. Han, D., Kim, J.: Unsupervised simultaneous orthogonal basis clustering feature selection. In: CVPR, pp. 5016–5023 (2015)
10. He, X., Cai, D., Niyogi, P.: Laplacian score for feature selection. In: NIPS, pp. 507–514 (2006)
11. Ikizler, N., Cinbis, R.G., Pehlivan, S., et al.: Recognizing actions from still images. In: ICPR, pp. 1–4 (2008)
12. Kumar, A., Rai, P., Daume, H.: Co-regularized multi-view spectral clustering. In: NIPS, pp. 1413–1421 (2011)
13. Lee, D.D., Seung, H.S.: Learning the parts of objects by non-negative matrix factorization. Nature **401**(6755), 788 (1999)
14. Li, Z., Yang, Y., Liu, J., et al.: Unsupervised feature selection using nonnegative spectral analysis. In: AAAI, vol. 2, pp. 1026–1032 (2012)
15. Naikal, N., Yang, A.Y., Sastry, S.S.: Informative feature selection for object recognition via sparse PCA. In: ICCV, pp. 818–825 (2011)
16. Niu, D., Dy, J.G., Jordan, M.I.: Iterative discovery of multiple alternativeclustering views. IEEE T-PAMI **36**(7), 1340–1353 (2014)
17. Qian, M., Zhai, C.: Robust unsupervised feature selection. In: IJCAI, pp. 1621–1627 (2013)
18. Shi, J., Malik, J.: Normalized cuts and image segmentation. IEEE T-PAMI **22**(8), 888–905 (2000)
19. Tang, B., Kay, S., He, H.: Toward optimal feature selection in naive Bayes for text categorization. IEEE T-KDE **28**(9), 2508–2521 (2016)
20. Wang, H., Nie, F., Huang, H.: Identifying quantitative trait loci via group-sparse multitask regression and feature selection: an imaging genetics study of the ADNI cohort. Bioinformatics **28**(2), 229–237 (2011)
21. Wang, H., Nie, F., Huang, H.: Multi-view clustering and feature learning via structured sparsity. In: ICML, pp. 352–360 (2013)
22. Winn, J., Jojic, N.: LOCUS: learning object classes with unsupervised segmentation. In: ICCV, vol. 1, pp. 756–763 (2005)
23. Yang, Y., Shen, H.T., Ma, Z.: L2, 1-norm regularized discriminative feature selection for unsupervised learning. IJCAI **22**(1), 1589 (2011)
24. Zhao, Z., Liu, H.: Spectral feature selection for supervised and unsupervised learning. In: ICML, pp. 1151–1157 (2007)
25. Zhao, Z., Wang, L., Liu, H.: Efficient spectral feature selection with minimum redundancy. In: AAAI, pp. 673–678 (2010)
26. Zhu, P., Hu, Q., Zhang, C., et al.: Coupled dictionary learning for unsupervised feature selection. In: AAAI, pp. 2422–2428 (2016)

Performance Anomaly Detection Models of Virtual Machines for Network Function Virtualization Infrastructure with Machine Learning

Juan Qiu[✉], Qingfeng Du[✉], Yu He, YiQun Lin, Jiaye Zhu, and Kanglin Yin

Tongji University, Shanghai 201804, China
juan_qiu@tongji.edu.cn, du_cloud@tongji.edu.cn

Abstract. Networking Function Virtualization (NFV) technology has become a new solution for running network applications. It proposes a new paradigm for network function management and has brought much innovation space for the network technology. However, the complexity of the NFV Infrastructure (NFVI) impose hard-to-predict relationship between Virtualized Network Function (VNF) performance metrics (e.g., latency, throughput), the underlying allocated resources (e.g., load of vCPU), and the overall system workload, thus the evolving scenario of NFV calls for adequate performance analysis methodologies, early detection of performance anomalies plays a significant role in providing high-quality network services. In this paper, we have proposed a novel method for detecting the performance anomalies in NFV infrastructure with machine learning methods. We present a case study on the open source NFV-oriented project, namely Clearwater, which is an IP Multimedia Subsystem (IMS) NFV application. Several classical classifiers are applied and compared empirically on the anomaly dataset which is built by ourselves. Considering the risk of over-fitting issue, the experimental results show that neutral networks is the best anomaly detection model with the accuracy over 94%.

Keywords: NFV · Performance anomaly detection · Machine learning

1 Introduction

The paradigm of Network Function Virtualization (NFV) has immediately been an emerging paradigm which is a new vision of the network that takes advantage of advances in dynamic cloud architecture, Software Defined Networking (SDN), and modern software provisioning techniques. The topic about NFV bottlenecks analysis and relevant hardware and software features for high and predictable performance have been already highlighted in the Group Specification (GS) by European Telecommunications Standards Institute (ETSI) industry Specification (ISG) Network Functions [1].

© Springer Nature Switzerland AG 2018
V. Kůrková et al. (Eds.): ICANN 2018, LNCS 11140, pp. 479–488, 2018.
https://doi.org/10.1007/978-3-030-01421-6_46

The purpose of this paper aims to detect performance anomalies by modeling the various performance metrics data collected from the virtual machines of the NFV platform. We conduct an experiment with an open source NFV-oriented project, namely Clearwater, which has been designed to support massive horizontal scalability and adopts popular cloud computing design patterns and technologies, to demonstrate how the proposed method can be applied to the detection performance anomalies. The main contributions of this paper are as follows:

1. Present an approach on how to build the performance anomaly dataset for NFVI.
2. Put forward an approach for detecting performance anomalies in NFVI with machine learning models.

The paper is organized as follows: The next section discusses the related works; Methodology and implementation are presented in Sect. 3, then we conduct a case study on Clearwater in Sect. 4; Sect. 5 concludes and provides the conclusion.

2   Related Works

Reliability studies for NFV technology including performance and security topics are also hot research areas for both academia and industry. In order to guarantee high and predictable performance of data plane workloads, a list of minimal features which the Virtual Machine (VM) Descriptor and Compute Host Descriptor should contain for the appropriate deployment of VM Images over an NFV Infrastructure (NFVI) are presented [1]. NFV-Bench [2] is proposed by Domenico et al. to analyze the faulty scenarios and to provide joint dependability and performance evaluations for NFV systems. Bonafiglia et al. [3] provides a (preliminary) benchmark of the widespread virtualization technologies when used in NFV, which means when they are exploited to run the so-called virtual network functions and to chain them in order to create complex services. Priyanka et al. presents the design and implementation of a tool, namely NFVPerf [4], to monitor performance and identify performance bottlenecks in an NFV system. NFVPerf runs as part of a cloud management system like OpenStack and sniffs traffic between NFV components in a manner that is transparent to the VNF.

Anomaly detection is an important data analysis task that detects abnormal data from a given dataset, it is an important data mining research problem and has been widely studied in many fields. It can usually be solved by statistics and machine learning methods [5–8]. In recent years, anomaly detection literature in NFV has also begun to emerge. Michail-Alexandros et al. [9] presented the use of an open-source monitoring system especially tailored for NFV in conjunction with statistical approaches commonly used for anomaly detection, towards the timely detection of anomalies in deployed NFV services. Domenico et al. [10] proposed an approach on an NFV-oriented Interactive Multimedia System to detect problems affecting the quality of service, such as the overload, component crashes, avalanche restarts and physical resource contention. EbAT [11] is an automated online detection framework for anomaly identification and tracking in data center systems. Fu [12] proposed a framework for autonomic anomaly detection on cloud systems and the proposed framework could select the most relevant among the large number of performance metrics.

We have been actively participating in the OPNFV[1] Yardstick project[2]. Especially, we continuously and deeply involved in the HA Yardstick framework architecture evolution, and the fault injection techniques used in the this paper are based on our previous research works [13, 14]. Recently we are participating in the OPNFV Bottlenecks project[3] which is a testing project aims to find system bottlenecks by testing and verifying OPNFV infrastructure in a staging environ- ment before committing it to a production environment. Most cloud operators identify performance bottlenecks by monitoring hardware resource utilization, or other application-specific metrics obtained from instrumenting the application itself. In this paper, we are trying to detect performance anomalies by modeling the various performance metrics data collecting from the virtual machines of the NFV platform.

3   Methodology and Implementation

3.1   Classification Problem

The performance anomaly detection method studied in this paper is based on the classification methods. The essence of the anomaly detection problem is to train and get a detection model by using the performance metrics data collected from the virtual machine in the NFV infrastructure layer. The virtual machine state characterized by the performance metrics collected in real time is divided into multiple classes based on the anomaly detection model.

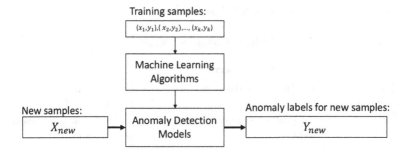

Fig. 1. The training and testing processes of anomaly detection model

---

[1] https://www.opnfv.org/.

[2] https://wiki.opnfv.org/display/yardstick/Yardstick/.

[3] https://wiki.opnfv.org/display/bottlenecks/Bottlenecks/.

As shown in Fig. 1, given the training performance metric samples: $T = \{(x_1, y_1), (x_2, y_2), ..., (x_k, y_k)\} \in (R^n \times Y)^k$ *where* $X_i = [x_{1i}, x_{2i}, ..., x_{ni}]^T \in R^n$ is the input vector, the component of the vector represents the performance metrics. y_i is the output which is the accordingly anomaly label for x_i and (x_i, y_i) represents a sample of the training set and k is the sample size of the training set. For the multi classification problem, we need not only to determine whether there is an anomaly, but also to further determine which kind of anomaly it belongs to. $y_i \in Y = \{1, 2, ..., c\}, i = 1, 2, ..., k$, where c is the size of anomaly classes. We agree on that $y_i = 1$ means normal status, the other value y_i represent abnormal status. thus the solution is to explore a decision function in R^n: $y = f(x) : R^n \rightarrow Y$ and this function could be used to infer the corresponding value Y_{new} of any new instance X_{new}. It performs detection with localization of an anomalous behaviour by assigning one class label to each anomalous behaviour depending on its localization.

Machine learning is a famous field to be extremely relevant for solving classification problems. with respect to the machine learning models that we aim to build for detection classifiers, samples of labeled monitoring data are needed to train them to discern different system behaviours. There are a large pool of classification-based techniques available, we will try to introduce some of the well known classifiers in this paper, such as support vector machines (SVM), K-Nearest Neighbors (KNN), Random Forests, Decision Tree and Neural Networks (NN).

The measures of classification efficiency could be built from a confusion matrix that could provide results of counting correctly and incorrectly detected instances for each class of events. The confusion matrix, also known as an error metrics is a specific table layout that allows visualization of the performance of a classifier in the field of machine learning. In a binary classification task, the terms 'positive' and 'negative' refer to the classifier's prediction, and the terms 'true' and 'false' refer to whether that prediction corresponds to the external judgment (sometimes known as the 'observation'). Given these definitions, the confusion matrix could be formulated as Table 1.

Table 1. Confusion matrix

	Actual class (observation)	
Predicted class (expectation)	TP (True Positive) correct result	FP (False Positive) Unexpected result
	FN (False Negative) Missing result	TN (True Negative) correct absence of result

accuracy, *precision* and $F - measure$ are the well known performance measures for machine learning models. Intuitively, $accuracy = \frac{TP+TN}{TP+FP+TN+FN}$ is easy to understand, that is, the proportion of correctly categorized samples accounted for all samples. Generally speaking, the higher the accuracy, the better the classifier. $precision = \frac{TP}{TP+FP}$ is the ability of the classifier not to label as positive a sample that is negative, and $recall = \frac{TP}{TP+FN}$ is the ability of the classifier to find all the positive samples. The $F_\beta = (1 + \beta^2) \frac{precision \times recall}{\beta^2 precision + recall}$ (F_β and F_1 measures) can be interpreted as a weighted harmonic mean of the precision and recall. A F_β measure reaches its best value at 1 and its worst score at 0. With $\beta = 1$, F_β and F_1 are equivalent, and the recall and the precision are equally important.

3.2 Implementation

Performance Anomaly Detection Framework. We implement an anomaly detection framework which includes a system perturbation module, a cloud platform monitoring module and a data processing and analysis module. The perturbation module generates workload and faultload to simulate performance issues or bottlenecks. At the same time, the monitoring module can collect relevant performance data, it performs the monitoring process according to the Key Performance Indicator (KPI), the goal of monitoring is to gather data samples from the target system via performance counters which is so-called monitoring metrics, then the anomaly datasets could be built. As shown in Table 2, the anomaly dataset is composed of three parts of data, the performance metrics, the anomalous behavior labels and the miscellaneous features. $Schema = \{Metrics \cup AnomalyLabels \cup MiscFeatures\}$, where $Metrics$ are composed of the specific performance metrics such as cpu_usage, $memory\_usage$. The $AnomalyLabels$ imply the type of a performance anomaly, the value of '1' represents the underlying anomaly happens, and '0' represents no such anomaly happens. The dataset also contain some miscellaneous features such as $location$ where the VNF located, and the $timestamp$ feature of the record. Finally, the data processing and analysis module is responsible for creating models that are trained offline for performance anomaly detection based on the anomaly dataset.

Table 2. The schema of the anomaly dataset

location	timestamp	metric_1	...	metric_n	anomaly_label_1	...	anomaly_label_k

Bottlenecks Simulation. In order to better engage in the research of NFV performance anomaly detection, performance anomalies and bottlenecks could be simulated by the perturbation module as implemented in Algorithm1, and the performance related data in the NFVI layer could be collected by the data monitoring module. Both workload and faultload could be generated by the perturbation module.

Algorithm 1. Bottlenecks injection controller

Input: $vm\_list, bottleneck\_type\_list,$
        $injection\_duration, user\_count, duration$
1: $timer = start\_timer()$
2: **while** $timer < duration$ **do**
3:    $sip\_simulate(user\_count, duration)$
4:    $bottleneck\_type = random\,(bottleneck\_type\_list)$
5:    $vm = random\,(vm\_list)$
6:    $injection = new\ injection\,(bottleneck\_type)$
7:    $inject(vm, injection\_duration)$
8:    $sleep(pause)$
9: **end while**

Performance Metric Model. Classification-based techniques highly reply on expert's domain knowledge of the characteristics of performance issues or bottlenecks status. The work in this paper particularly focuses on the identification of performance anomalies from monitoring data of VMs OSs of the NFVI such as CPU consumption, disk I/O, and memory consumption. A classic Zabbix[4] OS monitoring template[5] is adopted as the performance metric model in this paper.

4 Case Study

4.1 Experimental Environment Setup

The testbed is built on one powerful physical server DELL R730 which is equipped with 2x Intel Xeon CPU E5-2630 v4 @ 2.10 GHz, 128 G of RAM and 5 TB Hard Disk. The vIMS under test is the Clearwater project which is an open-source implementation of an IMS for cloud computing platforms. The Clearwater application is installed on the commercialized hypervisor-based virtualization platform (VMware ESXi). 10 components of Clearwater are individually hosted in a docker container on a virtual machine(VM), and the containers are managed by Kubernetes. Particularly there is an attack host for injecting bottlenecks into the Clearwater virtual hosts, a tool for the fault injection runs on the inject host, and the Zabbix agents are installed on the other hosts, finally the performance data of each virtual host could be collected by the agent when the faultload and workload are injected.

An open source tool SIPp[6] is used as the workload generator for IMS. Fault injection techniques could be applied to bottlenecks simulation refers to the Algorithm 1 presented in the previous section.

---

[4] https://www.zabbix.com/.
[5] https://github.com/chunchill/nfv-anomaly-detection-ml/blob/master/data/
   Features-Description-NFVI.xlsx.
[6] http://sipp.sourceforge.net/.

The monitoring agent could collect the performance data from each virtual host for each round, the timestamp would be record in the log file once there is a bottleneck injection, so that the performance data could be labeled with related injection type according to the injection log. Finally, the performance dataset could be built for data analysis in the next section.

4.2   Experimental Results

There were three kinds of bottlenecks in the data: CPU bottlenecks, memory bottlenecks, I/O bottlenecks, in addition, if there is no bottleneck injection, the data is labeled as 'normal', and we extracted a total of 3693 records from the experiment, including 2462 with normal class, 373 with CPU bottlenecks class, 266 with memory bottlenecks class and 592 with I/O bottlenecks class. The schema of a record consists of two identification fields ($host, timestamp$), 45 monitoring metrics feature fields, and 4 labels ($normal, CPU$ $bottleneck,$ $memory$ $bottleneck,$ and I/O $bottleneck$).

We used the following machine learning classifiers to perform comparative experiments: Neural Networks, Combined Neural Networks with SVM, K-Nearest Neighbors, Linear SVM, Radial Basis Function (RBF) SVM, Decision Tree and Random Forests.

Table 3. Accuracy comparison results of machine learning classifiers

Models	Training set	Testing set
NN	0.94	0.90
NN+SVM	0.93	0.89
KNN	0.92	0.87
Linear SVM	0.80	0.83
RBF SVM	0.80	0.83
Decision Tree	0.77	0.80
Random Forrest	0.90	0.89

As shown in the comparison results in the Table 3, the effect of the neural networks is the best for both in training set and testing set. Table 4 shows the specific results of the neural networks. As the epoch history trend of neural network learning shown in Fig. 2, we can see that the trend of accuracy and loss on the training set and the validation set is almost the same, indicating that there is no over-fitting situation in the training process. It is proved that the effect of neural networks is ideal and effective to detect the performance anomalies.

All of the experiment artifacts are available on this github repository[7], including the fault injection tools, datasets and the python codes.

---

[7] https://github.com/chunchill/nfv-anomaly-detection-ml.

Table 4. The results by neural network

Accuracy on training set: 0.94			
Labels	Precision	Recall	F1-Score
Normal	0.97	0.95	0.96
cpu	0.90	0.93	0.92
Memory	0.91	0.85	0.88
I/O	0.87	0.95	0.91
avg/total	0.94	0.94	0.94

Accuracy on testing set: 0.90			
Labels	Precision	Recall	F1-Score
Normal	0.96	0.92	0.94
cpu	0.81	0.90	0.86
Memory	0.86	0.78	0.82
I/O	0.75	0.88	0.81
avg/total	0.91	0.90	0.90

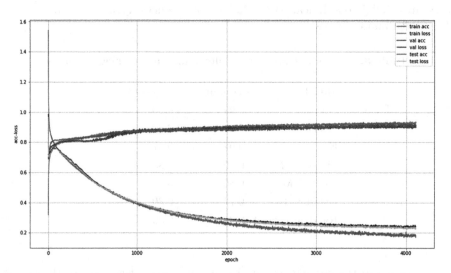

Fig. 2. The accuracy and loss trend of Neural Networks for both training set and validation set

5   Conclusion

This paper have proposed a machine learning based performance anomaly detection approach for NFV-oriented cloud system infrastructure. Considering that it is difficult for researchers to obtain comprehensive and accurate abnormal behaviors data in a real NFV production environment, system perturbation technology to simulate faultload and workload is presented, and the monitoring module is integrated into the anomaly detection framework to monitor and evaluate the platform, it is responsible for constructing anomaly dataset consisting of abnormal labels and multi-dimensional monitoring metrics. Finally, the effective machine learning models are fitted by training the statistical learning model on the anomaly dataset. The experiment results show that machine learning classifiers could be effectively applied to solve the performance anomalies problem, and the neural networks model is the best detection model with the precision over 94%.

Acknowledgement. This work has been supported by the National Natural Science Foundation of China (Grant No. 61672384), part of the work has also been supported by Huawei Research Center under Grant No. YB2015120069. And we have to acknowledge the OPNFV project, because some of the ideas come from the OPNFV community, we have obtained lots of inspiration and discussion when we involved in the activities on OPNFV projects Yardstick and Bottlenecks.

References

1. ETSI GS NFV-PER 001. https://www.etsi.org/deliver/etsi_gs/NFV-PER/. Accessed 1 July 2018
2. Cotroneo, D., De Simone, L., Natella, R.: NFV-bench: a dependability benchmark for network function virtualization systems. IEEE Trans. Netw. Serv. Manag., 934–948 (2017)
3. Bonafiglia, Roberto, et al.: Assessing the performance of virtualization technologies for NFV: a preliminary benchmarking. In: European Workshop on Software Defined Networks (EWSDN), pp. 67–72. IEEE (2015)
4. Naik, P., Shaw, D.K., Vutukuru, M.: NFVPerf: Online performance monitoring and bottleneck detection for NFV. In: International Conference on Network Function Virtualization and Software Defined Networks (NFV-SDN), pp. 154–160. IEEE (2016)
5. Liu, D., et al.: Opprentice: towards practical and automatic anomaly detection through machine learning. In: Proceedings of the Internet Measurement Conference, pp. 211–224. ACM (2015)
6. Li, K.-L., Huang, H.-K., Tian, S.-F., Wei, X.: Improving one-class SVM for anomaly detection. In: IEEE International Conference on Machine Learning and Cybernetics, vol. 5, pp. 3077–3081 (2003)
7. Shanbhag, S., Gu, Y., Wolf, T.: A taxonomy and comparative evaluation of algorithms for parallel anomaly detection. In: ICCCN, pp. 1–8 (2010)
8. Yairi, T., Kawahara, Y., Fujimaki, R., Sato, Y., Machida, K.: Telemetry-mining: a machine learning approach to anomaly detection and fault diagnosis for space systems. In: Second International Conference on Space Mission Challenges for Information Technology(SMC-IT), p. 8. IEEE (2006)
9. Kourtis, M.A., Xilouris, G., Gardikis, G., Koutras, I.: Statistical-based anomaly detection for NFV services. In: International Conference on Network Function Virtualization and Software Defined Networks (NFV-SDN), pp. 161–166. IEEE (2016)
10. Cotroneo, D., Natella, R., Rosiello, S.: A fault correlation approach to detect performance anomalies in virtual network function chains. In: IEEE 28th International Symposium on Software Reliability Engineering (ISSRE), pp. 90–100 (2017)

11. Wang, C., Talwar, V., Schwan, K., Ranganathan, P.: Online detection of utility cloud anomalies using metric distributions. In: Network Operations and Management Symposium (NOMS), pp. 96–103. IEEE (2010)
12. Fu, S.: Performance metric selection for autonomic anomaly detection on cloud computing systems. In: Global Telecommunications Conference (GLOBECOM), pp. 1–5. IEEE (2011)
13. Du, Q., et al.: High availability verification framework for OpenStack based on fault injection. In: International Conference on Reliability, Maintainability and Safety (ICRMS), pp. 1–7. IEEE (2016)
14. Du, Q., et al.: Test case design method targeting environmental fault tolerance for high availability clusters. In: International Conference on Reliability, Maintainability and Safety (ICRMS), pp. 1–7. IEEE (2016)

Emergence of Sensory Representations Using Prediction in Partially Observable Environments

Thibaut Kulak and Michael Garcia Ortiz[(✉)]

SoftBank Robotics Europe - AI Lab, Paris, France
thibaut.kulak@gmail.com, mgarciaortiz@softbankrobotics.com

Abstract. In order to explore and act autonomously in an environment, an agent can learn from the sensorimotor information that is captured while acting. By extracting the regularities in this sensorimotor stream, it can build a model of the world, which in turn can be used as a basis for action and exploration. It requires the acquisition of compact representations from possibly high dimensional raw observations. In this paper, we propose a model which integrates sensorimotor information over time, and project it in a sensory representation. It is trained by preforming sensorimotor prediction. We emphasize on a simple example the role of motor and memory for learning sensory representations.

1 Introduction

Autonomous Learning for Robotics aims to endow agents with the capability to learn from and act in their environment, so that they can adapt to previously unseen situations. An agent can learn from this interaction by building compact representations of what it encounters in its environment, using information captured from a high dimensional raw sensory input and motor output.

Theories on sensorimotor prediction state that an agent learns the structure of its world by learning how to predict the consequences of its actions [2,12]. The sensorimotor approach proposes to learn sensor representations and motor representations by identifying the regularities in the sensorimotor stream. However, these regularities are hard to capture: a robotic agent acts and perceives in an environment which is usually partially observable (limited field of view), noisy and ambiguous. The sensory information is not sufficient to know the exact state of the agent in its environment (similar sensory states can originate from different situations in the environment). This is in particular true for navigation tasks where an agent can observe several occurrences of very similar portions of the scenes (wall, corners) at different locations in the environment (e.g. in a maze). For these reasons, we need representations that can help disambiguate the observations and the state of the agent.

In the case of an autonomous agent, without labeled data, unsupervised learning allows to learn compression for different data streams [6,13,16]. These representations, based on the statistics of the data, reduce the dimensionality

V. Kůrková et al. (Eds.): ICANN 2018, LNCS 11140, pp. 489–498, 2018.
https://doi.org/10.1007/978-3-030-01421-6_47

of the sensory stream, but do not inform the agent on the modalities of its potential actions in its environment, which is related to the problem of grounding knowledge in the experience of an agent [5]. In order to build representations, a classic approach is to learn forward internal models [3]: learning to predict the sensory consequences of actions. For instance a forward model of physics is learned for a real-world robotic platform in [1]. Recently, [4] proposed to build world models through learning forward models, and use them to train policies in different Reinforcement Learning environments. The authors of [9] present a complete overview of the current methods for learning representations in robotics.

In this paper, we propose to learn sensory representations using principles from sensorimotor prediction (or, forward models) and to study the properties of the learned representations. We show, on a navigation scenario, that using motor information as well as a short-term memory leads to sensory representations that correspond to richer classes of sensory stimuli encountered in the environment. Recent work also propose to learn sensory representation by sensorimotor prediction [4,17], and show that the representations learned could be successfully used for navigation or control tasks. In this paper we are interested in studying the nature of the representations that are learned.

2   Sensorimotor Predictive Model

We train a forward model, named Recurrent Sensorimotor Encoder (**Recurrent-SM-encoder**), shown in Fig. 1, and composed of three subnetworks: (i) A sensory encoding subnetwork takes as input the sensory state s_t and outputs an encoded sensory state z_t^s. It is composed of hidden layers followed by a stacked Long short-term memory (LSTM) network, which role is to provide a form of memory about the previous sensor states. (ii) A motor encoding subnetwork, which is a classical dense network composed of hidden layers, taking as input the motor command m_t and outputting the encoded motor command z_t^m. (iii) z_t^s and z_t^m are concatenated to form the encoded sensorimotor vector z_t^{sm}, used as an input for a dense network, which outputs a prediction of the next sensory state $\hat{s}_{t+1}$.

We use several baselines (see Fig. 2) to evaluate the role of motor information and memory: the Sensorimotor Encoder (**SM-encoder**), doesn't have a memory, the Recurrent Sensory Encoder (**Recurrent-S-encoder**) doesn't have motor input, and the Sensory Encoder (**S-encoder**) doesn't have memory or motors. We train the proposed networks using a loss to minimize the prediction error:

$$\mathcal{L}_2 = \sum_{t=1}^{T-1} \left(\hat{s}_{t+1} - s_{t+1} \right)^2 \tag{1}$$

where T is the size of the learning batch.

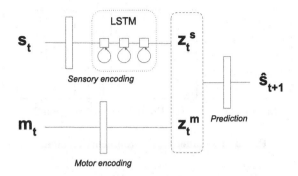

Fig. 1. Recurrent Sensorimotor Encoder

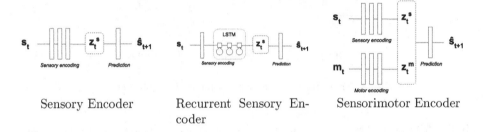

Sensory Encoder   Recurrent Sensory Encoder   Sensorimotor Encoder

Fig. 2. Architectures of the baselines

3   Experimental Setup

Our simulated agent (inspired from the Thymio-II robot [14]) is equipped with 5 distance sensors, evenly separated between -0.6 and 0.6 rad, with their range limited to 10 units of distance. The agent controls its translation forward (direction of the middle laser) and its rotation. One motor command (d, r) is the succession of a translation d and a rotation r. It is a planar agent moving without friction, and there is no noise on its distance sensors. We created 3 environments of size 50 units, shown on Fig. 3: **Square** is a square without walls or obstacles. **Room1** additionally contains one vertical wall and one horizontal wall. **Room2** contains one horizontal and three vertical walls.

The agent moves by random translations forward and random rotations, while avoiding collisions with the walls. At each timestep, if one distance sensor value is smaller than 1 unit, the agent rotates by $r \sim \mathbf{U}(\pi - \frac{\pi}{10}, \pi + \frac{\pi}{10})$ radians ($\mathbf{U}$ denoting the uniform distribution). If not, the agent moves forward by $d \sim \mathbf{U}(0, 1)$ units, and rotates by $r \sim \mathbf{U}(-\frac{\pi}{6}, \frac{\pi}{6})$ radians. Figure 4 displays the trajectory of the agent during 10 000 steps in the different proposed environments.

We generated a sequence of 1 000 000 timesteps for each environment (each point has 5 distance sensors values and 2 motor commands), split as such: the first 80% for training, the next 10% for validation, and the last 10% for testing.

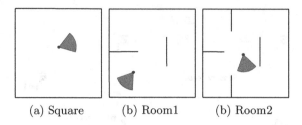

(a) Square   (b) Room1   (b) Room2

Fig. 3. The different environments created.

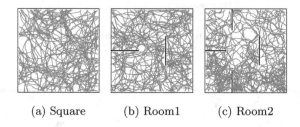

(a) Square   (b) Room1   (c) Room2

Fig. 4. Trajectories in the environments (10 000 points)

In Fig. 5 we reconstructed, for different situations, what the agent perceives based on its sensors. Note that the agent doesn't have access to the position and angles of its distance sensors, it only receives as input a 5-dimensional real vector.

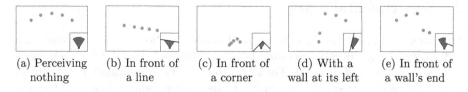

| (a) Perceiving nothing | (b) In front of a line | (c) In front of a corner | (d) With a wall at its left | (e) In front of a wall's end |

Fig. 5. Examples of different sensory stimuli perceived by the agent. The 5 red dots represent the distance perceived by the agent, projected in top-view. (Color figure online)

4   Results

4.1   Numerics

Our models are trained with the Adam optimizer [8] (learning rate of 0.001). The training is stopped if the loss on the validation set doesn't decrease by 5% for 10 consecutive epochs. We use a mini-batch size of 64, and ReLUs for the activation functions. We choose arbitrarily the sensory representation space to be 10-dimensional and the motor representation space to be 5-dimensional. The number and size of layers in the different architectures are as follow: In

SM-encoder, the sensory encoding and motor encoding subnetworks have 3 hidden layers of size 16, 32 and 64, while the prediction subnetwork has one layer of size 128. **S-encoder** is identical to the SM-encoder, without the motor encoding subnetwork. In **Recurrent-SM-encoder**, the sensory encoding and motor encoding subnetworks have 1 hidden layer of size 16, while the prediction subnetwork has one layer of size 128. The (stacked) LSTM has 3 layers with 32 units at each layer, and a truncation horizon of 20. **Recurrent-S-encoder** is identical to Recurrent-SM-encoder, without the motor encoding.

4.2   Sensorimotor Prediction Results

We report in Table 1 the $\mathcal{L}_2$ prediction error of the models trained on the Square environment, and tested on the three environments. First we verify that models using motor information largely outperform those without, which makes sense because motors are necessary to predict the next sensory state. We also see that models using a memory perform better compared to their memoryless counterpart, confirming that a memory is useful for accurate sensorimotor prediction. Finally, we note that the Recurrent-SM-encoder model performs best. It is to be expected, as it benefits from additional information. We verified that these observations hold when trained on Room1 and Room2.

Table 1. Sensorimotor prediction $\mathcal{L}_2$ error of the models trained on Square tested on the test dataset of the three environments.

Model	Square	Room1	Room2
S-encoder	0.0374	0.0430	0.0729
SM-encoder	0.0056	0.0145	0.0257
Recurrent-S-encoder	0.0359	0.0407	0.0697
Recurrent-SM-encoder	**0.0024**	**0.0105**	**0.0181**

4.3   Representation Spaces

We plot on Fig. 6 the representation spaces learned by our models, projected on the first two principal components extracted with a Principal Component Analysis (PCA) [7]. We color-code those spaces by the minimum value of the 5 lasers, as this gives information about the distance to the wall the agent perceives.

We observe that the models without motors group states where the agent doesn't see anything with states where the agent sees a wall from a very short distance, because its behavior (avoiding collision, see Sect. 3) makes it experience sensory transitions from seeing a wall very close to seeing nothing. Without access to motor commands, the model brings those states close to each other, while in reality those states are fundamentally different. We see that the portion of the representation space corresponding to the agent perceiving nothing is larger with the Recurrent-SM-encoder than with the Recurrent-S-encoder.

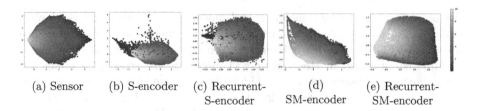

| (a) Sensor | (b) S-encoder | (c) Recurrent-S-encoder | (d) SM-encoder | (e) Recurrent-SM-encoder |

Fig. 6. Representation spaces learned on the Square environment, colored by the minimum value of the lasers. (Color figure online)

We can interpret it as memory and the information about motor commands helping to create different states for points where the agent doesn't see anything.

4.4 Clusters Extraction

We cluster the sensory representation spaces learned for each model, and visualize the activation of the different clusters in the environments, in order to estimate if the sensory encoding learns spatial features. We sample random sensorimotor transitions and use a kMeans algorithm [10] to extract 20 clusters from each sensory representation space. We plot for each cluster the ground truth position and orientation of 500 random data points associated with this cluster.

We show on Fig. 7, as a baseline, the 20 clusters extracted from the S-encoder representation space. We see that there are clusters corresponding to different distances/angles to the wall. As there is no memory in this model all of the configurations when the agent doesn't perceive anything are in the same cluster.

We see on Fig. 8 that the Recurrent-SM-encoder representation space trained on the Square environment contains clusters corresponding to different distances to a wall, and also a cluster corresponding to corners. We observe that we have different clusters corresponding to an absence of visual stimuli, but at different distances from a wall (when the wall is behind the agent). LSTM provides the agent with a memory of previous events, and it contains a form of spatial information. However this memory is short-term as it is relative to the previous wall that has been seen, and there is no global notion of position in the environment.

We show on Fig. 9 the clusters extracted from the Recurrent-SM-encoder model trained on the Room1 environment. We observe that in addition to clusters similar to those appearing in Square environment, there is now a cluster corresponding to wall's ends. We note, however, that when training on Room2, the cluster corresponding to wall's ends is not visible with 20 clusters extracted. We hypothesize that the layout causes the agent to be stuck in the different rooms, reducing the number of appearance of wall's ends in the database.

4.5 Robustness to Testing Environment

In this experiment, we evaluate if the representations learned in one environment transfer to other environments. We train the Recurrent-SM-encoder as well as

Fig. 7. S-encoder representation space clusters

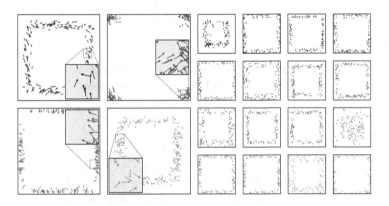

Fig. 8. Recurrent-SM-encoder representation space clusters

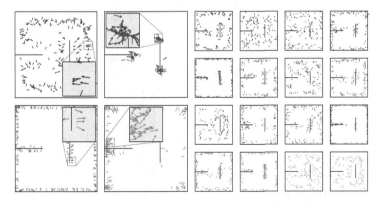

Fig. 9. Recurrent-SM-encoder representation space clusters, trained on Room1

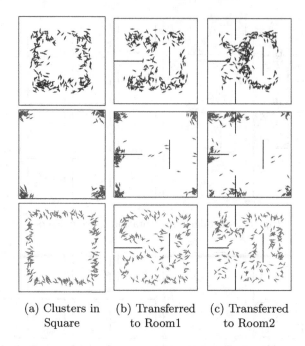

(a) Clusters in   (b) Transferred   (c) Transferred
    Square   to Room1   to Room2

Fig. 10. Transferring some Square clusters

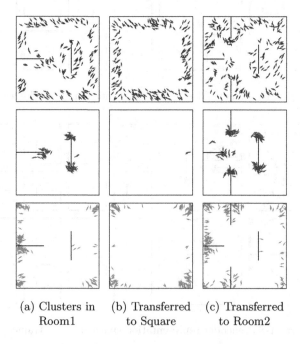

(a) Clusters in   (b) Transferred   (c) Transferred
    Room1   to Square   to Room2

Fig. 11. Transferring some Room1 clusters

our clustering algorithm on one environment, then apply the learned representations and clusters in other environments. We show the transfer of some clusters of interest learned on Square on Fig. 10. We show on Fig. 11 the transfer of a few clusters of interest learned on Room1 to other environments. We observe that the representations learned in one environment can be used in other environments, with different spatial layouts. This is to be expected as the LSTM only captures and retains short-term information, which represents sensorimotor transitions, but do not represent different spatial layouts of the environments.

5   Conclusion

In this paper we proposed to use an unsupervised learning method based on sensorimotor prediction that allows an agent to acquire sensory representations by integrating sensorimotor information using recurrent neural networks.

We observed that our model extracts classes of interaction with the environment that seem qualitatively meaningful, and which contain temporal information through short-term memory of previous experiences. In particular we verified that the motor commands and memory are very beneficial to learn sensory representations through prediction. We note that the clusters of the sensory representation are similar to particular cells observed in mammals, such as distance, orientation, and border cells [11]. We noticed that the representation learned on an environment can be used in other environments with different spatial layouts.

We used a generic approach, inspired from recent proposals about the nature and emergence of autonomy and intelligence through sensorimotor prediction [2]. It uses only raw data, and requires (in our simple experiment) very few engineering biases. In future works we want to investigate whether it scales to more complex environments and sensory streams, and if it can be applied on a robotic platforms in a real human environment.

One interesting possible extension would be to use the representations to learn a map of the environment. We plan to investigate how to build a graph where the nodes would correspond to particular activations of the representation, and the edges would correspond to motor commands necessary to transition from one representation to the other. We want to study the compression of this graph to obtain compact spatial representations, as proposed in [15,17].

In general, the proposed approach deals with very low level processing of sensorimotor streams in order to build meaningful representations. The usefulness of these representations, and how they can integrate in a cognitive architecture, would have to be demonstrated. We plan to use the learned representations in a Reinforcement Learning task. On the one hand, the success rate at the task gives a clear quantitative evaluation. On the other hand, it will allow us to evaluate the benefits of learning representations in terms of generalization, abstraction, and transfer of knowledge across different environments.

References

1. Agrawal, P., Nair, A.V., Abbeel, P., Malik, J., Levine, S.: Learning to poke by poking: experiential learning of intuitive physics. In: Advances in Neural Information Processing Systems, pp. 5074–5082 (2016)
2. Friston, K.: The free-energy principle: a unified brain theory? Nat. Rev. Neurosci. **11**(2), 127–138 (2010)
3. Ghahramani, Z., Wolpert, D.M., Jordan, M.I.: An internal model for sensorimotor integration. Science **269**, 1880–1882 (1995). http://citeseerx.ist.psu.edu/viewdoc/summary?doi=10.1.1.57.74
4. Ha, D., Schmidhuber, J.: World models (2018). https://worldmodels.github.io
5. Harnad, S.: The symbol grounding problem (1990). http://cogprints.org/3106/
6. Hinton, G.E., Salakhutdinov, R.R.: Reducing the dimensionality of data with neural networks. Science **313**(5786), 504–507 (2006)
7. Hotelling, H.: Analysis of a complex of statistical variables into principal components. J. Educ. Psychol. **24**(6), 417 (1933)
8. Kingma, D.P., Ba, J.: Adam: a method for stochastic optimization. arXiv preprint arXiv:1412.6980 (2014)
9. Lesort, T., Díaz-Rodríguez, N., Goudou, J.F., Filliat, D.: State representation learning for control: an overview. ArXiv e-prints, February 2018
10. Lloyd, S.: Least squares quantization in PCM. IEEE Trans. Inf. Theory **28**(2), 129–137 (1982)
11. Moser, M.B., Rowland, D.C., Moser, E.I.: Place cells, grid cells, and memory. Cold Spring Harb. Perspect. Biol. **7**(2), a021808 (2015)
12. O'Regan, J.K., Noë, A.: A sensorimotor account of vision and visual consciousness. Behav. Brain Sci. **24**(5), 939–973 (2001)
13. Radford, A., Metz, L., Chintala, S.: Unsupervised representation learning with deep convolutional generative adversarial networks. arXiv preprint arXiv:1511.06434 (2015)
14. Riedo, F., Rétornaz, P., Bergeron, L., Nyffeler, N., Mondada, F.: A two years informal learning experience using the Thymio robot. Adv. Auton. Mini Robot. **101**, 37–48 (2012)
15. Stachenfeld, K.L., Botvinick, M.M., Gershman, S.J.: The hippocampus as a predictive map. Nat. Neurosci. **20**(11), 1643–1653 (2017). https://doi.org/10.1038/nn.4650
16. Tenenbaum, J.B., De Silva, V., Langford, J.C.: A global geometric framework for nonlinear dimensionality reduction. Science **290**(5500), 2319–2323 (2000)
17. Wayne, G., et al.: Unsupervised predictive memory in a goal-directed agent. CoRR abs/1803.10760 (2018). http://arxiv.org/abs/1803.10760

Signal Detection

Change Detection in Individual Users' Behavior

Parisa Rastin[1,2]([⊠]), Guénaël Cabanes[1,2], Basarab Matei[1,2],
and Jean-Marc Marty[1,2]

[1] LIPN-CNRS, UMR 7030, Université Paris 13,
99 Avenue J-B. Clément, 93430 Villetaneuse, France
{rastin, cabanes, matei}@lipn.univ-paris13.fr
[2] Mindlytix, 10 Rue Pergolèse, 75116 Paris, France

Abstract. The analysis of a dynamic data is challenging. Indeed, the structure of such data changes over time, potentially in a very fast speed. In addition, the objects in such data-sets are often complex. In this paper, our practical motivation is to perform users profiling, i.e. to follow users' geographic location and navigation logs to detect changes in their habits and interests. We propose a new framework in which we first create, for each user, a signal of the evolution in the distribution of their interest and another signal based on the distribution of physical locations recorded during their navigation. Then, we detect automatically the changes in interest or locations thanks a new jump-detection algorithm. We compared the proposed approach with a set of existing signal-based algorithms on a set of artificial data-sets and we showed that our approach is faster and produce less errors for this kind of task. We then applied the proposed framework on a real data-set and we detected different categories of behavior among the users, from users with very stable interest and locations to users with clear changes in their behaviors, either in interest, location or both.

Keywords: Time series · Change detection · Signal-based approaches
Users profiling

1 Introduction

With the current progress of technology, the amount of recorded data is perpetually increasing and the need of fast and efficient analysis algorithms is more important than ever. One of the major challenge in data mining is the detection of change in dynamic data-sets. Indeed, as new data are constantly recorded, the structure of the data-set can vary over time. This phenomenon is known as "concept drift" [9, 18]. One direct application, which is our practical interest in this paper, is the detection of change in users' behavior and interest based on data recorded during their online navigation. This task is known as "user profiling" and has a high economic importance for companies in the field of online advertising. Profiling tasks aim at recognizing the "mindset" of users through their navigation on various websites or their interaction with digital "touch points" (varying ways that a brand interacts and displays information to prospective customers and current customers). It intervenes in the international market for

© Springer Nature Switzerland AG 2018
V. Kůrková et al. (Eds.): ICANN 2018, LNCS 11140, pp. 501–510, 2018.
https://doi.org/10.1007/978-3-030-01421-6_48

"programmatic advertising" tasks, by assigning a profile to users connecting to a site that can offer advertising, so that the displayed advertising corresponds best to the needs of the users. Indeed, being able to detect when a user changes his interest or when he moves to another city or country is very important to adjust the advertising strategy regarding this user. These profiles are computed from a very large database of internet browsing which lists URL sequences or touch points visited by a large number of people. Each URL of a "touch point" is characterized by contextual and semantic information.

In this context, each user is described as a time series of URL categories and physical locations. The URL categories are computed using a clustering approach adapted to complex data [16, 17]. The locations are recorded using geolocation information collected during the user's navigation but are restricted to a series of postal codes. The detection of changes in time series involves the extraction of "stable" periods, separated by usually short period of variation. There are therefore two main strategies: either the algorithm focuses on detecting the different period of stability in the time series, or it focuses on detecting the period of variation [1, 3, 4, 6, 10, 11]. Detecting stability or homogeneity is related to the task of data stream clustering. The detection of variation in the series can be related to signal analysis approaches. In both case, the time series must be segmented into several time windows that will be compared to find either similarities or variations [9, 18].

In this paper we consider a sliding time windows with a step of one day, in order to obtain for each window a distribution of location or interest. Most clustering approaches are not adapted to distributional data and cannot be applied without costly adaptations. However, it is not difficult to compute the pairwise dissimilarities between adjacent windows, using an adapted metrics, in order to produce a signal representing the variations in each user behavior. The main challenge in this case is to discriminate meaningful variation in the signal to random noise. The usual approach is to apply a smoothing function to the signal in order to retain only the significant variations [2, 5, 7, 12]. The main advantages of such algorithms are the computation speed and the absence of user-defined parameter, which are usually difficult to tweak.

We propose in this paper a new signal-based approach, described in Sect. 2, adapted to the profiling task. This algorithm is based on a multi-scale smoothing of the computed signal, allowing a better elimination of non-significant variations in the signal. We then tested the algorithm on simulated data to validate its quality in comparison to traditional approaches; results are presented in Sect. 3. Finally, we applied the proposed framework on a real industrial data-set, as shown in Sect. 4. A conclusion is given in Sect. 5.

2 General Framework

The detection of change in behavior of users is a very interesting information which can help marketing companies to send and sell the right product to users based on their needs. In this work we used the users' geographic location to detect changes in their geographic habits, and the users' navigation logs to detect variation in their interests. We first created a signal for each user based on distributions representing his behavior.

Similarities between distributions are computed by the Jenson-Shannon metric. Then, by using a change detection algorithm, we detected the dates where there was a change in the user's behavior.

2.1   Signal Computation

In order to detect changes in the users' behavior, we applied a change detection algorithm described below. This algorithm detects unusual "jumps" in a signal characterizing behavioral variations. To construct such signal, were a change in behavior is characterized by a jump, we defined the distribution of labels or postal codes in the first time-windows as the reference behavior. Then, the window is shifted one day at a time, in order to produce a series of distribution. For example, if in a time window a user has been detected in France 7 times in Strasbourg (Postal code 67000) and 3 times in Nancy (postal code 54000), the distribution for this user and this time window will be {67000: 70%, 54000: 30%}. The signal is created from the dissimilarities between the distributions in the sliding time window and the distribution of reference. The signal thus obtained represents the evolution of the differences with respect to the reference window and makes it possible to detect significant changes in distributions: a move or a change of interest. The similarity between two probability distributions (reference window and shifted windows) is computed by a metric called Jensen-Shannon divergence [8, 15]. It is based on the Kullback-Leibler divergence, with some notable (and useful) differences, including that it is symmetric and it is always a finite value. The Jensen-Shannon divergence (JS) is a symmetrized and smoothed version of the Kullback-Leibler divergence $D(P \text{ k } Q)$ between two discrete distributions. It is defined by

$$JS(P||Q) = \frac{1}{2}D(P \parallel M) + \frac{1}{2}D(Q \parallel M)$$

Where $M = \frac{1}{2}(P+Q)$. For discrete probability distributions P and Q, the Kullback-Leibler divergence from P to Q is defined [14] to be

$$D_{KL}(P \parallel Q) = -\sum P(i) \log \frac{Q(i)}{P(i)} = \sum_i P(i) \log \frac{P(i)}{Q(i)}.$$

Note that any zero probabilities in P or Q are ignored in the computation, meaning that two totally different distributions will have a JS value of 1. The proposed approach has been tested on the artificial data-set for validation, then applied on the real data-sets to analyze the changes in users' behaviors.

2.2   Proposed Multi-scale Change Detection Algorithm

Algorithm 1 describe the multi-scale change detection approach. The idea is: an iterative smoothing process eliminates random fluctuations in the signal, then unusually high variations are detected. The signals are piece-wise continuous functions having discontinuities at some locations x_i, i.e., $v(x_i^+) \, 6 = v(x_i^-)$. For that type of functions, there exist many approaches to locate the singularities. These can either be signal based (i.e., one detects large amplitude variations using an appropriate threshold) or multi-scale coefficients based. Again, we consider that v_k^j are the averages of some function v discretized on the intervals $I_{j,k} = 2^{-j}[k, \; k+1[$. In multi-scale coefficients-based approach, a strategy to detect the singularities at level j is based on a criterion that uses the first or the second order differences of v^j. In these approaches, the jump singularities detection is carried out at each level independently.

Algorithm 1. Changes Detection in Behavior Signal

    Input: Signal vector v of length N.
    Output: List of detected changes.
1: Initialize $j = \lceil \log_2(N) \rceil$
2: Initialize global list of jumps $L_g = \emptyset$
3: **while** $j > \lceil \log_2(N) \rceil - 4$ **do**
4:     *Smoothing*
5:     **for** $i \leftarrow 1, length(v^j)$ **do**
6:         $v_k^{j-1} = \frac{v_{2k-1}^j + v_{2k}^j}{2}$
7:     Initialize local list of jumps $L_e = \emptyset$
8:     *Compute cost function dv based on first order of finite differences:*
9:     **for** $k \leftarrow 1, length(v^{j-1})$ **do**
10:        $dv_k^{j-1} = |\Delta v_k^{j-1}| + |\Delta v_{k+1}^{j-1}|$
11:     *Compute local maxima of cost function dv:*
12:     **for** $k \leftarrow 1, length(v_k^{j-1})$ **do**
13:        **if** $dv_k^{j-1} > \max(dv_{k-2}^{j-1}, dv_{k-1}^{j-1}, dv_{k+1}^{j-1}, dv_{k+2}^{j-1})$ **then**
14:           $L_j \leftarrow L_j + \{k\}$
15:     $j \leftarrow j - 1$
16: Define L_g as the intersection of all L_j: $L_g = \cap_{j=\lceil \log_2(N) \rceil - 4}^{\lceil \log_2(N) \rceil} L_j$

However, we propose a strategy to locate the jump singularities at a given level j by taking into account the detection at other levels. We detect intervals $I_{j,k}$ potentially containing a jump singularity as those containing the local maxima of $dv_k^j = |\Delta v_k^j| + |\Delta v_{k+1}^j|$ where Δ is the first order finite difference operator $\Delta v_k^j = v_{k-1}^j - v_k^j$, and where v^j is obtained by successive averaging of v^J, J is considered at the finest level of discretization. We then compute the number N_j of singularities at level j, and we define j_{max} as the largest level j such that $N_{j-1} = N_j$. We also define the level j_{min} as the smallest j such that $N_j = N_{j max}$.

A singularity detected in $I_{j,k}$ for $j_{min} < j < J$ is called admissible if there exists a singularity inside $I_{j+1,2k}$ or $I_{j+1,2k+1}$. This definition implies that admissible singularities make up chains when j varies. In that context, the singularities at level j must be separated by more than 2 intervals at the finest level.

3   Experimental Validation

In this section we will present the experimental protocol we used to validate the proposed algorithm. To validate the quality of our algorithm in a controlled environment, we tested the proposed algorithm on artificial data-sets and compared the results with the quality of the state-of-the-art algorithms. The computations are tested on a Windows 10 (x64) machine, 16G RAM, with a dual-core CPU clocked at 2.50 Ghz (i5-2450 M).

3.1   Artificial Data-Sets

To generate the artificial data-set we considered three categories of behavior: The user's behavior changes over time into a totally new behavior, the user's behavior changes over time into a partially different behavior, and the user do not change its behavior. We generated 10000 signals for each of these categories of users. To construct a signal, we first generated two sets of 1 to 5 random labels each, representing the possible behaviors before and after the change. Only one set is created to simulate the absence of change and to simulate partial change we forced the two set to share 1 or 2 labels. We simulated a period of two months. A hundred random time-stamps were generated over this period. Each time-stamp were associated to a label from the first or the second set, depending on a randomly chosen date of change.

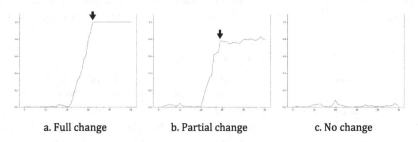

| a. Full change | b. Partial change | c. No change |

Fig. 1. Example of simulated signals of user's behaviors. The arrows indicate the detected changes (if any).

Figure 1a is an example of simulated signal for a user who expressed a full change of behavior. The horizontal axis is the time-stamp (days) and the vertical axis is the JS dissimilarity for the reference window. As you see, the JS increases from the 22th to the 29th day. Then the signal keeps a value of 1 from the 30th day onward, as there is no intersection between the reference distribution and the distributions from the 30th day. In the case of a partial change, the user express new behaviors in addition to some of its previous. For example, a user who relocate into a new house but keep the same work in its previous location. Figure 1b shows such case. This time, the signal never reaches 1 as there are still some similarities before and after the changes. The change is nonetheless correctly detected by the algorithm. The last case is when there is no detection of change for a user. In this case there is no significant different between the reference window and the shifted windows and the signal stays steady over the time. The example showed in Fig. 1c demonstrates that the similarity computed by the Jensen-Shannon divergence is low. The signal created is stable all over the time with no notable change. This case can describe users who keep a regular activity without any notable variations.

3.2 Experimental Results

To demonstrate the effectiveness of the proposed approach, we evaluated its performances in terms of computation time. In addition, to validate the quality of detected changes, we computed the means of absolute differences between the detected and the predicted date of change and we compared it to a set of state-of-the-art algorithms: Jump penalty, PWC bilateral, Robust jump penalty, Soft mean-shift, Total variation, Robust TVD and Medfiltit (see [13]). Table 1 presents the results of comparison between the proposed algorithm and the 7 state-of-the-art algorithms. This table has 6 columns which describe 3 different categories: the first, third and fifth columns describe respectively the time computed for detection of no change, detection of full change and the partial change in user's behavior. As you see, the proposed algorithm has the minimum value in comparison to the other algorithms: it is (usually by far) the fastest approach for this task. Moreover, the error of the proposed method is the lowest among all. This is especially true for stable signals, when there is no change to detect. In that case, the multi-scale approach performs very well at smoothing the whole signal and removing all random variation. Overall the quality of the proposed approach is very satisfying and it should be able to deal with real data in more complex applications.

Table 1. Experimental results

Algorithm	No change time (s)	error	Full change time (s)	error	Partial change time (s)	error
Proposed	0.85	2.78	0.94	1.67	0.87	2.07
Jump penalty	29.4	14.33	25.26	4.11	31.93	4.47
PWC bilateral	83.87	14.31	12.83	3.77	18.71	4.19
Robust jump penalty	8.43	14.26	93.48	4.02	90.63	4.57
Soft mean-shift	8.57	16.57	21.99	3.6	21.5	4.56
Total variation	45.55	13.12	103.44	3.27	116.8	4.02
Robust TVD	7016.69	14.82	4405.04	3.8	4390.13	4.61
Medfilt.it	1.32	13.92	0.98	2.95	1.29	3.93

4   Application

To follow the real changes in individual interest based on the data provided by our project partner, Mindlytix, we used a data-set of the navigation log of 142794 users giving for each user a list of time-stamps associated to the URL visited at this time, over a period of 30 days. Based on the result of the URLs clustering presented in the previous section (using the contextual similarity), each URL were substituted by a cluster label. This step allows a user navigating between different URLs from the same topics to be considered having stable interest. The time windows for this data-set is fixed to 5 days, meaning that the distribution of URLs' labels visited during a 5 days period defines a user behavior. Finally, to follow the change in users' physical location habits, Mindlytix provided a dataset of geolocations (postal codes) associated to time-stamps over a period of 74 days for 598 users. The objective for these data is to be able to detect when a user relocates to a different location or spend some time outside its usual area. Here, we chose a size of 10 days for the time windows to avoid detecting very short trips and unusual displacements.

4.1 Geolocation

In this section we will describe the results obtained on the geolocation data-sets provided by Mindlytix. We analyzed the change behavior for 598 users during 74 days. In the signal creation step we used a window with a size of 10 days. We observe some variety in the signals, but there are still some characteristic patterns. Figures 2a and b illustrates some examples of signals characteristic of a clear relocation. In Fig. 2a the Jensen-Shannon dissimilarity increases sharply for two days, stays stable for three days, then again rises suddenly. Two changes are detected, the first being a partial change. This kind of signal can be interpreted as a move in two steps, with a period where the user spend time in both locations before moving definitively. Figure 2b is another example for relocation of a user and it is a good example of simple change in the user's location. However, this time we observe a small period where the user spends some time in its previous location.

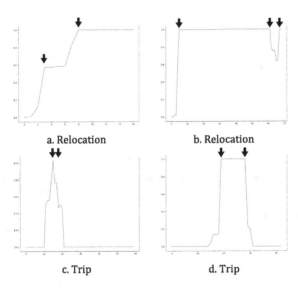

a. Relocation   b. Relocation

c. Trip   d. Trip

Fig. 2. Example of obtained signals during a user's relocation or a temporary displacements (trip). The arrows indicate the detected changes.

Users from another category do not move at all, neither to relocate nor to go to trip or vacations during the recorded period. The dissimilarity between the reference window and the shifted windows stays low all the time. Another interesting case is when the user leaves for a vacation or work for some time, before returning to the place he/she used to live. Figures 2c and d shows two examples for this case. As you see in Fig. 2c, around the 10th day the user starts to move. The dissimilarity between the reference window and the shifted window rises sharply until the 15th day. Then, this dissimilarity decreases rapidly to reach the same distribution as the reference window. It means that this user spent 10 days (the size of the time windows) in another place before coming back. Another example is presented in Fig. 2d, which shows a clear example of a user leaving for a 3-week travel and return to his/her initial place. In both examples, the two changes are correctly detected.

4.2   Individual Interest

To follow the change of users' interest we used users' navigation log information. We have the URLs visited during 30 days for 142794 users. Each URL have been associated to a cluster in the previous section, and the user's navigation can be expressed into a distribution of visited clusters varying over time.

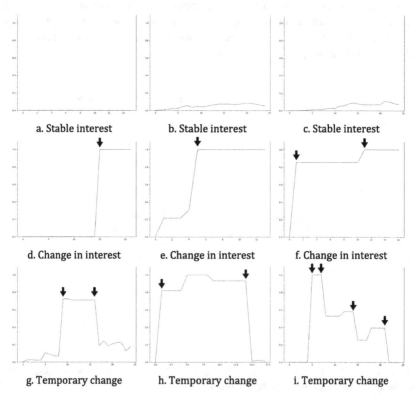

Fig. 3. Examples of stable interest, change in interest and temporary change in interest of users, based on their navigation logs.

Figures 3a to c illustrate the behavior of users who do not change their interest during one month. All three figures the signal is either stable or with only minor variations (undetected by the algorithm). Figure 3d to f is an example of results for the detection of change in individual interest, where the users change their interest over time. As can be seen, in Figs. 3d the signal of this user remains stable for 14 days, then starts to rise sharply as the user start to navigate in other categories of URLs. In Figs. 3e and f, the change is more gradual before reaching a state of interest fully different from the window of reference. These three figures are typical examples of the different pattern of change in a user's interest. A third category of observed behavior is a group of users who change their interest for a limited period and then return to their initial interest. Figures 3g to i illustrate this type of users. As you see, these signals go up and stay stable over a period of time and then go down. It means that the dissimilarity between the reference window and the shifted windows increase for a period of time, but at the end of the recorded period the distribution of visited categories of URL returns to a distribution similar to the distribution of reference. Figure 3i shows a particular example of temporary change, were the user return to its initial interests in several steps.

5 Conclusion

In this paper, we proposed a new multi-scale algorithm of change detection to analyze the change in individual behavior of users based on their navigation and geolocation data. We first created, for each user, a signal of the evolution in the distribution of online user's interest and another signal based on the distribution of physical locations recorded during their navigation. Then, by using the signal-based jump detection algorithm, changes in interest or locations were detected automatically. We detected different scenarios: during the analyzed period, some users kept the same behavior, some had a clear change in their behaviors and some showed a change in their behavior which lasted only a short period of time. Experimental tests performed on simulated signals showed that the proposed approach is faster and makes less errors for this task than state of-the-art algorithms.

References

1. Aggarwal, C.C., Han, J., Wang, J., Yu, P.S.: A framework for clustering evolving data streams. In: Proceedings of the 29th International Conference on Very Large Data Bases, VLDB 2003, VLDB Endowment, vol. 29, pp. 81–92. (2003)
2. Arandiga, F., Cohen, A., Donat, R., Dyn, N., Matei, B.: Approximation of piecewise smooth functions and images by edge-adapted (ENO-EA) nonlinear multiresolution techniques. Appl. Comput. Harmonic Anal. **24**(2), 225–250 (2008). Special Issue on Mathematical Imaging – Part II
3. Bifet, A.: Adaptive stream mining: pattern learning and mining from evolving data streams. In: Proceedings of the 2010 Conference on Adaptive Stream Mining: Pattern Learning and Mining from Evolving Data Streams, pp. 1–212. IOS Press, Amsterdam (2010)

4. Cao, F., Estert, M., Qian, W., Zhou, A.: Density-based clustering over an evolving data stream with noise, pp. 328–339. Society for Industrial and Applied Mathematics (2006)
5. Chan, T.F., Zhou, H.M.: ENO-wavelet transforms for piecewise smooth functions. SIAM J. Numer. Anal. **40**(4), 1369–1404 (2002)
6. Chen, Y., Tu, L.: Density-based clustering for real-time stream data. In: Proceedings of the 13th ACM SIGKDD International Conference on Knowledge Discovery and Data Mining, KDD 2007, pp. 133–142. ACM, New York (2007)
7. Claypoole, R.L., Davis, G.M., Sweldens, W., Baraniuk, R.G.: Nonlinear wavelet transforms for image coding via lifting. IEEE Trans. Image Process. **12**(12), 1449–1459 (2003)
8. Dagan, I., Lee, L., Pereira, F.: Similarity-based methods for word sense disambiguation. In: Proceedings of the Eighth Conference on European Chapter of the Association for Computational Linguistics, EACL 1997, pp. 56–63 (1997). Association for Computational Linguistics, Stroudsburg
9. Gama, J.: Knowledge Discovery from Data Streams, 1st edn. Chapman & Hall/CRC, Boca Raton (2010)
10. Han, J.: Data Mining: Concepts and Techniques. Morgan Kaufmann Publishers Inc., San Francisco (2005)
11. Last, M.: Online classification of nonstationary data streams. Intell. Data Anal. **6**(2), 129–147 (2002)
12. Lipman, Y., Levin, D.: Approximating piecewise-smooth functions. IMA J. Numer. Anal. **30**(4), 1159–1183 (2009)
13. Little, M.A., Jones, N.S.: Generalized methods and solvers for noise removal from piecewise constant signals, i. background theory. Proc. Roy. Soc. A **467**(2135), 3088–3114 (2011)
14. MacKay, D.J.C.: Information Theory, Inference and Learning Algorithms. Cambridge University Press, New York (2002)
15. Manning, C.D., Schutze, H.: Foundations of Statistical Natural Language Processing. MIT Press, Cambridge (1999)
16. Rastin, P., Matei, B.: Prototype-based clustering for relational data using Barycentric coordinates. In: Proceeding of the International Joint Conference on Neural Networks (IJCNN), IJCNN 2018 (2018)
17. Rastin, P., Zhang, T., Cabanes, G.: A new clustering algorithm for dynamic data. In: Hirose, A., Ozawa, S., Doya, K., Ikeda, K., Lee, M., Liu, D. (eds.) ICONIP 2016. LNCS, vol. 9949, pp. 175–182. Springer, Cham (2016). https://doi.org/10.1007/978-3-319-46675-0_20
18. Silva, J.A., Faria, E.R., Barros, R.C., Hruschka, E.R., de Carvalho, A.C., Gama, J.: Data stream clustering: a survey. ACM Comput. Surv. **46**(1), 13–31 (2013)

Extraction and Localization of Non-contaminated Alpha and Gamma Oscillations from EEG Signal Using Finite Impulse Response, Stationary Wavelet Transform, and Custom FIR

Najmeddine Abdennour[1]([⊠]), Abir Hadriche[1,2]([⊠]), Tarek Frikha[3]([⊠]),
and Nawel Jmail[4]([⊠])

[1] Department of Electronics and Telecommunication, Institute of Computer Science and Multimedia. ISIMG, University of Gabes, Gabes, Tunisia
najemabdennour@gmail.com, Abir.hadriche.tn@ieee.org
[2] REGIM Lab, ENIS, Sfax University, Sfax, Tunisia
[3] CES Lab, ENIS. Sfax University, Sfax, Tunisia
tarek.frikha@enis.tn
[4] MIRACL Lab, Sfax University, Sfax, Tunisia
naweljmail@yahoo.fr

Abstract. The alpha and gamma oscillations derived from EEG signal are useful tools in recognizing a cognitive state and several cerebral disorders. However, there are undesirable artifacts that exist among the electrophysiological signals which lead to unreliable results in the extraction and localization of these accurate oscillations. We introduced, three filtering techniques based on Finite Impulse Response filters FIR, Stationary Wavelet transform SWT method and custom FIR filter to extract the non-contaminated (pure) oscillations and localize their responsible sources using the Independent Component Analysis ICA technique. In our obtained results, we compared the effectiveness of these filtering techniques in extracting and localizing of non-contaminated alpha and gamma oscillations. We proposed here the accurate technique for the extraction of pure alpha and oscillations. We also presented the accurate cortical region responsible of the generation of these oscillations.

Keywords: EEG signal · Oscillation · FIR · SWT · Custom FIR
Source localization

1 Introduction

In order to study the human brain activity, we relied on analyzing electrophysiological signals; among this recording technique the electroencephalogram EEG signal remains one of the reliable ways to investigate the neurons activity response and their impact on our daily tasks, conscious state and medical disorders. Based on the EEG frequency variation, this physiological signal is generally classified into five waves: delta band (0.5–4 Hz), theta waves (4–7.5 Hz), alpha (8–13 Hz), beta (14–26 Hz) and gamma

© Springer Nature Switzerland AG 2018
V. Kůrková et al. (Eds.): ICANN 2018, LNCS 11140, pp. 511–520, 2018.
https://doi.org/10.1007/978-3-030-01421-6_49

(30–45 Hz) [1]. The alpha waves are generally located in the occipital area, considered as the most important cortical waves, it reveals the states of relaxation, awareness and absence of concentration. For the gamma waves they are much more identified as active level of cognition state and mostly used for confirmation of serval neurological diseases and malfunctions [2], especially in epilepsy. The extraction of these frequency bands in a pure way was and remains a challenging task notably when the EEG recorded frequencies covers a wide range (from 0.5 Hz up to 45 Hz and above). With a variety of different filtering techniques, [3–6], the consensus filtering method remain in negotiation versus several constraints: the signal to noise ratio, the overlapped level, the width of spikes and oscillations…. An effective separation of cortical frequency band would produce non-contaminated oscillatory activities (neurons generators) with a much better analysis of the responsible sources and generators of these activities.

2   Filtering Techniques

2.1   Finite Impulsive Response (FIR): Kaiser Window

The Finite Impulse Response filter is a classical technique that conservers both the causality and stability aspects. The FIR is preferred then Infinite Impulsive Response IIR (difficult to implement mainly for the instability in higher orders) [7–9].

In fact, the FIR is always applied with windowing method. Hence, we used the Kaiser window to control the passband ripples stability with a smother manner [10]. The Kaiser window (Kaiser function in Matlab), defines the window shape by the β parameter. In our study, we settled the filter order to N = 100, the passband frequencies Fc1, Fc2 respectively set to 8 and 12 Hz for the extraction of the alpha wave and for the gamma wave were set to 30 and 46 Hz. (fir1 function in matlab), and the β window parameter to 3.

2.2   A Custom Designed FIR Filter Derived from Parcks-MacClellan Algorithm

The Parcks-MacClellan algorithm is as fundamental way to design Equiripple FIR filters [11], based on the Chebyshev approximation [12].

The main advantage of this filter is its ability to minimize errors both in passband and stopband frequencies [10].

We defined in our study, the filter order to N = 100, the stop and pass weights to Wstop1 = 100, Wpass = 80 and Wstop2 = 120. The passband and stopband frequencies were the same as the FIR filter settings for both alpha and gamma waves extractions.

2.3   Stationary Wavelet Transform (SWT)

The stationary Wavelet Transform SWT is a wavelet transform filter based on the Discrete Wavelet Transform (DWT) with the advantage, of surpassing binary decimation step, of the wavelet transform [3, 13] that allows a retention of the real signal properties. The SWT also has a better performance than the Classical Wavelet Transform (CWT) by overcoming the frequency bands overlapping. The SWT has been also proven very useful in EEG signal analysis [3, 14]. In fact, this technique, decomposes a signal s(t) at each scale j and step k, then project it on the mother wavelet function ϕ by the Eq. (1):

$$\phi_{j,k(t)} = 2^{-j}\phi\big(2^{-j}(t-k)\big), C_{j,k} = \big\langle s(t), \phi_{j,k(t)} \big\rangle \tag{1}$$

with $C_{j,k}$ is the value of the approximated or detailed coefficients at level j decomposition depending on the reconstruction.

In our case, we applied the SWT to extract the alpha using 7 levels of decomposition while the gamma rhythms require only a decomposition of 6-levels (the decomposition level increases when the selected frequency band decreases). We applied, in this study, the wavelet family symlets 4 and the SWT Matlab function for the decomposition with the iswt functions of Matlab for the reconstruction of pure alpha and gamma oscillations.

3 Database

Our real EEG signal used in this work is a registration of one subject, the acquisition and preprocessing phases were applied in the Clinical Neurophysiology Department of 'La Timone hospital' in Marseille as in Jmail and colleagues [6] and validated by an expert neurologist. This particular EEG recording was chosen because it presented clear alpha and gamma patterns with regular spiking and visible epileptic oscillations as validated by the expert. The EEG data was recorded on a Deltamed System, sampled at 2500 Hz, with anti-aliasing low-pass analog filter set to 100 Hz. Our dataset is composed of 74 epochs each with 6 s duration, 62 channels and 148 events.

4 Results

4.1 Extraction of Alpha and Gamma Rhythms for Real EEG Signal

In Fig. 1, we depicted the three-filtering methods response for the reconstruction of the alpha rhythm against the EEG signal. It is noticeable that the FIR and the SWT methods have a relatively similar result with a visually confirmed proof of match to the ideal alpha wave, while the Custom FIR could not dispose the higher frequency oscillations which leads to a contaminated signal more related to the real EEG signal.

In Fig. 2, we compared the robustness of our adopted filtering methods versus the real EEG signal. Similar to the alpha case, it is perceptible that the FIR and SWT methods are relatively similar results in the extraction of the gamma band, however the Custom FIR still present a corrupted oscillation.

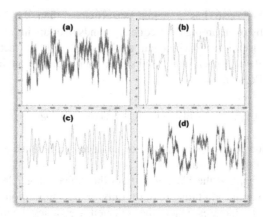

Fig. 1. A comparison of (a) original EEG dataset, with the extracted alpha band by (b) FIR (c) SWT (d) Custom FIR.

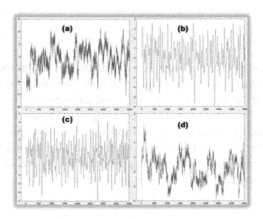

Fig. 2. A comparison of (a) original EEG dataset, with the extracted gamma band by (b) FIR (c) SWT (d) Custom FIR.

4.2   Evaluation of the Three Extraction Methods

The GOF for the Extraction of Pure Alpha and Gamma Rhythm
The reconstructed simulated signals using three filtering techniques were compared to the simulated signals. See Eq. (2):

$$GOF = 1 - \left(\frac{\sum_{t=1}^{r} (s(t) - s_f(t))^2}{\sum_{t=1}^{r} s(t)^2} \right) \tag{2}$$

With s(t) is the theoretical power and $S_f(t)$ is the power of the filtered signal that depends on the adopted filtering technique (FIR, SWT, Custom designed FIR).

The GOF value for these different SNR measurements is gathered in the Fig. 3.

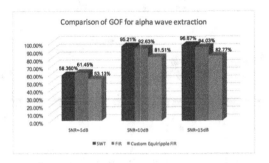

Fig. 3. Comparison of GOF values for the recovered alpha simulated signal by SWT, FIR and custom FIR.

It is clear that the SWT provides the best result in the extraction of alpha wave for different SNR values. Hence the SWT is the accurate filtering technique for the recovery of pure alpha signal even in a noisy signal.

We depicted in Fig. 4 the GOF results for the recovery of gamma wave.

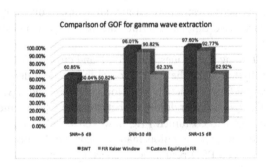

Fig. 4. Comparison of GOF values for the recovered gamma simulated signal by SWT, FIR and custom FIR.

We have similar results as the alpha extraction values, furthermore the GOF values has been widened between the filtering techniques in high SNR values.

The Topographies and DSP for the Extraction of Pure Alpha and Gamma Rhythms.

The topographies and power spectral density (PSD) mapping for the alpha rhythm extraction versus the real EEG signal was depicted in Figure [15] (Fig. 5).

The FIR filter improves the scalp map depolarization, compared to real EEG map, in fact the recovered alpha has a clearer dipolar topography. The SWT shows a much more dipolar and clearer results than the FIR and the original signal. For the Custom FIR has slightly depolarized the scalp map topography.

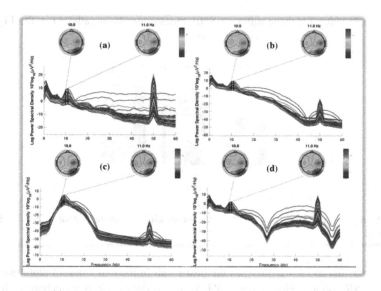

Fig. 5. Comparison of the Topographies and PDS of (a) real EEG signal and the extracted alpha signal by (b) FIR (c) SWT (d) Custom FIR.

There are two clear activities: a parietal and an occipital one, a typical location of alpha rhythms, in fact these dipolar activities are much clear and pure by the SWT filtering technique.

All the adopted filtering techniques: FIR, SWT and custom FIR, have been able to bring out the alpha rhythm since they did valorize the spectral density energies.

For the gamma rhythm extraction, the topographies and PSD evaluation are depicted in Fig. 6. There is no clear difference between the topographies of original and extracted gamma by FIR and costumed FIR, however the SWT topography showed a slight improvement in the depolarization map (a clear dipolar mapping that reflect a physiological activity). The PSD results are increasingly improved (Custom FIR then FIR and finally SWT) in terms of valorizing the gamma band.

The Source Localization of the Pure Alpha and Gamma Rhythm.
To define the accurate sources responsible of the generation of alpha and gamma band, we resolved the forward and inverse problem, using the EEGLAB [15] and the fieldtrip toolbox.

For the resolution of the source localization, we used in this work the BEM technique as a solution for the Forward problem, and the ECD technique (simple in implementation with good results in estimation of the responsible sources) as a solution for the inverse problem. We also set the Residue Variance to RV = 15% (to reduce the low sources effect on the high sources).

Furthermore, we computed the Independent Component Analysis (ICA) for our original signal to keep only one generator per activity (one with 10 Hz for alpha and one with 45 Hz for gamma). We set the number of component equal to the number of channels (captors) to emphasis the number of independent components. We used the

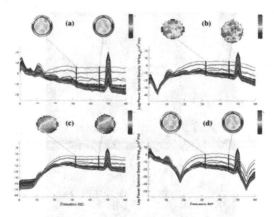

Fig. 6. Comparison of the Topographies and DSP of the (a) real EEG signal and extracted gamma by (b) FIR (c) SWT (d) Custom FIR.

ICA function on Matlab implemented in the EEGLAB toolbox for each filtered dataset (pure alpha/gamma by FIR, pure alpha/gamma by SWT, pure alpha/gamma by custom FIR). Finally, we applied the source localization algorithms on the ICA component depicting a pure alpha oscillator then a pure gamma oscillator.

The choice of the involved components to be localized was based on the topographies results (studied in the previous section). In fact, we selected the components 6 and 8, (dipolar map) for alpha band and the components 13 and 14 for gamma activities.

Figure 7 illustrates the source localization of the involved alpha components 6,8 by our proposed filtering technique (FIR, SWT, custom FIR) versus our real EEG signal.

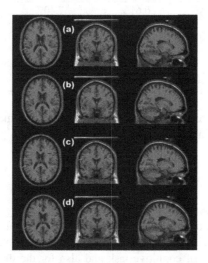

Fig. 7. Source localization of component 6 and 8 for (a) real EEG signal and pure alpha signal using (b) FIR (c) SWT (d) Custom FIR.

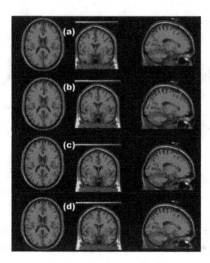

Fig. 8. Source localization of component 13 and 14 for (a) real EEG signal and extracted gamma by (b) FIR (c) SWT (d) Custom FIR.

In Fig. 8 we compared the source localization results as in the Fig. 7 for the gamma rhythms.

The Residual Values RV after localization for all the components are gathered in Table 1, the more the RV value is lower the more the results are accurate.

Table 1. Components RV values for the real EEG signal, FIR, SWT and Custom FIR.

	Component 6 RV%	Component 8 RV%	Component 13 RV%	Component 14 RV%
Real EEG signal	2.45%	6.61%	7.40%	>15%
FIR	7.31%	14.52%	>15%	14.22%
SWT	2.45%	6.61%	1.98%	3.99%
Custom FIR	2.46%	12.26%	>15%	>15%

The RV value indicates that SWT is the efficient filtering method for the extraction of non-contaminated alpha and gamma rhythms.

5   Discussion

In this study, we compared the performance of three filtering methods (FIR, custom FIR and SWT) in the extraction of two frequency bands (the alpha and the gamma wave) among a real EEG signal. In fact, these activities (alpha and gamma) are very important in the analysis of cognitive task and also for the diagnosis of neurological disease as epilepsy. Hence, we proposed to define the best filtering method to recover in a resalable way a pure alpha and gamma activity in order to locate their responsible sources. These productions are useful to help different neurological decisions for both normal and epileptic cases.

We also evaluated the robustness of our adopted filtering methods against the noise and we proved that the SWT technique is the best method for the extraction of both alpha and gamma waves. Furthermore, the SWT has shown its efficiency in the topographic mapping especially for the alpha band and for the source localization of the gamma extracted signal. In order to help neurologist during the analysis and diagnosis of electrophysiological signal, we propose in the further work to embed our processing chain as a monitoring and neurofeedback system.

Acknowledgements. This work was supported by 18 PJEC 12-21, 2018: Hatem Ben Taher project, Minister of Higher Education and Scientific Research in Tunisia.

References

1. Sanei, S.: Adaptive Processing of Brain Signals, pp. 10–14. Wiley, Chichester (2013)
2. Nariai, H., et al.: Scalp EEG Ictal gamma and beta activity during infantile spasms: Evidence of focality. Epilepsia **58**(5), 882–892 (2017)
3. Jmail, N., et al.: A comparison of methods for separation of transient and oscillatory signals in EEG. J. Neurosci. Methods **199**(2), 273–289 (2011)
4. Hadriche, A., et al.: The detection of Evoked Potential with variable latency and multiple trial using Consensus matching pursuit. In: 1st International Conference on Advanced Technologies for Signal and Image Processing (ATSIP). IEEE (2014)
5. Jmail, N., et al.: Despikifying SEEG signals using a temporal basis set. In: 15th International Conference on Intelligent Systems Design and Applications (ISDA). IEEE (2015)
6. Jmail, N., et al.: Despiking SEEG signals reveals dynamics of gamma band preictal activity. Physiol. Meas. **38**(2), N42 (2017)
7. Singh, V., et al.: Comparative study of FIR and IIR filters for the removal of 50 Hz noise from EEG signal. Int. J. Biomed. Eng. Technol. **22**(3), 250–257 (2016)
8. Frikha, T., et al.: Adaptive architecture for medical application case study: evoked Potential detection using matching poursuit consensus. In: 15th International Conference on Intelligent Systems Design and Applications (ISDA). IEEE (2015)
9. Frikha, T., et al.: Embedded application for evoked potential detection. J. Inf. Assur. Secur. 11(4) (2016)
10. Kumar, M., et al.: Design of band pass finite impulse response filter using various window method. Int. J. Eng. Res. Appl. **3**(5), 1057–1061 (2013)
11. Filip, S.I.: A robust and scalable implementation of the Parks-McClellan algorithm for designing FIR filters. ACM Trans. Math. Softw. (TOMS) **43**(1), 7 (2016)
12. Parks, T., McClellan, J.: Chebyshev approximation for nonrecursive digital filters with linear phase. IEEE Trans. Circuit Theory **19**(2), 189–194 (1972)
13. Jmail, N., et al.: Integration of stationary wavelet transform on a dynamic partial reconfiguration for recognition of pre-ictal gamma oscillations. Heliyon **4**(2), e00530 (2018)

14. Jmail, N., et al.: Separation between spikes and oscillation by stationary wavelet transform implemented on an embedded architecture. J. Neurol. Sci. **381**, 542 (2017)
15. Delorme, A., Makeig, S.: EEGLAB: an open source toolbox for analysis of single-trial EEG dynamics including independent component analysis. J. Neurosci. Methods **134**(1), 9–21 (2004)

Long-Short Term Memory/Chaotic Complex Models

Chaotic Complex-Valued Associative Memory with Adaptive Scaling Factor

Daisuke Karakama, Norihito Katamura, Chigusa Nakano, and Yuko Osana[(⊠)]

Tokyo University of Technology, 1404-1, Katakura, Hachioji, Tokyo 192-0982, Japan
osana@stf.teu.ac.jp

Abstract. In this paper, we propose a Chaotic Complex-Valued Associative Memory with Adaptive Scaling Factor which can realize dynamic association of multi-valued pattern. In the proposed model, the scaling factor of refractoriness is adjusted according to the maximum absolute value of the internal state up to that time as similar as the conventional Chaotic Associative Memory with Adaptive Scaling Factor. Computer experiments are carried out and we confirmed that the proposed model has the same dynamic association ability as the conventional model, and the proposed model also has recall capability similar to that of the conventional model, even for the number of neurons not used for automatic adjustment of parameters.

Keywords: Chaotic complex-valued neuron · Associative memory
Adaptive Scaling Factor

1 Introduction

Recently, various researches on neural networks have been carried out as a method which has flexible information processing ability found in brain. Among them, a lot of associative memory models have been proposed.

On the other hand, chaos is drawing much attention as one of methods which have flexible information processing ability. Chaos is a phenomenon that can not be predicted over a long term occurring in a nonlinear system with deterministic time evolution. It is observed in brain and nervous system of living organisms and is thought to play an important role in memories and learning in brain [1]. In a chaotic neuron model [1], chaos is introduced by considering spatio-temporal summation, refractoriness of neuron, continuous output function seen in real neurons. The chaotic associative memory is an auto-associative memory composed of the chaotic neuron model and it has the same structure as the Hopfield network [2]. It is known that it can recall the stored binary/bipolar patterns dynamically [1,3]. Moreover, it is known that dynamic association ability improves by temporally changing scaling factor of refractoriness which is a parameter of chaotic neuron model [4]. However, dynamic association ability depends on parameters of chaotic neuron model such as damping factors and a scaling factor of refractoriness. Since appropriate parameters vary depending on

© Springer Nature Switzerland AG 2018
V. Kůrková et al. (Eds.): ICANN 2018, LNCS 11140, pp. 523–531, 2018.
https://doi.org/10.1007/978-3-030-01421-6_50

the number of neurons, the number of training patterns and so on, there is a problem that appropriate parameters have to be determined by trial and error.

As the model which can adjust parameters automatically in the Chaotic Associative Memory, we have proposed the Chaotic Associative Memory with Adaptive Scaling Factor [5]. In this model, automatic parameter adjustment method are determined based on the relationship between the internal state and the parameters in which the high dynamic association ability is obtained in the Chaotic Associative Memory with Variable Scaling Factor. In this model, the connection weights are normalized by dividing by the number of neurons so that the range that internal value does not depend on the number of neurons. However, this model can deal with only binary/bipolar patterns.

On the other hand, a complex-valued neural network has been proposed as a model that can deal with multi-valued patterns. This model consists of the complex-valued neuron model, and realizes association of multi-valued patterns by expressing multi-value using complex-values. In this model, the unit circle on the complex plane is equally divided by S, and the point at the equally divided position is made to correspond to multiple values to represent a multivalued pattern.

Furthermore, a chaotic complex-valued neuron model [6] has been proposed in which a chaotic neuron model is extended to deal with complex values as an internal state or output. This is a model combining a complex-valued neuron model and a chaos neuron model. In the chaotic complex associative memory [6] which is an auto associative memory model consisting of chaotic complex-valued neuron models, dynamic association of multi-valued patterns can be realized. Chaotic complex-valued associative memory has a structure in which neurons are mutually coupled as similar as the Hopfield network, and consists of chaotic complex-valued neuron model. In this model, as similar as the complex-valued neural network, multi-valued patterns are represented by assigning points on the unit circle in the complex plane to multi values, and the state of the network is changed by chaos, dynamic association of multi-valued patterns.

In this paper, we propose a Chaotic Complex-Valued Associative Memory with Adaptive Scaling Factor which can realize dynamic association of multi-valued pattern. In the proposed model, the scaling factor of refractoriness is adjusted according to the maximum absolute value of the internal state up to that time as similar as the conventional Chaotic Associative Memory with Adaptive Scaling Factor.

2   Chaotic Complex-Valued Associative Memory with Adaptive Scaling Factor

Here, we explain the proposed Chaotic Complex-Valued Associative Memory with Adaptive Scaling Factor. This model is an auto-associative memory composed of a chaotic complex-valued neuron model having a scaling factor of refractoriness that varies with time and internal states of neurons. It can realize dynamic association of multi-valued stored patterns by internal state change by chaos.

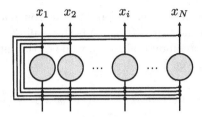

$$x_1 \quad x_2 \qquad x_i \qquad x_N$$

Fig. 1. Structure of proposed model.

2.1 Structure

The proposed model has the similar structure as the Hopfield network [2] as shown in Fig. 1. Each neuron is a chaotic complex-valued neuron model with a scaling factor of refractoriness that varies with time and are coupled to each other.

2.2 Learning Process

In the learning process of the proposed model, the connection weights are determined using correlation learning as similar as the Hopfield network. When P patterns are memorized into the network consisting of N neurons, the weight matrix $\boldsymbol{w}$ is determined as follows:

$$\boldsymbol{w} = \frac{10}{\beta(S)N + \gamma(S)} \sum_{p=1}^{P} \boldsymbol{X}^{(p)} \boldsymbol{X}^{(p)*} - P\boldsymbol{I}_N \tag{1}$$

where N is the number of neurons, $\boldsymbol{x}^{(p)}$ is the p-th stored complex-valued pattern vector, $\boldsymbol{I}_N$ is a unit matrix $(N \times N)$, and $*$ represents conjugate transposition. $\beta(S)$ and $\gamma(S)$ are is the normalization parameters when the number of states is S ($\beta(4) = 6.6375$, $\beta(6) = 6.6241$, $\beta(8) = 6.6211$, $\gamma(4) = -0.6618$, $\gamma(6) = 0.832$, $\gamma(8) = 4.1951$).

2.3 Recall Process

The recall process of the proposed model has following four steps.
Step 1 : Input of Pattern
    A pattern is given to the network.
Step 2 : Calculation of Internal States

The internal states of the neuron i at the time $t + 1$, $u_i(t+1)$ is given by

$$u_i(t+1) = \sum_{j=1}^{N} w_{ij} \sum_{d=0}^{t} k_m^d x_j(t-d) - \alpha(t, I(t)_{max}) \sum_{d=0}^{t} k_r^d x_i(t-d) \tag{2}$$

$$(u_i(t), x_i(t), w_{ij} \in \mathbb{C}, \quad k_m, k_r, \alpha(t, I(t)_{max}) \in \mathbb{R})$$

where N is the number of neurons, k_m is the damping factor of the mutual coupling term, k_r is the damping factor of the refractoriness term, w_{ij} is the connection weight between the neuron i and the neuron j, and $x_j(t)$ is the output of the neuron j at the time t. $\alpha(t, I(t)_{max})$ is the scaling factor of refractoriness at the time t when the maximum absolute value of the internal state up to the time t is $I(t)_{max}$. It is given by

$$\alpha(t, I(t)_{max}) = a(I(t)_{max}) + b(a(I(t)_{max})) \cdot \sin\left(c \cdot \frac{\pi}{12} \cdot t\right) \tag{3}$$

where $I(t)_{max}$ is the maximum absolute value of the internal state up to the time t, and it is given by

$$I(t)_{max} = \max\{I(t), I(t-1)_{max}\} \tag{4}$$

where, $I(t)$ is the average of the absolute values of internal states excluding the refractoriness term at time t, and it is given by

$$I(t) = \frac{1}{N}\left|\sum_{j=1}^{N} w_{ij} \sum_{d=0}^{t} k_m^d x_j(t-d)\right|. \tag{5}$$

$a(I(t)_{max})$, $b(a(I(t)_{max}))$, c are parameters that determine how to change the scaling factor of refractoriness. $a(I(t)_{max})$ is the average value when the maximum absolute value of the internal state up to the time t is $I(t)_{max}$, $b(a(I(t)_{max}))$ is the amplitude when the maximum absolute value of the internal state up to the time t is $I(t)_{max}$, and c affects the cycle.

In the case of $S = 4$,

$$a(I(t)_{max}) = \begin{cases} 21.504I(t)_{max} - 17.259 & (I(t)_{max} \leq 1.401405) \\ 13 & (1.401405 < I(t)_{max}) \end{cases} \tag{6}$$

is used. In the case of $S = 6$,

$$a(I(t)_{max}) = \begin{cases} 47.919I(t)_{max} - 50.094 & (I(t)_{max} \leq 1.345291) \\ 15 & (1.345291 < I(t)_{max}) \end{cases} \tag{7}$$

is used. In the case of $S = 8$,

$$a(I(t)_{max}) = \begin{cases} 49.539I(t)_{max} - 53.057 & (I(t)_{max} \leq 1.404302) \\ 17 & (1.404302 < I(t)_{max}) \end{cases} \tag{8}$$

is used.

$b(a(I(t)_{max}))$ is given by

$$b(a(I(t)_{max})) = a(I(t)_{max}). \tag{9}$$

These equations are determined based on the relationship between the internal state and the parameters a and b in the parameter in which the high dynamic association ability is obtained in the Chaotic Complex-Valued Associative Memory with Variable Scaling Factor composed of 300 to 600 neurons.

Step 3 : Calculation of Output

The output of the neuron i at the time $t+1$, $x_i(t+1)$ is given by

$$x_i(t+1) = f(u_i(t+1)) \tag{10}$$

where $f(\cdot)$ is output function. Here, we use the following function:

$$f(u) = \frac{\eta u}{\eta - 1.0 + |u|} \tag{11}$$

where, η is a positive constant.

Step 4 : Repeat

Steps 2 and **3** are repeated.

3   Computer Experiment Results

Here, we show the computer experiment results to demonstrate the effectiveness of the proposed model under the condition shown in Table 1. The following experiments are the average of 10 trials.

3.1   Comparison of Dynamic Association Ability with Proposed Model and Conventional Model

Here, we compare the recall rate of the proposed model with the well-tuned conventional Chaotic Complex-Valued Associative Memory with Variable Scaling Factor. The coefficients a, b and the damping factors k_m and k_r of the conventional model use values obtained when the highest recall rate is obtained. Figures 2, 3 and 4 shows the recall rate when 2 to 20 patterns are memorized in each model.

From these results, it can be seen that the proposed model has the same dynamic association ability as the well-tuned conventional model (adjusted model).

Table 1. Experimental conditions

The Number of Neurons	N	100–2000
The Number of Patterns	P	1–20
S-valued Pattern	S	4, 6, 8
Damping Factor	k_m	0.86
Damping Factor	k_r	0.88 $(S=4,6)$ 0.87 $(S=8)$
Parameter in Output Function	η	1.000001
Coefficient in Scaling Factor of Refractoriness	c	2.0

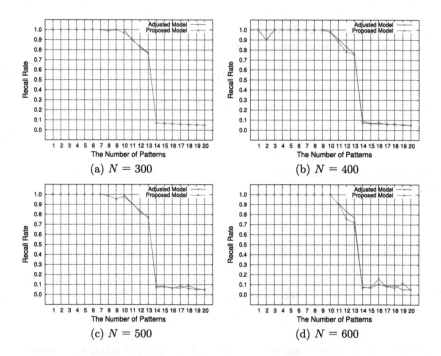

Fig. 2. Dynamic association ability of the proposed model and the conventional model ($N = 300$–600, $S = 4$).

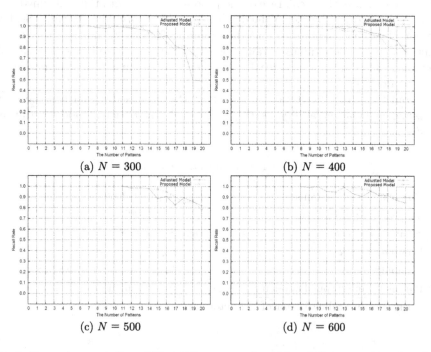

Fig. 3. Dynamic association ability of the proposed model and the conventional model ($N = 300$–600, $S = 6$).

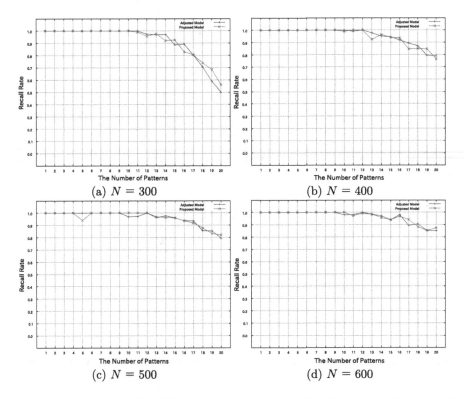

Fig. 4. Dynamic association ability of the proposed model and the conventional model ($N = 300$–600, $S = 8$).

3.2 Dynamic Association Ability of Proposed Model Composed of More Neurons

Here, we investigated whether a high recall rate can be obtained also in the case of the number of neurons not used for determining the parameter automatic adjustment method in the proposed model. Figures 5, 6 and 7 show the recall

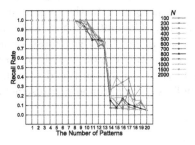

Fig. 5. Dynamic association ability of the proposed model composed of more neurons ($S = 4$)

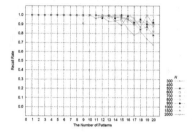

Fig. 6. Dynamic association ability of the proposed model composed of more neurons ($S = 6$)

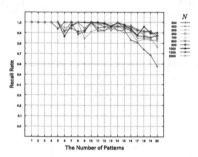

Fig. 7. Dynamic association ability of the proposed model composed of more neurons ($S = 8$)

rate when 2 to 20 patterns are memorized in each model. From these figures, it can be seen that the proposed model also has recall capability similar to that of the conventional model, even for the number of neurons not used for automatic adjustment of parameters.

4   Conclusions

In this paper, we have proposed the Chaotic Complex-Valued Associative Memory with Adaptive Scaling Factor. In the proposed model, the scaling factor of refractoriness is adjusted according to the maximum absolute value of the internal state up to that time. Computer experiments are carried out and we confirmed that the proposed model has the almost same dynamic association ability as the well-tuned conventional model, and the proposed model also has recall capability similar to that of the well-tuned conventional model, even for the number of neurons not used for automatic adjustment of parameters.

References

1. Aihara, K., Takabe, T., Toyoda, M.: Chaotic neural networks. Phys. Lett. A **144**(6 & 7), 333–340 (1990)
2. Hopfield, J.J.: Neural networks and physical systems with emergent collective computational abilities. Proc. Natl. Acad. Sci. USA **79**, 2554–2558 (1982)
3. Osana, Y., Hagiwara, M.: Separation of superimposed pattern and many-to-many associations by chaotic neural networks. In: Proceedings of IEEE and INNS International Joint Conference on Neural Networks, Anchorage, vol. 1, pp. 514–519 (1998)
4. Osana, Y.: Recall and separation ability of chaotic associative memory with variable scaling factor. In: Proceedings of IEEE and INNS International Joint Conference on Neural Networks, Hawaii (2002)
5. Okada, T., Osana, Y.: Chaotic associative memory with adaptive scaling factor. In: Lintas, A., Rovetta, S., Verschure, P.F.M.J., Villa, A.E.P. (eds.) ICANN 2017. LNCS, vol. 10614, pp. 713–721. Springer, Cham (2017). https://doi.org/10.1007/978-3-319-68612-7_81
6. Nakada, M., Osana, Y.: Chaotic complex-valued associative memory. In: Proceedings of International Symposium on Nonlinear Theory and its Applications, Vancouver, pp. 16–19 (2007)

Computation of Air Traffic Flow Management Performance with Long Short-Term Memories Considering Weather Impact

Stefan Reitmann$^{(\boxtimes)}$ and Michael Schultz

Department of Air Transportation, Institute of Flight Guidance,
German Aerospace Center (DLR), Braunschweig, Germany
{stefan.reitmann,michael.schultz}@dlr.de
http://www.dlr.de/fl/

Abstract. In this paper we compute the impact of weather events to airport performance, which is measured as deviation of actual and scheduled timestamps (delay). Weather phenomena are categorized by the Air Traffic Management Airport Performance weather algorithm, which aims to quantify weather conditions at European airports. A comprehensive dataset of flights of 2013 for example airport Hamburg and accompanied weather data result in both a quantification of the individual airport performance and an aggregated weather-performance metric.

To model complex correlations between weather and flight schedule data we use advance machine learning procedures as Long Short-Term Memories are. Various structured models are applied to certain simulation scenarios considering differences in weather affected air traffic dynamics.

Keywords: Neural networks · LSTM · RNN · Time series analysis
Sequence prediction

1 Introduction

1.1 Ease of Use

From an air transportation system view, a flight could be seen as a gate-to-gate or an air-to-air process, where the gate-to-gate is more focused on the aircraft trajectory flown, the air-to-air process concentrates on the airport ground operations to enable efficient flight operations proving reliable departure times. Typical standard deviations for airborne flights are 30 s at 20 min before arrival [1], but could increase to 15 min when the aircraft is still on the ground [6]. To evaluate these deviations in an economic context, [2] provide reference values for the cost of delay to European airlines. The average time variability (measured as standard deviation) during the flight phase (5.3 min) is higher than in the

© Springer Nature Switzerland AG 2018
V. Kůrková et al. (Eds.): ICANN 2018, LNCS 11140, pp. 532–541, 2018.
https://doi.org/10.1007/978-3-030-01421-6_51

taxi-out (3.8 min) and in the taxi-in (2.0 min) phases but it is still significantly lower than the variability of both the departure (16.6 min) and arrival (18.6 min) phases [3]. The changes experienced during the gate-to-gate phase are comparatively small, leading to a translation of departure variability into arrival one [11]. Thus, the arrival punctuality is driven by the departure punctuality [3]. This is why current research in the field of flight operations primarily addresses the economic and ecological efficiency [7, 10].

As the Air Traffic Management (ATM) is a weather-sensible system, the influence of different meteorological conditions on ATM performance - and so on economical and ecological efficiency - needs to be discussed. This paper provides a data-based approach for identification of linkages between delay and weather phenomena by training advanced artificial models with task relevant input data of both, flight schedules and aggregated weather datasets. The knowledge, which is learned by the neural network driven model (*system identification*), is possibly contrary to the one represented by the given time series emitting ATM system (in our example Hamburg airport, HAM), but recreates a valid description of delay-weather-dynamics on data level. The amount of relevant time series, the data aggregation and the setup of the model have a huge effect on the learning process and are discussed extensively in this paper.

1.2 Structure of the Document

The document provides a fundamental analysis of the impact of specific weather phenomena on the performance of the airport. In this context, the performance is measured as deviation of actual and schedule timestamps (delay). The weather phenomena are categorized by the ATM Airport Performance (ATMAP) weather algorithm, which aims to quantify weather conditions at European airports [4]. This aggregation results in both a quantification of the individual airport performance and an applied performance metric, which can be used in comprehensive neural network studies to evaluate the meteorological impact on local performance deterioration.

In Sect. 2, the operational data set (flight plan) is introduced followed by description of the weather data (METAR). These data are used as input for the airport performance metric and the ATMAP algorithm. Then, an exemplary, detailed analysis of Hamburg airport (HAM) is shown to emphasize our general approach of the weather/performance evaluation with Long Short-Term Memory (LSTM). Finally, a set of applications for a LSTM is provided to model the performance behavior of a categorized airport as a function of weather (Sect. 3). The document closes with a conclusion and outlook (Sect. 4).

2   Datasets and Evaluation Metrics

The following section outlines the basic data sources and their comprising information, which are either relevant or non-relevant for an artificial approach. Therefore we take a view at requirements for both data aggregation and ensuing system identification.

As shown in Fig. 1, the usage of several data sources in ATM may increase or change the level-of-detail in the aggregated data. To describe the relevant performance indicator delay, general ATM indicators from FlightStats, Eurocontrol Demand Data Repository (DDR) or radar data. These sources can be merged (e. g. to add information about flight pathes to raw scheduled times), which we want to apply in further studies. This first approach includes basic indicators of FlightStats (grey colored).

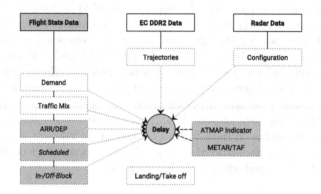

Fig. 1. Data overview to show ATM and weather indicators from different sources with certain level-of-detail. Used indicators are grey colored.

2.1   Flight Plan

A flight performance assessment is typically based on a data set of aircraft movements including scheduled and actual timestamps. This flight schedule was derived and aggregated in a local database (see Table 1) using data from online available sources of FlightStats. A single data entry contains the actual/scheduled arrival and departure times, arrival/departure delay, origin and destination airport, aircraft category (heavy, medium, light), and callsign. Time stamp fields in the database can also be filled with qualified statements: no delay reported *(on-time = −30000)*, indicates qualitatively a deviation from the schedule smaller than 15 min, no value reported *(no-time = −31000)*, identifies recorded flights without time stamps for actual or scheduled at arrival or departure, and flight *(cancellation = −32000)*, identifies canceled flights.

Table 1. Segment of data set of airport related flights (HAM 2013).

Date	From	To	Type	AC	Flight	Sched.	Act.	ARR	DEP
10.6.	STR	HAM	ARR	319	4U2046	670	683	13	−31000
10.6.	HAM	LHR	DEP	319	BA965	675	672	−30000	−3
10.6.	LHR	HAM	ARR	320	LH3391	680	678	−2	−31000
10.6.	HAM	BRU	DEP	319	SN2624	680	686	−30000	6

Concerning the upcoming analysis, recorded flights considering qualified statements are not taken into account for the sequence prediction, but the on-time statement could be integrated as a measure of punctuality. The used data set contains 122987 flights in 2013 between *HAM* and European airports or airports in the world. These flights are not linked to a specific aircraft tail number, which does unfortunately not allow us to analyze the reactionary delays of the European air traffic network.

2.2   Weather Data/ATMAP Algorithm

Weather data are usually recorded at each airport in form of *METAR (Meteorological Aviation Routine Weather Report)* also in combination with a *Terminal Area/Aerodrome Forecast (TAF)*. While *TAF* provides forecast values (6 h horizon), *METAR* data are measured values. In addition to information about the location, the day of the month and the UTC-time the *METAR* contains information about wind, visibility, precipitation, clouding, temperature, and pressure which are relevant for the air traffic, especially for the airport operations. In this paper, *METAR* data of HAM were analyzed for the year 2013.

But instead of integrating single meteorological elements of *METAR*, we use the *ATMAP* algorithm [4], which offers an approach to quantify and aggregate the available weather data focusing on the impact to the air traffic. This algorithm differentiates five weather classes (ceiling & visibility, wind, precipitations, freezing conditions, dangerous phenomena) and also considers different degrees of severity per weather class.

2.3   Dataset Merge

For all experiments one basic dataset is used: the original ATMAP dataset is combined with the corresponding flights, which means the ATMAP time slot serves as time index (35 each day). This dataset is characterized by a constant Δt of 30 min and comprising flight data, like average ARR or DEP delay for the given ATMAP time slot (absolute delay per time slot number of flights).

The merged datasets of Sects. 2.1 and 2.2 contain the features = {Date, time, score_total, score_visibility, score_wind, score_precipitation, score_freeze, score_danger, Flow, Flow Scheduled, Delta, nARR, nDEP, nCANC, ARR Delay, DEP Delay}.

Table 2 contains the used features of the upcoming experiments and their descriptive statistics. The statistics summarize the central tendency, dispersion and shape of the dataset's distribution. 25%, 50% and 75% represent the 25th, 50th and 75th percentile.

The 122987 flights in 2013 are distributed over 12762 ATMAP time frames. The *mean* weather condition (represented by the score total) is 1.08, which indicates basically good weather at HAM, with a *std* of 2.49. The deviations of delay are much higher, which represent a wide spectrum of possible weather-delay interdependencies. It is important to consider the *max*-value of the delay indicators, because their sizes outreach the ATMAP time frame size of 30 min.

Table 2. Descriptive statistics of used features in experiments.

	ATMAP score total	Flow	ARR Delay [min]	DEP Delay [min]
n	12762	12762	12762	12762
$mean$	1.08	7.49	1.65	3.07
std	2.49	3.80	13.43	8.95
min	0.00	0.00	−75.00	−37.50
25%	0.00	5.00	−2.00	0.00
50%	0.00	7.00	0.00	1.00
75%	1.00	10.00	3.00	4.54
max	32.00	20.00	674.00	348.00

This results in a back-lock effect, as these scheduled flights are re-mapped to other time frames and create entropy.

3   Application

In the following section we want to give an overview about the simulation preparation and the results. Other machine learning applications for sequence learning showed up, that a data pre-analysis is useful to transfer statistical knowledge to the LSTM modeling process [8, 12], which we want to apply in further investigations on this topic.

3.1   Scenario Definition

The mentioned dataset is used for two major scenarios A and B (see Table 3). They differ in their way of defining training and testing data for the neural network (no validation data were used). As usual, a supervised learning problem is addressed by splitting into 2/3 training and 1/3 testing data [5]. Through the isolation of daily ATM operations at HAM (interpretable as reset), given by the ban on night flights, we use whole days as separated input sets and simulate the ATM dynamics for certain, non-trained days (e.g. training on 7 winter days under normal weather conditions to describe the behavior on 3 non-trained days).

Table 3. Scenario definitions for training and testing data splitting

	Training data	Testing data
A	254 $days_{normal}$ (130 S, 124 W)	
	168 days	86 days
B	111 $days_{irregular}$ (53 S, 58 W)	
	73 days	38 days

Related to the weather-delay correlations, the major split of the datasets is done by differentiating in *normal* and *irregular* weather situations. As it showed up in a descriptive analysis on ATMAP total score distributions ($\mu = 1.08$ and $\sigma = 2.49$), irregular conditions encompassing days containing at least one ATMAP total score ≥ 6, which leads in 254 normal conditioned days (130 in summer, 124 in winter) and 111 irregular days (53 in summer, 58 in winter). A segmentation into season and weekdays is not applied as we do not want to characterize daily dynamics, but overall effects of weather to ATM performance, which are observable on every day (certainly in various dynamics).

3.2 Experimental Setup

The input data for the LSTM model is provided by the sources described in Sect. 2. We implemented the given LSTM structures in *Python 3.6* using the open-source deep learning library *Keras 2.1.3* (frontend) with open-source framework *TensorFlow 1.5.0* (backend) and *Scipy 1.0.0* (routines for numerical integration and optimization). Training and testing were performed on GPU (NVIDIA Geforce 980 TI) using CUDA as parallel computing platform and application programming interface.

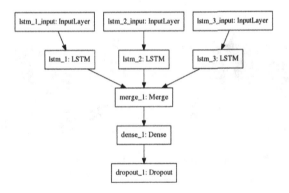

Fig. 2. Model conception in KERAS.

Figure 2 shows up the basic structure of the implemented network in KERAS. The general network structure includes 3 input layers (flow, weather, delay), 3 separate LSTM layer (like in [9] we used independent LSTM layer before merge layer), one dense layer for output and one dropout layer with a dropout rate of 0.1 to prevent overfitting.

Table 4 shows up the basic setup of the simulation network covering various properties of the LSTM (based on [9]). The optimizer derived by the KERAS frontend defines the size of the learning rate, the number of hidden layers the complexity of the network. The window size defines two arguments: the width of the sliding window and the initial value of the prediction. Value 10 covers

Table 4. Network parameter for structure and learning behavior

Parameter	Description	Value
$optimizer$	Predefined set of learning parameter	Adam ($\eta = 10^{-2}$)
$n_{hiddenlayer}$	Number of LSTM hidden layers	40
$batchsize$	Number of samples per gradient update	50
$windowsize$	Width of the sliding window	10
n_{epochs}	Number of learned epochs per samples set	50

a prediction starting after 10 ATMAP time steps, which means $10 * 30\,\text{min} = 5\,\text{h}$, which implies a starting time of 11.00 am (when considering regular ATM conditions) and so a prediction horizon of 12 h.

3.3   Simulation Results

The two following subsections offer 3D-plot representations of flow-weather-delay dependencies for both ARR and DEP. Every section comprises the results of all scenario related prediction data. It is important to keep in mind, that under

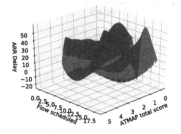

(a) Arrival delay, normal days

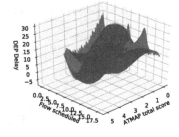

(b) Departure delay, normal days

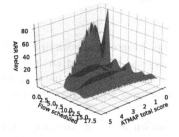

(c) Arrival delay real, normal days

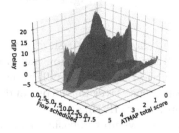

(d) Departure delay real, normal days

Fig. 3. Results scenario A.

the given circumstances the network is forced to describe delay with only two indicators (flow and weather), but there might be a wide set of reasonable sources for deviations in scheduled times.

Scenario A. In A only days under regular weather conditions are used for training and testing.

This model calculates the basic dynamics of the DEP delays by reaching a peak cluster in the middle section of flow spans (7.5 to 12.5, Fig. 3). Nevertheless, the ARR delay could not be recreated in a sufficient way. As ARR delays, especially under normal meteorological conditions, are mainly reasoned by reactionary delays from other airport's ATM, the model is not able to compute basic ARR delay behavior because of missing data from airport networks. The model is forced to identify a dynamic truth for ARR delays by just using the inputs flow and weather. The overall average deviation of ARR is 29.3 min, of DEP 11.9 min. The KERAS accuracy level is 36.5% for ARR and 61.3% for DEP.

Scenario B. Similar to scenario A, B comprises a simulation of data of one certain meteorological type - irregular weather conditions.

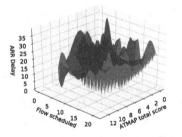
(a) Arrival delay, irregular days

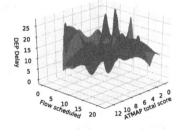
(b) Departure delay, irregular days

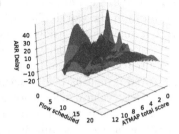
(c) Arrival delay real, irregular days

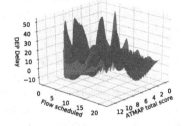
(d) Departure delay real, irregular days

Fig. 4. Results scenario B.

In contrast to A, this model is able to rebuild DEP and partly ARR in their basic dynamical behavior (Fig. 4). The fact, that also ARR could be identified, is describable by the fact, that ARR show a higher weather dependency than in Scenario B. Nevertheless, this model is not able compute negative delays and does not reach bottoms of the test data. Peaks (especially for ARR delay at ATMAP total scores of 5–7) are reached with small deviations. The average error of ARR is 24.4 min and of DEP 12.7 min. KERAS accuracy levels are 57.0% for ARR and 81.8% for DEP.

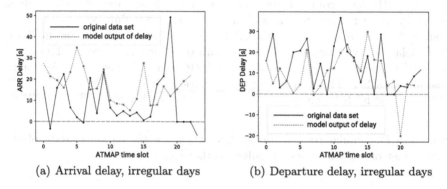

(a) Arrival delay, irregular days   (b) Departure delay, irregular days

Fig. 5. Results scenario B, diurnal variation lines (black - original, red - model). (Color figure online)

The mentioned errors in the system identification process are represented in Fig. 5 for one exemplary test day. The basic dynamics of the original datasat are learned and used in a sufficient way to predict delay for DEP. At $ATMAP = 20$ one can see a dynamical behavior, which was predicted by the model based on the given data, but propably indicated by different points of measurement.

4   Conclusion

This study is based on an analysis of a data set containing about 120.000 flights in 2013 between HAM and European airports or airports in the world. The delay values are not limited to airport-related delays but may also consider delays caused by increased distances in the en-route sector or reactionary delays, which differentiates the computed data based reality from real ATM system behavior. Additional the flight schedules comprise data prepared 6 months before actual flights, so a lot of effects are reproduced by the delay values, which do not represent the actual ATM performance. An extension of the flight schedules by using more relevant schedules (e. g. EC DDR2 data) seems to be useful. Besides this study is especially designed for HAM, as meteorological conditions and their influence strongly differ from region to region.

The use of LSTM offers opportunities for an advanced data based approach for recreation system dynamics like weather and delay correlations in certain cases. The learning behavior hardly depends on the given input data and their inner structure as well as the understanding of arrival and departure dependencies. As we used ATMAP related flights in this study, we will focus our research on computing sequence prediction with flight related ATMAP scores. Furthermore, the increase of details of the datasets (e. g. calculating particular ATMAP scores instead of ATMAP total score) might lead to more accurate results. Nevertheless, the network parametrization and learning algorithm need to be specified for these extended use cases.

Another possible option would be, to turn the precisely prediction of delay values to a classification problem for delay groups. Basing on both data and logical clustering of delays (depending on the impact on the ATM system), a mapping of the ATM and weather to delay groups would decrease the level of detail, but possibly decrease the overall errors, especially of scenarios A and B.

References

1. Bronsvoort, J., McDonald, G., Porteous, R.: Study of aircraft derived temporal prediction accuracy using FANS. In: Proceedings of 13th ATRS World Conference (2009)
2. Cook, A.J., Tanner, G.: European airline delay cost reference values. EUROCONTROL Performance Review Unit (2015)
3. EUROCONTROL Performance Review Report. An Assessment of Air Traffic Management in Europe During the Calendar Year 2014, 2015, 2016 (2017)
4. EUROCONTROL Performance Review Unit. Algorithm to describe weather conditions at European airports (2011)
5. Greff, K., Srivastava, R.K., Koutník, J., Steunebrink, B.R., Schmidhuber, J.: LSTM: a search space odyssey. IEEE Trans. Neural Netw. Learn. Syst. (2016)
6. Mueller, E.R., Chatterji, G.B.: Analysis of aircraft arrival and departure delay. In: AIAA ATIO Conference (2002)
7. Niklaß, M., Lührs, B., Luchkova, T., Gollnick, V., et al.: Potential to reduce the climate impact of aviation by climate restricted airspaces. Transport Policy (2017)
8. Reitmann, S.: Ableitung eines mathematischen Wirkungsmodells durch systematische Analyse von Leistungsindikatoren. Deutscher Luft-und Raumfahrtkongress (DLRK), Munich, Germany (2017)
9. Reitmann, S., Nachtigall, K.: Applying bidirectional long short-term memories (BLSTM) to performance data in air traffic management for system identification. In: Lintas, A., Rovetta, S., Verschure, P.F.M.J., Villa, A.E.P. (eds.) ICANN 2017. LNCS, vol. 10614, pp. 528–536. Springer, Cham (2017). https://doi.org/10.1007/978-3-319-68612-7_60
10. Rosenow, J., Lindner, M., Fricke, H.: Impact of climate costs on airline network and trajectory optimization: a parametric study. CEAS Aeronaut. J. 8(2), 371–384 (2017)
11. Tielrooij, M., Borst, C., van Paassen, M.M., Mulder, M.: Predicting arrival time uncertainty from actual flight information. In: 11th ATM Seminar (2015)
12. Yu, L., Wang, S., Lai, K.K.: An integrated data preparation scheme for neural network data analysis. IEEE Trans. Knowl. Data Eng. 18(2), 217–230 (2006)

Wavelet/Reservoir Computing

A Study on the Influence of Wavelet Number Change in the Wavelet Neural Network Architecture for 3D Mesh Deformation Using Trust Region Spherical Parameterization

Naziha Dhibi[(✉)], Akram Elkefai, and Chokri Ben Amar

REGIM Laboratory, ENIS, University of Sfax, Sfax, Tunisia
dhibi.naziha@gmail.com, elkefiakram@gmail.com,
chokri.benamar@ieee.org

Abstract. The 3D deformation and simulation process frequently include much iteration of geometric design changes. We propose in this paper a study on the influence of wavelet number change in the wavelet neural network architecture for 3D mesh deformation method. Our approach is focused on creating the series of intermediate objects to have the target object, using trust region spherical parameterization algorithm as a common domain of the source and target objects that minimizing angle and area distortions which assurance bijective 3D spherical parameterization, and we used a multi-library wavelet neural network structure (MLWNN) as an approximation tools for feature alignment between the source and the target models to guarantee a successful deformation process. Experimental results show that the spherical parameterization algorithm preserves angle and area distortion, a MLWNN structure relying on various mother wavelets families (MLWNN) to align mesh features and minimize distortion with fixed features, and the increasing of wavelets number makes it possible to facilitate the features alignment which implies the reduction of the error between the objects thus reducing the rate of deformation to have good deformation scheme.

Keywords: 3D mesh deformation · Spherical parameterization
Trust region algorithm · Wavelet neural network

1 Introduction

One of the characteristics of a geometric mesh is the locations of key feature points. Moreover, the disfigurement of the mesh is the result of the displacements of these feature points that give a geometric mesh with control point locations. It is worth noting that there is a pressing need to compute the regions affected by each of the control points. The mesh needs a good definition of the feature points for the purpose of getting realistic looking deformation and animation. This means that to define the control point locations, there are two variables that should be considered, namely the animation properties and real-life topology of the object under consideration [1]. We used the Laplacian representation to define the mesh geometric details expressed by the

V. Kůrková et al. (Eds.): ICANN 2018, LNCS 11140, pp. 545–555, 2018.
https://doi.org/10.1007/978-3-030-01421-6_52

difference between a vertex and its one-ring neighbour vertices designed for large rotations, The differential coordinates of a mesh can be interpreted as the difference of the original mesh and a smoothed version of this mesh; these coordinates describe the detail of the surface, represent the geometric details. The deformation process computes the set of transformations brought by the deformation of the source mesh, maps the transformations through the correspondence between the source and the target mesh, and solves an optimization problem to regularly use for the transformations to the target mesh. Because of such specificities an initial stage, which consists of establishing a correspondence between the source and target meshes, is essential. The correspondence is achieved in an indirect manner with the help of spherical parameterization techniques. Our mesh deformation method applied in the domain for ROI (region of interest) based on Multi Library Wavelet Neural Network structure founded on several mother wavelets families (MLWNN) to align mesh features and minimize the rate of deformation with fixed features reducing the sum of the distances between all corresponding vertices [2], The wavelet neural networks architecture which use wavelets as basis function are found to have various interesting properties including fast training and good generalization performance, various methods have been proposed for structure selection and wavelet neural networks training. We describe in this paper the Influence of the wavelets number change in the hidden layer to have a good 3D deformation process.

2 Multi Library Wavelet Neural Network Architecture

The wavelet occurs in a family of functions define by each dilation d_i which controls the scale parameter and a translation t_i that controls the position of a single function, called mother wavelet and recorded. A wavelet network with one output y, N_i inputs $x_1, x_2, \ldots, x_{N_i}$ and N wavelets. WNN can reflect the time frequency properties of the function, the overall response of a WNN is:

$$\hat{y}(x) = \sum_{i=1}^{N_p} w_i \varphi_i + \sum_{k=0}^{N_i} a_k x_k \qquad (1)$$

The wavelets φ_i are dilated and translated versions of a single function φ termed the "mother wavelet": $\Re^d :\to \Re$

$$\varphi_i(x) = \varphi(d_i(x - t_i)) \qquad (2)$$

N_p is the number of wavelet nodes in the hidden layer, w_i is the synaptic weight of WNN, x is the vector of input, the output can be a component refines, with respect to variables coefficients a_k.

This network can be considered as being composed of three layers: the first is composed of N_i inputs, the second is a hidden layer with N_p wavelets and finally the output layer defined as a linear neuron collecting the weighted outputs of wavelets. The input and the output layers are definitely connected to the hidden layer: Thae input layer consists of simple vectors whose entries are equal to outputs: these are the values of input data. The hidden layer contains neurons wavelet type (or basis functions, also called hidden units). Between the hidden layer and output layer there are the connection weights. These are used to calculate the network output, which is a linear combination of wavelets in the hidden layer, weighted by the connection weights.

MLWNN structure is similar to the classic network, but it has some differences; the classic network uses dilation and translation versions of only one mother wavelet, besides the new version constructs the network by the implementation of several mother wavelets in the hidden layer. The new wavelet network structure with one output f can be expressed by the following equation:

$$
\begin{aligned}
f(x) &= \sum_{i=1}^{N_1} w_i^1 \Psi_i^1(x) + \sum_{i=1}^{N_2} w_i^2 \Psi_i^2(x) + \ldots + \sum_{i=1}^{N_M} w_i^M \Psi_i^M(x) + \sum_{k=0}^{N_i} a_k x_k \\
&= \sum_{j=1}^{M} \sum_{i=1}^{N_{Mw}} w_i^j \Psi_i^j(x) + \sum_{k=0}^{N_i} a_k x_k \\
&= \sum_{l(i,j)=1}^{N_{Mw}} w_l \Psi_l(x) + \sum_{k=0}^{N_i} a_k x_k
\end{aligned}
\tag{3}
$$

Where $N_{Mw} = \sum_{l=1}^{M} N_l$, $i = [1, \ldots, N], j = [1, \ldots, M], x_0 = 1$

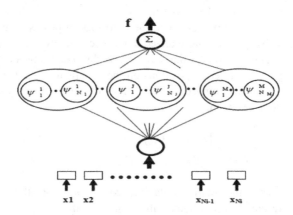

Fig. 1. Multi-mother wavelet neural network structure

MLWNN architecture is illustrated in Fig. 1.

The neuron in the input layer is connected to all the wavelets in the hidden layer that are not connected to each other. The output neuron is connected to all the wavelet in the hidden layer, as well. Each component of input vector is constituted of N_{MW} wavelets lets of M mother wavelets whose outputs are combined via a linear combination [3, 4]. This structure is realized in different steps:

- Initialization of the network: this step consists of developing a wavelet library made up of translated, dilated and rotated versions of a mother wavelet.
- Optimization of network parameters: obtained by combining a selection method OLS (Orthogonal Least Squares) and an optimization algorithm Levenberg-Marquardt. This algorithm determines the linear parameters of the network and iteratively optimizes the number and the parameters of wavelets by minimizing the rate deformation between the two objects.
- The initialization of weights, as well as translations and dilations of the wavelet network (generation of the Multi-mother).
- An automatic selection and increment of the wavelet in the hidden layer using improved version of OLS by employing the modified Gram-Shmidt orthogonalization [14].
- The choice of the optimal wavelet numbers N_{opt} using the GCV (Generalized Cross-Validation method).
- The update and construction of the wavelet network.

3   Our 3D Mesh Feature Alignment Based Multi Library Wavelet Neural Network Architecture

Uses of the characteristic points in 3D mesh modeling describe the 3D geometric mesh. We will take the position of the predefined feature points on the surface of the mesh to define the shape of the object. Therefore the movements of these characteristic points which are also called control points define the deformation process according to their neutral positions in absolute or in normalized units. The objective of our algorithm is to achieve a feature alignment process that reduces the distances between features points without modifying the local vertex positions on the spherical maps. If there is k input mesh and each mesh has n features defined, the transformation can be expressed as the following optimization problem:

$$\left\{ \begin{array}{ll} min \sum_{j=1}^{n} dist\{P_i(j) - P_1(j)\} & i = 1, 2, 3, \ldots, k \\ dist\{P_i'(j) - P_i'(l)\} = dist\{P_i(j) - P_i(l)\}, & \forall j, l = 1, 2, 3, \ldots, n \end{array} \right\} \quad (4)$$

Where P_i represents the matrix containing coordinates for all feature points on mesh i and P_i' represents the coordinates after transformation.

3.1   Trust Region Spherical Parameterizations

First, the optimized trust region spherical parameterizations are computed for both models (this step can be carried out as preprocessing and the mapping can be stored along with the mesh representation) [5]. Then, feature regions are detected on both models using region of interest and matched between the two models.

Next, feature point pairs are extracted and an optimized spherical parameterization is computed for the second model with respect to the feature point pairs. In order to obtain good fitting results, we need the triangles in the parameterization domain to have good shapes as well. Hence, we should propose a mapping from the given mesh to a unit sphere preserving the shapes of the triangles. Significantly reducing the computation distortion is required for the procedure of mesh parameterization in a sphere, since all calculations are performed in the space of the sphere to reduce the distortion angle and region: ratio of inverted triangle (IT) at the mapping of each triangle. Spherical energy minimization problem can be resolved by an algorithm of optimization. Actually, our approach is based on trust region algorithm (TRSP) that preserves angle and area distortion. Our Spherical parameterization algorithm based trust region algorithm is illustrated in Fig. 2.

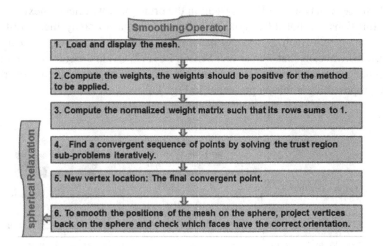

Fig. 2. Spherical parameterization based trust region algorithm

3.2   3D Feature Alignment-Based MLWNN Algorithm

Our proposed approach computes deformed ROI, updates and optimizes it to align features of mesh based on a Multi Library Wavelet Neural Network structure founded on several mother wavelet families (MLWNN) and spherical parameterization configuration to compute the corresponding feature region sets using Laplacian representation to preserve the mesh detail (Fig. 3).

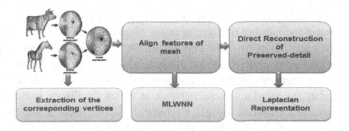

Fig. 3. Block diagram of deformation training

Our idea is to prove that wavelet networks structure founded on several mother wavelet families are capable of reconstructing and representing 3D deformed objects used in computer graphics, a wavelet network approximation using to optimize the alignment feature of mesh, minimize distortion with fixed features and to minimize the sum of the distances between all corresponding vertices.

We can try to characterize the wavelet selection based on dilation, translation and rotation parameters. We use a training algorithm based on the OLS method to specify the wavelet selected number for each mother wavelet family, and Levenberg-Marquardt method to optimize the network settings.

Several choices of the wavelets are available. Best known wavelets (and older) are certainly those which are the Haar system in the orthogonal wavelet context. The Haar system functions are not differentiable; it is not possible to apply the algorithms to estimate parameters, such as wavelet networks. Therefore, in our work, to construct networks, the wavelets that we use are: SLOG, POLYWOG and Beta wavelet families. These functions are differentiable and have the universal approximation property.

Our proposed algorithm is presented in Fig. 4.

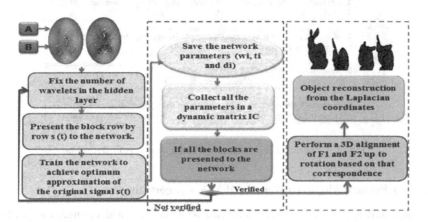

Fig. 4. Overview of the feature alignment-based MWNN algorithm

4   Implementation and Result

We will present the efficiency of our 3D spherical parameterization method and the 3D deformation approach based on three-dimensional wavelet neural network architecture when we increase the number of wavelet in the hidden layer. This approach uses the information of each 3D point with coordinates (x, y, z) to construct a 3D object modeling from the original object. From 3D points, we applied the training algorithm. To evaluate the performance of the wavelet networks structure, in terms of a 3D object modeling capacity, we used a wavelet network in which the library is made up of six mother wavelets (MexicanHat, Slog1, Polywog 1, Beta1, Beta 2 and Beta 3). To evaluate on the basis of the wavelet number in the hidden layer.

The following Fig. 5 shows the original objects that we used.

(Bunny, 29299 vertex)   (Horse, 19851 vertex)   (Elephant, 84642 vertex)   (Face ; 58895 vertex)

Fig. 5. Original objects

4.1 Trust Region Spherical Parameterization Result

We tried to develop a map that minimizes either angle distortion, area distortion; or a balancing between both of them. The angle distortion per triangle can be measured [6] on the map of each triangle f: T → t by:

$$E_D(T) = cot\,\alpha\,|a|^2 + cot\,\beta\,|b|^2 + cot\,\gamma\,|c|^2 \qquad (5)$$

Where T and t represent respectively the triangle of mesh M and its image on the parametric sphere S: α, β, γ are the angles in T and a, b, c stand for the corresponding opposite edge lengths in t. The area distortion can be measured as follows:

$$E_A(T) = \frac{Area(t)}{Area(T)} \qquad (6)$$

To perform side-by-side comparisons, we implemented the harmonic spherical mapping [7], curvilinear spherical parameterization [8], the progressive spherical parameterization of [9] and we obtained mapping results from the Spherical Parameterization using progressive optimization [10].

We also parameterized various input models using our Trust region spherical parameterization algorithm (TRSP) under different weights. In the above-mentioned experiments, we use $\lambda = 0.1$ and $\mu = 1.0$. Numerically, the spherical mapping results of Bunny, Elephant and Horse, computed by [7–10] are compared with our approach in Tables 1, 2, and 3.

Table 1. Comparative study based on angle and area distortions for Bunny object.

Bunny object	[8]	[7]	[9]	[10]	Our TRSP
E_D	63.6	50.8	78.1	61.4	27.7
E_A	25.5	22.8	14.0	14.2	11.3
Time(s)	91	2397	600	58	68

Our approach introduces smaller angle and area distortions. Hence it better preserves the facial features on the sphere, generates a bijective and lowly distorted mapping, and converges efficiently thus creating a good 3D spherical geometry image.

Table 2. Comparative study based on angle and area distortions for Elephant object.

Elephant object	[8]	[7]	[9]	[10]	Our TRSP
E_D	51.7	78.8	81.2	81.8	43.6
E_A	93.6	141.7	41.5	47.7	39.5
Time(s)	75	150	88	70	52

Table 3. Comparative study based on angle and area distortions for Horse object.

Horse object	[8]	[7]	[9]	[10]	Our TRSP
E_D	78.2	65.3	80.1	60.2	56.4
E_A	55.1	77.5	49.6	44.2	40.1
Time(s)	82	77	150	89	41

Simulation results show that it is possible to achieve a considerable correspondence between the angle and area perspective distortion.

Our method overcome the limitation of parameterization for shapes containing many extremities, for example for Bunny object we see that the angle distortion (E_D) is decreased from 78.1 in [9], 63.6 in [8], 61.4 in [10], 50.8 in [7], to 27.7 in our work, and the area distortion (EA) is decreased from 25.5 in [8], 22.8 in [7], 14.2 in [10], 14.0 in [9], to 11.3 used our proposed TRSP.

4.2   3D Mesh Deformation Results

To evaluate the quality of the reconstructed object we use the MSE (Mean-Square Error). Generally the performance of mesh deformation is based on the two following criteria: the deformation rate and the quality of the reconstructed object. In our approach, the performance of mesh deformation depends on other criteria: the type of wavelets used in the hidden layer.

$$MSE = \frac{1}{N_i} \sum_{k=1}^{N_i} \left(M_N(x_{Nk}, y_{Nk}, z_{Nk}) - M(x_k, y_k, z_k) \right)^2 \tag{7}$$

M is the mesh to be deformed; K is the number of observations. We used the minimal distance of fixed vertices to compute the measured rate deformations.

The ratio $r(\vec{x})$ is defined as the distance of the neighbour vertex x to the next handle vertex x_h divided by the minimal distance of a fixed vertex to a handle one.

$$r(\vec{x}) = \frac{|\vec{x} - \vec{x}_h|}{min\left(|\vec{x}_f - \vec{x}_h|\right)} \tag{8}$$

The simulation results are reserved to compare the proposed approaches with MLWNN in term of MSE, and wavelet number in hidden layer in Table 4.

The selected wavelet number for every mother wavelet on bunny object present in Table 5:

Table 4. MSE for 3D objects deformation using MLWNN

Object	15 wavelets	40 wavelets	100 wavelets	150 Wavelets	300 Wavelets
Bunny	0.000139	1.012e$-$4	1.071e$-$7	1.002e$-$8	1. 022e$-$10
Elephant	0.000578	3.569e$-$5	2.455e$-$7	1.251e$-$8	1.021e$-$10
Horse	0.000323	4.754e$-$4	3.214e$-$5	2.012e$-$6	1.020e$-$10
Face	0.000875	8.675e$-$4	1.744e$-$6	1.612e$-$7	1.002e$-$10

Table 5. Selected wavelet number for every mother wavelet on bunny object

N	MexicanHat	Slog1	Polywog 1	Beta1	Beta 2	Beta 3
15	2	2	3	5	1	2
40	8	3	20	4	2	3
100	26	20	2	50	1	1
150	55	40	50	2	1	2
300	35	100	20	50	55	40

From these simulation results we notice that the MSE is reduced with increasing the number of wavelets in the hidden layer from 15 to 300 wavelets; however, the object becomes increasingly well reconstructed. Besides, for 300 wavelets in the hidden layer for the object bunny, the MSE is equal to 1. 022e$-$10 compared to 0.000139 using 15 wavelets. We see that increasing the wavelet number improves the modeling quality. In order to get a better modeling, we will use MexicanHat, Slog1, Polywog 1, Beta1, Beta 2 and Beta 3 wavelets for 3D modeling objects in order to improve the wavelet network performances when trained with a signal that contains a large number of samples, we used a Multi Library Wavelet Neural Network structure as an approximation tools for feature alignment between the source and the target models. The 3D deformed object complexity is directly related to the selected wavelet number and to the training iteration number to construct the network. The Variation of deformation rate in terms of wavelet library using MLWNN architecture compared to other works presents in Table 6.

Table 6. The variation of deformation rate

Object	Deformation rate in other work	Our deformation rate
Bunny	92 [11]	52
Horse	59.52 [12]	14.89
Elephant	75 [13]	45
Face	42 [13]	23

The simulation test achieved the robustness and speed considerations when developing deformation methodologies. The ratio of deformation is low compared to other works from the state of the art. We demonstrate that representing the geometric information of a triangle mesh in differential form enables detail-preserving interactive mesh modeling.

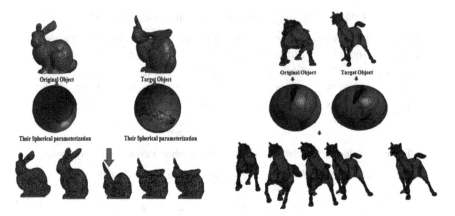

Fig. 6. Deformation processes based on MLWNN on the Bunny and Horse objects

Our deformation technique for Bunny and Horse objects is shown in Fig. 6.

5   Conclusion

The features alignment process is necessary in order to guarantee a successful deformation process that minimizes the sum of the distances between all corresponding vertices. We propose to use a Multi Library Wavelet Neural Network structure as an approximation tools for feature alignment between the source and the target models. We solve this problem in the spherical parametric domain with the help of Laplacian mesh editing techniques using estimated rotations and trust region algorithm which lead to a minimum mesh distortion. From the simulation results we clearly see that increasing the wavelet number in the hidden layer increases the approximation capacity. This network architecture ensures the use of several mother wavelets to solve the problem of high dimensions using the best wavelet mother that well models the signal [2]. Also to ameliorate these criteria (MSE) we can increase the iterations number in the training stage, but in the same way, time cost also increase considerably, we are trying to solve this problem in the future work.

References

1. Kshirsagar, S., Garchery, S., Magnenat Thalmann, N.: Feature point based mesh deformation applied to MPEG-4 facial animation. In: Magnenat-Thalmann, N., Thalmann, D. (eds.) The International Federation for Information Processing, vol. 68. Springer, Boston (2001). https://doi.org/10.1007/978-0-306-47002-8_3
2. Dhibi, N., Elkefi, A., Bellil, W., Amar, C.B.: 3D High resolution mesh deformation based on multi library wavelet neural network architecture. 3D Res. **7**, 31 (2016). https://doi.org/10.1007/s13319-016-0107-6

3. Othmani, M., Bellil, W., Amar, C.B., Alimi, M.A.: A novel approach for high dimension 3D object representation using multi-mother wavelet network. Int. J. Multimedia Tools Appl. MTAP **59**(1), 7–24 (2012). https://doi.org/10.1007/s11042-010-0697-6
4. Dhibi, N., Bellil, W., Amar, C.B.: Study implementation of a new training algorithm for wavelet network based on genetic algorithm and multiresolution analysis for 3D objects modeling. In: IEEE Mediterranean Electrotechnical Conference (2012)
5. Dhibi, N., Elkefi, A., Bellil, W., Amar, C.B.: A trust region optimization method for fast 3D spherical configuration in morphing processes. In: Battiato, S., Blanc-Talon, J., Gallo, G., Philips, W., Popescu, D., Scheunders, P. (eds.) ACIVS 2015. LNCS, vol. 9386, pp. 541–552. Springer, Cham (2015). https://doi.org/10.1007/978-3-319-25903-1_47
6. Floater, M.S.: Parameterization and smooth approximation of surface triangulation. Comput. Aid. Geom. Des. **14**(3), 231–250 (1997)
7. Gu, X., Yau, S.T.: Global conformal surface parameterization. In: Proceedings of Symposium of Geometry Processing (2003)
8. Zayer, R., Rossl, C., Seidel, H.P.: Curvilinear spherical parameterization. In: Proceedings of IEEE International Conference on Shape Modeling and Applications (2006)
9. Praun, E., Hoppe, H.: Spherical parametrization and remeshing. ACM Trans. Graph. **22**(3), 340–349 (2003)
10. Wan, S., Ye, T., Li, M., Zhang, H., Li, X.: Efficient spherical parametrization using progressive optimization. In: Hu, S.-M., Martin, R.R. (eds.) CVM 2012. LNCS, vol. 7633, pp. 170–177. Springer, Heidelberg (2012). https://doi.org/10.1007/978-3-642-34263-9_22
11. Gao, Y., Hao, A., Zhao, Q.: Skin-detached surface for interactive large mesh editing. In: Pan, Z., Cheok, A.D., Müller, W., Chang, M., Zhang, M. (eds.) Transactions on Edutainment VII. LNCS, vol. 7145, pp. 99–109. Springer, Heidelberg (2012). https://doi.org/10.1007/978-3-642-29050-3_9
12. Blanco, F.R., Manuel, M.: Instant mesh deformation. In: I3D 2008 Proceedings of the Symposium on Interactive3D Graphics and Games, pp. 71–78 (2008)
13. Sumner, R.W., Popovicn, J.: Deformation transfer for triangle meshes. In: ACM Transactions on Graphics (TOG) Proceedings of ACM SIGGRAPH (2004)
14. Golub, G.H., Van Loan, C.F.: Matrix Computations, 2nd edn. John Hopkins University Press, Baltimore (1989)

Combining Memory and Non-linearity in Echo State Networks

Eleonora Di Gregorio, Claudio Gallicchio$^{(\boxtimes)}$, and Alessio Micheli

Department of Computer Science, University of Pisa,
Largo B. Pontecorvo, 3, 56127 Pisa, Italy
`gallicch@di.unipi.it`

Abstract. Echo State Networks (ESNs) represent a successful method-ology for efficient modeling of Recurrent Neural Networks. Untrained recurrent dynamics in ESNs apparently need to comply a trade-off between the two desirable features of implementing a long memory over past inputs and the ability of modeling non-linear dynamics. In this paper, we analyze such memory/non-linearity trade-off from the perspective of recurrent model design. In particular, we propose two variants to the standard ESN model, aiming at combining linear and non-linear dynamics both in the architectural setup of the recurrent system, and at the level of recurrent units activation functions. The proposed models are experimentally assessed on ad-hoc defined tasks as well as on standard benchmarks in the area of Reservoir Computing. Results show that the introduced ESN variants can grasp the proper trade-off between memory and non-linearity requirements, at the same time allowing to improve the performance of standard ESNs. Moreover, the analysis of the employed degree of non-linearity in the reservoir system can provide useful insights on the characterization of the learning task at hand.

Keywords: Echo state networks · Reservoir computing
Memory non-linearity trade-off

1 Introduction

Reservoir Computing (RC) [13,16] represents a paradigm for efficient modeling and training of Recurrent Neural Networks (RNNs). Essentially, RC is based on the separation between a randomized dynamical recurrent component, which is left untrained after initialization, and a simple feed-forward readout part, which is the only trained part of the RNN architecture. Within the umbrella of RC methods, the Echo State Network (ESN) [10,12] is one of the most widely known models, which in the last decade has attested itself as a state-of-the-art approach for efficient learning in the temporal domain. ESNs showed excellent performance on computational tasks in several application domains, ranging from chaotic time-series modeling [5,12] to complex real-world problems, e.g. in the areas of speech processing (e.g. [15]), human activity recognition (e.g. [1,14]), robotics (e.g. [3]) and forecasting of economic time-series (e.g. [2]).

© Springer Nature Switzerland AG 2018
V. Kůrková et al. (Eds.): ICANN 2018, LNCS 11140, pp. 556–566, 2018.
https://doi.org/10.1007/978-3-030-01421-6_53

Besides the application success, the ESN model presents a number of interesting research questions [4,7], among which one of the most intriguing one is related to the estimation of the quality of randomized reservoir dynamics. In this context, the short-term memory capacity [11] has been identified as having a prominent role. Fundamental literature results in this direction showed that memorization skills of RC models are generally optimized in the case of reservoir units with linear activation functions [11]. Using reservoir units with non-linear activation functions has the effect of degrading the memorization ability of the ESN, as recently analyzed from the information theory viewpoint in [9]. However, the ability to model non-linear recurrent dynamics is very important in practical applications of ESNs. Essentially, linear reservoirs are better at memorization tasks, while non-linear reservoirs are preferable for modeling complex real-world tasks, which led to the well known *memory versus non-linearity trade-off* dilemma [17]. While this trade-off has been subject of analytical and theoretical studies [9,17], simple design strategies to conjugate both the desired properties of memorization and ability to approach non-linear tasks still need to be investigated.

In this paper we deal with the problem of combining memorization skills and non-linearity of reservoir units in ESNs, proposing two simple ways to realize a mixture of linear and non-linear reservoir dynamical behavior. Specifically, such a mixed linear/non-linear dynamics is implemented both at an architectural level, through a decomposition of the reservoir into decoupled systems with qualitatively different non-linear behaviors, and at the level of individual recurrent reservoir units, by driving the system dynamics using a combination of linear and non-linear activation functions. The proposed variants to the standard ESN approach are comparatively assessed both on controlled scenarios, using artificial datasets, and on standard RC benchmarks for chaotic time-series modeling.

The rest of this paper is organized as follows. In Sect. 2 we recall the basics of the ESN model. We introduce the proposed ESN variants in Sect. 3, and we experimentally analyze their effectiveness in suitably combining memorization capabilities and non-linear behavior in Sect. 4. Finally, we draw conclusions in Sect. 5.

2   Echo State Networks

An ESN [10,12] is a dynamical recurrent network composed of a hidden recurrent layer, called *reservoir*, and a feed-forward output layer, called *readout*. The reservoir implements an input-driven discrete-time dynamical system, expanding the input temporal signal into a typically high-dimensional state space by means of a pool of randomized filters. Essentially, the reservoir component encodes the recent history of the driving input signal into a temporal representation that contextualizes each new input and gives a memory to the overall system. The basic idea behind the ESN approach is that if the set of randomized dynamics provided by the reservoir is rich enough and representative enough of the driving input, then the temporal task is likely to be satisfactorily solved in the reservoir state space by using a simple linear readout tool. Accordingly, the reservoir is left untrained after initialization (subject to stability constraints), and the readout is the only trained component of the network.

The architecture of an ESN is illustrated in Fig. 1. At each time-step t, we denote the external input as $\mathbf{u}(t) \in \mathbb{R}^{N_U}$, the reservoir state as $\mathbf{x}(t) \in \mathbb{R}^{N_R}$, and the output of the network as $\mathbf{y}(t) \in \mathbb{R}^{N_Y}$. Input, state and output dimensions are respectively indicated by N_U, N_R and N_Y. The reservoir operates by updating the network's state according to a state transition function, described by the following equation:

$$\mathbf{x}(t) = \mathbf{f}(\mathbf{W}_{in}[\mathbf{u}(t); b] + \hat{\mathbf{W}}\mathbf{x}(t - 1)), \tag{1}$$

where $\mathbf{W}_{in} \in \mathbb{R}^{N_R \times N_U + 1}$ is the input-to-reservoir weight matrix, $[\mathbf{u}(t); b]$ denotes the (column) concatenation of the input $\mathbf{u}(t)$ with a constant input bias b, and $\hat{\mathbf{W}} \in \mathbb{R}^{N_R \times N_R}$ is the recurrent weight matrix of the system. The symbol $\mathbf{f}$ is used here to denote the element-wise applied activation function of the reservoir units f, where for linear reservoirs the identity function is used, i.e. $\mathbf{f} \equiv \mathbf{id}$, while in the case of non-linear reservoirs the hyperbolic-tangent activation function is commonly adopted, i.e. $\mathbf{f} \equiv \mathbf{tanh}$. Typically, a null state is used as initial condition at $t = 0$, i.e. $\mathbf{x}(0) = \mathbf{0} \in \mathbb{R}^{N_R}$.

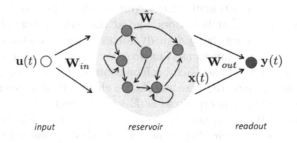

Fig. 1. Architecture of an ESN.

The reservoir is randomly initialized based on the constraints imposed by the Echo State Property (ESP) [10], which essentially states that the orbits of the reservoir system should be asymptotically stable under the influence of the driving input, i.e. the temporal representations developed by the reservoir should depend only on the driving input and the influence of initial conditions should progressively vanish. Based on the ESP, the stability of reservoir dynamics is commonly controlled by studying the spectral properties of the recurrent weight matrix $\hat{\mathbf{W}}$. In particular, following the necessary condition for the ESP, the elements in $\hat{\mathbf{W}}$ are randomly initialized from a uniform distribution e.g. over $[-1, 1]$ and then are re-scaled such that $\rho(\hat{\mathbf{W}}) < 1$, where $\rho(\cdot)$ denotes the spectral radius operator[1]. The elements of the input-to-reservoir weight matrix $\mathbf{W}_{in}$ are

---

[1] The spectral radius of a matrix is the maximum among its eigenvalues in modulus.

randomly initialized from a uniform distribution over $[-scale_{in}, scale_{in}]$, where $scale_{in}$ in an input scaling parameter.

The readout computes the output of the ESN through a linear combination of the reservoir units activations, i.e. as $\mathbf{y}(t) = \mathbf{W}_{out}\mathbf{x}(t)$, $\mathbf{W}_{out} \in \mathbb{R}^{N_Y \times N_R}$ is the readout weight matrix. The elements in $\mathbf{W}_{out}$ are adapted on a training set to solve the resulting least squares problem, typically exploiting direct methods such as pseudo-inversion [13].

3   Mixture ESN Variants

Here we introduce two ESN variants aiming at combining linearity and non-linearity in reservoir dynamics. The first model that we propose implements the linear/non-linear combination at the architectural level, decomposing the reservoir into two sub-systems, one made up of linear units and the other composed of recurrent units with tanh non-linearity. In this case, reservoir dynamics are split into a linear system, with state $\mathbf{x}^{(L)} \in \mathbb{R}^{N_L}$, and a non-linear one, with state $\mathbf{x}^{(NL)} \in \mathbb{R}^{N_{NL}}$, evolving according to the following equations:

$$
\begin{aligned}
\mathbf{x}^{(L)}(t) &= \mathbf{W}_{in}^{(L)}[\mathbf{u}(t); b] + \hat{\mathbf{W}}^{(L)}\mathbf{x}^{(L)}(t-1), \\
\mathbf{x}^{(NL)}(t) &= \tanh(\mathbf{W}_{in}^{(NL)}[\mathbf{u}(t); b] + \hat{\mathbf{W}}^{(NL)}\mathbf{x}^{(NL)}(t-1)),
\end{aligned}
\tag{2}
$$

with $[\mathbf{W}_{in}^{(L)}; \mathbf{W}_{in}^{(NL)}] = \mathbf{W}_{in}$ and $[\hat{\mathbf{W}}^{(L)}\, \mathbf{0}; \mathbf{0}\, \hat{\mathbf{W}}^{NL}] = \hat{\mathbf{W}}$ respectively representing the input-to-reservoir and the recurrent weight matrix of the whole system (for a formulation similar to the one in Eq. 1). The ESN variant in Eq. 2 implements an *architectural mixture* of linear and non-linear reservoirs and it is referred as *ESN-MixArch* in the rest of this paper. Given a total number of reservoir units N_R, the degree of non-linearity in ESN-MixArch can be expressed in terms of the amount of non-linear units in the system, hence through the value of a parameter $\alpha_{Arch} = 1 - (N_L/N_R)$. Differently from the mixture model analyzed in [9], the two sub-reservoir systems in ESN-MixArch are not connected between each other, enabling to study the resulting network's dynamics as decoupled into a purely linear component and a purely non-linear one. In this case, the resulting memorization skills of the network increase with decreasing values of α_{Arch}, and thus can be directly controlled.

A second variant to the standard ESN model is proposed with the complementary aim to shift the focus of the linear/non-linear combination to the dynamics of individual reservoir units. Accordingly, we introduce an ESN with *mixture of activation functions*, referred as *ESN-MixAct* in what follows, and in which the state dynamics are ruled by the following state transition function:

$$
\begin{aligned}
\mathbf{x}(t) = {}&(1 - \alpha_{Act})(\mathbf{W}_{in}[\mathbf{u}(t); b] + \hat{\mathbf{W}}\mathbf{x}(t-1)) \\
&+ \alpha_{Act}\tanh(\mathbf{W}_{in}[\mathbf{u}(t); b] + \hat{\mathbf{W}}\mathbf{x}(t-1)),
\end{aligned}
\tag{3}
$$

where the value of the α_{Act} parameter determines the degree of non-linearity in the reservoir dynamics.

Note that both the non-linearity degree parameters α_{Arch} and α_{Act} assume values in the range $[0, 1]$, where the case of standard tanh ESNs corresponds to $\alpha_{Arch}, \alpha_{Act} = 1$, while linear ESNs are achieved in correspondence of $\alpha_{Arch}, \alpha_{Act} = 0$.

4   Experiments

In this section we experimentally assess the ability of the proposed ESN variants to appropriately combine memory and non-linearity. Such ability is first analyzed in controlled conditions on ad-hoc defined tasks, i.e. a Mixture task (in Sect. 4.1) and a non-linear Memory Capacity task (in Sect. 4.2), for which the trade-off between memorization and non-linear requirements can be directly modulated. Then, the proposed models are comparatively assessed on well known RC benchmarks related to chaotic time-series prediction (in Sect. 4.3).

4.1   Mixture Task

With the aim of explicitly and directly controlling the competing requirements for memorization skills and non-linearity we introduce an ad-hoc designed task, called *Mixture* task, defined as a combination of known target functions. Specifically, given an univariate input signal $u(t)$ sampled from a uniform distribution in $[0, 0.5]$, the target of the Mixture task is defined by:

$$y^{tg}(t) = (1 - \alpha_{Task})\, u(t - 10) + \alpha_{Task}\, y_N^{tg}(t), \qquad (4)$$

where $y_N^{tg}(t)$ is the target function of the 10-th order NARMA task[2] and $\alpha_{Task} \in [0, 1]$ controls the degree of the task non-linearity. In particular, for $\alpha_{Task} \to 0$ the task tends to a pure memorization characterization, requiring to recall a 10-steps delayed version of the input signal. For $\alpha_{Task} \to 1$ the task tends to a non-linear moving average of the 10th order. We generated 10400 time-steps, where the first 5400 samples were used for training, and the remaining 5000 samples for test. We ran experiments with reservoirs with 100 recurrent units, $\rho \in \{0.1, 0.5, 0.9\}$, $scale_{in} \in [0.1, 1.3]$ with steps of 0.3 and input bias $b \in \{0, 0.5, 1\}$. For ESN-MixArch we considered $\alpha_{Arch} \in \{0, 0.1, 0.2, 0.3, \ldots, 0.8, 0.85, 0.9, 0.95, 1\}$, while for ESN-MixAct we explored values of $\alpha_{Act} \in [0, 1]$, with steps of 0.1. The values of hyper-parameters were selected (individually for ESN, ESN-MixArch and ESN-MixAct) on a validation set comprising the last 1000 time-steps of the training data, according to an hold-out cross-validation scheme. For each network hyper-parameterization, we averaged the results over 50 repetitions. For all the models, training was performed by using pseudo-inversion.

Table 1 shows the Mean Squared Error (MSE) on the test set achieved by ESN, ESN-MixArch and ESN-MixAct for increasing non-linearity of the Mixture task. Results show that both ESN-MixArch and ESN-MixAct are able to outperform the standard ESN with *tanh* non-linearity in all the cases (slightly

---

[2] $y_N^{tg}(t) = 0.3y_N^{tg}(t-1) + 0.5y_N^{tg}(t-1)(\sum_{i=1}^{10} y_N^{tg}(t-i)) + 1.5u(t-10)u(t-1) + 0.1)$.

better results are obtained by the ESN-MixArch model). The performance gain is more evident for smaller values of α_{Task}, up to 8 orders of magnitude for the case $\alpha_{Task} = 0$. Overall, results on the Mixture task indicate that ESN-MixArch and ESN-MixAct can appropriately model the trade-off between memory and non-linearity required by the task, resulting in a performance that is optimized with respect to the one that can be provided by a standard ESN. It is also interesting to inspect the degree of non-linearity selected on both the proposed ESN variants. Figure 2 shows the degree of models non-linearity, i.e. α_{Arch} for ESN-MixArch and α_{Act} for ESN-MixAct, plotted for increasing non-linear characterization of the target (i.e. for increasing values of α_{Task}). We can observe that both models are able to catch the progressive trend of increasing task non-linearity, where higher values of α_{Task} correspond to higher values of α_{Arch} and α_{Act}. In particular, Fig. 2 indicates a nearly linear relation between α_{Task} and α_{Act}, which can then be considered as a good estimate and a convenient indicator of the degree of non-linear influence on the task dynamics.

Table 1. Test set MSE (and std) acheved by ESN, ESN-MixArch and ESN-MixAct for increasing non-linearity of the Mixture task.

α_{Task}	ESN	ESN-MixArch	ESN-MixAct
0.0	$2.52\ 10^{-6}(\pm 1.99\ 10^{-6})$	$9.81\ 10^{-14}(\pm 8.38\ 10^{-14})$	$7.62\ 10^{-14}(\pm 6.25\ 10^{-14})$
0.3	$4.94\ 10^{-5}(\pm 8.10\ 10^{-6})$	$4.71\ 10^{-5}(\pm 8.60\ 10^{-6})$	$4.46\ 10^{-5}(\pm 6.47\ 10^{-6})$
0.7	$2.95\ 10^{-4}(\pm 5.71\ 10^{-5})$	$2.76\ 10^{-4}(\pm 4.07\ 10^{-5})$	$2.58\ 10^{-4}(\pm 3.91\ 10^{-5})$
1.0	$1.52\ 10^{-3}(\pm 1.75\ 10^{-4})$	$1.52\ 10^{-3}(\pm 1.75\ 10^{-4})$	$1.11\ 10^{-3}(\pm 1.23\ 10^{-4})$

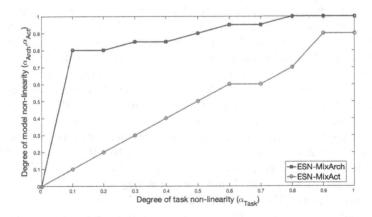

Fig. 2. Selected degree of ESN-MixArch and ESN-MixAct non-linearity in correspondence of increasing degree of non-linearity of the Mixture Task.

4.2 Non-linear Memory Capacity

As a second task we take into consideration a variant of the well known Memory Capacity (MC) task [11], in which the purely memorization problem is modified to introduce the influence of non-linearities by composing a delayed input reconstruction problem with a non-linear function [9]. Here we adopt a sine function to this purpose and refer to the resulting task as to *sinMC*. Specifically, assuming an univariate i.i.d. input signal $u(t)$ sampled from a uniform distribution over $[-0.8, 0.8]$, the target output is given by the following formula:

$$y_k^{tg}(t) = \sin(\nu\, u(t-k)),\tag{5}$$

where the value of the parameter k determines the length of required memory, while the value of ν modulates the frequency of the sine function and impacts on the non-linearity of the task, with smaller (resp. higher) values of ν corresponding to weaker (resp. stronger) non-linear characterization. As a general observation, we can note that the role of non-linearity is more relevant for smaller values of the delay k, with the extent of such influence being ruled by the value of ν. For higher values of k, the role of non-linearity progressively vanishes and leaves room to the memorization requirement. We generated a dataset with a total number of 6000 time-steps, the first 5000 of which were used for training, leaving the last 1000 for test. For this task, we adopted the same experimental setting as for the Mixture task in Sect. 4.1, exploring the same ranges of reservoir hyper-parameterizations, with the exception of $\alpha_{Arch} \in \{0, 0.1, 0.25, 0.5, 0.75, 0.9, 0.95, 1\}$. The values of the hyper-parameters were selected on a validation set comprising the last 1000 time-steps of the training data. For each hyper-parameterization, the results were averaged over 10 repetitions.

Figure 3 shows the Normalized Mean Squared Error (NMSE) achieved on the test set of the sinMC task by standard ESN, ESN-MixArch and ESN-MixAct for increasing values of the delay k, and for two choices of the ν parameter, i.e. $log\nu = -1$ (in Fig. 3(a)) and $log\nu = 0$ (in Fig. 3(b)). As it can be seen, while the performance of standard ESNs progressively degrades for increasing delays (i.e. as the memorization requirement sets in), both the ESN-MixArch and ESN-MixAct models are able to catch a good trade-off between the competing needs of memory and non-linearity of the task, outperforming the ESN for all the values of k. Slightly better quantitative results are achieved also in this case by ESN-MixAct. Figure 4 shows the values of the selected non-linearity of ESN-MixArch and ESN-MixAct models for increasing values of the delay k in the two considered cases ($log\nu = -1$ in Fig. 4(a), and $log\nu = 0$ in Fig. 4(b)). We can observe that in the cases in which the target has a non-linear influence (i.e. for smaller values of k) the progressiveness of such influence is better represented by the degree of non-linearity in the ESN-MixAct model (i.e. the value of α_{Act}), which for both the choices of ν shows a linear degradation from non-linear to linear (i.e. memorization) task dominance, confirming the results found in Sect. 4.1 on the Mixture task. When the task shifts to a clear memorization problem (i.e. for higher values of k) the increasing extent of the required memory is progressively

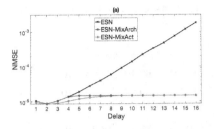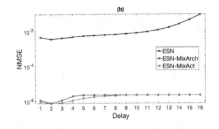

Fig. 3. Test set NMSE (in log scale) achieved by ESN, ESN-MixArch and ESN-MixAct on the sinMC for increasing values of the delay. (**a**): $\log \nu = -1$. (**b**): $\log \nu = 0$.

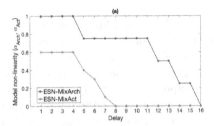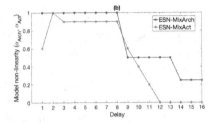

Fig. 4. Selected degree of non-linearity for ESN-MixArch (i.e. α_{Arch}) and for ESN-MixAct (i.e. α_{MixAct}) on the sinMC task, for increasing value of the delay. (**a**): $\log \nu = -1$. (**b**): $\log \nu = 0$.

matched by the decreasing non-linearity degree of the ESN-MixArch model (i.e. by the value of α_{Arch}).

4.3 Chaotic Time-Series Prediction

In this section we assess the performance of the proposed ESN variants on two well known tasks involving chaotic time-series modeling, namely the *Laser* and the *Mackey-Glass* tasks. In the former case, the considered time-series is obtained by sampling the intensity of an infrared laser in chaotic regime, while in the latter case it is obtained as an iterated map approximation of the dynamics of a Mackey-Glass system in chaotic regime[3]. Both the tasks consist in a next-step prediction on the corresponding time-series, with a total number of time-steps of 10093 and 10000 for the Laser and the Mackey-Glass tasks, respectively. In both cases, the first 5000 time-steps were used for training and the remaining for test. We adopted the same experimental setting and model selection scheme as in previous tasks, exploring the same ranges for hyper-parameters as in Sect. 4.2, with the exceptions of $scale_{in} \in [0.1, 1.2]$ with steps of 0.1. For each hyper-parameterization, the results were averaged over 50 repetitions.

---

[3] We used a value of $\tau = 17$ as control parameter for the Mackey-Glass equation, as common in the RC literature.

Table 2. Test set MSE (and std) achieved by ESN, ESN-MixArch and ESN-MixAct on the Laser and Mackey-Glass tasks.

Model		Laser	Mackey-Glass
ESN		$1.12\ 10^{-3}(\pm 1.56\ 10^{-4})$	$1.93\ 10^{-9}(\pm 2.98\ 10^{-10})$
ESN-MixArch		$1.06\ 10^{-3}(\pm 1.88\ 10^{-4})$	$1.89\ 10^{-9}(\pm 1.84\ 10^{-10})$
	α_{Arch}	0.95	0.75
ESN-MixAct		$9.75\ 10^{-4}(\pm 9.12\ 10^{-5})$	$1.85\ 10^{-9}(\pm 2.43\ 10^{-10})$
	α_{Act}	0.80	0.50

Table 2 reports the MSE on the test set of the Laser and Mackey-Glass tasks obtained by ESN, ESN-MixArch and ESN-MixAct. For the sake of results presentation, in the same table we also report the values of the models degrees of non-linearities selected in the different cases. As results show on both the tasks, ESN-MixArch and ESN-MixAct are able to improve the already good performance of standard ESNs. Again, ESN-MixAct results in a slightly better predictive performance. Moreover, in light of the previous analysis on the controlled tasks in Sects. 4.1 and 4.2, the selected degrees of model non-linearity, especially for the case of ESN-MixAct, can be used to get insights on the memory/non-linearity trade-off that is intrinsic to the tasks. In our case, the chosen values of $\alpha_{Act} = 0.80$ for the Laser task and of $\alpha_{Act} = 0.50$ for the Mackey-Glass one, indicate a strong non-linear characterization for the former task and a more pronounced memorization requirement for the latter.

5   Conclusions

In this paper we have investigated the memory/non-linearity trade-off in RC from a model design perspective. Specifically, we have introduced two variants to the standard ESN model, aiming at realizing a combination between a linear and a non-linear behavior. For the ESN-MixArch model this is done at the architectural level, through an explicit decoupling of reservoir dynamics into a linear and a non-linear sub-systems, while in the case of the ESN-MixAct model the combination is achieved by using a mixture of linear and non-linear activation functions. The proposed ESN variants have been experimentally analyzed on artificial tasks for which the degree of target non-linearity can be directly controlled, as well as on standard RC benchmarks for chaotic time-series modeling. Results pointed out that both the proposed variants are able to catch the right trade-off between the competing requirements of memorization and non-linearity of the target functions, through appropriate values of non-linearity degree parameters, with the ESN-MixAct model providing an easier and more natural way to control the trade-off. At the same time, the proposed ESN variants showed an optimized performance with respect to standard ESNs with tanh reservoir units, and in particular the ESN-MixAct model resulted in the best performance on all the considered tasks.

Overall, the analysis of the combination between linear and non-linear reservoir dynamics reported in this paper paves the way to further studies aiming at an automatic setting of the degree of reservoir non-linearity in a task-dependent fashion. As future research directions, we also foresee to analyze the dynamical regime of reservoirs characterized by a mixture of linear/non-linear behaviors under a dynamical system perspective, and to extend the advantages of such mixtures to the recently introduced deep RC framework [6,8].

References

1. Bacciu, D., Barsocchi, P., Chessa, S., Gallicchio, C., Micheli, A.: An experimental characterization of reservoir computing in ambient assisted living applications. Neural Comput. Appl. **24**(6), 1451–1464 (2014)
2. Crisostomi, E., Gallicchio, C., Micheli, A., Raugi, M., Tucci, M.: Prediction of the italian electricity price for smart grid applications. Neurocomputing **170**, 286–295 (2015)
3. Dragone, M., Gallicchio, C., Guzman, R., Micheli, A.: RSS-based robot localization in critical environments using reservoir computing. In: Proceedings of the 24th European Symposium on Artificial Neural Networks (ESANN), pp. 71–76 (2016)
4. Gallicchio, C., Martin-Guerrero, J., Micheli, A., Soria-Olivas, E.: Randomized machine learning approaches: recent developments and challenges. In: 25th European Symposium on Artificial Neural Networks, Computational Intelligence and Machine Learning (ESANN 2017), pp. 77–86 (2017). i6doc.com
5. Gallicchio, C., Micheli, A.: Architectural and markovian factors of echo state networks. Neural Netw. **24**(5), 440–456 (2011)
6. Gallicchio, C., Micheli, A., Pedrelli, L.: Deep reservoir computing: a critical experimental analysis. Neurocomputing **268**, 87–99 (2017)
7. Gallicchio, C., Micheli, A., Tiňo, P.: Randomized recurrent neural networks. In: 26th European Symposium on Artificial Neural Networks, Computational Intelligence and Machine Learning (ESANN 2018), pp. 415–424 (2018). i6doc.com
8. Gallicchio, C., Micheli, A.: Deep Echo State Network (DeepESN): A brief survey. arXiv preprint arXiv:1712.04323 (2017)
9. Inubushi, M., Yoshimura, K.: Reservoir computing beyond memory-nonlinearity trade-off. Sci. Rep. **7**(1), 10199 (2017)
10. Jaeger, H.: The "echo state" approach to analysing and training recurrent neural networks - with an erratum note. Technical report, GMD - German National Research Institute for Computer Science (2001)
11. Jaeger, H.: Short term memory in echo state networks. Technical report, German National Research Center for Information Technology (2001)
12. Jaeger, H., Haas, H.: Harnessing nonlinearity: predicting chaotic systems and saving energy in wireless communication. Science **304**(5667), 78–80 (2004)
13. Lukoševičius, M., Jaeger, H.: Reservoir computing approaches to recurrent neural network training. Comput. Sci. Rev. **3**(3), 127–149 (2009)
14. Palumbo, F., Gallicchio, C., Pucci, R., Micheli, A.: Human activity recognition using multisensor data fusion based on reservoir computing. J. Ambient. Intell. Smart Environ. **8**(2), 87–107 (2016)

15. Triefenbach, F., Jalalvand, A., Demuynck, K., Martens, J.P.: Acoustic modeling with hierarchical reservoirs. IEEE Trans. Audio Speech Lang. Process. **21**(11), 2439–2450 (2013)
16. Verstraeten, D., Schrauwen, B., d'Haene, M., Stroobandt, D.: An experimental unification of reservoir computing methods. Neural Netw. **20**(3), 391–403 (2007)
17. Verstraeten, D., Dambre, J., Dutoit, X., Schrauwen, B.: Memory versus non-linearity in reservoirs. In: International Joint Conference on Neural Networks (IJCNN), pp. 1–8. IEEE (2010)

A Neural Network of Multiresolution Wavelet Analysis

Alexander Efitorov, Vladimir Shiroky, and Sergey Dolenko$^{(\boxtimes)}$ (iD)

D.V. Skobeltsyn Institute of Nuclear Physics,
M.V. Lomonosov Moscow State University, Moscow 119991, Russia
{a.efitorov,shiroky,dolenko}@sinp.msu.ru

Abstract. Wavelet transformation is a powerful method of signal processing which uses decomposition of the studied signal over a special basis with unique properties, the most important of which are its compactness and multiresolution: wavelet functions are produced from the mother wavelet by transition and dilation. Wavelet neural networks (WNN) are a family of approximation algorithms that use wavelet functions to decompose the approximated function. If only approximation and no inverse transformation is needed, the values of transition and dilation coefficients may be determined during network training, and the windows corresponding to various wavelet functions may overlap, making the whole system much more efficient. Here we present a new type of a WNN – Adaptive Window WNN (AWWNN), in which window positions and wavelet levels are determined with a special iterative procedure. Two modifications of AWWNN are tested against linear model and multi-layer perceptron on Mackey-Glass benchmark prediction problem.

Keywords: Wavelet neural networks · Wavelet analysis · Multiresolution
Group method of data handling

1 Introduction

The task of processing signals of measuring equipment is a very important task for ensuring the results of scientific research. Machine learning techniques and especially neural networks have been successfully used for a long time to solve inverse problems (determination of the target value from indirect measurements, e.g. [1, 2]). However, recent advances in the field of deep learning are often not applicable to solving the above-described problems, for example, for spectral measurements of biological samples. Typically the amount of data obtained during such studies is very small (often hundreds of patterns), because of the high cost of measurement, complicated process of preparing samples etc. In this case, the initial number of features of the original signal can reach thousands (e.g., for spectral data), while using simple techniques for decreasing the dimension (e.g., taking average over some window) may lead to loss of

---

This study has been performed with financial support from the Ministry of Education and Science of Russia, agreement no.14.604.21.0163, project ID RFMEFI60417X0163.

V. Kůrková et al. (Eds.): ICANN 2018, LNCS 11140, pp. 567–574, 2018.
https://doi.org/10.1007/978-3-030-01421-6_54

information, for example, if narrow peaks of proper frequencies of the object are encountered in these spectra. Signal conversion techniques reducing the dimensionality of data, such as PCA [3], describe only linear interactions in the data, and therefore some of the information useful for solving the problem can be spread over several high number PCs that will be excluded after selecting only some number of first components.

An alternative is using the methods of selecting significant features [4]. However, as practice shows, simple techniques such as cross-correlation are also ineffective in the presence of complex internal interrelations in the data, and more complex methods such as cross-entropy calculations or analysis of neural network weights are only valid with a significant number of patterns. Thus, when observing high-dimensional signals with the emerging nonlinearity and a small number of patterns, there is lack of a more or less universal methodology.

Note that one of the techniques that demonstrate high efficiency in processing of real signals and compression of such signals is the technique of wavelet transform [5]. There are many families of wavelet functions to decompose the signal, as well as many strategies for carrying out multi-resolution analysis (MRA) [6]: discrete wavelet transform (DWT), continuous wavelet transform (CWT), batch algorithms etc. The problem is that even using the simplest technique (DWT), the main question is the choice of essential wavelet-coefficients, because using all the coefficients of all levels yields the same number of input variables as there was before DWT. Note that using the technique of CWT generates the number of features similar to the number of variables of the original signal, at every scale of the transform.

In this paper, we propose a model of a wavelet neural network (WNN) that performs MRA. Note that this model seriously differs from the classical WNN, proposed in 1992 [7] and developed in the following years, however not so actively as dense, recurrent and convolution neural networks. The point is that a neuronal element of a usual multi-layer perceptron (MLP) performs the transformation by the activation function taken of the weighted sum of its inputs, whereas a neural element of the classical WNN is a product of wavelet functions, the argument of which is an input variable, and the wavelet transfer function has 2 parameters of delay and scaling. Next, the result of the product of the elements is fed to the next layer and a response is formed from the weighted sum. Obviously, this network is much more complicated than the classical MLP, and therefore, WNN are not so widely spread as MLP.

Here we report an alternative architecture that uses as input features the results of convolution of signal sections with wavelets of different scales and different families. This peculiarity makes it possible to carry out a MRA relevant to the solved inverse problem. Also, the concept of using wavelets of only one family is given up, since the model does not involve reconstruction of the signal, which means that there is no need to observe the orthogonality conditions of the wavelets participating in the decomposition. In our new type of a WNN – Adaptive Window WNN (AWWNN), window positions and wavelet levels are determined with a special iterative procedure.

2   A New Type of Wavelet Neural Network: A Neural Network of Multiresolution Wavelet Analysis

Our model performs simultaneous transformation of various parts of the signal by functions of various scales. The training strategy of such model is partly similar to the strategy of polynomial approximation by the multi-row Group Method of Data Handling (GMDH) [8], which improves (complicates) at the next iteration ("row") of the algorithm the best polynomial models selected at the preceding iteration. In our algorithm, the improvement of the model means the transition to the next detail level of decomposition, i.e. the reduction of the scale parameter of wavelet functions and, accordingly, of the areas of the signal within which the convolution operation is performed. We call this model Adaptive Window Wavelet Neural Network – AWWNN.

Detailed description of the AWWNN model with comments can be found in [9]. Here we give a brief description of the algorithm.

Our task is elaboration of an approximation that maps the observed physical parameters (signal) to the given desired value, based on a superposition of the wavelet representations of the fragments of the signal.

The developed model consists of the following structural elements:

(1) The input layer units performing wavelet transform.
(2) The weight coefficients connecting the input layer units with the neurons of the hidden layer.
(3) Neurons – neuronal elements performing the conversion of the weighted sum of the inputs according to the transfer functions defined for these neuronal elements.

The proposed model and the procedure of its training are much different from the existing modern developments in this area by the following features:

(a) The problem of working with high-dimensional input data is solved by using signal regions rather that separate signal values as input features of the model;
(b) The model structure is formed dynamically by construction of competing options. This approach is easily parallelized.

The main stages of work with Adaptive Window Wavelet Neural Networks are the following.

Stage 1: Determine the model structure and the method of its training. The following options need to be defined to set up the structure of the AWWNN model.

1. Wavelet functions to be used in the blocks of the input layer. To select the optimal wavelet functions, the MRA-analysis procedure (multiresolution analysis) [10] is performed using various candidate functions. This procedure is computationally cheaper using the Mallat algorithm [11]. The functions that showed the lowest value of the error function are selected.
2. The detail levels (i.e. the values of the dilation (scale) parameter), for which the training will be conducted. The corresponding levels are chosen similar to the

classical multiscale DWT and correspond to a twofold increase in the width of the wavelet window.

3. The degree of overlap between adjacent wavelet blocks d. This is an alternative to the parameter of the wavelet transition (shift): the purpose of the proposed definition of this parameter is to minimize the loss of information at the edges of the wavelet function window in the process of convolution. The degree of overlap can vary from 0 to 1, the recommended value of d is 0.5, which provides the minimum number of input features guaranteeing no loss of information at the edges of windows.

4. The number of wavelet blocks, which directly depends on the selected scale parameter, the degree of their overlap and the number of wavelet function families.

5. The number of neurons in the hidden layer, which should be chosen empirically. An important recommendation here is to choose the number of neurons greater than the number of desired outputs of the AWWNN.

Stage 2: Form the training sample and define model training parameters. The following training parameters should be defined to train the AWWNN.

1. The optimization algorithm that will be used to determine the weights between neuronal elements. The possible candidates are Stochastic Gradient Descent (SGD), Adam, and Rmsprop algorithms [12]. Their internal optimal parameters are determined empirically.

2. The criterion for stopping the training of each local candidate model. We use stopping the training after 100 training epochs without improving the value of the objective function on the validation set.

3. The objective function to assess the quality of local models and of the aggregate model for a given level of detail. It is recommended to use the mean squared error for regression and prediction problems and binary cross entropy for classification problems.

Stage 3: Train the AWWNN model.

1. Determine the windows of the current detail level, corresponding to the preset values of the parameters of their width s_i and of the position of their centers t_i, with the degree of overlap of adjacent windows d.

2. For each pattern from the training array, process it with wavelet transform, convolving the signal with wavelet functions in Fourier space [13] over the overlapping windows of the given detail level L, obtaining as many wavelet coefficients $a_1^L...a_n^L$ as there were windows.

3. Using the parameters defined at Stage 2, construct a family of K models solving the problem under study. The set of input features for each of the models of the family is a unique subset (combination) of wavelet coefficients included in the full set of wavelet coefficients $\{a_1...a_n\}$. (In this implementation, all the wavelet coefficients correspond to the same detail level L as specified in step 2.) The recommended type of models is MLP type ANN.

4. Train each of the K models of the family of step 3 on the training set (sample), obtaining the values of weight coefficients of the model. Select a pre-defined

number K_0 of best models according to the criterion calculated on the validation set.

5. Test the set of K_0 models selected at step 4 on the test sample by calculating the criterion to assess the convergence of the algorithm.
6. Consider the windows of the current level of detail corresponding to the best models using wavelet coefficients a_i previously calculated inside these windows to be the signal areas significant for solving the problem, and to be used for further construction of the model.
7. Go to the next level of detail: for each window of the significant areas defined at detail level L, calculate the corresponding wavelet transform with twice smaller scale parameter (detail level $L + 1$), thus obtaining a detailed representation of the set of significant areas.

Steps 3–7 are repeated until the convergence criterion determined by the value of the objective function on the test set is reached.

The results of the algorithm are: the value of detail level L_{fin} (scale parameter s) and a set of values of transition (shift) parameters $\{t_i\}$ corresponding to the significant areas of the measured signal; a set of input wavelet blocks with the wavelet functions specified in them; a hidden layer of neurons, and weight coefficients linking the neuronal elements.

3 Results

The algorithm was tested at the examples of a well-known benchmark time series (TS) prediction problem (Mackey-Glass TS) [14]. All numerical experiments were performed in Python programming language on the basis of *Keras* machine learning library [15] and *Tensorflow* library for efficient mathematical operations with large arrays of data [16]. Parallel computations on multiple computers with multiple cores/threads were maintained by *GNU Parallel* [17]. The results are compared with logistic regression and classical MLP.

For all the algorithms, 50 consequent values of the TS were taken to predict 10 next values of the same TS (i.e. delay embedding depth was 50 steps, and the prediction horizon ranged from 1 to 10). The criterion for comparison was the coefficient of multiple determination R^2 on the test set of data. R^2 grows with decreasing mean squared error and approaches unit when the mean squared error approaches zero.

Table 1 presents the results of four methods.

For small prediction horizon values, all the methods demonstrate performance close to absolute. For prediction horizon greater than 3, the worst results are demonstrated by linear regression, due to the fact that the studied dependence is non-linear.

Significantly better results are obtained by an MLP when it is fed directly with 50 consequent values of the TS as described above, i.e. with simple delay embedding. The MLP had two hidden layers with 200 neurons each, it was trained with Adam optimization algorithm with *learning rate* = 0.001, $\beta_1 = 0.9$, $\beta_2 = 0.999$, ε = none, *decay* = 0, *amsgrad* = false [15], and using Dropout [18] with the parameter 0.5.

Table 1. Comparison of performance (multiple determination coefficient R^2) for various prediction methods on Mackey-Glass benchmark problem.

Prediction horizon	Feature+ AWWNN	AWWNN	MLP	Linear regression
1	0.996	0.996	0.997	1.000
2	0.997	0.997	0.998	0.999
3	0.997	0.997	0.997	0.998
4	0.997	0.995	0.993	0.992
5	0.996	0.989	0.984	0.968
6	0.995	0.978	0.968	0.872
7	0.993	0.958	0.944	0.776
8	0.991	0.930	0.913	0.724
9	0.987	0.893	0.874	0.707
10	0.980	0.850	0.831	0.689

Use of AWWNN brings further improvement. For the first type of AWWNN (simply "AWWNN" in Table 1) the MLP at its output is fed only with wavelet convolved features which were extracted according to the algorithm described in the preceding section of this paper. The following parameter values were used: wavelet family – real-valued Morlet, scale parameter values $s_i = 4$, 8, 16, 32 points (corresponding to the input variables), degree of overlapping $d = 50\%$. The MLP at the output had the same parameters as described above for MLP only model.

For the second type of AWWNN ("feature+ AWWNN" in Table 1) the MLP at its output is fed both with extracted wavelet convolved features and with the 50 consequent values of the TS. This architecture demonstrates additional significant improvement in the results for all values of horizon; it is especially important that the prediction degrades much slower with increasing horizon that for all the other models.

Such behavior of MLP, AWWNN, and feature+ AWWNN makes the authors suppose that the performance of AWWNN can be improved if simultaneous use of different scale wavelet coefficients is allowed like in usual DWT. When windows are split in two at step 7 of the described algorithm, significant wavelet coefficients of the preceding level L should be also preserved and included into the full set of wavelet coefficients $\{a_1...a_n\}$. Then the subsets of the full set extracted for each candidate model at step 3 of the algorithm could include wavelet coefficients of various scales, best combinations selected at step 4 by the criterion.

In this way, wavelet coefficients could better describe the situation when the important changes of the signal in its different parts (differing by the shift parameters t_i) may have different scales. This is a very realistic situation e.g. in spectroscopy, where some parts of a spectrum can be characterized with wide peaks and some with narrow. Implementation and test of this improvement of the algorithm should be the subject of the next study.

4 Conclusions

In this study, we demonstrate a new type of a wavelet neural network – a neural network with multiresolution wavelet analysis called Adaptive Window Wavelet Neural Network (AWWNN). In AWWNN, window positions and wavelet levels are determined with a special iterative procedure.

Two modifications of this new type of WNN were tested against linear model and multi-layer perceptron on Mackey-Glass benchmark problem. The new WNN architecture demonstrated its efficiency, outperforming a linear regression model and a multi-layer perceptron with two hidden layers fed with delay embedded data.

Direction of future improvement of the algorithm has been formulated.

References

1. Efitorov, A., Dolenko, T., Burikov, S., Laptinskiy, K., Dolenko, S.: Solution of an inverse problem in raman spectroscopy of multi-component solutions of inorganic salts by artificial neural networks. In: Villa, A.E.P., Masulli, P., Pons Rivero, A.J. (eds.) ICANN 2016. LNCS, vol. 9887, pp. 355–362. Springer, Cham (2016). https://doi.org/10.1007/978-3-319-44781-0_42
2. Gorbachenko, V.I., Lazovskaya, T.V., Tarkhov, D.A., Vasilyev, A.N., Zhukov, M.V.: Neural network technique in some inverse problems of mathematical physics. In: Cheng, L., Liu, Q., Ronzhin, A. (eds.) ISNN 2016. LNCS, vol. 9719, pp. 310–316. Springer, Cham (2016). https://doi.org/10.1007/978-3-319-40663-3_36
3. Wehrens, R.: Chemometrics with R: Multivariate Data Analysis in the Natural Sciences and Life Sciences. Springer, Heidelberg (2011). https://doi.org/10.1007/978-3-642-17841-2. p. 288, ISBN: 3642178405
4. Efitorov, A., Burikov, S., Dolenko, T., Laptinskiy, K., Dolenko, S.: Significant feature selection in neural network solution of an inverse problem in spectroscopy. Procedia Comput. Sci. **66**, 93–102 (2015)
5. Strang, G., Nguyen, T.: Wavelets and Filter Banks, 2nd edn. Wellesley-Cambridge Press, Wellesley (1996). 520 pp
6. Mallat, S.G.: A theory for multiresolution signal decomposition: the wavelet representation. IEEE Trans. Patt. Recogn. Mach. Intell. **11**(7), 674–693 (1989)
7. Zhang, Q., Benveniste, A.: Wavelet networks. IEEE Trans. Neural Netw. **6**, 889–898 (1992). https://doi.org/10.1109/72.16559
8. Malada, H.R., Ivakhnenko, A.G.: Inductive Learning Algorithms for Complex Systems Modeling. CRC Press (1994)
9. Efitorov, A., Dolenko, S.: A new type of a wavelet neural network. Opt. Mem. Neural Netw. (Information Optics) **27**(3), 152–160 (2018). http://doi.org/10.3103/S1060992X18030050
10. Ouahabi, A. (Ed.): Signal and Image Multiresolution Analysis. Wiley (2012). 301 pp
11. Mallat, S.: A Wavelet Tour of Signal Processing. Academic Press, San Diego (2008). 832 pp
12. Kingma, D.P., Ba, J.L.: Adam: a Method for Stochastic Optimization. Conference paper ICLR 2015 (2015). arXiv:1412.6980
13. Hramov, A.E., Koronovskii, A.A., Makarov, V.A., Pavlov, A.N., Sitnikova, E.: Wavelets in Neuroscience. Springer, Heidelberg (2015). https://doi.org/10.1007/978-3-662-43850-3. 318 pp

14. Mackey, M., Glass, L.: Oscillation and chaos in physiological control systems. Science **197** (4300), 287–289 (1977). https://doi.org/10.1126/science.267326
15. Keras: The Python Deep Learning Library. https://keras.io/
16. TensorFlow™: An open source machine learning framework for everyone. https://www.tensorflow.org/
17. Tange, O.: GNU Parallel 2018, March 2018. ISBN 9781387509881. https://doi.org/10.5281/zenodo.1146014
18. Srivastava, N., Hinton, G., Krizhevsky, A., Sutskever, I., Salakhutdinov, R.: Dropout: a simple way to prevent neural networks from overfitting. J. Mach. Learn. Res. **15**, 1929–1958 (2014). http://jmlr.org/papers/v15/srivastava14a.html

Similarity Measures/PSO - RBF

Fast Supervised Selection of Prototypes
for Metric-Based Learning

Lluís A. Belanche[✉]

Computer Science Department, Technical University of Catalonia,
Jordi Girona, 1-3, 08034 Barcelona, Catalonia, Spain
belanche@cs.upc.edu

Abstract. A crucial factor for successful learning is the finding of more
convenient representations for a problem, such that subsequent processing can be delivered to linear or non-linear modeling methods. Similarity
functions are a flexible way to express knowledge about a problem and to
capture meaningful relations of data in input space. In this paper we use
similarity functions to find an alternative data representation which is
then reduced by selecting a subset of relevant prototypes, in a supervised
way. The idea is tested in a set of modelling problems, characterized by
a mixture of data types and different amounts of missing values. The
results demonstrate competitive or better performance than traditional
methods in terms of prediction error and sparsity of the representation.

Keywords: Similarity representations · Similarity measures
Metric learning

1 Introduction

A non-written principle in learning systems states that *similar inputs should
have similar outputs* for a model to be successful. While this is no guarantee of
good performance –specially near class boundaries, where the principle could be
violated– it certainly is a *sine qua non* condition. If the principle is not true,
generalization becomes almost impossible. For a learning system to be successful,
the trick is then to capture (that is, to *learn*) meaningful similarity relations.

Similarity-based learning systems do not directly learn from the data but
first transform them into a similarity representation from which learning a target concept can be facilitated. Although a relatively little studied area within
machine learning, similarity functions have been used with great success since
the early days of pattern recognition. The relation to kernel-based methods [4] is
clear but there are obvious differences: in the latter the change of representation
is implicit rather than explicit, and the kernel functions (acting as similarity
measures) must comply with the positive semi-definiteness property.

Modern modelling problems are difficult for a number of reasons, including
dealing with mixtures of data types and varying amounts of missing information.
For example, in the well-known UCI repository [5], over half of the problems

© Springer Nature Switzerland AG 2018
V. Kůrková et al. (Eds.): ICANN 2018, LNCS 11140, pp. 577–586, 2018.
https://doi.org/10.1007/978-3-030-01421-6_55

contain explicitly declared nominal variables, let alone other data types (*e.g.*, ordinal), usually unreported. Although there is often enough domain knowledge to characterize the nature of the variables, in many cases this *heterogeneous* information is encoded (and sometimes forced) as real-valued quantities, in order to be processed by the learning model.

The aim of this paper is to demonstrate the learning abilities of simple layered architectures, where the first layer computes a user-defined *similarity function* between training data and prototypes. The basic idea is that a combination of partial similarity functions, comparing variables independently, is more capable at capturing the specific properties of an heterogeneous dataset than other methods, which require *a priori* data transformations. In order to develop the idea, we propose to compute the similarities among the elements in the learning dataset, and then use a *reduction* method to select a small subset thereof. These selected observations are the *centers* of the first layer. In other words, the first layer is a change of the representation space from the original feature space to a similarity space [6], while the second layer takes the form of a learner.

The paper is organized as follows. Section 2 further motivates of the approach and gives the technical details thereof. Section 3 presents an experimental study that puts forward the presented ideas. Section 4 reviews previous work. The paper ends with the conclusions and suggestions for future work.

2   Proposed Method

2.1   Preliminaries

We depart from a training data matrix $X_{n \times d}$ composed of n observations $\mathbf{x}_i$ described by d variables, plus a vector $\mathbf{t}$ containing the known targets of the n observations. Given a similarity function, we first compute the similarities between the observations and turn them into Euclidean distances, thus obtaining a new metric representation for the data. Another algorithm then selects a number d' of *prototypes*, that best represent the learning data in the following sense: *i)* the prototypes are a subset of the known training observations; and *ii)* d' should be much smaller than n. More formally, the steps followed by the proposed method are as follows:

1. **Computation of the distance matrix** from the training data matrix $X_{n \times d}$: given a similarity measure and a transformation function, a $D_{n \times n}$ distance matrix (symmetric with null diagonal) is created.
2. **Selection of prototypes.** From the matrix of distances $D_{n \times n}$ and the vector $\mathbf{t}$ of targets we obtain a submatrix $D'_{n \times d'}$, where $d' \ll n$.
3. **Modeling.** In this last step, any desired learner can be used, fed with D' as inputs and $\mathbf{t}$ as targets.

The chosen measure for the first step is Gower's similarity score [9], conveniently turned into a metric distance. For the second, the idea is to exploit the fact that D is symmetric: instead of using a costly search mechanism, we propose to use a *supervised learning* method, specifically one that can be made to select either a subset of the rows or a subset of the columns, effectively performing prototype selection, as explained below (Sect. 2.3).

2.2   The Similarity Measure

We next describe specific similarity measures for different types of variables, defined in the common codomain $I_s = [0, 1]$. We use s_{ijk} to mean $s_k(x_{ik}, x_{jk})$, the similarity of observations $\mathbf{x}_i, \mathbf{x}_j$ according to variable k.

A basic but very useful general similarity coefficient is Gower's score, well-known in the literature on multivariate data analysis [9]. For any two vector objects $\mathbf{x}_i, \mathbf{x}_j$ to be compared on the basis of feature k, the score s_{ijk} is defined as follows. First, set $\delta_{ijk} = 0$ when the comparison of $\mathbf{x}_i, \mathbf{x}_j$ is not meaningful on the basis of feature k for some reason[1], and $\delta_{ijk} = 1$ otherwise; if $\delta_{ijk} = 0$ for all k, then $s(\mathbf{x}_i, \mathbf{x}_j)$ is undefined. The partial measures s_k considered in this work include the real, nominal, ordinal, binary asymmetric, binary symmetric and circular types, computed as follows:

Real (or quantitative) variables are compared with the standard metric in $\mathbb{R}$: $s_{ijk} = 1 - |x_{ik} - x_{jk}|/R_k$, where R_k is the *range* of feature k (the difference between the maximum and minimum values).

Binary variables indicate the presence/absence of a trait, represented by the symbols $+$ and $-$. In case of asymmetry (only $+/+$ matches should contribute), then $s_{ijk} = 1$ iff $x_{ik} = x_{jk} = +$ and $\delta_{ijk} = 0$ iff $x_{ik} = x_{jk} = -$, leading to a measure well-known in numerical taxonomy as the Jaccard Coefficient [10].

Categorical variables can take a finite number of discrete values, which are commonly known as *modalities*. For these variables no order relation can be assumed. Their similarity is $s_{ijk} = 1$ if $x_{ik} = x_{jk}$ and $s_{ijk} = 0$ if $x_{ik} \neq x_{jk}$. This formula covers also the case of binary symmetric variables (which are identified with categorical ones with two modalities).

Ordinal variables take on one of m possible levels, numbered for convenience as $\{1, \ldots, m\}, m \geq 2$. These variables are not defined in Gower's original work, but can be easily incorporated. Their similarity is computed as:

$$s_{ijk} = 1 - \frac{|z_{ik} - z_{jk}|}{max(z_k) - min(z_k)}, \qquad \text{where } z_{ik} := \frac{x_{ik} - 1}{m - 1}.$$

Circular variables are also considered as given in $\{1, \ldots, m\}$; these values can be imagined as located equally-spaced in the perimeter of a unit circle[2]. In this work we make use of the extension introduced in [13]:

$$s_{ijk} = \begin{cases} | 1 - \frac{2}{m} | x_{ik} - x_{jk} ||, & m \ odd \\ | 1 - \frac{2}{m-1} | x_{ik} - x_{jk} ||, & m \ even \end{cases}$$

---

[1] For example, by the presence of missing values, by the feature semantics, etc.
[2] Such variables are increasingly common, especially when they refer to a time periodicity, such as the month in a year.

The overall coefficient of similarity between observations $\mathbf{x}_i$ and $\mathbf{x}_j$ is defined as the average score over all meaningful partial comparisons:

$$s(\mathbf{x}_i, \mathbf{x}_j) = \frac{\sum_{k=1}^{d} s_{ijk}\delta_{ijk}}{\sum_{k=1}^{d} \delta_{ijk}} \in I_s = [0,1] \tag{1}$$

As a side note, the "ignorance" of the absent values and normalization by the number of the present ones has been found superior to other missing value treatments in standard data analysis experiments [11].[3]

One can then form a symmetric $n \times n$ similarity matrix S with entries $S_{ij} = s(\mathbf{x}_i, \mathbf{x}_j)$. To convert this similarity matrix into a distance matrix D, we use the formula $D_{ij} = \sqrt{1 - S_{ij}}$. For this type of similarity matrices, it is known that D is Euclidean if and only if S is positive semi-definite (PSD) [12]. A sufficient condition for S to be PSD is the absence of missing values.[4]

2.3   The Selection of Prototypes

An immediate question is derived when carrying the proposed method forward: how the prototypes should be selected. Our conjecture is that this task should be performed in a *supervised* way, something that discards, among others, clustering methods. It should also be relatively fast – in comparison to alternative methods– and linked with the learning method to be applied afterwards. A natural choice is to use precisely a learning method, but adapted to the prototype selection task. We are interested in selecting a supervised learner able to perform variable (*i.e.*, column) selection. Alternatively, since D is symmetric, one can pick a supervised learner able to perform instance (*i.e.*, row) selection and then transpose the resulting submatrix.

We consider in this work three different learners for the prototype selection task: the Lasso [2], a Random Forest (RF) [19] and a Support Vector Machine (SVM) [4]. The use of the Lasso as prototype selector is straightforward, given that the columns are the new features. The SVM is more tricky: once it is trained using D as data, we remove the non-support vectors from D and transpose the result. In both cases, one obtains $D'_{n \times d'}$, where d' is the selected number of prototypes. To use a RF as prototype selector, we train an initial model with D as features, and iterate a backward-selection process guided by the OOB (Out-of-Bag) error, in which the δ worst variables are removed until no further removal is possible. The value of δ is set as the number of features below the 10%-quantile of the distribution of importances, as calculated by the RF at every step.

---

[3] It is not difficult to check that this is equivalent to the replacement of the missing similarities by the average of the non-missing ones. Therefore, the conjecture is that the missing values, if known, would not change the overall similarity significantly.

[4] This property is not used in this work but it is interesting in other contexts, such as optimization.

3   Experiments

In this section we detail the experimental procedure and report the results of experimental work in which the previous ideas are applied to a set of modeling problems. As mentioned above, the method entails the selection of two chained techniques, one for selecting the prototypes and another to learn from the reduced distance matrix. We study the following prototype selector/learner combinations: `Lasso/glm`, `Lasso/RF`, `Lasso/SVM`, `RF/RF` and `SVM/SVM`.

In addition to these five combinations, we also test the learners acting on the input space (*i.e.*, without the similarity layer), to see the effect. To this end, we perform a pre-process in which variable types are properly identified; in particular, non-numerical information is binarized with a standard dummy code [16]. For the missing values, we use the Multivariate Imputation by Chained Equations (MICE) method [15], which generates multiple imputations for incomplete multivariate data by Gibbs sampling. This method is attractive because, if the data contains categorical variables, these are also used in the regressions on the other variables. Finally, in order to test the need of a reduction, we consider a method computing steps 1 and 3 but not 2 –see Sect. 2.1– where the learner is glm (which should be directly compared to Lasso/glm) and call it `dist-glm`.

In all cases, the `SVM` uses the RBF kernel, where the smoothing parameter in the kernel is estimated using the *sigest* method, averaging the 10% and 90%-quantiles of the sample distribution of $\|\mathbf{x}_i - \mathbf{x}_j\|^2$ [14]; the cost parameter C is set to 1. The RF uses 500 trees and the square-root rule for the number of features explored at each tree node [19].

Several problems have been selected displaying some characteristics of modern modeling datasets: data heterogeneity and presence of missing values. The problems are not large in size to keep running times low and be able to perform a significant number of resampling repetitions. In all cases, the available documentation from the UCI repository [5] has been analyzed for an assessment on the more appropriate data treatment. Missing information is also properly identified. The main characteristics are displayed in Table 1.

Table 1. Basic characteristics of the studied problems. Task: BC (binary class) or MC (multiclass) classification, R (regression). Variables: (Q)uantitative, (N)ominal, (O)rdinal, binary (S)ymmetric, binary (A)symmetric and (C)ircular. Missing? is the percentage of missing values.

Problem	Task	Size	Variables	Missing?
HORSE COLIC	BC	368	21 [7Q,6N,8O]	28%
HEPATITIS	BC	155	19 [6O,13N]	6%
CREDIT APPROVAL	BC	690	15 [6O,9N]	5%
HEART DISEASE	BC	270	13 [6Q,3S,3N,1O]	–
AUDIOLOGY	MC	226	31 [7O,1N,23A]	2%
CONTRACEPTIVE	MC	1473	10 [3Q,4N,3O]	–
SERVO	R	167	4 [2Q,2N]	–
AUTOMOBILE	R	201	25 [14Q,11N]	3%

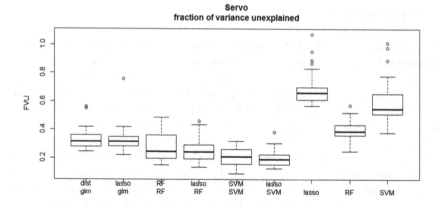

Fig. 1. Generalization errors for the SERVO problem.

All datasets are split into learning and test parts, using half of the data for each task (learning the model and making independent predictions). In the training part, 3×5-CV is used to select the hyperparameters (three times 5-fold cross validation). This training/test partition and modelling process is iterated 50 times, generating a distribution of test results.

3.1   Discussion of the Results

Our performance criteria include computational cost (measured in CPU seconds[5]), sparsity (measured as the percentage of training data points not used by the model) and generalization ability –measured as test error rate for classification and fraction of variance unexplained (FVU) for regression. A grand summary of the results for the classification problems described in Table 1 (the first 6) is displayed in Table 2.

The two regression problems (SERVO and AUTOMOBILE) are presented separately. For space reasons, we show only a sample of the results –those of generalization error– in Figs. 1 and 2, respectively.

As could be reasonably expected, no single absolute winner exists. Methods lasso/glm and RF are the best in terms of generalization errors; lasso/glm, lasso/RF and lasso/SVM in terms of sparsity; and lasso, RF and SVM in terms of training time, although the largest time is below half a minute. In view of these numbers, if one wants a good compromise between the three quality measures, possibly lasso/glm would be the chosen method. It is also noteworthy that this combination generates a completely linear model, which may be interesting in terms of interpretability. The second observation is that the selection of columns (*i.e.* distances to prototypes) is absolutely necessary (dist/glm is the worst method except in training time). The third remark is that the change of representation space favours sparsity, even for the lasso.

---

[5] The experiments were run on a HP laptop with 2GB of RAM and an Intel(R) Core(TM)2 Duo CPU T7500 at 2.20GHz.

Table 2. Average generalization errors, sparsity and execution time for the 9 methods studied applied to the classification problems described in Table 1. All the reported figures are the average of the medians of the 50 test error distributions.

Method	Error	Sparsity	Time (s)
dist/glm	0.261	0%	9.9
lasso/glm	0.209	88.7%	12.3
RF/RF	0.229	76.9%	28.0
lasso/RF	0.231	88.5%	24.9
SVM/SVM	0.230	53.2%	5.3
lasso/SVM	0.217	87.8%	21.2
lasso	0.220	32.8%	1.7
RF	0.205	0%	0.6
SVM	0.213	36.8%	1.6

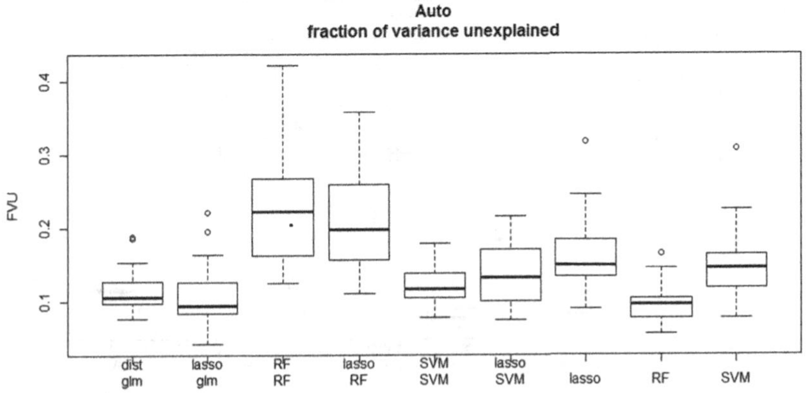

Fig. 2. Generalization errors for the AUTOMOBILE problem.

3.2 The Bank Marketing Problem

A further, challenging problem is studied: the two-class BANK MARKETING dataset (also from the UCI repository [5]), dealing with a marketing campaign where potential customers –who might be interested in a term deposit– are called. The task is to predict whether the called person will be interested in the offer of the bank. This dataset is markedly larger than the rest (in excess of 45,000 observations and 18 variables), displays a great data heterogeneity –including several circular variables– and a severe class imbalance (11.26% vs 88.74%). Specifically, the variables types[6] are [9Q,1S,1A,4N,1O,2C], and the percentage of missing values is around 10%. It is important to remark –for comparison purposes– that we decided to eliminate two predictive variables: duration, because it

---

[6] See the caption of Table 1 for a description.

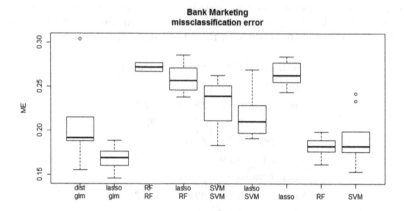

Fig. 3. Generalization errors for the BANK MARKETING problem.

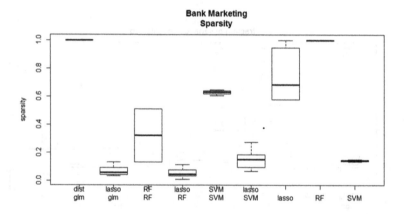

Fig. 4. Sparsity for the BANK MARKETING problem.

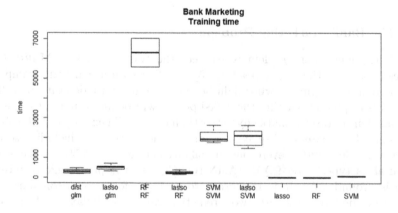

Fig. 5. Training times for the BANK MARKETING problem.

represents *a posteriori* information (the duration of the call); and `default`, describing whether the called person has personal debts (only 3 observations of the total have a non-zero value). For this problem we display the full results, in Figs. 3, 4 and 5. This time the `lasso/glm` combination stands out even more markedly as the method giving the best compromise; it also exhibits a low variance in comparison to other combinations, pointing to a good stability.

4   Related Work

Purely similarity-based techniques have been used with great success in fields like Case Based Reasoning [1] or Information Retrieval [3] and interest has never faded way; on the contrary, it has grown considerably since the appearance of kernel-based methods [4]. A large portion of the literature is concerned with learning either a Mahalanobis distance $(\mathbf{x} - \mathbf{x}')^{\top}\mathbf{M}(\mathbf{x} - \mathbf{x}')$ or a generalised dot product $\mathbf{x}^{\top}\mathbf{M}\mathbf{x}'$, where $\mathbf{M}$ is a PSD matrix. In both cases, this requires estimating $O(d^2)$ parameters, which is highly undesirable, specially in a small sample size setting.

The selection of prototypes is also a field of study *per se* –particularly linked to nearest neighbour classifiers [21]. Methods include clustering algorithms [18], artificial immune systems [8], genetic algorithms [17] –even extreme methods like random selection or no selection at all [7]. The results are most often inconclusive [20], [6]. The majority of these methods –if not all– focus on unstable search mechanisms, are unsupervised or work with dissimilarities showing no metric properties, which greatly difficults drawing valid conclusions.

5   Conclusions and Future Work

Selecting prototypes for learning in a similarity/distance space remains largely an open and interesting problem. We have presented and explored a different approach to similarity-based learning via prototype selection. This step is carried out in a fully supervised way, avoiding search methods, which are costly and likely to be unstable. The idea has been shown to be viable, delivered acceptable results in terms of computational cost, and very satisfactory in terms sparsity and generalization ability. The `lasso/glm` combination stands out as the best tradeoff between these three aspects of learning. An attractive advantage is found in the capacity of handling mixed variable types and missing information.

Current lines of research include the extension to new data types (*e.g.* fuzzy variables), the addition of weights to alter the contribution of each partial similarity, and the efficient extension to larger and more challenging problems.

References

1. Osborne, H., Bridge, D. Models of similarity for case-based reasoning. In: Interdisciplinary Workshop on Similarity and Categorisation, pp. 173–179 (1997)
2. Tibshirani, R.: Regression Shrinkage and Selection via the lasso. J. R. Stat. Soc. Ser. B. Wiley **58**(1), 26788 (1996)
3. Baeza-Yates, R., Ribeiro, B.: Modern Information Retrieval. ACM Press, New York (1999)
4. Shawe-Taylor, J., Cristianini, N.: Kernel Methods for Pattern Analysis. Camb. Univ Press, Cambridge (2004)
5. UCI Machine Learning Repository. http://archive.ics.uci.edu/ml
6. Pekalska, E.: The Dissimilarity representations in pattern recognition. Concepts, theory and applications. (Ph.D. Thesis) Delft University of Technology (2005)
7. Duin, R.P.W., Loog, M., Pekalska, E., Tax, D.M.J.: Feature-based dissimilarity space classification. In: Ünay, D., Çataltepe, Z., Aksoy, S. (eds.) ICPR 2010. LNCS, vol. 6388, pp. 46–55. Springer, Heidelberg (2010). https://doi.org/10.1007/978-3-642-17711-8_5
8. Garain, U.: Prototype reduction using an artificial immune model. Pattern Anal. Appl. **11**(3–4), 353–363 (2008)
9. Gower, J.C.: A general coefficient of similarity and some of its properties. Biometrika **27**(4), 857–871 (1971)
10. Sokal, R.R., Michener, C.D.: Principles of Numerical Taxonomy. W.H. Freeman, San Francisco (1963)
11. Dixon, J.K.: Pattern recognition with partly missing data. IEEE Trans. Syst. Man Cybernet. **9**, 617–621 (1979)
12. Gower, J.C., Legendre, P.: Metric and Euclidean Properties of Dissimilarity Coefficients. J. Classification **3**, 5–48 (1986)
13. Pavoine, S., Vallet, J., Dufour, A.B., Gachet, S., Daniel, H.: On the challenge of treating various types of variables: application for improving the measurement of functional diversity. Oikos **118**(3), 391–402 (2009)
14. Caputo, B., Sim, K., Furesjo, F., Smola, A.: Appearance-based object recognition using SVMs: which kernel should I use? In: NIPS Workshop on Statistical methods for Computational Experiments in Visual Processing and Computer Vision (2002)
15. van Buuren, S., Groothuis-Oudshoorn, K.: mice: multivariate imputation by chained equations in R. J. Stat. Softw. **45**(3), 1–67 (2011)
16. Ripley, B.: Pattern Recognition and Neural Networks. Camb. Univ Press, Cambridge (1996)
17. Ravindra Babu, T., Narasimha Murty, M.: Comparison of genetic algorithm based prototype selection schemes. Pattern Recognit. **34**, 523–525 (2001)
18. Belanche, L.l., Hernández, J.: Similarity networks for heterogeneous data. In: Proceedings of the ESANN: European Symposium on Artificial Neural Networks, Computational Intelligence and Machine Learning (2012)
19. Breiman, L.: Random forests. Mach. Learn. **45**(1), 5–32 (2001)
20. Kuncheva, L., Bezdek, J.: Nearest prototype classification: clustering, genetic algorithms, or random search? IEEE Trans. Syst. Man Cybern. Part C **28**(1), 160–164 (1998)
21. Lipowezky, U.: Selection of the optimal prototype subset for 1-NN classification. Pattern Recognit. Lett. **19**, 907–918 (1998)

Modeling Data Center Temperature Profile in Terms of a First Order Polynomial RBF Network Trained by Particle Swarm Optimization

Ioannis A. Troumbis[1], George E. Tsekouras[2(✉)],
Christos Kalloniatis[2], Panagiotis Papachiou[3],
and Dias Haralambopoulos[1]

[1] Department of Environment, University of the Aegean, Mytilene, Greece
envm615001@env.aegean.gr, dharal@aegean.gr
[2] Department of Cultural Technology and Communication,
University of the Aegean, Mytilene, Greece
gtsek@ct.aegean.gr, chkallon@aegean.gr
[3] ICT Sector, University of the Aegean, Mytilene, Greece
pnp@aegean.gr

Abstract. In this paper a polynomial radial basis function neural network is trained to model and predict the temperature profile-energy proxy of a highly complex data center located at the University of the Aegean, Greece. A number of input variables are identified that directly quantify the rack's air temperature. The corresponding data set is generated through an experimental monitoring system used over a two-week period. The network's structure encompasses three distinct levels. The first level involves a number of hidden nodes with Gaussian activation functions, while the second level generates first order polynomial functions of the input variables. Finally, the third level aggregates the outputs of the above two levels and generates the network's output. The network's training process is based on using the particle swarm optimization algorithm. For comparative reasons, a typical radial basis function and a feed-forward network were developed. The results indicate that the proposed network is very effective in predicting the server rack's air temperature, outperforming the other two networks.

Keywords: Polynomial radial basis function neural network
Particle swarm optimization · Data center · Temperature

1 Introduction

The ever increasing high-performing data centers equipped with advanced information technology frameworks to process network data, user profiles, information personalization, internet data traffic and communications, has made the energy consumption a central design parameter [1]. As a result, a number of studies have been conducted to investigate the above problem. In [2] an adaptive evolutionary approach was proposed

V. Kůrková et al. (Eds.): ICANN 2018, LNCS 11140, pp. 587–595, 2018.
https://doi.org/10.1007/978-3-030-01421-6_56

to minimize energy consumption in cloud computing data centers. Beloglazov et al. [3] stated the need for software solutions in deciding when to move resources to minimize the cooling requirements of the data center, while in [4] stochastic neural models were developed to predict the data center network's load, providing an optimized schedule of task allocations. Derakhsan et al. [5] used machine learning to predict the resource consumption of service requests, by dividing them into distinct consumption categories. Matsunaga and Fortes [6] compared various machine learning techniques, such as k-nearest neighbor, linear regression, artificial neural networks, decision trees and support vector machines for their suitability in predicting the resource consumption of different applications. The continuous monitoring enabled vast improvements in cooling efficiency. Xu and Fortes [7] used a genetic algorithm with fuzzy multi-objective evaluation to optimize the virtual machine placement problem in terms of resource wastage, power consumption and thermal dissipation.

Each data center is more or less unique and obeys certain peculiarities regarding location, room layout, usage load etc., rendering the modeling process of the electricity demand a highly nonlinear problem. An effective approach to capture the resulting nonlinearities is to use polynomial neural networks (pNNs). PNNs are constructed by modifying the network's structure using polynomial functions [8, 9]. Typical training mechanisms involve fuzzy clustering [10], and/or evolutionary computation [9]. In [11], the well-known Chebyshev polynomials are employed to form the neuron activation functions. However, as the number of input variables increases the number of neurons also increases and the resulting computational cost becomes too expensive for high dimensional problems. Rigos et al. [12] developed a Chebyshev polynomial RBF network to resolve the shoreline extraction problem.

In this paper, we propose to use a first order polynomial radial basis function (RBF) neural network to predict the rack's temperature profile of the data center, located at the University of the Aegean, Mytilene, Greece. The center supports a significant number of units and users. After analyzing the structure of the units and the related services and facilities, a number of input-output variables were identified that directly define the rack's air temperature. Among others the input variables include the internet traffic, and CPU and memory usage.

The material is organized as follows. Section 2 describes the experimental setup and the data acquisition process. Section 3 presents the analytical structure of the proposed neural network. The simulation study is presented in Sect. 4. Finally, the paper concludes in Sect. 5.

2 Problem Description and Data Extraction

Energy consumption is a determinant of low-carbon modernization of economy in the sense of internalizing economic externalities. Stemming from this elementary assumption within the broader ICT industry, the targets of SMART ICT 2020 [13] encapsulate the dynamics of transformation of both the vast and disparate domains of wise-use of knowledge, technology, energy and natural resources as well as the informatization of non-ICT per se production processes (e.g. education and research, agriculture, transports, logistics, etc.). Within the well-known asymmetric sigmoidal "Cost–GHG emissions abatement" curves, energy consumption management in data centers is among the prominent levers for significant mitigation policies regarding C-emissions [14]. Contrary to the positive linear hypothesis of ICT-driven "optimization" –in the sense of C-emissions' minimization or abatement- of a long series of ICT governed production processes, a rebound effect of coupled energy consumption/C-emissions is haunting ICT and environmental strategists.

In this paper, we study the ICT data center of the University of the Aegean, Mytilene, Lesvos Island, Greece. The University' s campus comprises a number of buildings and the data center is equipped with two clusters, split into three racks, which are cooled using three AC units having a cooling capacity 21.4 KWh. The first cluster is comprised of 6 IBM HS23 servers, housed in an IBM Blade Center and is designated for High Performance Computing (HPC) applications. Each of the HPC cluster's cores has 24 cores running at 2.9 GHz, 64 GB of memory, 2 × 200 GB SSD disks, 2 × 1 Gbit network connections and 2 × 10 Gbit FCoE network connections. The second cluster is comprised of 12 IBM HS23 servers in a second IBM Blade Center and is designated for general purpose (GP) use. Each server has 32 cores at 2.5 GHz, 256 GB of RAM memory, 2 × 200 GB SSD disks, 2 × 1 Gbit network connections and 2 × 10 Gbit FCoE network connections.

The experimental methodology consists of the collection and analysis of the server room usage data and the outside environmental temperature for a period of 2 weeks, starting from the middle of March 2018 (19/3/18-30/3/18). The data were obtained at a three-minute interval using the IT service's monitoring system. A server was set-up to enable constant data gathering, using Python 3.6 and the Django framework. The input variables were identified as follows. (a) The internet traffic (upload/download) in Bytes, for the HPC and GP clusters, the backup server, the university's connection to the central authority (GRNET), and for the five buildings of the campus. In order to reduce the number of variables in the neural networks, these data were aggregated, using arithmetic progression, into two variables: Upload (U) and Download (D). (b) The current CPU usage (Q), which is directly responsible for temperature rise. (c) The current memory usage (M) which is a metric of the current workload. (d) The CPU temperature (T_{CPU}). (e) The memory bank's temperature (T_{MEM}). Finally the system's output is the air temperature inside the server' s rack (T_{air}). By using the symbolization $x_1 = U$, $x_2 = D$, $x_3 = Q$, $x_4 = M$, $x_5 = T_{CPU}$, $x_6 = T_{MEM}$, and $y = T_{air}$, the experimental setup generated $N = 4811$ input-output data of the form $\{x_k; y_k\}|_{k=1}^{N}$ with $x_k = [x_1, x_2, \ldots, x_6] \in R^6$ and $y \in R$.

3   Structure and Training of the Polynomial RBF Network

The proposed network comprises three major operational levels (see Fig. 1) namely, Level 1, Level 2, and Level 3. Given p input variables, Level 1 includes a hidden layer of nodes with Gaussian activation functions [9],

$$g_\ell(x) = \exp\left(-\left(\frac{\|x - v_\ell\|}{\sigma_\ell}\right)^2\right) \tag{1}$$

where v_ℓ is the center element of the Gaussian function, σ_ℓ is the corresponding standard deviation, $\ell = 1, 2, \ldots, c$, with c being the number of hidden nodes, and x the input vector. Level 2 creates the polynomial regression part of the network, which aggregates the input variables in terms of a first order polynomial functions [9],

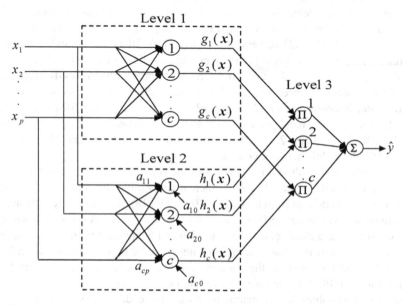

Fig. 1. Graphical representation of the first order polynomial RBF neural network.

$$h_\ell(x) = a_{\ell 0} + a_{\ell 1} x_1 + \ldots + a_{\ell p} x_p = a_{\ell 0} + \sum_{j=1}^{p} a_{\ell j} x_j \tag{2}$$

To this end, Level 3 generates the network's output as follows,

$$\hat{y} = \sum_{\ell=1}^{c} g_i(x) h_i(x) = \sum_{\ell=1}^{c} \exp\left(-\left(\frac{\|x - v_\ell\|}{\sigma_\ell}\right)^2\right)\left(a_{\ell 0} + \sum_{j=1}^{p} a_{\ell j} x_j\right) \tag{3}$$

Given a set of input-output data $\{x_k; y_k\}|_{k=1}^{N}$ with $x_k \in R^p$ and $y \in R$, the training process is based on minimizing the corresponding square error,

$$J = \sum_{k=1}^{N} |y_k - \hat{y}_k|^2 \tag{4}$$

To accomplish this task, we propose to use two sequential steps. In the first step, the particle swarm optimization (PSO) algorithm is applied to determine the parameters v_ℓ and σ_ℓ $(1 \leq \ell \leq c)$. The second step implements a ridge regression procedure to estimate the parameters $a_{\ell 0}, a_{\ell 1}, \ldots, a_{\ell p}$ with $1 \leq \ell \leq c$.

The particle swarm optimization (PSO) involves a swarm of Np vectors $p_i \in R^q (1 \leq i \leq Np)$, called particles [14]. Each particle is assigned a velocity $z_i \in R^q$. The positions with the best solution obtained so far by the particle p_i and by all particles are denoted as p_i^{best} and p_{best}, respectively. Then, the velocity is,

$$z_i(t+1) = \omega h_i(t) + \varphi_1 U(0, 1) \odot \left(p_i^{best}(t) - p_i(t) \right) + \varphi_2 U(0, 1) \odot \left(p_{best}(t) - p_i(t) \right) \tag{5}$$

where $\odot$ is the vector point-wise product, $U(0, 1)$ is a vector with elements randomly generated in $[0, 1]$; ω, φ_1, and φ_2 are positive constant numbers called the inertia, cognitive and social parameter, respectively. Finally, the position of each particle is updated as,

$$p_i(t+1) = p_i(t) + z_i(t+1) \tag{6}$$

The elements of the particle are confined in the range $p_j^{min} \leq p_{ij} \leq p_j^{max}$ [15], where p_j^{min} and p_j^{max} are the boundaries of the domain of values in the jth dimension of the particles' search space. To implement the PSO, each particle codifies the parameters v_ℓ and σ_ℓ $(1 \leq \ell \leq c)$. Therefore, the dimension of the particles' search space is equal to $q = c(p+1)$ (i.e. $p_i \in R^q \ \forall i$). All particles are randomly initialized.

On the other hand, there are $c(p+1)$ polynomial parameters $a_{10}, a_{11}, \ldots, a_{1p}, a_{20}, a_{21}, \ldots, a_{2p}, \ldots, a_{c0}, a_{c1}, \ldots, a_{cp}$ are estimated using the well-known ridge regression [16], where the regularization parameter is adjusted manually.

4 Simulation Study

Based on the analysis described in Sect. 2, the data set includes $N = 4811$ input-output data pairs of the form $\{x_k; y_k\}|_{k=1}^N$ with $x_k \in R^6$ and $y_k \in R$. The data set was randomly divided into a training set consisting of the 60% of the original data, and a testing set consisting of the remainder 40%.

Parameter setting for the PSO was as follows: $\varphi_1 = \varphi_2 = 2$, ω was randomly selected in $[0.5, 1]$, and the population size was $Np = 20$.

For comparison, two more neural networks were designed and implemented. The first one is a radial basis function neural network (RBFNN). The basis functions parameters as well as connection weights were estimated in terms of the PSO algorithm.

The second one is a feedforward neural network (FFNN) with activation functions

$$f(x) = \tanh \frac{x}{2} \tag{7}$$

The network's parameters of the FFNN were determined using once again the PSO algorithm. In both of the above networks, the parameter settings for PSO were the same as in the proposed network. All networks were implemented using the Python software. The performance index was the root mean square error:

$$RMSE = \sqrt{\frac{1}{N} \sum_{k=1}^{N} (y_k - \hat{y}_k)^2} \tag{8}$$

For the three networks, we considered various numbers of nodes. For each number of nodes we run 10 different initializations. The results are shown in Table 1 for the training data and in Table 2 for the testing data. The proposed network appears to have the best performance compared with the other two networks. The best result for both the training and testing data sets is obtained by the proposed network for $c = 9$. The results reported in the above tables are visualized in Fig. 2. There are some interesting observations related to this figure. First, the superiority of the proposed method is clear, in comparison with the other two tested networks. Second, the behaviours of the FFNN and the RBFNN appear to be similar, but with the latter achieving a slightly better performance in both the training and testing data. Third, in all networks, the general tendency is a decrease of the RMSE as the number of nodes increases.

With regard to the effectiveness of the proposed network the following should be noted. The RMSEs found, although smaller are still considered closed to the respective errors obtained by the other two networks. Taking into account the high variability of the data, it seems that the obtained RMSEs reflect the highly nonlinear nature of the overall process during the period of observations.

Table 1. RMSE mean values and the corresponding standard deviations obtained by the three networks for various numbers of nodes for the training data set

No of nodes (c)	RBFNN	FFNN	Proposed Polynomial RBF Network
2	0.99089 ± 0.04554	1.02675 ± 0.01785	0.92275 ± 0.04692
3	0.97380 ± 0.05496	0.98982 ± 0.01541	0.86041 ± 0.04520
4	0.96124 ± 0.02184	0.97438 ± 0.00767	0.83386 ± 0.05102
5	0.95858 ± 0.01604	0.96971 ± 0.01642	0.85830 ± 0.05313
6	0.95419 ± 0.01122	0.97841 ± 0.00977	0.79190 ± 0.03304
7	0.92386 ± 0.01793	0.98349 ± 0.01175	0.76170 ± 0.02352
8	0.93199 ± 0.01369	0.96833 ± 0.04979	0.77992 ± 0.01539
9	0.93363 ± 0.01342	0.96910 ± 0.01324	0.75779 ± 0.02254
10	0.92118 ± 0.03202	0.95349 ± 0.01157	0.77104 ± 0.01297

Table 2. RMSE mean values and the corresponding standard deviations obtained by the three networks for various numbers of nodes for the testing data set

No of nodes (c)	RBFNN	FFNN	Proposed Polynomial RBF Network
2	0.99810 ± 0.03451	1.05889 ± 0.01221	0.94464 ± 0.04468
3	0.97032 ± 0.03631	0.98055 ± 0.01015	0.89804 ± 0.03555
4	0.95734 ± 0.01441	0.97730 ± 0.00517	0.89473 ± 0.02327
5	0.95441 ± 0.01075	0.96925 ± 0.01107	0.87134 ± 0.01616
6	0.95831 ± 0.01422	0.97966 ± 0.00638	0.85364 ± 0.03070
7	0.95369 ± 0.01129	0.97203 ± 0.00787	0.84447 ± 0.04264
8	0.94564 ± 0.01607	0.98847 ± 0.03542	0.83688 ± 0.01323
9	0.93799 ± 0.04792	0.98172 ± 0.00970	0.82566 ± 0.01580
10	0.92718 ± 0.00798	0.97530 ± 0.01134	0.83648 ± 0.01286

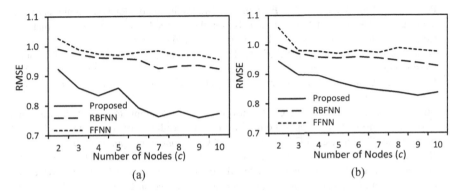

Fig. 2. Mean values of the RMSE as a function of the number of nodes for: (a) the training, and (b) the testing data.

5 Conclusions

In the present contribution we have presented a systematic methodology that uses an experimental setup and a novel polynomial neural network to predict the server rack's temperature of the data center located at the University of the Aegean, Greece. A set of input variables were identified that affected that temperature, which together with experimental observations taken on a three-minute interval basis over a period of two weeks were used to generate the input-output training data. The network's structure involves three levels. Level 1 comprises a typical RBF hidden layer. Layer 2 generates first order polynomials of the input variables, where the polynomial factors play the role of the regression parameters in the network's inference mechanism. Finally, in Level 3 the outputs of the above two layers are aggregated to produce the estimated output. The training procedure was carried out by applying in sequence the particle swarm optimization and ridge regression. Simulation experiments were conducted and the results were compared with those obtained by two other neural networks: a radial basis function neural network and a feedforward neural network. The comparison showed that the proposed network performs better in all cases as far as the modeling process of the above-mentioned server rack's temperature is concerned.

References

1. Ham, S.-W., Kim, M.-H., Choi, B.-N., Jeong, J.-W.: Simplified server model to simulate data center cooling energy consumption. Energy Build. **86**, 328–339 (2015)
2. Ibrahim, H., Aburukba, R.O., El-Faki, K.: An integer linear programming model and adaptive genetic algorithm approach to minimize energy consumption of cloud computing data centers. Comput. Electr. Eng. (2018). doi:https://doi.org/10.1016/j.compeleceng.2018.02.028
3. Beloglazov, A., Abawajy, J., Buyya, R.: Energy-aware resource allocation heuristics for efficient management of data centers for cloud computing. Fut. Gener. Comput. Syst. **28**(5), 755–768 (2012)
4. Prevost, J.J., Nagothu, K., Kelley, B., Jamshidi, M.: Prediction of cloud data center networks loads using stochastic and neural models. In: the Proceedings of the 6th International Conference on System of Systems Engineering, pp. 276–281 (2011)
5. Derakhshan, F., Roessler, H., Schefczik, P., Randriamasy, S.: On prediction of resource consumption of service requests in cloud environments. In: The Proceedings of the 20th International Conference on Innovations in Clouds, Internet and Networks (ICIN), pp. 169–176 (2017)
6. Matsunaga, A., Fortes, J.A.B.: On the use of machine learning to predict the time and resources consumed by applications. In: The Proceedings of the 10th IEEE/ACM International Conference on Cluster, Cloud and Grid Computing, pp. 495–504 (2010)
7. Xu, J., Fortes, J.A.B.: Multi-objective virtual machine placement in virtualized data center environments. In: The Proceedings of the IEEE/ACM International Conference on Green Computing and Communications & International Conference on Cyber, Physical and Social Computing, pp. 179–188 (2010)
8. Ivakhnenko, A.G.: Polynomial theory of complex systems. IEEE Trans. Syst. Man Cybernet. **4**, 364–378 (1971)
9. Oh, S.-K., Kim, W.-D., Pedrycz, W., Park, B.-J.: Polynomial-based radial basis function neural networks (P-RBF NNs) realized with the aid of particle swarm optimization. Fuzzy Sets Syst. **163**(1), 54–77 (2011)
10. Tsekouras, G.E.: A simple and effective algorithm for implementing particle swarm optimization in RBF network's design using input-output fuzzy clustering. Neurocomputing **108**, 36–44 (2013)
11. Lee, T.-T., Jeng, J.-T.: The Chebyshev-polynomials-based unified model neural networks for function approximation. IEEE Trans. Syst. Man Cybernet. Part B: Cybernet. **28**(6), 925–935 (1998)
12. Rigos, A., Tsekouras, G.E., Vousdoukas, M.I., Chatzipavlis, A., Velegrakis, A.F.: A Chebyshev polynomial radial basis function neural network for automated shoreline extraction from coastal imagery. Integr. Comput.-Aided Eng. **23**, 141–160 (2016)
13. GeSI: SMART 2020: Enabling the low carbon economy in the information age (2008)

14. Kaplan, J., Forrest, W., Kindler, N.: Revolutionizing Data Center Energy Efficiency, Technical Report. McKinsey & Company (2008)
15. Kennedy, J., Eberhart, R.C.: Swarm Intelligence. Morgan Kaufmann, Berlin (2001)
16. Tikhonov, A.N., Goncharsky, A.V., Stepanov, V.V., Yagola, A.G.: Numerical methods for the solution of ill-posed problems. Kluwer Academic Publishers, Dordrecht (1995)

Incorporating Worker Similarity for Label Aggregation in Crowdsourcing

Jiyi Li[1,4(✉)], Yukino Baba[2,4], and Hisashi Kashima[3,4]

[1] University of Yamanashi, Kofu, Japan
jyli@yamanashi.ac.jp
[2] University of Tsukuba, Tsukuba, Japan
baba@cs.tsukuba.ac.jp
[3] Kyoto University, Kyoto, Japan
kashima@i.kyoto-u.ac.jp
[4] RIKEN Center for AIP, Tokyo, Japan

Abstract. For the quality control in the crowdsourcing tasks, requesters usually assign a task to multiple workers to obtain redundant answers and then aggregate them to obtain the more reliable answer. Because of the existence of the non-experts in the crowds, one of the problems in the label aggregation is how to differ experts with higher ability from non-experts with lower ability and strengthen the influences of these experts. Most of the existing label aggregation approaches tend to strengthen the workers who provide majority answers and regard them with high ability. In addition, we find that the similarity among worker labels is possible to be effective for this issue because two experts are more probable to reach consensus than two non-experts. We thus propose a novel probabilistic model which can incorporate the similarity information of workers. The experimental results on a number of real datasets show that our approach can outperform the existing models including a probabilistic model without incorporating the similarity. We also make an empirical study on the influence of worker ability, label sparsity and redundancy to the performance of label aggregation approaches, and provide a suggestion on the strategy of collecting the labels in crowdsourcing.

Keywords: Crowdsourcing · Quality control · Worker similarity

1 Introduction

Crowdsourcing has been successfully applied to various areas of computer science including computer vision, natural language processing, machine learning and so on. Crowdsourcing platforms such as Amazon Mechanical Turk offer human intelligence tasks to a large group of unspecified workers who can be non-experts. One kind of important tasks is multiple choices. Workers are asked to select one answer from multiple candidates on a given task, for example, a label of an image, or an answer to a scientific question.

© Springer Nature Switzerland AG 2018
V. Kůrková et al. (Eds.): ICANN 2018, LNCS 11140, pp. 596–606, 2018.
https://doi.org/10.1007/978-3-030-01421-6_57

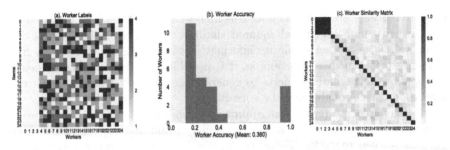

Fig. 1. A Toy Example of Worker Label, Similarity, and Accuracy Distribution. In (a) and (b), there are four experts in 25 workers for 25 items. The experts always select correct choices. The non-experts always randomly select the choices. In (c), the label similarity between two experts is prominently higher than that between two non-experts, thus it is possible to be used for differ experts from non-experts.

Quality control is one of the essential problems in crowdsourcing. Workers may fail to provide correct answers because of their lack of ability or mistakes. One of the major approaches to cope with this quality problem is to introduce redundancy, i.e., assigning the same task to different workers and aggregating them to obtain a reliable answer. Besides the simple aggregation approaches like majority voting, there have been proposed various more sophisticated probabilistic models such as GLAD [13], DARE [1] and so on.

Because of the existence of the non-experts in the crowds, one of the problems in the label aggregation is how to differ experts with higher ability from non-experts with lower ability and strengthen the influences of these experts. Most of the existing approaches are based on the assumption that workers with high ability are likely to give correct answers, and correct answers are likely to be given by workers with high ability. They tend to strengthen the workers who provide majority answers and regard them with high ability.

In addition to this assumption in existing work, we find that the similarity among worker labels may be effective on this problem because two experts are more probable to reach consensus than two non-experts. Figure 1 illustrates a toy example which can explain the benefits of worker similarity in the answer aggregation. In Fig. 1(a), the items are four-choice questions with candidate labels {1, 2, 3, 4}. There are 25 items in total. Among the 25 workers, there are four experts who can always assign the correct label "1" to all of the items. The other 21 workers always provide random labels. Figure 1(b) shows the worker accuracy distribution in this example. In this example, the accuracy of aggregation results by the majority voting approach is 0.72.

We find that the similarity of two workers on their labels may be able to differ experts from non-experts. Figure 1(c) shows the similarity of each pair of workers in Fig. 1(a) by computing the square of Jaccard similarity of their labels. The squared similarity of two experts is much higher than that of two non-experts or that between an expert and a non-expert. If we integrate this squared similarities between a given worker and all other workers to represent this worker, a weighted majority voting approach which assigns high weights to the labels provided the workers with high integrated squared similarity can achieve 1.0 accuracy. In other words, the worker similarity information can distinguish the experts from the non-experts in this toy example. It is possible to be used for strengthening the opinions of potential experts to generate the aggregated labels which may have the higher probability to be correct.

In this paper, we propose an approach which implements the above idea by building a probabilistic model. We use similarity information among answers of different workers to model the worker abilities. We assume that the workers which have high similarity with other workers may have high abilities and implement this notion in the model. The contributions of this paper are as follows.

- We find that worker similarity is effective for differing experts from non-experts. We propose an approach which incorporates the similarity with a probabilistic model and has better aggregation results than existing work including a probabilistic model without incorporating worker similarity.
- We propose a solution to tune the hyperparameter with a perplexity measure in the unsupervised scenario and tune on a subset to decrease the time cost.
- We make an empirical study on the influence of worker ability, label sparsity and redundancy to the performance of label aggregation approaches, and provide a suggestion on the strategy of collecting the labels.

2   Related Work

In the approaches for aggregating multiple labels into a reliable label, majority voting [10] is a widely used and effective one which assigns equal weights to all workers. The more sophisticated approaches can be divided into two categories, i.e., using the auxiliary information or not.

The approaches without using the auxiliary information only leverage the distributions of answers by different workers on different questions. Some approaches jointly estimate worker ability and true answer with sophisticated probabilistic models, such as [2,3,13] and so on. Some other approaches are based on the Bayesian graphical model [1], belief propagation on bipartite graphical model [6], minimax Entropy [14] and so on. Our approach can be regarded as an extension to the probabilistic models like GLAD by incorporating the worker similarity. We verify that the worker similarity is effective for improve the performance of such models. How to incorporating the worker similarity with other types of models will be addressed in future work.

Most of these approaches basically strengthen the opinions of the majority workers in some ways, and do not address the cases where only a few capable workers (i.e. experts) are available; therefore, they do not work well in such cases where majority voting fails in most questions. [5] focused on the cases of a few experts without utilizing auxiliary information by a notion of the hyper question. Our label aggregation approach can also be extended to an approach integrating with the hyper question, like the hyper-question based GLAD proposed in [5].

In addition, there are existing approaches using the auxiliary information such as worker profile [4] and task description [7]. In contrast, our approach only uses the worker answers and does not rely on any auxiliary information. It is practical to assume that the auxiliary information is not available.

3   Our Approach

3.1   Definitions and Notations

We focus on the *c-Choice task* in crowdsourcing. We define a task assigned to a worker as an *item*. We assume there is a set of workers $\mathcal{A} = \{a_i\}_i$, a set of items $\mathcal{M} = \{b_j\}_j$, and a set of candidate labels $\mathcal{C}$ where $|\mathcal{C}| = c$. For each item, we ask each worker to select a label from $\mathcal{C}$. Let l_{ij} denote the label given by worker a_i to item b_j. We denote the set of all labels by $\mathcal{L} = \{l_{ij}\}$, the set of labels given to b_j as $\mathcal{L}_{*j} = \{l_{ij}|a_i \in \mathcal{A}\}$ and the set of labels given by a_i as $\mathcal{L}_{i*} = \{l_{ij}|b_j \in \mathcal{M}\}$.

Given the worker set $\mathcal{A}$, the item set $\mathcal{M}$, the label set $\mathcal{L}$, our goal is to estimate the correct label z_j for each item b_j.

3.2   Probability Model

We model the probability that a label l_{ij} is equal to the correct label z_j for item b_j using the worker similarity. Our key assumption is that a worker has a higher probability to give a correct label if the worker has a high ability and if the worker tends to provide the same answer as other workers with a high ability. We utilize the similarity between workers to implement this idea.

On one hand, in our assumption, the ability of different workers are diverse and needs to be contained in our model. We assume that each worker has an ability parameter $\tau_i \geq 0$. The ability of a random worker is equal to 0. The ability of an expert is a high positive value. We regard a worker who shows lower accuracy than a random worker on labels as a malicious worker. The true ability of such worker is actually not lower than a random worker or as good as an expert ($\tau_i \geq 0$).

On the other hand, to utilize the similarity information of two workers, we assume that a worker with higher integrated similarity with all other workers is more probable to be an expert and thus has the higher probability to provide the correct labels. Our probability model is thus as follows.

$$p(l_{ij} = z_j|\tau_i) = \frac{1}{1 + (c-1)e^{-\gamma_i}} = \xi_{ij},$$

$$\gamma_i = \tau_i\phi_i, \quad \phi_i = (\lambda + \sum_{i' \neq i} s_{ii'}^2 \tau_{i'}), \quad \tau_i \geq 0,$$

where $s_{ii'}$ is the similarity between worker a_i and worker $a_{i'}$, and λ is a hyper parameter. $(c-1)$ is used in this model to ensure that when $\tau_i = 0$, the label l_{ij} is selected randomly, i.e., $p(l_{ij} = z_j|\tau_i = 0) = 1/c$. The square on the similarity measure is to strengthen the influence of workers with high similarity.

We further assume uniform probability over incorrect answers, namely,

$$p(l_{ij} \neq z_j | \tau_i) = \frac{1 - p(l_{ij} = z_j)}{c - 1} = \frac{1}{e^{\gamma_i} + (c - 1)}$$

3.3 Inference

In the probability model, l_{ij} is observed variable, and our target is to estimate the correct labels $\{z_j\}$ as well as worker ability $\{\tau_i\}$ which are unobserved variables. We use EM algorithm for the inference process. In the iterations, in the expectation step, we estimate z_j; in the maximization step, we update τ_i.

Initialization: We set Gaussian prior with $\mu = 1$ and $\sigma = 1$ as the prior of worker ability τ_i. The prior probability $p(z_j)$ is set to equal to $1/c$.

Expectation Step: We compute the posterior probabilities z_j based on the observed labels $\mathcal{L}$ and worker ability τ which values are from the initialization or the last maximization step. We assume that τ is conditional independent with z_j. δ_{ij} is a Kronecker delta function on l_{ij} and z_j. The computation is as follows.

$$p(z_j | \mathcal{L}, \tau) \propto p(z_j) \prod_i p(l_{ij} | z_j, \tau_i).$$

where $p(l_{ij} | z_j = k, \tau_i) = \xi_{ij}^{\delta_{ij}^k} \left(\frac{1 - \xi_{ij}}{c - 1} \right)^{(1 - \delta_{ij}^k)}$, $\delta_{ij}^k = \begin{cases} 1, l_{ij} = z_j = k \\ 0, l_{ij} \neq z_j = k \end{cases}$.

Maximization Step: We set the object function as the joint log-likelihood of all worker labels $\mathcal{L}$ and all correct label $\mathcal{Z}$. It is computed based on the posterior probability $p_j^k = p(z_j = k | \mathcal{L}, \tau)$ which is the result of previous expectation step.

$$\mathcal{Q} = E[\log p(\mathcal{L}, \mathcal{Z} | \alpha)] = E[\log \prod_j (p(z_j) p(\mathcal{L}_{*j} | z_j, \tau)))]$$

$$= \sum_j \sum_k p_j^k \log p(z_j = k) + \sum_{ij} \sum_k p_j^k \log p(l_{ij} | z_j = k, \tau_i)$$

We solve a constrained optimization problem for inferring parameter τ,

$$\max_\tau \mathcal{Q}, \text{ subject to } \tau_i \geq 0.$$

Finally, we use p_j^k to estimate the correct label $\{z_j\}$, $z_j^* = \arg\max_k p_j^k$.

3.4 Hyperparameter Selection

Since we set our work in the unsupervised scenario, we cannot use the ground truth to tune the hyperparameters and improve the performance. It is a rational setting because golden labels are always unknown in real crowdsourcing applications. Because we simplified the design of our approach, there is only one hyperparameter which needs to be selected, i.e., the λ in the probability model.

We propose a measurement named *perplexity* based on the estimated probability of candidate labels for an item, which is computed based on the entropy of a discrete probability distribution and represents how well a probability model predicts a sample. In details, we define the perplexity on a dataset as follows. It is the sum of the perplexity on an item. We use the λ which can generate minimum $perplexity_M$. Although the hyperparameter with minimum $perplexity_M$ maybe not the best hyperparameter which can generate estimated labels with the highest accuracy, it can generate good and rational results.

$$perplexity_M = \sum_j perplexity_j = \sum_j 2^{-\sum_k p_j^k \log p_j^k}.$$

This tuning method computes t times for our approach on the entire dataset where t is the number of groups of parameters. When the entire dataset is very large and the number of candidate values of the hyperparameter is not small, it increases the computation a lot. To decrease the time cost, instead of tuning the hyperparameter on the entire dataset, our idea is only using a selection of the data when tuning the hyperparameters. We thus propose a non-expert filtering solution to select the workers who have the higher probability to have higher ability than other workers in the datasets. In details, we first utilize the integrated worker similarity and select a worker subset with top-r similarity, i.e., $r = 10$. After that, we tune the hyperparameter of our approach based on the subset of labels which are only generated by this worker subset.

3.5 Similarity

In this work, the similarity of workers can be defined by various measures, e.g., cosine similarity or normalized mutual similarity, and so on. However, the problem is that many of them require that any two workers label same items. In other words, they require that all workers label all items. When the dataset is large scale, the requirement of labeling all items is not feasible.

In the implementation in this paper, we thus utilize a similarity measure which does not require that any pair of workers label same items. It is the Jaccard similarity. The Jaccard similarity between two workers a_i and $a_{i'}$ is formulated as $s_{ii'} = (|\mathcal{L}_{i*} \cap \mathcal{L}_{i'*}|)/(|\mathcal{L}_{i*} \cup \mathcal{L}_{i'*}|)$.

4 Experiments

4.1 Experimental Settings

In our approach, for tuning the hyperparameter λ in the probability model, we set the range of its values in $\{0.1, 0.2, 0.5, 1, 2\}$. In the subset of workers with top-r similarity for hyperparameter tuning, r is set to 10.

We compare our approach with the existing label aggregation approaches including Majority Voting (MV) [10], GLAD [13] which is based on a probabilistic model by the EM algorithm, and DARE [1] which is based on a Bayesian

Table 1. Statistics of Datasets. lmr (label matrix ratio) is the ratio of labels in the worker-item matrix showing the sparsity of labels in the dataset; lpi (label per item) is the number of workers for each item showing the redundancy of labels for an item.

Dataset	#choices	#items	#workers	#labels	lmr	lpi
wsd [10]	3	177	34	1770	0.294	10.00
popularity [9]	2	500	143	10000	0.140	20.00
temporal [10]	2	462	76	4620	0.132	10.00
rte [10]	2	800	164	8000	0.061	10.00
weather [11]	5	300	110	6000	0.182	20.00
smile [13]	2	159	17	1950	0.721	12.26
duck [12]	2	108	39	4212	1.000	39.0
face [8]	4	584	27	5242	0.332	8.98

graphical model. The reasons that we select these approaches is that they are well-known and widely-used ones.

The evaluation metric is the accuracy of the aggregated labels. $accuracy = m_c/m$, where m_c is the number of the correct aggregated labels and m is the number of the items.

We utilize several datasets proposed in existing work on the topic of label aggregation to verify our approach. We select the datasets with diverse factors to show the performance of our approach in different cases. Table 1 lists the statistical factors of these datasets including the number of choices (binary or multiple), the number of items, the number of workers and the number of labels.

In addition, We also list the information of two factors, i.e., label-matrix-ratio (*lmr*) and label-per-item (*lpi*). label-matrix-ratio (*lmr*) is the ratio of labels in the worker-item matrix and represents the sparsity of labels considering the number of items and workers in the dataset. It is equal to $\#labels/(\#worker * \#items)$. label-per-item (*lpi*) is the number of workers for each item and shows the redundancy of labels for an item. Most of these datasets contain a large number of incomplete labels.

We also show the worker accuracy distribution in Fig. 2. We sort these datasets based on the mean accuracy of the workers, from high accuracy to low accuracy. It shows that the mean accuracy for the first four datasets (wsd, popularity, temporal and rte) is high (>80%) and that for the other four datasets (weather, smile, duck, and face) is not high (<70%). We can investigate the performance of our approach in both high and low accuracy cases.

4.2 Experimental Results

Table 2 lists the results on these datasets. First, the bold values represent the cases that an approach performs best in all approaches for comparisons. It shows that our approach can perform best in most of these datasets. In all these approaches, each approach performs best on at least one of the datasets, our approaches can perform best on more datasets than others.

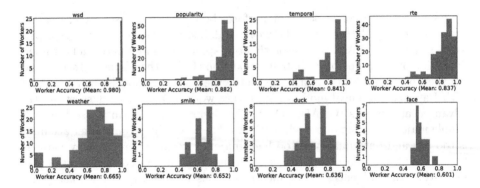

Fig. 2. Worker Accuracy Distribution in the Datasets. We sort them based on the mean accuracy of the workers, from high accuracy to low accuracy. The first four datasets have relatively higher accuracy and the latter four have relatively lower accuracy.

Table 2. Comparison between our approach and the baselines. Bold values represent the cases that an approach performs best in all approaches. The underline values represent the cases that our proposed approach does not perform worse than GLAD.

Dataset	MV	GLAD	DARE	Our
wsd	**0.9944**	**0.9944**	0.9887	**0.9944**
popularity	0.9440	**0.9460**	0.9440	**0.9460**
temporal	**0.9394**	0.9351	0.9351	**0.9394**
rte	0.9187	0.9263	0.9250	**0.9275**
weather	0.8467	0.8533	**0.8567**	0.8533
smile	0.7233	0.7610	0.7170	**0.7673**
duck	0.7593	0.7222	0.7593	**0.7685**
face	**0.6301**	0.6284	0.6216	0.6284

Second, on one hand, in the cases that the experts are relatively more or the accuracy of workers are relatively higher (wsd, popularity, temporal and rte), our approach can at least perform as well as the best approach in the three baselines. On the other hand, in some cases that the experts are relatively fewer or the accuracy of workers are lower (duck and smile), our approach is also possible to generate best label aggregation results in all these approaches for comparison.

Third, the underline values represent the cases that our approach perform better than GLAD or as well as it in all datasets, even in the two datasets (face and weather) that our approach does not perform best in all approaches. Our approach performs better than GLAD in four of the eight datasets. It thus illustrates that the worker similarity is effective for differing experts from non-experts and improving the label aggregation results when incorporating it with existing probabilistic models like GLAD.

Fourth, our approach does not perform best on two datasets, i.e., weather dataset and face dataset. For the weather dataset, because our approach performs same with GLAD, the reason that our approach cannot perform best is the limitation of such type of probability model on the weather dataset. Incorporating the worker similarity information into other types of models such as DARE with Bayesian graphical models is in future work. For the face dataset, all the advanced approaches (GLAD, DARE, Our approach) perform worse than the simple majority voting approach. It shows that when the mean worker accuracy is too low and data quality is too bad, majority voting approach may perform better than the advanced approaches. Because these advanced approaches try to strengthen the influences of the incorrect labels from low-ability workers, they thus generate worse results than majority voting.

In summary, our approach is effective not only for general cases in which majority of workers have good ability but also for the special cases that only a few experts are available in the crowd workers. However, if the data quality is very low and there are no distinct experts in the datasets, our approach cannot perform well. Other quality control mechanism such as roughly worker selection should be utilized to avoid the extremely low data quality.

4.3   Sparsity, Redundancy and Worker Accuracy

On one hand, in the results in Table 2, we arrange the datasets following the mean accuracy of workers which is shown in Fig. 2 based on the order from high to low mean worker accuracy. It shows that for all these approaches, the performance generally decrease when the mean worker accuracy decreases. It shows that mean worker accuracy harm the performance of the label aggregation.

On the other hand, a special case is the duck dataset. It has better results on three of the four approaches than the smile dataset, though it has lower mean worker accuracy than the smile dataset. In Table 1, it shows that duck dataset has much lower label sparsity (much higher lmr, no incomplete labels) and higher label redundancy on lpi than the smile dataset. It shows that lower label sparsity and higher label redundancy can improve the performance of the label aggregation approaches.

Furthermore, although the duck dataset has no unlabeled items and has very high label redundancy ($lpi=39$), the accuracy of the label aggregation approaches still cannot be higher than 0.80. This observation shows that the worker accuracy is more important than sparsity and redundancy for generating better label aggregation results. In other words, when using crowdsourcing for collecting data, because lower sparsity and higher redundancy lead to higher budget cost, it is better to select potential high ability workers who can provide high-quality labels rather than assigning the tasks to more workers without taking care of their ability. The research list in the existing work which are proposed to selecting high-quality workers can be utilized for this issue.

5   Conclusion

In this paper, we find that worker similarity is effective for the label aggregation problem. We propose an approach which can incorporate the similarity with a probabilistic model and can generate better aggregation results than existing work. We propose a solution to tune the hyperparameter with a perplexity measure in the unsupervised scenario. We also provide an empirical discussion that finding high ability workers is more important than collecting more labels without taking care of worker ability when in the crowdsourcing applications.

For the future work, We will consider the solution to utilize the similarity information to extend other type of models such as DARE.

Acknowledgments. This work was partially supported by JSPS KAKENHI Grant Number 15H01704.

References

1. Bachrach, Y., Minka, T., Guiver, J., Graepel, T.: How to grade a test without knowing the answers: a bayesian graphical model for adaptive crowdsourcing and aptitude testing. In: Proceedings of the 29th International Conference on International Conference on Machine Learning ICML 2012, pp. 819–826 (2012)
2. Dawid, A.P., Skene, A.M.: Maximum likelihood estimation of observer error-rates using the EM algorithm. J. R. Stat. Soc. Ser. C (Appl. Stat.) **28**(1), 20–28 (1979)
3. Karger, D.R., Oh, S., Shah, D.: Iterative learning for reliable crowdsourcing systems. In: Proceedings of the 24th International Conference on Neural Information Processing Systems NIPS 2011, pp. 1953–1961 (2011)
4. Li, H.W., Zhao, B., Fuxman, A.: The wisdom of minority: discovering and targeting the right group of workers for crowdsourcing. In: Proceedings of the 23rd International Conference on World Wide Web, pp. 165–176 (2014)
5. Li, J., Baba, Y., Kashima, H.: Hyper questions: unsupervised targeting of a few experts in crowdsourcing. In: Proceedings of the 2017 ACM on Conference on Information and Knowledge Management CIKM 2017, pp. 1069–1078 (2017)
6. Liu, Q., Peng, J., Ihler, A.: Variational inference for crowdsourcing. In: Proceedings of the 25th International Conference on Neural Information Processing Systems NIPS 2012, pp. 692–700 (2012)
7. Ma, F.L., et al.: Faitcrowd: fine grained truth discovery for crowdsourced data aggregation. In: Proceedings of the 21th ACM SIGKDD International Conference on Knowledge Discovery and Data Mining KDD 2015, pp. 745–754 (2015)
8. Mozafari, B., Sarkar, P., Franklin, M.J., Jordan, M.I., Madden, S.: Active learning for crowd-sourced databases. CoRR abs/1209.3686 (2012)
9. Pang, B., Lee, L.: A sentimental education: sentiment analysis using subjectivity summarization based on minimum cuts. In: Proceedings of the 42nd Annual Meeting on Association for Computational Linguistics ACL 2004 (2004)
10. Snow, R., O'Connor, B., Jurafsky, D., Ng, A.Y.: Cheap and fast–but is it good?: evaluating non-expert annotations for natural language tasks. In: Proceedings of the Conference on Empirical Methods in Natural Language Processing EMNLP 2008, pp. 254–263 (2008)

11. Venanzi, M., Teacy, W., Rogers, A., Jennings, N.R.: Weather sentiment-amazon mechanical turk dataset (2015)
12. Welinder, P., Branson, S., Belongie, S., Perona, P.: The multidimensional wisdom of crowds. In: Proceedings of the 23rd International Conference on Neural Information Processing Systems NIPS 2010, pp. 2424–2432 (2010)
13. Whitehill, J., Ruvolo, P., Wu, T., Bergsma, J., Movellan, J.: Whose vote should count more: optimal integration of labels from labelers of unknown expertise. In: Proceedings of the 22nd International Conference on Neural Information Processing Systems NIPS 2009, pp. 2035–2043 (2009)
14. Zhou, D.Y., Platt, J.C., Basu, S., Mao, Y.: Learning from the wisdom of crowds by minimax entropy. In: Proceedings of the 25th International Conference on Neural Information Processing Systems NIPS 2012, pp. 2195–2203 (2012)

NoSync: Particle Swarm Inspired Distributed DNN Training

Mihailo Isakov[✉] and Michel A. Kinsy

Adaptive and Secure Computing Systems (ASCS) Laboratory,
Department of Electrical and Computer Engineering, Boston University,
Boston, MA, USA
{mihailo,mkinsy}@bu.edu

Abstract. Training deep neural networks on big datasets remains a computational challenge. It can take hundreds of hours to perform and requires distributed computing systems to accelerate. Common distributed data-parallel approaches share a single model across multiple workers, train on different batches, aggregate gradients, and redistribute the new model. In this work, we propose *NoSync*, a particle swarm optimization inspired alternative where each worker trains a separate model, and applies pressure forcing models to converge. NoSync explores a greater portion of the parameter space and provides resilience to overfitting. It consistently offers higher accuracy compared to single workers, offers a linear speedup for smaller clusters, and is orthogonal to existing data-parallel approaches.

Keywords: Deep learning · Artificial neural network
Distributed systems · Evolutionary algorithm
Particle swarm optimization

1 Introduction

Deep neural networks have shown excellent results on a number of tasks such as image recognition [8], machine translation [2], question answering [1], and game playing [16]. In his 2014 keynote on "Large Scale Deep Learning" [4], Jeffrey Dean makes the point that DNN researchers want the results of experiments quickly, and that there is a "patience threshold" they are willing to pay. As state-of-the-art networks require weeks to train with a single GPU on the ImageNet dataset, many researchers are turning to distributed systems for training. This distributed training ranges from running a model on a single machine outfitted with multiple GPUs, to using clusters with thousands of cores, novel architectures, and special interconnects [19].

Two common approaches for distributing neural networks across multiple workers are model parallelism and data parallelism. In model parallelism, network layers are split across multiple workers, and workers communicate neuron activations and gradients. In data parallelism, networks are cloned between

© Springer Nature Switzerland AG 2018
V. Kůrková et al. (Eds.): ICANN 2018, LNCS 11140, pp. 607–619, 2018.
https://doi.org/10.1007/978-3-030-01421-6_58

workers, workers work on different batches and communicate parameter updates after every batch. Data parallelism is better suited for convolutional neural net parallelization, as this approach requires less network bandwidth [12].

Data parallel distributed DNN training approaches are either synchronous or asynchronous. Synchronous approaches require that all the updates are aggregated before the next training batch can begin. They suffer from low worker utilization due to locking, and are typically only employed when high network bandwidth and homogeneous hardware is available [9]. Asynchronous DNN training aims to fix some of these issues by relaxing the requirement that all workers must finish their updates before the next batch can begin. This significantly raises utilization and reduces bandwidth requirements, but introduces staleness in the system. If left unchecked, the staleness of worker models can range in tens or even hundreds of iterations [5]. This staleness negatively impacts accuracy, prompting a number of researchers to attempt to counter this effect [7,13].

We propose an alternative to the conventional data-parallel approaches. Our intuition stems from the fact that in both synchronous and asynchronous training, a model is cloned across multiple workers, wasting the majority of worker memory. We ask whether using that memory to train individual workers may give us faster convergence, and how would it impact accuracy. We propose NoSync, a Particle Swarm Optimization (PSO) inspired deep neural network training algorithm.

We summarize our contributions here:

- We propose a new type of distributed neural network training, which offers both higher accuracy compared to synchronous and asynchronous data-parallel approaches, as well as lower bandwidth requirements and good scalability.
- We show that *model averaging* can work, as long as the models do not diverge too far, and we provide an insight into the learning happening during NoSync training.
- We verify the results by training common convolutional networks on simulated systems, and show that our training has equivalent utilization and bandwidth requirements as common synchronous approaches.

2   Related Work

Processing neural networks typically involves training, inference, or both (known as online training). In case of inference, distributing a neural network is trivial, as each example or batch can be processed independently. In the case of distributed training, there are two methods of parallelizing neural networks present in literature: (1) model parallelization [5,12], where different network layers or neurons are partitioned between machines and all machines work on the same data, and (2) data parallelization [9,15], where the same network model is present on all machines, but trains on different data.

Model parallelization splits a model between multiple workers, requiring the workers to transmit neuron activations for each batch. This approach is efficient in the case of fully-connected layers, where models are large and activations are small, but is very inefficient in the case of convolutional neural networks where the convolution kernels are small, but activations are large [12].

While model parallelization exploits the fact that neural networks are highly parallelizable, data parallelization attempts to parallelize the training algorithm, in this case stochastic gradient descent (SGD). In data parallel distributed DNN training, multiple workers share the same model, but work on different data. Typically, we take a batch, split it amongst workers, aggregate the calculated gradients, and update all the models [5,14,17]. Data parallel approaches can be further broken down into synchronous and asynchronous. In synchronous data parallel training, a locking mechanism prevents each of the workers from working on stale models, requiring that all machines have identical models at all times. This approach leads to lower utilization, requiring either fast interconnects to achieve good performance [9], or a higher computation/communication ratio [19].

A simple way of increasing worker utilization is allowing the workers to work on batches independently of each other. In asynchronous training, each worker requests the newest model from a parameter server, calculates the gradients on a batch, and sends them back. These gradients are likely not applied to the same model the worker was given, but to a newer one updated by other workers, meaning that the applied update is stale. Asynchronous approaches, while faster than synchronous ones, suffer an accuracy penalty due to this staleness. Several works have attempted to minimize this loss in accuracy [7,13]. In [7], authors inversely weigh the updates by their staleness, meaning that staler updates will have less of an impact on training. While restoring accuracy, this approach does not fully utilize all the workers, as the slower workers might not contribute to training at all due to their lower learning rates. In [13], the authors show that staleness caused by asynchrony can be viewed as just an amount of implicit momentum. By tuning the momentum parameter, they restore the original accuracy while still valuing all updates equally.

Recently, several works have pushed the envelope on the minimum time required to train a network on the ImageNet dataset, ranging from 29 h on 8 NVidia P100 GPUs [8], down to 1 h using 256 P100 GPUs [6], and even 15 min using 1024 P100's [18]. All of these approaches use synchronous training and try to increase the computation to communication ratio, for example by using batches as large as 32k samples. Similar to our work, but in parallel, the authors in [20] propose training an individual model on every worker and applying elastic averaging between workers as means to prevent divergence. This development serves as further validation of the proposed approach.

3 NoSync Training

Particle Swarm Optimization: Particle Swarm Optimization [10] (PSO) is a biology-inspired optimization algorithm imitating the movement of flocks of birds or swarms of insects. It searches for a function extreme by having a population of particles, each of which samples the function at a certain position. Each particle has a position and velocity, and repeatedly moves in the parameter space searching for a better extreme. PSO is gradient-insensitive, easy to parallelize, and is a good global search algorithm.

In PSO, each particle with index j at time t consists of a position x_t^j and velocity v_t^j. A particle keeps track of the best position it has encountered during the search p_t^{ij} and the swarm stores the position p_t^g of the best solution any particle has encountered during the search. PSO introduces two metaparameters: the cognitive parameter c_1 and the social parameter c_2, along with the random values $r_1, r_2 \in [0, 1]$ determined at each iteration.

Each iteration, a particle j updates its position and velocity as:

$$\begin{aligned} x_{t+1}^j &= x_t^j + v_t^j \\ v_{t+1}^j &= v_t^j + c_1 r_1 (p_t^{ij} - x_t^j) + c_2 r_2 (p_t^g - x_t^j) \end{aligned} \tag{1}$$

From Eq. 1, a particle maintains its speed across iterations, and accelerates towards the best local and global solution. The goal of the cognitive and social parameters is to control the amount of 'pull' applied towards the best individual and swarm solution, respectively. Initially, the swarm should give more freedom to the particles by having a small value of $c2$. Later in the search, PSO increases $c2$, forcing the particles to converge and explore the area around the best solution.

Particle Swarm Optimization and Gradient Descent: Classic gradient descent is often prone to overfitting and does not generalize very well. Adding momentum has been shown to help the search escape local minima and find good solutions. For some parameters θ, iteration t, a learning rate α, objective $J(\theta)$, and a batch of input-output pairs x_i and y_i drawn from a dataset, we can write one update as:

$$\begin{aligned} \theta^{t+1} &= \theta^t - v^t \\ v^{t+1} &= \mu v^t + \alpha \nabla_\theta J(\theta; x_i, y_i) \end{aligned} \tag{2}$$

By observing Eqs. 1 and 2, we notice some similarities: (1) both equations maintain a position and speed, and (2) in PSO, each particle is pulled towards the best solution it has encountered $(c_1 r_1 (p_t^{ij} - x_t^j))$, while in gradient descent, a model calculates and applies the gradient, arriving at a better solution $(\alpha \nabla_\theta J(\theta; x_i, y_i))$. The third component $c_2 r_2 (p_t^g - x_t^j)$ of a PSO velocity update has no counterpart in gradient descent - it is used to pull the swarm towards the best solution any particle in the swarm has encountered. Since gradient descent only trains one solution, there is no global solution for it to be pulled towards. From this observation, we introduce a new type of neural network training which trains multiple solutions, and applies a force for them to converge.

Introducing NoSync: In NoSync, for a distributed system of w workers, we train w models, one on each worker. Each worker is trained with classic stochastic gradient descent with momentum. After every batch, we gather the n best performing models, and calculate their mean model c_m, i.e., their 'center of mass'. We then perform pulling - we move each of the w models towards this center of mass c_m. The amount of pull depends on the distance between the model and the center of mass, multiplied by the pull coefficient β. With the metaparameter β set to 0, models will freely diverge. Interpolating two models will typically produce a model whose accuracy is worse than either of the two. This is because the error function on the linear path between them is highly nonconvex. There is no reason to assume that two distant models can gain anything by being interpolated. For that reason, we apply pulling from the very start, forcing the models not to stray too far. If the models are close enough, we can safely assume that the error function between them is convex.

Pulling Models: In order to prevent models from diverging, we introduce 'pulling' between workers. In a cluster of w workers, each worker i trains its model W^i on a separate batch, and afterwards sends it over the network to the parameter server. The parameter server computes the average of the models, and pulls all the workers' models towards it by a parameter β as:

$$W_{t+1}^i = (1 - \beta)W_t^i + \frac{\beta}{w} \sum_{k=1}^{w} W_t^k \qquad (3)$$

Parameter β is chosen so that the models do not diverge to far, but also do not converge to a single point, rendering the parallelization useless. While there is no reason to think that combining different trained models results in a network with comparable accuracy, in Sect. 6 we show that combining or pulling models from the very start results in higher accuracies than that of single machine implementations. There exists an obvious connection between the learning rate α and the pull β: higher learning rates will permit models to diverge further, possibly breaking the above assumption about interpolating loss, and lower learning rates will lead to the models converging and not usefully exploring the parameter space.

In a one-dimensional system, let us assume that there are w particles at time t have positions p_i^t and gradients g_i^t drawn from a normal distribution $g_i^t = \mathcal{N}(0, \sigma_g^2)$. Each iteration, particle i updates its position as:

$$p_i^{t+1} = (1 - \beta)(p_i^t + \alpha g_i^t) + \frac{\beta}{w} \sum_{k=1}^{w} p_k^t \qquad (4)$$

Assuming that particles are initialized from a normal distribution $\mathcal{N}(0, \sigma_w^2)$, in case when the pull parameter β is $\beta = 0$, one can model the position of a particle as a random walk:

$$p_i^t = p_i^0 + \sum_{t=1}^{t} \alpha g_i^t$$

$$= \mathcal{N}(0, \sigma_w^2) + \alpha \sum_{t=1}^{t} \mathcal{N}(0, \sigma_g^2) \qquad (5)$$

$$= \mathcal{N}(0, \sigma_w^2 + t\alpha^2 \sigma_g^2)$$

$$= \mathcal{N}(0, t\alpha^2 \sigma_g^2), \quad \sigma_w^2 \ll t\alpha^2 \sigma_g^2$$

It follows that two particles m and n at time t will have a distance of:

$$|p_m^t - p_n^t| = |\mathcal{N}(0, t\alpha^2\sigma_g^2) - \mathcal{N}(0, t\alpha\sigma_g^2)| \tag{6}$$
$$= |\mathcal{N}(0, 2t\alpha^2\sigma_g^2)|$$

The absolute value of normal value is a half-normal distribution, with the mean $\mu = \frac{\sigma\sqrt{2}}{\sqrt{\pi}}$. Hence, the average distance can be calculated as:

$$E(|p_m^t - p_n^t|) = \frac{\sqrt{2}\sqrt{2t\alpha^2\sigma_g^2}}{\sqrt{\pi}} = \frac{2\sqrt{t}\alpha\sigma_g}{\sqrt{\pi}} \tag{7}$$

From Eq. 7 it follows that the average distance between two points grows with the square of time. To prevent different models from diverging, we apply the pull coefficient $\beta \in [0, 1]$. With $\beta \neq 0$, the Eq. 7 becomes:

$$p_i^{t+1} = (1 - \beta)(p_i^t + \alpha g_i^t) + \frac{\beta}{w}\sum_{k=1}^{w} p_k^t$$

$$= (1 - \beta)(\mathcal{N}(0, \sigma_{p_i^t}^2) + \alpha\mathcal{N}(0, \sigma_g^2)) + \frac{\beta}{w}\sum_{k=0}^{w}\mathcal{N}(0, \sigma_{p_i^t}^2) \tag{8}$$

$$= \mathcal{N}(0, (1 - \beta)^2(\sigma_{p_i^t}^2 + \alpha^2\sigma_g^2)) + \mathcal{N}(0, \frac{\beta^2}{w^2}w\sigma_{p_i^t}^2)$$

$$= \mathcal{N}(0, \alpha^2\sigma_g^2(1 - \beta)^2 + \sigma_{p_i^t}^2((1 - \beta)^2 + \frac{\beta^2}{w}))$$

$$\psi = (1 - \beta)^2, \quad w = (1 - \beta)^2 + \frac{\beta^2}{w} \tag{9}$$

$$p_i^{t+1} = \mathcal{N}(0, \psi\alpha^2\sigma_g^2 + w\sigma_{p_i^t}^2) \tag{10}$$

In order to determine $\sigma_{p_i^t}^2$, we monitor p_i^t from time-step 0 onwards:

$$p_i^0 = \mathcal{N}(0, \psi\alpha^2\sigma_g^2)$$
$$p_i^1 = \mathcal{N}(0, \psi\alpha^2\sigma_g^2 + w\psi\alpha^2\sigma_g^2)$$

$$\vdots \tag{11}$$

$$p_i^t = \mathcal{N}(0, \psi\alpha^2\sigma_g^2\sum_{k=0}^{t} w^k) = \mathcal{N}(0, \psi\alpha^2\sigma_g^2\frac{1 - w^t}{1 - w})$$

The distance of two particles pulled by coefficient β is:

$$E(|p_i^t - p_j^t|) = E(|\mathcal{N}(0, \psi\alpha^2\sigma_g^2\frac{1 - w^t}{1 - w}) - \mathcal{N}(0, \psi\alpha^2\sigma_g^2\frac{1 - w^t}{1 - w})|)$$

$$= \frac{2(1 - \beta)\alpha\sigma_g\sqrt{\frac{1 - w^t}{1 - w}}}{\sqrt{\pi}} \tag{12}$$

Therefore, the distance between particles will grow with bigger gradient deviation σ_g, greater learning rate α, and will decrease with increasing pull β. It is also worth noting that this distance will approach infinity when $\beta \to 0$ and $t \to \inf$. Assuming that the number of workers w is large and $t \to \inf$, the distance becomes:

$$E(|p_i^t - p_j^t|) = \frac{2(1-\beta)\alpha\sigma_g}{\sqrt{\pi}\sqrt{2\beta - \beta^2}} \tag{13}$$

Assuming $\beta \ll 1$, the distance changes into:

$$E(|p_i^t - p_j^t|) = \frac{\sqrt{2}\alpha\sigma_g}{\sqrt{\pi}\sqrt{\beta}} \tag{14}$$

With the coefficient $\beta \neq 0$, the mean distance from the center of mass will stabilize, as the random gradients force the particles to diverge irrespective of the mean distance from the center, while the pull grows linearly with the distance. By increasing β, one can reduce the size of the swarm, and by decreasing β more freedom of movement will be given to the particles. This formulation gives the user the ability to directly control the relative size of the swarm compared with weight updates. One can make sure that the each particle on average is not more than n steps from every other particle.

Dropping Models: In classic PSO, each particle is pulled towards a single or multiple best optima encountered. In the above section, NoSync applies pull to the 'center of mass', for which all particles contribute. We explore the possibility of calculating the center of mass from only the n best particles, which might allow the swarm to follow the leaders and faster escape local minima. Given a set N of the n best models, we rewrite Eq. 3 as:

$$W_{t+1}^i = (1 - \beta)W_t^i + \frac{\beta}{n}\sum_{k \in N} W_t^k \tag{15}$$

An additional benefit of this approach is bandwidth reduction - only the particles that are in the top n solutions transmit their model every iteration.

4   Exploring Learning in NoSync

Source of the Accuracy Increase: NoSync modifies the original synchronous training approach in three ways: (1) It does not synchronize models. Each worker trains a separate model, and periodically sends updates to the parameter server. (2) Instead of synchronizing models, effectively taking their "center of mass", NoSync only pulls them closer. This means that at any point during training, we have w different models, which allows exploring w points in the parameter space, instead of just 1. (3) While synchronous data-parallel training integrates updates from all batches, regardless of how poorly a training model performs, we only integrate the n best performing models, $n \in [1, w]$. This aggregation approach does not mean that low-performing models stop contributing to subsequent training rounds, but rather that their states are disregarded during the current iteration.

These modifications raise the question: does the accuracy increase stem from dropping bad gradients, or from training multiple models in parallel? In order to find the source of the increase in accuracy, we compare several systems:

1. A baseline single worker system;
2. A synchronous model distributed over w workers;
3. 10 models on 10 machines, where after every batch we keep only the last batch's best performing model and redistribute it. This is equivalent to setting $n = 1$ and $\beta = 1$;
4. 10 NoSync trained models, with the n parameter set to 10, i.e., we pull all workers towards the "center of mass";
5. 10 NoSync trained models, with the n parameter set to 3.

In Fig. 1, we present the training and test accuracy after 30 epochs of all 5 systems. The three best performing systems are NoSync with $n = 10$, $n = 3$, and $n = 1$, in that order. Evidently, sharing more models between the workers is ideal (no drop), but sharing only the best performing model still allows the system to give a higher accuracy compared to the single-machine and distributed synchronous systems. These results corroborate the fact that accuracy stems from the number of parallel models rather than model dropping. This fact also highlights the trade-off opportunity between accuracy and network communication.

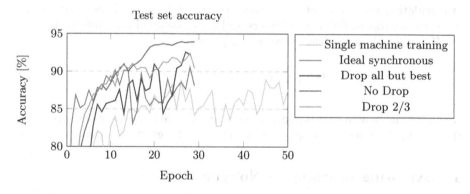

Fig. 1. Training and test accuracy of 5 systems: (green) training with a single worker, (red) classic synchronous training with 10 workers, (blue) dropping all but one, (cyan) pulling all 10 models, (orange) pulling top 3, and dropping 7 models. (Color figure online)

We attribute the accuracy increase to three effects: (1) by training many models, a greater amount of the loss function is explored and there is a higher chance that a good solution will be found. (2) NoSync acts as a regularizer, i.e., though some models may get stuck in local optima or saddle points, other models will get the opportunity to pull out the underperforming ones. (3) Similarly as in PSO, while individual particles may follow local gradients, the whole swarm is less sensitive to nonlinearities of the loss function, and shows more stability.

Saddle Points, and Broad Minima: Another way of understanding NoSync speedup is by observing saddle points during training. In [3], the authors argue that while saddle points will not prevent gradient descent from finding a good local minimum, getting trapped in a saddle point will significantly slow down training. This is due to the fact that, similarly to minima, the gradients in saddle points approach close to zero. Several approaches try to solve this, either by cycling the learning rate as a triangular wave, or by periodically resetting the gradient back to the staring value. NoSync combats this problem by having multiple particles. With a low enough value of β, the particles will have enough freedom and some of them will quickly fall off the saddle point. Particles which fall off will have a larger gradient than that of those trapped in the saddle point, and will pull the trapped ones out.

Next, we test out the quality of NoSync solutions compared to those acquired by conventional training. In [11], authors argue that "broader" local minima are better at generalizing than "narrow" minima. Given a minimum, we would prefer one that is robust to random changes in the parameters, which equates to it being broad. We compare the resilience of two networks to random parameter changes, one network trained with classic stochastic gradient descent, and the other with NoSync. In Fig. 2, we vary the amount of noise applied to the parameters and measure the accuracy and loss on the test set. The NoSync models trained with smaller learning rates (0.01) are more sensitive to perturbations compared with models with larger learning rates. We attribute this effect to multiple particles early on clustering on a single minimum, and fine-tuning it instead of exploring the area. This effect is not present when the learning rate is higher (0.1), as particles will more easily diverge and populate different solutions.

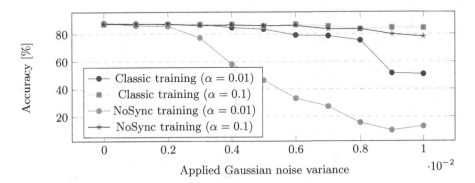

Fig. 2. Robustness to noise of networks trained with classic stochastic gradient descent, and with NoSync. Classic networks are trained for 30 epochs, and NoSync network is trained with 10 workers for 10 epochs. We vary the learning rate (0.1 and 0.01), and set the pull as $\beta = 0.1$.

5 System Design

As shown above, the NoSync method converges to higher accuracies compared to conventional approaches. In this section we propose a distributed training architecture and explore techniques for reducing network bandwidth and increasing worker utilization. A typical synchronous data-parallel system uses a number of workers and either parameter servers [5] or reduction trees [9]. Following the work in FireCaffe [9] we design a synchronous training system with $log_2 w - 1$ reduction tree levels. We pick a synchronous over an asynchronous architecture in order to simplify training and not have to consider staleness of the system.

In NoSync, each worker computes the forward pass individually and calculates the accuracy on its batch, requiring no network communication. Each worker then sends its accuracy to a parameter server, which sorts the models based on their accuracies. The parameter server requests the models of the n best workers, takes their average, and broadcasts it to all workers on the network. Each worker is tasked with calculating the weighted average of its model and the broadcasted model, and uses this newly calculated model in the next batch.

NoSync and Synchronous Training: The NoSync method has the same performance as the classic synchronous training when we integrate all the models. NoSync can further reduce traffic by: (1) decreasing the number of integrated models by dropping the worst performing ones, and (2) introducing stride, i.e., pulling models only every n iterations. Furthermore, if one allows some small staleness, each worker can have full utilization during training.

6 Evaluation

In the case of synchronous data-parallel training, we can prove that if randomness is removed, the system will behave exactly as a single machine implementation. This allows authors to independently monitor speedup and accuracy. In NoSync, however, our speedup stems from a modified search algorithm, and not a purely parallelized implementation of backpropagation. This means that we cannot observe accuracy and speedup in a vacuum, but must measure both together in order to determine the overall benefit of NoSync. For example, a slower NoSync implementation may nonetheless overtake an optimized synchronous one, as it may compute less epochs per second, but have faster convergence per epoch.

NoSync Accuracy: We first focus on whether our search algorithm benefits or hurts overall accuracy. In Fig. 3, we compare a baseline single machine system, an ideal w-worker synchronous implementation with a w times larger aggregated batch size, and several different NoSync configurations with different numbers of workers. For testing NoSync, we train a conventional 18-layer ResNet18 network [8]. Due to GPU memory constraints, we did not train deeper networks, as multiple instances of larger networks are unable to fit into the memory of a single NVidia Titan Xp GPU.

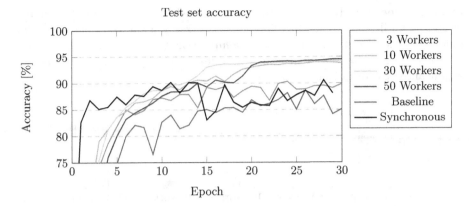

Fig. 3. Per epoch training and test accuracy of 6 systems: (red) NoSync, $w = n = 3$, (orange) NoSync, $w = n = 10$, (green) NoSync, $n = w = 30$, (blue) NoSync, $n = w = 50$, (cyan) Baseline single worker training, (black) Synchronous 10 worker training. (Color figure online)

NoSync offers a considerably higher accuracy compared to single machine or synchronous data-parallel approaches. Additionally, we notice that NoSync with 10 workers converges as quickly as the synchronous approach, but additional workers do not speed up convergence.

Metaparameter Exploration: We report that the choice of metaparameters greatly affects accuracy. In Fig. 4 we compare 3 systems of 10, 30, and 50 machines, and run a grid search on the learning rate α and the pull coefficient β.

Experiments show that the systems with smaller numbers of workers are less sensitive to the metaparameter settings. The amount of 'pull' is normalized for the number of workers, so it is reasonable that a larger cluster will occupy a larger portion of space. The larger the cluster is, the higher the chance that the loss function between each worker and the center of mass will be nonlinear, and pulling will negatively affect their performance. Therefore, we should increase the pulling force with the number of particles.

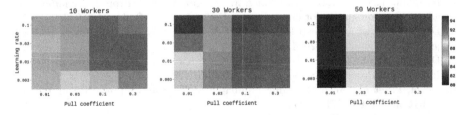

Fig. 4. Test accuracy for 3 different configurations of 10, 30, and 50 machines, training with learning rates $\alpha \in \{0.003, 0.01, 0.03, 0.1\}$ and pulls $\beta \in \{0.01, 0.03, 0.1, 0.3\}$. Each accuracy reported is the best seen on 20 epochs of training. We use a batch size of 512, momentum of 0.9.

Overall Speedup: To measure the overall speedup, we measure the number of epochs until convergence for different networks, and the time per epoch for different implementations. In Fig. 5, we compare the time to reach 87% accuracy for each of the systems. As we can see, adding more than 3 workers does not significantly speed up convergence.

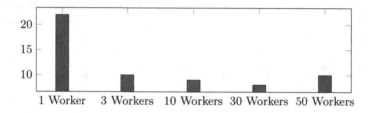

Fig. 5. Epochs until each system achieves 87% test set accuracy.

7   Conclusion

In this work, we presented an alternative distributed DNN training strategy that outperforms synchronous distributed training in terms of both accuracy and performance. We analyzed how this approach converges, and showed experimental results for it. We further proposed a system implementation, and introduced several modifications to it like adding stride and staleness. Future work will focus on providing a strict theoretical backing to the NoSync learning and an architecture exploration exploiting dropping and striding to reduce network contention.

References

1. Andreas, J., Rohrbach, M., Darrell, T., Klein, D.: Learning to compose neural networks for question answering. CoRR abs/1601.01705 (2016)
2. Bahdanau, D., Cho, K., Bengio, Y.: Neural machine translation by jointly learning to align and translate. CoRR abs/1409.0473 (2014)
3. Dauphin, Y.N., de Vries, H., Chung, J., Bengio, Y.: RMSProp and equilibrated adaptive learning rates for non-convex optimization. CoRR abs/1502.04390 (2015)
4. Dean, J.: Large scale deep learning (2014). https://research.google.com/people/jeff/CIKM-keynote-Nov2014.pdf
5. Dean, J., et al.: Large scale distributed deep networks. In: Advances in Neural Information Processing Systems, pp. 1223–1231 (2012)
6. Goyal, P., et al.: Accurate, large minibatch SGD: training ImageNet in 1 hour. CoRR abs/1706.02677 (2017)
7. Gupta, S., Zhang, W., Wang, F.: Model accuracy and runtime tradeoff in distributed deep learning: a systematic study. In: Proceedings of IEEE International Conference on Data Mining, ICDM, pp. 171–180 (2017)
8. He, K., Zhang, X., Ren, S., Sun, J.: Deep residual learning for image recognition. CoRR abs/1512.03385 (2015)

9. Iandola, F.N., Ashraf, K., Moskewicz, M.W., Keutzer, K.: FireCaffe: near-linear acceleration of deep neural network training on compute clusters. CoRR abs/1511.00175 (2015)
10. Kennedy, J., Eberhart, R.: Particle swarm optimization. In: Proceedings of IEEE International Conference on Neural Networks, vol. 4, pp. 1942–1948 (1995)
11. Keskar, N.S., Mudigere, D., Nocedal, J., Smelyanskiy, M., Tang, P.T.P.: On large-batch training for deep learning: Generalization gap and sharp minima. CoRR abs/1609.04836 (2016)
12. Krizhevsky, A.: One weird trick for parallelizing convolutional neural networks. CoRR abs/1404.5997 (2014)
13. Mitliagkas, I., Zhang, C., Hadjis, S., Re, C.: Asynchrony begets momentum, with an application to deep learning. In: 54th Annual Allerton Conference on Communication, Control, and Computing, Allerton 2016, pp. 997–1004 (2017)
14. Niu, F., Recht, B., Re, C., Wright, S.J.: HOGWILD!: a lock-free approach to parallelizing stochastic gradient descent, pp. 1–22 (2011)
15. Paine, T., Jin, H., Yang, J., Lin, Z., Huang, T.S.: GPU asynchronous stochastic gradient descent to speed up neural network training. CoRR abs/1312.6186 (2013)
16. Silver, D., et al.: Mastering the game of go without human knowledge. Nature **550**, 354 (2017)
17. Strom, N.: Scalable distributed DNN training using commodity GPU cloud computing. In: Proceedings of the Annual Conference of the International Speech Communication Association, INTERSPEECH 2015, pp. 1488–1492 (2015)
18. Akiba, T., Suzuki, S., Fukuda, K.: Extremely large minibatch SGD: training ResNet-50 on ImageNet in 15 minutes (2017)
19. You, Y., Zhang, Z., Hsieh, C., Demmel, J.: 100-epoch ImageNet training with AlexNet in 24 minutes. CoRR abs/1709.05011 (2017)
20. Zhang, S., Choromanska, A., LeCun, Y.: Deep learning with elastic averaging SGD. CoRR abs/1412.6651 (2014)

Superkernels for RBF Networks Initialization (Short Paper)

David Coufal$^{(\boxtimes)}$

Institute of Computer Science, Czech Academy of Sciences,
Pod Vodárenskou věží 2, 18207 Prague, Czech Republic
david.coufal@cs.cas.cz

Abstract. One of the basic tasks solved using artificial neural networks is the regression task. In its canonical form, one seeks for adjusting network's parameters so that its response on input training data fits the desired outputs reasonably well. Training data $\{\boldsymbol{x}_i, y_i\}_{i=1}^n$, $n \in \mathbb{N}$ consists of points from $\mathbb{R}^{d+1}$ Euclidean space, i.e., $\boldsymbol{x}_i \in \mathbb{R}^d$, $y_i \in \mathbb{R}$. The quality of the fit is typically measured in terms of the mean integrated squared error (MISE). Various regularization techniques are considered to prevent from overfitting. Optimal setting of parameters can be specified analytically in the linear model (linear computational units), however, for the nonlinear units, the network's parameters are set using different variants of stochastic optimization [1].

The formulation and solution of the regression task is relatively straightforward in the realm of probability theory. Training data are considered being a random sample from the distribution of the random vector $(\boldsymbol{X}, Y) : (\Omega, \mathcal{A}) \rightarrow (\mathbb{R}^{d+1}, \mathcal{B}(\mathbb{R}^{d+1}))$. It is well known that the optimal MISE estimator of Y given $\boldsymbol{X}$ is the conditional expectation $\mathbb{E}[Y|\boldsymbol{X}]$. That is, given $\boldsymbol{X} = \boldsymbol{x}$, the regression function writes $\mathbb{E}[Y|\boldsymbol{X} = \boldsymbol{x}]$.

An explicit form of $\mathbb{E}[Y|\boldsymbol{X} = \boldsymbol{x}] : \mathbb{R}^d \rightarrow \mathbb{R}$ is computed using the joint density f of the distribution of $(\boldsymbol{X}, Y)$. Having access to $f(\boldsymbol{x}, y) : \mathbb{R}^d \rightarrow [0, \infty)$, it is the classical result that the conditional distribution of Y given $\boldsymbol{X}$ has the density $f(y|\boldsymbol{x}) = f(\boldsymbol{x}, y)/f(\boldsymbol{x})$ and

$$\mathbb{E}[Y|\boldsymbol{X} = \boldsymbol{x}] = \int y f(y|\boldsymbol{x})\, dy = \int y \frac{f(\boldsymbol{x}, y)}{f(\boldsymbol{x})}\, dy = \frac{\int y f(\boldsymbol{x}, y)\, dy}{\int f(\boldsymbol{x}, y)\, d\boldsymbol{x}}.$$

Thus the regression function can be at least theoretically computed in the closed form (of course analytical integration can make problems). The key to this computation is the joint density $f(\boldsymbol{x}, y)$. Theory of nonparametric estimation [2] deals with the approximation of $f(\boldsymbol{x}, y)$ on basis of a random sample $\{\boldsymbol{x}_i, y_i\}_{i=1}^n \sim (\boldsymbol{X}, Y)$.

Namely, we work with the nonparametric approximation of $\mathbb{E}[Y|\boldsymbol{X} = \boldsymbol{x}]$ known as the Nadaraya-Watson estimator f_n^{NW}, [2, Sec. 1.5]. Given the data $\{\boldsymbol{x}_i, y_i\}_{i=1}^n$, the kernel estimate $\hat{f}(\boldsymbol{x}, y) = 1/(nh^{d+1}) \sum_{i=1}^n K((\boldsymbol{x} - \boldsymbol{x}_i)/h_n)\, K((y - y_i)/h_n)$ of f is constructed for a suitable function $K : \mathbb{R}^{d+1} \rightarrow \mathbb{R}$ known as a *kernel* and a bandwidth $h_n > 0$, which depends on the number of data $n \in \mathbb{N}$. Approximating capabilities of the kernel are related to its order $\ell \in \mathbb{N}$. The

© Springer Nature Switzerland AG 2018
V. Kůrková et al. (Eds.): ICANN 2018, LNCS 11140, pp. 621–623, 2018.
https://doi.org/10.1007/978-3-030-01421-6

Nadaraya-Watson estimator f_n^{NW} uses $\hat{f}$ to approximate f and consequently $\mathbb{E}[Y|\boldsymbol{X} = \boldsymbol{x}]$ as follows:

$$f_n^{NW}(\boldsymbol{x}) = \frac{\int y\hat{f}(\boldsymbol{x},y)\,dy}{\int \hat{f}(\boldsymbol{x},y)\,d\boldsymbol{x}} = \frac{\sum_{i=1}^{n} y_i\,K((\boldsymbol{x}-\boldsymbol{x}_i)/h_n)}{\sum_{i=1}^{n} K((\boldsymbol{x}-\boldsymbol{x}_i)/h_n)}.$$

We presents the idea of using f_n^{NW} to initialize shallow RBF networks for further training to meet some regularization criterions. The straightforward approach to regularization is to limit the number of computation units. In RBF networks, selecting $N \ll n$ units, their centers and widths can be specified on basis is of clustering the training data. Instead of setting the coefficients of a linear combination in the network using the training data, we linearly regress with respect to $\{\boldsymbol{x}_k, f_n^{NW}(\boldsymbol{x}_k)\}_{k=1}^{N'}$, $N' \in \mathbb{N}$s, where $\{\boldsymbol{x}_k\}_{k=1}^{N'}$ regularly spans some region of interest, for example, $[\min_i\{x_i^1\}, \max_i\{x_i^1\}] \times \cdots \times [\min_i\{x_i^d\}, \max_i\{x_i^d\}]$ with $\boldsymbol{x}_i = (x_i^1, \ldots, x_i^d)$. The granularity of the span then determines the number of points N'. Other schemes for utilizing f_n^{NW} in initializing and learning RBF networks can be presented.

The main issue discussed is how to deal with convergence of $\hat{f}$ to f in dependence on properties of f. The following upper bound applies on the MISE of the presented kernel density estimate [3, Theorem 3.5]:

$$\mathbb{E}\left[\int_{\mathbb{R}^{d+1}} (\hat{f}(\boldsymbol{x},y) - \hat{f}(\boldsymbol{x},y))^2 \, d\boldsymbol{x}dy\right] \leq C \cdot n^{-\frac{2\beta}{2\beta+d}},$$

where C is constant w.r.t. n and $\beta \in \mathbb{N}$ refers to the Sobolev character of the density f that relates to its smoothness. To have the bound valid, it is assumed that the order of kernel K meets β, i.e., that $\ell = \beta$.

Whilst the above upper bound increases with d, it decreases with β and $\lim_{\beta \to \infty} n^{-\frac{2\beta}{2\beta+d}} = n^{-1}$ for the dimension d fixed. So, increasing smoothness can in some sense override the curse of dimensionality. However, the substantial issue here is that the Sobolev character of f is unknown when working with empirical data, and in consequence one cannot use some kernel K with the corresponding order $\ell = \beta$ to construct f_n^{NW}.

In the contribution, we discuss using the *superkernels* [2, p. 27] for constructing density kernel estimates and f_n^{NW} for RBF networks initialization. The superkernels are kernels which enjoy simultaneously all orders $\ell \in \mathbb{N}$. If a superkernel is used to construct $\hat{f}$, then the maximal rate of convergence applies in the upper bound without exact specification of β, which overcomes the mentioned problem of the unknown Sobolev character. We discuss the construction of multidimensional superkernels, a relation to the Fourier transform and results from experiments showing performance in concrete tasks.

Keywords: Regression task · Nonparametric estimation · Superkernel

Acknowledgments. This work was supported by the Czech Grant Agency grant GA18-23827S and institutional support of ICS CAS RVO 67985807.

References

1. Haykin, S.S.: Neural Networks and Learning Machines, 3rd Ed. Prentice Hall (2009)
2. Tsybakov, A.B.: Introduction to Nonparametric Estimation. Springer, New York (2009)
3. Coufal, D.: On convergence of kernel density estimates in particle filtering. Kybernetika **52**(5), 735–756 (2016)

Author Index

Printed in the United States
By Bookmasters